PRINCIPLES OF QUANTITATIVE
BIOLOGY
LABORATORY

2016–2017

JAMES E. ALEXANDER, JR.
JOSEPH M. STEFFEN
UNIVERSITY OF LOUISVILLE

Principles of Quantitative Biology Laboratory

James E. Alexander, Jr.
Joseph M. Steffen
University of Louisville
2016–2017

Printed in the United States of America
10 9 8 7 6 5 4 3 2 1
ISBN: 978-1-61740-102-2

Van-Griner Publishing
Cincinnati, Ohio
www.van-griner.com

CEO: Mike Griner
President: Dreis Van Landuyt
Project Manager: Brenda Schwieterman
Customer Care Specialist: Julie Reichert

Alexander 102-2 Su16
165855
Copyright © 2017

Table of Contents

UNIT 1 — Experimental Design

Key Words

hypothesis
proof
disproof
independent variables
dependent variables
controlled variables

null hypothesis
alternative hypothesis
control treatments
experimental treatments
prediction
experiment

theory
law
adaptation
acclimation
oxygen dissociation curves

Learning Objectives

When finished with this unit, you should be able to:

1. Describe the basic steps of the scientific method;

2. Describe the basic attributes of a valid hypothesis;

3. Suggest hypotheses based on prior observations, and make predictions based on these hypotheses;

4. Understand the difference between the phrases 'proving hypotheses' and 'disproving hypotheses';

5. Identify and contrast null and alternative hypotheses;

6. Develop an experimental test of a scientific hypothesis;

7. Identify and contrast dependent, independent, and controlled variables;

8. Identify and contrast control and experimental treatments;

9. Compare and contrast the following concepts: facts, observations, hypotheses, theories, and laws; and

10. Generate conclusions based on experimental results.

The Scientific Method

Scientists generally follow certain established procedures in obtaining and analyzing data. We call this approach **the scientific method.** Contrary to popular belief (perhaps you have been exposed to the scientific method in high school or in other college classes), there is no single scientific 'method' that must be strictly followed in order to 'do' science. However, the sequence listed below (consisting of six 'steps') is usually what we refer to as "The Scientific Method":

Step 1 Make initial observations about some phenomenon;

Step 2 Ask questions and generate tentative answers (hypotheses) to these initial questions;

Step 3 Design and conduct tests of the hypotheses (experiments);

Step 4 Collect data from the experiments, summarize the data into results, and analyze the results;

Step 5 Draw conclusions from the results; and

Step 6 Suggest and conduct further observations and tests.

All scientists follow a general sequence of steps to investigating and understanding some natural phenomenon. Why do scientists follow the above basic steps to 'do' science? One important reason is that the knowledge acquired in everyday life can differ from that knowledge gained by science. Some assertions made by various people and organizations are not testable in the same way as scientific conclusions are. For example, religious assertions are based on faith, cultural mores, and personal values. Religion is a belief system (you basically take it on a matter of faith that something happened the way you were told it happened), but science is based more on testing hypotheses about natural phenomena.

Science does not rely on any belief system, on dogmatic assertions, or even on a consensus when it comes to creating or accepting hypotheses. Even logic, by itself, is not completely reliable as the sole basis for science. Scientists assume natural events follow predictable patterns, and that these patterns can be discerned through careful observation and the use of proper, established methods of scientific analysis. Scientists believe that fellow scientists are truthful in their description, execution, and analysis of experiments and their discoveries increase our understanding of the physical universe. Because of the checks and balances involved (for example, the process of publishing one's work and the subsequent replication of experiments and verification by others), fraudulent science or bad science can be discovered and corrected.

Scientists often form generalizations, or models, of how nature works. By using various models (mathematical models, physical models, and mental models), scientists can predict future changes in systems based on the outcomes of the models without having to spend the vast sums of money needed to run large-scale experiments. Often, the phenomenon we wish to examine (for example, the possibility of global warming and its impacts) takes place over time and spatial scales that are much too large for us to conduct a 'real-life' experiment. Instead, scientists can manipulate a model's parameters and observe the subsequent results of the manipulations, and then make useful predictions and explanations (i.e., hypotheses) on how the real world would behave if it was under the same conditions as the model system. These models then can be used as the basis for subsequent empirical experiments to be conducted later, which can yield 'real-life' results.

Not every question can be answered scientifically. Science does not and cannot answer all questions. Certain questions you may have posed can be answered by other 'ways of knowing,' where personal opinions, consensus, faith, tradition, and moral/ethical considerations may play important roles. However, the questions asked and the answers obtained by relying on faith, consensus, and tradition may have no basis in science. Science asks questions of the natural, observable world, not of the supernatural.

The Steps to the Scientific Method

Step 1 **Make initial observations and pose questions.** You make an initial observation, and then ask questions about what you saw, such as "why or when or how?" First, a scientist may make an initial observation, where he or she notes some interesting fact of nature. A fact in science is an observation that is confirmed typically by several observers and believed to exist or to be true. The scientist then asks 'why' or 'how' this particular fact of nature occurred.

For example, let's say you are taking care of your parents' house while they are on a month-long vacation. Among other duties, you are to water your mom's favorite plant while she is away. However, she did not tell you when or how to water the plant. You watered it once every three days by pouring a cupful of water on the plant. After a week or so, your mother's favorite plant dies. After your panic attack is over, if you wanted to think about the event 'scientifically,' you then may consider why the plant died.

Scientists are not naive in making initial observations and suggesting initial hypotheses. Through a long period of learning and experience, scientists personally accumulate considerable knowledge about the physical universe, particularly in their specialty areas, and thus can make appropriate initial observations. In addition, scientists know the previously published scientific literature in their fields and can use the results found in the literature as the starting point for generating more observations and hypotheses. This knowledge of prior research saves a large amount of time and money that would be spent if a scientist has to 'reinvent the wheel,' so to speak, every time they start a new experiment.

The scientific method and critical thinking skills. The ability to think 'scientifically' is not limited to scientists, however. All people should be able to observe some natural phenomenon and, after some thought, pose and answer 'how and why' questions concerning the phenomenon's cause(s). You will hear a lot of discussion about **'critical thinking skills'** in many classes. In the sciences, critical thinking is essential and necessary. **The scientific method is one very important approach to thinking critically.**

In order to be an effective scientist, you must be able to:

1. Recall or access prior knowledge about the world (terms, concepts and prior history of your research field);

2. Describe the assumptions needed to understand how or why a phenomenon occurred;

3. Execute clearly defined experiments;

4. Draw valid conclusions from your experimental results, typically based on mathematical analysis; and

5. Judge the validity of your experimental designs and experimental outcomes.

All of these ideas listed above form crucial parts of 'critical thinking' in the sciences.

Step 2 **Develop answers to these questions by proposing hypotheses. A hypothesis is a tentative explanation of some observation of the physical universe.** In our hypothetical example, you may make the hypothesis that you watered the plant too much, which then caused the roots to become waterlogged. The soil became anoxic, and the plant died.

A hypothesis is a tentative explanation of why certain observations about the physical universe are the way they are. Note that all hypotheses are 'tentative' explanations. After making initial observations, scientists often pose questions on how or why the phenomenon under observation occurred, or why the phenomenon being observed had a particular value or state. The answers to these questions are potential hypotheses that can be tested.

Often, science is depicted (mistakenly) as always working toward the 'truth' of the universe, and that doing science well means that you are always correct. In reality, science is an ongoing process that continually changes our notions on how the universe works. Scientists have made many hypotheses about the universe, and many of these hypotheses subsequently have been shown to be false and eventually discarded. Some hypotheses, on the other hand, have been shown to have great explanatory power, and these supported hypotheses help explain a wide variety of observations.

Scientists can propose many types of hypotheses, but there are **five crucial attributes of hypotheses.**

Valid scientific hypotheses must have the following attributes:

1. They are **predictable** (potential outcomes can be produced from them);

2. They are **testable** (they can be examined either directly or indirectly);

3. They are **falsifiable** (they can be shown to be false);

4. They are **repeatable** (you can replicate the experiment and get similar results); and

5. They are **verifiable** (someone else can replicate your experiment and get similar results).

You should think about each of these attributes and determine why each is important.

All experiments involve two (or more) hypotheses. The null hypothesis (H_0) usually states that the observed phenomenon is due to random causes or factors. The null hypothesis also typically says there is no effect or difference among the different treatments. The null hypothesis usually is constructed as a negative statement: "the independent variable under examination has no impact on the dependent variable."

The alternative hypothesis (H_A or H_1), in its most general form, covers all other outcomes not explained by the null hypothesis. The alternative hypothesis states that there is a significant difference between treatments. The alternative hypothesis is usually presented in the form of a positive statement: "there is some effect of the independent variable on the dependent variable." In addition, the alternative hypothesis may predict the direction, magnitude, or intensity of the independent variable's effect.

In our example, H_0 is "watering schedule has no effect"; H_A is "watering schedule has an effect."

For some experiments, there are two competing hypotheses: one null and one alternative. However, as we will discuss later, there can be more than two hypotheses. There may be several competing alternative hypotheses that can be created and tested.

Hypotheses make predictions about future observations. Null and alternative hypotheses typically make opposite or contrasting predictions about the outcomes of subsequent experiments. In other words, the competing hypotheses should be **mutually exclusive.**

Scientists establish their null and alternative hypotheses before doing an experiment. These hypotheses are thus called *a priori* hypotheses ("from the former"). If the hypotheses are created after the experiment is conducted, it is highly likely that their selection is biased by the outcome of the experiment. Responsible scientists thus create their hypotheses first, before doing any experimentation.

This does not mean that additional analyses cannot be done on the experimental results after the experiment has been conducted. Additional *post hoc* ("after this") analyses may be conducted after an experiment has been completed, in order to examine additional details related to the basic analysis. For example, you may have tested to see if three different types of pesticides were effective in killing some pest insects. The null hypothesis is that "there is no effect of the pesticide on insect mortality," versus the alternative hypothesis "there is an effect on mortality." Let's say that your results support the alternative hypothesis, and now you wish to know which pesticide was more efficacious. Additional *post hoc* analyses of the data could identify (if there was an effect) which pesticide (if any) was better than the others in eliminating the pest.

Step 3   **Develop and execute a test (experiment) of the hypotheses.** Scientists design an **experiment** (where subsequent observations are made under controlled conditions) to test the validity of competing hypotheses. Experiments are designed to determine which hypothesis best 'fits' all of the known observations—all of the previous ones made in the past, as well as the new observations made during the experiment. Hypotheses are typically generated before the experiment is conducted; however, further *post hoc* analyses can be done on data once the data have been gathered.

The best experiments are designed so that their outcomes will falsify predictions made by all but one of the competing hypotheses. As mentioned above, there may be multiple alternative possibilities. Several alternative hypotheses may be made. Experiments may be examining two, three, or more competing hypotheses simultaneously, and, if set up correctly, the experiment will reject the false hypotheses.

Scientists run experiments to collect and analyze **data** (singular: datum; plural: data). **Data are the quantitative or qualitative values of one attribute of the phenomenon observed.** In biology, examples of useful data include molecular weight, molecular concentration, an organism's height or weight, time of death or birth, death rates and birth rates, population growth rates, temperature, light wavelength (color), pH, absorption spectra, or some other attribute of the biological world (at the level of molecule, cell, organism, population, or ecosystem being studied).

Scientists usually set up experiments to disprove the null hypothesis. Scientists do not go about 'proving' hypotheses (although you will occasionally hear someone say this). Newspaper stories, television articles, or commercials often state (incorrectly) that some scientist or doctor has proven something. Scientists generally proceed by conducting experiments that permit the predictions made by the various competing hypotheses to be tested. Those hypotheses whose predictions are not confirmed by the test are **rejected** (or disproved). The term 'disproof' refers to the experimental evidence that disproves some hypothesis—that hypothesis is refuted or shown to be false. These false, unsupported hypotheses subsequently are discarded and a new hypothesis is proposed as an explanation. If a hypothesis is supported by the experiment, the hypothesis is **accepted** as a statement that sufficiently explains all of the observations.

The accepted hypothesis usually is viewed as **tentatively** accepted because it may be rejected later with additional, more refined, experiments. Science has a number of built-in features that help to detect inaccurate or fraudulent claims, to correct errors, and to reject false hypotheses.

In a biological experiment, the objects being examined are grouped into different treatments. There can be two treatments (one experimental treatment and one control treatment, see below), or there can be three or more treatments, depending on the design of the experiment. In all of these treatment groups, scientists generally try to keep all **variables** (variables are the factors that could differ among treatments) constant except one. Procedures, treatments, and variables are explicitly defined by the scientists, so that other scientists can replicate the procedures precisely and accurately in subsequent independent experiments.

There are two basic types of treatments.

1 Experimental treatment (group): The treatment in which the examined biological objects—molecules, cells, organisms, populations, communities, or ecosystems—are subjected to a change of (or manipulation of) one variable. Often, several variables are manipulated in experiments. This manipulated variable (the experimental variable, see below) could be a change in the concentration of a chemical, pH, body temperatures, population densities, food levels, the presence of toxic compounds, and so on. As the experimental variable is changed by the scientist, the scientist strives to keep all other variables constant among the treatments.

2 Control treatment (group): The treatment where all variables are kept at their initial values at the beginning of the experiment, including the variable that was allowed to change in the experimental treatment.

In testing hypotheses, a good experiment typically allows the **independent** (manipulated) **variable** to change in a systematic way in order to observe its effect on the **dependent** (responding) **variable.** In our plant watering example, the experimental treatment is "water weekly," the control treatment is "water every three days." The independent variable is the frequency of watering. The growth or survival of the plants in each treatment is the dependent variable. The independent variable is part of the experimental design, and the dependent variable is the phenomenon measured or monitored.

To give you an example of what is meant by an experimental and control treatment, suppose you wanted to know the effectiveness of a given drug (let's call the drug 'Happitude') on general mood. You have two groups of human test subjects. One subject group (= experimental treatment) will receive a 3 cc injection of a saline solution containing 'Happitude'; the other group (= control treatment) will receive a 3 cc injection of the same saline solution, but without the drug included. Prior to the experiments, you tried to make the two subject groups as similar as possible, with respect to age, gender, race, and other variables. In addition, your procedure also helps account for any effect of the injection itself. If you see a significant difference in the behavior or attitude of the two treatment groups, you can be somewhat confident that the drug itself accounts for the differences, and not some other variable.

There are three basic types of variables in an experiment: Independent variables, dependent variables, and controlled variables.

1 Independent variables are variables that can be manipulated (changed), measured, or selected by the scientist. Scientists view the independent variable(s) as the cause of the change in some observed outcome or event, in other words, the change in the responding, dependent variable(s). Scientists view the independent variables as those that are not affected by the other variables under study.

In many cases, scientists wish to observe the effect of one variable (for our example, water) on a second variable (survival). There are many variables that are affected by other variables; the state or value of each of these variables is said to be 'dependent upon' the values of the other variables. For example, as you have grown older, you have increased in height. Age is an **independent variable** (not affected by height) but height is a **dependent variable** (height is affected by age, sex, health, food, genes, and many other things).

2 **Dependent variables** are variables that are not under the scientist's direct control; they are not to be manipulated by the experimenter. They are variables that are observed and measured in response to changes in the independent variable(s). The values of dependent (responding) variables are thought to be predicted by, or caused by, changes in the values of one or more independent variables.

3 **Controlled variables** are those variables that have not been allowed to vary among treatments. Controlled variables have been kept constant among the replicates. For example, if you are examining the effect of water on plant survival, you would not want air temperature also to differ among the treatments (as well as light, pH, age, size, sex, or initial health of the individual plants, the presence of household pets and insect pests, and so on). If these other extraneous variables do differ in a dramatic way among the replicate groups or treatments, their effects may **confound** the effects of water on plant survival (in other words, these uncontrolled variables minimize your ability to determine the impact of water on survival). You also would want to use individuals of one species throughout your experiment because different species often have very different responses to variables.

Do not confuse controlled variables with control treatments. Controlled variables exist in both control and experimental treatments, but the controlled variables are not allowed to vary or differ between the two treatments. For example, suppose we were examining the effect of nitrogen on plant growth, and we started out with 10 seedlings in each of two groups: a control group (no extra nitrogen is added to the soil) and an experimental group (extra nitrogen is added). The age and size of the plants are controlled variables, in that all 20 plants (from both treatments) initially should be of the same size and age.

The importance of keeping all variables (other than the independent variables) constant: For example, suppose we wanted to see the effect of temperature on the growth rate of zebra mussels. We would not want the light intensity or food quality to vary among the treatments. If we saw a difference in growth rates in our treatment groups, but we allowed light or food quality to vary as well in an uncontrolled fashion, we would not know if it was the change in temperature that caused a change in the zebra mussels' growth rates, or if the change in light levels or food quality caused the change. In addition, the change in growth rates may be due to some complex interaction between temperature and light/food quality.

In summary, the **independent variable** usually serves as a point of reference, where the **dependent variable** is related to the independent variable in some predictable way. In a cause-and-effect relationship, the independent variable is the cause, and the dependent variable is the outcome or effect. The controlled variables are those variables or factors whose impacts are not under immediate study. The controlled variables are kept constant, so that they do not affect the outcome of an experiment and thus prevent us from identifying the cause-and-effect relationship between the independent and dependent variables (if one exists).

Step 4 **Make conclusions based on the experimental data.** After finishing the experiment, scientists analyze the data and make summaries; these summaries are called **results.** Scientists then draw conclusions from the experimental summaries, by determining if the results support or reject each hypothesis.

Scientists usually attempt to disprove (reject) the null hypothesis, which is usually the simplest of all of the competing hypotheses. In our example, suppose you watered 10 plants (replicates) per treatment, and you observed all 20 plants dying after two weeks. You have to accept the null hypothesis of 'no effect of watering schedule,' and that death was due to some other reason.

Another alternative hypothesis with respect to watering exists, however. You may have watered the plants too infrequently, or with not enough water! You must do another experiment with **three treatments:** a) water daily, b) water every three days, and c) water weekly. In this second experiment, the outcome shows that only the plants watered daily survived. You now reject the null hypothesis (no effect) and accept this new alternative hypothesis (you initially watered too little).

There are many other potential reasons that may also help to explain the results. In our example, plant survival may depend on the quantity of water provided at each time (instead of one cup, perhaps two or more cups of water were needed), on water quality (polluted or fresh, warm/cold, acidic/basic) or on the ionic composition of water (salty or fresh, or the absence/presence of trace minerals and nutrients). Other experiments must be conducted in order to rule out the relative importance or impact of these other variables, particularly if you cannot rule them out with the results of your first experiment.

Step 5 **Communicate your results, determine potential weaknesses of your results, make additional hypotheses, and run further tests.** The last step of the scientific method is to start over and propose new hypotheses to test. Further tests are conducted to provide additional support for or refinement of some hypothesis. Professional scientists typically write up their results and present their conclusions to the general scientific audience via papers published in **refereed journals.** The editor of a scientific journal receives a manuscript and then sends copies of this manuscript out to several knowledgeable scientists for their (typically) anonymous review. These referees or reviewers critique the manuscript and then either recommend that the manuscript: a) not be published, b) be published as is, or c) be resubmitted once comments and criticisms listed by the reviewers have been addressed by the authors. Reviewers may make suggestions on improving the format or style of the paper—for example, how to present the results more clearly.

Reviewers thus provide important feedback on the experimental design and the scientific method. Reviewers constructively criticize the generalizations made from the results. Reviewers thus act as an important check in preventing poorly written manuscripts (or poorly conducted experiments) from being published.

Once published, other scientists then can read the papers with a critical eye, and in turn, they create new hypotheses and experiments to verify earlier results. Papers that are not verified by other scientists fade in importance, whereas verified hypotheses often lead to new avenues for exploration. In this way, scientific knowledge increases over time, and we more clearly understand how the universe works.

Only testable and falsifiable hypotheses are in the realm of science. As stated earlier, scientists do not rely on authority, faith, or even a consensus, but on falsification of hypotheses and on replication. **Replication** is essential to science, especially independent replication **(verification)** by other scientists. This verification process is why the experimental design and methods must be described in detail when scientists communicate their findings.

Hypotheses are not just picked out of a hat. Scientists, historians of science, and philosophers agree that scientists also use creative and imaginative processes in formulating hypotheses. These creative processes are based on prior knowledge, curiosity, insight, and intuition. Luck and chance may play a role in discovering a new phenomenon, but it is the scientist's training and curiosity that allow him or her to note interesting observations and reexamine results that may be confusing or paradoxical.

Why do scientists try to disprove hypotheses, and not try to prove them? We disprove hypotheses because both true and false hypotheses can make predictions that appear to come true, because of unforeseen factors. To illustrate the crucial importance of disproving hypotheses, we could make two different competing hypotheses about the relationship of the Sun and Earth (as was done centuries earlier): 1) the Sun revolves around the Earth, or 2) the Earth circles around the Sun (see Figure 1.1). We can logically make a prediction that is the same for both hypotheses! The identical prediction is as follows: "The Sun will be observed rising from the horizon at dawn, passing overhead, and setting on the opposite horizon at dusk." Both hypotheses make this prediction, and it thus takes a different set of observations to distinguish them.

The debate about the correct orbital relationship between the Earth and the Sun is just one of many examples that demonstrate why science attempts to disprove hypotheses, not prove them. The Earth/Sun relationship shows how a false hypothesis and a true hypothesis both may make a true prediction. A false hypothesis may appear true because some assumption is wrong, or because some important factor has not been taken into account. This example also demonstrates why logic, by itself, is insufficient in making valid hypotheses, because both competing hypotheses were 'logical,' based on the evidence at the time. The 'fact' that the Sun is observed rising in the east is not sufficient to 'prove' the Earth-centered universe. In this case, the Earth, as it revolves around the Sun, also rotates on its axis. The planet's rotation causes the apparent revolution of the Sun, the stars, and the other planets around the Earth. By examining the movement of other planets, placing spacecraft into orbit, observing eclipses, and by many additional observations, scientists have long accepted the fact that the Earth is a sphere that both rotates on its axis and revolves around the Sun. Actually, the Earth and the Sun revolve around their common center of gravity, which is basically near the center of the Sun. We now know that hypothesis 1 above (the Earth-centered solar system) is false.

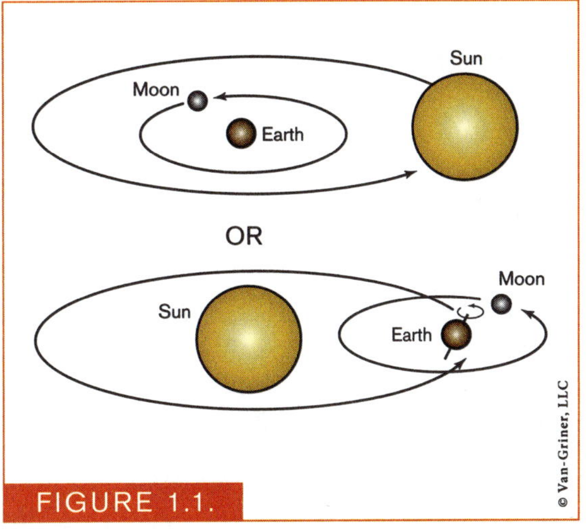

FIGURE 1.1.

The orbital relationship between the Earth and the Sun: two possible hypotheses.

Because hypotheses are accepted or rejected by experimental observations, only hypotheses that can produce some type of repeatable, verifiable prediction (and can subsequently be **tested**) are considered valid hypotheses. If a hypothesis relies solely on the faith in (or existence of) the supernatural, or for some reason cannot be tested directly or indirectly, that hypothesis is considered outside the realm of science and thus is not scientifically valid. Nonscientific questions (and their answers) are not necessarily less important to human society, but these nonscientific questions cannot be answered by the process of scientific inquiry.

Scientists often use statistics to make decisions on accepting or rejecting hypotheses. A statistical analysis is based on probability theory and on the data collected in experiments. If the data of a given experiment was affected by random variation (or it is not affected by our independent variable), the data would exhibit a particular frequency or distribution that can be examined by mathematical analysis. We will use and describe specific statistics throughout the semester.

Scientific Theories

A hypothesis accepted after repeated tests becomes a theory. A theory is composed of one or more hypotheses (that have been often tested and never rejected) that adequately explain some phenomenon. A theory is not a half-baked idea, as you probably have used the term 'theory' in everyday speech. In science, a theory is a powerful set of explanations that adequately accounts for a large body of observations. Theories are typically composed of a cluster of verified, rigorous hypotheses, but facts, laws and logical inferences can be included as well. A theory is a well-substantiated explanation of a phenomenon; a theory has been repeatedly tested over time and was **not** shown to be false.

However, even theories can be disproved with further experiments. Established theories can come into conflict with the results of new experiments that have rigorously been conducted. The theory can either be discarded, and a new hypothesis is put in its place, or the theory could be modified. A modified theory can become a powerful, more inclusive theory that explains all of the observed phenomena and experimental results. **The new theory, however, is not one discarded earlier; the new theory must also explain all previous results of the earlier valid experiments.** Science cannot provide absolute proof of the truthfulness of theories, but scientists can state with a high degree of confidence that a theory is true, due to the reliability of its predictions.

Scientific Laws

A **scientific law** is different from a theory. Laws are descriptions of what we observe in nature; laws typically are mathematical generalizations describing the precise relationships between two or more variables. For scientific laws, if you know the value of all but one of the variables, you can state the value of the unknown variable, without exception.

For example, we have a law of gravity, where we know that there is a gravitational attraction between two objects. This attraction varies as a function of the masses of the objects and the distance between them. If we know the bodies' masses and the distance separating them, we know the value of the gravitational attraction between the two objects. If we know the mass of one object, and the distance between the two objects, and the strength of the gravitational force, we can infer the mass of the second object. However, this law does not explain why or how gravity works this way. The law of gravity is a statement that describes the attraction (there are hypotheses posited about gravity that describe how or why this attraction occurs). A theory describes or explains the mechanisms underlying the nature of collected data and laws.

We typically describe laws in chemistry and physics (the ideal gas law, the laws of thermodynamics, the law of gravity), but laws exist in biology as well. For example, the law of segregation and the law of independent assortment are but two of the biological 'laws' you will see later in the semester.

Exercises

1 In today's lab, you will set up hypotheses and test them in the following model. The data you will collect are hypothetical, yet they are based on actual research. The following papers provide some further information on the subject: Chappell and Snyder, (1981); Chappell et al. (1988); and Snyder et al. (1988).

Your group will act as a 'research team.' Your team will 'sample' populations of the deer mouse *Peromyscus*. These populations live at a variety of altitudes in the mountains of the American West. Hemoglobin is the major oxygen-carrying molecule in many organisms. The mammalian hemoglobin molecule consists of four protein chains linked together: two alpha hemoglobins and two beta hemoglobins. For the deer mouse, there are two major forms of the alpha hemoglobin, a_1 and a_0. These different alpha hemoglobins differ in their amino acid sequence, and their amino acid sequence is coded for by two different versions (alleles) of the alpha hemoglobin gene, a_1 and a_0. It is somewhat more complicated than this in reality, so we have simplified the actual situation slightly.

The degrees to which these alpha hemoglobins bind to oxygen vary as a function of the concentration of oxygen in the atmosphere (measured as the partial pressure of oxygen gas). At low altitudes near sea level, the air is 'thicker,' and there is more oxygen. At higher altitudes, there is less atmospheric pressure, and thus less oxygen. Animals that live in high altitude environments typically have adaptations that can be observed by changes in the **oxygen dissociation curves** of their blood (see Figure 1.2). The oxygen dissociation curves relate the saturation of the hemoglobin to the oxygen partial pressure in the blood. Above some partial pressure, the hemoglobin is totally saturated with oxygen (the hemoglobin is carrying the maximum amount of oxygen), and below a certain partial pressure, the hemoglobin is carrying little oxygen, or the hemoglobin releases the oxygen. The shape of this curve is related to the degree to which the hemoglobin can carry oxygen. In animals that live in higher altitudes, the curve often is shifted to the left, which shows that the hemoglobin 'loads up' more oxygen at lower partial pressures. The shape of the curve does not change, the unloading and loading of oxygen still occurs in about the same way, regardless of the position of the curve. The higher oxygen affinity of the hemoglobin of these high altitude animals thus aids the uptake of oxygen from the air (this higher oxygen affinity is thus an **adaptation** to the higher altitude and thinner air).

A beneficial trait is called an **adaptation.** An adaptation is a change in structure, behavior, or physiology that increases the chances of an organism's survival and reproduction in a particular environment, at one point in time. It is assumed that the underlying cause of the adaptation is at least in part heritable (it has a genetic basis). These favorable adaptations increase the chances for that individual to survive and reproduce, thus greater numbers of the next generation may also possess the adaptation (and the underlying gene that encodes for the beneficial trait). In this class, we will refer to many different adaptations organisms use in response to their environments.

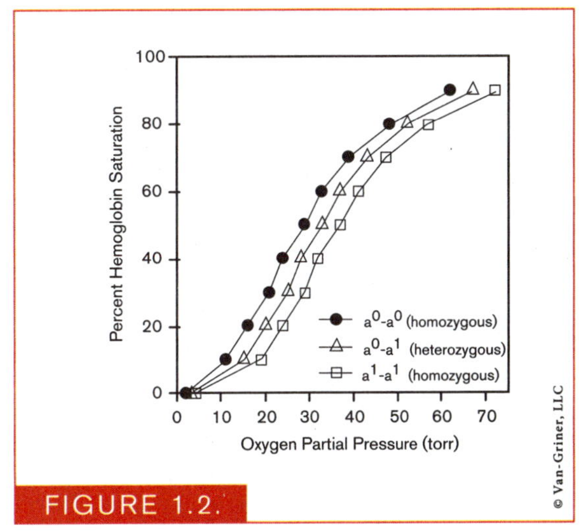

FIGURE 1.2.

The hypothetical oxygen dissociation curves for the a_1 and a_0 alpha hemoglobins.

The various hemoglobins in this exercise represent physiological adaptations to changes in environmental oxygen concentrations. The a_1 hemoglobin (coded for by the a_1 allele) has a lower affinity for oxygen than the a_0 hemoglobin (coded for by the a_0 allele). The relative frequencies of these two alleles thus may differ in *Peromyscus* populations at different altitudes.

2 First, your research team should suggest what independent variables and specific hypotheses (null and alternative) you would like to examine, given the information above. Talk amongst yourselves about specific questions and hypotheses you would test, and how you would test them. After this time, your lab instructor will ask for each group to provide some ideas.

3 State specific null and alternative hypotheses below. List the independent and dependent variables, as well as control variables.

Null hypothesis:

Alternative hypothesis:

Independent variable(s):

Dependent variable(s):

Variables that should be controlled:

④ Experimental design. Each research team is given $15,000 'dollars' from a 'granting agency' to run their experiment (some teams may be 'awarded' more or less money). You must spend this money wisely in order to answer your question well.

a It costs you $500 to travel to and sample on any given mountain. If you travel to another mountain, you must spend an additional $500. There are three mountains: Red Mountain, Blue Mountain, and Green Mountain. It takes money to travel to these different mountains and to transport personnel and equipment.

You are not allowed to go up ahead of time and look at the cards. All of the facts you are allowed to know, ahead of time, are that there are three different mountains and ten different 'sites' on each mountain. At your table, your research team must first make decisions on how many mountains (one, two, or all three) you will sample, and you must also decide upon how many altitudes (sites) you may wish to sample. The ten sites could range from near sea level (at the mountain's base) to near the mountain's peak.

b It also costs $100 per card that you pick up at each site. You must make the decision on how many cards you will collect before going up to choose the cards. Part of the cost is due to the fact you have to capture the mouse, remove a small amount of its blood, release the mouse, and take the blood sample back to the lab for analysis. It takes money to process the DNA of the sample and determine the alleles that particular mouse possesses. In addition, it costs money to travel to each site and set up the live traps.

It is possible that you may not catch a mouse at some sites (some cards may be blank). Some of the sites may not have many mice. **However, for each card you pick up, it costs you $100, even if the card is blank, or has some other animal or event listed on it. You are not allowed to pick up another card. If you run out of money, you cannot continue collecting data.** In addition, you cannot talk to the other research teams for information.

c The 'deer mice' are represented by the 3×5 cards. On one side of the card is the altitude and mountain range where the deer mouse was caught. The back of the card lists the 'hemoglobin a' alleles for that deer mouse. The deer mouse is diploid (two complete sets of genes, like humans), thus they have three possible allele combinations. These three allele combinations are called the **genotypes:** a_1-a_1 (homozygous for a_1), a_1-a_0 (heterozygous), and a_0-a_0 (homozygous for a_0). A blank card means that you did not catch a mouse in that trap.

d You sample the population by picking up a card and noting the mountain, altitude, and genotype. Remember, you only have $15,000 to spend. Record your data in Table 1.1. Keep track of your blank cards as well.

⑤ Results. Once you have sampled all of the mice you wish to sample, calculate the relative percentage of the a_1 and a_0 alleles at each altitude, and add these results to Table 1.2. Plot the 'frequency of the a_1 allele' as a function of altitude on Figure 1.3. If you sampled different mountains, you may wish to use different colors to represent the data of different mountains. Label your axes!

As you summarize your data as results in tables and figures, you should always provide information that allows the reader to make their own conclusions, based on your data. Any units that are used should be provided, as well as sample sizes (N) and statistical summaries, if produced.

⑥ Are there any conclusions you can make about the results? Which hypothesis is supported?

⑦ What are the weaknesses of your design? How would you repeat the experiment? Discuss your answers to these questions in your group and with the entire class.

Good science always leads to further studies. Suggest some additional hypotheses and experiments, extending your knowledge on this particular line of research. What other factors may be influencing the allele frequencies?

You may be tempted to draw some sort of straight line through your data. Are you sure the relationship between altitude and allele relative frequencies is linear? If you drew some sort of curve, are you sure the relationship is a curvilinear one? What other possible curves could you draw?

Can you identify any other potential adaptions that these mice may have with respect to altitude and oxygen concentrations? Are there any possible adverse side effects or costs for mice to have certain adaptations at different altitudes?

FIGURE 1.3.

The frequency of the a_1 allele as a function of altitude.

TABLE 1.1. Data collection: the frequency of the a_1 and a_0 alleles.

Mountain	Altitude (m)	Mouse Genotype: a_1-a_1, a_1-a_0, or a_0-a_0	Mountain	Altitude (m)	Mouse Genotype: a_1-a_1, a_1-a_0, or a_0-a_0

TABLE 1.2. The results of your experiment.

Mountain	Altitude (m)	Percent of Alleles of the Deer Mouse Population that were a_1

Descriptive Statistics and Measurements in Biology

Keywords

sample

population

variable

replicate

scientific notation

parameter

statistic

mean

median

mode

range

outlier

variance

standard deviation

Learning Objectives

When finished with this unit, you should be able to:

1. Distinguish between the following terms: sample and population;

2. Discuss the importance of variation and replication;

3. Recognize the base units in the metric system for temperature, length, mass, and volume;

4. List the metric unit prefixes and convert from one unit to the next;

5. Convert measurements from English to metric, or from metric to English, when given the conversion factors;

6. Round off numbers correctly;

7. Use scientific notation;

8. Contrast the following descriptive statistics concerning the 'average' value of a set of data: mean, median, mode;

9. Calculate the mean, median, and mode of a data set;

10. Contrast the following various types of descriptive statistics concerning the dispersion of a set of data around a mean value: range, standard deviation, variance; and

11. Calculate the range, standard deviation, and variance of a data set.

Variables

When we make measurements on some object or phenomenon, our observations are made on the values of certain properties of the phenomena we are studying. Recall from Unit 1 that a **variable** is some feature or attribute about the objects or phenomena we are observing. This observed attribute can have different values among the different objects in our sample.

For example, if we are examining a **population** of whitetail deer, we could go out and tranquilize some individual animals, and then take a number of measurements about their appearance, status or condition. We could measure length, weight, age, and sex, take blood samples, or count the number of parasites on each deer's skin. We could tag each deer in the hopes that we recapture some of them in the future, in order to measure growth and survival rates. In a given geographical area, we could take estimates concerning the status of the deer population: population size, age class distribution, or sex ratios. We can observe what vegetation the deer feed upon, and we can make measurements about the community and the ecosystem in which the deer population lives. All of these attributes we are measuring about the whitetail deer and their environment are called variables.

Sampling and Replication

In order to know literally everything about a population (such as our deer population above), we would need to capture and examine every single individual. However, biologists rarely, if ever, capture all of the individuals of an entire population. Instead, biologists can take a **sample** (a representative subset) of a population, and then make inferences about the entire population from the sample. Let's say we were omnipotent and knew that there were currently 1,204 whitetail deer in a given forest, and we knew the lengths of their right ears. All of the 'right ears' of these deer would represent the **population.** In statistics, a population is the entire collection of measurements of some variable about which we want to make a conclusion, generalization, or summary.

However, we could never be sure that we counted every single deer and measured their ears. Because the deer population may be large in size, and the difficulty and expense in catching all deer in order to measure their ears may be so prohibitive, we could not be certain we measured them all. Instead, we could capture a subset of the deer and measure the ears of this subset. This subset of the population (a **sample**) then provides us with an **estimate** of the variable we are measuring.

The 'population' thus can be a somewhat imaginary entity. Suppose we measured growth rates of 50 rats over several weeks, during which time they have been consuming a given food. The 50 animals represent a sample of all possible rats on Earth that could eat the food under similar conditions (in other words, the hypothetical population). Even though there are millions of rats that could conceivably have been selected for the study, we still have a certain degree of confidence that our sample reflects the true average growth rate that all of the rats currently in existence would show if we could measure them all. In a related way, we may not ever know what the total number of rats in the population is at any one time, but we can suggest (again with a varying degree of certainty) that another sample of rats would exhibit a similar growth rate, if both samples were randomly selected subsets of the entire rat population.

Because the individuals of the sample are determined largely by chance, successive sampling can produce very different estimates. Multiple sampling will tend to even out the variation in the samples due to chance. **Replication** (repeated sampling or repeated experiments) thus is very important in biology experiments.

Random Variation and the Use of Replicates

You may wonder why we have to measure so many replicates in order to feel confident about any generalizations you may make. As you take quantitative measurements on both inanimate and living objects, you may note that there are many small differences among the individual objects. A large number of factors may affect the objects under study in a myriad of small ways. By taking a large enough sample (i.e., using a number of replicates), you would be 'evening out' the minor random variation inherent among the objects, and you can have some degree of confidence that you have a reliable estimate of the population.

For example, suppose you were an alien scientist from another world and you wanted to know the average height and weight of humans in a large city. Right away, you would see that humans come in two sexes and the two sexes have different average heights/weights. Age, health, activity levels, income level, genes—all of these variables affect height/weight as well. If you examined only five people that you met on the street, you could not state with confidence that you know the 'true average' height and weight of the city's population. If you measured 5,000 people, however, you have much more confidence that you know the 'true average' for that city, and that you can account for much of the observed variation on the basis of the independent variables you measured. Even then, if you only sampled one location in a major city, you still will end up with a biased sample because many cities are segregated with respect to age, race, income, and other socioeconomic factors.

How many replicates should one take to see if there is a difference between two populations? This question is not so easily answered; it depends upon what you desire to know, and on the actual differences that exist between two populations. Statisticians have various ways of determining the appropriate answer. The amount of time or money involved in collecting data also is important; for some analyses, a scientist may only be able to obtain a limited number of data points.

Biologists usually determine what major factors affect the objects under study, and then later examine the effects of minor factors. When first examining some phenomenon, we typically do not examine the effects of factors that we think are of little importance to our study question, unless some prior study suggested that such an examination is necessary. Biologists use their knowledge of the published literature and past history of their field to select what variables are important.

Think about the sampling and replicate numbers you obtained in Unit 1. Do you now think your research team used the most effective sampling procedure, as well as an appropriate sample size?

Magnusson and Mourão (2004) in their book *Statistics Without Math* describe a number of important points about statistics. One chapter deals with "how much evidence is enough?" Suppose you had measured the sizes of individual snails in several populations found in streams where predatory crayfish were present, and populations in streams where the crayfish were not present (this hypothetical scenario is based on data in Crowl (1990) and Crowl and Covich (1990)). You observed the snails' sizes when they first start reproducing. The null hypothesis would be that the presence of crayfish (a snail predator) has no impact on the snails' sizes at reproduction, and the alternative hypothesis is that crayfish do affect snail size.

Suppose you had measured one snail in a stream with crayfish, and one snail from a stream without crayfish. The sizes of the two individual snails are shown in Figure 2.1.

How comfortable are you in supporting either hypothesis? Obviously, one data point per treatment is not sufficient. Suppose we had taken the sizes of three snails in each treatment (Figure 2.2). You may only feel a little more comfortable about supporting the alternative hypothesis (the snails appear to be larger in the stream with crayfish; perhaps the snails delay reproduction and grow more rapidly, until they are larger and presumably more invulnerable to the predators). There still is considerable overlap in the two treatments.

Suppose you measured the sizes of 12 snails per stream (see Figure 2.3). In this case, you may feel more comfortable in rejecting the null hypothesis and accepting the alternative hypothesis, just by examining the data. The snails in the stream with crayfish appear to be considerably larger than those in the stream without crayfish, even though there is still overlap in size range.

However, although a replicate size of 12 snails seems to be sufficient, you still do not know if you can adequately answer the question about the impacts of crayfish on snails, depending on how you have worded the question. Your data

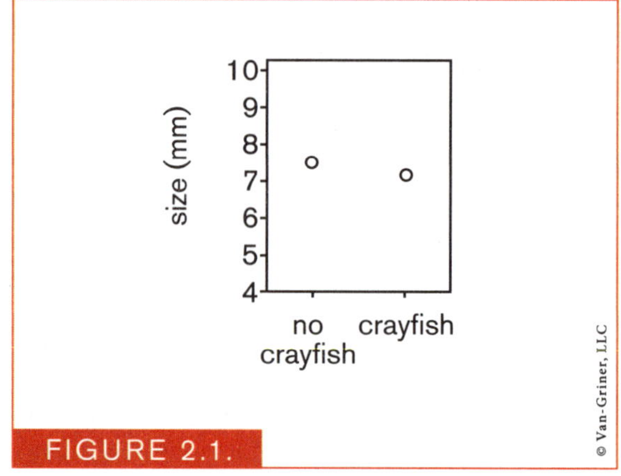

FIGURE 2.1.

Size at first reproduction for two snails: one from a stream with crayfish; one from a stream without crayfish.

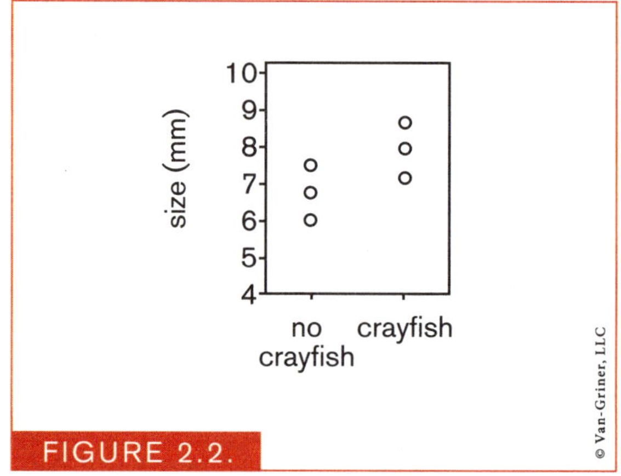

FIGURE 2.2.

Size at reproduction for three snails from each stream.

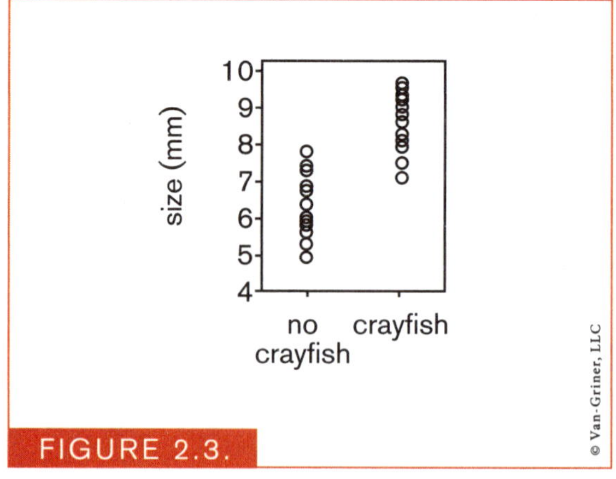

FIGURE 2.3.

Size at reproduction for 12 snails from each stream.

points are all from just two streams. Can you say in a general sense that crayfish affect snail sizes in all streams? What if you went to another set of streams? Instead of the crayfish affecting snail size, the effect could have been due to some unique impact (pollution, temperature or oxygen levels, food quality, other species) instead.

Examine Figure 2.4; it shows that four snails from each of six streams were measured: three streams had crayfish present, and three streams did not. The three 'columns' of points for each stream type represent snails from three different streams. Because the general pattern holds in all three streams of a given treatment, you may feel confident in supporting the alternative hypothesis. The pattern (crayfish affect snail sizes) appears to be consistent among streams. However, compared to the situation in Figure 2.3, your sample size for each stream is fairly low. For increased confidence, you would want to increase the sample size for each stream.

Figure 2.3 and Figure 2.4 point out that the specific design of your experiment, as well as the exact nature of your question and the specific set of hypotheses you are testing, are important factors in determining the numbers of replicates you will need to answer your question adequately. The amount of time and money you have available to conduct the experiment also are important factors.

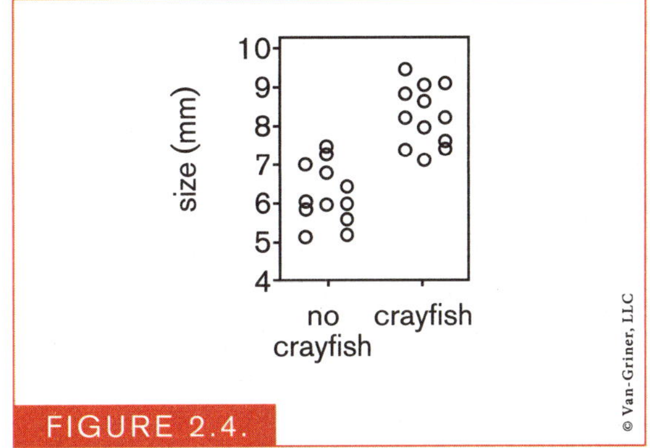

FIGURE 2.4.

Size at reproduction for snails in six streams: three with crayfish, and three without crayfish.

The Metric System

Most of the world uses the metric system, called the **International System of Units** or **SI,** when measuring things. The metric system is used universally by scientists. All persons in science, medicine, and technology therefore should understand the metric system. We will be using these measurements throughout the semester. The base units of SI (meter, gram, liter) are multiplied by factors of 10 and given the special names listed in Table 2.1 below:

TABLE 2.1.

Symbol	Prefix	Value
G	giga-	1,000,000,000 or 10^9
M	mega-	1,000,000 or 10^6
k	kilo-	1,000 or 10^3
h	hecto-	100 or 10^2
da	deca-	10 or 10^1
d	deci-	1/10 or 0.1 or 10^{-1}
c	centi-	1/100 or 0.01 or 10^{-2}
m	milli-	1/1,000 or 0.001 or 10^{-3}
μ	micro-	1/1,000,000 or 0.000001 or 10^{-6}
n	nano-	1/1,000,000,000 or 0.000000001 or 10^{-9}

Length and Area

base unit: one meter (m)

one m = 1,000 millimeters (mm) = 100 centimeters (cm), one kilometer (km) = 1,000 m

Length Conversions

1 mile = 1.609 kilometers (km)	1 kilometer = 0.621 miles
1 yard = 0.9144 meters = 91.4 cm	1 meter = 39.37 inches = 1.094 yards
1 inch = 2.54 centimeters = 25.4 mm	1 cm = 0.394 inches

Mass

Mass is measured by the weight of an object on earth, due to gravity's effect on mass.

base unit: one gram (g)

one gram = 1,000 milligrams (mg) = 10^6 micrograms (µg), one kilogram (kg) = 1,000 g

Weight Conversions

1 pound = 0.454 kilograms = 453.6 grams	1 kg = 2.205 pounds = 35.3 ounces
1 ounce = 28.35 grams	1 g = 0.035 ounce
1 microgram (µg) = 10^{-6} grams = 10^{-3} milligrams	

Volume

base unit: one liter (l or L), 1,000 milliliters (ml) = 1 L

Liquid Volume Conversions

1 gallon = 3.785 L (liquid)	1 L = 0.264 gallons = 1.057 quarts = 33.8 fluid ounces
1 fluid ounce = 29.574 ml	1 ml = 0.0338 fluid ounces

Volume Conversions

1 cubic centimeter (cc or cm³) = 1 ml (for water, 1 ml of water also weighs 1 g)

1 cubic inch = 16.387 cc	1 cc = 0.061 cubic inch
1 cubic yard = 0.765 m³	1 cubic meter (m³) = 1.308 cubic yards
1 cubic foot = 0.028 m³	1 m³ = 35.315 cubic feet

Temperature

There are three units for temperature.

1 degrees Celsius (°C),   **2** degrees Fahrenheit (°F),   **3** kelvin (K).

Degrees Celsius (centigrade) (°C): water freezes at 0°C, boils at 100°C at sea level.

Water freezes at 32°F, boils at 212°F (**degrees Fahrenheit**) at sea level.

°C = 5 / 9(°F − 32)   °F = [(9 / 5)(°C)] + 32

Actually, in SI units, temperature is measured in **kelvins** (K), which is (°C +273.15), but biologists typically use °C.

Energy

base unit: 1 calorie (cal) = energy required to raise 1 g of H_2O 1°C.

1 kilocalorie = 1 kcal = 1,000 cal = 1 Calorie C

Actually, energy in SI units is measured as **joules** (1 J = 0.239 cal), but many biologists typically report energy values in Calories.

Time

seconds (sec), **minutes** (min), and **hours** (h) are used in both SI and English (American) systems.

Scientific Notation (Exponential Notation)

Because science deals with very large and very small numbers, a shorthand method of number notation was developed. This method is called **scientific notation** or **exponential notation.** Scientific notation is a method that makes large and small numbers convenient to use because large or small numbers written in the conventional format are easy to misinterpret and difficult to write out. Scientific notation consists of a decimal number between 1 and 10, multiplied by a power of 10. The exponent is the number of times the coefficient (we usually use the base number of 10) is multiplied by itself.

We can convert the conventional number 454,000 into scientific notation, as shown in the figure to the right. Conventional numbers greater than 1 are converted into scientific notation by placing a decimal point after the first digit, and the number of digits after the decimal point are the exponent (in other words, when you multiply by 10, you move the decimal point one place to the right). Thus, 454,000 becomes 4.54, and there are five digits after the decimal point, so the exponent is 5, thus 4.54×10^5.

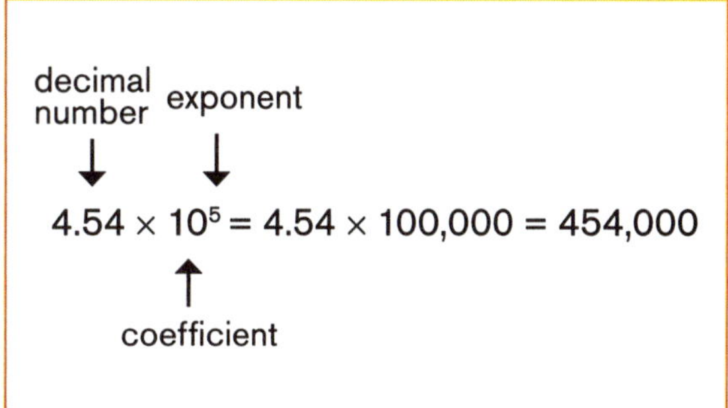

Likewise, 2,345 is 2.345×10^3, $10 = 1 \times 10^1$, 1 is 1×10^0, and 0 is 0.

Conventional numbers that are fractions (greater than 0 but less than 1) are converted into scientific notation by again placing the decimal point to the right of the first digit that is not a zero. The number of places skipped to get to the first nonzero digit is a negative value and is the exponent value (i.e., when you divide by 10 you move the decimal point one place to the left). 0.0021 can be written as 2.1×10^{-3}.

Negative numbers have a minus sign in front of the decimal number: $-24,800,000 = -2.48 \times 10^7$, and $-0.00000000006 = -6.0 \times 10^{-11}$.

Occasionally, you may see a scientific notation number without the decimal number in front: 10^4, for example. The number in this case is implied to be 1.0×10^4 or 10,000.

Rounding Off Numbers

Counts are usually whole numbers. For example, when you count five puppies in a litter, there are exactly five puppies, not 5.5 puppies. Many measurements, however, cannot be known exactly with a high degree of precision; it may be virtually impossible to make an exact measurement. For example, suppose a tick was found to be 6.236 mm (6,236 µm) long, using calipers. In any basic biology lab, you cannot determine the tick's length this precisely, because biologists do not have calipers with that degree of resolution!

Use the following guidelines for determining the number of **significant digits** and for **rounding off** numbers.

Rule 1   **The number of significant digits in a number is the number of digits known with certainty, plus one. In other words, the last digit is assumed to have been measured with some uncertainty.**

The degree of uncertainty in a measurement is reflected in the number of **significant digits** used. As an example, suppose you were measuring the length of a pine needle. The pine needle was between 9 and 10 cm long, and your ruler is calibrated in 1 cm delineations. You observe that the needle is longer than 9 cm, but shorter than 10 cm. When using significant digits, you then must estimate the length to the nearest tenth of the next smaller digit. You estimate that the needle is about 3 mm longer (0.3 cm) than 9 cm, so you would record 9.3 cm. There is a little uncertainty about the last digit (3), but the 'real answer' is nearer to 9.3 cm than it is to either 9 cm or 10 cm. The number 9.3 has two significant digits.

How many significant digits are in the number 20,000? Suppose a friend from another school asked how many students are at your school, and you say, "oh, about 20,000." In reality, there is only one significant digit (the 2). All of the zeroes are not significant because you did not measure them. Let's say there are exactly 21,304 students currently enrolled at the school at 2 pm today. This number (21,304) has five significant digits. By using scientific notation, you can see the precision of the two different estimates of the student population size (2×10^4 versus 2.1304×10^4).

Rule 2   **The last digit reported in any statistical value depends on the precision of your data measurements.**

This rule should make sense to you. If you measured seven bugs to the nearest 0.1 mm (they were 10.2, 8.7, 6.5, 12.6, 13.0, 9.7, and 6.9 mm in length), the mean should not be reported as 9.6571429 mm, but as 9.7 mm. Your calculator may give you the former number, but it is inappropriate to imply to your readers that much precision (to the ten millionth of a mm), when your measurements were to the nearest 0.1 mm.

Rule 3   **When you round off a number, you should round it off by first looking at the precision of the numbers that went into the calculation, and make the precision of the answer match the precision of the least precise measurement.**

First, determine what the last significant digit should be in your answer. Look at the digit to the right of that digit. If it is less than 5, round it and all digits to its right off ("if less than 5, round down"). If the digit to the right of the last reported digit is greater than 5, round it and all digits to its right off and increase the last reported digit by one ("if 5 or more, round up"). (There are more involved rules to rounding numbers, but this one will serve our purposes.)

In our example above, the calculator gave us an answer of 9.6571429 mm. There are two significant digits (the '6' is significant, the '5' to its right is not significant). However, because the '5' is "5 or greater," then the correct answer to write down is '9.7 mm.' If the mean answer instead was 9.6471429, then you would round down to '9.6 mm.'

Rule 4 **In calculations that involve multiplication or division, the answer must have the same number of significant figures as the measurement that has the least number of significant figures.**

For example, suppose you traveled 215 miles in three and a half hours. 215 miles / 3.5 hours = 61.428571 miles/hour, according to most calculators. However, there are only two significant digits to one of the initial measurements, so the answer should be rounded down to 61 mph. If the time was measured as 3.50 hours (3.50×10^0 hours, the zero was measured so there are three significant digits, like the mileage), then the answer could be listed as 61.4 mph.

Rule 5 **In calculations involving addition or subtraction, the results typically have the same number of digits to the right of the decimal point as the term with the least number of digits to the right of the decimal point.**

For example, add up the following numbers: 7.01, 13.5, 22.5, 14.567, and 18.2. You should have determined that the precision of the answer should be in tenths. The sum of the numbers prior to rounding was 75.777, but the sum should be reported as 75.8.

In simple addition and subtraction, you do not worry so much about the number of significant digits, but you look instead at the number of digits to the right of the decimal point. Suppose a scientist measured five insects, using the same instrument. The lengths of the five insects were 7.2 mm, 10.5 mm, 13.2 mm, 14.6 mm and 15.7 mm. The mean, as calculated by your calculator, would be 12.24. You look at the data, and see that the value '7.2' has two significant digits. From Rule 5, you would say that the mean was 12 mm (1.2×10^1). However, the insect 7.2 mm long was measured with the same degree of precision, using the same instrument. The scientist thus had the same **degree of resolution** (presumably his/her measuring tool could reliably measure lengths down to the nearest tenth of a mm) when he/she measured each insect. Therefore, the answer (12 mm) that you would obtain simply from going with the number of significant digits is not as accurate as it could reliably be reported. Under these conditions, it would be correct to report the mean length as 12.2 mm (three significant digits), instead of 12 mm (two digits) or 12.24 mm (four significant digits). With measurements taken from a variety of studies, where you do not know the degree of resolution of all measuring devices used, follow Rule 5.

Conversion Factors and Significant Digits

One point of confusion of significant figures concerns conversion of numbers from one scale of measurement to another (for example, feet to inches). If you were asked to determine the length (in inches) of a piece of wood that is 1.85 feet long (three significant digits) and you know that there are 12 inches to a foot (two significant digits), you may think that the answer should be 22 inches, instead of 22.2 inches. The original measurement (1.85 feet) has three significant digits, but there appears to be only two significant digits to the number of inches in a foot. Thus, it might seem that the answer should contain only two significant figures. We can clear up this confusion by remembering that only measurements involve error or uncertainty. Many unit factors are based on definitions. For example, one foot is defined as exactly 12 inches. **Conversion factors generally are assumed to have an infinite number of significant digits.** The answer therefore should be to three significant figures (22.2 inches).

Likewise, if you wanted to convert the length of a piece of wood that was 1.85 feet long into meters, recall that 1 yard = 0.9144 meters. Your piece of wood is 1.85 feet / 3 feet in a yard = 0.6166666 yards long. Thus, converting from yards to meters: 0.6166666 × 0.9144 = 0.56388 meters long. However, you had three significant digits in your original number, so you would round off the final answer to 0.564 meters.

Rule 6 **All nonzero numbers are significant, but zeroes are only significant if they occur between two nonzero numbers. Zeroes that indicate the position of the decimal point (leading zeroes to the left) are not considered significant. Trailing zeroes are considered significant only if the decimal point is specified; this means that these zeroes were measured with certainty.**

The following table (Table 2.2) gives several examples showing the importance of significant digits. In the fourth and fifth examples (300.0 and 0300.0), the zeroes to the right of the decimal point were measured exactly. We assume when using scientific notation, any zero to the right of the decimal point was measured with some certainty.

TABLE 2.2. Examples of significant digits.

Number	Significant Digits	Scientific Notation
00300	1	3×10^2
300	1	3×10^2
300.	3	3.00×10^2
300.0	4	3.000×10^2
0300.0	4	3.000×10^2
0.00682	3	6.82×10^{-3}
1.072	4	1.072×10^0
0.172	3	1.72×10^{-1}

The Importance of Scientific Notation

How many significant digits are there to this number?   54,000

If the three zeroes are known precisely (they were measured), then there are five significant digits (5.4000×10^4). If the zeroes are used only to indicate where the decimal point is, then there are only two significant digits (5.4×10^4). Note the importance of using scientific notation in this last example. Scientific notation helps to determine the number of significant figures to the measurement. If the scientist had measured 54,000 exactly, then the number in scientific notation would be reported as 5.4000×10^4.

Guidelines When Using Calculators

Rule 7　　When using a calculator, in a long calculation involving mixed operations on numbers with different significant digits, carry as many digits as possible through the entire set of calculations, and then round the final result appropriately.

> For example,
>
> $$(5.00 / 1.235) + 3.000 + (6.35 / 4.0) = 4.0485829959514170040485829959514... + 3.000 + 1.5875 = 8.6360829959514170040485829959514...$$

The first division should result in three significant digits; the value 3.000 has four significant digits, and the last division should result in two significant digits; the three numbers added together should result in a number that is rounded off to the last common significant digit occurring farthest to the right (which in this case means the final result should be rounded with one digit after the decimal point). The correct rounded final result should be 8.6 because of the more limited accuracy in the last division step. The calculator used for this example gave 32 significant digits, but in the final answer, only two significant digits should be used.

Rule 8　　When you are performing any statistical test, use the maximum number of digits in all intermediate steps, and only round off the final result.

Carrying all digits through to the final result is critical for many mathematical operations in statistics. Rounding off intermediate results can seriously compromise the accuracy of the statistical test.

Descriptive Statistics

Some measurable feature of a population, such as the population's mean size or the standard deviation of the size, is called a **parameter** of the population. These population parameters are the things we want to know in order to draw conclusions about the population. However, because we rarely know the entire population, we have to rely on one or more **samples** to estimate the parameters. An estimate of the population parameter is called a **statistic,** which we obtain from analyzing a sample.

As scientists, we try to collect data in a useful fashion. We try to make sense of the data by summarizing it into a simpler, more compact form. There are two main types of statistics: **descriptive statistics** and **inferential statistics.** We will study the descriptive statistics first. Inferential statistics are useful for hypothesis testing, and we will describe and use several types of inferential statistics later.

Descriptive statistics describe and summarize the data. Descriptive statistics can be further subdivided into two main types: **statistics of central tendencies** and **statistics of dispersion.**

Statistics of Central Tendencies

(A) There are three basic statistics of central tendencies useful to biologists: the mean (the arithmetic average), the median (the middle value of a series of values), and the mode (the most frequently occurring value of a series of values).

(1) Mean. The arithmetic mean is the arithmetic average of the data points. There are several types of means: the one typically used is the **arithmetic mean.** The mean is the sum of all of the observations, divided by the number of samples (the sample size). The mean $(\overline{X})$ is the arithmetic average of the individual measurements (Equation 2.1):

$$\textbf{Equation 2.1.} \quad \overline{X} = \left(\sum X_i\right) / N$$

where $\sum X$ is the sum of all measurements (X_i) and N is the number of specimens measured (the sample size).

Suppose you wanted to know the average length of a sample of skinks (a skink is a species of lizard), and measured the lengths of seven animals $(N = 7)$ of the population. There are seven X_i values for this sample: $X_1, X_2, X_3, X_4, X_5, X_6$, and X_7, with the length of the first skink represented by X_1, the second by X_2, and so on. Suppose we had seven skinks with the following lengths: 10, 12, 8, 13, 13, 7, and 6 cm. The mean length is 9.9 cm. However, note that in the example above, no skink was 9.9 cm long. The mean does not to have to be represented by an actual value in the sample. Suppose the following data are the number of children in the ten families living on your street: (0, 0, 2, 3, 4, 5, 1, 2, 2, 7). The average number of children is 2.6 children. Have you ever seen six-tenths of a child walking around?

Note: Following the rules of significant digits, you may think that the correct answer should be the integer '3.' However, you could hypothetically measure with some accuracy a 'tenth' of a child walking around, so the answer 2.6 is more precise.

(2) Median. When all of the observations are listed in order from smallest to largest, the median is the middle value with 50% of the observations higher in value, and 50% are lower in value. For an odd number of observations, the median is the middle value of the ranked observations. For example, the median value of the lengths of seven skinks (10, 12, 8, 13, 13, 7, 6 cm) is 10 cm.

If there is an even number of observations, the median is the midpoint between the two observations closest to the middle. The median of the following set of six skink measurements (4, 5, 6, 8, 9 and 4) is 5.5.

The median is less sensitive to extreme scores than the mean. This fact makes the median a better measure than the mean for highly skewed distributions. The median income is usually more informative than the mean income, for example. The following example describing the importance of mean, median, and mode is based on one by Huff (1954, see Figure 2.5). Suppose you were interviewing for a job at a company that had eleven employees: five employees made $10,000, one employee made $20,000, one employee made $30,000, one employee made $50,000, one employee (the boss' son) made $150,000, one employee (the boss' brother) made $300,000, and the boss made $500,000 (you know what each person makes as a salary). See Figure 2.5 below. The boss tells you that the average salary for the company is $100,000, but he will pay you the median salary. What is the median salary? How likely are you to take the job?

When should a median score be reported over a mean score? If you have a population that is highly skewed, you should report the median score (or report both mean and median). If the two measures are different, this tells the reader that the distribution of the data is highly skewed, one way or the other, and the median is more informative.

3 **Mode. The mode is the most frequently observed value in the observations.** The mode of the following set of observations (1, 2, 3, 4, 4, 4, 4, 5, 6, 10) is 4. The median value is also 4 in this case, and the mean is 4.3).

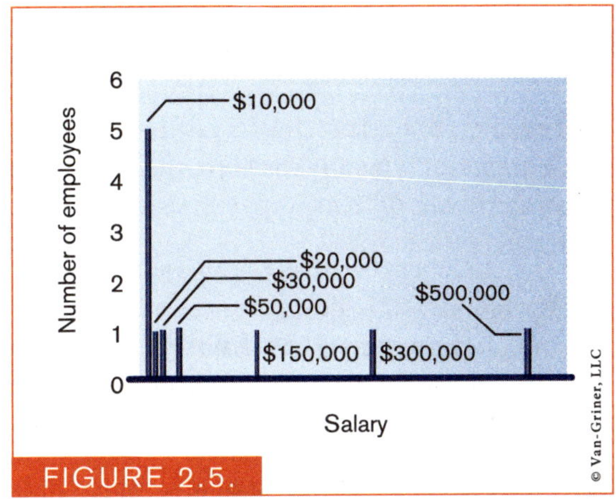

FIGURE 2.5.

Salary distribution of a hypothetical company.

There can be multiple modes to a data set. For example, in the following list of 15 numbers: 2, 2, 3, 3, 3, 3, 4, 7, 8, 8, 8, 8, 9, 9, and 10, there are two modes: 3 and 8.

For nominal data (which we will discuss later in the semester), a mode can be determined, but a mean and a median cannot be determined from the data. For example, in the local phone directory, there may be more people named 'Smith' than any other name; thus 'Smith' is the mode. It does not make sense to talk about a mean or median 'name.'

A mean and a median score can always be calculated for a sample, but there may not be a mode. For example, in the following list of 15 numbers (2, 3, 5, 6, 7, 8, 9, 11, 13, 14, 17, 20, 22, 24, 30), there is no distinct mode (although there is a median [11] and mean [12.7]).

In our hypothetical company salary question above, suppose the boss told you that you would be paid the modal salary. Now how likely are you to take the job? What is the modal salary?

The three measures of central tendencies have different uses, and are influenced by extreme scores in dramatically different ways. The mean can be influenced by extreme values, whereas the median and mode are not. For example, take the mean of the following numbers: 5, 6, 7, 7, 7, 8, 300. The mean for this sample is 48.6, the mode is 7, and the median score is 7. The mode and median scores do not change if we replaced the '300' observation with one of value '8,' but the mean drops to 6.9.

Statistics of Dispersion

There are three basic statistics of dispersion: range, variance, and standard deviation of the mean. These statistics typically measure the amount of variability (the amount of deviation of the samples) about the mean of the sample. There are other measures of the dispersion of samples; we will concentrate on these three.

1 **Range.** If you have a large sample of observations (the **sample size** is the number of observations), **the range is the difference between the smallest and largest value.** The range is more affected by outliers and by sample size, compared to other measures of dispersion. In general, a larger sample typically has a greater range.

2 **Variance. The variance of a sample (s^2) is the average squared deviation from the mean of all of the measurement observations.** It is equal to the sum of the squares of the deviations of each sample (X_i) from the average ($\overline{X}$), divided by sample size (N) minus 1 (the '$N-1$' statistic is called the 'unbiased estimate of the population variance'):

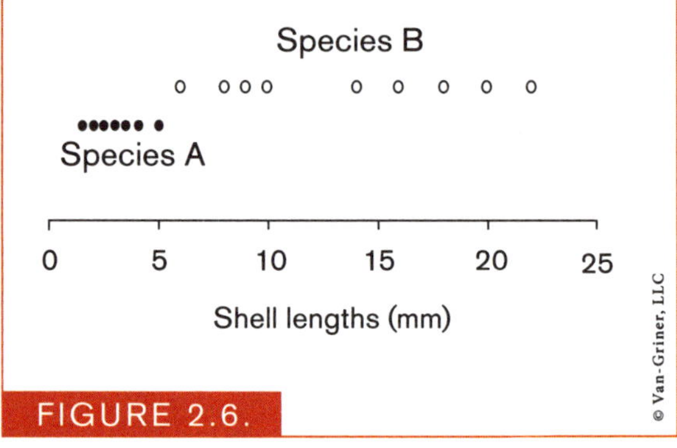

FIGURE 2.6.

Samples with high and low variance.

$$\textbf{Equation 2.2.} \quad s^2 = \frac{\Sigma\,(X_i - \overline{X})^2}{(N-1)}$$

If you calculate a high variance, this means that the observation measurements are spread out widely around the mean. Look at Figure 2.6. One sample (species B) has a high variance, the other sample (A) does not.

3 **Standard Deviation. The standard deviation (s or S.D.) is the square root of the variance** (s^2, Equation 2.3). One nice feature that a standard deviation has is that it is expressed in the same units as that of the mean (if you measured the shell lengths in millimeters [mm], then the standard deviation would be in mm). If the observations were measurements in meters, the mean and standard deviation would have units of meters.

$$\textbf{Equation 2.3.} \quad s = \sqrt{s^2}$$

Almost all calculators these days can provide means and standard deviations. You need to learn how to generate sample means and standard deviations, using your calculator. Most calculators have a button for the mean (usually marked by the "$\overline{X}$" symbol) and one or more buttons for standard deviations (usually marked by the "σ" or "s" symbol). For the sample standard deviation, use the button marked "σ_{n-1}," instead of the button marked "σ_n," which calculates the population standard deviation.

These statistics of dispersion are also dramatically affected by extreme scores. Recall our previous data sets of 7 numbers: sample A and sample B. See if you can obtain the same results that are shown in Table 2.3.

TABLE 2.3. Summary statistics of two hypothetical populations.

	Sample A	Sample B
observations	5, 6, 7, 7, 7, 8, 300	5, 6, 7, 7, 7, 10, 15
sample size (N)	7	7
mean	48.6	8.1
median	7	7
mode	7	7
range	5 to 300	5 to 15
variance (s^2)	12,293	11.5
standard deviation (s)	111	3.4

Observe the differences in the summary statistics in Table 2.3. You have probably noted that Sample A has a data point (300) that is far above the mean value; in fact, it is far above all of the other values. This data point is called an **outlier.** Outliers can have dramatic effects on statistical summaries of data, and methods exist to determine if outliers can and should be removed.

Examine the data points for the two samples in Table 2.3, and then examine the differences between the summary statistics for the two samples in Table 2.3. Which descriptive statistics are strongly influenced by outliers?

Exercises

Exercise 2.1.

a The dimensions of this page are _________ × _________ meters, or _________ × _________ mm.

b A 16 oz can is _________ ml, or _________ liters.

c Weight of a 220 lb football player: _________ g, or _________ kg.

d Length of a football field (100. yards): _________ meters.

e Weight of 10. grams of water: _________ ounces.

f The length of a 1 m long stick: _________ yards.

g 500 sec in standard time is _________ sec in metric.

h 10. ml of water was heated from 20 to 40°C. How many calories (cal) were needed? _________ cal.

i The volume of a butter cube 10 mm × 1 cm × 0.01 m? _________ cc.

j 55.6°C = _________ °F.

k 98.6°F (normal human body temperature) = _________ °C.

l Which is a greater temperature change: 5°F or 5°C? _________

m Which is greater: 22 meters or 25 yards? _________

n Which is faster: 50 kph (kilometers per hour) or 40 mph (miles per hour)? _________

Write the following numbers in scientific notation:

a 10,000 _____________

b 520. _____________

c 0 _____________

d 1 _____________

e 1 trillion _____________

f −84.21 _____________

g 54,321 _____________

h 0.00102 _____________

i −0.0000908 _____________

j human population now on Earth: 7.246 billion _____________

Write the following numbers in conventional form:

a 1.0×10^3 _____________

b 6.8×10^{-4} _____________

c -5.79×10^{-11} _____________

d 10^3 _____________

e 1×10^0 _____________

f 2.111×10^4 _____________

g -9.456×10^3 _____________

h 1.2×10^0 _____________

i -56×10^{-1} _____________

j 6.1×10^6 _____________

Rounding

a If you were measuring the length of a house, and you used a long stick that was marked off in one-tenths of a meter (10 centimeters), you could estimate the length of the house by what level of precision? ____

b You have the lengths of four ants, which were measured in different studies. The lengths were: 10.65 mm, 22.0 mm, 17.346 mm, and 2.6789 mm. The average length for the four ants would be reported as: ____

c Round 90.43679 to the first decimal place (tenths) ____

d Round 90.43679 to the second decimal place (hundredths) ____

Exercise 2.2.

Your lab instructor will have two sets of objects (shells, bones, etc.) for you to sample and measure. Collect 15 specimens from the first set of objects. Measure the length of these 15 specimens to the nearest tenth of a millimeter, using the vernier calipers provided. Your lab instructor will show each table how to read the calipers. Record your data in Table 2.4.

TABLE 2.4. Lengths of 15 specimens of set 1

Object or species name: ____

Specimen	Length (mm)	Specimen	Length (mm)	Specimen	Length (mm)
1		6		11	
2		7		12	
3		8		13	
4		9		14	
5		10		15	

In addition, collect 15 specimens of a second set of objects. Measure the length of these 15 specimens to the nearest tenth of a millimeter, using the vernier calipers provided. Put the data of this second species in Table 2.5.

TABLE 2.5. Lengths of 15 specimens of set 2

Object or species name: ____

Specimen	Length (mm)	Specimen	Length (mm)	Specimen	Length (mm)
1		6		11	
2		7		12	
3		8		13	
4		9		14	
5		10		15	

Determine the range, the standard deviation, and the variance of your sample of lengths.

TABLE 2.6. Comparison of sample and population statistics.

	N	Mean (mm)	Median	Mode	Range	Standard Deviation	Variance
Set/Species 1 your sample							
Set/Species 1 the entire population							
Set/Species 2 your sample							
Set/Species 2 the entire population							

Your lab instructor has the 'true' or grand mean for both populations, as well as the medians, modes, ranges, standard deviations, and variances. These statistics represent the population parameters. Add these values to Table 2.6. How do your sample results compare with that of the entire population?

For each set/species, how do the median and mean scores compare?

Is your estimate of the sample mean similar to the population mean?

How does your sample estimate agree with those of the other students?

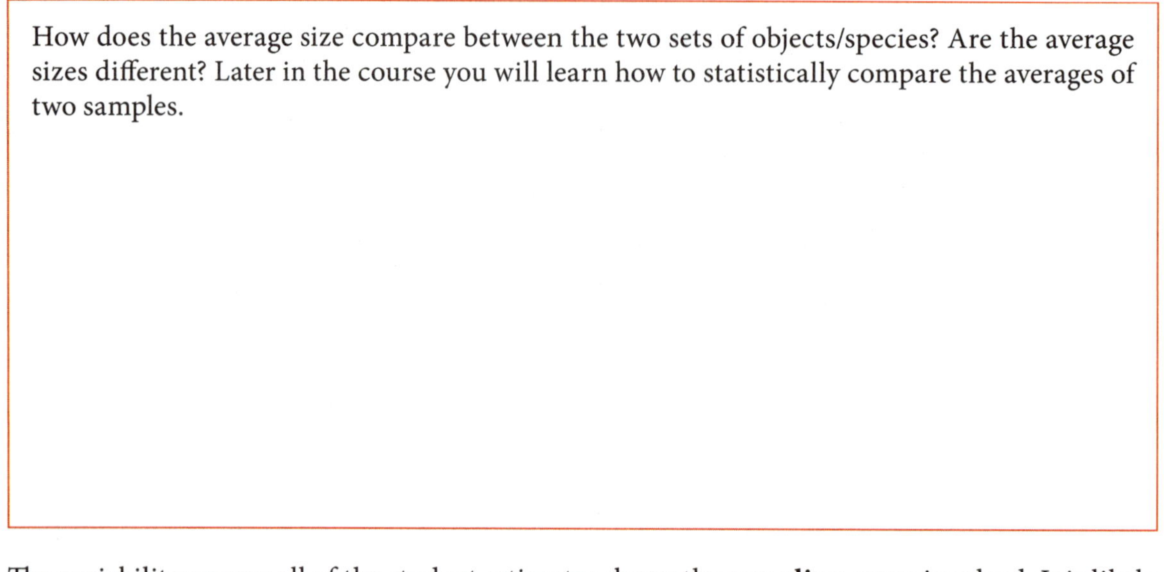

How does the average size compare between the two sets of objects/species? Are the average sizes different? Later in the course you will learn how to statistically compare the averages of two samples.

The variability among all of the student estimates shows the **sampling error** involved. It is likely that all student estimates do not agree very well for several reasons, some of which should be obvious to you. All of you are attempting to make a generalization about the large collection of objects; however, each of you is making this generalization using only 15 specimens. Your individual sample size is small. Secondly, due to chance, some or all of you may not have a representative sample of the objects. For example, perhaps you picked up 15 small specimens, which skewed your sample's estimate of the mean to lie far below the actual population mean.

Did you see any effect of sampling error in your specific sample? How can you minimize the effect of sampling error?

Exercise 2.3.

Compare Figure 2.3 and Figure 2.4. Which sampling procedure is better, in your opinion? Why? Can both be valid samples?

Examine Figures 2.1 through 2.4 in light of your sampling procedure from the exercise in Unit 1. Did you collect data from just one mountain or from all three mountains? Could you have done a better job? If you could repeat the sampling procedure, would you have changed how you sampled? Why or why not?

Biological Data and Inferential Statistics

UNIT **3**

Keywords

quantitative variable	ratio-scale data	correlation
qualitative variable	parametric	slope
discrete variable	nonparametric	intercept
continuous variable	median	correlation coefficient (r)
nominal-scale (categorical) data	normal distribution	square of the correlation coefficient (r^2)
ordinal-scale data	probability (p) value	type I and type II errors
interval-scale data	degrees of freedom	outlier
	regression	

Learning Objectives

When finished with this unit, you should be able to:

1. Distinguish between qualitative and quantitative data;

2. Distinguish between discrete and continuous data;

3. Identify to which measurement scale a given set of data belongs (ratio-scale, interval-scale, ordinal-scale, or nominal-scale). Know the key characteristics for each type of measurement scale data;

4. Distinguish between type I and type II errors in hypothesis testing;

5. Statistically analyze experimental results using a t-test. Be able to determine the number of degrees of freedom, and be able to use a statistical table listing critical test values (like Tables 3.1, 3.2, and 3.3)

6. Statistically analyze experimental results using a chi-square analysis; and

7. Statistically analyze experimental results using a regression or a correlation analysis. Know the three assumptions implied when using a regression. Know how to interpret r and r^2 values and how to distinguish between direct versus inverse relationships between variables.

Quantitative Variables versus Qualitative Variables

Observations can be **quantitative** or **qualitative** in nature. When you were younger, you probably lumped objects into discrete classes. As an example, objects were either bigger than you or smaller than you. 'Big' and 'small' are **qualitative** descriptions. As a child, you may have noticed that grass is green (the greenness is a qualitative character; you can distinguish green from blue and red and yellow).

However, as you got older, you may have noticed that grass is not always green (it is brownish in the winter) and even when it is green, it may have different 'shades' of green. When you make quantitative measurements on grass, you are measuring the 'greenness' or the degree of greenness of the grass. Grasses that have had fertilizer recently applied to the soil appear 'greener' than adjacent plots of grass, as shown both by your eye and by using scientific instruments to measure the greenness (which in turn is related to the relative amount of chlorophyll present in the grasses' leaves and/or the presence of other pigmented compounds).

A **quantitative variable** is one in which the data may differ in **magnitude** (for example, a mouse 10 cm in length is 2 cm longer than a mouse 8 cm in length). With quantitative data, you can rank the data on some measurement scale, and determine how far apart on the scale each data point is from each other. Size, age, height, speed—all of these variables can be quantified in some fashion. As a scientist, you usually will make quantitative measurements of biologically important phenomena.

In contrast, a **qualitative variable** is one in which the data differ in **kind** rather than in magnitude. There is no measurement scale on which to rank the data in any meaningful way. Examples of qualitative data include colors (green, blue, red) or gender (male or female).

Continuous Variables versus Discrete Variables

Continuous variables. Continuous variables are those where a measurement could be of any conceivable value along a continuum. One common example of a continuous variable is length. Let's say you have a number of snail shells in front of you. You pick up one shell and measure it with a meter stick (one that had millimeter gradations), and you estimated that it is 12 mm long. Using a more precise pair of vernier calipers, you estimate that the shell is 12.04 mm long. You pick up a second shell that appears to be 12 mm in length when you used the meter stick, but when you use the calipers, you found that the second shell is slightly longer than the first; the second shell is 12.06 mm long. Suppose you had even finer calipers, perhaps you could measure the lengths to 0.001 mm. Extending this example further, you find that there are an infinite number of measurements that could be made between 12 and 13 mm, and thus shell length is a continuous variable.

Discrete variables. A discrete variable is one with a countable number of numerical values, categories or codes. The number of leaves on a plant, the number of red blood cells in a mm^3 of blood, the number of children in a family—all these things are discrete (integer) measurements. You cannot find any family in your neighborhood with exactly 2.4 children (although the average number of children in the families that live in your neighborhood could be 2.4 children per family: for example, suppose there are 24 children and 10 families on your street). What is 4/10th of a person? Likewise, there are two categories for pregnancy: pregnant versus nonpregnant. You cannot be 'a little pregnant!' You are either pregnant, or you are not pregnant.

Objects that can be counted as integers (whole numbers) are discrete objects. The possible values of discrete variables generally are the consecutive integers (1, 2, 3, 4, 5, …), but not necessarily. For example, arthropods typically have three, four, five, six, or more **pairs** of legs, so only the even integers are possible values (2, 4, 6, 8, …). An insect could have five legs, but it has lost a leg (as a result of an accident or from a predator attack). In addition, an insect could have a part of a leg (the rest of that leg has been lost); however, would it make sense to refer to an insect as having 5.6 legs?

Ratio-scale, interval-scale, and ordinal-scale data can be either continuous or discrete, but nominal-scale data are only discrete in nature (see below).

Four Basic Types of Biological Data

In order to do statistical analysis, one has to collect data. Different types of statistical analyses require different classifications of data. Data are the observations that you have made on some phenomenon, collected into a set. You have to identify what type of data you have collected before you can begin to do any of the math (statistics) to describe and compare the data. There are four basic kinds or types of data collected in the biological sciences; these four types differ in their characteristics. All four types can be graphed and analyzed, but the methods by which one graphs and analyzes each can be different.

1 **Nominal (= Categorical) Data**

A The key characteristics of nominal-scale data are as follows:

1 Nominal data are qualitative, discrete variables. Using the nominal scale, objects (data) are named or categorized by some attribute they have rather than by any quantitative, numerical measurement. The value of the data points are typically names ('green,' 'blue,' 'male,' 'female').

2 Nominal data can be measured only in terms of whether the individual items belong to certain distinct, nonoverlapping categories (nominal data thus are sometimes called categorical data), but the categories cannot be quantified. Nominal data can be assigned numbers for purposes of graphing; however, the assignment of numbers to categories is totally arbitrary (for example, blue eyes = 1, green eyes = 2, brown eyes = 3). One way to think of a nominal scale is that it is a classification system.

3 A nominal/categorical scale establishes no explicit ordering on the category labels. For example one could list eye color data as: brown/blue/green, or as: green/brown/blue. There may be a temporal sequence to the categories, for example, the larval stage of insects follows the egg stage, but ordering is not required.

4 Because of lack of order and the lack of equal intervals on any measurement scale, one cannot perform arithmetical operations ($+$, $-$, $/$, $\times$) or logical operations ($>$, $<$, $=$) on nominal data. In addition, you cannot apply many types of statistical operations to nominal data, as you can to other three types of data (ordinal, interval, and ratio data).

5 With nominal data, you cannot compute averages, because nominal data lack order (ranking) and equal measurements on some measurement scale. Even if you assign numbers to eye color, as described above, taking a mean of the eye colors for a population does not make sense. One could generate percentages of nominal data; one could state that 40% of a population are brown-eyed and 60% are green-eyed, but you could not say the population, on average, has greenish-brown eyes.

B Examples of nominal-scale data include:

1 sex ('male' or 'female');

2 genotypes ('AA,' 'Aa,' or 'aa');

3 taxonomic categories (genus *'Felis'* [cats] or genus *'Canis'* [dogs], including names of species or individuals);

4 colors ('green,' 'brown,' or 'blue' eyes);

5 life cycle stage ('egg,' 'larva,' 'pupa,' 'adult'); and

6 passing or failing a course (you may have a total number of points you received in a class [ratio-scale], but if you took the course pass/fail, you either 'passed' or 'failed' [nominal scale]).

2 Ordinal Data

A The key characteristics of ordinal-scale data are as follows:

1 Ordinal data are quantitative variables that are often discrete, but they can be continuous.

2 Unlike nominal data, ordinal data are ordered (can be ranked in order of small to big, slow to fast, low to high, and so on). Data consisting of a ranking or ordering of the measurements are on the ordinal scale.

3 The objects or attributes of the objects are ordered but the distances between the points of the measurement scale are not equal. For example, wind speed could be listed as high, medium, or low, but we would not say that the difference between high and medium wind speed is equal to the difference between a medium and low wind speed. As another example, many restaurants serve small, medium, and large drinks. In different restaurants, these may contain very different amounts. There may not be an equal difference in size among the three. For example, they may be 10, 12, and 20 ounce drinks at one place, but another restaurant has the three sizes as 16, 20, and 24 ounces. The distances between points on an ordinal scale are not meaningful. Compare this with a nominal scale in which values cannot be ranked relative to each other (red, green, blue), and interval scales and ratio scales in which values can be ranked and in which the distances between points are meaningful.

4 The lack of equal distances between successive points on an ordinal scale makes many arithmetic operations impossible with ordinal data (how do you multiply 'fast' with something). However, unlike nominal data, you can perform logical operations on ordinal data. You can say something is 'smaller than' or 'greater than' something else. In other words, there is a directionality to the ordinal scale: you can state if one data point value is less than or greater than another data point value.

B Examples of ordinal-scale data include:

1 rankings: preferences, or degrees of satisfaction with a product or service (student evaluations), class grades ('A', 'B', 'C', 'D', 'F'), or the finish in a race (1st, 2nd, 3rd place finish);

2 relative locations: shallow, middle, and deep water;

3 relative sizes: large, medium, and small colonies would be ordinal scale (note that the absolute sizes of the colonies would be ratio scale but the information has been lost when creating the rankings of colony size), river/stream order (first-order stream, second-order stream, etc.), and the rankings given to tornadoes (the Fujita Tornado Scale, ranging from F0 to F5) and hurricanes (the Saffir-Simpson Hurricane Scale, ranging from category 1 to 5) as a consequence of their wind speeds; and

4 relative rates: fast or slow animals, fast/slow chemical reactions, and so on.

3 Interval Data

A The key characteristics of interval-scale data are as follows:

1 Interval data are ordered, quantitative data, and they may be either continuous or discrete.

2 Like ordinal data, there is a directionality to interval data (small to large, slow to fast).

3 Interval data can have negative or positive values.

4 There is a constant interval or distance between any two units on the ratio scale, which is an important distinction between ordinal and interval data. The 1°C increments are identical between each degree. In measuring lengths in cm, the 1 cm increments are identical in length between any two adjacent units. It is meaningful to say that a temperature increase of 5°C is similar, whether or not the initial temperature was 20°C or 4°C.

5 Unlike the ratio-scale data described below, however, there is no physically meaningful zero point. For example, temperature data (measured in °C or °F) are interval-scale data. There is a zero point, but it is not physically meaningful. A temperature of 0°C is not the coldest it can get. The Fahrenheit temperature scale is not ratio-scale, because a temperature of 0°F does not indicate an absence of temperature. A temperature of 20°C is not twice as warm as 10°C; thus it does not make sense to say that a temperature of 20°C is twice as warm as a temperature of 10°C; you cannot make ratios out of these data. (However, temperature measurements in K are ratio-scale; 0K is a physically meaningful point [compared to 0°C], and 100K may be considered twice as warm as 50K).

6 With interval data, one can perform both logical and arithmetic operations $(+, -, /, \times)$. For instance, if a compass direction is 270° (due west), adding 15° would cause the direction to be 285° (slightly north of west). Subtracting 15° would cause the direction to be slightly south of west (255°).

B Examples of interval-scale data include:

1 Temperature (in degrees Celsius and degrees Fahrenheit, but not Kelvin);

2 Compass directions (for example, the direction birds fly when released from a given point, from 0° to 360°) are interval-scale data. True North (0°) is an arbitrary zero point; due south, east, or west could as easily been considered to be the zero point; and

3 Measurements of time, including the time of day (from 0:00 to 24:00). Midnight (0:00 or 24:00) is an arbitrary-defined zero point, compared to noon (12:00) or 3 pm (15:00); we could set any time of the day as zero. Time of day and compass directions are also considered circular data, and are analyzed by specific statistical analyses. Dates and years also are interval data (March 21, 2000, for example).

4 Ratio Data

Many observations in biology produce ratio-scale data. For example, suppose you have measured the individual heights of plants in an experiment. You are looking at two plants. One plant was 20 cm high, and another plant was 16 cm high. These height measurements are ratio-scale data. At the same time, you measured the number of leaves and flowers produced by each plant; the number of leaves and flowers are also ratio-scale data.

A The key characteristics of ratio-scale data are as follows:

1 Ratio data are ordered, quantitative data, and they can be continuous or discrete.

2 There is a constant interval size between any two units on the ratio scale. For example, the difference in the height between a 16 cm high plant and 20 cm high plant is the same as the difference between a 25 cm high plant and 29 cm high plant. The difference between a plant with 10 leaves and a plant with 13 leaves (a three leaf difference) is the same as the difference in the number of leaves between a plant with 100 leaves and a plant with 103 leaves.

3 There is a zero point on the ratio scale, and this zero is meaningful in a physical way. The ratio scale incorporates all of the characteristics of the interval scale with one important addition: there is an absolute zero or 'natural zero point.' Because of the absolute zero point, with ratio scale data, you can say absolutely nothing exists.

4 Because ratio scale data use an absolute zero point, you can make statements involving ratios of two observations, such as "object A is twice as fast as object B" or "object C is half as long as object D." As an example, you measured the running speeds of two species of mice: species X and species Y. Species X can run at a maximum speed of 7.5 miles per hour, and species Y can move at 15 mph. You can state that "species Y is twice as fast as species X." In our plant example above, the 20 cm plant is 25% taller than the 16 cm high plant.

5 You can perform both arithmetic and logical operations with ratio-scale data. If you multiply the height of something by 2, the object is now twice as tall, and is larger than it was earlier. Some ratio-scale data can take on negative or positive values (for example, acceleration of objects is on a ratio scale—you can have deceleration [negative] or acceleration [positive]).

B Examples of ratio-scale data include:

1 The number of things (pups in the litter, population sizes, the number of leaves on a plant);

2 Physical, numerical measurements of objects (population sizes, lengths, weights, volumes of lungs or volumes of lakes, the number of mitochondria in cells, the sizes of cell nuclei);

3 The length of elapsed time for a phenomenon to occur (measured in minutes, hours); and

4 Rates (population growth rates, chemical reaction rates, velocity or speed of locomotion, changes in speed, and so on).

Hypothesis Testing

As we test hypotheses, we have to have some set of rules on when we will accept or reject hypotheses that is based on probability of obtaining results purely by chance. For example, the probability of flipping a fair coin and getting heads is 0.5. The probability of flipping a coin and getting five heads in a row is $(0.5)^5$ or 0.03125, or about 3 times out of 100.

Statistics is based on the probability of obtaining certain values if the null hypothesis is correct (there is no effect of the independent variable used in an experiment, or the observed differences between groups are due to chance events). If you simultaneously flip five coins, and all five were 'fair' coins, all five coins would land heads up only about 3 times out of 100 tries. This also means that about 97 times out of 100, you would **not** get five heads. If you flipped 10 coins, and got 10 heads, there is a very small probability of getting this result (0.0009765625, or about 1 in a 1,000). Alternatively, the probability of getting any other combination (other than 10 heads) when you flip 10 coins is about 999 times out of a 1,000. If all 10 coins come up heads, this does not necessarily mean that the coins are unfair, but it does mean that the probability of getting such as result by chance alone is very small.

In the scientific literature, you will see something referred to as the **probability value** (or **p-value**) of a given statistic. The p-value is a measure of the likelihood of the **deviation** of some observed results from the value that was expected if the null hypothesis was true. A very small p-value suggests that the alternative hypothesis (in this case, the coins are not fair) is probably true.

There are two types of inferential statistics that are used in hypothesis testing. These are called **parametric** and **nonparametric** statistics. The two types of statistics have different assumptions about the data they analyze. In the lab, we will conduct several parametric tests, the t-test, regression (and correlation), and the chi-square (symbolized as χ^2) test.

Two important assumptions for parametric analyses are: 1) the data were randomly and independently sampled from the population, and 2) the data were sampled from a specified distribution. The **normal distribution** is the one distribution often assumed for parametric tests, but there are other specific distributions that are possible. Normally-distributed data, if plotted on a graph, generally form what is called a **normal curve.** A normal curve is depicted in Figure 3.1. The data form a symmetrical bell-shaped curve, with 50% of the values below the mean, and 50% of the values above the mean (the median and mode are assumed to equal the mean in a normal distribution). In addition, about 68.3% of the data points are within one standard deviation (S.D. or s) of the mean, about 95.5% of the data is within 2 S.D. of the mean, and 99.7% of the data are within 3 S.D. of the mean (Figure 3.1).

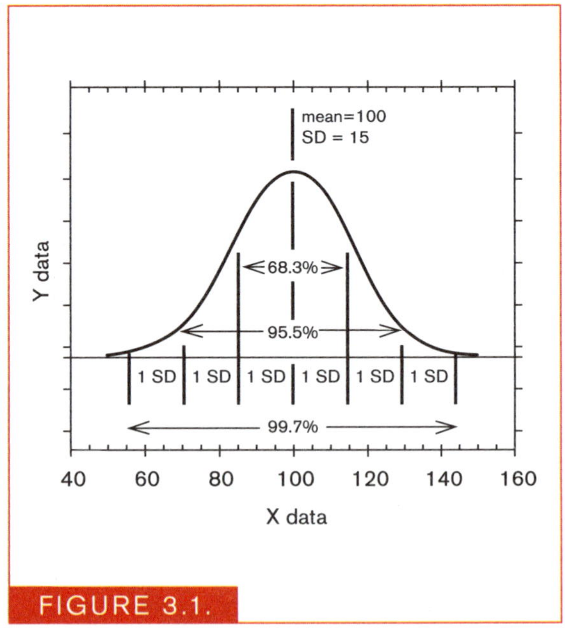

FIGURE 3.1.

The normal distribution.

As long as the underlying population distribution is normal (or at least approximates the normal distribution), parametric tests can be used, even if the sample is only approximately normal. However, the underlying population distribution may not be normally distributed. In these cases, nonparametric tests should be used, which do not assume that the data have a normal distribution (nonparametric tests also can be used on data that are normally distributed).

In the sciences, we use hypothesis testing to decide one of two options:

❶ Accept the null hypothesis (which usually is stated as "no difference between treatments"), or

❷ Accept the alternative hypothesis ("there is a significant difference between treatments").

Statistical tests provide a probability value (p), as discussed above. For each statistical test, there is a table of critical values (**alpha values, α,** which range from 0 to 1) for obtaining a particular statistic value due to chance. Your calculated probability value will lie between two alpha levels.

For most biologists, we generally use the **alpha value of 0.05** as a cutoff point for deciding if we accept the null hypothesis. If your p-value of the calculated test statistic is equal to 0.05, then this means that the observed or greater difference between treatments would occur by chance once out of twenty times. If a biologist obtains such as result, he or she rejects the null hypothesis and **tentatively accepts** the alternative hypothesis. If the p-value was $p = 0.75$, you would see the observed (or greater) difference 75 percent of the time if the difference is due to chance. Likewise, if the p-value is 0.01, this means that we would see that the observed (or greater) difference due to chance only once out of 100 times. In other words, as the p-value becomes smaller, the probability of seeing the observed difference between treatments due to random or chance factors becomes smaller.

If you have a p-value of 0.05, and you reject the null hypothesis, you are making a 'bet,' in a sense. Under these conditions, nineteen times out of twenty you would reject the null hypothesis, when the null hypothesis indeed is false, and only one time out of twenty would you be rejecting the null hypothesis when in fact the null hypothesis is true (you would commit a type I error, see below). Biologists generally view an alpha value of 0.05 as the maximum 'risk' we will take to reject a null hypothesis. Accepting the alternative hypotheses with a higher p-value is generally considered unacceptable to most scientists. For example, if you had a p-value of 0.75, and reject the null hypothesis (and thus accept the alternative hypothesis), you could be making a mistake three out of four times—a very risky strategy.

Type I and Type II Errors

As we discussed in Unit 1, when we test hypotheses, it involves either rejecting or accepting the null hypothesis (the hypothesis that usually states that the observed deviation from an expected outcome is due to random causes or factors). In addition, we talked about the fact that testing the null hypothesis involves probability. Testing null hypotheses thus is subject to **two** different types of potential errors: type I errors, and type II errors.

A type I error occurs when we reject a null hypothesis, when in fact the null hypothesis is true. A type I error is when we conclude that a relationship exists between two variables, when a relationship does not exist. This relationship may be a causal relationship: one variable has an effect on another variable. In Unit 1, our alternative hypothesis was that there was a relationship between altitude (the independent variable) and allele frequencies (the dependent variable). You probably rejected that null hypothesis and accepted the alternative hypothesis that there is a causal relationship. However, if altitude actually had no effect on allele frequencies (the change in allele frequencies was due to predators, or to something else) and you rejected the null (you think altitude does have an effect), you have committed a type I error.

In biology, the probability of a type I error is usually held at 5% (by selecting $\alpha = 0.05$) or less. If our p-value that we determine from our statistical analysis is less than 0.05, then we report that we have rejected the null hypothesis with an α of 0.05.

A type II error occurs when we accept the null hypothesis as true, when in fact the null hypothesis is false. In Unit 1, if you had accepted the null hypothesis (altitude has no effect on allele frequencies), but altitude indeed had an effect on allele frequencies, then you have committed a type II error.

The t-Test

Suppose you have two samples of numbers and you wish to determine if the means of the two samples are significantly different from each other. Comparing the means of two samples is one of the most common statistical analyses that are done in biological experiments. The Student's t-test (named after "Student," the pen name of the statistician W.S. Gosset who first described this method early in the 20th century) can be used to determine if the two means are different.

There are two major assumptions for the t-test. They are as follows:

1 The two samples are normally distributed around their means; and

2 The variances of the two samples are roughly equal.

The following steps are used to calculate the t-statistic:

1 First, calculate the sample means ($\bar{x}_A$ and $\bar{x}_B$) and sample variances (s_A^2 and s_B^2) for each sample (sample A and sample B).

2 Second, calculate the **pooled estimate of the standard deviation (s_p)** (see Equation 3.1)

$$\textbf{Equation 3.1.} \quad s_p = \sqrt{\frac{(N_A-1)s_A^2 + (N_B-1)s_B^2}{N_A + N_B - 2}}$$

where N_A and N_B are the sample sizes (number of observations) in the two samples.

3 After you have calculated the two sample means and their variances, and the pooled estimate of the standard deviation, you then calculate the t-test statistic, using Equation 3.2. with ($N_A + N_B - 2$) degrees of freedom.

$$\textbf{Equation 3.2.} \quad t = \frac{\bar{x}_A - \bar{x}_B}{s_p \sqrt{(1/N_A) + (1/N_B)}}$$

If you are testing the null hypothesis that the two sample means do not differ significantly, compare the t-test statistic with the critical t-value in the following table (Table 3.1) under the appropriate degrees of freedom. If the **absolute value** of your t-statistic is greater than the t-value in the table for (two-tailed test), then you reject the null hypothesis (the two means are equal) and tentatively accept the alternate hypothesis that the means do differ significantly (one mean is greater than another mean). Note that this test does not tell you which mean is greater.

If you predicted that one specific mean should be greater (one-tailed test), read the second table (Table 3.2) and read the tabulated critical t-value in Table 3.2 under the appropriate degrees of freedom.

Degrees of Freedom

We have used the phrase "degrees of freedom" several times, both in Unit 2 and today. What does "degrees of freedom" mean? The "degrees of freedom" number refers to the number of values in the final calculation of a statistic that are free to vary.

What do we mean by the phrase "free to vary?" As an example, suppose you had measured four lengths of frog legs. The frogs had rear legs that were 5, 10, 20, and 25 mm (small frogs!). The mean length is 15 mm. If we subtract the mean length from each measurement (we generate the deviations from the mean for each leg length), the sum of the deviations from the mean must add up to 0. Once we determine three of the deviation values, the value of the fourth deviation value is restricted by the exact value of the mean.

Consider, for example the sample variance statistic, s^2, from Unit 2 (Equation 3.3):

$$\textbf{Equation 3.3.} \quad s^2 = \frac{\sum (x_i - \overline{x})^2}{(N-1)}$$

To calculate the s^2 of a random sample, we must first calculate the mean ($\overline{x}$) of that sample and then compute the sum of the several squared deviations $[\sum(x - \overline{x})^2]$ from that mean. While there will be N such squared deviations, only ($N - 1$) of them are free to assume any value. The last deviation, however, cannot vary; its value is fixed by the sum effects of the others.

In general, the degrees of freedom of an estimate of a parameter (like the sample variance, s^2) is equal to the number of independent values used, minus the number of parameters used as intermediate steps in the estimation of the parameter itself. For example, the number of intermediate steps to variance is one, because the sample mean is the only intermediate step needed. For this reason, the s^2 statistic is said to have only ($N - 1$) degrees of freedom.

A general rule is that the degrees of freedom decreases when we have to estimate more statistical parameters. As we mentioned earlier, before you can compute the variance of a sample, you had to first estimate the mean ($\overline{x}$) of that sample. You thus 'lose' a degree of freedom when you generate the variance, and you should divide by ($N - 1$) rather than N. For the t-test statistic described above, we have to calculate a mean of each of two samples, so we have to subtract two degrees of freedom from the total of the sample sizes ($N_1 + N_2$) when we generate the t-test statistic. The total degrees of freedom in the t-test is thus equal to ($N_1 + N_2 - 2$).

An Example of the t-Test

As an example, calculate the *t*-statistic for the following hypothetical data on the body lengths of male frogs that had been found amplexed ('holding onto,' the males grasp and hold onto females for mating) with a female and the males found without a female. The null hypothesis is that there is no difference between the two groups, and the alternative hypothesis is that there is a difference between the two groups.

Size of Male without a Female (mm)	Size of Male Amplexed with a Female (mm)
10, 12, 11, 15, 15, 17, 16, 9	9, 18, 13, 14, 15, 17, 17, 16

$\overline{x}_A = 13.13$, $\overline{x}_B = 14.88$, $N_A = 8$, $N_B = 8$, $s_A = 3.00$, $s_B = 2.90$, $s_p = 2.95$

$t = 1.19$ with 14 d.f. Because $t <$ the critical *t*-value of 2.15 (see Table 3.1), then the null hypothesis (no difference between the two groups of frogs) is accepted.

TABLE 3.1. Critical *t*-values (two-tailed) for testing the null hypothesis of "no difference between means" versus the alternative hypothesis "difference between the two means," but you do not predict which mean should be higher, $\alpha = 0.05$.

d.f.	*t*	d.f.	*t*	d.f.	*t*	d.f.	*t*	d.f.	*t*	d.f.	*t*
1	12.7	6	2.45	11	2.20	16	2.12	21	2.08	26	2.06
2	4.30	7	2.37	12	2.18	17	2.11	22	2.07	27	2.05
3	3.18	8	2.31	13	2.16	18	2.10	23	2.07	28	2.05
4	2.78	9	2.26	14	2.15	19	2.09	24	2.06	29	2.05
5	2.57	10	2.23	15	2.13	20	2.09	25	2.06	30	2.04

TABLE 3.2. Critical *t*-values (one-tailed) for testing the null hypothesis of "no difference between means" versus "mean of sample 1 is higher than the mean of sample 2, or vice versa," but you do predict which mean should be higher, $\alpha = 0.05$.

d.f.	*t*	d.f.	*t*	d.f.	*t*	d.f.	*t*	d.f.	*t*	d.f.	*t*
1	6.31	6	1.94	11	1.80	16	1.75	21	1.72	26	1.71
2	2.92	7	1.90	12	1.78	17	1.74	22	1.72	27	1.70
3	2.35	8	1.86	13	1.77	18	1.73	23	1.71	28	1.70
4	2.13	9	1.83	14	1.76	19	1.73	24	1.71	29	1.70
5	2.01	10	1.81	15	1.75	20	1.73	25	1.71	30	1.70

The Chi-Square Test

One statistical test that we often use in biology is the chi-square test (χ^2). This test is used to analyze the distribution of observations among different categories. In general, we are looking for differences in expected distributions versus observed distributions. The chi-square statistic that you calculate is the sum of all of the ([observed value – expected value]^2 / expected value) of all categories (Equation 3.4).

$$\textbf{Equation 3.4.} \quad \chi^2 = \sum \frac{(O-E)^2}{E}$$

Do not be confused by symbols. The 'sigma' symbol ("Σ") above is a symbol that means "sum." The 'chi' symbol ("χ") is referring to the value you obtain from the calculation.

For example, suppose we looked at the distribution of snails over three types of habitat in a stream. The three types of habitat were sandy areas, muddy areas, and cobble, and each type represented about a third of the surface area at the bottom of the stream. If there was no effect of the substrate type on the distribution of the snails, then we would expect an equal number of snails to be in each habitat.

TABLE 3.3.

Habitat Type	Observed	Expected	$(O-E)^2/E$
mud	6	30	19.2
sand	4	30	22.5
cobble	80	30	83.3
totals	90	90	$\Sigma = \chi^2 = 125.0$

The degrees of freedom for the chi-square test is the number of categories minus 1.

In this case: d.f. = (3 − 1) = 2.

We are assuming that there would be an equal number of snails in each of the three types of substrate. We counted 90 snails, and there are three types of substrate, so we assume there should be (90 / 3) = 30 snails on each substrate. However, we found that 80 snails were on cobble, 4 on sand, and 6 on mud. As we will see later in the semester, the expected number of objects do not necessarily have to be the same in all categories. For example, in a Mendelian dihybrid genetic cross for two nonlinked genes, there are four distinct phenotypes possible. However, we would expect a $9:3:3:1$ phenotypic ratio among the F_2 offspring (not a $1:1:1:1$ ratio).

Your null hypothesis is that there is no difference between the observed and expected values, and the alternative hypothesis is that there is a difference. The critical χ^2-value is found in a table (Table 3.4), and you look under the appropriate degrees of freedom. If your calculated chi-square statistic is greater than the critical χ^2-value shown in Table 3.4 for the appropriate degrees of freedom, then you reject the null hypothesis (the snails are randomly distributed) and accept the alternative hypothesis (there is a significant difference in the distribution of the snails). This test does not tell you what exactly are the factors that cause the non-random distribution, however.

In our example, the calculated χ^2 test statistic value is 125.0, which is greater than the critical χ^2-value of 5.99 listed for 2 degrees of freedom in Table 3.4 below. The results thus are highly significant (p-value < 0.05). We conclude that the snails are not randomly distributed on the substrates, but that they are concentrating one type (cobble).

TABLE 3.4. Critical χ^2-values for testing the null hypothesis of "no difference between categories" versus "significant difference among the categories," $\alpha = 0.05$.

d.f.	χ^2	d.f.	χ^2	d.f.	χ^2	d.f.	χ^2	d.f.	χ^2	d.f.	χ^2
1	3.84	6	12.59	11	19.68	16	26.30	21	32.67	26	38.89
2	5.99	7	14.07	12	21.03	17	27.59	22	33.92	27	40.11
3	7.82	8	15.51	13	22.36	18	28.87	23	35.17	28	41.34
4	9.49	9	16.92	14	23.69	19	30.14	24	36.42	29	42.56
5	11.07	10	18.31	15	25.00	20	31.41	25	37.65	30	43.77

Linear Regression and Correlation

When you wish to describe the relationship between two variables, you will run a regression or correlation. In many biological experiments, we often wish to determine how much of the variation of one variable (the 'dependent variable') is explained by variation in the other variable (the 'independent variable'). This is done by running a **regression**. With a regression, you assume that there is some cause-and-effect relationship between the two variables. Recall the equation of a straight line (Equation 3.5):

Equation 3.5. $y = mx + b$

where y = the value of the dependent variable, m = the **slope** of the line, x = value of the independent variable, and b = the **intercept** of the line (the point at which the line crosses the y-axis). The dependent variable is plotted on the y-axis, and the independent variable is plotted on the x-axis (see Figure 3.2). The intercept need not cross the y-axis at 0; for example, the size of a baby at birth is not zero pounds.

The line (called the **best-fit line**) that you see drawn among data points on such a graph is typically the one produced by a method called the **least-squares method.** Using this method, the best-fit line is one that minimizes the sum of the squares of the differences of each dependent data point (the y-axis data) and the calculated y-value of the regression line.

We will not discuss the regression calculations in detail today. A linear regression calculates a straight line that runs through the cloud of points in such a way that minimizes the distance all of the data points are from that line, the line thus is a generalization about the relationship between the two variables. Once you have the equation for this line, you can estimate a y-value given an x-value, and vice-versa. If the regression is significant, this means that the value of the independent variable affects the value of the dependent variable, to some degree. If the regression is not significant, then there is little or no effect of the independent variable on the dependent variable.

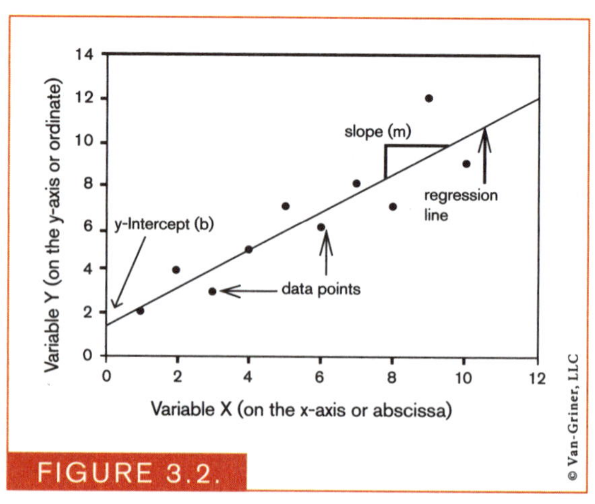

FIGURE 3.2.

Linear regression.

A related concept to regression is **correlation.** A **correlation analysis** tells you the degree of association between the two variables, but it is not used to examine a cause-and-effect relationship between the two variables (it does not tell you that X causes Y to occur). A correlation analysis can tell you the type of relationship (positive or direct relationship: as one variable increases, so does the other), or an inverse or negative relationship (as one variable increases, the other decreases). In a correlation analysis, because there is no cause-and-effect assumed, it does not make sense to produce a regression line.

There are two important statistics that a regression or correlation analysis provides scientists.

1 The **correlation coefficient r** describes the kind of relationship that exists between two variables. This statistic is useful for both correlation and for regression. The correlation coefficient r varies from –1.0 (a perfect one-to-one negative relationship) to 0 (no relationship) to 1.0 (a perfect positive relationship). A **positive correlation** indicates that there is a **direct relationship** between the two variables: a high value of variable X corresponds to a high value in variable Y, and a low X-value corresponds to a low Y-value. A **negative correlation** indicates that there is an **inverse relationship** between variables X and Y: a low X corresponds to a high Y, and a high X corresponds to a low Y. In addition to a indication of a direct or inverse relationship, the correlation coefficient gives you an idea of the 'scatter' of the data. A correlation coefficient near 0 means that there is no discernible relationship between X and Y; the two variables are independent of each other. There are several types of correlation coefficients: we will usually use one called the 'Pearson r' on interval-scale or ratio-scale data. See Figure 3.3 to compare the various correlation coefficient values.

Note in Figure 3.3.A a perfect one-to-one positive relationship ($r = 1.0$). An increase in X is perfectly matched with an increase in Y. Figure 3.3.B shows a perfect negative relationship ($r = -1.0$), where an increase in X is matched perfectly with a decrease in Y. When $r = 1.0$ or $r = -1.0$, the data would fall on a straight line.

Figure 3.3.C shows no correlation between X and Y ($r = 0$). As r approaches 0, there is less of a relationship between X and Y. When $r = 0$, there is no systematic relationship between X and Y, and we say the two variables are independent of each other.

Figure 3.3.D shows a negative relationship between X and Y ($r = -0.77$), and the other two figures (Figure 3.3.E and Figure 3.3.F) show positive relationships: ($r = 0.95$ and $r = 0.70$, respectively). The r-values are not 1.0 or –1.0, so there is some scatter in the points. A positive correlation coefficient occurs between $0 < r \leq 1.0$. This suggests a direct relationship between the two scores: a high X-value is generally related to a high y-value, and a low X-value is related to a low Y-value. The higher the r, the stronger the relationship is. A negative correlation coefficient occurs between $1.0 \leq r < 0$. This suggests an inverse relationship between the two scores: a high X-value is generally related to a low Y-value, and a low X-value is related to a high Y-value. The higher the r, the stronger the relationship is.

2 The **square of the coefficient** (r^2) in a regression equation will tell you the percentage of the variation of the dependent variable is explained by the variation in the independent variable. In Figure 3.3, the r-squared values are also given for some of the regressions. For the graphs where there is a perfect relationship (Figure 3.3.A and 3.3.B, $r = -1.0$ or 1.0), the r^2-value is near 1 or 100%. In other words, 100% of the variation in the Y-value is explained by the X-value. If r^2 is 0 (Figure 3.3.C), then no variation of Y is explained by X. In Figure 3.3.D, Figure 3.3.E, and Figure 3.3.F, the amount of variation in Y explained by X is 60% ($r^2 = 0.60$), 90% ($r^2 = 0.90$), and 49% ($r^2 = 0.49$), respectively.

Although correlation is useful to show that a relationship exists between the two variables being examined, it does not necessarily demonstrate that a cause-and-effect relationship exists. In correlation research, the experimenter usually has no direct control over either variable. The r- and r^2-values allow us to assign the degree to which the two variables are related, but further research is needed to see if a cause-and-effect relationship is occurring, or if both are affected by a third variable. For example, your height and weight are correlated, but one does not cause the other. Both variables are affected by your age and a number of other variables.

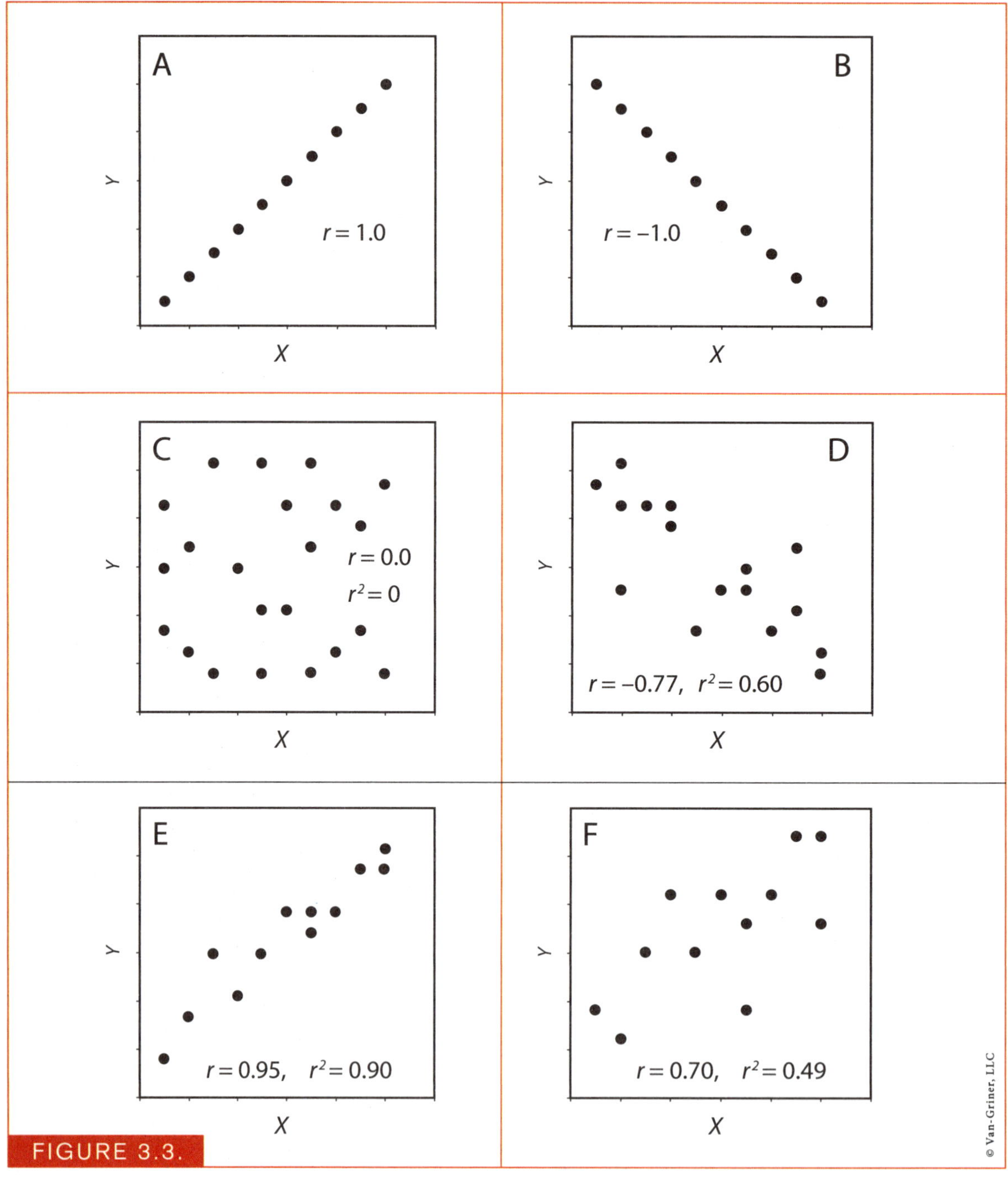

FIGURE 3.3.

Depictions of several regressions. Part A: a perfect positive correlation. Part B: a perfect negative correlation. Part C: no correlation exists between *X* and *Y*. Part D: a negative correlation. Parts E and F: two different positive correlations.

For regression analyses, several things are assumed. First, the experimenter randomly assigned subjects to different treatment groups. Second, he or she has direct control over the X variable (the experimenter can manipulate X). Third, the 'cause' (change in X) must precede the 'effect' (the change in Y) by some period of time. If we are measuring two variables that exist simultaneously, it is difficult to assign which change (X or Y) came first.

To show the value of a correlation analysis, the data below are plotted on a scatter plot (see Figure 3.4).

TABLE 3.5.

Animal	Body Length	Leg Length	Animal	Body Length	Leg Length
1	3	10	14	52	44
2	5	8	15	60	59
3	10	10	16	60	52
4	10	6	17	60	68
5	15	14	18	75	75
6	18	13	19	78	72
7	20	21	20	80	83
8	22	18	21	80	88
9	22	20	22	100	82
10	25	27	23	150	170
11	30	29	24	15	28
12	30	34	25	80	60
13	50	50			

For the data, the regression equation is: leg length = 1.02(body length) − 1.02. The coefficient for the analysis (r) is 0.97, which indicates a very close positive relationship.

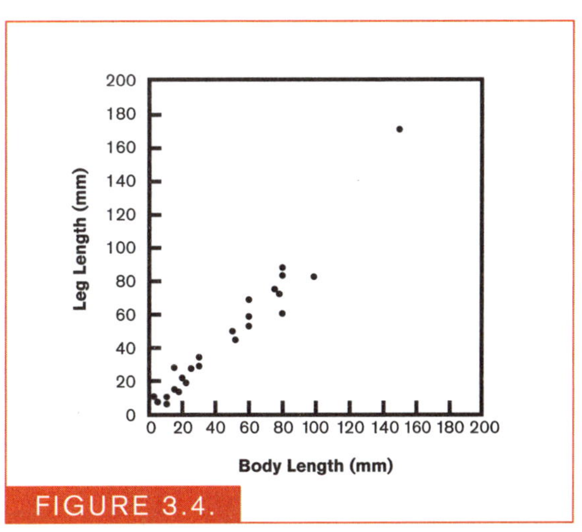

FIGURE 3.4.

Scatter plot of body length (mm) and leg length (mm) of hypothetical animals.

Outliers

However, as you may have guessed from Figure 3.4, we have one animal that is very large, compared to the other animals (body length of 150 mm). What if that single data point is inaccurate, or very rare or odd? An **outlier** is an observation that lies an 'abnormal' distance from other values in a random sample from a population.

Nonlinearity of Data

What if the data are nonlinear (in other words, what if the data appear to follow a curved line, not a straight line)? In a normal linear regression analysis, it is assumed that the relationship between the two variables is a linear one. If we look at the relationship between some variables (for example, zebra mussel shell length and mussel weight), the relationship is not linear, but curvilinear. See Figure 3.5 for an example of a nonlinear (curvilinear) relationship. In this case, we may be able to perform a **transformation** of the x-axis (independent) data to make the best-fit line more linear. A variety of transformations exist for such nonlinear data; you will study them in later classes.

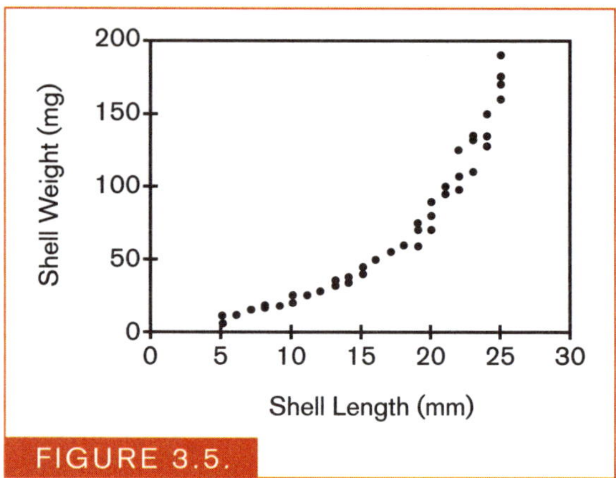

FIGURE 3.5.

A nonlinear relationship: zebra mussel length and weight.

Exercises

Exercise 3.1.

For each of the following situations listed in Table 3.6 below, identify if the variables or data observations as belonging to which category.

TABLE 3.6.

Variable/Data Observation	Qualitative or Quantitative	Discrete or Continuous	Nominal, Ordinal, Interval or Ratio Scale
you have a litter of kittens, and counted 6 kittens in the litter			
2004 USA population consisting of 292,686,306 humans			
three sexes in a species of snail: male, female, or hermaphroditic individuals			
a female frog with a male holding onto her (amplexed) or a female without a male (not amplexed)			
lizards that are either red-tailed or blue-tailed			
the pigmentation class or pattern of a species of salamander: 0 (no black pigmentation), 1 (a few black speckles), 2 (moderately speckled), 3 (heavily speckled), and 4 (completely black)			
an Olympic sprinter running the 100 yard dash in 14.5 seconds			
March 23, 1997			
27° (compass direction)			
27°C (temperature)			
27K (temperature)			
an average of 4.3 eggs laid in the nest of the local population of robins			
three snapdragon genotypes: RR, Rr, or rr			
first, second, or third degree burns			
the heights of the three large trees in your back yard: 23 m, 28 m, and 31 m high			
1,530 hours			

Exercise 3.2.

Using the data you collected in Unit 2 (where you measured the lengths of 15 specimens of two groups of objects), conduct a *t*-test on the data.

First, what is your null hypothesis? Your alternative hypothesis?

What are some of the critical assumptions that you should make concerning the data collected on the two groups?

Calculate the value of *t*. How many degrees of freedom do you have? Are the results significant?

Now, describe a situation in which you would commit a type I error.

Now, describe a situation when you would commit a type II error.

Exercise 3.3.

Examine the following hypothetical data on the number of caterpillars on tomato plants that have been treated with four different treatments. Suppose you wanted to know the efficacy of several types of treatments that are used to kill of caterpillar pests on tomato plants in your backyard garden. You had 24 plants. You sprayed six plants with a pesticide called 'bug-b-gone.' You also sprayed six other plants with a pesticide called 'super zapper ultra mega death lotion.' For six other plants, you simply added a solution of dishwashing liquid and water. You sprayed the last six plants (the controls) with water, to equalize handling effects. A week later, you counted the total number of caterpillars on your plants. The results are in the Table 3.7.

TABLE 3.7.

Treatment	Number of Caterpillars on the Plants in the Treatment (Observed)	Expected	$(O - E)^2 / E$
no treatment	90		
bug-b-gone	36		
common soap and water	6		
super zapper ultra mega death lotion	79		
totals			$\chi^2 =$

Calculate the χ^2 statistic using Equation 3.4, and determine the appropriate degrees of freedom. Compare your calculated χ^2-value against the critical χ^2-value listed in Table 3.4. Are your results significant?

State the null hypothesis.

State the alternative hypothesis.

According to the statistical analysis, which hypothesis do you reject, and which do you accept? Why?

What do you think is the best treatment to use, if any? Why?

Now, describe a situation in which you would commit a type I error.

Now, describe a situation when you would commit a type II error.

Exercise 3.4.

Yarrow Plants and Altitude

Examine the following hypothetical data (in Table 3.8 below) based on the work by J. Clausen and his collaborators (Clausen et al. 1940; Clausen et al. 1958; Nunez-Farfan and Schlichting 2001). They examined the clinal variation of the yarrow plant (*Achillea*) as one moved from low altitudes to higher altitudes. As one generally moved up in altitude, the average height of the plants decreased.

TABLE 3.8.

Location	Altitude (meters)	Plant Height (cm)
A	1,200	75, 72, 80
B	1,700	50, 52, 60
C	2,000	47, 44, 48
D	2,300	33, 37, 40
E	2,500	22, 25, 28
F	3,100	16, 20, 17
G	2,800	20, 19, 25
H	2,400	25, 28, 29
I	2,100	45, 38, 48

How do you think altitude would affect plant height?

State your null and alternative hypotheses.

Plot the data from Table 3.8 on Figure 3.6. Draw in what you think is the regression line. Later on in the semester, you will run a regression on the data, and calculate the best-fit line, r and r^2.

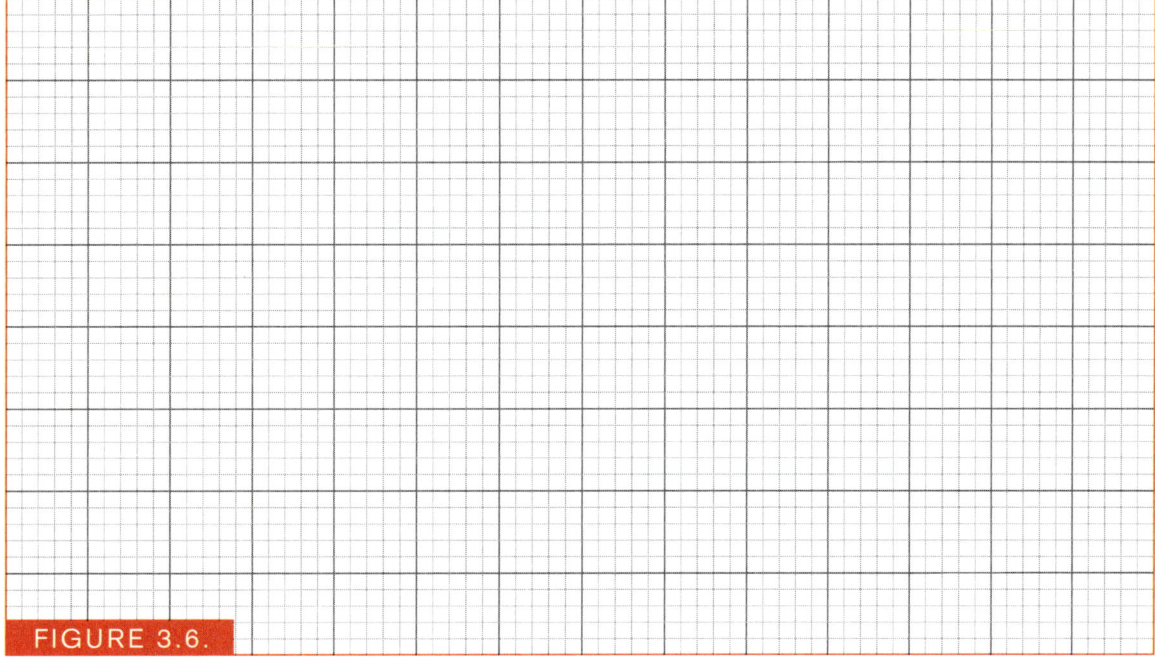

FIGURE 3.6.

The relationship between *Achillea* plant height and altitude.

Describe the relationship between the two variables. What would you estimate is the value of the correlation coefficient? (If you have a calculator that does regression, try to calculate the regression equation and the r-values.)

Now, describe the situation in which you would commit a type I error.

Now, describe the situation when you would commit a type II error.

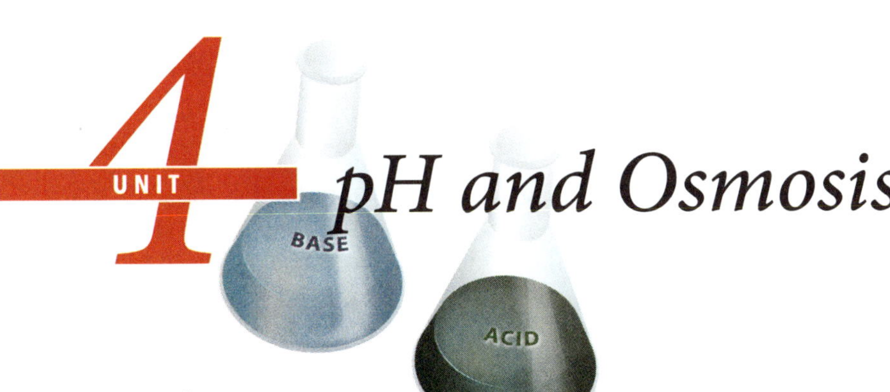

pH and Osmosis

Keywords

logarithms
exponential functions
natural logarithms
common logarithms
antilogs
pH
serial dilutions
acids
bases
salts
ions
membranes

plasma membrane
tonoplast
fluid mosaic model
lipid bilayer
phospholipids
cholesterol
proteins
polar
nonpolar
diffusion
facilitated diffusion
semipermeable

active transport
osmosis
hypertonic
hypotonic
isotonic
osmotic pressure
turgor pressure
hydrostatic pressure
accuracy
precision
resolution

Learning Objectives

When finished with this unit, you should be able to:

1. Understand the concepts of logarithms and antilogarithms;

2. Create a serial dilution;

3. Understand the logarithmic nature of pH and interpret the pH scale;

4. Describe the importance of cell membranes and describe the fluid mosaic membrane model;

5. Compare and contrast the following cellular activities: diffusion, osmosis, facilitated diffusion, active transport;

6. Estimate the relative osmotic strength of unknown samples using serial dilutions and regression;

7. Compare and contrast accuracy, precision, and resolution; and

8. Understand the impact of the degree of resolution on precision.

The pH of Solutions

The pH scale is logarithmic. There are many different logarithmic functions that have been described, but two specific logarithms (abbreviated as 'logs') are used often by biologists: **natural logs** and **common logs** (base 10). The button on your calculator for the natural log is identified as [ln] and the button for the common log is identified as [log].

Before the evolution of powerful calculators and computers, scientists used slide rules and tables to calculate logarithms. The use of logs allowed scientists to make calculations with large numbers easier. The basic idea is that the logarithm of a product of two numbers is the sum of their logarithms, and adding two or more numbers together is easier than multiplying two or more numbers together. In mathematics, the **logarithm functions** are the inverses of the **exponential functions.** Let us discuss the exponential functions first.

An **exponential function** is one where a number 'x' is equal to a positive number 'a' raised to a power 'y' (Equation 4.1).

> **Equation 4.1.** $x = a^y$

The **logarithmic function** (Equation 4.2) is the inverse of the exponential function.

In Equation 4.2, y is the **logarithm** of x in the base a. The logarithm 'y' is the power we have to raise 'a' by in order to get 'x' as the answer. For instance, $\log_{10}100 = 2$ (because $10^2 = 100$).

> **Equation 4.2.** $y = \log_a x$

First, find the [log] and [ln] buttons on your calculator. In addition, find the buttons that are the **inverse functions** for these logarithms: [e^x] is the inverse function ('**antilog**') for the natural log function [ln], and [10^x] is the inverse function ('antilog') for the common log function [log]. There may be separate buttons for the exponential and logarithmic functions, or the inverse functions are listed above the functions, which means that you have to hit an [inverse] or [INV] or [shift] or [second function] button first. For some of you, your calculator may have a [y^x] button, where you would first have to type in '10', then hit [y^x], then hit the number for 'x' to create the answer.

① **Natural Logarithms.** The natural logarithm (ln) of a given number (Equation 4.3) is the exponent ('y' below) that indicates the power to which the **base e** (e is approximately 2.718, rounded to four significant digits) must be raised to obtain a given number 'x.' Equation 4.4 is the inverse function of the exponential function. We will see this logarithm later in the semester. For example, the natural log of 10 is 2.302 ($e^{2.302} = 10$) and the antilog of 2.302 is approximately 10.

The number e ($e \approx 2.718$) has useful properties. When dealing with the logarithms to the base e, it is common in biology to denote '$\log_e$' as 'ln,' especially if there is any likelihood that the reader might think that base 10 or base 2 logarithms might be meant by the word 'log.'

> **Equation 4.3.** $y = \log_e(x) = \ln(x)$

Equation 4.4. $x = e_y$

2 Common Logarithms. The common logarithm of a given number (log) is the exponent that indicates the power to which a base of 10 must be raised to obtain a given number. For example, the common log of 100 (10^2) is 2, and the common log of 110 is 2.041. The antilog of 2 is 100, and the antilog of 2.041 is about 110 (rounded to the nearest whole number). A pH value is based on this type of logarithm. Examine the logarithmic (Equation 4.5) and exponential functions (Equation 4.6) using common logs below.

Equation 4.5. $y = \log_{10}(x) = \log(x)$

Equation 4.6. $x = 10^y$

The Logarithmic Function of pH

The concentration of the hydrogen ion [H^+] in an acidic or basic solution is often indicated by the pH. The term "pH" is actually a shorthand version of the expression, $-\log_{10}[H^+]$.

The equation for pH (Equation 4.7) and its inverse function (Equation 4.8, which calculates the molar concentration of hydrogen ions in a solution with that pH value) are listed below.

Equation 4.7. $pH = -\log_{10}[H^+]$

Equation 4.8. $[H^+] = 10^{-pH}$

Note the minus sign in front of the log symbol in Equation 4.7 and the minus sign in front of the exponent in Equation 4.8.

If you were to compare the results using pH paper (which changes color when placed in acidic or basic solutions) versus a pH electrode which displays the pH as a number:

A which is qualitative and which is quantitative data;

B which uses nominal or ordinal scales; and

C which uses interval or ratio scales?

Examine the following table (Table 4.1) to see the relationship between a given number and its common logarithm.

TABLE 4.1.

Number	Exponential Expression	Logarithm
1,000	10^3	3
100	10^2	2
10	10^1	1
1	10^0	0
1/10 or 0.1	10^{-1}	−1
1/100 or 0.01	10^{-2}	−2
1/1,000 or 0.001	10^{-3}	−3

On most calculators, you obtain the log (or ln) of a number by entering the number, then pressing the log (or ln) button.

Example 4.1.
Find the common log of the following number: 6.54×10^5

Input 6.54×10^5 into your calculator and then find its log: $\log 6.54 \times 10^5 = 5.8155777$

Most calculators will give you way too many significant digits. Some calculators display '5.8156' as the answer, while others may display even more significant digits ('5.8155777483242267267709280 1055935…').

Example 4.2.
Find the log of the following number: 2.5×10^{-7}

$\log 2.5 \times 10^{-7} = -6.60205999132796\ldots$ (again, too many significant digits).

How many significant digits should be used when dealing with logarithms? In Unit 2, we dealt with some aspects of rounding off numbers and using the correct number of significant digits. Let us examine the logarithms we calculated above more closely and figure out how to determine the correct number of significant digits.

For any log, the number to the left of the decimal point is called the **characteristic,** and the number to the right of the decimal point is called the **mantissa.** The characteristic locates the position of the decimal point of the number, so it is not included when determining the number of significant figures. The mantissa has as many significant digits as the number whose log was generated.

Example 4.3.
$\log (6.54 \times 10^5) = 5.816$

The characteristic of the number "5.816" ("5") has one significant digit and the mantissa has three (".816"). The mantissa has three significant digits because the number that generated the log has three significant digits ("6.54"). We also have rounded the number up to 5.816 from 5.8155.

Example 4.4.
$\log (2.5 \times 10^{-7}) = \log (0.00000025) = -6.60$

The number ("2.5") has two significant digits, so the mantissa of the log ends up with two significant digits.

We will find that the natural logarithms work in the same way:

Example 4.5.
Find the natural log of 3.95×10^6.

$\ln (3.95 \times 10^6) = 15.18922614\ldots$ (again, too many significant digits). There are three significant digits to the number, so the correct way to state the natural log of 3.95×10^6 is:

$\ln (3.95 \times 10^6) = 15.189$ (use three significant digits in the mantissa).

Example 4.6.
Find the natural log of 42.36.

$\ln (42.36) = 3.7462045 = 3.7462$ (four significant digits in the mantissa).

Example 4.7.
You cannot take the log of a negative number!

Try to take the common log of –2.3.

Your calculator will give an error message: "—E—," "Error," or something similar.

Finding the Antilogarithms (the Inverse Logarithms)

If you know the logarithm of a number, you can determine the number itself. This process is called finding the **antilogarithm** (or inverse logarithm or antilog) of the number. The steps involved in finding the antilog:

First, enter the appropriate function (hit the [shift] button), and then the [log] button;

Then enter the value; and finally press the [=] sign.

On some calculators, you may be able to determine the antilog directly, with the push of one button: first enter the log number, then press the $[10^x]$ button for the common base 10 log, or $[e^x]$ button for the natural log. For other calculators, you press the $[10x]$ or $[e^x]$ button first, then enter the log number.

Note: Your calculator may operate differently; your lab instructor can help you.

Example 4.8.
Find the base 10 antilog of 4.203.

$\log_{10} x = 4.203$

$\log x = 4.203$; so, $x =$ inverse log of $4.203 = 15{,}958.79147\ldots = 1.595879147 \times 10^4$ (note that once again we have too many significant digits. Most calculators provide too many digits.). There are three significant digits in the mantissa of the log, so the number is to have three significant digits. The answer, with the correct number of significant digits is 1.60×10^4. (Note that we had to round up to 1.60, and the zero, because it was included on the scientific notation number, is significant.)

Example 4.9.
Find the base 10 antilog of −15.3.

$\log x = -15.3$; so, $x = \text{inv log}\,(-15.3) = 5.011872336\ldots \times 10^{-16} = 5 \times 10^{-16}$ (note that this time there is one significant digit).

The antilogarithms of natural logarithms work in the same way.

Example 4.10.
Find the natural antilog to $\ln x = 2.56$.

$x = e^{(2.56)} = 12.93581732\ldots = 13$ (with two significant digits, because of the two significant digits of the mantissa and because of subsequent rounding).

Example 4.11.
What is the concentration of the hydrogen ion concentration in an aqueous solution with pH = 13.22?

$\text{pH} = -\log\,[\text{H}^+] = 13.22$ $\qquad\qquad\qquad\qquad$ $\log\,[\text{H}^+] = -13.22$

$[\text{H}^+] = 10^{(-13.22)}$ $\qquad\qquad\qquad\qquad$ $[\text{H}^+] = 6.0 \times 10^{-14}$ M (two significant digits to the hydrogen concentration)

Calculations Involving Logarithms

Because logarithms are exponents, mathematical operations involving them follow the same rules as those for exponents (see Table 4.2 below).

TABLE 4.2.

Common Logarithm	Natural Logarithm
$\log\,(xy) = \log x + \log y$	$\ln\,(xy) = \ln x + \ln y$
$\log\,(x\,/\,y) = \log x - \log y$	$\ln\,(x\,/\,y) = \ln x - \ln y$
$\log x^y = y \log x$	$\ln x^y = y \ln x$

Example 4.12.
$\log\,(5.0 \times 10^6) = \log\,(5.0) + \log\,(10^6) = 0.70 + 6 = 6.70$ (two significant digits)

Hint: This is an easy way to estimate the log of a number written in scientific notation.

Example 4.13.
$\log\,(154\,/\,25) = \log 154 - \log 25 = 2.188 - 1.40 = 0.788 = 0.79$ (two significant digits maximum, because of the number 25).

Example 4.14.
$\log\,(5.46 \times 10^{-3})^6 = 6 \times (\log 5.46 \times 10^{-3}) = 6 \times (-2.263) = -13.576$ [there are three significant digits in the number $(5.46 \times 10^{-3})^6$].

The pH of Solutions

Many molecules, when dissolved in water, dissociate into **ions.** Water itself will dissociate (ionize) into two ions: a **hydrogen ion** (H^+, consisting of a single proton), and a **hydroxyl ion** (OH^-).

An **acid,** by definition, is any compound that **releases** hydrogen ions when dissolved in water:

Carbonic acid [$H_2CO_3 \rightarrow H^+ + HCO_3^-$ (bicarbonate)]
Nitric acid [$HNO_3 \rightarrow H^+ + NO_3^-$ (nitrate)]
Sulfuric acid [$H_2SO_4 \rightarrow 2H^+ + SO_4^{2-}$ (sulfate)]

A **base** is a compound that **accepts** hydrogen ions while in water:

Ammonia [$NH_3 + H^+ \rightarrow NH_4^+$]

Salts, like NaCl and $CaCO_3$ (calcium carbonate, found in limestone) are salts because they dissociate in water and do not release or absorb hydrogen ions:

$NaCl \rightarrow Na^+ + Cl^-$
$CaCO_3 \rightarrow Ca^{+2} + CO_3^{-2}$

Pure water has a pH of 7, which means that there are 10^{-7} moles of hydrogen ions per liter of pure water (1×10^{-7} M). Water with a pH of 6 is 10 times more acidic (there are 10 times more hydrogen ions per liter (10^{-6} M) than in pure water. Water with a pH of 8 is 10 times more basic (less acidic) than pure water, because there are 10 times fewer hydrogen ions present per liter (10^{-8} M) than in pure water.

The pH Scale

TABLE 4.3. The pH scale.

H^+ (in moles/liter)	pH	Examples
10^{-14}	14	drain cleaner, lye (very alkaline)
10^{-13}	13	bleach
10^{-12}	12	ammonia
10^{-11}	11	
10^{-10}	10	milk of magnesia
10^{-9}	9	
10^{-8}	8	baking soda, seawater
10^{-7}	7	distilled water, blood (slightly alkaline), milk (slightly acidic)
10^{-6}	6	
10^{-5}	5	strong coffee
10^{-4}	4	orange juice, acid rain
10^{-3}	3	vinegar
10^{-2}	2	lemon juice, stomach acids, water leachate from some mines
10^{-1}	1	lab acids (very acidic)

We can measure the pH of a solution and compare it to the pH scale (Table 4.3). Acidic solutions have lower pH values (pH < 7), whereas basic solutions have higher values (pH > 7). Remember, because of the logarithmic nature of the pH scale, if solution A's pH is 5, and solution B's pH is 6, then the acidity of A is 10 times higher than B. If there was a 2 pH unit difference between the two solutions, this means that one solution is 100 times more acidic than the other.

Serial Dilutions

In biology, many experiments involve the use of **serial dilutions.** For example, one may need to adjust concentrations of chemical solutions for different purposes. Another reason may be to save on the amount of solvents used to create solutions. Another reason to use serial dilutions is that you wish to determine the concentration of some solution; you can compare it against a range of solutions of known concentrations.

Serial dilutions are often used in many fields, including molecular biology, microbiology, chemistry, and environmental science. The dilution factor is usually either by 1/10th or 1/100th. A rough approximation of the original solution and the desired concentration will determine how great the dilutions need to be and how many serial dilutions are required.

Using a series of serial dilutions is one method for making solutions of low molar concentrations. A stock solution with a molarity greater than that which is required is diluted using a suitable solvent. Suppose you had a stock solution of 1 molar (1 M) glucose, and you wanted to make a 1 mM (millimolar, 0.001 M) solution. Instead of taking one ml and adding it to 999 ml of distilled water, you may first want to dilute the 1 M stock to 0.1 M, by taking 10 ml of the stock solution and adding it to 90 ml of water, then stirring or agitating the solution to thoroughly mix it. You then would take 10 ml of the 0.1 M solution and add it to 90 ml of water, creating a 0.01 M solution. Finally, you could then add 10 ml of the 0.01 M solution to 90 ml of water. This method often gives you a more accurate 0.001 M solution, compared to taking 1 ml of stock (especially if you were trying to do this with graduated cylinders) and adding it to 999 ml of water.

Another common use of serial dilutions is to determine the concentration of bacteria or yeast (or some other organism) in a aqueous medium. You would make a series of 1:10 or 1:100 dilutions and culture these dilutions, then count the number of colonies. You would remove a small amount of an original solution to another container which is then brought back up to the original volume, using the required buffer or water. You would repeat this several times, until you have diluted the original stock greatly, perhaps by 1 million fold.

Suppose you had a solution of yeast that numbered around 2×10^5 cells/ml of water (which would be cloudy). If you plated 1 ml of this solution, you would get a thick lawn of colonies, which would be impossible to count. However, after you diluted the original sample by a series of 1 : 10 dilutions, you see the results depicted in Figure 4.3 and Table 4.4.

TABLE 4.4.

Dilution	Number of Colonies
original stock solution	too many to count (TMTC)
1 : 10	TMTC
1 : 100	TMTC
1 : 1,000	207
1 : 10,000	23
1 : 100,000	2

Based on the result for the 1 : 100,000 dilution, you would multiply 2 times the dilution factor (100,000) to give you an estimate of 2×10^5 cells/ml in the original stock solution. Using the data for the 1 : 10,000 dilution factor gives you an estimate of 2.3×10^5 cells/ml. If you made several replicate dilutions, you could provide a mean and standard deviation of your estimate.

Exercises

Exercise 4.1.

TABLE 4.5. Calculate the pH values, given the hydrogen ion concentrations (using Equation 4.7).

$[H^+] = 1.0 \times 10^{-5}$	pH =
$[H^+] = 1.0 \times 10^{-11}$	pH =
$[H^+] = 6.5 \times 10^{-3}$	pH =
$[H^+] = 1.0 \times 10^{-7}$	pH =
What is the pH of a solution when the concentration of hydrogen ions is 5.0×10^{-4} M?	pH =

Exercise 4.2.

Now if the pH is given, how does one find the $[H^+]$ (in other words how do you find the antilogarithm)? Equation 4.8 above provides you the answer: $[H^+] = 10^{-pH}$. Note the minus symbol in front of the exponent in Equation 4.8.

Thus, if the pH of a particular acid solution is 8.0, then the $[H^+] = 10^{-8}$ or 1×10^{-8} M.

If the pH is not a whole number, then the value of the decimal number will not be 1.0. For example, pH = 4.50, then $[H^+] = 10^{-4.50} = 0.0000316 = 3.2 \times 10^{-5}$ M (we use two significant digits to the concentration, because of the two significant digits in the mantissa of the pH). Try this conversion with your calculator.

Note: Do not leave your answers for molarity as $10^{-4.50}$, for example; you must give the hydrogen ion concentration in correct scientific notation (3.2×10^{-5}). Depending on your calculator, you may have to input your number (-4.5) and then press the $[10^x]$ button, or you may need to type the exponent value in and then press the [INV] (for "inverse") or [shift] button, and then press the [log] button. If you have difficulty see your lab instructor, and also check your calculator's manual.

TABLE 4.6. Convert these pH values into hydrogen ion concentrations (in scientific notation), using Equation 4.8.

pH = 3.0	$[H^+]$ =
pH = 4.9	$[H^+]$ =
pH = 5.0	$[H^+]$ =
pH = 12.76	$[H^+]$ =
If the pH of a solution is 7.9, what is the hydrogen ion concentration (in M)?	$[H^+]$ =

Exercise 4.3.

Serial Dilutions and pH

Each pair of students will do the following exercise. **Your lab instructor will first go over the use and care of the pH equipment.**

1 First, measure 100 ml of vinegar with the graduated cylinder and pour into a 250 ml beaker and measure the pH. With graduated cylinders, you take your measure from the bottom of the meniscus (the concave [curved] upper surface of the column of liquid inside the cylinder).

2 Next, measure 100 ml of tap water with a second cylinder and place into a separate 250 ml beaker. Measure the pH of tap water. Record these numbers in Table 4.7.

3 Using your graduated cylinder or measuring beaker, measure 90 ml of tap water, and add it to the third beaker.

4 Measure 10 ml of vinegar in the graduated cylinder (the vinegar is from the grocery store; it contains 5% acetic acid) and add it to the water in the third beaker. Rinse your cylinder out with distilled water afterwards. Stir gently, using a stirring rod.

5 As you make this dilution, estimate what you think will be the resulting pH of the 1/10 dilution solution. What is your estimate? Place your estimates of each dilution in the left-hand column of Table 4.7.

6 Measure the pH of this diluted vinegar solution (1/10 dilution), and record it in Table 4.7. How does it compare to your predicted pH?

7 Repeat Step 3, adding 90 ml of tap water to another beaker. Now, measure 10 ml of your 1/10 vinegar dilution and place into a 250 ml beaker. This will create a 1/100 dilution. Measure the pH. Record your data in Table 4.7.

8 Repeat 7 to create a 1/1,000 dilution, and a 1/10,000 dilution, a 1/100,000 dilution, and finally a 1/1,000,000 solution. Make estimates of the pH and then measure the pH.

9 Your lab instructor will ask for you to place your data on the board. Take the average pH value for a given dilution and add the data to Table 4.8. Plot the predicted and actual data you filled in Table 4.8 on Figure 4.1.

TABLE 4.7. Your pH measurements:

Cylinder volume used: _____ ml or measuring beaker used: _____ ml

pH of distilled water:	
pH of vinegar (undiluted):	
predicted pH of 1/10 solution:	actual pH of 1/10 solution:
predicted pH of 1/100 solution:	actual pH of 1/100 solution:
predicted pH of 1/1,000 solution:	actual pH of 1/1,000 solution:
predicted pH of 1/10,000 solution:	actual pH of 1/10,000 solution:
predicted pH of 1/100,000 solution:	actual pH of 1/100,000 solution:
predicted pH of 1/1,000,000 solution:	actual pH of 1/1,000,000 solution:

What do you think will be the correlation coefficient values? Is the relationship linear? (Remember, you are looking at a logarithmic scale, and the serial dilutions are of a factor of 10.) Your lab instructor will tell you the 'ideal' pH values over the range of dilutions.

What is the asymptote (the ultimate) pH value that your data would trend to? Why? Why can't the pH value be higher with subsequent dilutions?

TABLE 4.8. pH measurements

Solution	Replicate Values from the Entire Class										Mean	Ideal Value
	1	2	3	4	5	6	7	8	9	10		
distilled water												
vinegar												
1/10 solution												
1/100 solution												
1/1,000 solution												
1/10,000 solution												
1/100,000 solution												
1/1,000,000 solution												

FIGURE 4.1.

The effects of serial dilutions in the pH experiment.

Diffusion and Osmosis

One common principle of life is that living things exchange energy and matter with their environment. We will talk about several ways life exchanges materials with the physical environment.

1. **Simple Diffusion (Diffusion).** Diffusion is the movement of matter (in the form of atoms or molecules) from areas of high concentration to low concentration. The diffusing molecules (the small circles in Figure 4.2 and Figure 4.3) are said to 'move down their concentration gradients.' No energy use (in the form of ATP) is required by the cell for diffusion to occur. All molecules, if they are at temperatures above absolute zero, have some kinetic energy of motion. The movement is random, but because more molecules are in one spot (high concentration), they tend to move away from that spot rather than towards it. Oxygen and carbon dioxide move across cell membranes in the lining of the lungs and other respiratory surfaces because of diffusion.

   Diffusion occurs through both air and liquids. Molecules can also diffuse through barriers, such as membranes, if the membrane allows the molecules to pass through it. A **semipermeable membrane** (also called a selectively permeable membrane) is a membrane that allows certain molecules or atoms to pass through it by diffusion. If the molecules can pass through relatively easily, the membrane is considered to be **permeable** to that molecule. Other molecules, however, cannot pass through the semipermeable membrane (the membrane is considered **impermeable** with respect to these molecules). The rate at which the molecules move depends on the molecule's concentration, the molecule's size and charge, and on several physical factors, such as pressure and temperature. In addition, the relative permeability of the membrane is important.

2. **Facilitated diffusion** (or facilitated transport). The diffusion of molecules facilitated by a protein carrier across the membrane (Figure 4.3). One example of facilitated diffusion involves the movement of glucose into cells; glucose uses a carrier to cross the membrane of many cells. The molecules diffuse from areas of greater concentration to the opposite side of the membrane, where the concentration is lower, by moving through the pore in the transport protein. In facilitated diffusion, no ATP energy is needed.

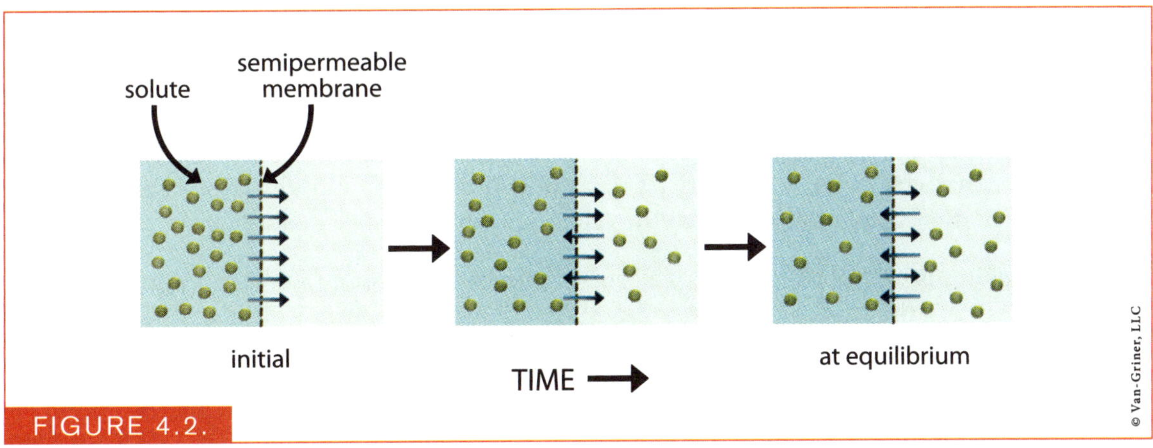

FIGURE 4.2.

Diffusion through a permeable membrane.

The **cell membrane** of living things consists of a lipid bilayer, composed of phospholipids and cholesterol, with a variety of proteins embedded in and lying on the membrane. Large molecules, polar molecules, and/or charged molecules (such as ions, and various carbohydrates and proteins) cannot easily cross most cellular membranes. In contrast, nonpolar molecules (lipids), and gases (such as oxygen and carbon dioxide) can cross the bilayer easily.

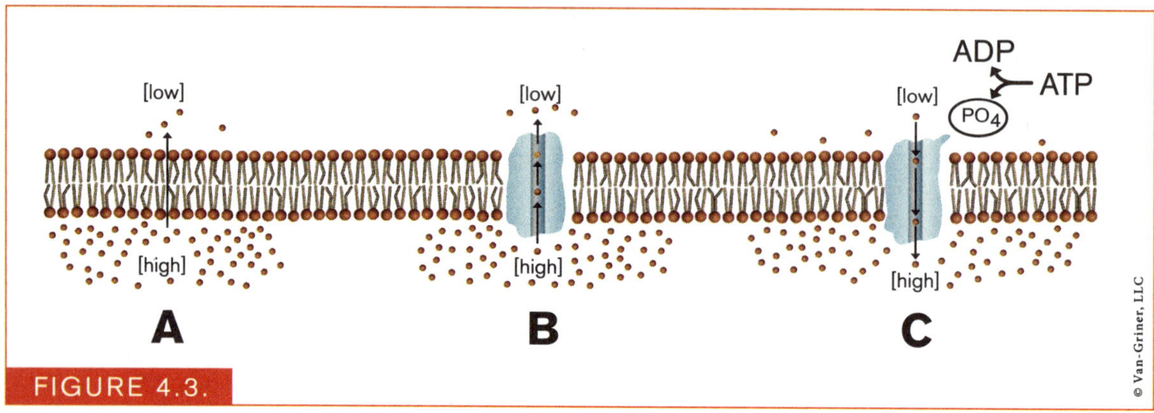

FIGURE 4.3.

Transport through cell membranes: A) diffusion, B) facilitated diffusion, and C) active transport.

❸ **Osmosis.** Osmosis is the diffusion of water across a semipermeable membrane. Osmosis refers only to the movement of water.

The diffusion of large amounts of water into and out of cells creates very big problems for both cells and organisms. Cells can be damaged if they swell or shrink, and could possibly die because of the stress caused by the shrinking or swelling. A solution can exert a 'force' against a membrane (this 'force' is called **osmotic pressure**), because of the movement of water across a membrane into the solution. The osmotic pressure of a solution increases as the number of particles dissolved in solution increases.

The term **'tonicity'** refers to the relative concentrations of solutes inside and outside the cell's plasma membrane.

a Cells lose water when placed in **hypertonic** solutions (Figure 4.4).

b Cells gain water when placed in **hypotonic** solutions (Figure 4.4).

c Solutions that contain the same concentration of solute particles as a cell are called **isotonic**. There can be movement of particles into and out of the cell into the isotonic solution, but the net movement of water inside the cell is equal to the movement of water outside.

If two solutions on opposite sides of a semipermeable membrane differ in tonicity, osmosis continues until the solutions are isotonic. When two solutions are isotonic, water molecules move at equal rates from one side to the other, with no net movement occurring (Figure 4.4).

The direction of osmosis is determined only by a difference in **total** solute concentration. The kinds of solutes in the solutions do not matter. The phenomenon of osmosis relies upon the principles of diffusion and facilitated diffusion.

The highly polar water molecules are an exception to the basic rule that polar molecules cannot easily pass cell membranes. To an extent, water can diffuse across the phospholipid membranes. However, there are special channels (made from proteins called **aquaporins**) that greatly facilitate the movement of water.

All cells, including plant cells and animal cells, respond to the tonicity of their environment (see Figure 4.4). However, plant cells and animal cells respond differently.

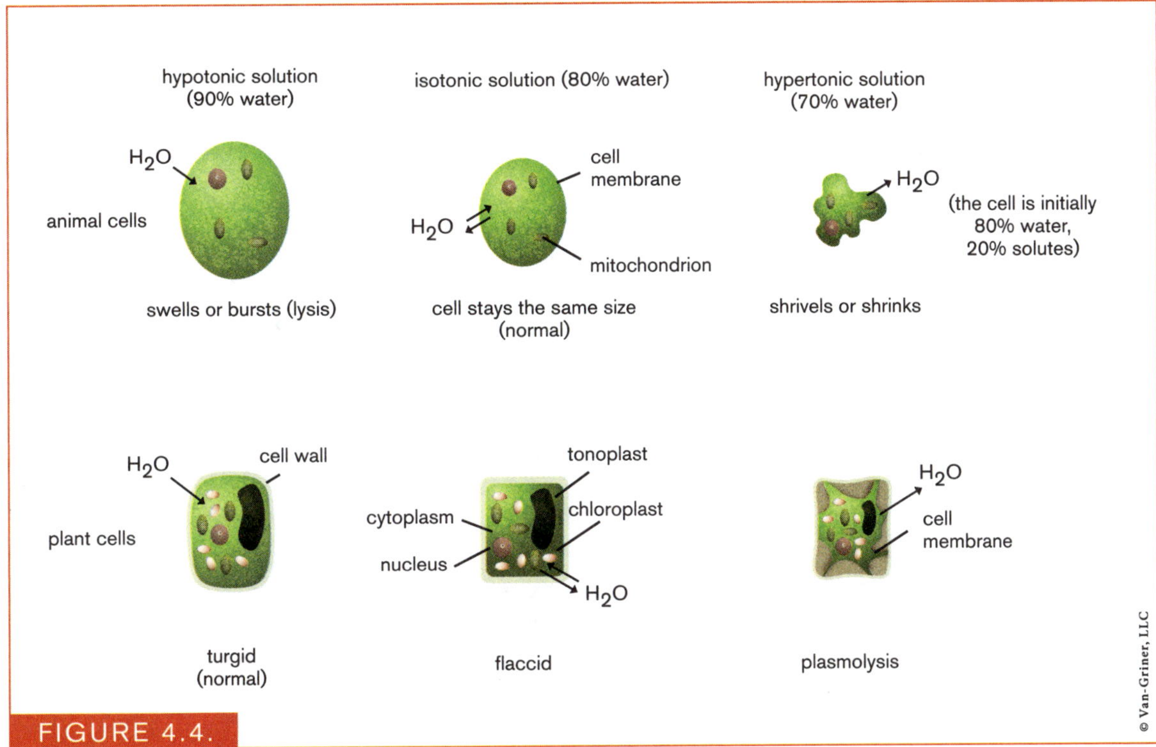

FIGURE 4.4.

Hypotonic, isotonic, and hypertonic solutions.

Hypotonic Environments

If a cell is placed in a **hypotonic solution,** it would swell by increasing in size (Figure 4.4). Water would diffuse into the cell from the extracellular fluid, causing the cell to swell. This inflow of water increases the pressure that the cytoplasm exerts on the membrane (called the hydrostatic pressure). If the membrane was strong enough, the cell could reach an equilibrium where the osmotic pressure (which is causing the water to move inside the cell) would be counterbalanced by the hydrostatic pressure (which is driving water back out of the cell). However, if a cell membrane is not strong enough, by itself, to hold up to this internal pressure, an isolated animal cell would **lyse,** or burst, like an overinflated balloon or rubber tire. Lysis subsequently kills the cell.

Because of the negative effects of hypotonic and hypertonic environments, it is important for most animal cells to be under isotonic conditions. Animal cells cannot tolerate excessive swelling or shrinking due to the uptake or loss of water. The problem is solved if the cell lives in an **isotonic environment** (for example, the interstitial fluids surrounding your cells). Terrestrial animals bathe many of their cells in an isotonic interstitial fluid. Seawater is isotonic to the tissues of most marine invertebrate animals. However, as animals (without cell walls) are exposed to dramatic changes in the tonicity of their environment, they must have various adaptations for **osmoregulation** (the regulation of water balance, in order to maintain the tonicity of the cells near a constant, optimal level). The large multicellular animals have a variety of organs (kidneys, salt glands, the lining of the digestive tract, gills and lungs, the skin) that regulate the degree of water gain/loss. Smaller animals and unicellular protists also have important adaptations for water gain/loss; for example, many protists that live in hypotonic environments have contractile vacuoles that force excess water out of the cell as fast as it enters by osmosis.

Marine organisms live in a **hypertonic** environment (greater concentration of water inside than outside the organism), thus water tends to move by osmosis out of the body into the environment. Some of the marine animals have adaptations to retain water and salts. For example, sharks have a special adaptation where they retain urea in their blood in order to raise their osmotic potential to that of seawater, stopping the net loss of water.

Many freshwater animals live in a **hypotonic** environment (greater concentration of water outside compared to inside the organism), where freshwater has a higher water concentration than the body fluids, thus they have the opposite problem of marine animals. Water is diffusing in constantly, and the animals also could lose a lot of salts with the active excretion of water, unless they have developed kidneys that can retain salts while excreting excess water.

Plant cells (as well as the cells of other organisms with cell walls) are **turgid,** or firm, when placed in hypotonic environments (Figure 4.4). The turgid state is generally considered to be the normal, healthy condition for plant cells. The osmotic uptake of water (the osmotic pressure) is counteracted in large part by pressure (**turgor pressure**) exerted on the elastic cell wall by the hydrostatic pressure inside the turgid cell. The cell wall can expand only so far, then it creates a 'back pressure' on the cell that opposes additional water uptake. In the case of plants and other organisms with cell walls, the cell wall is strong enough to hold up to hydrostatic pressures that the cell membrane cannot tolerate. In isotonic environments, the osmotic strength of the plant cell cytoplasm and their surroundings are equal, and the cells become **flaccid,** or limp. The plant as a whole then droops, or appears wilted.

Hypertonic Environments

If any cell is placed in hypertonic solutions, it loses water by osmosis and shrinks. Animal cells shrivel when kept in hypertonic environments. The loss of water can be deadly for animal cells because of the disruption of many cellular functions (Figure 4.4).

If plant cells are kept under hypertonic conditions for a long period of time, the plant cell shrivels, and the cell will **plasmolyze,** where the cell membrane begins to pull away from the cell wall (Figure 4.4). Plasmolyzed cells eventually die. This phenomenon, rare or absent in animals, occurs in plants and also in the other organisms with cells walls: fungi, plantlike protists, and bacteria.

4 **Active Transport.** Active transport is the movement of materials against their concentration gradients, opposite of the way they would move by diffusion. Active transport is the movement of molecules from areas of low concentration to areas of high concentration (Figure 4.3). We will not be examining active transport today, but you are to compare and contrast active transport with the processes of diffusion and osmosis.

a Active transport is important for the functioning of all cells, such as nerve cells and muscle cells in animals.

b Active transport is critical for a cell to maintain its internal concentrations of small molecules that would otherwise diffuse across the membrane.

c Active transport is performed by specific **transport proteins** embedded in the membranes.

d Active transport requires energy expenditures (ATP) by the cell. ATP powers active transport by shifting a phosphate group from ATP (forming ADP) to the transport protein. This **phosphorylation** induces a conformational change in the transport protein that then translocates the solute across the membrane.

Exercise 4.4.
The Effect of Osmotic Strength on Potato Tubers

In this experiment, you will measure the effect of different osmotic concentrations (using different sucrose solutions) on the volume of potato pieces ('fries') in order to determine the osmotic strength of the cytoplasm of the plant cells.

A potato cell has an outer cell membrane (**plasma membrane**) and a large central vacuole with a membrane (the membrane around the central vacuole is called the **tonoplast**). The cytoplasm is mostly water. When a potato cell is placed in water or a sucrose solution, water will move across the selectively permeable membranes of the plasma membrane and the tonoplast. How much water moves and the direction of movement will depend on the relative osmotic strength of the potato cell. Water will always move from areas of higher water potential (relatively more water molecules, higher free energy) to areas of lower water potential (relative fewer water molecules, and lower free energy). The water potential is influenced by the relative solute concentrations inside and outside of the cell and the physical pressure exerted on the cell walls from the outside and inside.

In this exercise, you will determine the osmolarity of the potato tuber tissues, based on their change in weight in response to immersion in different solutions. This exercise allows you to determine an unknown (the osmotic strength of the potato tissues) by comparing the behavior of potato tissues under a range of known conditions (immersing the potato tissue in solutions of known osmotic strengths).

Carry out the procedure below, in small groups.

Step 1 Obtain six beakers. Fill one beaker with 100 ml of distilled water. Fill the other five beakers with 100 ml of each of five sucrose solutions: 0.1, 0.2, 0.3, 0.4, and 0.5 Molar (a 1 M solution contains one mole of solute in a liter of water).

Step 2 Obtain six potato pieces from your lab instructor. Gently blot your potato pieces on paper towels to remove excess moisture. Line up all of the pieces, and cut them all to equal lengths (as close as you can) using the razor blades. **BE CAREFUL WITH THE RAZORS!** The pieces should be small enough to be immersed in the solutions, but large enough to provide measurable data over the time period allowed.

Step 3 Weigh the pieces using the weigh scale (to milligrams) and place your data in Table 4.9. Your lab instructor will direct you in this exercise. If you are measuring weights using the weigh scale, be very careful and keep the scale clean and dry. Do not set heavy weights on the scale. Work quickly through Steps 2 to 4, so your potato pieces do not dry out.

Step 4   Add one potato piece to each beaker containing the solutions.

Step 5   Incubate these potato pieces for at least one hour (**work on the rest of the lab exercises while you wait!**). The longer you can wait before taking the potato pieces out of the solution, the better.

Step 6   After the end of the hour, remove each potato piece and gently dry it by blotting with paper towels.

Step 7   Weigh your potato pieces again. Add your data to Table 4.9.

Step 8   Calculate the percentage change (increase or decrease) in the weights of your potato pieces. Place your results (percent change as a function of molarity) on the board with the rest of the class's data. Add the results of the entire class to Table 4.10. Calculate the average percent change of potato tissue for each molarity, using the data obtained by the entire class.

Step 9   **Before** examining the final results of the experiment, make a prediction on what the results would be. Draw your predicted curve relating the percent change as a function of molarity in Figure 4.5. Label this line "predicted results."

What, exactly, is the alternative hypothesis of this experiment? What would be a null hypothesis?

What is the dependent variable in this experiment? The independent variable? What variables should be held constant (in other words, control variables)?

dependent variable:

independent variable:

control variables:

Once you have obtained the average percent change of potato tissue at each sucrose concentration, plot the observed results. Label this line as "observed results."

How can you estimate the osmotic strength of potato tissue? Looking at your data in Table 4.10 and Figure 4.5, what is your estimate of the molarity of the potato tissue? How did your predicted results compare with your observed results?

TABLE 4.9. Results of the osmosis experiment using weight change as the dependent variable.

Sample	Solution	Initial Weight (mg)	Final Weight (mg)	Change in Weight (mg)	Percent Change
	0 (water)				
	0.1 M				
	0.2 M				
	0.3 M				
	0.4 M				
	0.5 M				

TABLE 4.10. Class results of the osmosis experiment.

Molarity	Replicate Values from the Class: The Percent Change in Potato Tissues										Average
	1	2	3	4	5	6	7	8	9	10	
0											
0.1 M											
0.2 M											
0.3 M											
0.4 M											
0.5 M											

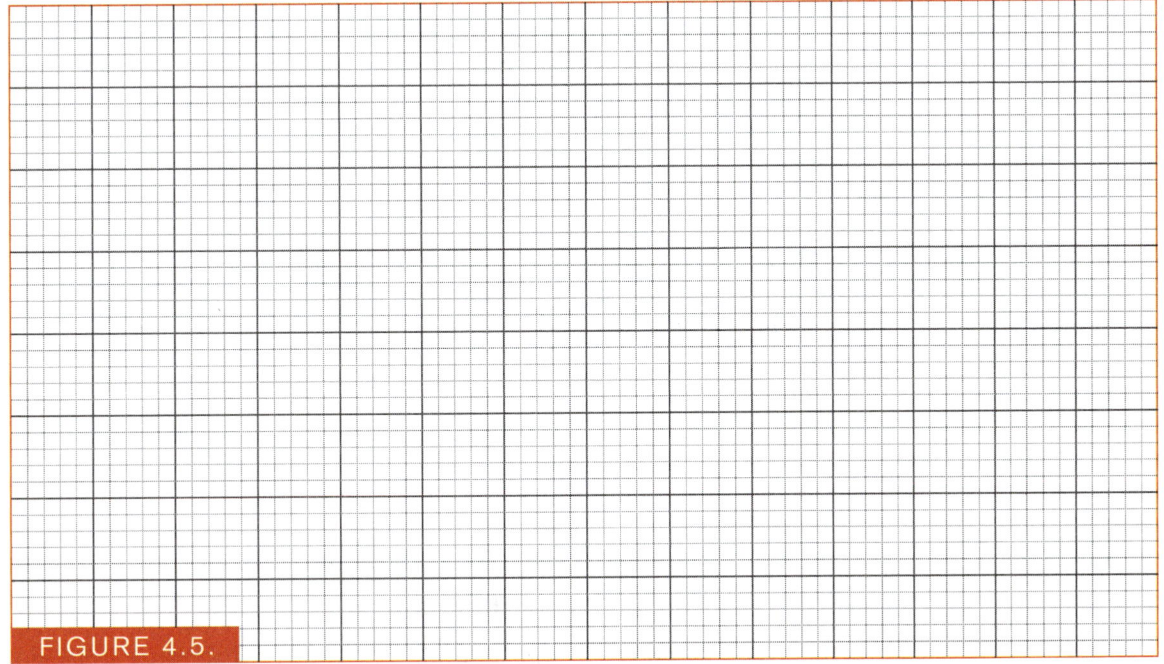

FIGURE 4.5. Percent weight change of potato tuber tissue as a function of sucrose concentration.

Exercise 4.5.

Accuracy and Precision

Sampling Error

You will discover that your estimates can be different from the true values for the phenomena you will observe in this class. The variability in the estimates made by you and your classmates represents the **sampling error**—where the samples' estimates cluster about the true value of the thing you are measuring. Sampling errors can be reduced by sampling a population a larger number of times (increasing the replicate size) and standardizing the procedure used in the making the measurements, as well as attempting to not violate any of the assumptions of the measuring procedure. Sampling errors can also be minimized by using more precise instruments.

Measurements and Uncertainty: Accuracy and Precision

Scientists realize every measurement is an approximation. There is a degree of uncertainty to every measurement, but scientists strive to minimize uncertainty with high accuracy and high precision.

Let's say you may make dinner tables for a living, and to your eye, all ten of the tables you made this week look identical in height. However, in reality, no two tables are the same in height; they are only approximately the same size. Measurements are limited by the **accuracy** (which is affected by the reliability of the instrument or the observer) and by the **precision** of the instrument used (which is affected by the degree of exactness with which something is measured). In addition to accuracy and precision, a third limitation of measurements is the degree of **resolution** (or resolving power) of the instrument being used.

❶ **Accuracy** is an indication of how closely a measurement or statistic made by the observer is to the true value. In Unit 2, you measured the lengths of a sample of snails or some other species. Your accuracy was indicated by the degree your estimate was close to the 'true' mean.

❷ **Precision** is a measure of how closely repeated measurements of the same thing agree with one another. The degree of exactness or reproducibility of a measurement is a measure of its precision. One way to think about precision is that precision thus is a measure of the 'scatter' in the data. Data with less 'scatter' would be considered more precise. Precision also shows how repeatable the results of a measurement are. A precise measuring instrument will give very nearly the same result each time it is used. One important distinction between accuracy and precision is that accuracy can be determined by only one measurement, while precision can only be determined with multiple measurements.

Precision has nothing to do with the true or accepted value of a measurement, so it is quite possible to be very precise and totally inaccurate. If a balance or a thermometer is not working correctly, then the instrument might consistently give inaccurate answers, resulting in high precision, but low accuracy.

High accuracy is obtained by using the appropriate correct method or procedure with instruments that give reliable results. High precision is obtained by using a given method or procedure correctly and consistently, using equipment that has a higher or finer **degree of resolution.** For example, a ruler stick marked off in centimeters is not as precise (it does not have as fine of a degree of resolution) as a ruler stick marked off in millimeters. Review the section in Unit 2, when we discussed the concept of rounding off numbers and the importance of precision.

It is important in science, technology and engineering to understand the difference between accuracy and precision. For example, an engineer states that the rubber O-ring used to seal fuel in the space shuttle becomes brittle at –1°C (30°F). Is it safe to fly the shuttle at 0°C? Is the ring partially brittle? Is the temperature at which the O-ring actually fails equal to 0°C? Is the degree of uncertainty ±1°C (the shuttle is unsafe to fly) or ±0.1°C (the shuttle is safe to fly)? The ± symbol means "plus or minus" and gives the reader an indication of the level of uncertainty (this level of uncertainty may be the range of the measurements, or the standard error of the mean measurement, or some other descriptive statistic).

In biology, many examples exist concerning uncertainty. As an example, a rare species has been found to live only in one location. If the habitat in which the species lives is cut in half (the other half has been developed into housing subdivisions), will this cause the population to go extinct? What if the habitat is cut by 10%? Does it matter if the population size is 500 ± 100 individuals? 500 ± 10 individuals? 5,000 ± 100 individuals?

Does reducing the habitat of a threatened species by 10% dramatically increase the chance of extinction? Will increasing the wildlife area by 10% ensure long term survival of a threatened species? How does this change in the area set aside for preservation affect the sustainability of local economies? In order to make a sound decision, you must know the ranges of the uncertainty of the measurement (for example, the population size, life history, and range of the species in question).

If a particular drug appears to increase the survival rate by 1%, is this increase 'real?' Understanding uncertainty is crucial because not taking the level of uncertainty into account may cost a large amount of money or time or lives. Not understanding the level of uncertainty may cause the loss of the species or habitat you are trying to protect, or it may cause patients to suffer from an uncertain application of a drug that was not adequately tested.

Figure 4.6 and Figure 4.7 depicts two different examples that distinguishes accuracy from precision. Note that you can have low or high precision with either low or high accuracy. The bull's-eye represents the actual or true value; the *X* symbols represent sample measurements. Their clumping represents precision, whereas their exact position relative to the bull's-eye represents accuracy.

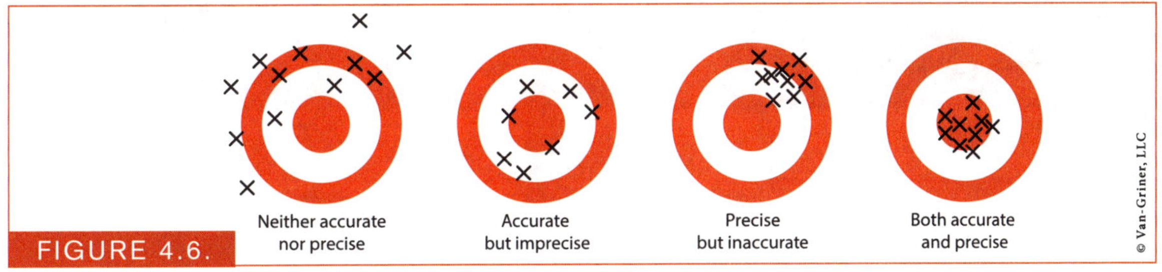

FIGURE 4.6.

A target analogy of the difference between accuracy and precision.

Every measurement contains a degree of uncertainty due to the limits of instruments that are used to make the measurement and the people using them. In general, a measurement is reported with one or more digits that are known with certainty and a final digit that is estimated. For example, suppose you are reading a thermometer that reads a temperature that has lines to mark each degree Celsius (°C), then you

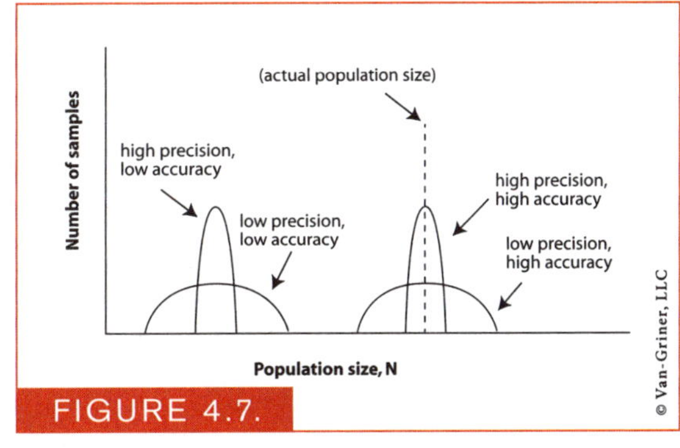

FIGURE 4.7.

The difference between accuracy and precision: population size estimation.

should report the temperature to the nearest tenth of a degree, if possible (i.e., 22.5°C). This would show that the 22°C is certain and the 0.5°C is an estimate. If you have trouble, review the concepts of significant digits back in Unit 2.

Procedure. There is a small block on the center table. The class will be divided into two groups: A and B. Group A will measure the block using the calipers from Unit 2. Group B will be using a large meter stick. Estimate the value to the nearest 0.1 mm (if using calipers) and to the nearest mm (if using the meter stick). At least ten students from each group measure the length, width, and the height of the block and place the class data on the front board. Copy the class data into Table 4.11 and Table 4.12.

TABLE 4.11.

Dimension	Replicate Values from the Entire Class, Using the *Calipers*										Mean	S.D.
	1	2	3	4	5	6	7	8	9	10		
length												
width												
height												
volume												

TABLE 4.12.

Dimension	Replicate Values from the Entire Class, Using the *Meter Stick*										Mean	S.D.
	1	2	3	4	5	6	7	8	9	10		
length												
width												
height												
volume												

Compare the average volume values calculated from using both measuring devices (the calipers versus the meter stick). Your lab instructor will give you the 'true volume.' Which device provided the greatest accuracy? The greatest precision?

In Unit 2, suppose you took measurements of each object with two measuring devices: electronic calipers that went to hundredths of millimeters, and a meter stick divided into millimeters. Suppose you measured each object five times with each device and took an average. Which estimate would be more precise, and which estimate would be more accurate?

5 UNIT
Respiration and Photosynthesis

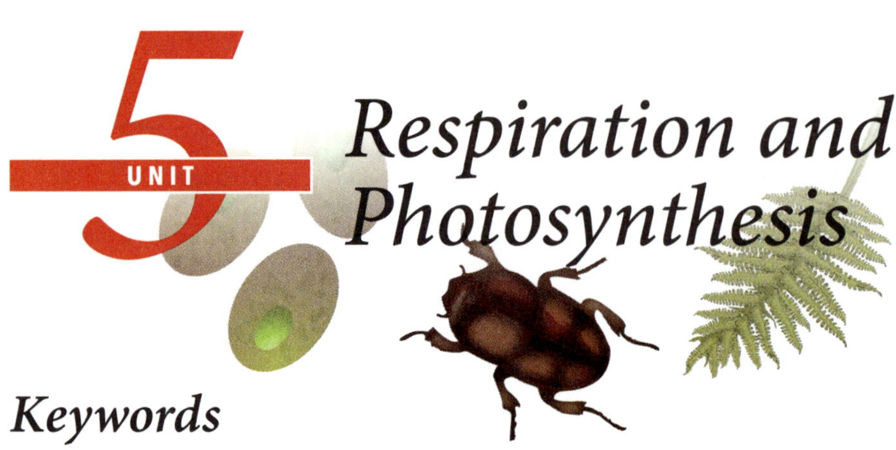

Keywords

glycolysis
oxidized
reduced
Krebs cycle
electron transport chain
chemiosmosis
ATP
NADH
$FADH_2$
pyruvate

alcoholic fermentation
lactic acid (lactate) fermentation
anaerobic respiration
aerobic respiration
chlorophyll
light reactions (light dependent reactions)
Calvin cycle (light independent reactions)

NADPH
mitochondria
chloroplasts
stroma
matrix
intermembrane space
photons
cristae
inner membrane
outer membrane

Learning Objectives

When finished with this unit, you should be able to:

1. Describe the basic processes that occur in glycolysis and fermentation (lactic acid fermentation and alcoholic fermentation);

2. Discuss the basic steps of aerobic respiration and state the specific cellular location where each step occurs: glycolysis, Krebs cycle and electron transport;

3. Describe the structure of the mitochondrion and relate its structure to aerobic respiration;

4. Compare and contrast fermentation and aerobic respiration, in terms of the products and the net ATP yield;

5. Describe the basic chemical equations for aerobic respiration, anaerobic respiration (fermentation), and photosynthesis, listing the reactants and products of each reaction;

6. Name the major photosynthetic pigments and their functions;

7. Interpret the absorption spectrum for the photosynthetic pigments;

8. Discuss the basic steps of photosynthesis (light reactions, Calvin cycle) and the specific location in which each step occurs;

9. Describe the structure of the chloroplast and relate its structure to photosynthesis;

10 Use gas sensors to measure the amount of oxygen and carbon dioxide consumed or produced by organisms; and

11 Correctly produce and evaluate figures and tables.

Respiration

All living things use energy to do work and maintain order: grow, repair, move, and reproduce. Cellular respiration and photosynthesis are the two major metabolic pathways found in living things. By using photosynthesis, plants (as well as the photoautotrophic algae and bacteria) capture and store energy from the sun in the form of chemical bonds that hold sugars together. When they require energy for cellular work, plants then can tap this stored energy by the process of cellular respiration. In addition to the autotrophs, all other living organisms respire. Cellular respiration refers to the process by which living organisms convert the chemical energy stored in organic molecules into a form immediately usable by organisms, in the form of ATP. All organisms (plants, animals, fungi, protists, and bacteria) oxidize glucose (as well as other organic compounds) for energy. In aerobic respiration, glucose is oxidized completely to water and carbon dioxide if there is oxygen available.

The overall equation for aerobic respiration is shown below.

$$\textbf{C}_6\textbf{H}_{12}\textbf{O}_6 + \textbf{6O}_2 \rightarrow \textbf{6CO}_2 + \textbf{6H}_2\textbf{O} + \textbf{approximately 30 to 32 ATP + heat}$$

Glucose, ATP, and water molecules are more reduced molecules compared to O_2 and CO_2 molecules, which are more oxidized.

When scientists refer to the process of oxidation, this means that a molecule has lost one or more electrons to another molecule. The process of reduction is one in which a molecule gains an electron from another molecule. In the generalized equation above, glucose ($C_6H_{12}O_6$) molecules are oxidized to carbon dioxide molecules, and oxygen atoms are reduced to water molecules. The basic idea of both respiration and photosynthesis is the movement of these electrons (which represent energy) from one molecule to another through a series of chemical reactions, where molecules pass the electrons from one to another. Each molecule thus alternates between its oxidized and reduced state as it loses or gains electrons.

Organic molecules (such as fat, glucose, and starch) contain many electrons and associated hydrogen ions (protons) and thus, contain a lot of stored energy that can be 'harvested.' Respiration and photosynthesis are the pathways that 'harvest' this energy.

There are three main steps to aerobic respiration in living things. We will talk briefly about each step:

a **Glycolysis,**

b **Krebs cycle (also called the TCA [tricarboxylic acid] cycle, also called the citric acid cycle),**

c **Electron transport chain (ETC) and the chemiosmotic production of ATP.**

Glycolysis

Glycolysis is a pathway that occurs in the cytoplasm of the cell. In glycolysis (see Figure 5.1), **glucose** (a six-carbon sugar, 6C) is partially oxidized, or broken down, to two three-carbon molecules (3C) called **pyruvate.** No carbon dioxide is produced by glycolysis. Glycolysis occurs regardless of the presence or absence of oxygen; oxygen is not needed.

During glycolysis, a series of enzymes, found in the **cytosol** (the fluid portion of the cytoplasm), sequentially breaks down glucose to pyruvate.

In order for glycolysis to occur, 2 ATP ("**Ad**enosine **Tri**Phosphate") are actually needed to start the process. A total of four ATP are produced by glycolysis by the end, thus a net of 2 ATP is produced.

Glycolysis also produces two **NADH molecules** ("**N**icotinamide **A**denine **D**inucleotide") from the oxidized form of NAD (NAD$^+$). NAD acts as a **coenzyme** for several enzymes that are involved in the oxidation of glucose. As NAD is reduced, it picks up two electrons and two protons. NADH can be viewed as a second type of 'energy carrier' that is produced by glcolysis. As glucose is broken down, it is oxidized slowly by a series of enzymatic steps, with hydrogens and electrons being stripped from the molecule.

Anaerobic Respiration, or Fermentation

In plant and animal cells, the energy in NADH can be further harvested by the ETC and associated proteins to produce more ATP (more on this later). However, in some cells, glycolysis is the end of the harvesting of energy. For example, you will observe yeast performing glycolysis followed by a process called **fermentation** (see Figure 5.2).

Yeast use glycolysis to produce ATP, but they do not have to take the next two steps of aerobic respiration: the Krebs cycle and the ETC. In order to recycle the NADH molecules back to their oxidized states (NAD$^+$), so that the yeast may continue glycolysis, yeast reoxidize the NADH back to NAD$^+$ by transferring the electrons and protons back to pyruvate, forming ethanol.

The overall chemical reaction for alcoholic fermentation is shown in the upper portion of Figure 5.2. The reactants and end products are in the boxes. Ethanol is the end product of **alcoholic fermentation.** In addition, carbon dioxide (CO_2) is an important by-product of this reaction. Fermentation is an important process; many of the foods you enjoy are made by yeast undergoing **fermentation.**

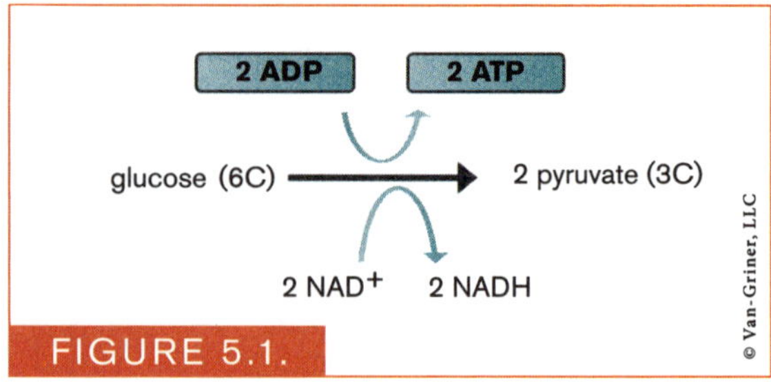

FIGURE 5.1.

Overview of glycolysis.

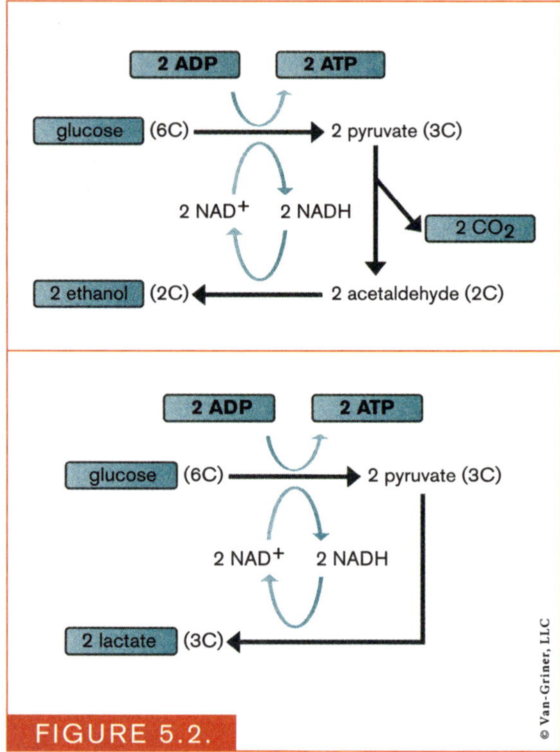

FIGURE 5.2.

Two forms of fermentation.

Your muscle cells use a related process called **lactic acid (lactate) fermentation** (in the lower portion of Figure 5.2). Muscle cells, in the absence of oxygen, can continue glycolysis by a 'fermentation' process that differs slightly from alcoholic fermentation. Even with little oxygen around (for example, during times when you are undergoing strenuous exercise), your muscle cells can continue producing a small amount of ATP for a brief period of time.

In lactic acid fermentation, the pyruvate is reduced to lactate (the acid form is lactic acid). Note that no CO_2 gas is created in lactic acid fermentation, gas that would eventually leave the cell. This process is important because, like alcoholic fermentation, the NADH molecules are reoxidized back to NAD^+, and your muscle cells thus can continue breaking down glucose anaerobically for a while. Later on, once in the presence of sufficient oxygen, the lactate produced by lactic acid fermentation can be converted back into pyruvate and aerobic respiration can then resume.

ATP molecules are central to metabolism. The chemical bonds that hold ATP together contain large amounts of energy, which can be used for work in the cell. Cells perform work in many ways, typically by transferring a phosphate group from ATP to enzymes and other molecules, thus activating them. This process of tacking on a phosphate to a molecule, which then energizes the molecule, is called **phosphorylation.**

At any given point in time, cells contain only a very small store of ATP. Cells thus must have some way to recycle ADP back into ATP. The re-synthesis of ATP is an important function of all major metabolic pathways, including glycolysis, fermentation, aerobic respiration, and photosynthesis.

Aerobic Respiration: Krebs Cycle and ETC/Chemiosmosis

Compared to the energy extracting capability of many plant and animal cells, alcoholic fermentation in yeast cells is not as efficient at obtaining energy from glucose. Pyruvate and ethanol still contain a considerable amount of energy (pyruvate possesses several more 'extractable' electrons and associated hydrogens) that could be tapped to produce ATP. After glycolysis, plant and animal cells can extract more energy from glucose by the process of **aerobic respiration.**

Glycolysis is the first step in both fermentation and aerobic respiration (Step A in Figure 5.3). However, your cells take the pyruvate formed from glycolysis and break it down further via the **Krebs cycle** to carbon dioxide and water. The energy (electrons) in pyruvate has been transferred to various energy carriers (NADH, $FADH_2$, and ATP). The energy carriers NADH and $FADH_2$ ("**F**lavin **A**denine **D**inucleotide") are reoxidized by the **electron transport chain** ('ETC').

After glucose has been broken down to pyruvate, pyruvate then enters the mitochondrion. In order for pyruvate to enter the Krebs cycle, pyruvate first is converted to acetyl coA (Step B in Figure 5.3). At this preparatory step, for each pyruvate (remember that **two pyruvates are made from one glucose**), another NADH is reduced and a carbon dioxide molecule is released. The enzyme that catalyzes this step removes the CO_2 and adds the coenzyme A to the pyruvate.

Both the Krebs cycle and the ETC occur inside the mitochondrion, whereas glycolysis and fermentation occur in the cell's cytoplasm. To be specific, the Krebs cycle occurs inside the inner membrane of the mitochondrion, in the **matrix** (see Figure 5.3), whereas the ETC complex (and the associated ATP synthetase enzyme complex, which creates ATP) is embedded in the membranes of the **cristae** (singular: crista), which are a series of infoldings of the inner membrane that extend into the matrix (see Figure 5.4).

The **Krebs cycle** oxidizes acetyl coA to two carbon dioxide molecules over a series of steps (Step C in Figure 5.3). First, acetyl coA is transferred from the cytosol into the matrix (the inner compartment of the mitochondrion, see Figure 5.4). In the matrix, enzymes of the Krebs cycle break up the relatively reduced two-carbon acetyl coAs to two completely oxidized carbon dioxides. There is a series of eight enzymatic steps to the cycle. The acetyl group is added to a four carbon molecule (oxaloacetate, or OAA). OAA is subsequently rearranged, and over the next steps, two carbon dioxides removed, and the cycle finally reforms OAA so that the cycle can accept another acetyl group again. For the two acetyl coA molecules that were produced from one glucose molecule, 4 carbon dioxide molecules, 2 ATP, 6 NADH, and 2 $FADH_2$ (another energy carrier, similar to NADH) are produced from the oxidation of the two acetyl groups (Figure 5.3).

The **electron transport chain** and the production of ATP by **chemiosmosis** make up the last step of aerobic respiration (Step D in Figure 5.3). The reduced energy carriers NADH and $FADH_2$ are reoxidized back to NAD and FAD by transferring high energy electrons to a series of proteins in the inner mitochondrial membrane (see Figure 5.3). The energy that is in these electrons is slowly 'removed' as the electrons are transferred from one protein to the next in the chain.

However, the cytochromes have to eventually get rid of these electrons, or electrons would clog the system and shut down the ETC. The final electron acceptor is an oxygen atom from an oxygen molecule. An oxygen atom picks up two electrons and two hydrogen ions from the medium and thus is reduced to water. The energy supplied by the electrons helps to create a hydrogen ion (proton) gradient across the inner mitochondrial membrane. **The intermembrane space** (Figure 5.4) between the two mitochondrial membranes thus has a low pH, because of the high hydrogen ion concentrations.

This high hydrogen ion concentration inside the intermembrane space is a form of **potential energy.** As these protons flow back across the inner membrane into the matrix, some of their energy is captured and used to produce ATP (and the protons are captured by oxygen to produce water). **Chemiosmosis** refers to the energy-coupling mechanism that uses the energy stored in the hydrogen ion gradient (created by the activities of the ETC) with ATP production (by a complex of proteins associated called **ATP synthetase**). **Oxidative phosphorylation** refers to the whole process of the electron transport chain and chemiosmosis working together to eventually generate ATP. This type of ATP phosphorylation is different from the **substrate-level phosphorylation** of ATP that occurs in glycolysis and in the Krebs cycle, where an enzyme attaches a phosphate to ADP directly. Like the proteins of the ETC, the ATP synthetase complex is embedded in the inner mitochondrial membrane near the proteins of the ETC. As the protons diffuse through a cylindrical protein channel (which is part of the ATP synthetase complex) across the inner mitochondrial membrane, they cause part of the molecule to spin, and this **kinetic energy** is used by ATP synthetase to create ATP from ADP and phosphate, found in the matrix.

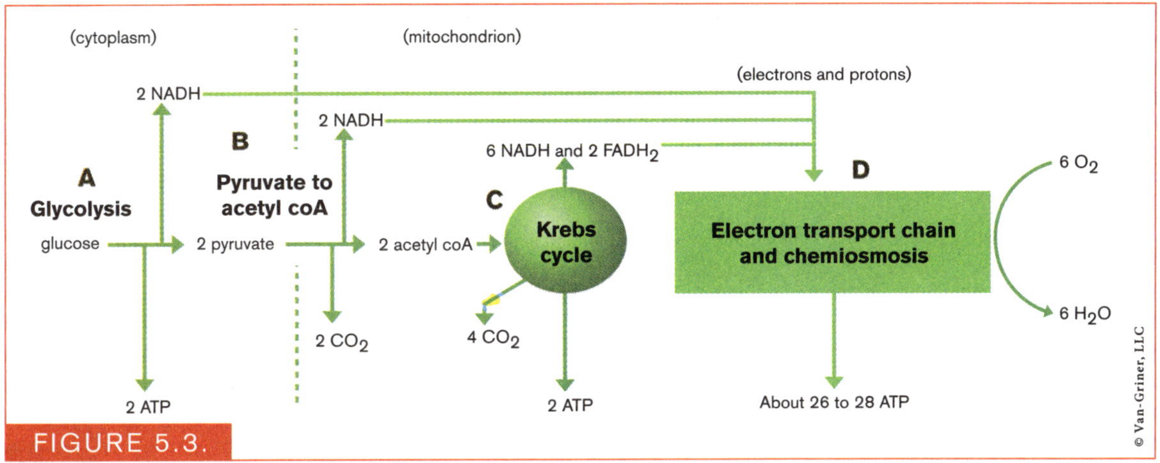

FIGURE 5.3.

Overview of cellular respiration.

The final electron acceptor of the ETC is oxygen, which is reduced to water (Figure 5.3). Oxygen is thus essential for cells using aerobic respiration.

The yield of ATP is much greater in aerobic respiration (Table 5.1), compared with fermentation (a net production of 2 ATP).

In older texts, the number of ATP produced for electron carrier was thought to be about 3 ATP per NADH, and 2 ATP per $FADH_2$. However, new research suggests that only about 2.5 ATP are produced per NADH, and 1.5 ATP per $FADH_2$ (the adjusted totals are shown in the brackets in Table 5.1). In addition, in some animal cells, an additional ATP is used per molecule of NADH that was reduced by glycolysis and whose electrons are shuttled into the mitochondrion. **Therefore, per glucose molecule, a net of about 30 to 32 ATP are produced by aerobic respiration.** This ATP yield is still considerably higher than that of anaerobic respiration.

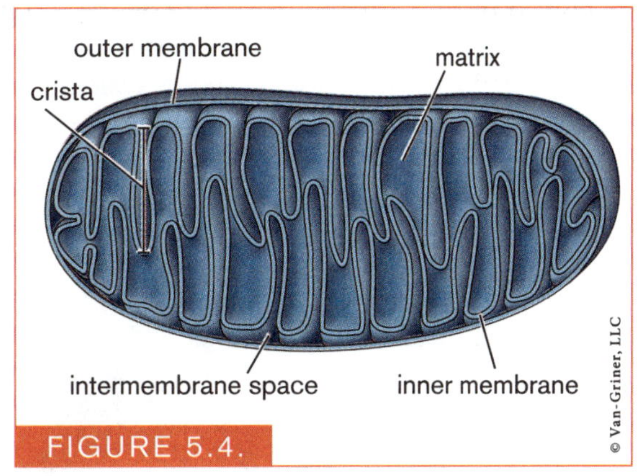

FIGURE 5.4.

Mitochondrial structure.

TABLE 5.1.

Energy Yields in the Steps of Respiration	Net Number of ATP Produced, per Glucose	Number of NADH Produced	Number of FADH₂ Produced
glycolysis	2 ATP	2 NADH	
pyruvate to acetyl coA		2 NADH	
Krebs cycle	2 ATP	6 NADH	2 FADH₂
totals	4 ATP	10 NADH	2 FADH₂
ATP equivalents	4 ATP	30 ATP [25 ATP]	4 ATP [3 ATP]

Photosynthesis

We will leave respiration for now and talk about the other major metabolic pathway: the pathway plants and other autotrophic organisms use to capture light energy from the sun and convert it into chemical energy. This process is called **photosynthesis.** First, we will examine the characteristics of light.

Visible light is a form of electromagnetic energy or radiation. **Electromagnetic radiation** (EMR) can be viewed as traveling in a rhythmic wave-like pattern through space. The distance between the crests of the electromagnetic waves is called the **wavelength** (which can be measured in units ranging from nanometers to a kilometer or more). The entire range of wavelengths is called the **electromagnetic spectrum** (see Figure 5.5). **Visible light,** the range of wavelengths important for photosynthesis, ranges from roughly 380 to about 750 nm. This range of wavelengths also is the same range that most humans and many animals perceive as visible light. Compared to visible light, ultraviolet radiation has a shorter wavelength (and x-rays and gamma rays are shorter still), and wavelengths that are longer than the reddish portion of visible light make up the infrared, micro-wave, and radio wave portion of the spectrum. Our sun puts out most of its EMR energy in the form of visible, ultraviolet, and infrared wavelengths (some infrared wavelengths we sense as heat).

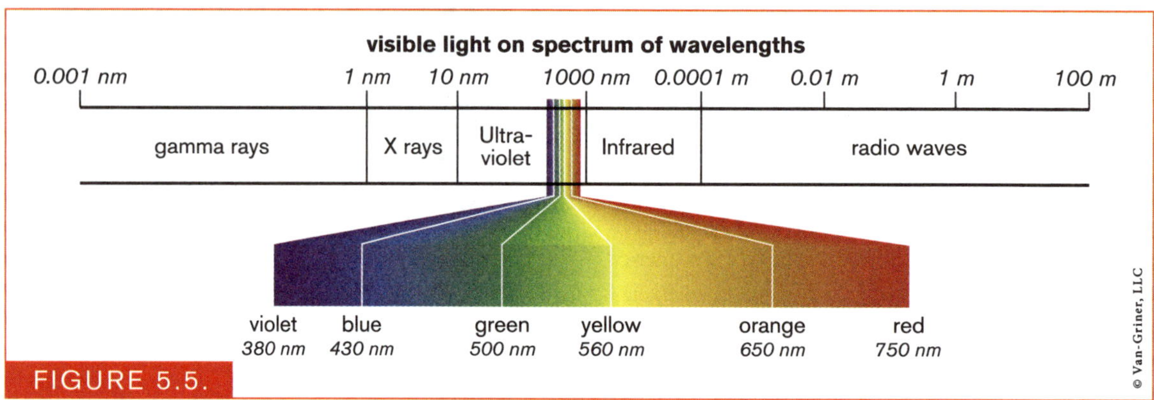

FIGURE 5.5.

The electromagnetic spectrum.

In addition to being viewed as waves, light and other forms of EMR can also be viewed as consisting of discrete particles, or **photons,** with a fixed quantity of energy, depending on wavelength. There is an **inverse** relationship between wavelength and energy, so that violet light (the shortest visible light) has about twice as much energy per photon as red light (the longest visible wavelengths).

The overall reaction of photosynthesis is shown in the equation below and the process is diagrammed in Figure 5.6.

$$6CO_2 + 6H_2O + \textbf{light energy} \rightarrow C_6H_{12}O_6 + 6O_2$$

Observe that the reaction for photosynthesis is very similar to what would be the 'reverse' of respiration. Again, the carbon dioxide and oxygen molecules are more oxidized compared to the water and glucose molecules. Light energy is captured by the chlorophyll molecules (the pigments that make plants appear green). This light energy is used to essentially combine carbon dioxide and water and form glucose, the simple carbohydrate that is used in the respiratory pathways. The chemical bonds holding the atoms of glucose together contain the energy that was originally from the sun. Also note that oxygen is an important by-product of photosynthesis. Plants give off oxygen, which in turn is used by all organisms for aerobic respiration.

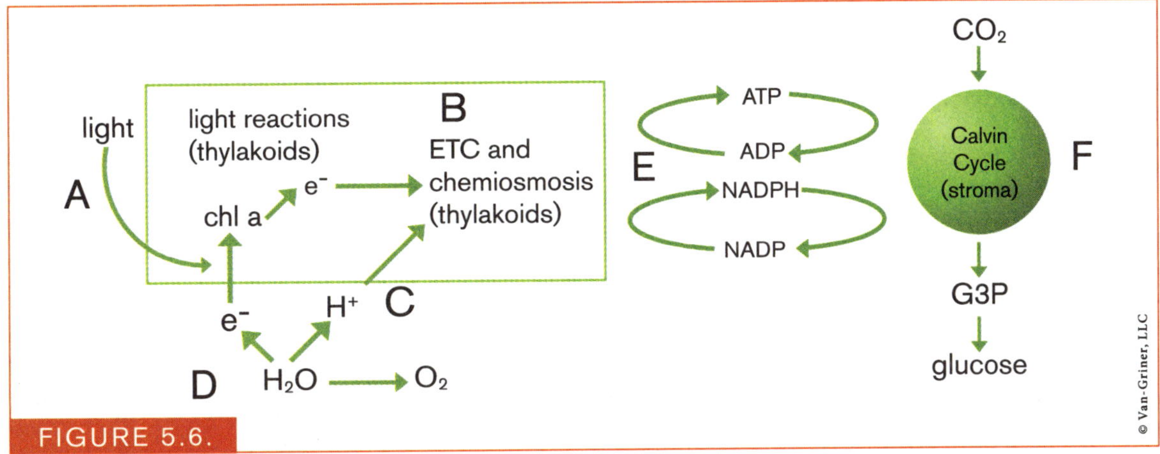

FIGURE 5.6.

Overview of photosynthesis.

Photosynthesis occurs in two major parts, the **light dependent reactions** and the **Calvin cycle** (Figure 5.6). These steps both occur in the **chloroplast** (see Figure 5.7). The first step, the **light dependent reactions,** captures light energy for the synthesis of ATP from ADP and the production of NADPH from NADP. NADPH ('**Nicotinamide Adenine Dinucleotide Phosphate**') is an energy carrier very similar to NAD. These energy carriers then act as intermediates that transport energy to the next step of photosynthesis, called the **Calvin cycle,** sometimes referred to as the **light independent reactions.** Years ago, the Calvin cycle was also called the '**dark reactions,**' but, because the Calvin cycle occurs both day and night, this term is not ap-

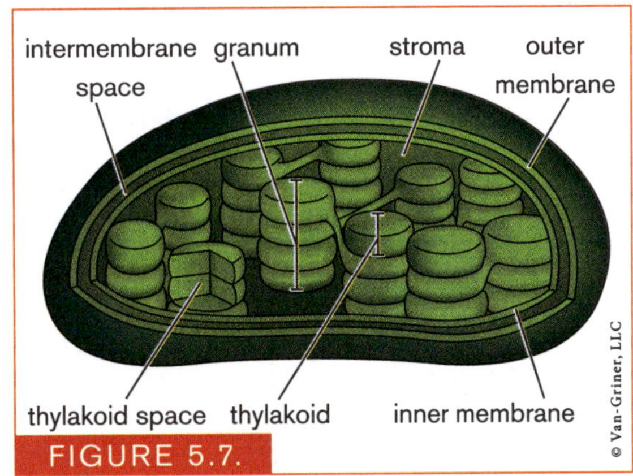

FIGURE 5.7.

The structure of a chloroplast (in cross section).

propriate. In the Calvin cycle, carbon dioxide is reduced to glucose and other sugars, using the energy supplied by NADPH and ATP. **Oxygen** is the major by-product of photosynthesis because water molecules are oxidized to provide electrons to the chlorophyll molecules in the light reactions.

The various compartments and membranes of a chloroplastid are shown in Figure 5.7. The organelle is surrounded by **two membranes,** with a fluid-filled space called the **intermembrane space** in between them. The dense, fluid-filled space inside the inner membrane is called the **stroma.** A series of membranes that form many interconnected flattened discs are called the **thylakoids.** A single stack of these thylakoids is called a **granum** (plural: grana). Inside the thylakoids is another fluid-filled space, called the **thylakoid space.**

The Light Dependent Reactions

Let's examine the light dependent reactions and Calvin cycle in more detail. The chlorophylls capture light energy and transfer this energy to electrons, which become 'high energy' electrons (Step A in Figure 5.6). Some of the energy is then used to produce ATP from ADP, and to produce NADPH. The molecules that capture this light energy are the **chlorophylls,** which form (along with various accessory pigments) an assemblage of molecules called a **photosystem.** The photosystems, as well as the molecules involved in the **electron transport chain** and **chemiosmosis,** are located in the **thylakoid membranes** (Figure 5.6).

Like mitochondria, chloroplasts produce ATP by using an electron transport chain (which is embedded in the thylakoid membranes near the photosystems) coupled with the chemiosmotic production of ATP. These high energy electrons originally from the chlorophyll molecules are then transferred to another electron transport chain (this ETC is similar to that found in mitochondria, in that the ETC in chloroplasts include cytochromes). Electrons in both chains (in the mitochondria and in chloroplasts) are involved in a series of oxidation-reduction reactions and are gradually stripped of potential energy (Step B in Figure 5.6).

As the electrons move from one cytochrome to another down the electron transport chain, this movement causes hydrogen ions to be pumped across the thylakoid membrane from the stroma to the thylakoid space (similar to that seen in mitochondria) and thus the hydrogen ion concentration increases in the fluid of the thylakoid space (Step C in Figure 5.6).

What replaces the electrons in the photosystems? An enzyme embedded in the thylakoid membrane releases electrons from water molecules by 'splitting' water into electrons, hydrogen ions (protons), and oxygen atoms. The oxygen gas then leaves the chloroplast and eventually diffuses from the cell (Step D in Figure 5.6). We will see the outcome of this process in Exercise 5.3. The electrons replace the ones that eventually end up in NADPH and subsequently in glucose.

The thylakoid space contains a high concentration of protons (and thus a low pH), similar to the condition seen in the intermembrane space of mitochondria. As these protons are allowed to flow back into the stroma, some of their energy is captured and used to produce ATP, by the process of chemiosmosis discussed earlier. The hydrogen ions are picked up by NADPH, which helps provide the reducing power needed for the Calvin cycle (Step E in Figure 5.6).

The Calvin Cycle

The final electron acceptor of the ETC is **$NADP^+$,** which is reduced to **NADPH.** NADPH is similar to NADH of aerobic respiration. Along with ATP, NADPH helps to drive the second part of photosynthesis, the **Calvin cycle. The Calvin cycle occurs in the stroma of the chloroplast.** Carbon (in the oxidized form of CO_2) enters the Calvin cycle and leaves the cycle in the form of **glyceraldehyde-3-phosphate** (G3P), a reduced three-carbon compound that can be used to form glucose and other sugars. The Calvin cycle uses the ATP energy from the light reactions to power this reaction, and also uses the reducing power of NADPH (Step F in Figure 5.6). For every three CO_2 molecules, a molecule of G3P is produced, using the energy from 6 ATPs and 6 NADPH molecules. The NADPH molecules are reoxidized to $NADP^+$ in the process.

Exercises

Exercise 5.1.

The Production of CO_2

Step 1 Obtain five 100 ml glass jars and stoppers with pre-cut glass pipettes (already inserted into the stoppers) from your lab instructor. If the jars are not labeled, label each jar 1 through 5. Add to each jar the following solutions (Table 5.2), along with 1 g of yeast cells (*Saccharomyces*):

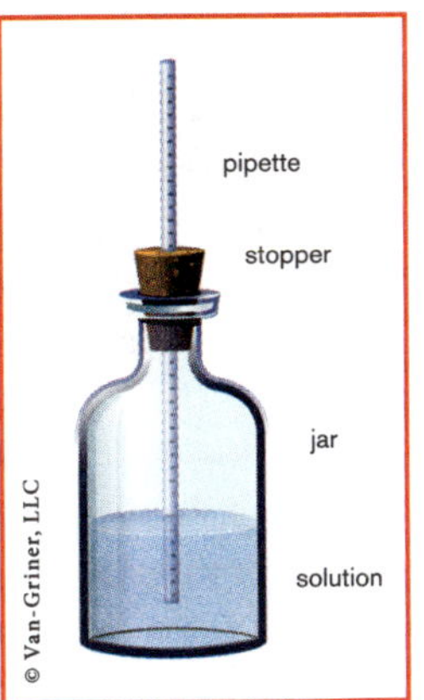

TABLE 5.2. The experimental setup for the yeast respiration exercise.

Jar	Solution
1	60 ml water, 1 g yeast,
2	60 ml of 1% dextrose, 1 g yeast
3	60 ml of 1% sucrose, 1 g yeast
4	60 ml of water with one packet of Equal®, 1 g yeast
5	60 ml of water with one packet of Splenda®, 1 g yeast

Step 2 Gently swirl the solutions until the yeast are suspended in the solution evenly. Note the time.

Step 3 Insert the stopper into each jar. Make sure that the end of the pipette is below the level of the solution, at least halfway down from the surface.

Step 4 Place the jars in the middle of the table. Be careful: do not knock them over.

Step 5 Record the initial volume of the fluid inside the pipette in Table 5.3.

Step 6 Now start the rest of the exercises. However, periodically observe (every five minutes) for at least 30 minutes.

FIGURE 5.8.

Molecular representations of the nutrients utilized in the yeast respiration exercise (Exercise 5.1).

What are the null and alternative hypotheses? What do you observe?

TABLE 5.3.

	Initial Volume in Pipette (ml)	Volume (ml) after 5 min	Volume (ml) after 10 min	Volume (ml) after 15 min	Volume (ml) after 20 min	Volume (ml) after 25 min	Volume (ml) after 30 min	Total CO_2 Volume (ml)	Rate of CO_2 (ml per hour)
water only									
1% dextrose									
1% sucrose									
Equal®									
Splenda®									

Step 7 Plot your data in Figure 5.9 below, indicating the rate of CO_2 produced as a function of time.

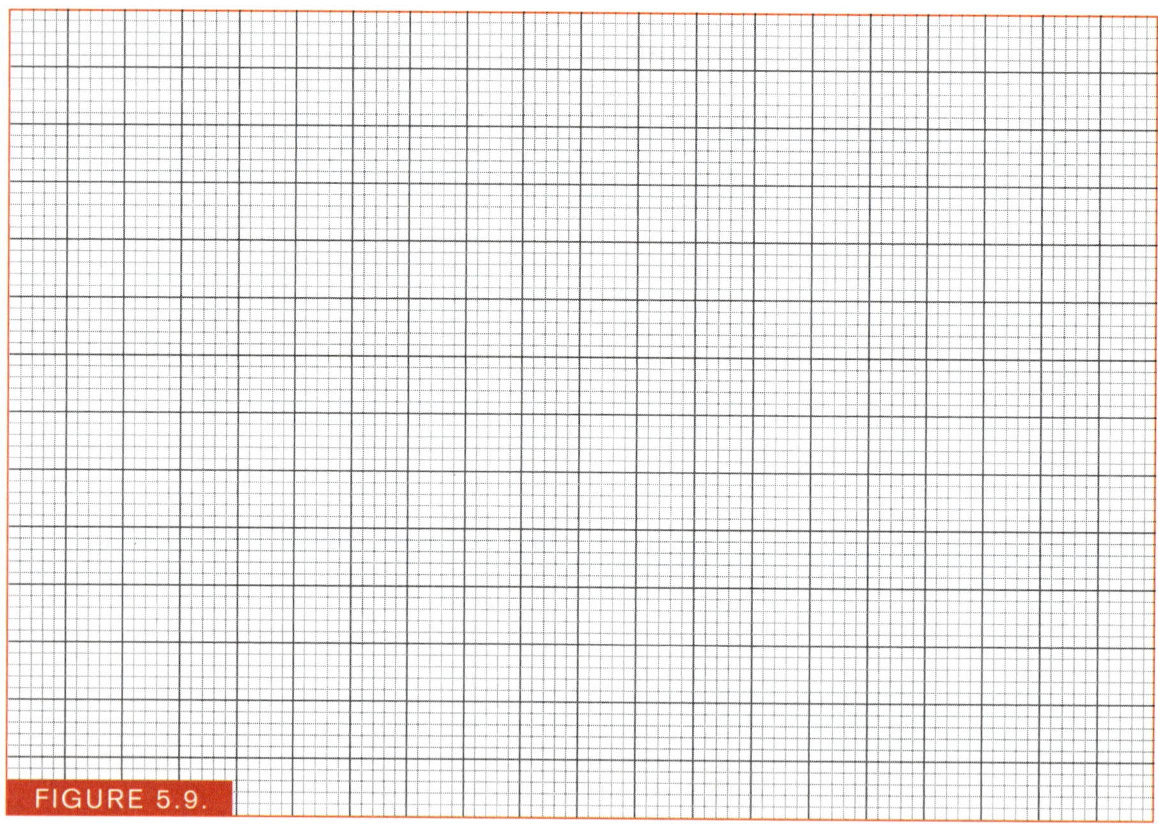

FIGURE 5.9.

The production of CO_2 by yeast, using different energy sources.

The yeast cells are using dextrose (**glucose**) and breaking it down (oxidizing) to two **pyruvate** molecules. The yeasts capture some of the energy (that was in the covalent bonds of glucose) in the form of a new chemical bond, the bond that holds the terminal phosphate to an **ATP (adenosine triphosphate)** molecule. This reaction is called **glycolysis;** it is the first step of both **aerobic respiration** and **anaerobic respiration.**

Because oxygen is available to the yeast in this exercise, they can use aerobic respiration; they oxidize the sugars completely to carbon dioxide and water. However, even when oxygen is present, if a large amount of sugars also are present, yeasts will mainly use anaerobic respiration. When oxygen is not available to the yeast, they would still create carbon dioxide as a by-product of alcoholic fermentation (in addition to ethanol molecules). For both aerobic and anaerobic respiration, the carbon dioxide gas then leaves the cell, forming the bubbles we see in the yeast suspension.

As the CO_2 is produced, it becomes a gas and enters the air above the solution. Inside the jars, as CO_2 increases, the pressure increases. The increased pressure of the air inside the jar forces the fluid to rise up into the pipette.

> Equal® (containing aspartame) and Splenda® (containing sucralose) are sugar replacements without caloric value (they cannot be metabolized) but they elicit a sweet taste sensation like sugar. You may have noticed some carbon dioxide produced; a small amount of sugar is added to the artificial sweetener packages. Can you see from the diagrams in Figure 5.8 how their molecular structures differ from dextrose? Why do they still taste sweet?

> Relate the fact of carbon dioxide production to the processes of cheese, wine, bread, and beer production.

Exercise 5.2.

The Effect of Temperature on CO_2 Production

Procedure

1. Obtain two glass jars and stoppers with pre-cut glass pipettes (already inserted into the stoppers) from your lab instructor. Add to each jar the following solutions, along with 1 g of yeast cells (*Saccharomyces*):

Jar	Solution
1	60 ml of 1% dextrose from the stock bottle in the refrigerator and add 1 g yeast
2	60 ml of 1% dextrose from the stock bottle on the front table and add 1 g yeast

2. Gently swirl the solutions until the yeast are suspended in the solution evenly. Note the time and record the initial temperatures.

3 Insert the stopper into each jar. Make sure that the end of the pipette is below the level of the solution, at least halfway down from the surface. See page 5-10 again to make certain you have correctly set up the apparatus.

4 Place the jars in the middle of the table. Place the cold jar within the Syracuse dish containing ice water. Be careful: do not knock them over.

5 Record the initial volume of the fluid inside the pipette in Table 5.4.

6 Periodically observe the two jars every five minutes, for at least 30 minutes. Record the final temperatures of the solutions.

TABLE 5.4.

	Room Temperature		Cold Jar	
	Initial °C ___ Final °C ___		Initial °C ___ Final °C ___	
initial volume in pipette (ml)				
volume (ml) after 5 min				
volume (ml) after 10 min				
volume (ml) after 15 min				
volume (ml) after 20 min				
volume (ml) after 25 min				
volume (ml) after 30 min				
total CO_2 volume (ml)				
rate of CO_2 (ml per hour)				

7 Plot your data in Figure 5.10 below.

FIGURE 5.10.

The effect of temperature on CO_2 production by the yeast *Saccharomyces*.

What are the null and alternative hypotheses? What do you observe?

If you used a yeast solution held at a much warmer temperature (for example 30°C), what rate of CO_2 production would you expect to see? Explain your reasoning.

Exercise 5.3.

Absorption Spectra of Photosynthetic Pigments

Scientists use a special instrument, called the **spectrophotometer,** to determine what wavelengths of light are reflected or absorbed by various molecules, including the plant pigments that are involved in photosynthesis. Light has three possible fates when it comes to the molecules of living things: it can pass through them **(transmission),** bounce off of them **(reflection),** or be absorbed by the molecules **(absorption).** A solution containing pigments can be examined at many wavelengths. At each wavelength, the amount of that wavelength that is absorbed is determined. We will come back to spectrophotometry in more detail when we use a spectrophotometer later this semester.

There are a number of **photosynthetic pigments** that absorb specific wavelengths of light. **Chlorophyll *a*** is a major molecule involved in the light reactions of photosynthesis. There are other chlorophylls, especially **chlorophyll *b*,** and several accessory pigments, such as **carotenoids** (carotene is one such example) that aid in capturing light.

Plot the data in Table 5.5 on Figure 5.11, with wavelength as the independent variable and percent absorption as the dependent variable.

TABLE 5.5.

Wavelength (nm)	Absorption (in percent) by:		
	Chlorophyll *a*	Chlorophyll *b*	Carotene
400	30	7	21
425	40	4	28
450	56	21	36
475	4	50	46
500	1	50	57
525	1	4	20
550	2	1	2
575	3	3	0
600	3	5	0
625	7	5	0
650	8	26	0
675	49	2	0
700	6	0	0

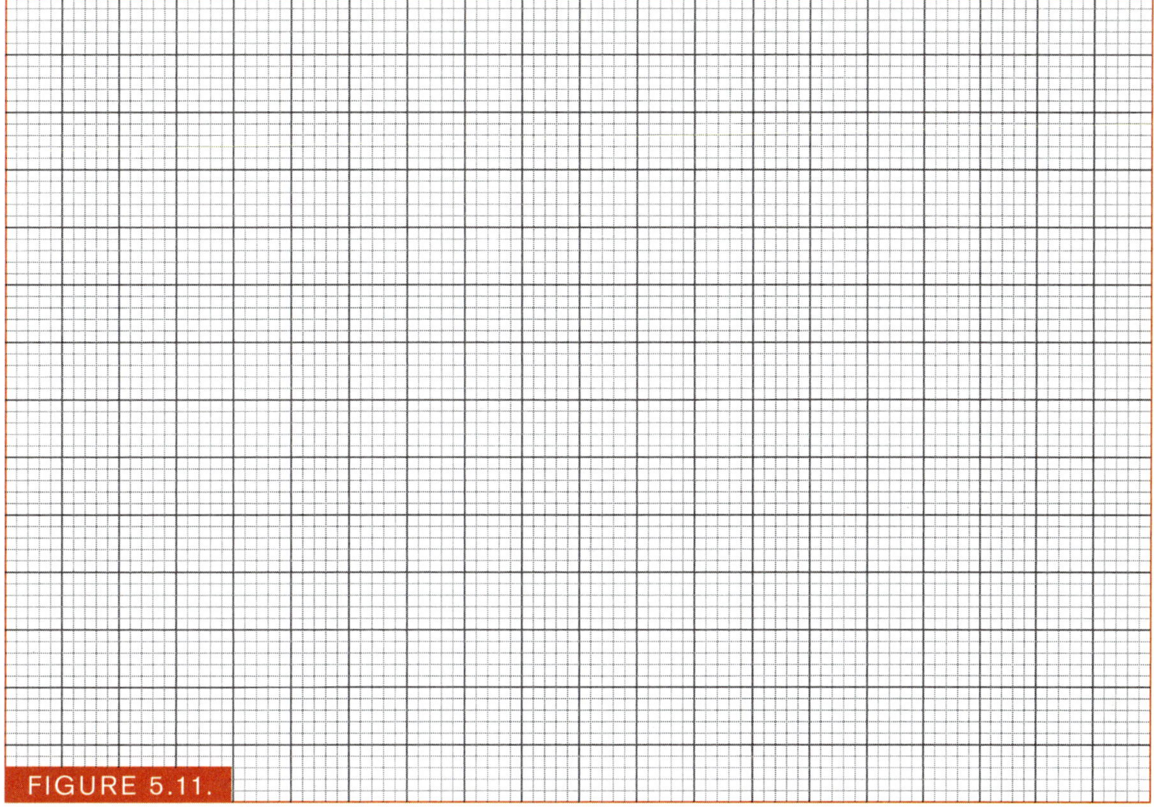

FIGURE 5.11.

The absorption spectrum for chlorophyll *a*, chlorophyll *b,* and carotene.

Examine Figure 5.11. What wavelengths (colors) does each pigment absorb best? Does this information make sense, concerning the fact that leaves are green? Can you guess what is one of the functions of accessory pigments (such as carotene)?

Suppose you were to grow plants under artificial light (most light bulbs do not produce the same light spectrum as that observed in sunlight). What would happen if you grew plants under green or yellow light?

Consider that fact that the **Photosynthetically Active Range** (the wavelengths of light used by plants to power photosynthesis) and the visual range (for most animals) are similar. In addition, much of the radiation put out by the sun is in the visible range. Discuss the significance of these facts. Discuss why UV and IR light are not used or perceived as readily as visible light is used by biological systems.

Exercise 5.4.

Photosynthesis in Elodea: *the Light Reactions and the Calvin Cycle*

We can qualitatively examine how light affects the amount of CO_2 used or the amount of O_2 produced by photosynthesis, by examining the aquatic plant *Elodea*. Remember, plants also use aerobic respiration to generate their ATP. When the plants are exposed to light, photosynthesis and cellular respiration both occur. However, in the dark, only cellular respiration occurs.

We can qualitatively measure the differences in the rates of photosynthesis and cellular respiration by measuring the amount of CO_2 given off or taken up by the plant, when the plant is in the light or in the dark.

How can we measure CO_2? Carbon dioxide combines with water to form carbonic acid (H_2CO_3) which dissociates into hydrogen ions (H^+) and bicarbonate ions (HCO_3^-). The pH drops due to the presence of hydrogen ions.

These reactions are reversible; if you add more CO_2, you will lower the pH of the water (more bicarbonate will form, along with more hydrogen ions); if you remove CO_2, the amount of bicarbonate and hydrogen ions also will decrease (and the pH will increase).

$$CO_2 + H_2O \rightleftharpoons H_2CO_3 \rightleftharpoons H^+ + HCO_3^-$$

All organisms that use aerobic respiration (including plants) release CO_2 into the water, and the pH decreases. During photosynthesis, autotrophic organisms (such as plants) take up CO_2 and the pH increases.

Step 1   Take the solution (provided by the lab instructor) and measure the pH of the solution, using pH meters. Gently blow into the solution with a straw for several minutes.

Note: **Wear the safety glasses while blowing into the straw! Do not blow hard into the straw, causing the fluid to splash out of the beaker.** Instead of blowing into the beaker, you may instead add a small amount of a sodium bicarbonate solution to the beaker.

Measure the pH after blowing into the solution. Did the pH change?

By blowing into the water (or after adding a small amount of sodium bicarbonate), we formed a weak solution of carbonic acid (H_2CO_3), which will dissociate into H^+ and HCO_3^- ions. Many aquatic plants can remove CO_2 and bicarbonate from the water. Therefore, as the plant removes CO_2 from the water, the pH should increase.

Step 2   Obtain four large test tubes. Put two of them in each of two test-tube racks.

Step 3   Pick two sprigs of *Elodea* from the aquarium housing the plants. These sprigs should be long enough to fill the entire length of the tubes without protruding from the water and they should be of equal length. The length of the stem can be adjusted by cutting a piece off from the base of the stem. Put one of the plants in one of the light tubes and a second sprig of *Elodea* in one of the dark tubes.

Step 4   Wrap a piece of aluminum foil completely around two of the tubes, so that no light is able to enter. These tubes are the 'dark' tubes. The dark tube should be entirely covered so that no light can enter the tube. The other tubes are called the 'light' tubes.

Step 5   Fill each tube with the solution containing bicarbonate, up to about 3 cm from the top.

Step 6   Cap both dark tubes with a piece of aluminum foil.

You have created a sample in each of four different treatments:

a 'Dark' control (tube without a plant, wrapped in foil, or placed in a closed cabinet);

b 'Light' control (tube without a plant, not wrapped);

c 'Dark' plant (tube containing an *Elodea* sprig, wrapped in foil) (or place in a closed cabinet); and

d 'Light' plant (tube containing an *Elodea* sprig, not wrapped).

Step 7 Place the test tubes in the test tube rack or beaker to hold them. Place the two uncovered tubes directly under a grow light. Place the test tube rack on top of a white piece of paper. Note the time.

Step 8 After about 45 minutes, test the pH of each of the tubes. Remove the sprigs of *Elodea* and return them to their home aquarium. Before measuring the pH, mix the contents of the test tube by inverting the tube several times, using a stopper to prevent water from spilling out. After mixing, insert the pH probe and wait until the reading stabilizes before recording your results. Record the pH (to the nearest 0.01 unit) for the entire class in Table 5.6, and calculate the mean pH for each treatment.

TABLE 5.6. Initial time:______; Final time:______; Elapsed time:______

Replicate	Dark Control		Dark Plant		Light Control		Light Plant	
	Initial pH	Final pH	Initial pH	Final pH	Initial pH	Final pH	Initial pH	Final pH
1								
2								
3								
4								
5								
6								
7								
8								
9								
10								
mean								

How did the pH change over the course of the experiment? Did the pH change after blowing into the solution? Why did it change again from the activities of the plants?

Hint: Think about the over all equations of respiration and photosynthesis. What is the purpose of the tube without a sprig of *Elodea*?

Did you see any gas bubbles on the leaves of *Elodea*? In which tube? What is the composition of the gas bubbles observed on *Elodea*?

Why did we need two different controls—one in the light and one in the dark?

Experiment 5.5.

Measuring Oxygen and Carbon Dioxide Production

You have observed that carbon dioxide gas is given off in respiration and alcoholic fermentation, and oxygen gas is released as a plant conducts the light reactions of photosynthesis. In this exercise, we will measure the amounts of both gases simultaneously produced and/or consumed by an animal (beetle larvae or 'mealworms,' *Tenebrio* sp.).

Note: Your laboratory instructor may be using another insect species.

You will use an O_2 gas sensor to record the rate of oxygen consumption/production by the insects as they respire. Likewise, you will use a CO_2 gas sensor to record the rate of carbon dioxide consumption/production. Your lab instructor will go over the use of the probes we used to measure CO_2 and O_2 production. Record your data in Table 5.7.

Your lab instructor will explain to each group how to hook up the probes and interface to the computers.

Step 1 Collect at least 15 mealworms (beetle larvae), or several beetle adults, from your lab instructor.

Step 2 Use the weigh scale to determine the total weight of the insects.

Step 3 Place the insects into the chambers and then place the probes into the chambers.

Important: Do not allow the probes to get wet. Do not breathe on the probes. Keep the oxygen sensor upright at all times.

Step 4 Record the data on the computer, and calculate the rates of production or consumption of both CO_2 and O_2, following your lab instructor's instructions.

Your lab instructor will show you how to determine the rate of CO_2 or O_2 consumption or production. You can convert %/min (parts per hundred) into parts per million (ppm) by multiplying %/min by 10,000. A concentration of 500 ppm for CO_2, for example, is the same as 0.5 ml per L of air. Dividing the rate (ppm/min) by the total weight of the beetles produces the weight-specific measure of respiration (ppm/min/mg).

Before conducting the exercise, predict what the insects' responses should be (i.e., describe the null and alternative hypotheses), and state your reasoning.

TABLE 5.7. Beetle respiration. Temperature: _______ °C

Number of Insects	Total Weight (mg) of Insects	Production of CO_2		Consumption of O_2		
		ppm/min	ppm/min/mg	%/min	ppm/min	ppm/min/mg

If the insects used up carbon dioxide and/or oxygen over time, indicate this by using a minus sign in front of the rate. If the insects produced excess carbon dioxide/oxygen over time, the number will be positive.

Calculate the mean carbon dioxide production and oxygen consumption from Table 5.7 above (columns 4 and 7). Write your answers in the box below. Discuss the significance of positive/negative rates. What is occurring?

Are the weight-specific rates of CO_2 production equal to the weight-specific rates of O_2 consumption? Why should they be similar?

There are a number of possible variables that may affect your results. Explain how each may affect the rates.

What would happen if you increased or decreased the temperature? How would this presumably affect the insects' respiratory rates?

Instead of the insects, suppose you added small plants into the chambers. You then shined a light from a bulb that emitted a light spectrum similar to that of the sun. What would have happened? If the plants are kept in the dark, what should happen?

Graphical Presentation of Results: Figures and Tables

After you have collected data, you may then graphically present the data for visual inspection. Visual summaries are important components to scientific presentations because readers may wish to decide for themselves what generalizations they may make from examining your results. There are two basic types of summaries: **figures** and **tables.** Figures and tables should be able to stand alone and be interpretable without the body of the text.

Figures

A figure is composed of two parts; the figure itself and the accompanying figure legend. The legend includes details to facilitate the reader's ability to understand the figure, such as location, the species involved, explanation of axes, units of measurement, and identification of symbols used in the figure.

There are various types of figures made by scientists. One common figure is the **line graph.** Construction of the line graph is easy. It consists of two perpendicular axes, the **abscissa** (the horizontal or *x*-axis) and the **ordinate** (the vertical or *y*-axis). Convention usually places the independent variable on the *x*-axis and the dependent variable on the *y*-axis to graphically illustrate the relationship between the two variables and the pattern of the relationship (see Figure 5.12). For example, the *x*-axis may be shell length, and the *y*-axis may be shell weight. As a snail's shell gets longer, it also becomes heavier.

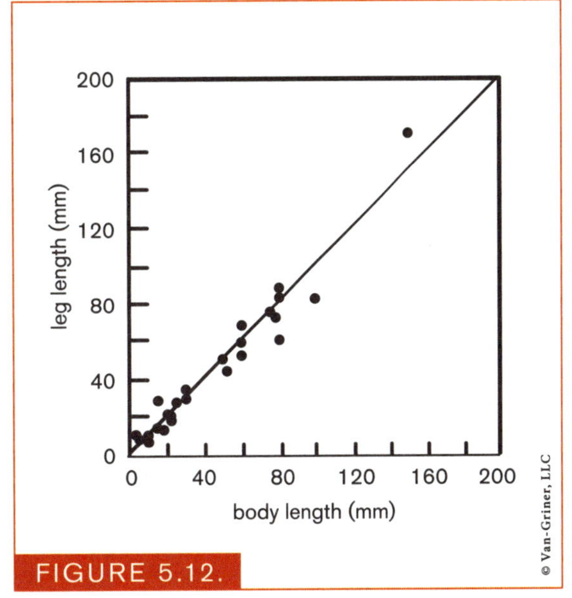

FIGURE 5.12.

Basic scatter plot graph showing the relationship of independent and dependent variables. The line shown is the best fit linear regression line, calculated from the data.

The figure then is a series of *x,y* coordinates (corresponding to the relationship between the independent and dependent variables). The figure's axes are then labeled with the variable name and the units in which the variable was measured (meters, seconds, grams, etc.).

Note that figures and tables have captions that briefly describe the contents of that table or figure. In order to receive full credit in this course, you will provide figure/table legends and captions for any materials turned in for credit.

Tables

Tables are similar to figures, in that they provide a visual inspection of the **data** (singular: datum; plural: data) which are the raw values obtained in the experiment for the variables, and/or the **results,** which are the descriptive statistics and inferential statistics of the data. Most tables inserted into scientific papers are tables describing the experimental results. A table lists the values (data or results) of the experiment in numerical form. For example, you have taken a test, and you know your score and the mean score of the class. Whether or not you are pleased with your score, you probably wish to see how it compares to the average. A large table of all scores would be of limited use if several thousand students took the test. It might take you hours to find your score, and it would not tell you where you stand in relation to the entire class.

Histograms

A **bar graph** or **histogram** is a common type of graphical representation of data we will use in this class. A histogram figure of the scores (listing the frequency of scores obtained for each grade) would be of greater use because it would be easier to interpret and generalize (in other words, it can tell you how you are doing in the class). In order to make a histogram, you first select a number of categories (size classes, for example), and count the number of individuals of your sample that fall into each category. The trick is to know what range one needs for each category of the independent variable; usually it is apparent what range you need. For example, let's say you had a number of shells that varied in length from 50 to 100 mm in maximum length. One useful range of categories then could be in 10 mm increments: 50–59 mm, 60–69 mm, 70–79 mm, and so on. You probably would not want to use increments of 1 mm (there would be too many bars to the figure), or increments of 25 mm (too few bars) because the important information about the distribution may be obscured. Traditionally, the independent variable is placed along the **abscissa** (*x*-axis), the dependent variable along the **ordinate** (*y*-axis). Examine the sample histograms shown in Figure 5.13.

Exercise 5.6.

Construct histograms for the data given in the tables below. The data are hypothetical data from beak sizes (beak depths) of two related species of birds (*Geospiza fuliginosa* and *G. fortis*) on three hypothetical islands in the eastern Pacific. These are two of the various species of related finch-like birds that Darwin observed on the Galapagos Islands, during his voyage on the *H.M.S. Beagle*. The observations he made concerning these birds was crucial to his formulation of his most famous hypothesis: the process of evolution by natural selection, and many scientists have examined these little birds ever since. The heads of the birds are depicted in Figure 5.14.

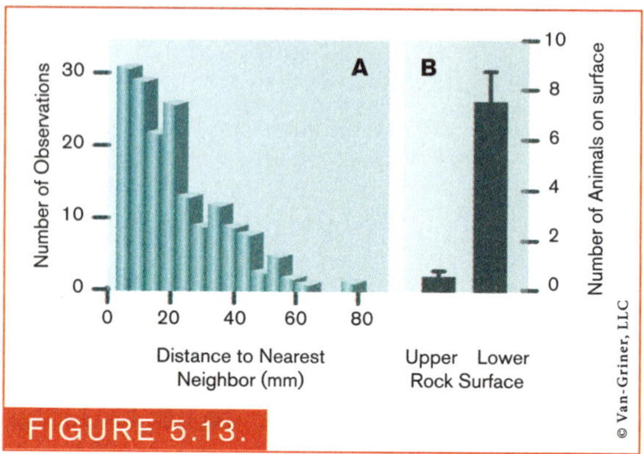

FIGURE 5.13.

Two examples of histograms: the frequency of nearest neighbor distance between zebra mussels in the Ohio River (the left-hand histogram labeled A) and the number of zebra mussels on the upper and lower surfaces of rocks in the Ohio River (B). The right-hand histogram also has error bars indicated (standard errors of means). (Data from Dr. J. Alexander.)

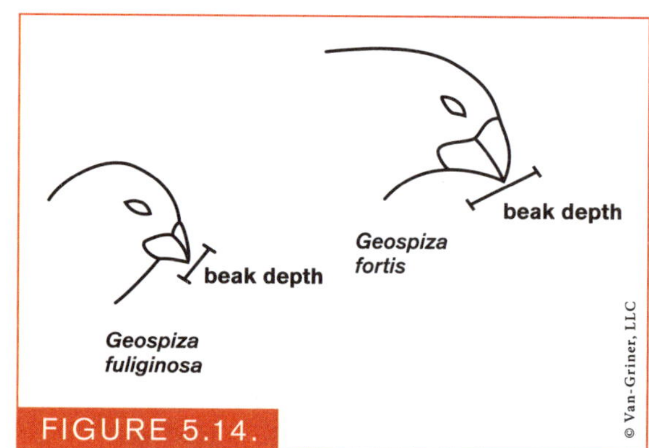

FIGURE 5.14.

The basic shape and size of the heads of *Geospiza fuliginosa* and *Geospiza fortis*.

The following data are hypothetical, yet they are based on real results. Read Lack (1947) for additional information on the subject. Determine what the proper number of size range categories are needed by looking at the data. Plot the histograms in Figure 5.15, Figure 5.16, and Figure 5.17.

Island: Los Gatos (only one species)

Species: *G. fuliginosa*	beak depths (mm): 8, 9, 9, 11, 8, 10, 10, 10, 10, 11, 9, 10, 11, 9, 8, 10, 10, 10, 9, 10, 9, 8, 8, 9, 11, 11, 11, 9

Island: Dos Perros (only one species)

Species: *G. fortis*	beak depths (mm): 9, 9, 11, 10, 10, 10, 10, 10, 10, 10, 11, 10, 11, 9, 12, 9, 10, 12, 11, 11, 9, 9, 9, 9, 12

Island: San Diego (both species coexist)

Species: *G. fuliginosa*	beak depths (mm): 8, 8, 8, 8, 8, 9, 7, 7, 8, 9, 7, 8, 9, 9, 9, 8, 7, 7, 7, 9, 7, 9, 9, 9
Species: *G. fortis*	beak depths (mm): 10, 10, 11, 13, 12, 13, 14, 11, 11, 10, 14, 13, 12, 11, 10, 12, 12, 13, 14

Calculate the mean beak depths of both species on each island. What do the results suggest to you concerning the relationship between these two species, when they are found alone and when they are found together (on San Diego Island)? What do you think is going on?

Island	Mean Beak Depth of *G. fuliginosa*	Mean Beak Depth of *G. fortis*
Los Gatos		not found
Dos Perros	not found	
San Diego		

Devise a hypothesis to explain these observations. Are there other possible explanations?

Null hypothesis:

Alternative hypothesis:

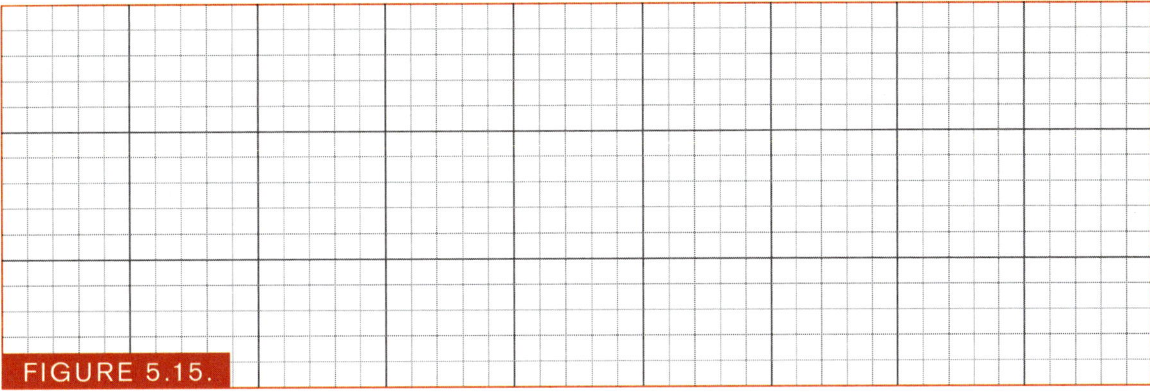

FIGURE 5.15.

Beak depth of *G. fuliginosa* on Los Gatos Island.

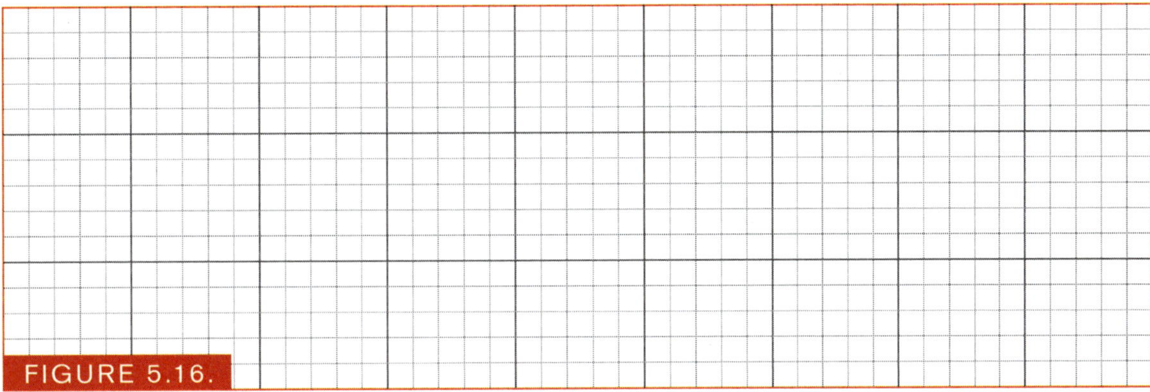

FIGURE 5.16.

Beak depth of *G. fortis* on Dos Perros Island.

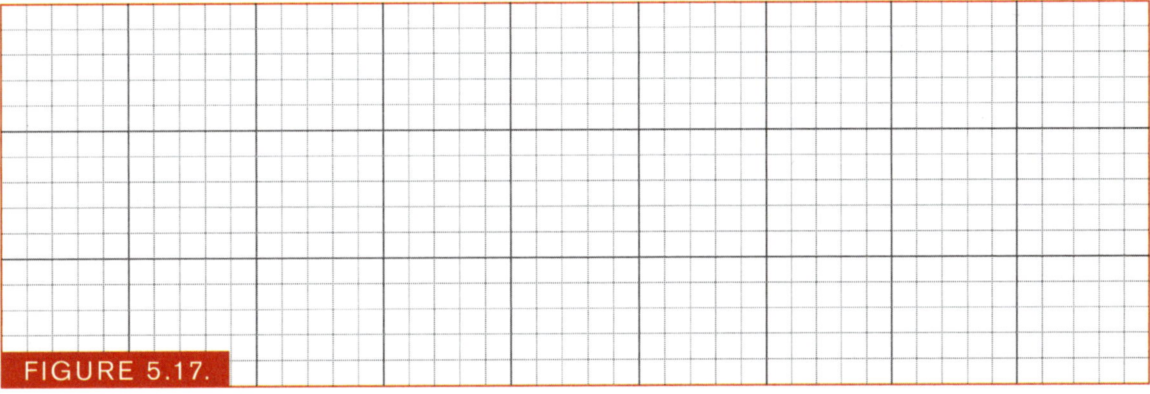

FIGURE 5.17.

Beak depth of *G. fortis* and *G. fuliginosa* on San Diego Island.

6 UNIT

The Microscope and Cells

Keywords

base
arm
stage
nosepiece
eyepiece (ocular)
objectives
iris
fine and coarse
 adjustments
parfocal
parcentered
field of view
depth of field
total magnification
SA : V
prokaryotic
eukaryotic
plasma membrane

cytoplasm
cytosol
cell walls
 (primary cell
 wall, secondary
 cell wall, middle
 lamella)
extracellular matrix
cellulose
collagen
nucleus
nucleolus
chromosomes
chromatin
nuclear envelope
mitochondrion
cristae
matrix

intermembrane
 space
lumen
cisternae
cisternal spaces
chloroplast
stroma
thylakoids
grana
thylakoid space
Golgi apparatus
 (cis and
 trans sides)
endoplasmic
 reticulum
membranous tubules
vesicles
ribosomes

lysosomes
food vacuole
central vacuole
tonoplast
phagocytosis
exocytosis
centrosome
centrioles
flagella
cilia
basal bodies
microtubules
cytoskeleton
interpolation
extrapolation
regression

Learning Objectives

When finished with this unit, you should be able to do the following:

1. Identify the major parts of both compound microscopes and dissecting microscopes and explain each part's function (base, arm, stage, nosepiece, eyepiece [ocular], body tube, objectives, iris diaphragm, fine and coarse adjustment knobs, slide manipulators);

2. Describe the proper use and care of microscopes;

3. Define parfocal and parcentered;

4. Find an object on a prepared slide, using a light microscope, and understand how both the depth of field and the diameter of the field of view changes with changes in magnification.

5 Determine the diameter of the field of view and determine the total magnification, as well as estimate the approximate sizes of objects under different magnifications;

6 Prepare a wet mount;

7 Describe the size ranges observed in cells of various taxonomic groups, and discuss what sets the upper and lower sizes of cells;

8 Discuss the importance of surface area to volume ratios ($SA : V$);

9 Compare and contrast bacterial (prokaryotic) cells with eukaryotic cells (plants and animals);

10 Identify structures and organelles (and their subcomponents and functions), both on slides and on available models and photographs (cell membrane-associated proteins, cell walls, nucleus, nuclear envelope (membrane), mitochondria, chloroplasts, Golgi apparatus, ribosomes, endoplasmic reticulum (both smooth and rough ER), lysosomes, food vacuoles, centrioles, flagella, cilia, DNA, microtubules and microfilaments, cytoskeleton);

11 Estimate the number of cells in multicellular organisms, based on the organism's weight, volume, and average cell size; and

12 Distinguish between interpolation and extrapolation.

Prokaryotic Cells and Eukaryotic Cells

Living things are made of one of two kinds of cells: **prokaryotic** cells ('before the nucleus') and **eukaryotic** ('true nucleus') cells.

Prokaryotic cells and eukaryotic cells share many things in common:

1 All cells are surrounded by a **plasma membrane.**

2 All cells contain **chromosomes** that are made of DNA and proteins.

3 All cells also have **ribosomes,** tiny structures made of protein and RNA. Ribosomes synthesize proteins, using the instructions contained in genes. The ribosome size and structure differs somewhat between the cytoplasmic ribosomes of the eukaryotes and the ribosomes of the prokaryotes.

4 All cells have a semifluid medium (the **cytosol**) located inside the plasma membrane.

5 Many metabolic pathways and many enzymes are shared by both prokaryotes and eukaryotes.

Prokaryotic and eukaryotic cells also differ in many respects:

1 A major difference between prokaryotic and eukaryotic cells is the **location of their chromosomes.**

In a eukaryotic cell, chromosomes are contained in a membrane-enclosed organelle, the **nucleus.** In eukaryotic cells, the contents of the nucleus are within a double membrane called the **nuclear envelope.** In a prokaryotic cell, the DNA is concentrated in the **nucleoid** region, but no membrane separates the chromosome from the rest of the cell.

2 The region between the nucleus and the plasma membrane of a eukaryotic cell is the **cytoplasm.** The cytoplasm of a eukaryotic cell consists of the cytosol and membrane-bound **organelles.** The various membrane-bound organelles have different specialized forms and functions. Membrane-bounded organelles are absent in prokaryotes.

3 Eukaryotic cells are generally much larger than prokaryotic cells. Most bacteria are 1 to 10 microns in diameter, but eukaryotic cells are typically much larger, about 10 to 100 µm in diameter (recall that one micron or micrometer is one-millionth of a meter long).

Surface Area to Volume Ratios

What limits the upper size of a cell? Could any single cell be huge—say, for example, 10 centimeters across? Obviously, as a cell gets bigger, the outer surface area and volume of the cell also increases. However, the volume increases as a factor of the cube of the length of the cell (length^3) whereas the surface area increases as the square of the length (length^2).

Suppose you had a block of wood that was 1 cm on a side; this block represents a standard-sized or typical cell (see Figure 6.1). The total surface area of the block of wood would be the surface area of its six sides, each side being 1 cm in length. There was thus 6 cm^2 of surface area.

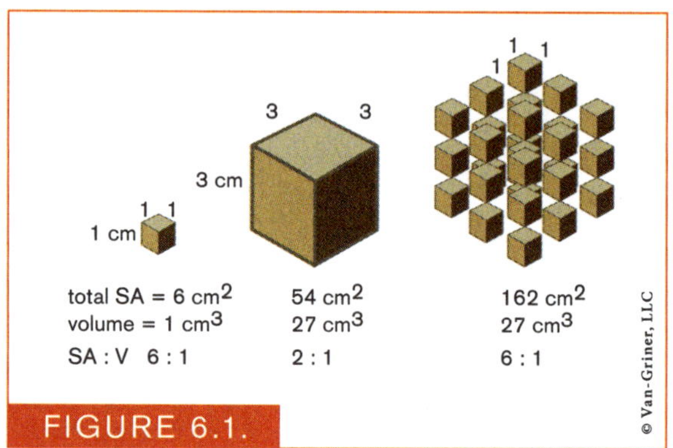

FIGURE 6.1.

The relationship between surface area (*SA*) and the volume (*V*) of hypothetical cells.

The volume is the (height × width × length) of the cell, thus the volume is 1 cm^3. The surface to volume ratio (*SA : V* or sometimes described as *SA/V*) is the surface area divided by the total volume. In this case, the *SA : V* of a cube 1 cm on a side is 6 : 1 (6 cm^2 of surface area is supporting 1 cm^3 of cell volume).

If the wooden cube's linear dimensions were increased to 3 cm on a side, the total *SA* is now 6 sides × 3 cm × 3 cm, or 54 cm^2 (Figure 6.1) However, the volume increased to 27 cm^3 (3 cm × 3 cm × 3 cm). Now, the *SA : V* is lower (2 : 1). This means that the amount of *SA* supporting each unit volume has declined by 67%, compared to the cell that was 1 cm on a side.

Now, if you divided the larger block of wood into 27 separate cubes, each 1 cm on a side, and separated them slightly to expose all of their surfaces to their environment, the total aggregate volume of the 27 smaller cubes stays the same (27 cm^3) as the larger cube, but the aggregate surface area has increased to 162 cm^2. In this case, the *SA : V* increases to 6 : 1.

Therefore, as the cell gets bigger, there is relatively less surface area supporting each unit of cell volume. Because materials have to get into the cell through its surface, and waste materials also must pass across this outer surface, metabolic requirements are one important limit to the upper size of a eukaryotic cell.

What sets the lower size limit of a cell? Each cell has to have a minimum amount of DNA, as well as a minimum number of cellular structures—membranes, ribosomes, mRNAs, proteins—to carry out transcription, translation, and metabolism. Some bacterial cells (the mycoplasmas) are only about one-tenth of a micron across; they are probably near the theoretical limit for the smallest cell size.

Parts of the Eukaryotic Cell

Plant and animal cells are examples of **eukaryotic cells**: they contain a membrane-bound nucleus and numerous **organelles** ("little organs") that are suspended in the cytosol. Biologists disagree on what constitutes an organelle; some argue that the term "organelle" only applies to "those membrane-bound structures that contain their own DNA and that presumably originated from prokaryotic organisms acquired by the larger cell via the evolutionary process of endosymbiosis." For this course, we will be more inclusive: the typical cell organelle is a "large assemblage of macromolecules that perform a specific cellular function; most organelles are enclosed by membranes, in which specific metabolic activities have been compartmentalized." This compartmentalization provides little compartments within one cell, thus facilitating specific biochemical reactions to occur. Some reactions are incompatible with other metabolic pathways, so the spatial isolation allows these different, antagonistic reactions to occur simultaneously in the same cell.

Most of these organelles are too small to be easily resolved by a compound microscope that uses visible light. Special staining techniques and very high magnification are needed. Scientists use **electron microscopes** in order to see the organelles and other fine details of the cell's internal structure. The following is a brief description of the main organelles found in living animal cells.

The Cell Membrane and the Nucleus

A The cell or plasma membrane (Figure 6.2, Figure 6.3, and Figure 6.4) separates the contents of the cell from the outside. Proteins imbedded in the plasma membrane act as channels for the movement of materials into and out of the cell. Some of these embedded proteins also act as receptors or enzymes for a variety of molecules, such as hormones, antibodies, or various substrates. Other membrane-associated proteins interact with the extracellular matrix (in animals) and with the cell's internal cytoskeleton (in all eukaryotes). These proteins thus are involved in the coordination of activity both within a cell and between cells. Membranes exist within the eukaryotic cell as well, particularly around various organelles (Figure 6.3, Figure 6.4). A few prokaryotic bacteria have internal membranes (thylakoids, Figure 6.2).

The plasma membrane is a **selective barrier;** it allows oxygen and nutrients to enter a cell and carbon dioxide and metabolic wastes to exit a cell. The volume of cytoplasm determines the need for this exchange of materials. As we discussed above, if a cell has a very large cytoplasmic volume, there may not be sufficient surface area to support the volume; the rates of chemical exchange may be inadequate to maintain a large cell.

The main structure of a cell membrane is the **phospholipid bilayer.** Hydrophilic ("water-loving") portions of phospholipids are oriented to the outside of the membrane, whereas hydrophobic ("water-hating") ends are on the inside of the membrane. The lipid cholesterol also is associated with membranes, as are a number of proteins.

B The **nucleus** (Figure 6.3, Figure 6.4) is a spherical or ovoid structure several μm in diameter that contains the chromosomes (which are in the form of chromatin) within the **nuclear envelope.** The nuclear envelope or **nuclear membrane** consists of a double membrane. One or more conspicuous **nucleoli** (singular: **nucleolus**) often can be observed inside the nucleus; the nucleolus is the site of RNA production. The chromosome(s) will appear as a grainy material (**chromatin**) within the nucleus of an active cell. The nucleus is similar in all eukaryotic organisms.

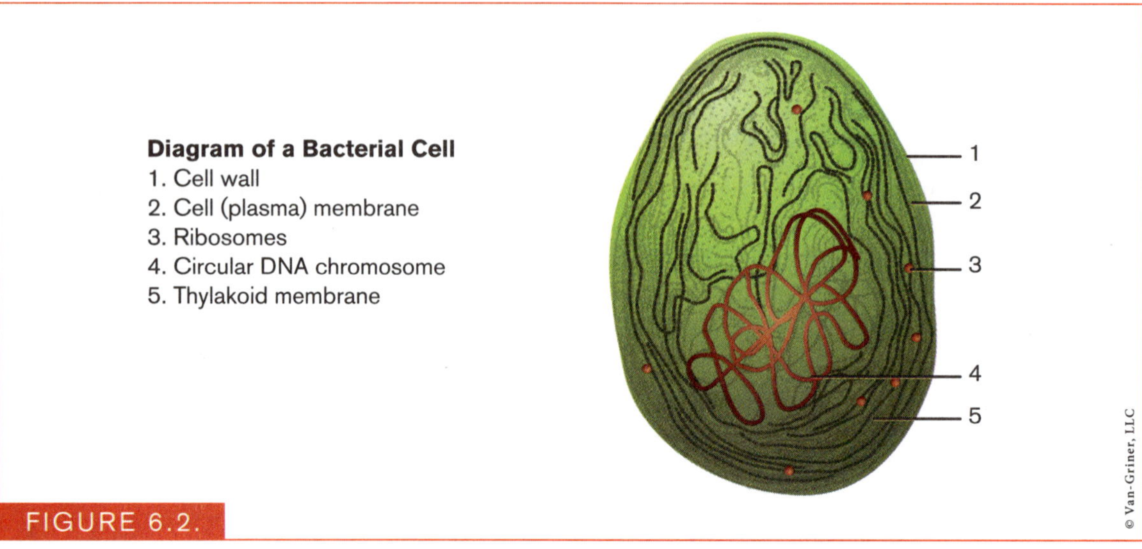

FIGURE 6.2.

An example of a prokaryotic cell.

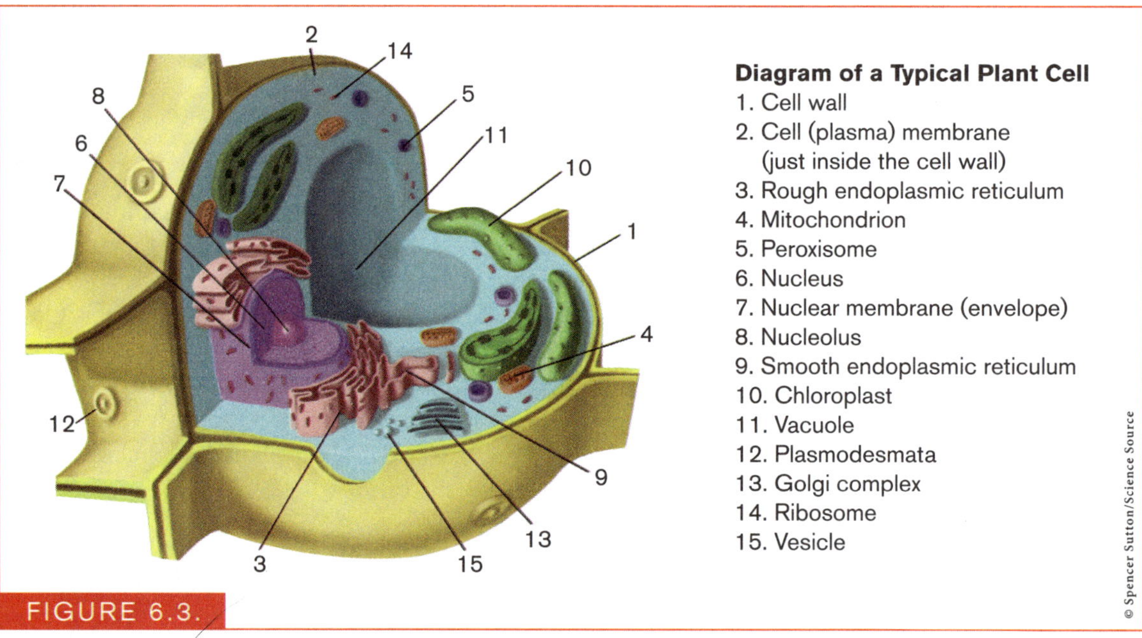

FIGURE 6.3.

An example of the eukaryotic plant cell.

Membrane-Bound Organelles

C **Mitochondria** (Figure 6.3, Figure 6.4) are small organelles (about 1 μm) involved in cellular respiration. Numerous mitochondria are found in most eukaryotic cells. Glucose and other compounds are broken down enzymatically in the cell's **cytoplasm** (by the process called **glycolysis**), and some ATP (the main energy carrier for the cell) is produced by this chemical pathway. The products of glycolysis can be broken down further in the mitochondrion, releasing more energy and creating more ATP.

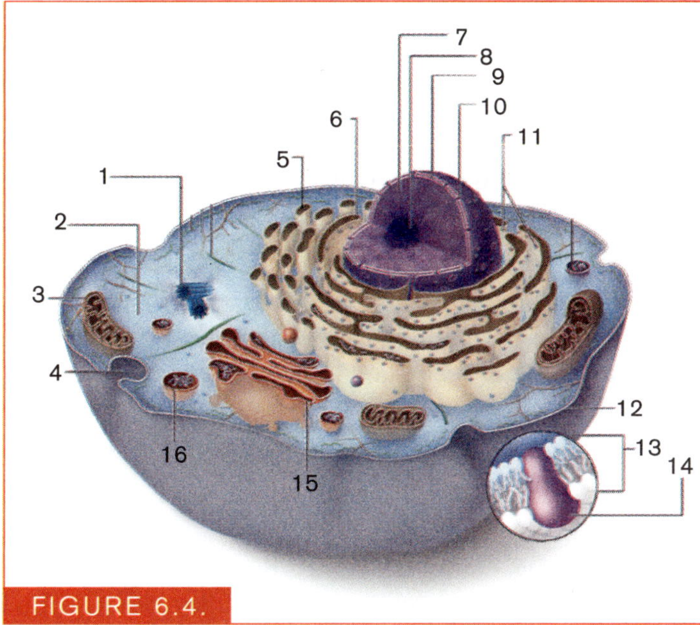

FIGURE 6.4.

An example of the eukaryotic animal cell.

D **Chloroplasts** (Figure 6.3) are organelles found in plants and algae. Chloroplasts are the sites where photosynthetic pigments are located. In both mitochondria and chloroplasts, the presence of multiple membranes and several different fluid-filled compartments were important in allowing various incompatible activities to occur during aerobic respiration and photosynthesis.

E There are a number of fluid-filled, membrane-bound vesicles in plant and animal cells. Examples include the central vacuole, lysosomes, food vacuoles, secretory vesicles, and transport vacuoles. Plant cells typically have large fluid-filled organelles called the **central vacuole** (Figure 6.3), which serve various functions. The functions of the central vacuole include storing water, ions, and other compounds, and supporting the rigidity of the plant cell by maintaining the turgor pressure inside the cell. The **tonoplast** is the membrane that surrounds the central vacuole. Vacuoles can be seen in some animal cells; these relatively small, short-lived structures are involved in temporary storage and transport of materials.

Other Membranous Organelles

F The **endoplasmic reticulum (ER)** (Figure 6.3, Figure 6.4) is a large structure that comes in smooth and rough forms. The ER accounts for about half the membranes of a eukaryotic cell. It helps to compartmentalize the cell cytoplasm so that diverse metabolic pathways can occur in isolation from other metabolic pathways. The ER is used in the transport of materials through the cell, and the ER is involved in the synthesis of other molecules.

The ER is made of **membranous tubules** and sacs called **cisternae.** The internal fluid-filled spaces (the internal **lumen**) inside the tubules and cisternae are called **cisternal spaces.** These cisternal spaces are separated from the cytosol of the cytoplasm by the membranes. The ER membrane is connected to the nuclear envelope and the cisternal space of the ER is continuous with the space between the two membranes of the nuclear envelope. There are two types of ER: smooth ER and rough ER. Rough ER is studded with numerous ribosomes, while smooth ER is not. The smooth

ER is involved in the synthesis of lipids, and in the detoxification of drugs and various poisonous compounds, as well as storing calcium ions and creating new membranes. Rough ER is involved in the production of secretory proteins and the production of cell membranes.

G The **Golgi complex** (also called the **Golgi apparatus** or **Golgi body**) (Figure 6.3, Figure 6.4) is composed of a series of flattened membranous sacs called **cisternae** (resembling a stack of porous pancakes). The Golgi membranes contain enzymes involved in the storage and packaging of various proteins, preparing them for secretion. Lysosomes, for example, are formed by the Golgi complex.

H Many **transport vesicles** from the ER travel to the **Golgi apparatus** for modification of their contents. One side of the Golgi, the **cis** side, receives material by fusing with vesicles from the ER, while the other side, the **trans** side, buds off **transport vesicles** that travel to other sites within the cell, and **secretory vesicles** that carry wastes, hormones, digestive enzymes, or neurotransmitters to the outside of the cell. Secretory vesicles fuse with the outer cell membrane, thus transporting their contents out of the cell.

I **Lysosomes** (Figure 6.4) are small (0.1 to 1 μm) membrane-bound vesicles that contain digestive enzymes in animals and possibly other organisms. Lysosomes recycle worn-out organelles, digest food particles, and kill and digest foreign materials, such as viruses or bacteria. They fuse with food vacuoles and chemically break down the food particles. Lysosomes contain hydrolytic enzymes that are active at low pH (around 4 to 5). Special proton pumps on the lysosome membrane pump hydrogen ions into the lysosome, making it turn acidic. After fusing with another vacuole (a food vacuole, for example), the lysosome's hydrolytic enzymes then break down the complex molecules, producing simple sugars, amino acids, and other monomers, which diffuse out of the food vacuole into the cytosol of the cell.

Amoebas and many other protists, along with a number of animal cells, take in food by engulfing it and forming small vesicles called **food vacuoles** (this process is called **phagocytosis**). Some of your immune cells (macrophages, for example) do the same thing; they engulf and destroy bacteria, viruses, and other materials.

The waste products exit the cell by the vacuole 're-fusing' with the outer cell membrane in a process called **exocytosis** (see Figure 6.4, where a vesicle has fused with the outer cell membrane). Exocytosis is also the process by which the cell releases digestive proteins, antibodies, materials of the extracellular matrix or cell walls (see below), hormones, and neurotransmitters. Cells also recycle cell membranes and transport plasma membrane receptors in this way.

Nonmembranous Organelles

J **Ribosomes** are complexes of enzymes and ribosomal RNA (Figure 6.4). Ribosomes are involved in protein synthesis. In eukaryotes, many ribosomes are embedded into the outer (cytoplasmic) surface of the **rough ER** (smooth ER has no ribosomes) and on the cytoplasmic surface of the outer nuclear membrane. Many 'free' ribosomes are present in the cytoplasm in all prokaryotic and eukaryotic cells (Figure 6.2, Figure 6.3, Figure 6.4).

K In animal cells, the **centrosome** (Figure 6.4) is a structure that contains two **centrioles,** oriented at right angles to each other. Centrioles are small organelles possibly involved in cell division in animals (and in the primitive plants, such as the mosses and ferns.) Higher plants lack centrioles. The centrosomes produce the mitotic spindle apparatus.

L **Cilia and flagella** are locomotory structures found in some animal cells, as well as in a few plant cells and in many protists. Cilia and flagella are associated with the outer plasma membrane. These are thin, hairlike organelles on the exterior of the cell that beat or whip, causing the cell to move about. The two organelles are similar in internal structure, but cilia are shorter than flagella. A cell may have only one or a few flagella per cell, but there are usually hundreds of cilia on a single cell's surface. Centriole-like **basal bodies** are at the base of all eukaryotic cilia and flagella.

Both eukaryotic cilia and eukaryotic flagella have the same structure: they have microtubules sheathed by the plasma membrane. In most eukaryotic cilia and flagella, nine doublets of microtubules are arranged in a circle around two single microtubules at the center (the "9 pairs + 2" pattern). Proteins connect the outer doublets to each other and to the center. The outer doublets are also connected by motor proteins.

M Animal cells and plant cells also have a **cytoskeleton.** The cytoskeleton is composed of a number of different protein fibers. The cytoskeleton is involved in internal support of the cell, the movement of organelles, cell division, and other processes. Mitochondria and chloroplasts, for example, move around the cells along specific 'tracks' of the cytoskeleton.

N **Cell walls.** Outside of the cell membrane, extracellular structures can be found in many cells, particularly bacteria, plants, fungi and many protists (Figure 6.2, Figure 6.3).

1 The cell wall helps maintain the cell's shape and prevents physical damage to the cell. The cell walls of plants are composed of cellulose or other materials, whereas other materials are found in the cell walls of fungi and protists. The **cell wall,** also found in prokaryotes, fungi, and some protists, has multiple functions. **Plasmodesmata** are cytoplasmic connections between two adjacent plant cells through pores in the cell walls (Figure 6.3).

A In plants (Figure 6.3), the cell wall protects the cell, maintains its shape, and prevents excessive uptake of water.

B Plant cell walls also support the plant against the force of gravity.

C The thickness and chemical composition of cell walls differ from species to species and among cell types.

D The basic cell wall design is analogous to fiberglass or reinforced concrete; it consists of **cellulose** embedded in a matrix of proteins and other polysaccharides.

E A mature plant cell wall consists of a **primary cell wall,** a **middle lamella** with sticky polysaccharides that holds two adjacent cells together, and layers of the **secondary cell wall** (the secondary wall is not found in some plant cells).

2 Unlike the plants and fungi, animal cells do not have cell walls; they instead produce, bind to, and maintain an extracellular matrix (ECM) found outside of the plasma membrane. The primary constituents of the **extracellular matrix** are glycoproteins (proteins with attached carbohydrates), including large **collagen** fibers that are embedded in a network of other proteins.

Exercises

Exercise 6.1.

Prior to class, read the appendix titled "Proper Microscope Usage and Care." Study the parts of the microscope at your station. Be able to identify each part of the microscope. If you have any questions concerning the use of any scope, please see your lab instructor. In this exercise, you are to become familiar with the microscope's parts as well as the microscope's use and care. Microscopes are fragile and expensive; even if you have used one before, please refresh yourself on their proper use.

Examine the slide labeled 'letter e.' This exercise will illustrate the use of coarse and fine adjustments and the orientation of the image. Look at the slide with the letter 'e' under low power (40×) then switch to high power (100×). What happened to the light intensity? As you move the slide to the left or right, which direction does the image move?

Is the image inverted (up and down reversed) and/or reversed (left and right sides are switched)?

What is the width of the letter 'e' (see the next page)?

Exercise 6.2.

Colored Threads

Examine the slide labeled 'colored threads.' (This slide will help you understand the concept of **depth of field.**)

Which colored thread is on top? _________   How thick (how wide across) is a thread? _________

How many threads can be in focus at one time under low power (40× total magnification)? _________

How many are in focus under high power (100× total magnification)? _________

How does the depth of field change with higher magnification?

Exercise 6.3.

How to Measure Size of Microscopic Objects

Examine one of the rulers under the microscope. Although many cells and objects you will be observing this semester are small, we can estimate fairly accurately the average sizes of cells and organelles by comparing their sizes with the diameter of the field of view and the size of the eyepiece pointer. The pointer has an apparent length and width that changes with each successive magnification. Examine the chart below. A micron (micrometer, μm) is 1/1,000th of a millimeter (10^{-3} mm) or one-millionth of a meter (10^{-6} m).

How many microns are in a meter? __________

The following are estimated lengths of the pointer and the diameter of the field of view at different magnifications (Table 6.1).

Note: Depending on your microscope, your lab instructor will provide other estimates of the pointer's length and width.

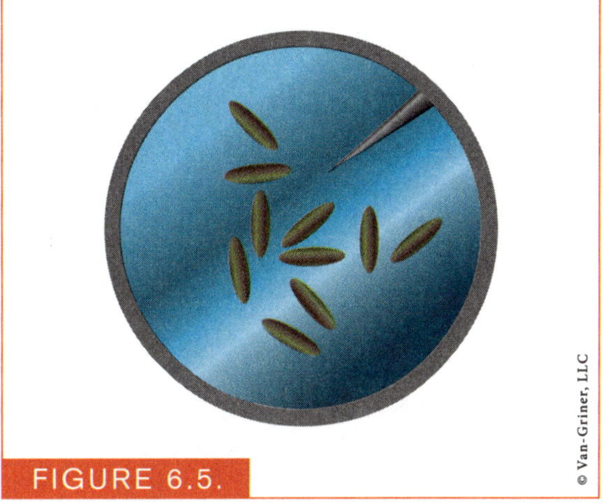

FIGURE 6.5.

Estimating the size of an organism under the microscope, using the pointer.

© Van-Griner, LLC

TABLE 6.1.

Magnification	Pointer Length (μm)	Pointer Width (μm)	Diameter of the Field of View (μm)
40×	2,500	60	4,500
100×	1,000	24	1,800
400×	250	6	450
1,000×	100	2.5	180

For an example, let's say you are looking at an organism under the microscope at 40× (see Figure 6.5). It is half as long as the pointer length. Therefore, the organism is approximately 1,250 μm long.

Exercise 6.4.

The Stereoscopic Dissecting Microscope

Go over the various parts of a stereoscopic dissecting scope. Your lab instructor will identify the various parts of a dissecting scope. Note that the dissecting scopes are **binocular** (they have two eyepieces). This scope is used for specimens that are too large for the compound scope. You can also see a three-dimensional view of the object at low magnification. For most dissecting scopes, the total magnification is 10× or 20×. However, a few dissecting microscopes have 15× eyepieces and 4× lenses, thus the total magnification can be as high as 60×.

Examine objects under the dissecting scope using both transmitted and reflected light. Your lab instructor will show you various materials that you may look at using the dissecting scopes. Note the total magnifying power of the specific scope you use.

Is the image inverted, like that seen with the compound microscope?

Exercise 6.5.

Bacterial Cells

The prokaryotic cells lack a membrane-bound nucleus (Figure 6.2). Typically, there is a single strand of DNA (deoxyribonucleic acid). There are no membrane bound organelles, such as mitochondria or chloroplasts. Smaller organelles, called ribosomes, are present. A rigid or semirigid (depending on the species) cell wall is present outside of the outer cell membrane. You will not be able to see these structures clearly with your microscope, because the bacteria are too small.

Examine the demonstration slide showing bacteria (under oil immersion, 1,000× total magnification). Estimate the cells' sizes, and notice the various bacterial shapes and make sketches of what you see in the space below (Figure 6.6). **Be careful! DO NOT ram the objective through the slide! Only use the fine focus and not the coarse focus when at high power.**

FIGURE 6.6.

Bacteria shapes and groups.

Exercise 6.6.
Making a Wet Mount

Take the small 'skin' off of a layer of onion, or a small piece of live *Elodea* leaf (see Figure 6.8). If you use *Elodea*, use only a small piece. Your lab instructor will assist you, if you need help.

If you are looking at onion epidermis, carefully place this piece of onion epidermis in a drop of water on a slide, and add a small drop of iodine (**Be careful! Iodine will stain clothing and skin. If you are looking at *Elodea*, no iodine is needed.**)

View the slide under 40× total magnification and draw what you see in the space provided below (Figure 6.7).

Estimate the approximate size (width and length, in μm) of your onion and/or *Elodea* epidermal cells. Assume the depth of the cells is similar to the width.

Cell width: ____________ μm

Cell length: _____________ μm

FIGURE 6.7.

Elodea or onion epidermis.

You should notice numerous green **chloroplasts** in the *Elodea* leaf.

Find a chloroplast and measure its size: _________ μm

The **nucleus** is several times larger than a chloroplast. It may have a slightly paler color, compared to the chloroplasts.

Find a nucleus and measure its size. _________ μm

When you are finished viewing the onion cells or *Elodea* leaves, please clean the slide by rinsing it under tap water in the front sink. Throw the cover slip away into the broken glass container next to the front table. **Do not throw any paper trash into the glass container. In addition, do NOT throw a cover slip, or a broken slide, or any other glass materials, in the trash barrels!** Do not leave any cover slips lying around on a table or bench. If you do so, you may injure a fellow student, lab instructor, or one of the custodians cleaning the lab.

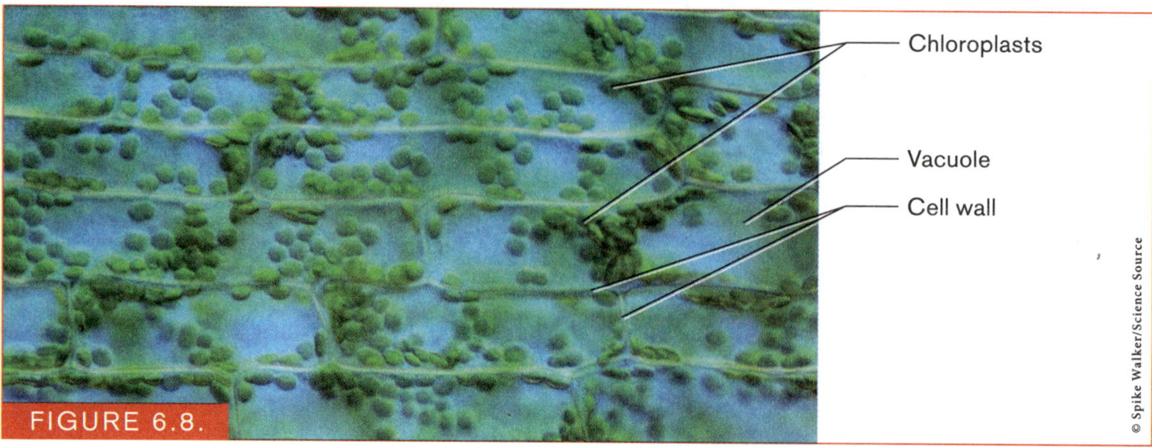

FIGURE 6.8.

Live *Elodea* cells.

Exercise 6.7.

The Size of Human Cheek Cells

Examine the slide labeled "human cheek cell" (or "human buccal cell") under 40× and 100× total magnification. These cells are the lining of the inside of your mouth. They have been stained with methylene blue and will appear as either isolated cells, or small clusters of flattened pancake-like cells. You will not be able to see much detail on any organelles other than the nucleus. Draw what you see in the space provided below (Figure 6.9). Be sure to label the nucleus and plasma membrane.

The diameter of a human cheek cell: _________ μm

The diameter of the cheek cell nucleus: _________ μm

The cheek cell is about 1 to 2 μm thick.

FIGURE 6.9.

Human cheek cells.

Exercise 6.8.

Sea Star Ovum

Examine the slide of the sea star egg under 40× and 100× total magnification. The sea star egg shows a stained spherical **nucleus,** the outer **plasma membrane,** the **cytoplasm,** the **nuclear envelope,** and the **nucleolus.** The DNA will appear as a grainy material (**chromatin**) within the nucleus.

Draw the egg in the space provided below (Figure 6.10), and indicate its size. Label as much structure as you can.

Average diameter of the egg: _________ μm

FIGURE 6.10.

Sea star egg.

Exercise 6.9.
Fungal Cells

Observe the fungal hyphae slide (*Rhizopus*) under 40× and 100× total magnification. Make a sketch of what you see in the space provided below (Figure 6.11). Like animals, fungi are eukaryotic heterotrophs, but fungi typically obtain their nutrients from dead organic matter. Except for the unicellular yeasts, fungi are multicellular. The body of a fungus consists of many elongated filaments, called **hyphae.**

Draw the fungal hyphae, and include a ruler bar for size:

Typical length of a hyphal cell: _________ μm

Typical diameter of a fungal hyphal cell: _________ μm

Diameter of a sporangium: _________ μm

FIGURE 6.11.

Fungal hyphae and cells.

Exercise 6.10.

Mitochondrial and Chloroplast Structure

The **mitochondrion** has two membranes: an **outer membrane** and a convoluted **inner membrane.** The infoldings of the inner membrane are called **cristae.** The inner membrane divides the mitochondrion's interior into two compartments: the **intermembrane space** (the fluid-filled compartment between the two membranes) and the **matrix** found within the inner membrane.

Like the mitochondria, chloroplasts have two membranes: the **outer membrane** and the **inner membrane.** The **intermembrane space** exists between the two membranes. These two membranes enclose additional membranes called **thylakoids.** The thylakoids are stacked into 'poker chip' stacks, called **grana.** The **stroma** is the fluid-filled compartment outside of all of the thylakoids, but inside the inner membrane. The **thylakoid spaces** are fluid-filled compartments within the thylakoids.

Label the parts of a typical mitochondrion and chloroplast in the drawings below (Figure 6.12).

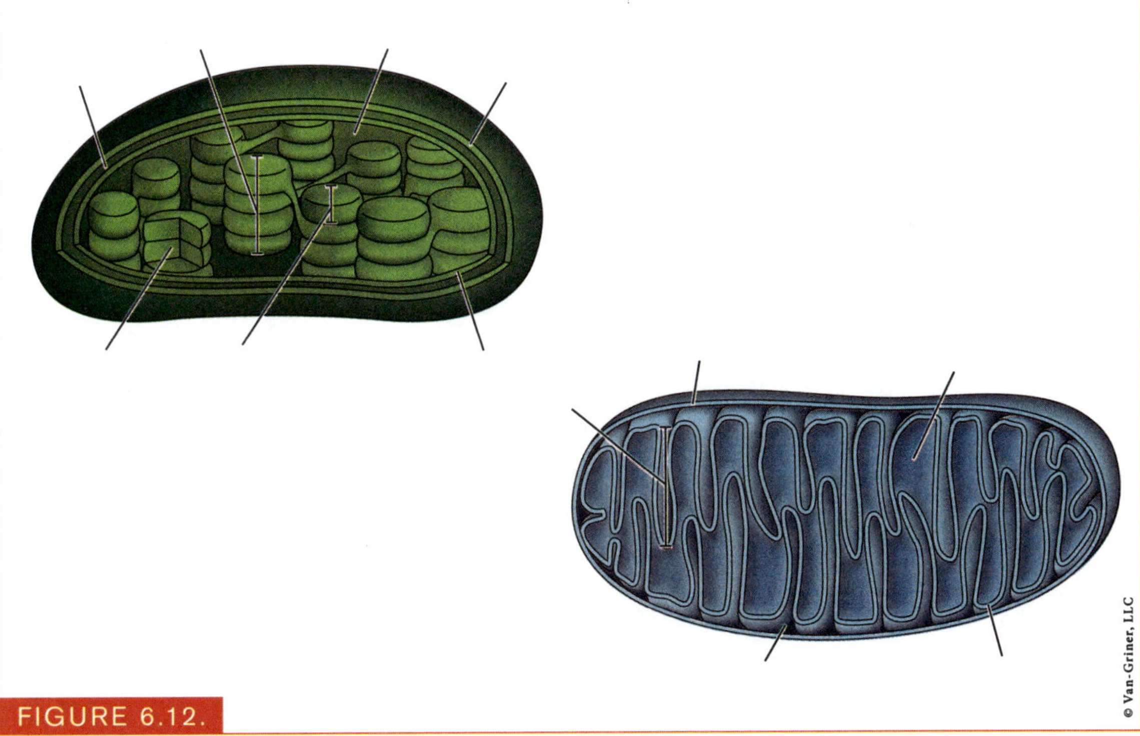

FIGURE 6.12.

Mitochondrion and chloroplast structure.

Exercise 6.11.

Estimate the number of cells in your body: you can make a rough estimate of the number of cells in your body by using the following equations and using the estimate of the size of a human cheek cell.

$$\text{number of cells} = \frac{\text{(your weight in pounds) (454 g/lb) (1 ml/g) (}10^{12}\ \mu m^3/ml)}{4/3\ \pi\ (\text{radius of the cheek cell})^3}$$

$$\text{number of cells} = \frac{\text{(your weight in pounds) (}1.08 \times 10^{14})}{(\text{radius of the cheek cell})^3}$$

Your estimate of the total number of cells of your body: _______________________

(If you have trouble understanding the above equation, talk it over with your lab instructor). This equation assumes several things: 1) you and your cells weigh the same as an equal-sized volume of water (1 g/ml); 2) the cheek cells are perfect spheres; 3) you are completely composed of cells, and thus have no non-living components; and 4) the cheek cell is an averaged-sized cell. Discuss these assumptions with your lab mates and the lab instructor.

Do you think the assumptions above are valid assumptions?

Ask your lab instructor for the average number of cells in the human body. Was your estimate close? How can you make this estimate more accurate?

Exercise 6.12.

Cell Sizes

Today you have looked at a variety of cells.

What is the range and average sizes for cells?

Do larger organisms have larger cells than smaller organisms?

Exercise 6.13.

Examine the relative sizes of various cells, and relate their sizes and shapes to constraints with $SA : V$ ratios.

Some equations concerning volumes that you may remember from grade school:

volume of a cube: $V = l^3$ 　　　　　　　　　volume of a sphere: $V = 4/3(\pi r^3)$

volume of a box or rectangular prism: $V = lwh$ 　　　volume of a cylinder: $V = \pi r^2 h$

where r = radius, π = pi, or 3.1416, l = length, d = diameter, w = width, h = height or depth.

Average diameter of a human cheek cell (it is like a shallow cylinder): _________ μm

Average length of a human cheek cell: _________ μm

Estimated volume of a human cheek cell: _________ μm^3

Average diameter of the fertilized sea star egg: _________ μm (a sphere)

Estimated volume of a sea star egg: _________ μm^3

Average diameter of the bacteria observed: _________ μm (they are like small spheres)

Estimated volume of a bacterium: _________ μm^3

Estimated length of a *Paramecium*: _________ μm^3 (like a box)

Estimated volume of a *Paramecium*: _________ μm^3

Average length of the *Elodea* cells: _________ μm

Average width of the *Elodea* cells: _________ μm

Average depth of the *Elodea* cells: _________ μm³

Estimated volume of an *Elodea* cell: _________ μm³

Are the volumes of these cells similar? Can you see any relationship?

Plot the average volume for the following organisms as a function of their length or diameter in Figure 6.13. What is the relationship between mass and body length? Can you explain what is going on?

FIGURE 6.13.

The relationship between volume and length among various cells.

Exercise 6.14.

Some cells obviously are larger than a few microns in diameter. For example, some of your nerve cells and muscle cells have lengths of centimeters, not microns. The human ovum is a large cell, relative to other human cells. Discuss with your lab partners several possibilities that could allow for these large cells to exist. Talk this over with your lab instructor after you have discussed several possibilities.

Exercise 6.15.

Making Predictions: Interpolation and Extrapolation

Interpolation

Interpolation is the process of obtaining a value from a figure or table at a point that is located between data points that have already been measured. A prediction made for a point between known values of data is called interpolation.

Extrapolation

Extrapolation is the process of obtaining a value from a figure or table that extends beyond the given data. The 'trend' of the data is extended past the last point given (either by eye, or better yet, by using statistical techniques) and an estimate is made of the value. A prediction made for a point beyond the range of known values of data is called extrapolation.

Examine Figure 6.14. It shows the weights and lengths of various snail shells. You are to predict additional points that would be at points A, B, and C. At points A, B, and C, are we extrapolating, or interpolating?

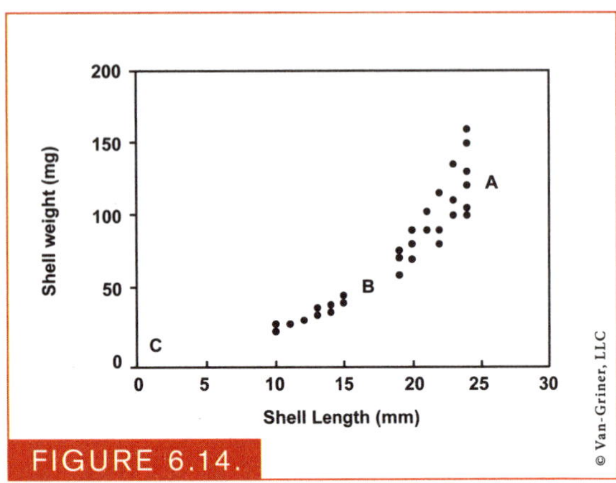

FIGURE 6.14.

Shell lengths and weights.

Estimate what shell length (mm) would be for a 100 mg shell. ________

Estimate what the shell weight (mg) would be for a 5 mm long shell. ________

Which method (interpolation or extrapolation) is more risky? Why?

Do you think points A, B, and C are equally 'risky' as predictions?

In the potato exercise in Unit 4, which method did you use to predict the potato tissue molarity: interpolation or extrapolation?

In some relationships, data follow a linear trend, and we can use a linear regression analysis to help make our predictions. Some biological phenomena are modeled more effectively with functions that are more complex than linear equations. Some nonlinear examples include quadratic, polynomial, exponential, and logarithmic functions.

In the osmosis exercise in Unit 4, were the results 'linear?

Look at Figure 6.14. Draw what you think would be the linear regression curve through the data. Do the data 'look' linear? Is there another type of line you would draw?

Although we have been talking about interpolation and extrapolation using linear regressions, we can use extrapolation and interpolation in nonlinear functions as well.

For example, examine Figure 6.15.

If you use extrapolation (using either a linear, exponential, or logistic function for population growth) what is the predicted total population size for humans in 2050? Why could this be somewhat unreliable? What assumptions are being made about this extrapolation?

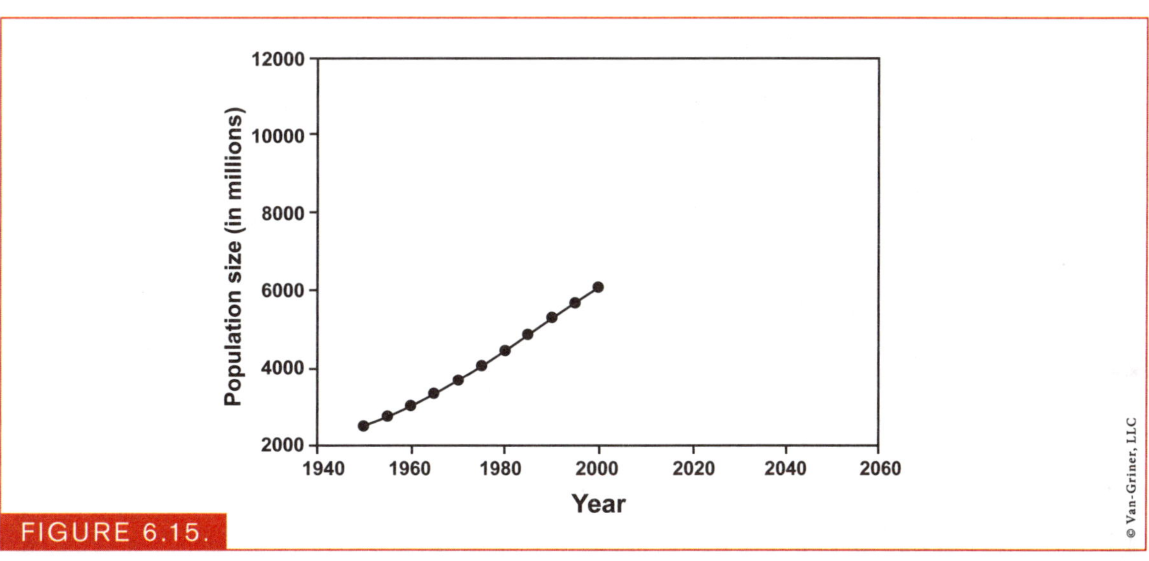

FIGURE 6.15.

Human population growth estimates.

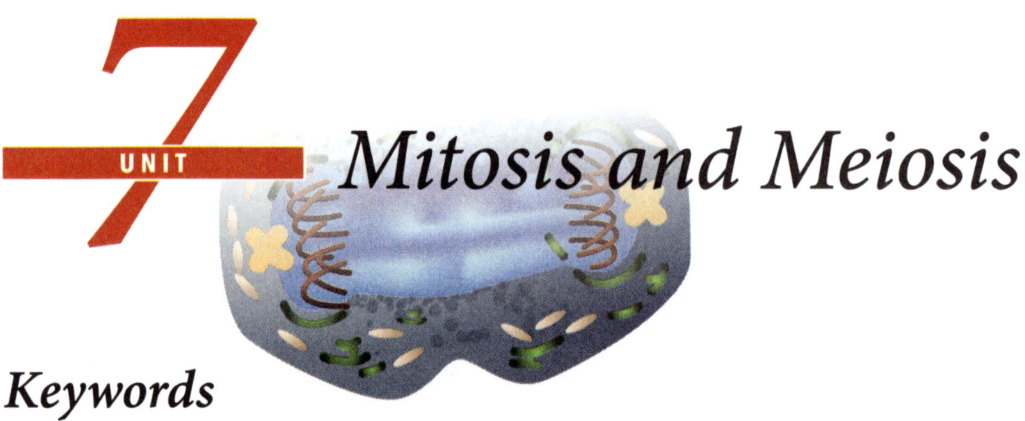

UNIT 7 — Mitosis and Meiosis

Keywords

cell cycle
interphase
mitosis
meiosis
prophase
metaphase
anaphase
telophase
cytokinesis
oogenesis
spermatogenesis
chromosomes
chromatids
chromatin

centromeres
kinetochore
centrioles
poles
equator (metaphase plate)
spindle
spindle fibers
aster
interkinesis
homologous chromosomes (homologues)
synapsis
crossing over

tetrads
chiasma (chiasmata)
cleavage
cleavage furrow
haploid
diploid
gametes
sperm
ova
primary and secondary oocytes
spermatogonia
oogonia
polar bodies

primary and secondary spermatocytes
spermatids
ootids
ovaries
testes
follicles
seminiferous tubule
interstitial cells
nurse cells
zygote
somatic cells
fertilization

Learning Objectives

When finished with this unit, you should be able to do the following:

1. Describe the events that occur in both mitosis and meiosis, in their correct sequence;

2. Estimate the relative length of time each phase of the cell cycle lasts (interphase, prophase, metaphase, anaphase, and telophase) from the examination of tissue slides;

3. Identify the phases of mitosis in drawings, photomicrographs, and slides;

4. Identify the phases of meiosis on drawings;

5. Compare and contrast oogenesis and spermatogenesis;

6. Describe the basic functions of mitosis and meiosis. In addition, compare sexual and asexual reproduction in terms of their function and the nuclear division involved. Describe how meiosis increases the potential for genetic variability;

7. State the relative turnover of cells (how many cells are lost each day from the typical animal);

8 Compare the daughter cells to each other and to the parent cell, both in terms of genetic similarity and the amount of genetic material, for cells completing mitosis or meiosis; and

9 Describe the differences in mitosis and cytokinesis between plant cells and animal cells.

The Cell Cycle

One common principle or theme in biology is that organisms are made of cells, and cells produce other cells. In this week's lab, you will examine the **cell cycle** (Figure 7.1) and the process of **cell division.** Normal cells do not divide continuously. When cells are not dividing, the cells are in the part of the cell cycle referred to as **interphase.** Interphase is not considered a phase of the two major types of nuclear division; **mitosis** and **meiosis.** Sometimes interphase is called the 'resting phase.' However, a cell in interphase is not resting at all; it is only 'resting' from cell division. During interphase, the cell is respiring, producing and secreting materials, contracting, moving, interacting with other cells, and doing all of the things living cells do.

Interphase is divided into three parts: G1 (for 'first gap'), **S** (for 'synthesis' of DNA), and **G2** ('second gap,' see Figure 7.1). During G1, the chromosomes are single, unreplicated structures. In G1, the cell prepares for the replication of DNA. During S, the cell duplicates its DNA; at the end of the S phase, each chromosome has been duplicated and thus consists of two **sister chromatids** joined together by various proteins (called cohesins). During G2, the cell prepares for cell division by producing the components for the spindle apparatus. By the end of G2, most of the cohesins are removed, except at a region called the **centromere,** where the two chromatids remain attached together until anaphase of mitosis. Throughout interphase, all of the cell's DNA is not tightly coiled into dense structures called **chromosomes.** However, as we will see during mitosis, DNA is tightly coiled.

A **chromosome** is a strand of DNA with a series of genes located along its length. The chromosome may be circular (with no ends) or linear (with two ends), depending on the organism. During the first phase (prophase) of mitosis and meiosis, various proteins (particularly histones and condensins) coil the DNA strands tightly into compact chromosomes, thus making the job of separating chromosomes that make their way into daughter cells easier.

Because many plants and animals increase in size over time, there must be some way to increase the number of cells during animal growth. In addition, in higher animals, many lose about 1 to 2% of their cells on a given day. Many cells are constantly being shed along the intestinal tract. The outer skin of all animals is composed of layers of dead cells that function as a mechanical barrier to disease organisms. Other cells wear out (like red blood cells) and they either die or are consumed by phagocytic cells of the immune system.

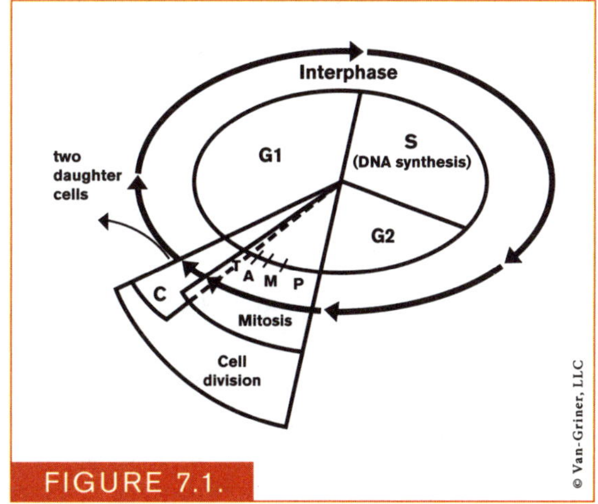

FIGURE 7.1.

The cell cycle. G1 = "gap 1" phase; S = "synthesis" phase when DNA is replicated; G2 = "gap 2" phase; C = "cytokinesis"; and P, M, A, and T = the four phases of mitosis. At the end of cytokinesis, two daughter cells are formed, and each enters G1. Note that cytokinesis typically begins during telophase of mitosis (note the overlap).

In plants, many cells die and form support structures (like the wood of woody plants), and as the plant grows, new leaves, stems, and flowers must be produced. Plants and animals are also damaged (damaged meaning that they lose cells) due to injury caused either by predators, by aggressive interactions with other individuals, by disease and accidents, or from exposure to the weather and the physical environment. Thus, at least some cells in all multicellular organisms must have the ability to increase their numbers by **cell division.** Cell division is composed of two parts: a nuclear division (**mitosis** and **meiosis**) and a cytoplasmic division (**cytokinesis**). All multicellular plants, animals, and fungi have this ability to increase in size.

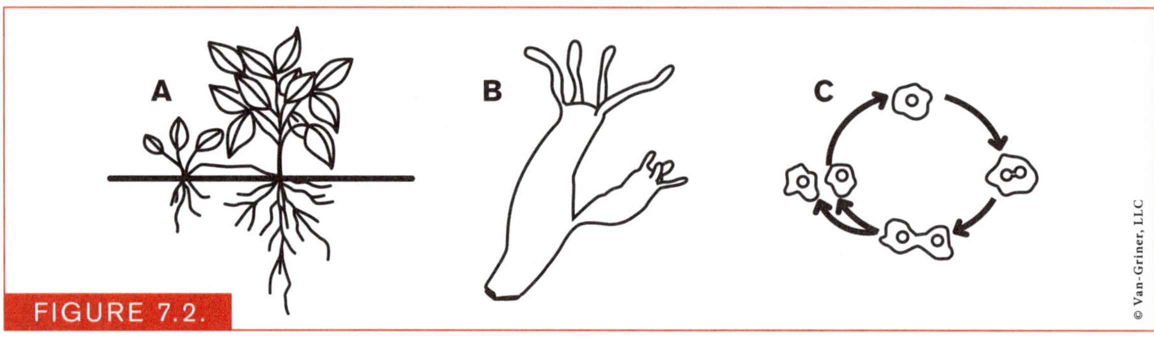

FIGURE 7.2.

Examples of asexual reproduction: A: plant runners/stolons, B: buds (in *Hydra*), and C: cell division (binary fission) in both protists and yeasts.

All multicellular organisms have the ability to grow and to replace cells by **mitosis.** In many animals, mitosis is also used for **asexual reproduction:** the production of offspring by one parent (Figure 7.2). This type of reproduction produces genetically identical offspring by budding, fragmentation, or the development of a single offspring by repeated mitotic divisions of a single unfertilized cell. In addition to being genetically identical to each other, offspring produced by asexual reproduction are genetically identical to the parent. The only genetic variation that is observed in asexual reproduction comes from mutation.

Like the animals, many plants and fungi reproduce asexually using mitosis (see Figure 7.2). Vegetative propagation, budding, fission, and fragmentation are all ways of increasing the numbers of individuals of a species, and mitosis is the nuclear process underlying all of these forms of asexual reproduction. In the unicellular protistans, mitosis is the basis of their mode of asexual reproduction as well.

A second important type of nuclear division is **meiosis** (see Figures 7.8 and 7.11, 7.12). Meiosis does not replace **somatic cells,** like mitosis. Somatic cells make up all of the cells of the animal's body, except the gamete-producing cells. Meiosis is a special form of nuclear division that occurs only in gamete-producing tissues. Meiosis is involved in the production of **gametes.** A gamete is a reproductive cell that fuses with another cell (this process of fusing two gametes together is called **fertilization**). After the cytoplasm of the two gametes fuse (called **plasmogamy**), the two gamete nuclei also will fuse (the fusion of the two nuclei is called **karyogamy**), producing a genetically unique cell (called the **zygote**). In multicellular organisms, the zygote undergoes repeated mitotic divisions to develop into a multicellular offspring.

Sexual reproduction is the process where two parents give rise to offspring through the fusion of gametes produced by meiosis; these offspring have a unique combination of genes inherited in the gametes formed by each parent. The offspring are not genetically identical to either parent, but each offspring does possess half of the genes of each parent. Because of meiosis, considerable genetic variation exists in the offspring of sexually reproducing species.

Offspring produced by sexual reproduction are not genetically identical to each other or to the parent, due to:

1 The 'scrambling' of genes by meiosis, and

2 The somewhat random process of which genetically unique gamete fuses with another gamete in fertilization.

The Phases of Mitosis

Phase 1 – Prophase

The first phase of mitosis is **prophase.** The DNA is condensed into microscopically visible chromosomes. In interphase, the chromosomes were thin and spread out. In this diffuse state, the DNA molecules are bound with a variety of proteins (this complex of DNA and proteins is called **chromatin**), and cannot be seen with an ordinary light microscope. Remember that last lab period you observed that the chromatin is inside the **nuclear membrane** or nuclear envelope. A **nucleolus** (the site of ribosomal RNA production) may be seen inside the nucleus. Prior to mitosis, each chromosome consists of two identical copies of DNA (due to DNA replication occurring in the S period of interphase). These two identical copies are called **sister chromatids,** which are joined together at the **centromere.**

There can be as few as two, or as many as several hundred, chromosomes in a cell of various eukaryotic organisms, depending on species. For example, there are 46 chromosomes in the nuclei of human cells. The more advanced animals do not necessarily have more chromosomes; there is no obvious pattern. For example, fruit flies have 8 chromosomes, cats have 32, sand dollars (an echinoderm) have 52, cattle have 60, horses and guinea pigs have 64, dogs have 78, whitefish have 80, and goldfish have 94 chromosomes. All of these animal species mentioned above are **diploid.** At the end of prophase, the **nuclear membrane** and the nucleolus disappear, allowing the condensed chromosomes to migrate somewhat freely within the cell (the centromeres attach to microtubules, which act as a scaffolding on which chromosomes move).

The two **centrioles** in the cell had duplicated themselves earlier in interphase, and they have moved to opposite sides (**poles**) of the cell. These centrioles are very small and are not easily seen with light microscopes. The centrioles (at least in animal cells) appear to direct the production of a series of microtubules: the **asters** and the **spindle fibers.** The microtubule spindle fibers form the scaffolding (the **spindle apparatus**) on which the chromosomes move. One difference between plant cells and animal cells is there are no centrioles present in plant cells and most fungi.

Note: In a number of texts, prophase has been divided into prophase and another phase, referred to as 'prometaphase.' In this course, we will concentrate on four phases, not five. However, remember that the phases of mitosis and meiosis run smoothly into each other.

Phase 2 – Metaphase

The chromosomes (made of two sister chromatids) move and line up at the center of the cell (the **cell equator** or the **metaphase plate**). The spindle fibers push the sister chromatids until they are all arranged at the metaphase plate. The metaphase plate (also called the **equatorial plate**) is an imaginary line that is equidistant from the two poles from which the spindle fibers originate. The **kinetochores** associated with chromatid centromeres attach to some of the microtubules of the spindle apparatus (these microtubules are referred to as kinetochore microtubules). Microtubules from one pole attach to one kinetochore of one chromatid, while microtubules from the other pole attach to the kinetochore of the other chromatid.

Phase 3 – Anaphase

At the start of anaphase, the sister chromatids separate from each other at the centromere. The chromatids now are called **daughter chromosomes,** to indicate that they are considered to be separate chromosomes. The two identical daughter chromosomes separate and travel to opposite poles, by the action of motor proteins associated with the kinetochore.

Phase 4 – Telophase

The fourth and last phase of mitosis, telophase, begins when the two groups of chromosomes reach the opposite poles. A nuclear membrane forms around each collection of chromosomes. The chromosomes begin to unwind and become **chromatin,** and the spindle disappears. The nucleolus reappears, signaling that the cell is beginning to produce RNA for protein synthesis.

Cytokinesis

Cytokinesis is the actual division of the cell's cytoplasm between the two daughter cells (Figure 7.3). Cytokinesis typically begins in telophase of mitosis. After the end of mitotic telophase and cytokinesis, you now have two genetically identical daughter cells. Each cell then re-enters interphase, either to specialize into certain types of cells, or to prepare to divide again.

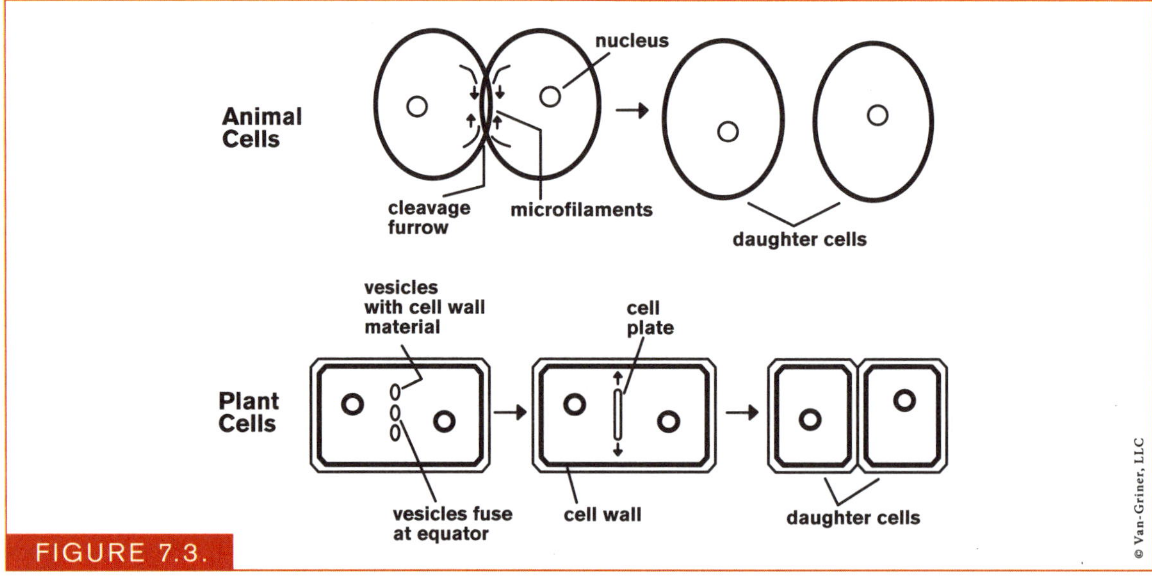

FIGURE 7.3.

Cytokinesis in animal and plant cells.

The process of cytokinesis differs slightly between animal cells and plant cells. During animal cell cytokinesis, a **cleavage furrow** forms, where the cell 'pinches' into two by a ring of microfilaments around the cell equator (Figure 7.3). In plant cells, a new **cell wall** eventually forms between the two new cells (Figure 7.5). No cell walls are formed in animals (Figure 7.4). Starting in the middle of the cell, the cell wall forms from a cell plate that is laid down along the equator of the cell by the fusion of vesicles produced by the Golgi apparatus. The fusion of vesicles forms cell membranes that eventually fuse with the outer plasma membrane, resulting in the production of two daughter cells that have their own plasma membranes. The contents of the vesicles form the **cell plate,** which eventually forms the new cell walls separating the two cells (see Figure 7.3).

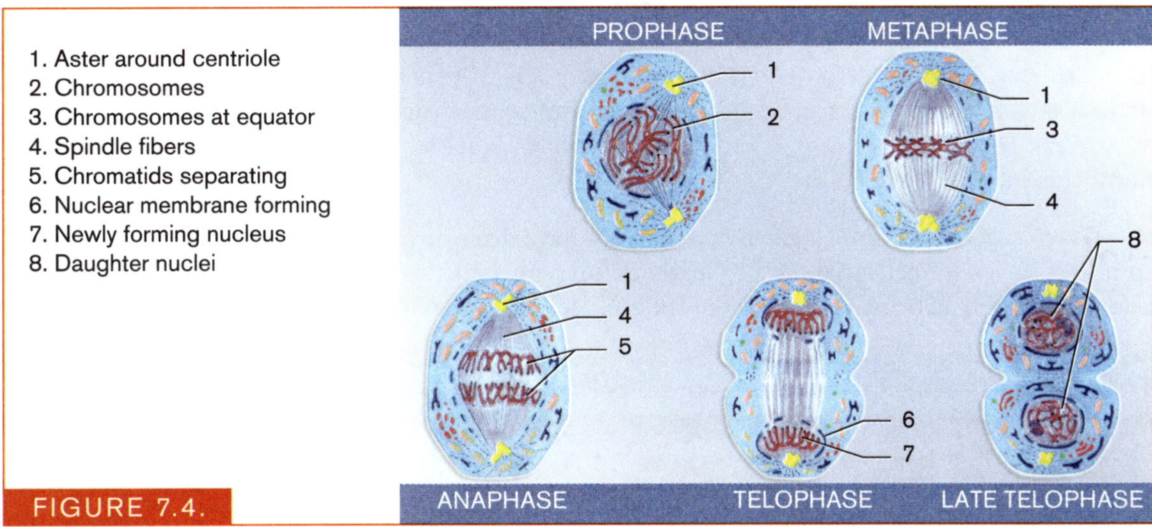

FIGURE 7.4.

Animal cell mitosis.

Exercises

Exercise 7.1.

How Long Does the Cell Stay in Each Phase of Mitosis?

You can estimate the relative amount of time each cell spends in each mitotic phase (as well as in interphase) by counting the number of cells observed in each phase. Look at the end of the onion root tip under low and high power. If you have problems finding cells that are in mitosis, ask your lab instructor for help. Use Figure 7.7 to guide you. Draw cells in each of the phases of mitosis and in interphase in the space provided below (Figure 7.5). If you see a cell undergoing cytokinesis, make a sketch of what you see. Count the number of cells in each phase in one field of view under 400×. Tally the number of cells in each phase in Table 7.1 below. Your lab instructor will collect all numbers and total them on the board.

Because the cross section of a given cell may not have been through the area of the nucleus or the spindle, only count cells that have a clearly defined nucleus (for interphase) or cells in which you clearly see stained chromosomes (for prophase, metaphase, anaphase and telophase).

TABLE 7.1. The number of onion root tip cells in various stages of the cell cycle.

	Interphase	Prophase	Metaphase	Anaphase	Telophase
your tally					
class totals					

The assumption is that at a given point in time, the number of cells in a given phase of division is proportional to the length of time of that phase (i.e., the fewer cells, the shorter the relative time). Is this a valid assumption? Which phase appears to be the longest? The shortest? In the onion root tip, does interphase last longer than all of the phases of mitosis combined?

FIGURE 7.5.

Plant cell mitosis: onion root tip.

Exercise 7.2.

View the whitefish blastula slide. In the young developing whitefish embryo, the cells early in development divide more or less simultaneously. However, later on, the cells undergo cell division at different rates. This slide was made by preserving the embryo and sectioning through it. The cells are killed and stained, thus frozen in the stage they were in at the time. Draw cells in each of the phases of mitosis and in interphase in the space provided below (Figure 7.6). If you see a cell undergoing cytokinesis, make a sketch of what you see.

FIGURE 7.6.

Animal cell mitosis: whitefish blastula.

What potential barriers to cell division occur in plant and animal cells?

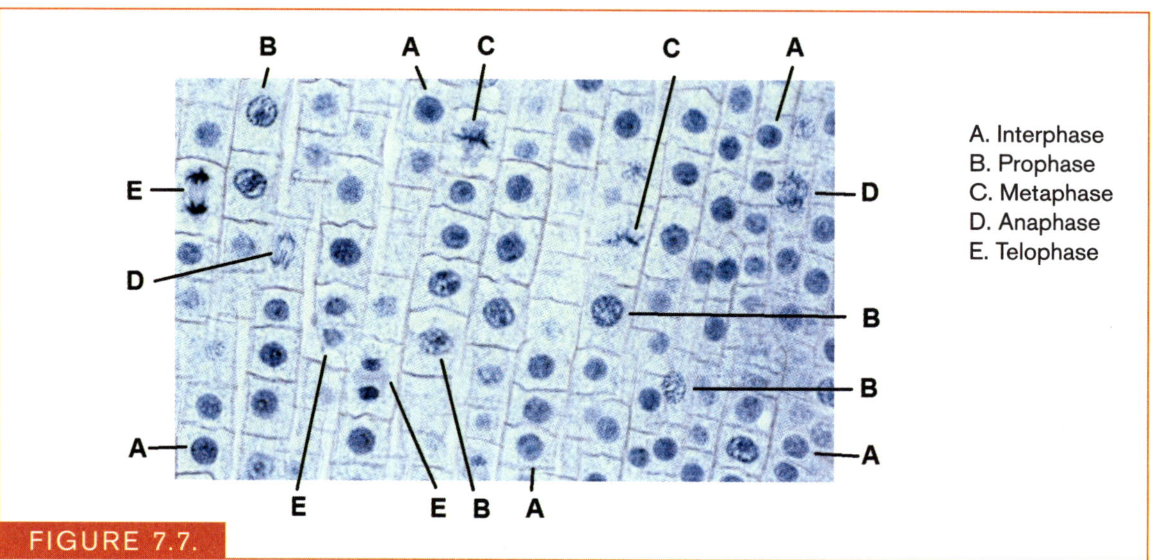

FIGURE 7.7.

Plant cell mitosis (onion root tip).

Exercise 7.3.

Differences between the process of cytokinesis and mitosis in plant cells and animal cells. Go to the demonstration station where pictures depicting the differences in cytokinesis are shown, and examine Figure 7.3, Figure 7.4, and Figure 7.7. Now, from memory, make a quick sketch/list in the space below (or use another sheet of paper) of the two types of cells (plant and animal) and their differences with respect to mitosis and cytokinesis. Check your answers, and correct any of your mistakes.

Do bacteria use mitosis? Why or why not?

Meiosis

Many aspects of the process we call meiosis resemble similar aspects of mitosis. Both processes are types of nuclear divisions, and both are preceded by the replication of chromosomes. However, in meiosis, there are two consecutive cell divisions, **meiosis I** and **meiosis II.** The process of meiosis is shown in Figure 7.8. At the end, there are four daughter cells (at least in males). Each final daughter cell has only half as many chromosomes as the parent cell. Meiosis reduces chromosome number by copying the chromosomes once, but dividing **twice.** The first division (meiosis I) separates homologous chromosomes. The second division (meiosis II) separates the two chromatids.

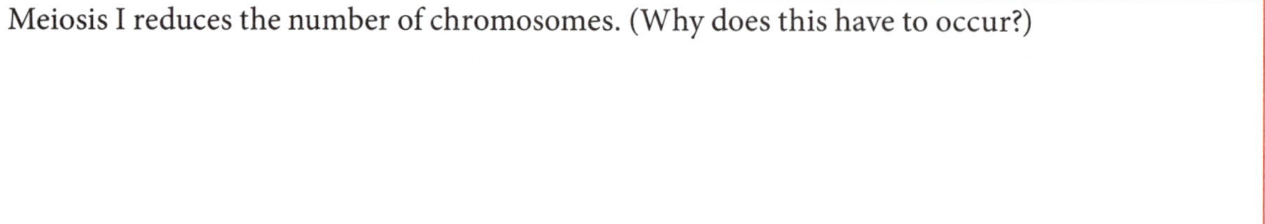

Meiosis I reduces the number of chromosomes. (Why does this have to occur?)

Meiosis I and II both occur in four phases: prophase, metaphase, anaphase, and telophase. During the preceding interphase, all chromosomes are replicated to form chromosomes that consist of two sister chromatids. The sister chromatids are genetically identical and joined at the centromere.

Meiosis I

Prophase I

At the beginning of meiosis, the chromosomes condense, just like mitosis. However, during prophase I, the homologous chromosomes pair up to form **tetrads.** A tetrad consists of two homologous chromosomes, and each **homologue** consists of two chromatids (See Figure 7.9). The homologous chromosomes are attached together by a set of special proteins. This process of attaching the homologues together is called **synapsis.** Note that synapsis does not occur in mitosis.

Once synapsis has occurred, an important phenomenon, called **crossing over,** can occur. **Crossing over** is the exchange of corresponding segments of chromatids of homologous chromosomes. When this exchange occurs, x-shaped attachment sites between two chromatids become visible (a single attachment site where crossing over is occurring is called a **chiasma;** plural: **chiasmata**).

One or more chiasmata can occur with each set of homologous chromosomes. The four chromatids align themselves closely gene by gene, and the chromatids then break at specific sites. Corresponding pieces of chromosomes (containing genes) then can be exchanged from one chromatid to another. One gene that was on a maternally inherited chromosome can now be found on a paternally inherited chromosome, and vice versa.

After crossing over, the four chromatids now are all genetically unique, in that they have different sequences of genes along their lengths.

A **spindle (spindle apparatus)** forms from microtubules that arise from each pole of the cell. Some of the spindle fibers attach to **kinetochores** located at the centromeres of the two chromatids of a chromosome. The kinetochore proteins connect the microtubules of the spindle to the chromosomes. Once the microtubules attach to the kinetochores, the spindle apparatus can begin to move the tetrad around.

Metaphase I

The tetrads are all arranged at the metaphase plate. Microtubules from one pole are attached to the kinetochore of one chromosome of each tetrad, while those from the other pole are attached to the other. During metaphase I, homologous pairs of chromosomes, not individual chromosomes, are aligned along the metaphase plate. In human cells, you would see 23 tetrads at metaphase of Meiosis I, whereas 46 chromosomes would line up in metaphase of mitosis.

Anaphase I

The homologous chromosomes separate and are pulled toward opposite poles. At anaphase I, it is homologous chromosomes, not sister chromatids, that separate. Note how this differs from mitosis: where the sister chromatids of each homologue separate and travel toward opposite poles. The homologues then are carried to opposite poles of the cell. The two chromatids remain attached at the centromere until anaphase II.

Telophase I

The movement of homologous chromosomes continues until there is a haploid set at each pole. Each chromosome still is composed of two linked chromatids; however, the two are now not identical (due to crossing over) and thus cannot be called sister chromatids.

Cytokinesis during Meiosis

Cytokinesis in meiosis occurs by the same mechanisms as mitosis. Cytokinesis usually begins in telophase I. After cytokinesis of meiosis I, the two cells each then may enter a brief resting phase unique to meiosis, called **interkinesis.** There is no replication of chromosomes in interkinesis. After interkinesis is over, the two cells enter meiosis II. Interkinesis does not occur in all organisms.

Meiosis II

The second part of meiosis, meiosis II, is very similar to mitosis.

Prophase II

During prophase II, a spindle apparatus forms, attaches to kinetochores of each of the chromatids, and moves them around. Spindle fibers from one pole attach to the kinetochore of one chromatid and those of the other pole to the other chromatid.

Metaphase II

The chromatids are arranged at the metaphase plate. The kinetochores of chromatids face opposite poles. Metaphase II appears identical to metaphase in mitosis, except that there are half the number of chromosomes present.

Anaphase II

The centromeres of the two chromatids or each chromosome separate and the separate chromatids travel toward opposite poles. Remember that the chromatids are not identical (unlike anaphase in mitosis, where the two chromatids are identical).

Telophase II

During telophase II, separated chromatids arrive (which can be called chromosomes composed of one chromatid) at opposite poles. The nuclear membranes reappear, forming around the chromatids. A second round of cytokinesis then divides the cytoplasm. Thus, at the end of meiosis, there are **four** haploid daughter cells.

Mitosis and meiosis have several key differences:

1 The chromosome number is reduced by half in meiosis, but not in mitosis.

2 Mitosis produces daughter cells that are genetically identical to the parent and to each other. Meiosis produces daughter cells that differ from the parental cell (they only have half of the parental cell's genes) and the daughter cells also are different from each other.

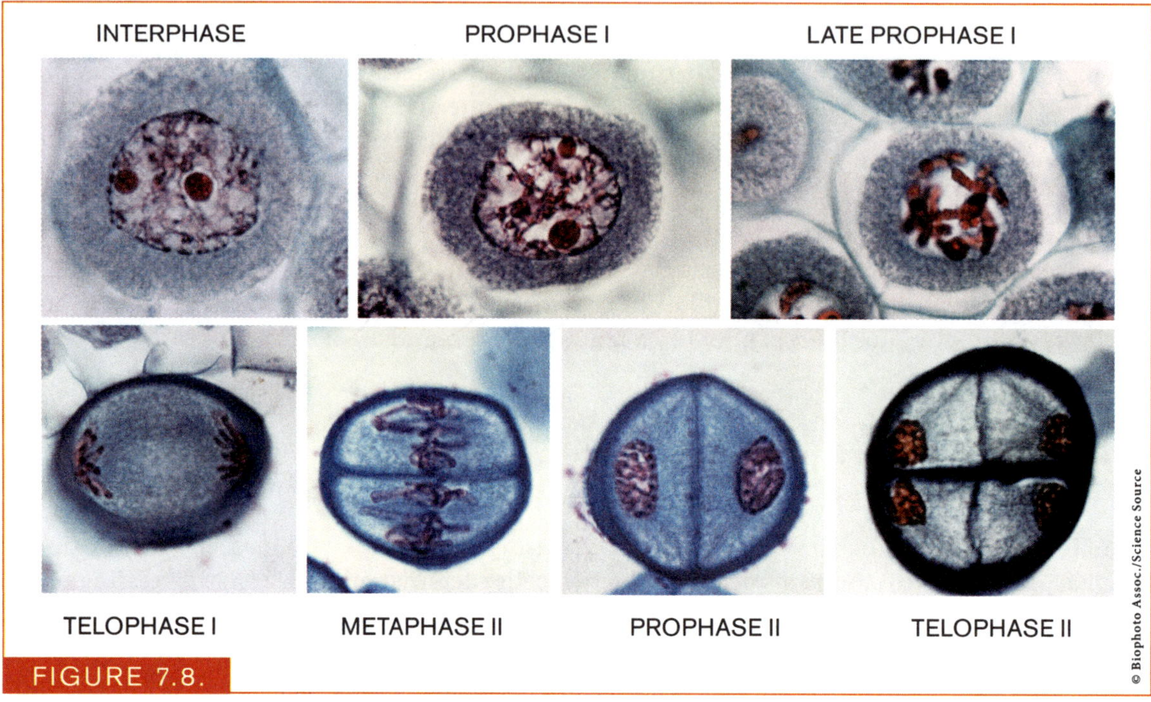

FIGURE 7.8.

Meiosis in lily microsporocytes. Each of the four microspores will produce a pollen grain (male gametophyte) that will produce sperm.

The Importance of Crossing Over

During prophase I, the two homologues have paired (**synapsis**). At this time, recall that each homologous chromosome is composed of two identical copies, the chromatids. **Crossing over** is the exchange of corresponding segments of any two chromatids (crossing over can occur between the sister chromatids of one homologue, or between chromatids of the other homologue, see Figure 7.9). When this exchange occurs, an x-shaped attachment site between two chromatids becomes visible; this x-shaped structure is called a **chiasma** (plural: **chiasmata**). If the chromatid pieces are exchanged, sister chromatids are no longer identical.

In summary, meiosis and crossing over cause an increase in genetic variability among the offspring. The genetic variability is from the creation of new gene combinations—combinations that did not exist in the original chromosomes inherited from each parent.

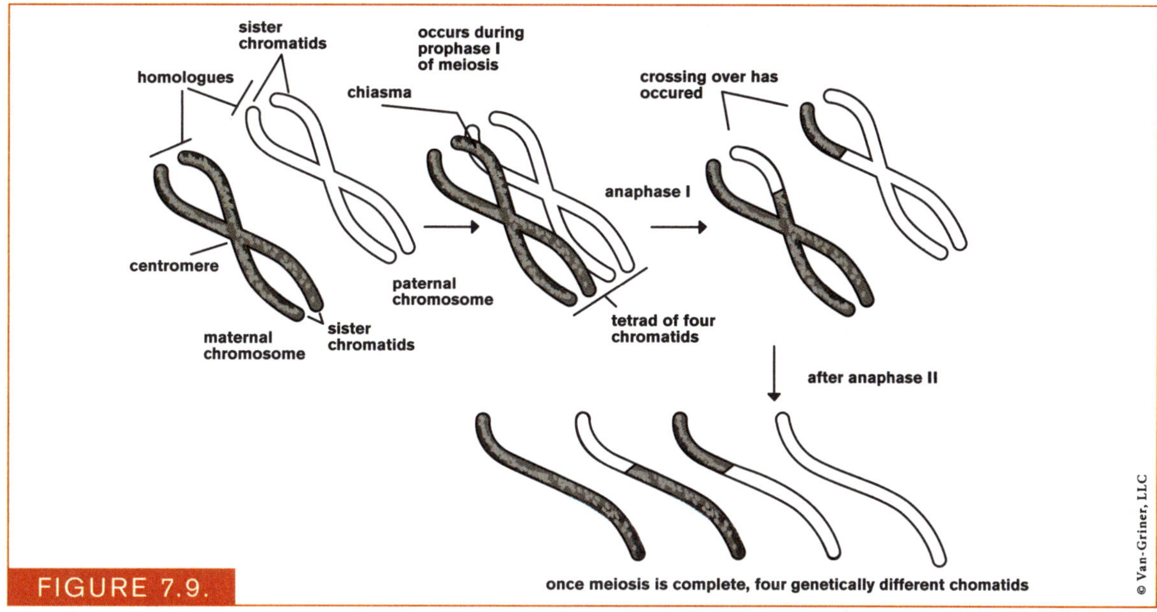

FIGURE 7.9.

Crossing over in meiosis.

Exercise 7.4.

Demonstration of the Importance of Crossing Over

Go to the demonstration table and examine the demonstration of crossing over, and examine Figure 7.9. Afterwards, attempt to make a sketch of what you saw, from memory, in the space below (Figure 7.10). On your sketch, label the following: tetrad, homologues, sister chromatids, chiasmata. Check your sketch with Figure 7.9, and correct any obvious mistakes.

FIGURE 7.10.

Your sketch of the process of crossing over.

Meiosis: Spermatogenesis and Oogenesis

In all animals, oogenesis differs from spermatogenesis in two basic ways. The first difference is due to a difference in the amount of cytoplasm partitioned to the daughter cells after cytokinesis. The partitioning of cytoplasm is unequal in oogenesis and equal in spermatogenesis. The second difference concerns the number of functional gametes produced at the end of meiosis. Four functional sperm are produced per spermatogonium, but only one functional ovum is produced from meiosis in an oogonium.

Inside the mammalian ovary, many **follicles** are present. Beginning at puberty, FSH (follicle stimulating hormone) periodically stimulates one or more follicles to grow and develop. A cell inside the follicle, the **oogonium,** will differentiate into a **primary oocyte** at the beginning of **oogenesis.** Adjacent cells (**nurse cells**) surround the developing oocyte. The diploid primary oocyte enters the first division of meiosis, meiosis I. After meiosis I, the primary oocyte undergoes cytokinesis, but one haploid daughter cell (the **secondary oocyte**) will receive most of the cytoplasm. The other haploid daughter cell (**primary polar body**) receives little cytoplasm; it basically receives the 'unused' chromosomes. After the second phase of meiosis (meiosis II), cytokinesis is again unequal, producing another haploid polar body (the **secondary polar body**) and a cell (the **ootid**) that will mature into the **ovum** (plural: **ova**). The ovum will be much larger than the typical human cell, containing yolk and other materials needed to support early development. A second reason ova tend to be quite large is because nurse cells transfer additional cytoplasmic materials to the ova while it is developing in the follicle.

At the end of oogenesis, you have one large functional ovum, and two or three polar bodies (depending on whether or not the primary polar body also finishes meiosis II). The polar bodies typically die, and because they have too little cytoplasm to presumably allow for early development of the zygote, they are not capable of being fertilized. However, in mammals, the second meiotic division occurs after penetration of the sperm; the sperm acts as a 'trigger' for the secondary oocyte to finish meiosis.

Sperm are produced inside the male gonads, the **testes.** In mammals, there are many spermatogonia near the outer wall of the seminiferous tubules. **Nurse cells** (Sertoli cells) also provide nourishment to spermatogonia as they enter spermatogenesis. **Interstitial cells** (Leydig cells) that are found between the seminiferous tubules produce testosterone under stimulation by luteinizing hormone (LH). Functional sperm are much smaller than ova, and contain little cytoplasmic material, other than mitochondria and a large nucleus. Cytokinesis occurs evenly during spermatogenesis, so that each daughter cell receives half of the cytoplasm. In addition, at the end of spermatogenesis, four spermatids are produced, and each one matures into one functional sperm. At the beginning of spermatogenesis, one **spermatogonium** differentiates into a **primary spermatocyte.** The primary spermatocyte undergoes meiosis I, producing two haploid **secondary spermatocytes.** Although there are 46 total chromatids present inside a secondary spermatocyte and secondary oocyte, these cells contain only 23 chromosomes: half of the diploid number of 46 chromosomes found in human cells. The chromosomes at this time are composed of two chromatids each. The secondary spermatocytes finish meiosis II, producing a total of four haploid **spermatids.** Each spermatid then matures into a **sperm** cell or **spermatozoan** (or **spermatozoon;** plural: **spermatozoa**), which are motile (sperm have flagella). Ova have little locomotory capabilities.

In humans and other mammals, oogenesis and spermatogenesis differ in a third way. In a human female, all of the oogonia have matured into primary oocytes and the primary oocytes begin the first part of meiosis, before she herself is born; but they stop in the middle of prophase I. She is born with all of the potential ova she will ever have (although some recent evidence suggests that there can be additional oogonia production after birth). When she reaches puberty years later, one or a few primary oocytes continue meiosis during each menstrual cycle. Thus, in human females, only about 400 oocytes will form functional ova over the course of her reproductive lifetime.

In males, spermatogonia can begin meiosis at puberty. In contrast to females, however, spermatogonia can replace themselves by undergoing mitosis throughout the male's adult lifetime. At any given instant in an adult human male, some of the spermatogonia are differentiating into spermatocytes, and other spermatogonia undergo mitosis. Billions of sperm thus can be made by a male over his lifetime.

Exercise 7.5.

Oogenesis (Figure 7.11) and **spermatogenesis** (Figure 7.12) are the two forms of meiosis observed in animals. View the cat ovary, rat seminiferous tubules, and human sperm demonstration slides. In addition, examine the charts on oogenesis and spermatogenesis on the demonstration table. Be sure to understand ovary structure and testis structure (follicle, seminiferous tubule, interstitial cells, nurse cells), and the cells formed in meiosis in males and females (spermatogonia, oogonia, primary and secondary oocytes, primary and secondary spermatocytes, spermatids, ootids, polar bodies, ova, sperm). Be able to compare and contrast oogenesis (production of ova via meiosis) with spermatogenesis (production of sperm via meiosis).

You will not be asked to distinguish various phases of meiosis on a prepared microscope slide, but you will be asked to understand and recognize the phases of meiosis on illustrations. You may also be tested on the materials shown in Figure 7.11 and Figure 7.12.

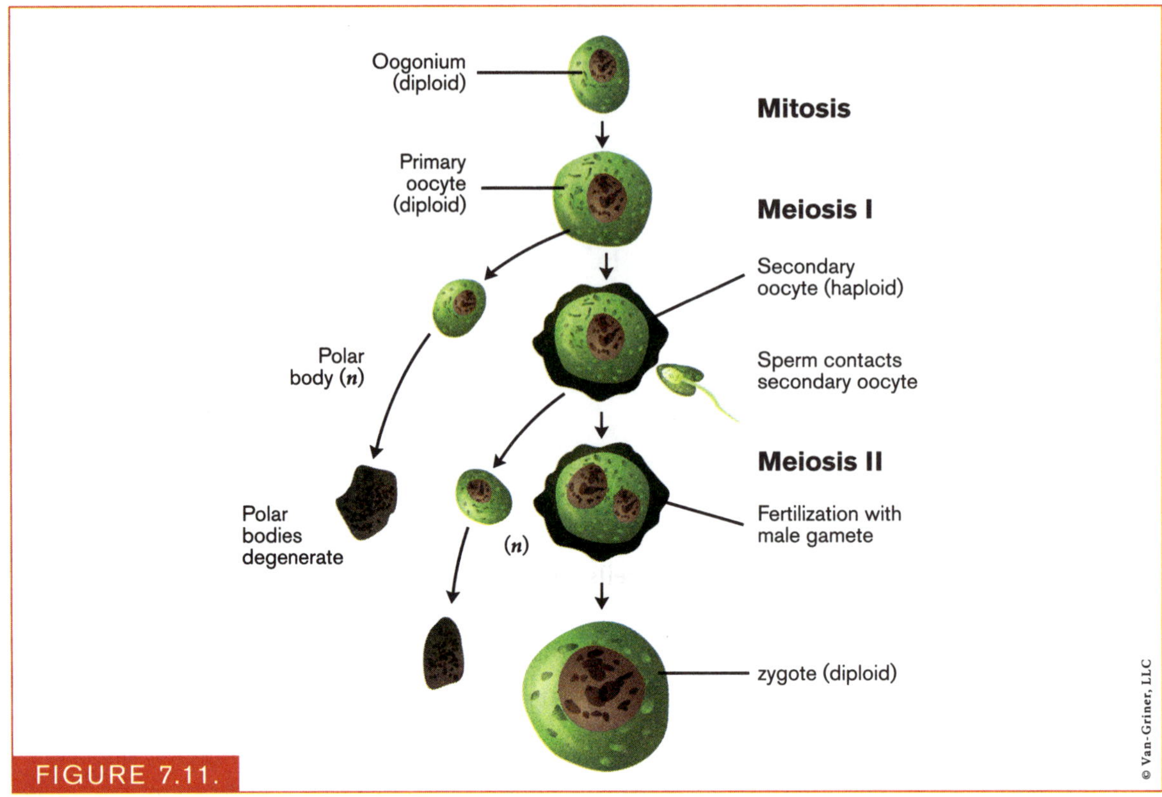

FIGURE 7.11.

Oogenesis in higher animals.

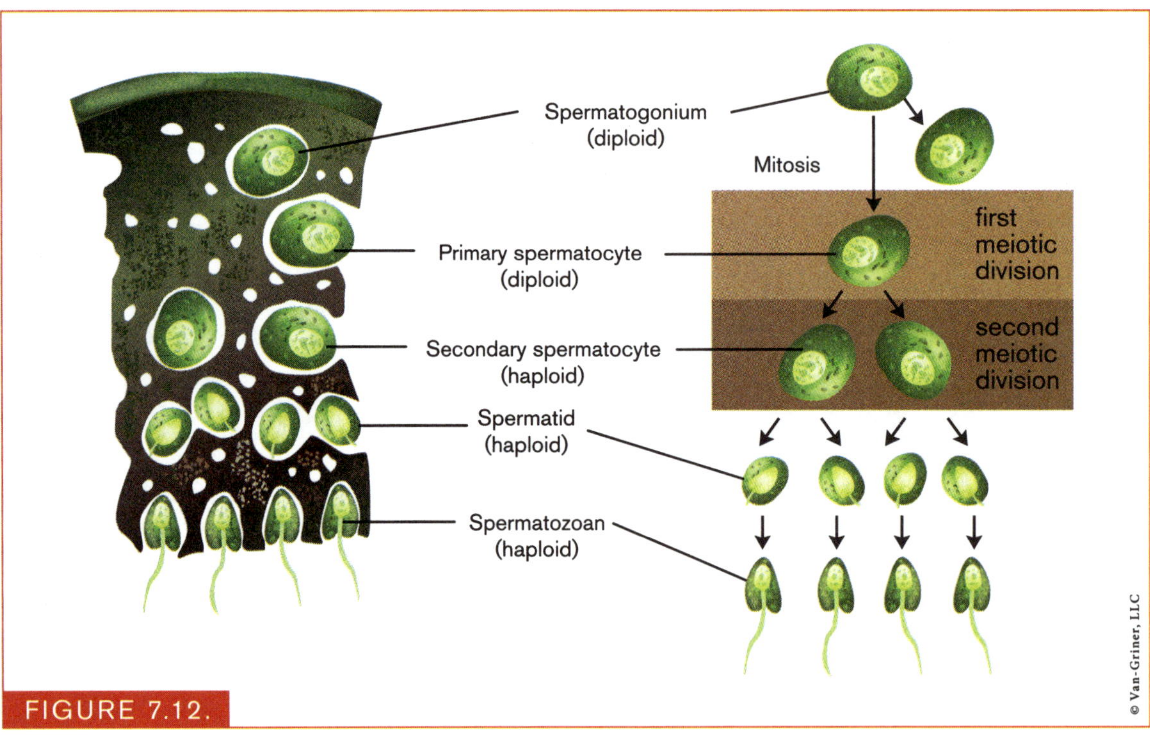

FIGURE 7.12.

Spermatogenesis in higher animals.

Exercise 7.6.

Mimic Mitosis

This hypothetical model organism has a total of six chromosomes, with a diploid number of 6 ($2n = 6$). Almost all animals (and many of the other eukaryotic organisms, such as plants, fungi, and protists) are **diploid,** meaning that they have two complete sets of chromosomes. Gametes in most animals have a haploid number of chromosomes (for example, in humans, the haploid number is 23 and the diploid number is 46), and so when the gametes fuse, the zygote has two sets.

Diploid: Two complete sets of chromosomes, two copies of each type of chromosome. Chromosome pairs that are of the same length and centromere position are called **homologous chromosomes.** The two copies of each distinct type of homologous chromosome have the same sets of genes located along their lengths. In humans, for example, there are 23 different pairs of homologous chromosomes, where one homologous chromosome of each pair is inherited from each parent.

Haploid: One complete set of chromosomes. A gamete contains a haploid set of chromosomes, as a result of meiosis.

Follow the following steps to illustrate the process of mitosis. First, divide up into small groups.

Step 1   *Interphase.* Match up identical pipe cleaners and slip a bead over each pair of identical pipe cleaners. The bead represents the centromere, and the pair of identical pipe cleaners represent the chromatids (one pipe cleaner = one chromatid). There are two sets of pipe cleaners (two different colors: black and white), with one large, one medium, and one small chromosome in each set. The pipe cleaners of one color represent chromosomes inherited from one parent (for illustration purposes, let's say that the black pipe cleaners represents maternal chromosomes from the egg nucleus, the white pipe cleaners represents paternal chromosomes from the sperm nucleus).

Step 2   *Prophase.* Put the homologues randomly on the table. This mimics that time during which the chromatin condenses into chromosomes.

Step 3   *Metaphase.* Line up the chromosomes on the 'equator' or center of the table. You do NOT have to necessarily line up the chromosomes by size or color.

Step 4   *Anaphase.* Separate each chromatid (remove the bead) and move the individual pipe cleaners of each homologue (representing the two identical copies, or chromatids) to opposite ends of the table ('poles'). Once they are separated, we call each chromatid a daughter chromosome.

Step 5   *Telophase.* At each end of the table, each chromosome group (6 pipe cleaners, one of each color and length) is now in a different daughter cell. Note that the two daughter cells are identical genetically.

Exercise 7.7.

Mimic Meiosis

Follow the following steps to mimic meiosis, using the pipe cleaners. Note how mitosis and meiosis are similar, and how they differ, while doing this exercise.

Step 1   *Interphase.* Match up identical pipe cleaners and slip a bead over each pair of identical pipe cleaners, exactly like you did in interphase of mitosis.

Step 2   *Prophase I.* Place each chromosome on the table. This time, pair up the homologous chromosomes (the pairs of pipe cleaners that are of the same size but different colors). This process of pairing homologues is called **synapsis.** (Note that synapsis does **not** occur in mitosis.) This collection of four pipe cleaners, consisting of two homologous pairs, is called a **tetrad.**

Step 3   *Metaphase I.* Line up each tetrad of pipe cleaners (chromosomes) at the center of the table. The center of the table can be viewed as the equator of the cell.

Note: The chromosomes of one color do not have necessarily have to be lined up on the same side of the table. The four chromatids can be mingled together in any order in each tetrad. If you have difficulty with this, ask your lab instructor to demonstrate.

Step 4   *Anaphase I.* Place two of the chromatids of each tetrad towards opposite poles (towards opposite ends of the table). The colors do not matter. This represents the separation of homologous chromosomes that occurs in anaphase I.

Step 5   *Telophase I.* You now have two cells (represented by the two ends of the table), but they contain different chromosomes (as evidenced by the pipe cleaners). These 'cells' represent the two secondary oocytes or spermatocytes formed by meiosis I.

After cytokinesis, these two cells each then may enter a brief resting phase unique to meiosis called **interkinesis.** In interkinesis, nuclear membranes may reappear and the chromosomes disappear. After interkinesis, the two cells enter meiosis II.

Step 6   *Prophase II.* The chromosomes 'reappear' in each cell.

Step 7   *Metaphase II.* Line up the chromosomes on the equator in each cell (the center of each end of the table).

Step 8   *Anaphase II.* Separate each chromatid and have them travel towards opposite poles (opposite corners of the table).

Step 9   *Telophase II.* You now should have four piles of pipe cleaners at different corners of the table. Each pile consists of three pipe cleaners (chromosomes), one large, one medium length, and one small. Note that all of the piles differ in their color make-up, but they all contain one chromosome of each type (one large, one medium, and one small). You now have four haploid 'gametes.'

Record the chromosome composition of the daughter cells. Are the daughter cells identical to each other? Are these the only combinations possible? Can you come up with another possible combination?

Hint: There are eight different combinations, consisting of one large, one medium, and one small pipe cleaner. Draw the various combinations in Figure 7.13.

If there were four sets of homologues ($2n = 8$) or even five sets of homologues ($2n = 10$), what are the number of gamete possibilities in each case, with just the independent assortment of chromosomes among the gametes? Can you determine the mathematical formula that tells you the possible numbers? How many unique gamete possibilities are possible in humans ($2 = 46$)?

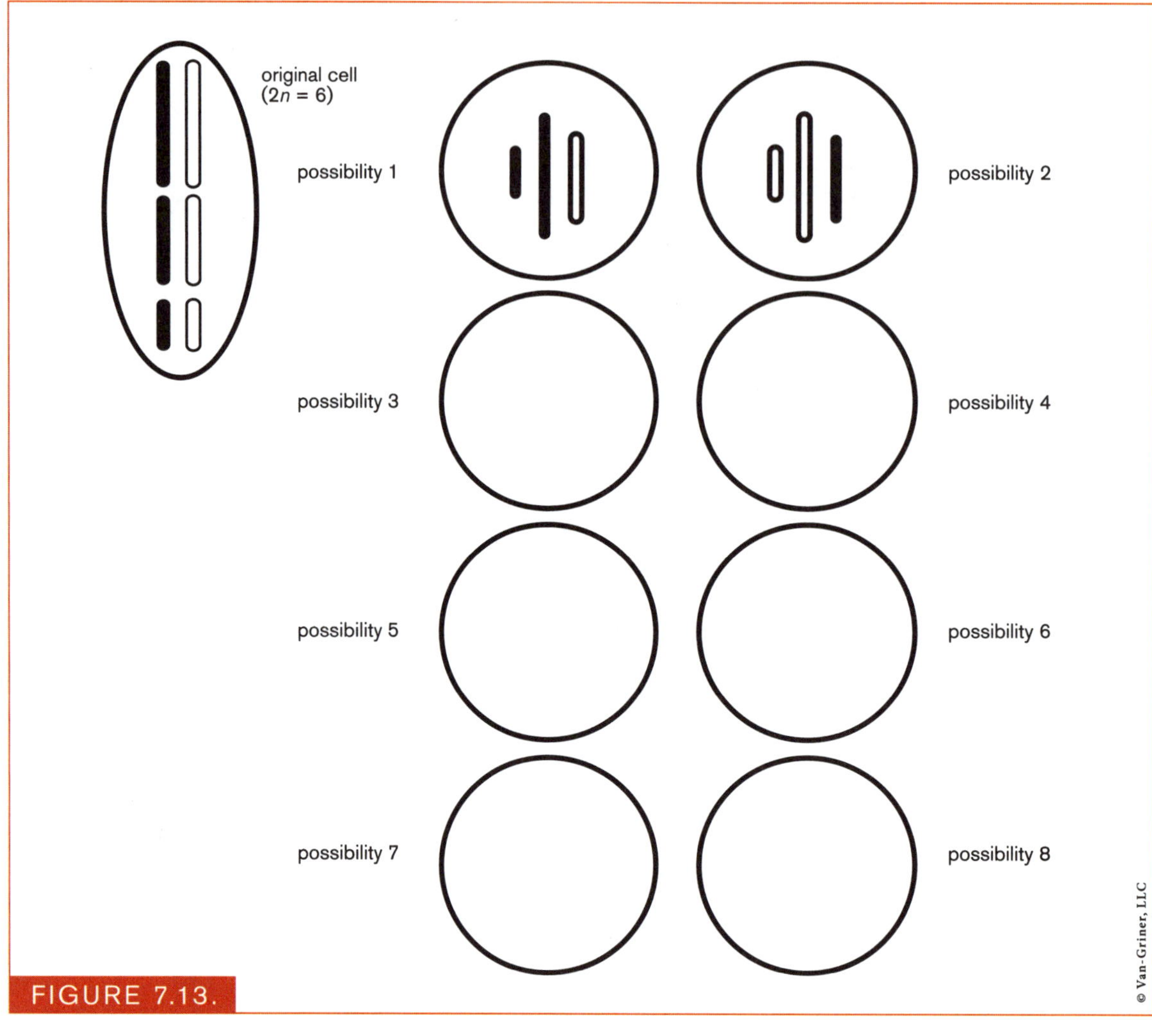

FIGURE 7.13.

The possible rearrangements of three different homologue pairs in the potential gametes that can be created by meiosis, where the homologues line up independently of each other. Use the pipe cleaner model to determine the possible arrangements (two possible arrangements are shown). The black pipe cleaner pieces represent the maternal chromosomes, the white pipe cleaner pieces represent the paternal chromosomes. Pipe cleaners of three different sizes represent three different sets of homologues.

Exercise 7.8.

Comparison of Mitosis and Meiosis

Work singly, or split into groups of two to four students. Fill in the Table 7.2 below, comparing mitosis and meiosis. After you are finished, have your lab instructor check your answers for accuracy.

TABLE 7.2. Comparison of mitosis and meiosis.

	Mitosis	Meiosis
The number of divisions [1 or 2] the original cell goes through to finish the process		
The number of daughter cells [2 or 4] produced, once the process is completed		
Is the original cell haploid [$1n$], or diploid [$2n$]?		
If the original cell was diploid [$2n$], are the daughter cells haploid [$1n$] or diploid [$2n$]?		
Where does each process occur? [throughout the body or only in the gonads]		
Does synapsis occur? [Yes/No]		
Does crossing over occur? [Yes/No]		
The genetic content of daughter cells is [the same as/different from] the original cell.		
The genetic content of daughter cells is [the same as/different from] each other.		

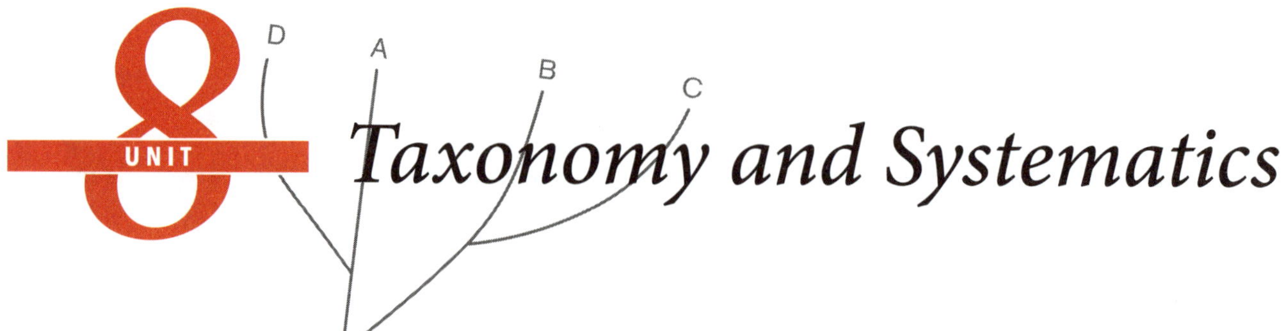

Taxonomy and Systematics

Keywords

extinct
extant
population
domain
kingdom
phylum
  (and division)
class
order
family
genus
species
taxa

taxon
sub- and super-
taxonomy
classification
systematics
phylogeny
homology
analogy
cladistics
phenetics
outgroup
clades
cladogram

plesiomorphy
apomorphy
symplesiomorphy
synapomorphy
polyphyletic
paraphyletic
monophyletic
dichotomous key
couplet
zygotic
gametic
sporic
sporophyte

sporangia
gametophyte
gametes
spores
syngamy
meiosis
mitosis
diploid
haploid
dikaryon
plasmogamy
karyogamy

Learning Objectives

When finished with this unit, you should be able to:

1 Write the proper scientific name of an organism;

2 Describe the concept of binomial nomenclature;

3 List, in order, the seven major taxonomic levels used to classify organisms, from kingdom to species. In addition, be able to list the other taxonomic levels (domain, subphylum, etc.) when they are used;

4 Understand the processes by which biologists classify organisms into taxonomic groups. Compare and contrast the following pairs of terms: artificial versus natural classification; subjective and objective classification; homologies and analogies; phenetic and cladistic classification;

5 Produce a cladogram;

6 Compare and contrast polyphyletic, paraphyletic, and monophyletic clades;

7 Produce and use a dichotomous key; and

8 Compare and contrast the three main life cycles observed in multicellular eukaryotes: zygotic, gametic, and sporic.

In this exercise, you will examine the diversity of living organisms. There are thought to be at least five to eleven million eukaryotic species now living on the planet; however, some estimates are five to ten times higher. To date, biologists have named and cataloged about 1.5 million living eukaryotic species and over a quarter million fossil eukaryotic species. The number of prokaryotes is unknown; it may range from tens of thousands to billions of species.

Taxonomy

Taxonomy is the field of biology that is involved in naming, describing, and classifying organisms, both fossil (**extinct**) species and living (**extant**) species. We use taxonomic principles to describe and give unique names to newly described species, and to identify and distinguish them from other organisms. The principles of taxonomy are also used to order species into categories based on their similarities and differences in morphology, physiology, biochemistry, behavior, or DNA sequence. Knowledge of the evolutionary relationships among species is not necessary for taxonomy, although most taxonomists try to use such data in classifying organisms.

Classification

Classification is one branch of taxonomy where various things (books, clouds, species, etc.) are identified and lumped together into groups. Classification orders and ranks things into a series of hierarchical levels (species into genera, genera into families, and so on).

Systematics

Systematics is the field of biology concerned with the identification of the evolutionary relationships among species through time. Species are classified into various groups, but then systematics elucidates the relationship of these taxa to each other through evolutionary time. To some scientists, the term "systematics" is a synonym for "classification," but some classification methods do not necessarily spell out evolutionary relationships.

Phylogeny

Phylogeny is the pattern of evolutionary descent of all of the taxa used in a classification of organisms. Biologists attempt to make the classification system evolutionary in nature. The goal of most taxonomists is to create an evolutionary classification scheme that reflects the evolutionary history of the listed organisms. In a perfect classification hierarchy, all of the species (both living and dead) that had a common ancestor would be grouped together. This classification then would describe the phylogeny of all organisms included in the classification. For a complete phylogeny, in addition to showing which species are more closely related, the times at which each species diverged from other species also would be included.

Taxa

In biology, taxa (singular: **taxon**) are monophyletic groups of organisms that can be recognized as members of the group on account of their shared characteristics.

Species

There are several different species definitions that you will be exposed to in different biology classes, but for this course, a species is a group of organisms (distributed into one or more separate, discrete populations) that potentially can interbreed and reproduce fertile offspring. This definition is called the **biological species concept.**

Population

A population is a group of organisms of one species living in a defined area (the area is often subjectively defined by the scientist, but a population may also be delineated by natural boundaries). After today, you will have an understanding of the basic concepts of how we name, classify, and identify living organisms, and how we infer evolutionary relationships from classification schemes.

Binomial Nomenclature

Each species has a unique **scientific name.** For example, the scientific name of human beings is *Homo sapiens* ('thinking man'), the house cat's name is *Felis catus*, and the dog's name is *Canis familiaris.* The concept of providing each species with a name, consisting of two parts, is called **binomial nomenclature.** Several hundred years ago, animals found in different geographical regions were called by a **common name** by the local people. This use of local common names led to confusion of just which animal was being referred to by people of different nations. For example, some common, wide ranging species had different names in different countries. Without a set of international rules to follow, the naming of species would be confusing. A 'robin' or a 'jay' are two birds commonly known to Americans, but a 'robin' or 'jay' refers to different birds for Europeans. Because of this naming problem, scientists now follow a procedure, first described by the Swedish biologist **Linnaeus,** for providing each newly described species with a proper and unique scientific name.

To this end, there are formal 'rules' used by scientists to name species. The rules of zoological nomenclature (naming animals) are contained in a document called the **"International Code of Zoological Nomenclature"** (ICZN). The ICZN provides the code by standardizing the names of animals and the animal-like protists (the 'protozoa'). Plants are named following the guidelines in a similar document, the **"International Code of Botanical Nomenclature"** (ICBN). In addition to the multicellular plants, the plant-like protists (the 'algae'), the fungi, and the bacteria (until recently) were also named using the rules in ICBN. Currently, bacteria are named following guidelines in the **"International Code of Nomenclature of Bacteria"** (ICNB). The object of these codes is to promote stability and universality in the scientific names generated for animals and other organisms.

The scientific name consists of two parts. These names are usually in Latin or Latinized form, because at the time taxonomy began several hundred years ago, the language used by many scholars was Latin. The first letter of the first name (the **genus**) is always capitalized, and the last name (the **specific epithet**) is always lower case. In addition, the entire name is either italicized or underlined to indicate that it is a proper scientific name. The scientific name of your dog is *Canis familiaris,* the name of the coyote is *Canis latrans,* and the wolf *Canis lupus.* These three doglike animals have the same genus name (i.e., they are closely related and thus in the same genus). However, the three animals each have a different species name, thus for some taxonomists, these three dog-like animals are different species in the genus *Canis.*

The specific epithet of the name can be used by more than one species. For example, the white-tailed deer's scientific name is *Odocoileus virginianus,* and the bobwhite quail's name is *Colinus virginianus.* The two animals have the same specific epithet, but they are two very different animals placed in different genera (actually they are in different vertebrate classes as well—one is a mammal, one is a bird).

In most scientific papers, the scientific name of a species is followed by a name of the taxonomist who first published a description of the species. Often, the authority name is abbreviated: for example, the letter "L." after a scientific name stands for "Linnaeus." A date may also be included after the authority name; the date refers to the year of the description. For example, the large pond snail *Lymnaea stagnalis* (L., 1758) was first described by Linnaeus in 1758.

Exercises

Exercise 8.1.

> Which of the following scientific names is properly written? For those that are incorrect, correct them. They are spelled correctly.
>
> *Procambarus Simulans*   *Physella* virgata   <u>homo sapiens</u>
>
> <u>Felis leo</u>   quercus Rubra   LEMNA <u>minor</u>
>
> (The above species are, respectively, a crayfish, a snail, humans, lions, red oaks, and duckweed).

Exercise 8.2.

> Which of the following organisms are most closely related (i.e., which are in the same genus)?
>
> *Ursus americanus*   *Quercus bicolor*   *Homarus americanus*
>
> *Parus bicolor*   *Parus carolinensis*   *Sitta carolinensis*
>
> *Sitta canadensis*   *Quercus rubra*   *Ursus arctos*
>
> (The above species are, from left to right, respectively, the American black bear, swamp oak, the lobster, tufted titmouse, Carolina chickadee, white breasted nuthatch, red breasted nuthatch, the red oak, and the polar bear).

Taxonomic Categories and Their Hierarchy

Most people can identify organisms in many cases as being grasshoppers, trees, birds, dogs, algae, and so on, but most do not know how to divide these groups further, nor do they know the key characteristics that scientists use to classify each group. Today's exercises will provide you with some basic understanding on how and why biologists classify organisms the way that they do.

Biologists today have seven basic taxonomic levels to name and classify organisms (Figure 8.1). The taxa are arranged in the following hierarchical sequence: the highest category, the **kingdom,** is the broadest category, containing perhaps millions of species, whereas the lowest category, the **species,** represents an individual species. One or more **species** are lumped into **genera** (singular: **genus**); one or more genera are in each **family;** one or more families are in an **order;** orders into **classes;** classes into **phyla** (singular: **phylum**); and several phyla are lumped together in one **kingdom.** For plants, the term **division** replaces the term phylum.

Recently, biologists have added the taxon **domain** to represent a taxon above that of kingdom. We currently recognize three domains: **Archaea** (a prokaryotic group), **Bacteria** (a second prokaryotic group), and **Eukarya** (all of the eukaryotes lumped together).

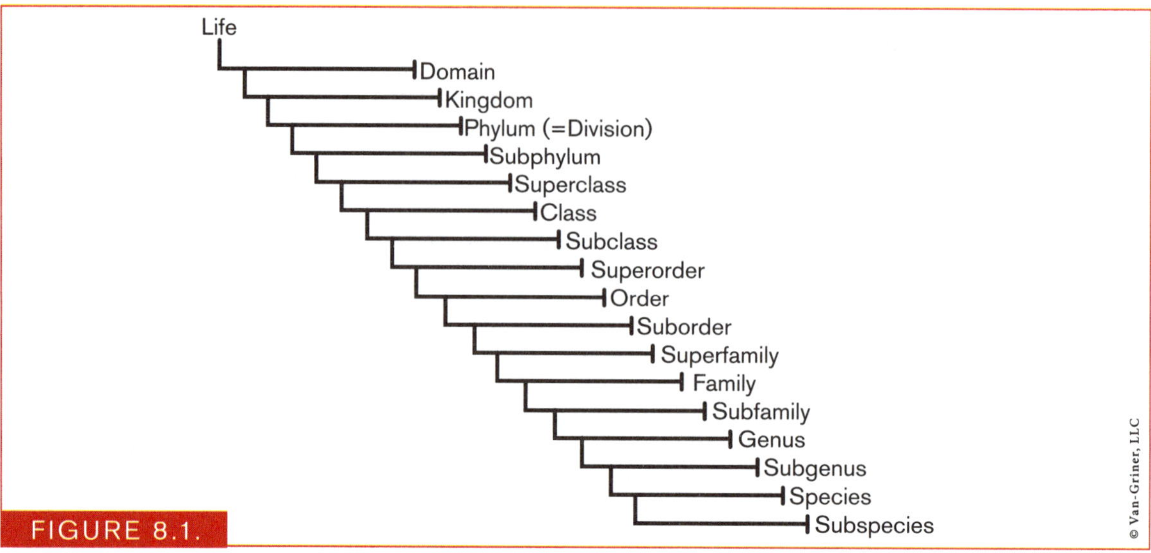

FIGURE 8.1.

The generally accepted hierarchical taxa (in descending order from upper left to lower right).

Additional taxonomic levels. Note that additional taxonomic categories exist as well for a number of taxa. The prefixes **super-** and **sub-** are common; they indicate a taxonomic level that is immediately above or below the suffix. For example, a superorder has one or more orders, while the order can have one or more suborders. **Subphylum, superorder, suborder, subclass, superclass,** and **subspecies** are examples. In addition, there are many other taxonomic categories used by various taxonomists for specific groups of organisms: **grades** (just below subkingdom), **cohorts** (just below subclass), **infraorders** (just below suborder), and **tribes** (just below subfamily) are a few examples.

Subspecies. To indicate a specific subspecies, a third name is used ('**trinomial nomenclature**'), for example, the scientific name *Homo sapiens sapiens* refers to a subspecies of humans called 'modern' humans.

There are many ways to classify organisms. If you were given a group of objects, one thing you would immediately do is group them together due to some criteria, often based on the **shared characteristics** of the objects. For example, if you emptied out your purse or your pockets, and you were asked to look at and categorize the contents, you probably would lump coins, writing instruments, cosmetics, and keys into their respective groups. The shared characteristics are based on easily recognizable features of the objects: their shapes, sizes, colors, or functions. In most forms of biological classification, shared characteristics are the basis by which we separate and recognize different species, genera, families, and higher taxa. These characteristics can also be used to infer common descent and how recently each group shared a common ancestor.

Exercise 8.3.

Which two of the five species listed in Table 8.1 are more closely related? Which three species are more closely related to each other, than to the other two species? Which species is not as closely related to the other four species? Explain.

TABLE 8.1. The hierarchical classification of five different animals.

Kingdom	Animalia	Animalia	Animalia	Animalia	Animalia
Phylum	Arthropoda	Chordata	Chordata	Chordata	Chordata
Class	Insecta	Mammalia	Mammalia	Mammalia	Mammalia
Order	Hymenoptera	Carnivora	Carnivora	Primata	Carnivora
Family	Apidae	Felidae	Canidae	Hominidae	Canidae
Genus	*Apis*	*Felis*	*Canis*	*Homo*	*Vulpes*
Species	*A. mellifera*	*F. catus*	*C. familiaris*	*H. sapiens sapiens*	*V. fulva*
(Common Name)	honeybee	house cat	dog	humans	red fox

Natural versus Artificial Classification

An **artificial classification** is based on one or a few shared features, which may not have any evolutionary significance. **Artificial classifications** may be constructed for convenience, using easily observed characteristics of organisms. A classification scheme that groups bats, robins, and butterflies together ('flying, winged creatures') as opposed to humans, penguins, and mites ('nonflying creatures') would be considered artificial. A **natural classification** groups together organisms descended from common ancestors, whereas an artificial classification probably will not group all related organisms together. In a natural classification, robins and other flying birds would be grouped with penguins and other flightless birds, butterflies would be grouped with mites and the other insects, and bats would be grouped with humans and the rest of the mammals.

In a natural classification scheme, two species are considered to be closely related if they share many features in common (in other words, they share many **homologies**). A natural classification is one where the members of a category are thought to share a common ancestor. These closely related species are going to be similar in many characteristics **not** used to define the group as well (in an artificial classification system, subsequent analysis may show that many characteristics that were not used to define the group are quite different among the group's members). An artificial scheme is one where the taxonomist perhaps has used one feature (like the presence or absence of wings). No matter how important wings may be, wings, by themselves, cannot be used to infer evolutionary relationships.

Homologies and Analogies

There are often many problems in telling what shared characteristics should be used to infer common descent. For example, bats, birds, and butterflies all have wings, but these three organisms' wings are what we call **analogous structures.** Analogous structures are similar in function, but the underlying structure (bones, blood vessels, muscles, tendons, and so on) and development (and thus evolutionary origin) of these structures are different.

Homology versus analogy. It is especially important to distinguish similarities that are based on shared ancestry or **homology** from those similarities that are based on **convergent evolution** or **analogy.** For example, the *Octotillo* cactus (America) and the *Allauidia* euphorb (Africa), which are two species classified in two different desert plant families, are not closely related but they look very similar. They owe their superficial resemblance to each other to analogous adaptations. Another example of convergent evolution is the white fur possessed by the arctic fox, the polar bear, the least weasel, and the arctic hare. White fur (as well as the white winter feathers of the ptarmigan and the snowy owl) presumably confer some protection in camouflaging both predators (bear, fox, weasel, owl) and prey (hare, ptarmigan).

So, a bird wing and butterfly wing are **analogous structures** for flight. *As wings,* a bird wing and bat wing are still viewed as analogous structures. However, *as forelimbs,* a bird wing and a bat wing are **homologous structures.** Homologous structures may have a different function (or a similar function), but the underlying structure, development, and physiology are the same. As forelimbs, a bat's wing, a whale's flipper, and your arm are homologous structures. The bones of your forearm are homologous with the bones of the bird's wing, as well as the bat's wing, a bear's forelimb, and the whale's flipper too. Therefore, you cannot infer that bats and butterflies are closely related on the basis of having wings, or that they had a common ancestor with wings.

Developmental patterns are very important in determining phylogenetic relationships. The developmental patterns of bat fetuses and human fetuses and whale fetuses are very similar, more similar to each other than any of them to the developmental pattern of the butterfly. Foreleg limb buds develop into wings, forearms and flippers in bats, humans and whales respectively. The wings of the butterfly do not develop from limb buds, but as extensions off of the outer exoskeleton. Forearms have always been used for locomotion, whereas the earliest function of the primitive wings of butterflies may have had more to do with thermoregulation than with flying.

As a general rule, the more homologous parts that two species share, the more closely related they are. The more complex two structures are, the less likely that they evolved independently. For example, the skulls of a human and chimpanzee are composed not of a single bone, but a fusion of multiple bones that match almost perfectly. It is improbable that such complex structures matching in so many details could have separate origins.

As discussed above, the distinction between homology and analogy is somewhat relative. The question of homology versus analogy often depends on the taxonomic level examined.

a At one level, the forelimbs of bats and birds are analogous adaptations for flight because the fossil record shows that both forelimbs evolved independently from the walking forelimbs of different ancestors. Their common specializations for flight are convergent features, not indications of recent common ancestry.

b However, at a different level, the presence of forelimbs in both birds and bats is a homology, at the level of tetrapods (a higher level in the classification). The bones, developmental patterns, muscles, blood vessels are the same. As wings the forearms of birds and bats are analogous (in part because the birds rely on lightweight feathers to form an airfoil, but the bats rely upon skin that is stretched between the arm, wrist, and finger bones to form the wing), but as appendages, the bat wing and bird wing are homologous features.

Classification

Objective versus subjective classification. Early humans probably classified organisms into categories based on some functional significance to them: for example, whether the animal approaching them was dangerous or not, edible or not, and so on. This is an example of **subjective classification,** where some characteristic is chosen arbitrarily, or is chosen because of some utilitarian reason (i.e., edible versus inedible, large versus small, nocturnal versus diurnal, dangerous versus safe). An **objective classification,** on the other hand, uses unambiguous features to classify animals. For example, unambiguous features include the presence or absence of fur, exoskeletons, feathers, scales, or shells, or the number of limbs and eyes. These traits do not necessarily confer some utilitarian purpose solely for human benefit.

The 'traditional' objective form of classifying species relied upon the examination of important **key characteristics.** We can separate out birds and mammals from the reptiles, for example, because of several key characters we think are important in the evolution of these species (fur, feathers, four-chambered hearts, and so on). However, by using phenetics, cladistics, or evolutionary classification (see below), our view may change.

Systematics: The Phenetic and Cladistic Principles of Classification

Working alongside the field of taxonomy, the field of **systematics** tries to group species into higher taxonomic groups in ways that convey meaningful biological information, often with an evolutionary context. Taxonomists wish to identify species; systematists group species together based their common similarities and their common ancestry.

Scientists attempt to use natural, objective methods to distinguish and relate groups of animals, instead of artificial and subjective methods. There are many ways to classify species into higher levels. The two main methods currently used in systematics are **phenetics** and **cladistics.** The big difference between these two approaches is how the classification of a group of organisms either reflects the overall similarity of the species (phenetics) or the closeness in terms of shared characteristics from common descent from older species (cladistics).

One discipline, called **phenetics,** examines many morphological and developmental characteristics (and, recently, genetic and biochemical characteristics), such as bone structure, body size, presence or absence of hair, feathers, and many other traits. Typically, all of these characters are equally weighted, with no regard to the phylogenetic history of the organisms examined. Those organisms that share the greatest number of similar characteristics are assumed to be more closely related to each other than to other species that did not share these common traits. However, as mentioned earlier, analogies and convergent evolution can cause species that are not closely related to look alike, and possibly be lumped together. Because of this, classifications that rely solely on similarities in outward characteristics *may* not reflect the true evolutionary history. In addition, this classification approach is based only on the overall similarity of the species, without regard to the evolutionary history of the species involved. This does not mean that pheneticists are creationists: it simply means that their classification scheme does not have to be evolutionary in context. Many pheneticists nonetheless are evolutionary in their outlook.

The phenetic method groups species together based on the **observed outer characteristics** (their **phenotypes**). Two species that most closely resemble each other will most likely be grouped together in a phenetic classification. For example, look at the five animals in Table 8.1. You would probably lump the dog and fox together as the most similar in a phenetic classification because they look very similar. Any and all observable characteristics may be measured: size, color, protein similarity, gene similarity, number of chromosomes, along with thousands of other characteristics. Nothing about the evolution of the species is necessarily needed to classify species using the phenetic method, although many pheneticists use evolutionary characters and are thinking in an evolutionary way. **Phenetics** can also be used to classify non-living things (books, languages, rivers, clouds, music, furniture).

In contrast, the **cladistic method** is more strictly viewed as evolutionary in nature; cladists seeks to illuminate the evolutionary relationships among living organisms. Music, furniture, books, and clouds cannot be classified easily using cladistics, but biological species can be so classified. The cladistic method relies on characteristics that are of two types: those traits shared by living species because they evolved from recent common ancestors (**synapomorphies**), and another set of traits that a larger group of organisms share because an ancient common ancestor had those traits, and passed them on to all descendant species (**symplesiomorphies**). Cladistics classifies species according to how recently they shared a common ancestor. Two species that share a very recent common ancestor will be in one taxon at a lower level (they are in the same genus) as opposed to two species that share a more distant common ancestor (they are in the same class). For example, dogs and foxes are in the same family and are more closely related to each other than they are to domestic housecats (which are classified in a different family); these three animals, in turn, are more closely related to each other than any of them to the human species (which is in a different order).

Both the phenetic approach and the cladistic approach produce the same classification scheme for most groups of organisms. However, they can disagree. For example, using phenetics, an adult barnacle (a crustacean) and a limpet (a snail) superficially may appear more similar to each other than either animal does to a crab (another crustacean), but a cladistic approach would put the two crustaceans (barnacle and crab) together in a group, with the mollusc (limpet) in a different group.

Monophyletic, Paraphyletic, and Polyphyletic Groups

In systematics, one goal is to arrange animals into **monophyletic** groups, where all of the members of the group are descendants of a common ancestral species (the ancestor often is considered extinct). A monophyletic group of related organisms (**clade**, 'tree') includes a single common ancestor species, and all of its descendant species, both living and extinct.

a A **monophyletic taxon** includes the single ancestor species and all species descended from that ancestral species. No unrelated species are included, and hopefully no related species has been left out and included elsewhere.

b A **polyphyletic taxon** is missing the common ancestor of all members of the identified group. It has grouped members that have descended from two or more ancestral forms not common to all members. The common ancestor has been left out. In addition, some descendent species that should be included are not.

c A **paraphyletic taxon** has the common ancestor and some, but not all, of the descendant species included in the clade. This lineage is not complete, usually because we have insufficient information about the group. In other words, some of the descendent species have been left out of the group, but not the common ancestor.

We do not have sufficient knowledge concerning all of the members of many taxonomic groups. In animal classification, taxonomists attempt to remove polyphyletic groups, once we obtain more data. Some of the recognized animal phyla, for example, may be polyphyletic. See Figure 8.2 for examples of monophyletic, paraphyletic, and polyphyletic groups.

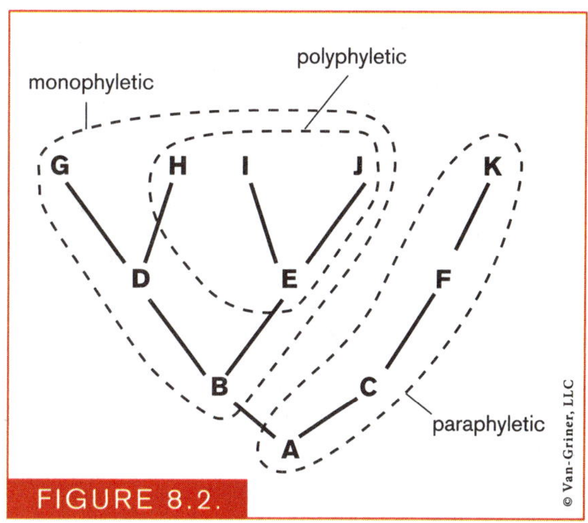

FIGURE 8.2.

Monophyletic, paraphyletic, and polyphyletic taxa.

Exercise 8.4.

The following diagrams in Figure 8.3 are similar to those of Figure 8.2. The 'actual' phylogenetic relationship is shown by the solid lines, with species 'A' as the common ancestor for all species. For each of the clades (within each dotted line), indicate whether or not it is a polyphyletic, paraphyletic, or monophyletic clade.

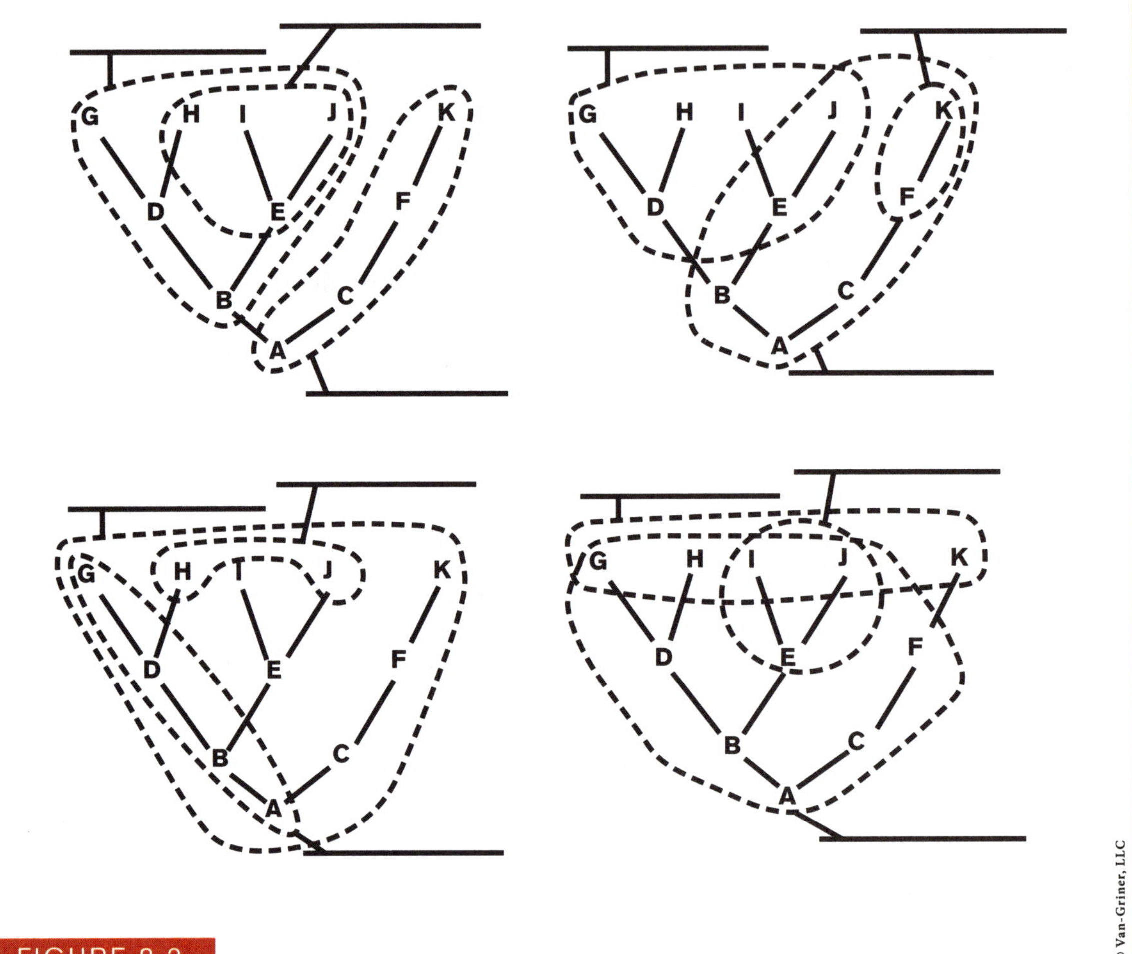

FIGURE 8.3.

Cladograms

The science of producing cladograms (**cladistics**) is a phylogenetic method of classification. In cladistics, a treelike diagram showing the clade is called a **cladogram** (see Figure 8.4). The ancestral species is at the bottom of the tree, and the living species are depicted at the top. A cladogram, if properly constructed, can suggest the evolutionary pattern of the clade and suggest new avenues of research. Scientists use **traits** (**characters**) to produce a cladogram.

You may wonder what traits should be considered 'ancestral.' An ancestral (most primitive) trait common to all of the members of the group is called a **symplesiomorphy.** A distinct head containing a brain and semicircular canals is the symplesiomorphy for all vertebrates (Figure 8.4).

A shared **derived trait** (**synapomorphy**) is a trait that has developed since common ancestry in one descendent group, with a related group not sharing this trait. The group that does not share the trait is called the **outgroup.** For example, in Figure 8.4, the presence of jaws separates the jawed animals (cartilaginous fish, bony fish, amphibians, reptiles, birds, and mammals) from the outgroup, consisting of the jawless lampreys and hagfishes. All vertebrate species still share the common trait of a head and brain. The outgroup for the vertebrates are the rest of the chordates, including tunicates and cephalochordates, which, along with the vertebrates, all share the same chordate traits—a notochord, a dorsal hollow nerve cord, pharyngeal gill slits, and a post-anal tail. Further up the cladogram, the presence of fur is a synapomorphy that separates mammals from all other species.

Primitive versus derived traits. Systematists must sort through the various traits observed in organisms in order to separate shared derived traits from shared primitive traits. Willi Hennig helped to develop **cladistics,** the systematic methodology that sought to emphasize objectiveness and reproducibility (in order to minimize the subjectivity of individual taxonomists) and be consistent with what scientists would refer to as "true" evolutionary patterns.

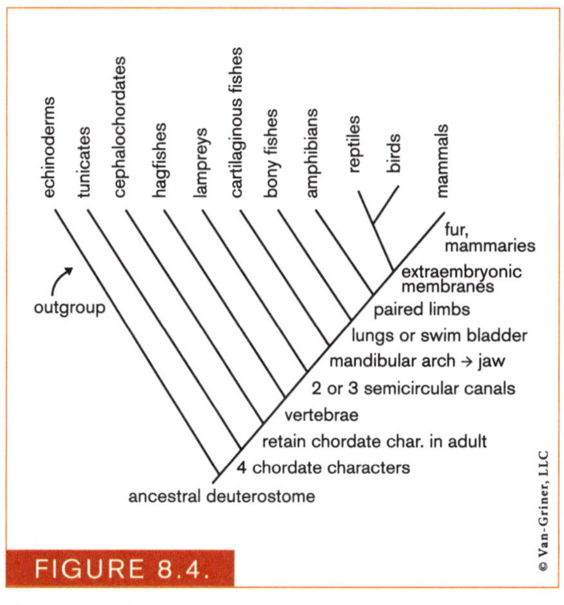

FIGURE 8.4.

The chordate cladogram.

A few terms used in cladistic analysis:

1. An **apomorphy** is a specialized or derived trait.

2. A **plesiomorphy** refers to a primitive or ancestral trait.

3. An **autapomorphy** is a derived trait that is unique to one group in a clade.

4. A **synapomorphy** is a derived trait shared by two or more groups in a clade.

5. A **symplesiomorphy** is a shared primitive trait. A symplesiomorphy can be found not only in the groups of the clade being analyzed, but it may be found in other clades as well.

These terms are defined relative to a particular node of the cladogram (e.g., representing a taxonomic level). This means that a trait can be a synapomorphy and a symplesiomorphy if different nodes are considered. For example, paired limbs are a synapomorphy of all tetrapods (compared to the fishes), but the 'paired limbs' trait is a symplesiomorphy for the reptiles and mammals, and thus is not as informative in separating the reptiles and mammals.

Shared derived traits are useful in establishing a phylogeny, but shared primitive traits are less useful. The presence of hair is a good trait to distinguish the clade of mammals from other tetrapods. Hair is a shared ancestral trait (symplesiomorphy) of non-cetacean mammals. Hairlessness is a unique derived trait (an autapomorphy) for the whales (cetaceans) whose ancestors were hairy (in reality, cetaceans are not totally hairless, they have sparse amounts of hair). Nonetheless, whale are considered mammals (they have mammary glands, for example). At the same time, hair does not indicate a close relationship of marsupial and placental mammals, nor does the presence of hair distinguish among the placental mammal orders (Carnivora, Primata, etc.).

Although the presence of a backbone is a shared trait for all mammals, it is a trait for other vertebrates as well, so the backbone is a symplesiomorphy for mammals. A backbone does not uniquely separate mammals from other vertebrates. For all vertebrates as a whole, compared to the related invertebrate animals, the vertebrae represent a synapomorphy because vertebrates all share this trait, and a backbone presumably evolved in the ancestor common to all living vertebrates. However, the presence of vertebrae is not a useful character to separate the various vertebrates because they all have them!

Ancestral, primitive traits are not 'inferior' or 'worse,' compared to derived characters. A backbone is a valuable trait to have, yet a backbone is a primitive trait for the advanced, more recently evolved mammals. Is a backbone less important than hair for a mammal? Are backbones in vertebrates better as skeletal supports than hydrostatic skeletons are in cnidarians?

Creating a Cladogram

1 A key step in cladistic analysis is called **outgroup comparison.** This step is used to differentiate shared primitive traits from shared derived ones. We first need to identify the **outgroup:** the species or group of species that is related to the various species that we are studying, but known to be less closely related than any study-group members are to each other. Take the following six taxa: lancelet, lamprey, tuna (a bony fish), salamander (an amphibian), turtle (a reptile), and leopard (a mammal). Find them on the clade shown in Figure 8.4. The five vertebrates are the **ingroup,** and the lancelet would be a good example of an outgroup. The outgroup is placed at the base of the clade.

a The lancelet is closely related to the most primitive vertebrates, based on other evidence.

b Taxonomic analysis shows that the lancelet is **not** more closely related to any of the ingroup taxa. Lancelets are thought to be equally related to all ingroup taxa.

c In an outgroup analysis, any homologies shared by the ingroup and outgroup must be primitive characters already present in the ancestor common to both groups, and thus they cannot be used to separate the outgroup from the ingroup.

d Homologies present in some or all of the ingroup taxa presumably must have evolved after the divergence of the ingroup and outgroup taxa.

2 In our example the notochord, present in lancelets and in the embryos of the ingroup, would be a shared primitive character (symplesiomorphy) and thus not useful to separate the different species any further apart.

a The presence of a vertebral column, shared by all members of the ingroup but not the outgroup (the lancelet), is a useful character (synapomorphy) if talking about the whole ingroup.

b However, for mammals, the vertebral column would be a symplesiomorphy that cannot be used to distinguish the various mammals.

c Similarly, the presence of jaws, which are absent in lampreys and present in the other vertebrate taxa, helps to identify the earliest branch in the vertebrate cladogram.

d Four walking appendages (paired limbs) separate the tetrapods (salamander, turtle, and leopard) from the fishes (the 'fishes' meaning the bony fish, along with the cartilaginous fish, the lampreys, and hagfishes). The amniotic egg separates the reptile and mammal from the amphibian.

e Finally, the presence of fur is an apomorphy which separates the leopard from everyone else.

3 This does not necessarily mean that living lampreys are extremely ancient species, compared to mammals. It also does not mean that lampreys are the ancestral species to the jawed animals. Lampreys have also been evolving all along. Recall that life is viewed as a tree, and each extant species is like a leaf on the tree. Cladistics is used to suggest that the group of organisms that eventually gave rise to lampreys diverged away from the group that gave rise to the chordates. Some living species go back many tens of millions of years, but most species do not. Likewise, the echinoderms are the outgroup comparison for all of the chordates (as shown in Figure 8.4 above), yet we do not think that the ancestral chordate was an echinoderm. Echinoderms have also evolved over the millions of years since the presumed shared common deuterostome ancestor for both chordates and echinoderms.

Which method is better: phenetics, cladistics, or something else?

Phenetics. The logic behind most phenetic analyses is that the more characters that are shared between two species, the more likely they are closely related. Pheneticists would make a tree (a **phenogram**) that may well be very similar to a cladogram generated on the same species or it may differ greatly.

There are problems with phenetics.

a One major problem with phenetics is that of convergent evolution of analogous traits. Because of convergent evolution, similar traits that are not due to common ancestry may cause mistakes to be made when classifying species together.

As an example, suppose you had a snail, a crab, and a squid to classify. You may think that the hard outer parts of the snail and crab would mean they were more closely related than either was to the squid, who was without a hard outer covering. However, the snail and squid are both mollusks, while the crab is an arthropod crustacean. Neither mollusk is considered more closely related to the crab than is the other.

b A second problem is that evolution can occur rapidly at some times and slowly at other times. Species may evolve phenotypically in one direction and then turn around and evolve back the other way. Because of these concerns, similarity thus is not necessarily a good prediction of how long ago two species shared a common ancestor. This shows the value of also using the fossil record to help elucidate the phylogenetic tree.

Cladistics. The logic behind cladistics is that if two species share derived characters, the more likely they are to be related. Just because two species share a number of primitive traits does not necessarily mean they are closely related.

There are problems with cladistics.

a One problem with cladistics is to determine what are derived traits and what are primitive traits. We may decide that a particular trait is a recent derived trait, but in order to know this, we have to have an idea of the relatedness of the species, which is precisely what we are trying to determine from cladistics.

b A second problem with cladistics is that cladograms, unlike the classical phylogenetic trees, do not directly tell which species arose from which species. Cladograms often are not very good at demonstrating all higher taxonomic levels (genera, families, orders, classes, and so on).

c Cladograms do not tell how long ago each group branched away from each other either; a cladogram gives no information on the absolute 'timing' of the splits depicted. A cladogram only portrays the relative relationships among groups. In addition, cladograms do not give any idea on the magnitude of similarity between any two groups.

In reality, most modern systematists use many methods to try to ascertain the evolutionary tree of life.

When you use both overall similarity and evolutionary relatedness, you can at times get conflicting answers. The difference between phenetics and cladistics is shown in Figure 8.5. The currently accepted phylogeny of the 20 extant species of apes (Superfamily Hominoidea: this groups includes humans, two species of chimpanzees, bonobo chimpanzees, chimpanzees, two species of gorillas, two species of orangutans, and the four genera/thirteen species of gibbons) is shown in Figure 8.5.F.

If we asked a cladist and a pheneticist to make their trees, the two approaches (phenetics and cladistics) may give different results (see Figure 8.5). First, some background information is needed.

All of the apes (superfamily Hominoidea) are different from the rest of the primate order: Old World monkeys, New World monkeys, tarsiers, and lemurs. Compared to the other primates, the apes are generally larger (except the gibbons, which are called the 'lesser' apes). Unlike the rest of the primates, the apes have no external tail. The arms of apes are relatively longer and the legs relatively shorter. The brain is relatively much larger in the apes.

The gibbons, orangutans, gorillas, and chimps have retained a number of the traits of early primates from millions of years ago, whereas humans have undergone an extensive change in morphology and behavior. All species have undergone evolution, but humans have diverged greatly, at least in terms of some aspects of our morphology and behavior.

Depending on the characters used, it is possible that the pheneticist would find a large number of similarities between gibbons, chimps, gorillas, and orangutans. Suppose you were acting as a pheneticist; depending on the characteristic traits you measured, you may have separated humans into a completely different group from all of the rest of the apes (Figure 8.5.A). Indeed, the phylogenetic trees of about 50 years ago placed humans in one family (Hominidae), and all of the other apes (chimps, gorillas, orangutans, and gibbons) were placed in the family Pongidae (Figure 8.5.E). The two families then were placed into one superfamily, Hominoidea. The phylogenetic tree then was more like the phenogram in Figure 8.5.C.

Cladists would note that the gibbons (the lesser apes) diverged away from the other species the great apes) earlier in time. Humans share a more recent common ancestor with chimps, and then humans and chimps share a more distant common ancestor with gorillas, and all three taxa share a common ancestor (in the distant past) with the orangutans, and then finally all of the above share a common ancestor with the gibbons. Further back in time, the apes as a group share a common ancestor with all of the Old World monkeys (baboons and rhesus monkeys), which lack a prehensile tail. Still further back, the Old World monkeys and apes share a common ancestor with the New World monkeys (howler monkeys, spider monkeys, and capuchin monkeys); the New World monkeys have a prehensile tail that can grasp objects and serve as an extra limb.

Today, cladists would lump humans and chimps together as a clade, then they would lump humans and chimps with the gorilla as yet a larger clade. The orangutan then would be lumped with the gorillas, chimps, and humans. Finally, the gibbons (the 'lesser apes') would be considered the outgroup to the great apes. Finally, cladists would lump the lesser apes and greater apes together as a group called 'the apes' (Figure 8.5.B). The cladogram is depicted in Figure 8.5.D.

Note that it can be very hard to classify species in the traditional way (species, genera, family, order) using cladistics. Indeed, some scientists want to do away with the traditional, hierarchical Linnean scheme of classification altogether (species, genera, families, and so on). For the cladistic view, the history of the system of branching is what is important. For the classical pheneticist, the structural similarity is what is important.

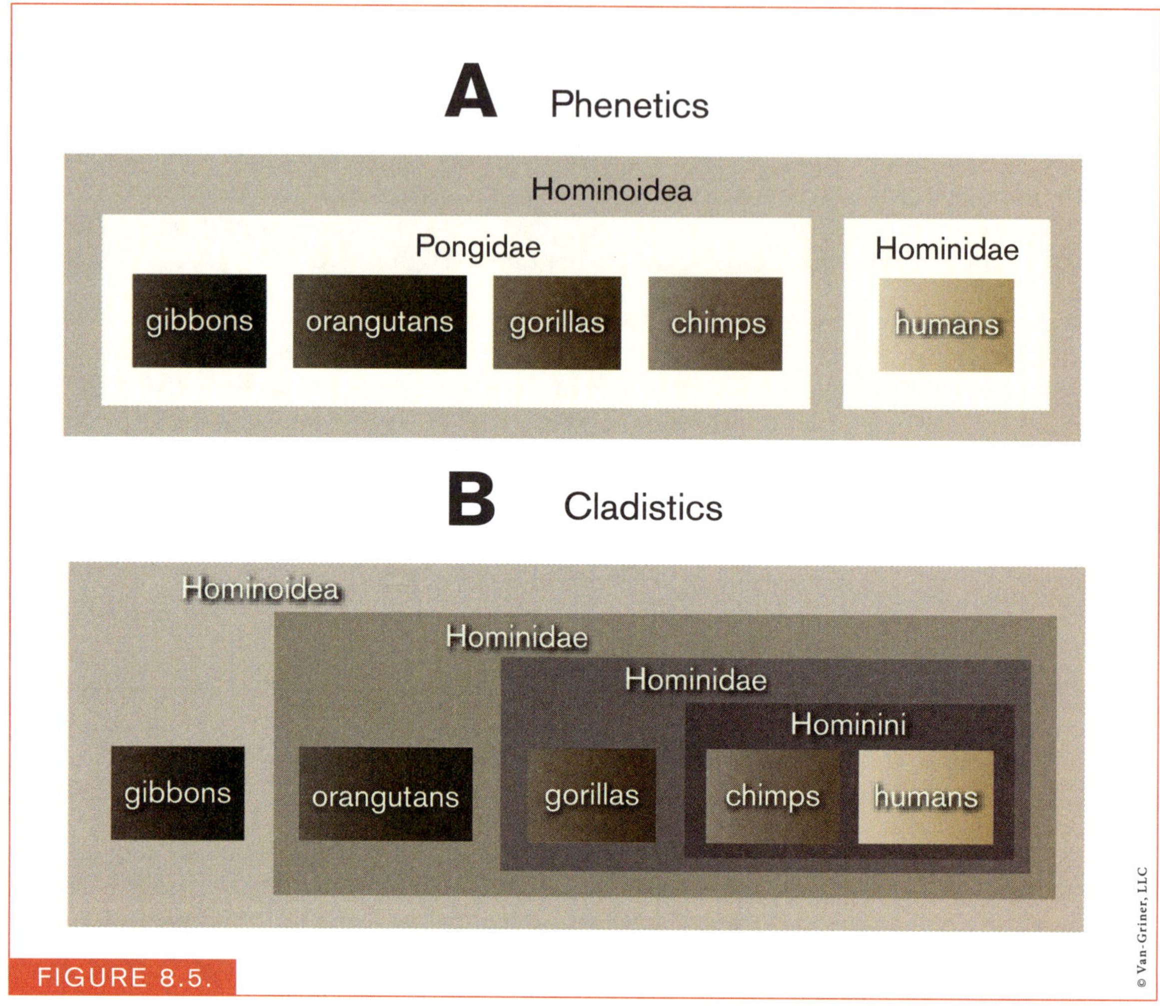

FIGURE 8.5.

A comparison of one phenetics classification (A) and cladistics (B). In both A and B, the smallest boxes represent the genera.

C PHENOGRAM
gibbons orangutans gorillas chimps humans
(ancestral ape)
D CLADOGRAM
gibbons orangutans gorillas chimps humans
(ancestral ape)
genus Homo Pan Gorilla Pongo Hyobates
family Hominidae Pongidae
superfamily Hominoidea E
order Primata
(1 sp.) (2 spp.) (2 spp.) (2 spp.) (13 spp.) (extant) species (present)
(humans) (chimpanzees) (gorillas) (orangutans) (gibbons)
Homo Pan Gorilla Pongo 4 genera genus
Hominini Gorillini tribe
Homininae Ponginae subfamily
Hominidae Hylobatidae family
F Hominoidea superfamily
Primata order
TIME
© Van-Griner, LLC

FIGURE 8.5.

(continued) One possible phenogram (C) is depicted, along with the commonly accepted cladogram today (D). In addition, two phylogenetic trees of the apes—circa 1950s (E) and the current version of the ape phylogenetic tree (F)—are depicted.

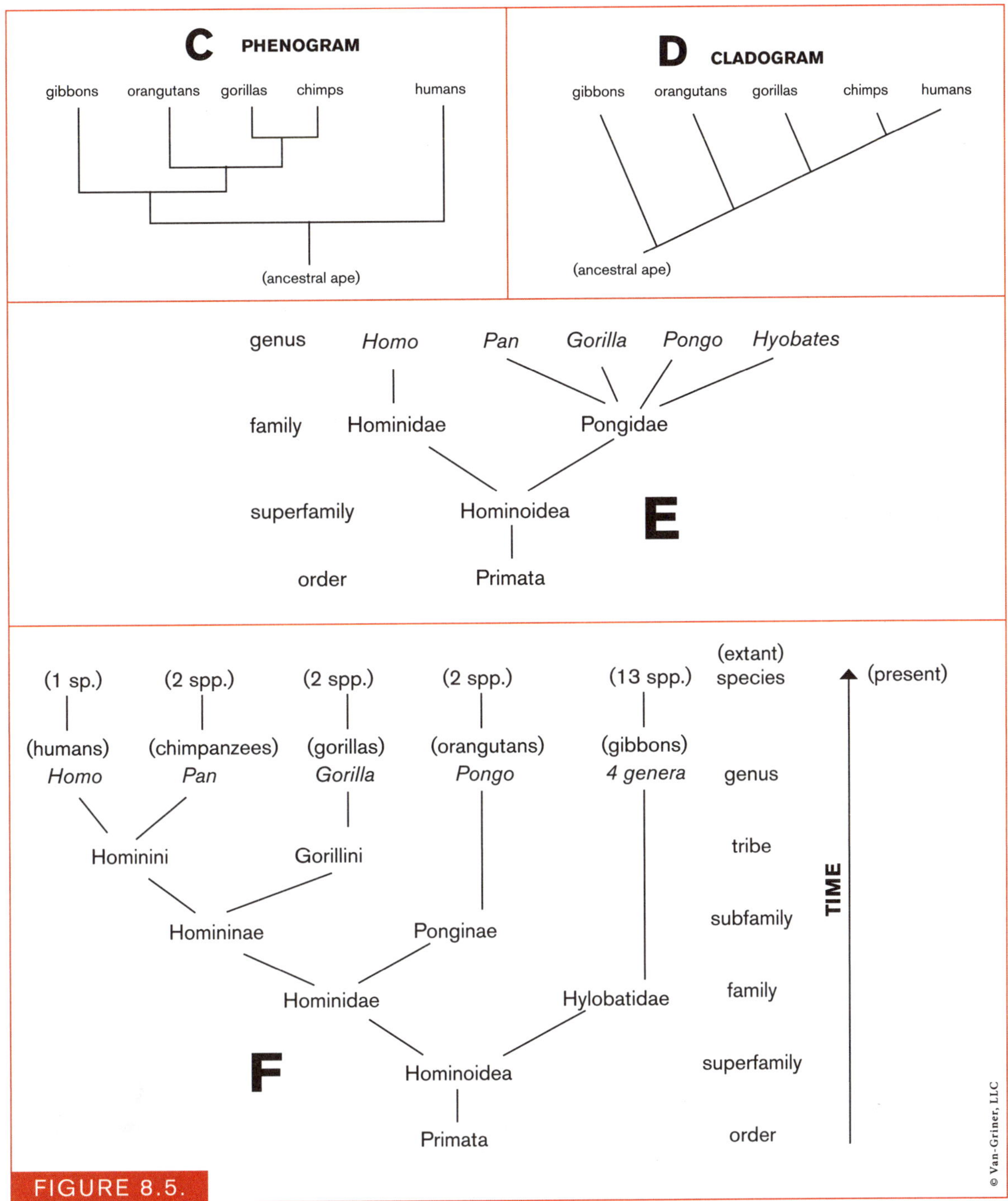

Exercise 8.5.

The Use of a Dichotomous Key

Scientists and naturalists use identification keys to help identify unknown plants and animals (this approach can also be used in other sciences, such as geology). Most identification keys are **dichotomous keys.** A dichotomous key consists of a series of sequential paired choices (couplets) that are arranged in a hierarchical fashion. A couplet consists of two (sometimes three or more) alternative descriptions of specific characteristics that the organism may or may not possess. The alternative descriptions ideally should be mutually exclusive choices. Both choices are read and compared with the specimen to be identified, and one choice is selected as the most accurate choice for your unknown organism.

Once you choose one of the alternatives, the choice determines the next step. Your chosen statement directs you to another couplet, either the couplet immediately following or to one further on in the key. The number at the end of your choice directs you to your next couplet. You then select another statement as true, and this process is repeated until you reach a successful identification of your organism. Eventually, if there is no number at the end of your choice, you have reached the end of your quest: your species has been identified. Your unknown specimen has been "keyed out."

Once you believe you have identified the organism, you should compare the unknown organism with any pictures or descriptions of the tentative identification. If you have identified your unknown correctly, the description should fit what you observe. If not, you either have an organism that cannot be 'keyed out' with your key (as it is constructed), or you made a mistake somewhere during the identification process. You then will need to 'back up' in the key to an earlier couplet, and start over.

It is possible that you may have an unknown specimen that does not fit a particular key, so that by using the key, you may end up misidentifying your unknown organism. Commonly used keys are in continuous revision in order to include new species and/or better identification choices.

Procedure to using a dichotomous key. Examine the cladogram for the chordates (Figure 8.4). Your lab instructor has placed some chordates on the front table, along with some echinoderms. Use the key on the next page, and try to identify each specimen. Place your answers in Table 8.2 and have your lab instructor confirm your answers.

TABLE 8.2.

Specimen Number	You Identified the Specimen as a(n)	Actual Identification of the Specimen

Taxonomic Key to the Chordates and Echinoderms

1 Specimen has a notochord, post-anal tail, and gill slits (Chordata) – go to 2

Specimen possesses a water vascular system and tube feet (Echinodermata) – go to 11

2 Retains notochord and tail as an adult – go to 3

Adult has no tail and notochord, but the adult possesses tough
outer tunic, enlarged pharynx – Urochordata (tunicates)

3 Has a distinct cranium (skull) around brain – go to 4

Does not have a cranium, body is 'pointed' on both ends – Cephalochordata (lancelets)

4 Lacks jaws, possesses a tubular body – go to 5

Possesses jaws and three pairs of semicircular canals (Gnathostomes) – go to 6

5 Has one pair of semicircular canals – Myxini (hagfishes)

Has two pairs of semicircular canals, and a circular mouth with
rasping tongue – Cephalaspidomorphi (lampreys)

6 Retains cartilaginous skeleton as adult, lacks lungs/swim bladders, nonflexible fins
that are not involved in propulsion – Chondrichthyes (sharks, rays, and skates)

Possesses lungs or swim bladders, along with flexible fins or limbs with feet – go to 7

7 Has protective flap (operculum) over gills, possesses flexible fins involved
in propulsion, but no limbs with feet – Osteichthyes (bony fish)

Has two pairs of limbs with feet – (Tetrapods) – go to 8

8 Extraembryonic membranes surround embryos – (Amniotes) – go to 9

Lacks extraembryonic membranes, eggs do not have a shell,
must reproduce in water – Amphibia (amphibians)

9 Presence of fur and mammary glands – Mammalia (mammals)

No fur is present, scales or feathers instead of fur – go to 10

10 Possesses feathers, wings and horned beak – Aves (birds)

Possesses scales, lacks fur and feathers – Reptilia (reptiles)

11 Specimen possesses distinct arms – go to 12

Does not possess distinct arms – go to 14

12 No anus, articulated snake-like arms that are set off from
distinct central disc – Ophiuroidea (brittle stars)

Possesses a complete digestive tract, five or more arms that are not articulated – go to 13

13 Five or more long feather-like arms, stalk may be present – Crinoidea (feather stars)

Five or more stout arms (not feathery) – Asteroidea (sea stars)

14 Ovoid or disc shaped body with spines – Echinoidea (sea urchins and sand dollars)

Tubular body, no spines or arms – Holothuroidea (sea cucumbers)

Exercise 8.6.

Making a Cladogram

Imagine you and your fellow lab mates are the exobiologists aboard the starship *Beagle.* You have landed on a new planet and your job is to identify, name, classify, and study the living animals on the planet. Your team examined a total of six mammal-like animals in the area around the ship (the animals are depicted below in Figure 8.6). You believe they are all in a monophyletic clade. You assign all of the species to one family: **Equimorphidae.**

Let us assume that all six species are alive at the time you landed. At each table, discuss how you would classify these species. Write down your 'classification scheme' in the box below. In Table 8.3, fill in the boxes with information: these data could help you determine what type of identification scheme you can come up with.

After your table has decided on a 'scheme,' call your instructor over to discuss your choice. Did you use a phenetic approach, a cladistic approach, or perhaps both? Did you lump your species into 'genera?' Did you make some sort of 'tree?' Did you think one or more species are ancestral? Why or why not? What are the shared characteristics that you believe are important? Are these characteristics homologies? What further information might you possibly want? What about fossil species?

Note that each species is identified by a letter (A–F). Try to determine which species, in your opinion, would be considered the most ancient species. Note which traits would be considered the ancestral traits for the clade (the symplesiomorphies) and which traits would be synapomorphies (new or derived traits).

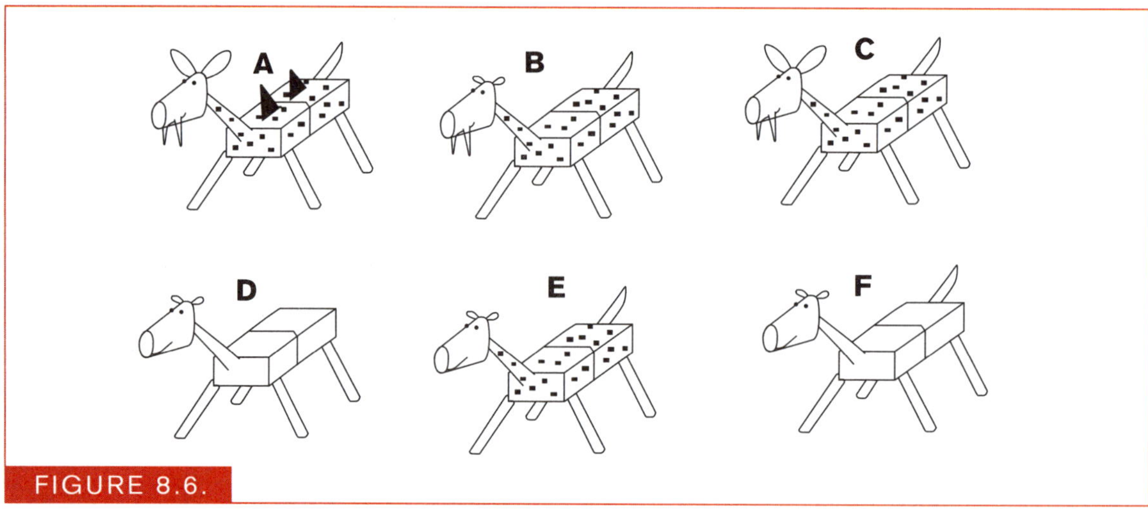

FIGURE 8.6.

The Equimorphs.

TABLE 8.3. The characteristics of the Equimorphs.

Animal	Tail/No Tail	Big Ears/ Small Ears	Fangs/ No Fangs	Spikes on Back/ No Spikes	Spots/ No Spots
A					
B					
C					
D					
E					
F					

You are to assign names to the six species in the family Equimorphidae. Recall that each species has a specific scientific name unique to that species, using the process of binomial nomenclature. There are specific rules to nomenclature:

1 The scientific name consists of two parts: *Genus species.*

2 These names are usually in Latin or Latinized form, although some names are from Greek roots.

3 The first letter of the first name (the genus) is always capitalized, and the last name (the specific epithet) is always lower case.

4 The entire name is either italicized or underlined to indicate that it is a proper scientific name. When writing out a scientific name by hand, don't try to use italics. **Underline the scientific name when writing out a scientific name by hand.** The scientific name of your dog is *Canis familiaris,* the name of the coyote is *Canis latrans,* and the wolf *Canis lupus.* These three dog-like animals have the same genus name (i.e., they are closely related and thus in the same genus). However, they each have a different species name—they are different species in the genus *Canis.*

5 The specific epithet part of the name can be used by more than one species. For example, the white tailed deer's scientific name is *Odocoileus virginianus,* and the bobwhite quail is *Colinus virginianus.* The two animals have the same specific epithet, but are two very different animals in different genera (actually they are in different vertebrate classes as well: one is a mammal, one is a bird).

6 A genus or family name is not typically used by more than one clade.

7 The family name in almost all groups ends in "-idae." The higher taxonomic categories do not officially have standard endings.

8 Assignment of taxonomic names can be somewhat subjective, above the species and genus level. See if you can assign species to genera and families, depending on how you grouped the species. Fill in the following table (Table 8.4), assigning names to the various taxa.

Here are some words (primarily Latin and Greek roots, prefixes, and suffixes) that you can use to describe your species.

alba = "white"
alpestris = "from mountains"
altissima = "tallest"
amphi- = "round"
anti- = "against"
arctica = "from the arctic"
arenaria = "from sandy places"
argentea = "silvery"
arthro- = "jointed"
armata = "prickly"
arvensis = "of the field"
aurantiaca = "orange"
aurea = "golden, yellow"
australis = "from the south"
autumnalis = "of autumn"
azurea = "blue"
barbata = "bearded, hairy"
bicolor = "two colored"
borealis = "from the north"
brad- = "slow"
brev- = "short"
calli- = "beautiful"
campestris = "of the field"
can- = "dog"
-caudatis = "tailed"
-cephalis = "head"
chrysantha = "yellow"
chloro- = "green"
circum- = "around"
co- = "together"
concolor = "same colored"
compacta = "compact"
crass- = "thick"
cyano- = "purple"
dactyl- = "finger" or "toe"
deca- = "ten"
dermis = "skin"
deut- = "second"
dolicho- = "elongated"
di- = "two"
dorsalis = "back"
edulis = "edible"
echino- = "spiny"
endo- = "inside"
epi- = "upon"
equi- = "horse" or "equal"
extra- = "beyond"
feli- = "cat"
foetida = "unpleasant smell"
furc- = "forked"

fuscus = "brown"
gastro- = "stomach"
gigantea = "giant"
glabra = "smooth"
gladi- = "sword"
glacialis = "from cold areas"
glutinosa = "sticky"
grandis = "big"
gymn- = "naked"
hemi- = "half"
hetero- = "different"
hirsuta = "hairy"
hispida = "bristly"
homo- = "same"
humilis = "short"
hydr- = "water"
hyemalis = "of winter"
hypno- = "sleep"
incana = "grey"
infra- = "under"
inodora = "unscented"
inter- = "between"
intra- = "within"
lanata = "woolly"
lateralis = "side"
lineatus = "striped"
major = "greatest"
lutea = "yellow"
macro- = "large"
maculatus = "spotted"
melanus = "black"
maritima = "near the sea"
maxima = "biggest"
micro- = "small"
minima = "small"
minor = "smaller"
mono- = "one"
montana = "from mountains"
-morph = "form"
myri- "many"
nana = "small"
neo- = "new"
nocturna = "nocturnal"
obscurus = "dark"
occidentalis = "western"
orientalis = "eastern"
odont = "tooth"
-oid = "like"
oligo- "few"
ortho- = "straight"

paleo- = "ancient"
ped = "foot"
penta- = "five"
phage = "eat"
platy- = "flat"
pallida = "cream"
palustris = "from marshes"
-phile = "love"
-phobe = "fear"
phoenicea = "purple"
pod = "foot"
poly- = "many"
pratensis = "field"
prot- = "first"
pulverulenta = "dusty"
purpurea = "deep pink"
pygmaea = "small"
quadra- = "four"
quint- = "five"
ram- = "branching"
rect- = "straight"
rivularis = "from near rivers"
rhynch- = "snout"
rubra = "red"
saxatilis = "of rocks"
schizo- = "split"
sex- = "six"
spicata = "spiked"
spinosa = "spiny"
stellata = "starry"
steno- = "narrow"
super- = "beyond"
sub- = "below"
supra- = "above"
sylvestris = "of the forest"
tachy- = "fast"
tetra= "four"
tormentosus = "furry"
tri- = "three"
trich- = "hair"
uni- = "one"
uro- = "tail"
velutina = "velvety"
vernalis = "of spring"
variegatus = "variegated"
villosa = "hairy"
violacea = "violet"
viridis = "green"
vulgaris = "common"
ventrus = "belly"

TABLE 8.4. Name the Equimorph species.

Animal (A–F)	Order	Family	Genus	Species
	Equimorpha	Equimorphidae		
	Equimorpha	Equimorphidae		
	Equimorpha	Equimorphidae		
	Equimorpha	Equimorphidae		
	Equimorpha	Equimorphidae		
	Equimorpha	Equimorphidae		

Did you have trouble assigning all species to various genera? Did you attempt to produce several families (instead of placing them into one family)?

Fill in the cladogram below. Place the letter of the Equimorph in the box provided, and on the lines to the right indicate the traits used to separate out each clade.

Exercise 8.7.

The Creation of a Dichotomous Key of the Equimorphs

Try to create a dichotomous key of the Equimorphs. Keep the following ideas in mind as you (either by yourself or as a group) attempt to construct a dichotomous key:

1 Use features that are distinct and unambiguous, and are constant. Try not to use variable features.

2 If possible, use distinct measurements of length, instead of ambiguous characters ('large' versus 'small').

3 If possible, use the same verb to start each alternative choice of a given couplet.

4 Look for the characteristics that are clearly either absent or present.

Previously, you filled out a table identifying the features of the Equimorphs (Table 8.3). Use that table to aid you in creating your own dichotomous key. List the couplets of your key on the next page, and ask your lab instructor to examine it.

> Compare your dichotomous key with those of the other groups? After discussing the strengths and weaknesses of the various keys produced in your lab section, which appears to be the best? What are the important attributes for a good key?

Taxonomic Key of the Equimorphs

1	
2	
3	
4	
5	
6	

Exercise 8.8.

Life Cycles

We will be examining the life cycles and biology of the multicellular eukaryotes this semester. The eukaryotes share many things in common, particularly at the molecular and cellular level. However, many things do differ among the eukaryotes with respect to form and function. In addition, the life cycles of the various eukaryotes differ dramatically. There are three major kinds of life cycles: **zygotic, gametic,** and **sporic** (see Figure 8.7 to Figure 8.9 below). See the demonstration table for further information.

❶ The **zygotic life cycle** (Figure 8.7) is observed in some of the algae and in the cellular slime molds, and the fungi. In some of the algae, the only diploid cell is the **zygote** itself. The zygote forms from the fusion of two haploid gametes (the gametes are produced by haploid individuals, using **mitosis**). The zygote then undergoes **meiosis,** creating haploid spore nuclei. These haploid spore nuclei in turn produce the haploid hyphae of new individuals. The zygote usually is a resistant overwintering stage.

There are several unique features about fungi with respect to sexual reproduction. First of all, there are no gamete cells (except for the flagellated gametes found in the primitive chytridomycetes). The fungi do not use gametes, in the sense of the fusion of two separate gamete cells. Instead of the fusion of two gametes, there is a fusion of two hyphae from two different individuals (**plasmogamy**), who have genetically different haploid nuclei. The two individual hyphae are of different mating types; there are two or more different mating types in a fungal species.

Secondly, in many fungi, the fusion of two hyphae is not immediately followed by the fusion of the haploid nuclei. The fusion of the nuclei in fungi is called **karyogamy.** We call this stage, where cells containing two different haploid nuclei, the **dikaryon** state. Eventually, specialized fruiting structures form, where the pairs of dissimilar gamete nuclei fuse (karyogamy), giving rise to zygotes long after the 'mating' occurred (the plasmogamy of two hyphae). Although the multicellular fungi grow primarily in moist places, the gamete nuclei are not released into the environment, so liquid water is not needed for fertilization (the exception is the primitive chytridiomycetes, who have flagellated gametes). In addition to the spores produced by meiosis, many fungi also produce **asexual spores** by mitosis.

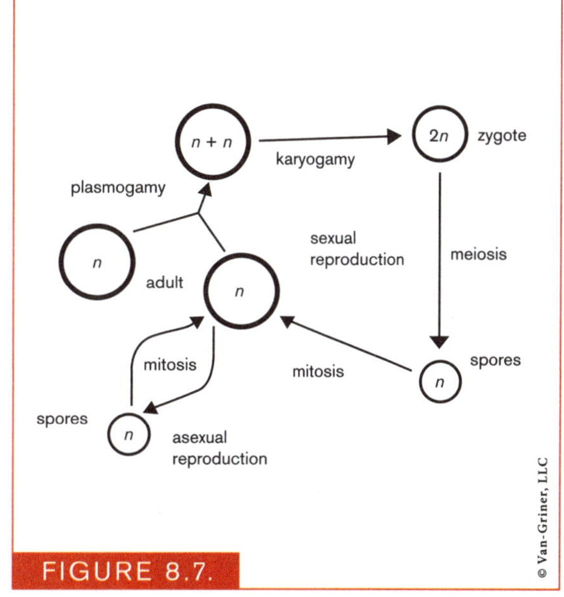

FIGURE 8.7.

The zygotic life cycle: fungi.

❷ The **gametic life cycle** is observed in animals (Figure 8.8). This is the life cycle you are probably most familiar with. The reproductive 'adult' stages are diploid. They produce haploid gametes (using meiosis) that fuse together (**syngamy** or **fertilization**) to produce a diploid **zygote.** The zygote then undergoes mitosis to produce a multicellular adult. The only life cycle stage that is haploid is the single-celled **gamete.**

3 The **sporic life cycle** is observed in some algae (for example, the kelps) and in the multicellular plants (Figure 8.9). Plants show a regular **alternation of generations,** where there is a multicellular haploid adult stage (the **gametophyte**) that alternates with a multicellular diploid adult stage (the **sporophyte**). Specialized cells in the sporophyte undergo meiosis to produce haploid spores, which then undergo mitosis to produce multicellular gametophytes. Reproductive cells in the gametophytes undergo mitosis to produce gametes, which subsequently fuse (syngamy) to form the zygote. The zygote then undergoes mitosis to produce the sporophyte.

Note that there are two distinct and different adults in the sporic cycle: gametophyte and sporophyte. They are not analogous to female and male.

Spores in both the zygotic and sporic cycles can give rise to adult stages directly, without having to fuse with another cell first (like gametes). Spores are long-lived cells, while gametes generally are short-lived.

Gametes must fuse with another cell in order to create the next life cycle stage; spores do not fuse with another spore in order to complete the cycle.

Spores can be produced both by mitosis and by meiosis. In fungi, spores are produced both mitotically and meiotically. In plants, spores are produced by meiosis, and gametes by mitosis.

Gametes also can be produced either by meiosis or mitosis, depending on the life cycle. Gametes are produced by mitosis in the sporic cycle, and gametes are produced by meiosis in the gametic life cycle of animals.

Fill in the following table (Table 8.5), which compares the three life cycles.

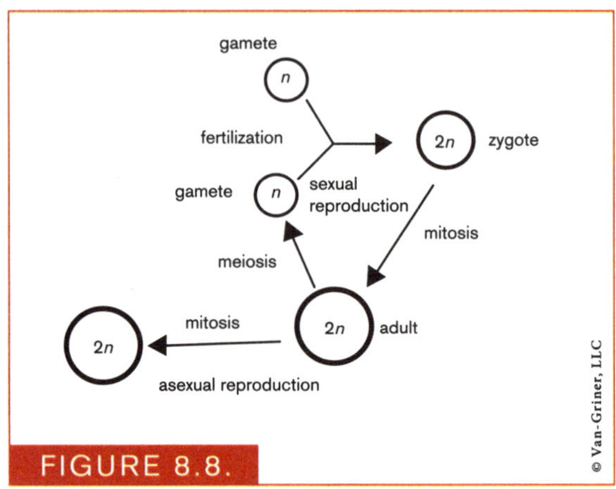

FIGURE 8.8.

The gametic life cycle: the animals.

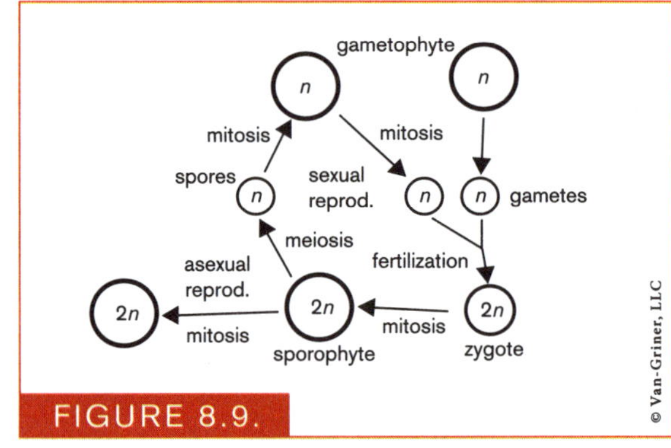

FIGURE 8.9.

The sporic life cycle: the higher plants.

TABLE 8.5. Comparison of the three life cycles of eukaryotic organisms.

	Zygotic	Gametic	Sporic
examples of representative multicellular groups			
meiosis produces haploid cells called [gametes or spores]			
cells called gametes present in life cycle [yes/no]			
gametes produced by [meiosis/mitosis/both]			
spores present in life cycle [yes/no]			
spores produced by [meiosis/mitosis/both]			
after the zygote is produced, it immediately undergoes meiosis to produce haploid cells [yes/no]			
after the zygote is produced, it immediately undergoes mitosis, producing a multicellular adult [yes/no]			
multicellular haploid adult phase present in life cycle [yes/no]			
multicellular diploid adult phase present in life cycle [yes/no]			
the presence of two different haploid nuclei in a cell (dikaryon state) [yes/no]			

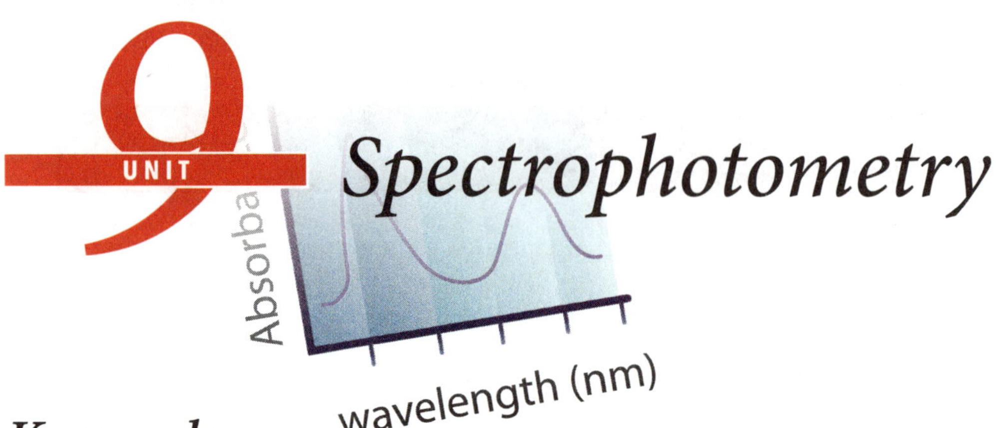

Spectrophotometry

Keywords

absorbance

transmittance

standard curve

absorbance spectrum

Learning Objectives

When finished with this unit, you should be able to:

1 Understand how to use a spectrophotometer;

2 Graph the absorbance spectrum for a compound; and

3 Determine the concentration of an unknown substance, using a spectrophotometer and a standard curve.

In many fields of biology, the spectrophotometer is an important analytical instrument. The concentration of specific compounds in a solution can be determined by measuring the amount of light (at a particular wavelength) that has been absorbed by a solution. The amount of absorbance depends on the concentration of the compound and the ability of that compound to absorb that particular wavelength of light. A beam of light of a single wavelength (we call this beam 'monochromatic light') is passed through a solution and some amount of the monochromatic light either is transmitted (passes through) or is absorbed by the solution. The **spectrophotometer** tells us the amount of the monochromatic light that is absorbed or transmitted.

In a spectrophotometer, a white light source (for visible wavelengths) is focused through a prism or diffraction grating (see Figure 9.1). The white light is then separated into its spectrum consisting of various wavelengths. A particular wavelength is selected by focusing the light through a narrow slit. The selected light wavelength (the incident beam) then passes through the solution containing the sample molecules dissolved in an appropriate solvent. The sample is contained within a special tube called a **cuvette,** which typically has a standard width, so that the light's path length is 1 cm.

As the incident beam passes through the sample in the cuvette, some of the light is absorbed by the solvent and by the sample molecules, and some passes through (transmitted). As the transmitted light (now called the transmitted beam or emergent beam) exits, it then strikes a photoelectric cell. As the emergent beam strikes the photoelectric cell, it generates an electrical current whose strength is proportional to the intensity of the emergent beam. If any of the incident light was absorbed, the total energy of the emergent light will be less than the incident beam. If the two beams are identical in intensity, then no energy was absorbed by the molecules in the solution and all of the light energy passed through the cuvette.

Because the molecules of interest are typically dissolved in a solvent prior to measurement, there must be a correction factor that takes into account the amount of the transmitted light that may be absorbed by the solvent. We can account for this by 'subtracting' the amount absorbed by the solvent by the use of a 'blank.' The blank is a cuvette that only contains the solvent. The blank is first inserted into the machine and then the spectrophotometer's absorbance reading is set to '0' absorbance. The sample cuvette is then inserted into the machine, and any reading above '0' absorbance is due to the absorbance of the sample molecules.

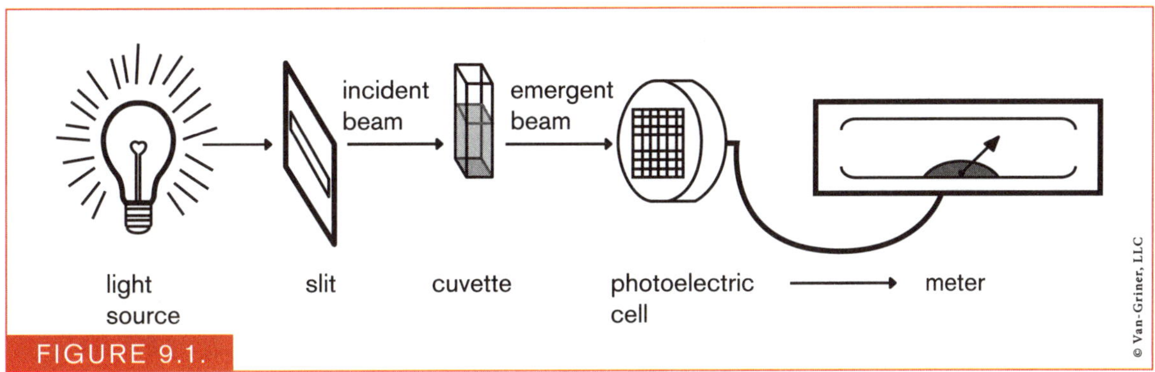

FIGURE 9.1.

The functional internal components of the spectrophotometer.

Exercises

Exercise 9.1.

Your lab instructor will go over the proper use and care of the spectrophotometer.

Two subgroups will measure the **absorbance spectrum** for the antibiotic compound tetracycline at one of two concentrations. The two concentrations you will use differ in concentration by 10-fold, therefore we will designate the solution with the greater concentration as 1.0 and that with the lesser concentration as 0.1.

We will measure the absorbance at 10 nanometer increments, from about 400 to 700 nanometers (λ, measured in nanometers). This range roughly brackets the visible spectrum of light.

After both groups have collected their data, copy the data from each group in Table 9.1 and Table 9.2. Plot the data in Figure 9.2. Label each line.

Do you see a pattern in the absorbance spectrum? At what wavelength is the absorbance greatest?

Examine the absorbance spectra of tetracycline. What effect does concentration have upon absorbance?

Exercise 9.2.

Using a Standard Curve

In addition to identifying compounds in solution, a spectrophotometer is useful in determining the concentrations of various solutes. You will be asked to determine the unknown concentration of tetracycline.

First, you need to generate a **standard curve.** The absorbance of a compound is in part determined by its concentration: the higher the concentration, the greater the amount of the light of the incident beam is absorbed.

Examine the absorbance curves you determined for tetracycline.

Note the shape of the curves for the two relative dilutions (1 and 0.1). Are the shapes of the curves related?

If you were to determine the relative concentrations of tetracycline using one wavelength, which wavelength would you use?

Generation of the standard curve. Your instructor will provide each group with a set of standard solutions containing known concentrations of tetracycline and three samples of unknown tetracycline concentration. Measure the absorbance of each of the standards and unknowns at the absorbance you determined above. Record the absorbance values for the standards and the unknown in Table 9.3. Plot the relationship between tetracycline concentrations of the standards and absorbance in Figure 9.3.

Examine your results and draw a straight line that you think best describes your data (refer to the section concerning regression analysis in Unit 3) and graph it. From the best-fit line, you can estimate the concentration of tetracycline in your unknown samples. This technique has many uses. For example, many farmers feed antibiotics (like tetracycline) to protect their livestock and enhance their growth. Suppose you worked for the state's Department of Water Quality. In order to respond to a mandate from the federal Environmental Protection Agency, you are sending out teams (the students) to assess the quality of water in rivers and lakes that border ranches in different parts of the state. These teams will determine if antibiotics are running off from any of these ranches' feedlots and entering the local water supplies for nearby towns. The students collect water samples and then compare the absorbance values of their samples to a standard curve, thus determining the extent of water pollution from tetracycline.

Using the results graphed in Figure 9.3, what is your estimate of the concentration of tetracycline in your unknown samples? (Your lab instructor will provide you with the answer later.)

Your estimates:

___________   ___________   ___________

How close were your estimates to the 'real' answers?

TABLE 9.1. Absorbance spectrum: tetracycline. Relative concentration: 1.

λ, nm	Absorbance	λ, nm	Absorbance	λ, nm	Absorbance
400		610		820	
410		620		830	
420		630		840	
430		640		850	
440		650		860	
450		660		870	
460		670		880	
470		680		890	
480		690		900	
490		700		910	
500		710		920	
510		720		930	
520		730		940	
530		740		950	
540		750		960	
550		760		970	
560		770		980	
570		780		990	
580		790		1,000	
590		800			
600		810			

TABLE 9.2. Absorbance spectrum: tetracycline. Relative concentration: 0.1.

λ, nm	Absorbance	λ, nm	Absorbance	λ, nm	Absorbance
400		610		820	
410		620		830	
420		630		840	
430		640		850	
440		650		860	
450		660		870	
460		670		880	
470		680		890	
480		690		900	
490		700		910	
500		710		920	
510		720		930	
520		730		940	
530		740		950	
540		750		960	
550		760		970	
560		770		980	
570		780		990	
580		790		1,000	
590		800			
600		810			

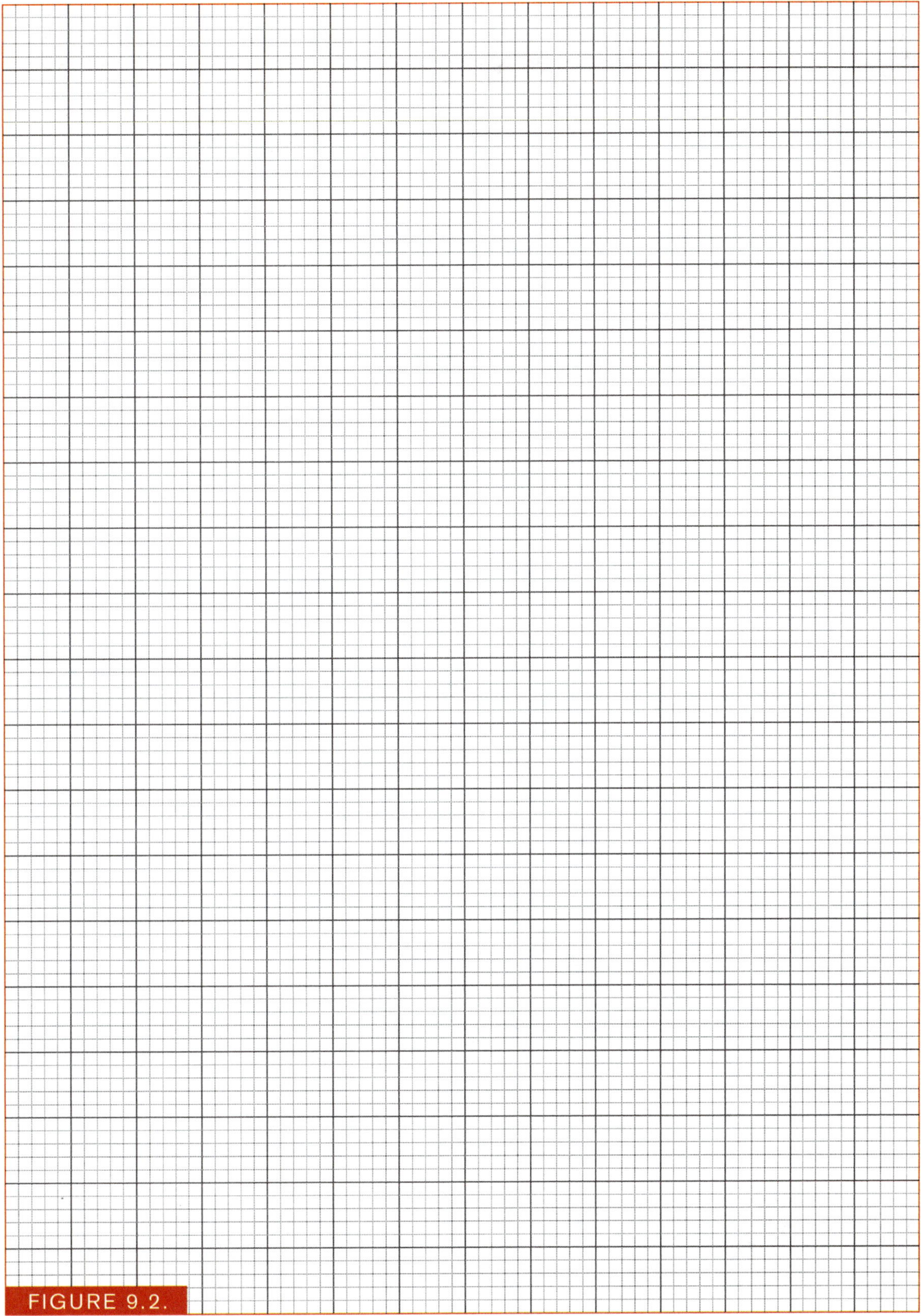

FIGURE 9.2.

Absorbance spectra for tetracycline at two relative concentrations.

TABLE 9.3. Tetracycline absorbance data.

Concentration	Absorbance at Wavelength ☐ nm
unknown 1 =	
unknown 2 =	
unknown 3 =	

FIGURE 9.3.

Standard curve for tetracycline.

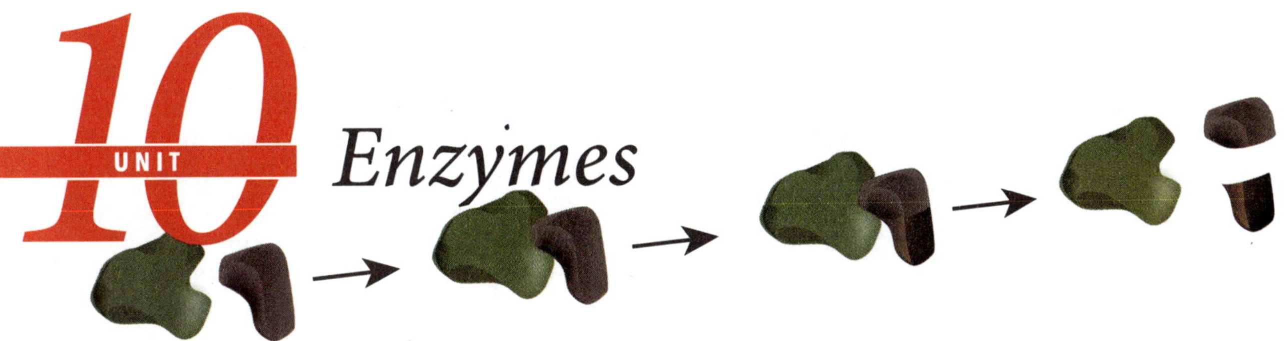

Keywords

enzyme

substrate

product

exergonic

endergonic

catalyst

activation energy

active site

induced fit

reversible

allosteric inhibitor

allosteric activator

cofactor

coenzyme

denaturation

Learning Objectives

When finished with this unit, you should be able to:

1. Understand the relationship between chemical reactions and energy gain/release;

2. Describe how ATP acts as a coupling agent between exergonic and endergonic reactions; and

3. Understand the role of enzymes as catalysts of chemical reactions.

Chemical energy is a type of potential energy. Chemical energy is stored in the covalent bonds of food molecules (lipids, carbohydrates, proteins) and energy carrier molecules (such as ATP). Chemical energy can be used for work in cells. In biology, **work** has the same meaning as in physics: most of the work (movement, maintenance of order, tissue repair, etc) done by living organisms involves the conversion of potential energy into kinetic energy. This stored energy can be tapped when bonds are broken and rearranged. **Chemical reactions** occur when molecules interact with each other, breaking and forming new bonds, storing or releasing energy.

Many chemical reactions that occur in cells are **exergonic:** they release energy (energy is lost into the system). Suppose we have the following reaction:

molecule A → molecule B + molecule C + energy

As molecule A breaks down into two products (B and C), the reaction releases energy stored in the covalent bonds that were broken.

Some reactions in living cells are **endergonic:** they have to be pushed 'uphill' by adding energy in from the system. Examine the following reaction:

molecule D + molecule E + energy → molecule F

Note that in this second reaction, D and E combine to form a larger molecule, F. In this case, additional energy is required for the second reaction (an endergonic reaction) to occur as new bonds (containing energy) have been formed.

What causes these endergonic reactions to occur? Cells can 'use' some of the energy released from exergonic reactions to drive endergonic reactions. Instead of having these reactions somehow occur close together in space or time, cells use energy carriers to temporarily store the energy. Adenosine triphosphate (**ATP**) is an energy-rich intermediate used by living things to couple endergonic and exergonic reactions together.

molecule A + ADP + phosphate → molecule B + molecule C + ATP

molecule D + molecule E + ATP → molecule F + ADP + phosphate

Another way to show these coupled reactions is depicted in Figure 10.1. The energy released from the exergonic reaction is temporarily stored in ATP. The energy can subsequently be released from ATP to provide energy needed for endergonic reactions to occur.

There are thousands of different chemical reactions that occur in living cells. Many occur as a series of reactions, one following another. In these pathways, molecules react by either breaking apart, rearranging, or combining, and in the process, they release energy or store energy (in chemical bonds). In addition, these pathways produce various molecules needed for life.

As we discussed earlier, some chemical reactions necessary for a cell's existence occur very slowly, if at all. Living cells carry out hundreds or even thousands of different chemical reactions very rapidly, using biological **catalysts** called **enzymes.** Catalysts are molecules that speed up chemical reactions. Catalysts do not 'cause' the reaction to occur, nor are they used up in the process. **Enzymes** are biological catalysts made of proteins.

For every chemical reaction that takes place in a living cell, a specific enzyme is used to speed up or **catalyze** the reaction. If the reaction involves splitting a molecule, or rearranging a molecule, it takes energy to stretch a bond to cause it to break. This energy is called **activation energy.** Enzymes do not alter the free energy change in the reaction, nor do they change the propor-

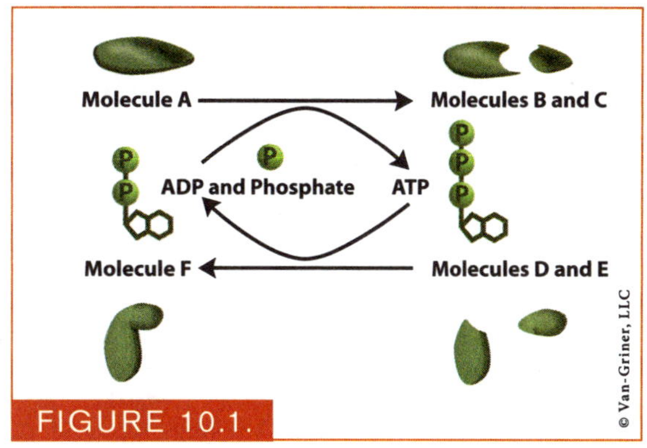

FIGURE 10.1.

Coupled reactions.

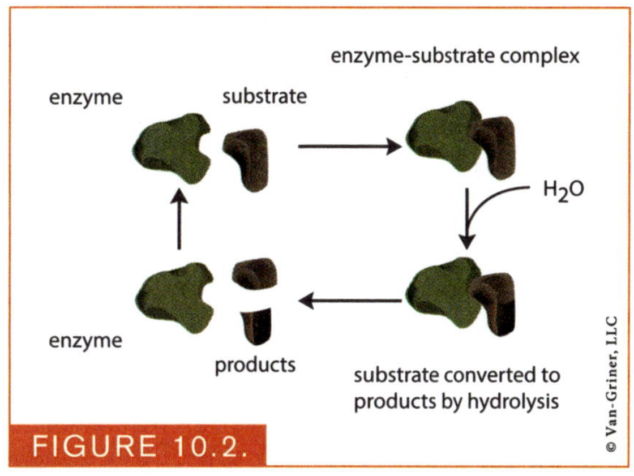

FIGURE 10.2.

Enzyme function: the enzyme-substrate complex.

tions of reactants and products (molecules at the beginning and end of the reaction). **Enzymes lower the activation energy** needed for the reaction to proceed, thus making it more likely for the reaction to occur.

Enzyme function. Enzymes bind in a specific way to the reactant molecules, the substrate(s). The substrate(s) bind to a specific three-dimensional site on an enzyme called the **active site.** Various bonds within the substrate then are distorted, and the product or products are formed either by splitting the substrate into two, by combining two substrates together, or by rearranging parts of the substrate (Figure 10.2).

Enzymes are very specific: they often only react with one substrate or perhaps a few substrates. The specificity is due to the specific three dimensional shape of both the active site and the substrates. The active site, when it has bound to the substrate, forms an **enzyme-substrate complex.** The binding of the substrate to the enzyme tends to slightly alter the shape of the enzyme (**induced fit**). This induced fitting of enzyme with substrate brings parts of the substrate into close contact with functional groups of different amino acids found at this specific part of the enzyme, helping to catalyze the reaction.

When this happens, the substrate is changed, resulting in a product molecule (or molecules, if the substrate split into two). The products then are released, but the enzyme emerges from the reaction unchanged, ready to bind more substrate and catalyze the reaction again. Enzymes work quickly, potentially at speeds of thousands of times per second. A small amount of enzyme thus can process a large amount of substrate in a short time.

You have thousands of different types of enzymes in your cells, and each enzyme catalyzes a specific reaction. The three-dimensional shape of the enzyme is due to the linear sequence of amino acids along the protein's length. This sequence is coded for by a specific gene in the organism's genome.

Many reactions are **reversible:** they can occur in both directions. These reactions often are shown by double-headed arrow, as shown in the chemical equation below. Those reactions where there is little free energy change are more easily reversible. Remember that endergonic reactions occur very slowly on their own, or not at all, because considerable amounts of energy has to be added.

$$\text{molecule A} \rightleftarrows \text{molecule B} + \text{molecule C}$$

Enzyme activity can be altered by many factors:

1. Many enzymes have associated **cofactors.** Many cofactors are **inorganic metal ions** (Fe, Mg, Cu, Se, Mn, and others) that usually help change a nonfunctioning active site to an active one. **Coenzymes** are organic cofactors that bind to enzymes and affect activity; many vitamins or their derivatives (particularly the B vitamins) act as coenzymes, as do ATP, NAD and FAD, and coenzyme A (we talked about these compounds in aerobic respiration in Unit 5). These organic cofactors often transfer electrons, protons, or various functional groups (for example, phosphate, acyl, methyl, amino, carbonyl, and carboxyl groups) from one molecule to another or from one chemical reaction to another. One possible adaptation to this process is increased efficiency from using a small set of metabolic intermediates to carry chemical groups between different reactions, particularly if these different reactions are occurring in different parts of the cell.

2. Changing the **pH** or **temperature** may speed up or inhibit enzyme activity by altering the three-dimensional structure (the tertiary or quaternary structure) of the enzymes. Altering the three dimensional structure of an enzyme may alter its active site, thus affecting the ability of the enzyme to bind with its specific substrate. Proteins can be permanently altered so that they are no longer active; the protein then is said to have been **denatured** (the process is called denaturation).

3. Various molecules (**inhibitors**) can bind to an enzyme, inhibiting its activity. These inhibitors may bind to the active site, thus competing with or interfering with the substrate's access to the active site, or the inhibitor binds to another site (referred to as an **allosteric site**), which consequently alters the shape (and thus the enzymatic activity) of the enzyme. Other compounds (including Ca ions) act as allosteric **activators,** which can activate enzymatic activity.

4 Changing enzyme and substrate concentrations also can affect the activity of enzymes. In today's lab, you will investigate the activity of a specific enzyme called **peroxidase.** This enzyme is found in many plant and animal cells; it functions to protect the cell by catalyzing the conversion of toxic hydrogen peroxide (H_2O_2) to water and a detoxified waste product (symbolized as P). Specifically, peroxidase catalyzes the reaction:

$$H_2O_2 + PH_2 \rightarrow 2H_2O + P$$

'P' stands for a compound that participates as a contributor of electrons and protons (in the form of hydrogen atoms) in the reaction, assisting the enzyme peroxidase in catalysis. In this lab you will take advantage of the fact that peroxidase can interact with different electron donors (including some not normally found in cells) that change color when they are oxidized (i.e., they lose electrons). Thus, the conversion of hydrogen peroxide to water can be quantified by the change in color of the mixture as the reaction proceeds.

We will use the electron donor **guaiacol** (a dye that turns brown when oxidized) to follow the rate at which hydrogen peroxide is broken down. Peroxidase, hydrogen peroxide, and the dye will be mixed in a test tube and then the solution will be poured into a cuvette. The cuvette then will be placed in a spectrophotometer, and the accumulation of brown color (measured at a wavelength of 500 nm) will provide a measure of the rate at which substrate is converted to product. You will record the absorbance values at timed intervals to measure the rate of the reaction. You will perform two exercises in today's lab: 1) increasing the amount of catalyst (peroxidase) while the amount of substrate remains constant, and 2) increasing the amount of substrate (hydrogen peroxide) concentration while the amount of the enzyme remains constant.

Exercises

Exercise 10.1.

1 You will be provided with 4 solutions containing variable amounts of the necessary components of the reaction: peroxidase, buffer (pH 5), hydrogen peroxide (10 mM), and guaiacol (25 mM). Note that for three different pairs of tubes (2 and 3, 4 and 5, 6 and 7) the enzyme (peroxidase) is separate from the substrate (hydrogen peroxide) and the dye (guaiacol).

2 Label seven test tubes 1 through 7. Fill the tubes as described below (Table 10.1) to test the effect of increasing enzyme concentration on the rate of the reaction.

TABLE 10.1.

Tube	Buffer (ml)	H_2O_2 (ml)	Peroxidase (ml)	Guaiacol (ml)	Total (ml)
1 (blank)	5	2	0	1	8
2	0	2	0	1	3
3	4	0	1	0	5
4	0	2	0	1	3
5	3	0	2	0	5
6	0	2	0	1	3
7	2	0	3	0	5

At this point, note that no tubes contain both the enzyme and the substrate. When you are ready to measure the reaction speed in each individual case, you will initiate the reaction by mixing two tubes together (the tubes containing substrate and enzyme).

3 Set the spectrophotometer to measure absorbance at 500 nm. Use the solution in tube 1 to zero or "blank" the spectrophotometer, so that the starting color of the mixture does not influence subsequent measurements.

4 Mix the contents of tubes 2 and 3 together (pour them back and forth several times). As soon as possible, carefully add the mixture to a cuvette (the special tube used in the spectrophotometer), wipe the outside surface of the cuvette, and place it in the chamber of the spectrophotometer. Record the absorbance value at 20 second intervals in Table 10.2 after placing the cuvette in the spectrophotometer. After taking six readings (2 minutes), remove the cuvette from the spectrophotometer and compare the color of the mixture to that in the blank tube.

5 After you have measured the reaction speed for tubes 2 and 3 mixed together, then repeat Step 4 for tubes 4 and 5. After you are done with the mixture of tubes 4 and 5, proceed to mix tubes 6 and 7 together and determine absorbance described in Step 4. Remember to 'blank' the spectrophotometer before each pair of tubes.

6 Plot the results (absorbance as function of time) of these three enzyme concentrations in Figure 10.3 (use different symbols for each of the concentrations). Draw a separate line connecting the points for each of the three enzyme concentrations.

State the null and alternative hypothesis for this experiment.

Did you draw a straight line through the points, or does a curved line better fit the data?

TABLE 10.2.

Enzyme Concentration	Absorbance Values at Time (sec):					
	20	40	60	80	100	120
blank						
1 ml						
2 ml						
3 ml						

Explain your results. Which hypothesis did you accept?

Do you accept or reject the null hypothesis you stated for this experiment?

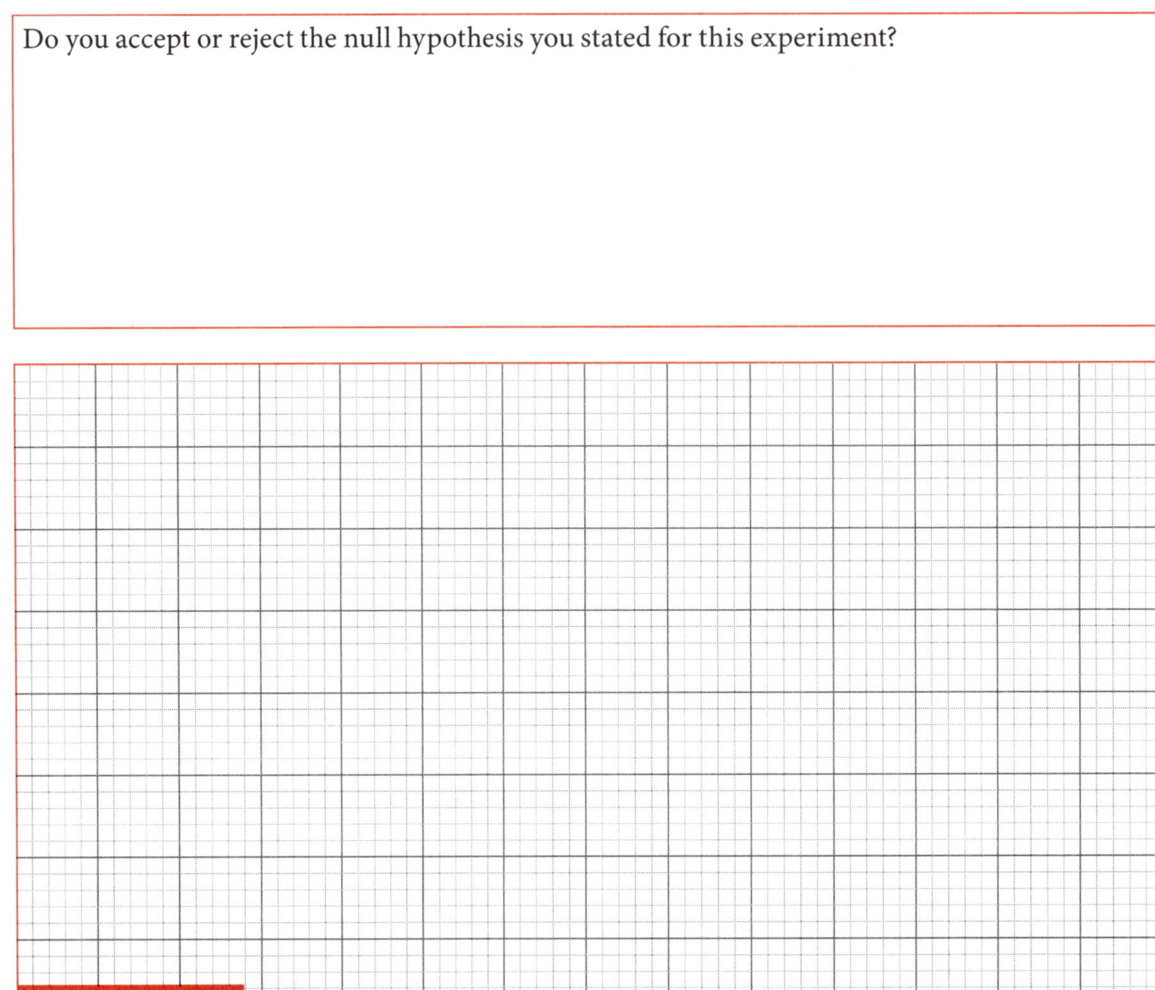

FIGURE 10.3.

Effects of peroxidase concentration.

Exercise 10.2.

You will use the results of the first experiment to determine the amount of enzyme to be used in this second activity. Looking at your graph from the first experiment, what amount of peroxidase would give a linear change in absorbance from 0 to a value approaching 1 in approximately 120 seconds? This is the amount of enzyme you should use in each of the experiments in this second exercise. The table below (Table 10.3) assumes that the results from tubes 2 and 3 in the first experiment fit this definition. However, your results may vary, and the exact amount of each solution may need to be modified.

1 Label nine test tubes 1 through 9. Fill the tubes as described to test the effect of increasing substrate concentration on the rate of the reaction.

TABLE 10.3.

Tube	Buffer (ml)	H_2O_2 (ml)	Peroxidase (ml)	Guaiacol (ml)	Total (ml)
1 (blank)	6	1	0	1	8
2	1.5	0.5	0	1	3
3	4	0	1	0	5
4	1	1	0	1	3
5	4	0	1	0	5
6	0	2	0	1	3
7	4	0	1	0	5
8	0	3	0	1	4
9	3	0	1	0	4

2 Set the spectrophotometer to measure absorbance at 500 nm. Like Experiment 10.1, use the solution in Tube 1 to zero or "blank" the spectrophotometer, so that the starting color of the mixture does not influence subsequent measurements.

3 When you are ready to measure the reaction speed in each individual case, you will initiate the reaction by mixing two tubes together (the tubes containing substrate and enzyme). Mix the contents of tubes 2 and 3 (pour them back and forth several times). Add the mixture to a cuvette, wipe the outside surface of the cuvette, and place it in the chamber of the spectrophotometer. Record the absorbance values at 20 second intervals after placing the cuvette in the spectrophotometer. Record your data in Table 10.4. After 6 readings (2 minutes) remove the cuvette from the spectrophotometer and compare the color of the mixture to that in the blank tube.

4 After you have measured the reaction speed for tubes 2 and 3, repeat Step 3 by mixing tubes 4 and 5 together, and measure. After you are done with tubes 4 and 5, repeat Step 3 with tubes 6 and 7. Finally, repeat Step 3 with tubes 8 and 9.

5 Plot the results of these four treatments (substrate concentrations) on Figure 10.4 (use different symbols for the 6 values in each individual treatment). The *x*-axis should be seconds (the independent variable) and the *y*-axis should be absorbance (the dependent variable). Draw a single straight line that best fits the data points for each of the four substrate concentrations (curves may plateau at the end of your measurements).

6 To help clarify the results, you will need to prepare a graph derived from the raw data, specifically, a graph of the slope of each of the lines representing the four substrate concentrations. For each of the six 20 second time segments (0 to 20 sec, 20 to 40 sec, 40 to 60 sec, 60 to 80 sec, 80 to 100 sec, and 100 to 120 sec) of data collected for the four substrate concentrations, calculate the slope of the line representing that segment by subtracting the absorbance reading at the start of the 20 second segment from the absorbance at the end of the 20 second segment. You will refer to this difference as ΔA (delta A), the change in absorbance, and then divide this value by 20 to give you a ΔA/second for that segment. Repeat that calculation for each of the six 20 second segments of each of the four substrate concentrations. For each of the substrate concentrations, select the ΔA/second that is the largest of the 6 values, and place this maximal 'ΔA' in Table 10.5. Graph the maximal ΔA value as a function of substrate concentration in Figure 10.5. You should end up with a graph that has 4 points (the highest ΔA/sec for the 0.5 ml substrate volume, the highest ΔA/sec for the 1.0 ml substrate volume, etc.).

What shape of curve do you get after you connect the data points? Explain.

Do you accept or reject the null hypothesis you stated for this test? Why?

TABLE 10.4.

Peroxide (Substrate) Concentration	Absorbance Values at Time (sec):					
	20	40	60	80	100	120
blank						
0.5 ml						
1.0 ml						
2.0 ml						
3.0 ml						

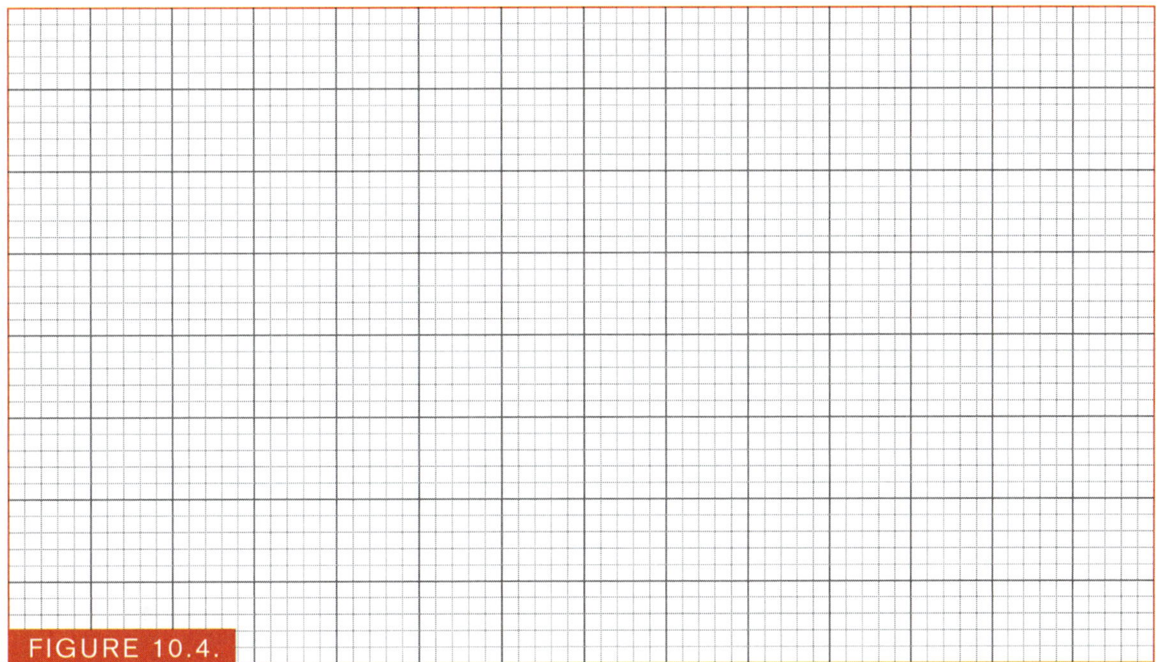

FIGURE 10.4.

Effects of peroxide (substrate) concentration on reaction speed.

TABLE 10.5. Impact of substrate concentration (volume) on maximal peroxidase velocity.

Substrate Volume	Maximal ΔA/sec
0.5 ml	
1.0 ml	
2.0 ml	
3.0 ml	

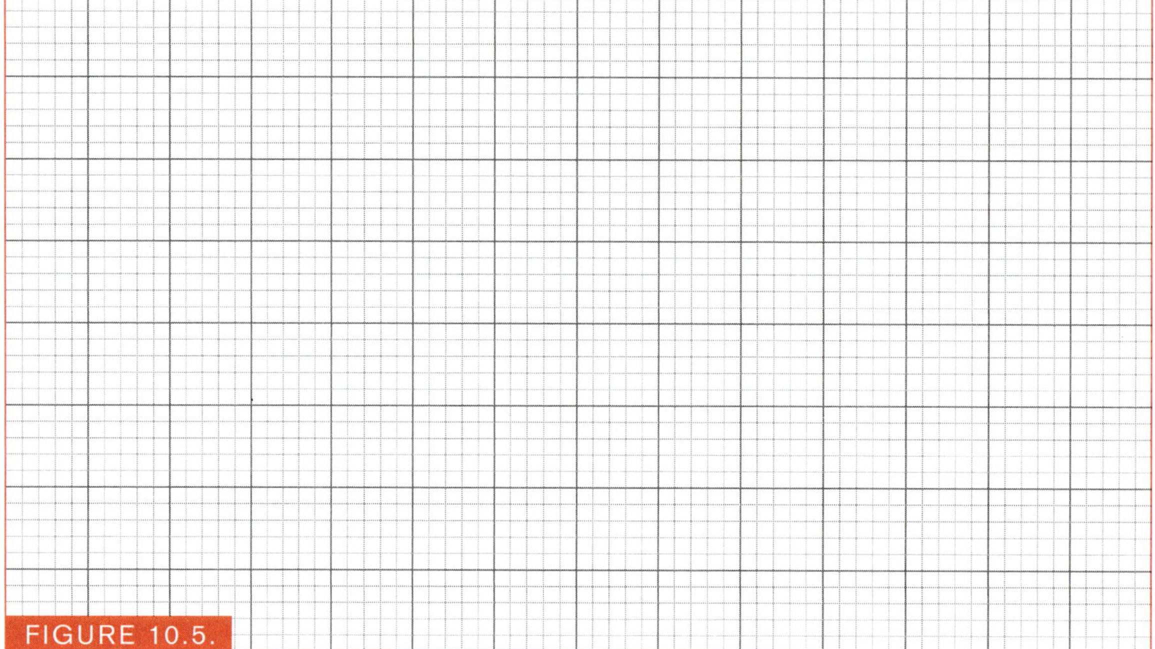

FIGURE 10.5.

Effect of substrate concentration on maximal velocity.

Exercise 10.3.

Suppose you had examined the effect of temperature on the activity of the enzyme acetylcholinesterase in two fish. One fish is a brook trout that lives in streams ranging in temperatures between 8 and 12°C, and a catfish that lives in streams that ranges from 25 to 30°C. Discuss with your classmates what the enzymatic activity curves for acetylcholinesterase would be under the normal temperature ranges for these two fish, and plot what you would predict would be the activity versus temperature in Figure 10.6. Check your answers with your lab instructor.

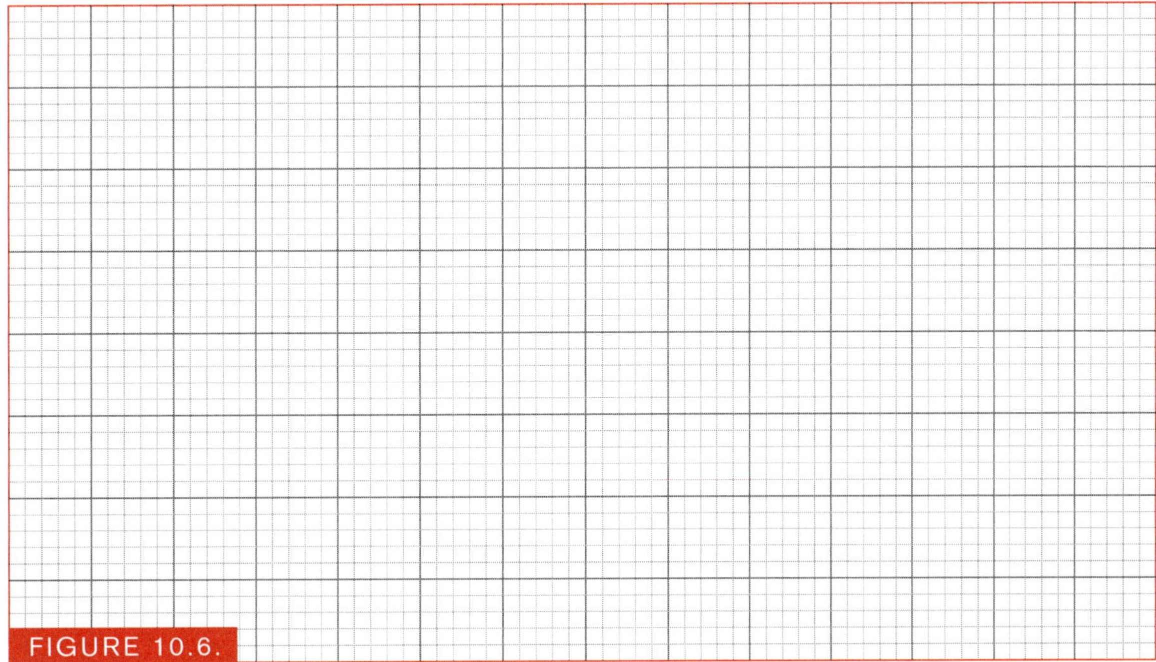

FIGURE 10.6.

The effects of environmental temperature on the enzymatic activity in two fish: the brook trout and the catfish.

With respect to the thermal optima for enzymes, what other possibilities exist for animals that are found in a wide range of environmental temperatures?

You have several hydrolytic proteases (enzymes that break down proteins). One protease is called pepsin; it works in the highly acidic (pH = 1.5 to 3) conditions of your stomach. Another protease, trypsin, works in the more alkaline conditions of your small intestine (pH = 7 to 8.5). Discuss with your classmates what the enzymatic activity curves for pepsin and trypsin under a range of pH values should look like, and plot what you would predict would be the activity under a range of pH in Figure 10.7. Check your answers with your lab instructor.

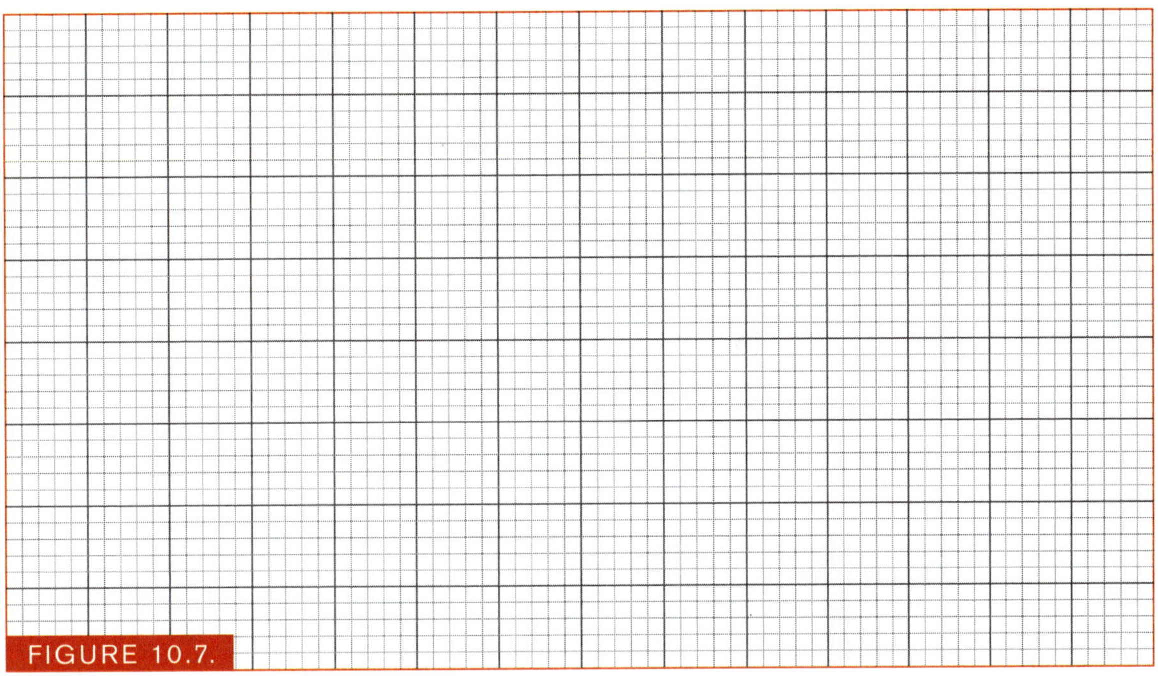

FIGURE 10.7.

The effects of pH on the enzymatic activity of two human proteases: pepsin and trypsin.

If you were taking large amounts of antacids, to the point that you changed the pH of your stomach from 2 to 7, could it have an effect on your digestion of proteins? Explain your answer.

Exercise 10.1 was based on a similar exercise described in W. D. Dolphin, D. Vleck, J. T. Colbert, L. M. Westgate (2011) *Biological Investigations: Form Function Diversity and Process.* 9th edition. McGraw-Hill, New York, NY.

UNIT 11 — Bacteria and Protists

Keywords

bacilli
cocci
spirillum
staphylo-
strepto-
diplo-
heterocyst
nitrogen fixation
mixotrophic
autotrophic
heterotrophic
spore
pellicle
oral groove
cilia

flagella
zygospore
isogametes
pyrenoids
stigma
chloroplasts
conjugation tubes
eyespots
contractile vacuoles
macronucleus
micronucleus
pseudopodia
cytostome
plasmalemma
binary fission

conjugation
undulating
  membrane
sporozoite
trophozoites
ookinete
gametocytes
isogamete
vegetative cell
unicellular
colony
red tide
sleeping sickness
amebic dysentery
malaria

intermediate hosts
definitive hosts
intracellular
extracellular
stipe
holdfast
floats (air bladder)
apical complex
gametophyte
antheridia
oogonia
sporophyte
haploid
diploid

Learning Objectives

When finished with this unit, you should be able to:

1. Describe the distinctive features of each group of unicellular prokaryotes and protists observed in lab;

2. Identify bacteria with respect to their shape, grouping (staphylo-, strepto-) and Gram stain response, and which organisms are capable of nitrogen fixation;

3. Describe the Gram stain procedure, and be able to distinguish gram-negative or gram-positive cells;

4. Compare and contrast the modes of sexual and asexual reproduction observed in unicellular organisms;

5. Identify the phylum and class of selected protistan specimens, and identify which organisms cause red tide, malaria, amebic dysentery, and sleeping sickness;

6 Determine the density of parasitic protozoans per unit of mammalian blood and the total parasitic load;

7 Determine the speed living protozoans can move;

8 Identify the following structures in algae and protozoa: cell walls, mucus sheaths, pseudopods, flagella, cilia, contractile vacuoles, food vacuoles, chloroplasts, zygospores, nucleus, undulating membrane, oral groove, pellicle, micronucleus, macronucleus, cytostome, apical complex;

9 Compare and contrast fission and conjugation in the protists; and

10 Compare and contrast intermediate and definitive hosts, and which type of host is usually harmed more often by parasites.

The following are various groups of bacteria and protists. In lab today, we will primarily concentrate on identifying the organisms and their distinctive features, as well as examining the life cycles of selected specimens. You will use the following taxonomic scheme to identify a given specimen to a 'group.' The taxonomic classification of both bacteria and protists are still in a state of flux because we are still discovering more about the evolutionary relationships among these organisms. For this lab, you will need to know these descriptive groups or phyla and their representative genera.

Classification

Domain Archaea (prokaryotic organisms)

Domain Bacteria (prokaryotic organisms)

    Proteobacteria (mostly gram-negative bacteria) (*Escherichia*)

    Gram-positive Bacteria (*Bacillus*)

    Spirochetes (*Spirillum*)

    Cyanobacteria, or the autotrophic "blue-green" bacteria (*Anabaena*)

Domain Eukarya (eukaryotic organisms, including the protists, fungi, plants, and animals)

    "Kingdom Protista"

    Phylum Dinoflagellata (the dinoflagellates, *Ceratium*)

    Phylum Bacillariophyta (the diatoms)

    Phylum Chlorophyta (the green algae: *Volvox, Spirogyra*)

    Phylum Phaeophyta (the kelps or seaweeds, brown algae)

    Phylum Euglenophyta (the euglenoids, *Euglena*)

    Phylum Rhizopoda (the amebas, *Amoeba*)

    Phylum Kinetoplastida (the trypanosomes, *Trypanosoma*)

    Phylum Apicomplexa (the apicomplexans, *Plasmodium*)

    Phylum Ciliata (the ciliates, *Paramecium*)

Exercises

One domain of living things is called **Archaea.** The Archaea have a number of unique characteristics with respect to their cell walls and metabolism. Many are what we call **extremophiles:** extremophiles live in stressful environments of high temperatures (thermophiles), saltiness (halophiles), or low oxygen. We have no representatives in lab today.

The **Eubacteria** or **Bacteria** are a second 'domain' of life. The Bacteria and Archaea are prokaryotes. We will examine a number of bacteria in lab today.

Bacterial Cell Shapes

As you observe the following bacterial slides (under oil immersion, 1,000× total magnification), note the various shapes of bacteria. Some bacteria are in the form of elongated rods (singular: **bacillus;** plural: **bacilli**), some appear circular (singular: **coccus;** plural: **cocci**), and some are curved spiral shapes. A variety of spiral shapes exist: comma-shaped rods (*Vibrio*), a thick nonflexible spirillum (*Spirillum*), or a flexible corkscrew shape (spirochaetes). If you look at the icon figure for the chapter (found at the top of page 11–1), you will note the three basic shapes. Some bacteria come in long chains of bacteria (prefix **strepto-**), some bacteria form clusters (**staphylo-**) and some are found as connected pairs (**diplo-**). A streptococcus thus is a chain of spherical-shaped bacteria.

Exercise 11.1.

Proteobacteria

The Proteobacteria are a large group of gram-negative bacteria. Observe the slide labeled '*Escherichia coli*' at the demonstration table. **Be careful! These slides are under oil immersion or high power! Do not use the coarse focus knob!** Draw what you see in the space provided below (Figure 11.1).

The very short rods or cocci that you see in the *E. coli* slide are common inhabitants of the intestines of many animals, including you. You have probably heard of or read about 'fecal coliform bacteria contamination' of water. These are the bacteria they are talking about. Many strains are harmless (although a few *E. coli* strains can cause serious illnesses), but their presence indicates that other pathogenic bacteria may be present as well. Note that *E. coli* varies in shape from cocci to short rod (bacilli) shaped cells.

FIGURE 11.1.

E. coli.

Exercise 11.2.
Gram-Positive Bacteria

This large group of bacteria includes species that produce many common antibiotics (like *Streptomyces*). However, a number of gram-positive bacteria are pathogenic as well. Observe the *Bacillus subtilis* slide (or similar slide) at the demonstration table. Draw what you see under the scope in the space provided below (Figure 11.2).

FIGURE 11.2.

The gram-positive bacteria.

Exercise 11.3.
Spiral Shaped Bacteria

Observe the *Spirillum* slide (or similar spirochete) at the demonstration table. Draw what you see in the space provided below (Figure 11.3).

The spirochetes are helical, or spiral, in shape and move in a corkscrew-like fashion. Some are well-known pathogens, like *Treponema* (the bacterium that causes syphilis).

FIGURE 11.3.

A spirochete bacterium (*Spirilum*).

Exercise 11.4.

The Blue-Green Bacteria or Cyanobacteria

The cyanobacteria are prokaryotic organisms that are **autotrophs** (capable of photosynthesis). One example that you will look at today are *Anabaena*. The blue-green bacteria grow in many different environments: marine, freshwater, and moist soils. Some species are **endosymbionts** (live inside other unicellular organisms or inside other cells) of lichens, plants, and various protists. They possess chlorophyll *a* (like the eukaryotic plants) and several of the other pigment molecules involved in photosynthesis. Cyanobacteria do not have chloroplasts, instead, they have a number of organized internal membranes containing the compounds involved in photosynthesis. Although many cyanobacteria are bluish-green in color, some are brownish or greenish. Cyanobacteria reproduce by binary fission and they create a mucus sheath around them. They often form **colonies,** typically in long strands. A bacterial **colony** is a cluster of organisms descended from a single cell, and thus all are genetically identical. Blue-green bacteria do not have flagella, but instead they glide through the medium. Nitrogen fixation is the production of organic nitrogen compounds from atmospheric inorganic nitrogen gas, N_2; this process occurs in the **heterocysts,** which have a special thickened cell wall separating the cytoplasm of the heterocyst from the oxygen-rich environment (high levels of oxygen inhibit the process of nitrogen fixation). This ability to fix atmospheric nitrogen gives blue-green bacteria an advantage over the various algal groups that may live in the same environment, when nitrogen is limiting.

Observe the *Anabaena* slide (or some similar blue-green bacterium) under the microscope. Draw what you see in the space provided below (Figure 11.4). You may see three different shaped cells. Most of the cells are typical vegetative cells that undergo photosynthesis. The specialized cells with a clear center and a thick multilayered cell wall are the **heterocysts** (see Figure 11.5); nitrogen fixation occurs within these cells. Strands often break at the heterocysts, and binary fission increases the strands' lengths. You may see much larger cells (**spores** or akinetes) that can resist harsh environmental conditions (temperature, desiccation); when favorable conditions reappear, the spore excysts and a new vegetative strand of vegetative cells is produced by binary fission.

FIGURE 11.4.

The cyanobacterium *Anabaena.*

Exercise 11.5.

The Gram Stain

The **Gram stain** is one of the most common techniques used to help classify and identify bacteria. It is based on differences in the structure and chemical composition of cell walls. There are two distinct types of bacteria that can be identified with the Gram stain: **gram-positive** and **gram-negative** bacteria. See Figure 11.6, which describes the Gram stain.

First, a purple dye (crystal violet) is added to the bacteria, followed by iodine. Then alcohol is used to remove the stain (from the gram-negative bacteria). The gram-positive bacteria retain the crystal violet. A reddish counterstain (safranin) is then added, staining the gram-negative bacteria red.

Gram-positive bacteria have a large amount of a compound called **peptidoglycan** in their cell walls, which can trap the purple crystal violet dye so that the alcohol cannot wash it away. Gram-negative bacteria have little peptidoglycan in their cell walls, but they do possess an additional outer membrane of phospholipids as part of their cell wall. This outer membrane of the cell wall does not retain the purple dye, which is easily washed away by the alcohol rinse. Gram-positive bacteria thus will appear bluish-violet, whereas the gram-negative bacteria appear reddish to reddish orange.

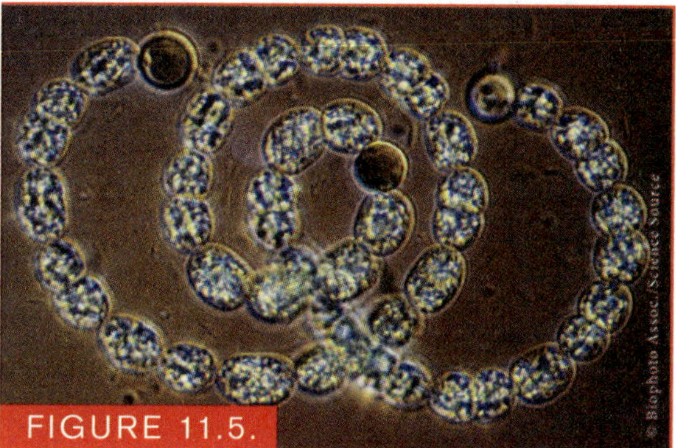

FIGURE 11.5.

Cyanobacteria.

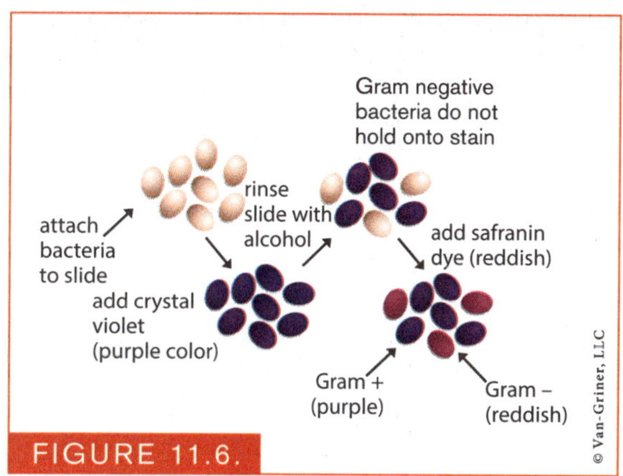

FIGURE 11.6.

Gram stain technique.

The gram-negative bacteria tend to be more pathogenic than the gram-positive bacteria because the outer membrane of the cell wall can be toxic and can prevent the movement of antibiotics and defensive compounds of their hosts into the bacteria.

What color are gram-negative bacteria?

What color are gram-positive bacteria?

Which type is generally considered more 'dangerous,' if you had an infection of one or the other type?

The Protists

The Eukarya is the third domain of living things. The domain Eukarya includes the protists, plants, fungi, and animals. **Protists** are unicellular, eukaryotic organisms. Many protists are aquatic, and some are parasites, living in the fluids and tissues of animal and plant hosts. These organisms are called eukaryotic ("true nucleus") because they have nuclei and membrane-bound organelles, as opposed to the less structurally complex prokaryotic organisms, the bacteria. Protists also show mitosis and meiosis, and are capable of both asexual and sexual reproduction. Eukaryotic protists go back in the fossil record at least 1.7 billion years.

The 'Algae'

We now will examine some of the unicellular autotrophic protists, collectively called the 'algae.' The algae is an artificial taxon not recognized by formal Linnean taxonomy. Algae live in a variety of habitats, and have both sexual and asexual reproduction. Many algae will form resistant spore-like resting stages that survive harsh environmental conditions.

Exercise 11.6.

Dinoflagellates

Dinoflagellates are primarily unicellular protists that live in marine and freshwater habitats. A few are endosymbiotes inside various protists and animals, including corals. The dinoflagellate cell wall is made of overlapping plates of cellulose, so dinoflagellates appear to possess 'armor.' They have a pair of dissimilar **flagella** by which they move in a sort of a whirling motion. These two flagella lie in two different, perpendicular **grooves** in the cell wall. The dinoflagellates often have arms or horns. The phenomenon called **'red tide'** is caused by a species of dinoflagellate. **Red tides** are dinoflagellate blooms that can be deadly to fish and many other organisms in shallow marine environments, due to toxins produced by the algae. Dinoflagellates are **autotrophic** (capable of photosynthesis), but they can act as **heterotrophs** (heterotrophs feed upon other organisms by predation or parasitism) by engulfing other small organisms. This ability to switch from autotrophy to heterotrophy for energy and/or carbon needs is called **mixotrophy.**

Observe the dinoflagellate *Ceratium* slide under high power and draw what you see in the space provided below (Figure 11.7). Use Figure 11.8 to guide you.

FIGURE 11.7.

The dinoflagellate *Ceratium*.

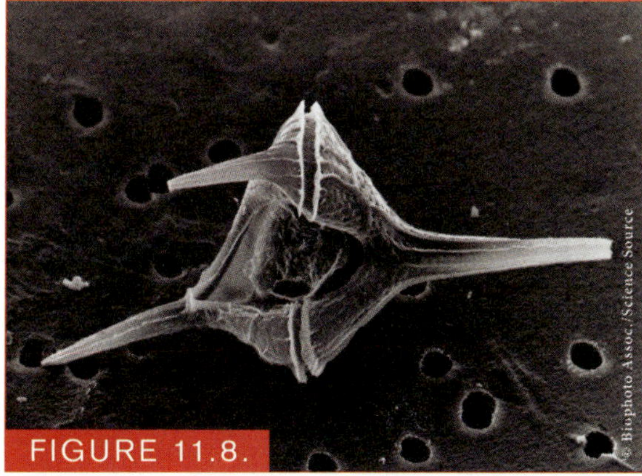

FIGURE 11.8.

The dinoflagellate *Ceratium*.

Exercise 11.7.

Diatoms

Diatoms (in the Phylum **Bacillariophyta**) are unicellular algae that are found in marine and fresh-water habitats, as well as in moist soils. They possess chlorophyll *a* and various xanthophyll pigments, which give them a golden color (they are sometimes called the 'golden-brown algae'). They have a **hard outer cell wall** made of **silicon dioxide,** or glass, and **calcium carbonates.** Diatoms often look like little disks, although some more resemble spines. The cell walls are often paired and overlapping, reminiscent of the two halves of a Petri dish.

Observe the slide marked 'diatoms' under the microscope and draw what you see in the space provided below (Figure 11.9). Use the figure of diatoms depicted in Figure 11.10 to guide you.

FIGURE 11.9.

Diatoms.

FIGURE 11.10.

Diatoms.

Exercise 11.8.

Chlorophyta

The **Chlorophyta,** or green algae, are either solitary unicellular species or they form **colonies** consisting of semi-independent cells. The green algae contain chlorophylls *a* and *b* and store starches for food (similar to the nonvascular and vascular land plants, which we will cover later). Most green algae live in freshwater habitats, but some green algae are marine. In addition, some species live in moist soils or are attached to moist rocks and tree trunks. Some of the lichens contain green algae instead of blue-green bacteria, and some chlorophytes are endosymbionts living within various protists and animals.

Volvox form hollow, spherical colonies composed of hundreds to thousands of haploid, biflagellated cells (vegetative cells) that have cytoplasmic connections between adjacent cells. The cells divide by mitosis, and the colony gets larger over time. The flagella extend outward, and as they beat, the colony moves around. For the most part, the cells are independent of each other; each cell has a cup-shaped chloroplastid. The cells are embedded in a gelatinous matrix. Throughout the spring and summer, *Volvox* produces daughter colonies asexually by mitosis (Figure 11.12, Figure 11.13). Daughter colonies develop within the parent colony and are released when the parent colony ruptures.

Volvox also reproduces sexually as well (Figure 11.12). Special germ cells undergo meiosis and produce haploid gametes. A germ cell produces either a number of motile sperm or a single large nonmotile egg. The sperm swim to and fuse with the eggs, forming a diploid **zygote.** The zygote enlarges and forms a spiny-walled **zygospore,** which will be released when the parent colony disintegrates later in autumn (Figure 11.12). The zygospore overwinters. In the spring, inside the zygospore, the diploid cell will undergo meiosis to produce haploid **spores;** these spores will leave the zygospore and produce new colonies.

Volvox is an example of the green algal group called the **Chlorophyta.** Examine the slide marked 'Volvox' under the microscope. Draw what you see in the space provided below (Figure 11.11). Use Figure 11.12 and Figure 11.13 to guide you. If you see daughter colonies, make certain to identify them. Look closely at the slides: if you can identify zygotes, eggs and sperm packets, or zygospores, sketch them as well.

FIGURE 11.11.

Volvox, an example of a green alga.

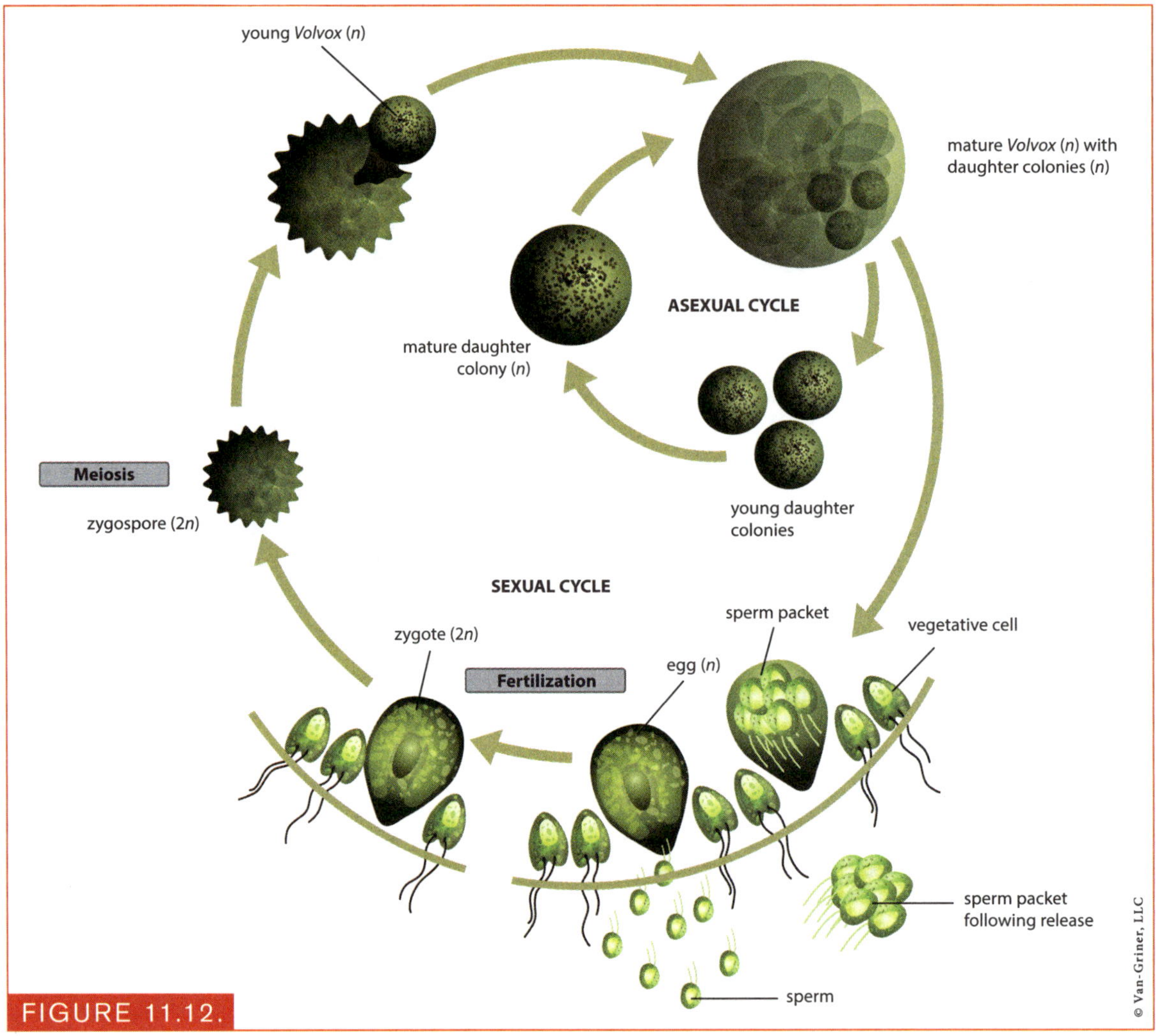

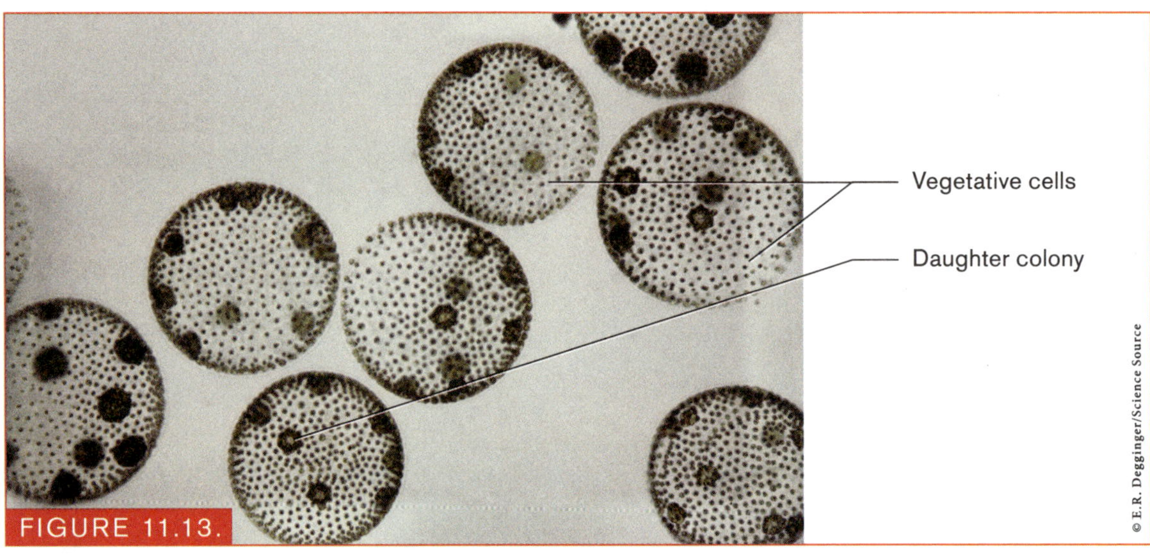

FIGURE 11.12.

The life cycle of the green alga *Volvox*.

FIGURE 11.13.

Asexual reproduction in the green alga *Volvox*.

Exercise 11.9.

Spirogyra

Spirogyra forms a mucus-like coating of pectins, similar to the cyanobacteria and the other green algae. The life cycle of *Spirogyra* is shown in Figure 11.15. *Spirogyra* forms nonmotile gametes. *Spirogyra* undergoes sexual reproduction using a process called **conjugation.** At the beginning of conjugation, two haploid filaments of opposite mating types (+ and –) line up side by side. Each cell then forms an extension that grows toward a cell on the opposite strand. The tubes fuse, forming the **conjugation tube.** The contents of the cells of the (–) strain travel through the tube and fuse with the cytoplasm of the cells of the (+) strain. The protoplasts (the entire living portion of the cell) of each individual organism thus act as an **"isogamete."** Unlike sperm and ova, isogametes are gametes that are indistinguishable in form, size, or behavior from another gamete with which it will fuse.

The resulting diploid zygote develops the **zygospore.** The zygospore has a tough resistant outer covering within the chambers of the (+) strain filament. The zygospore is released when the strands disintegrate, and the zygospores settle to the bottom of the stream in the fall. After winter is over, the zygote inside the zygospore undergoes meiosis.

When the zygospore undergoes meiosis, three of the four haploid nuclei disintegrate inside the zygospore. A spore cell containing the remaining haploid nucleus will leave the zygospore when it germinates, and a new filament develops from this cell from mitotic division.

Under the microscope, examine the slide labeled 'Spirogyra' and draw what you see in the space provided below, using Figure 11.15 to guide you. *Spirogyra* is a long filamentous green alga found on the surface of ponds, composed of a chain of elongated cells. Inside each cell is a long spiral of **chloroplastids** surrounding a large **vacuole.** The bead-like structures on a chloroplast are called **pyrenoids;** pyrenoids are sites of starch synthesis. The chloroplasts, nucleus, and the rest of the organelles are in a thin layer of cytoplasm sandwiched between the vacuole and the outer plasma membrane and cell wall. In addition, examine the slide labeled 'conjugation' and draw what you see on the slide in the space below (Figure 11.14).

FIGURE 11.14.

Spirogyra filaments (left), and *Spirogyra* conjugation (right).

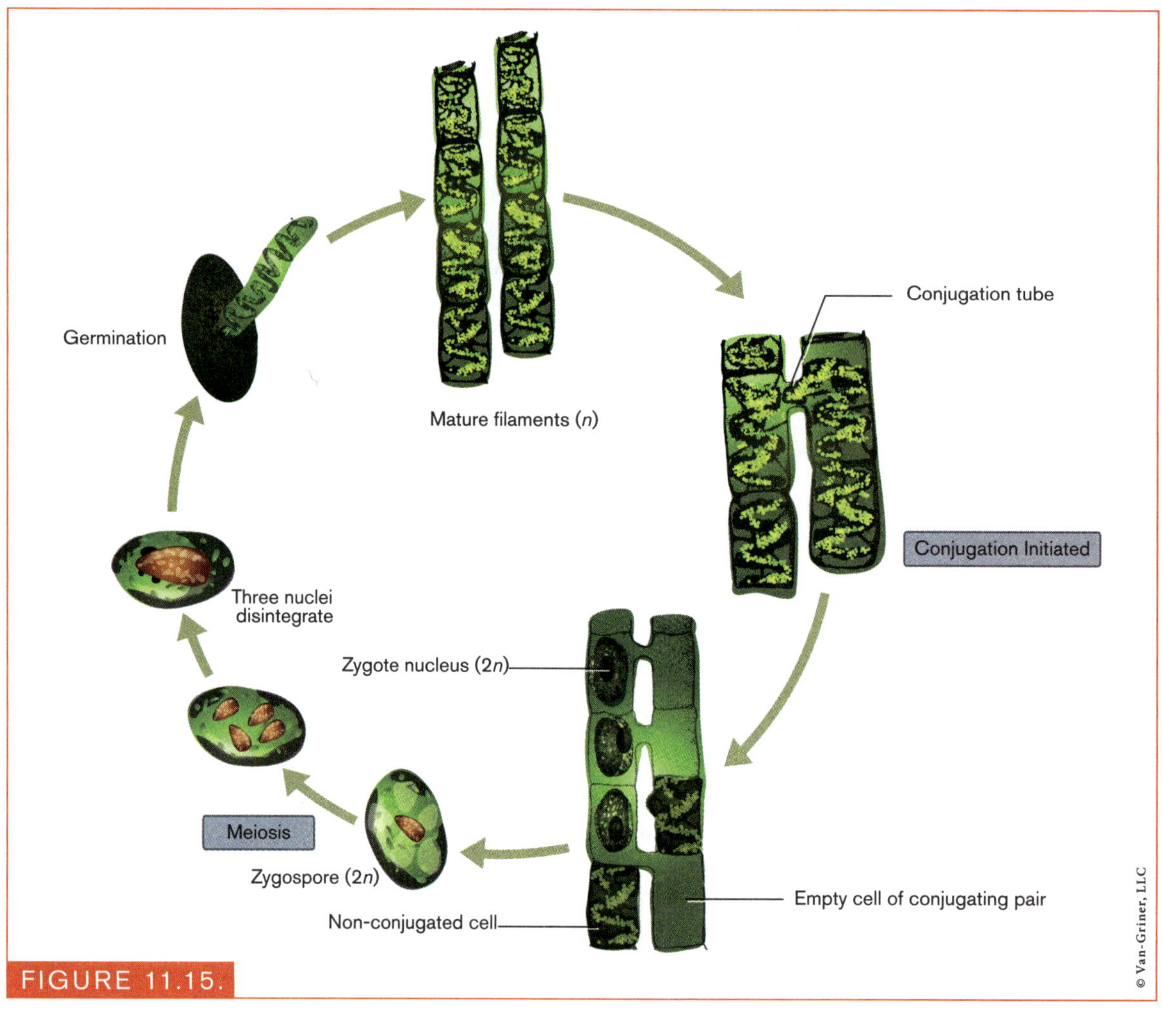

FIGURE 11.15.

The life cycle of the green alga *Spirogyra*.

Exercise 11.10.

The Kelps

The largest of the protists are the kelps or seaweeds, in the phylum **Phaeophyta** (brown algae). All of the species are **multicellular** and all are **autotrophic** (contain chlorophylls and undergo photosynthesis), and are found in shallow marine habitats.

The life cycle of the kelps is shown in Figure 11.17. It is similar to that of the plants, which we will cover in a few weeks. The diploid **sporophyte** has **sporangia** (meiosporangia) on the blades. Inside the sporangia, **meiosis** produces haploid flagellated **zoospores** (these zoospores are a type of spore called a **meiospore,** indicating that they are produced by the process of meiosis). Half of the spores produce a small haploid **male gametophyte** that are attached to rocks, and the other half of the spores produce a **female gametophyte.** Flagellated **sperm** (produced mitotically inside **antheridia** on the male gametophyte) swim and fertilize the haploid **eggs** found inside the **oogonium** on a **female gametophyte.** The diploid **zygote** then undergoes mitosis, producing the multicellular kelp sporophyte that stays attached to the female gametophyte until it develops holdfasts and stipes.

Kelps have a large body (**thallus**), with tissues and organs analogous to similar structures in plants: **holdfasts,** stem-like **stipes** and leaf-like **blades,** and air bladder **floats** (Figure 11.18). The gas-filled bladders help hold the blades close to the surface for photosynthesis, whereas the holdfasts hold the protist in place, despite the rough, turbulent, marine intertidal zones in which these organisms live. Some kelps form large 'forests' that are analogous to terrestrial forests with tall trees; kelps may extend up to 80 meters from the ocean bottom towards the surface. The kelps thus produce a large three-dimensional structure in which a variety of organisms live. Kelp is used for a variety of commercial products, including thickeners for many brands of ice cream, jellies, salad dressings, and toothpaste; as flavorings and vegetables for soups; and for other uses.

> Examine the various kelp examples displayed on the demonstration table. Draw what you see in the space below (Figure 11.16) labeling thallus, stipe, blade, holdfast, and bladders.

FIGURE 11.16.

The kelps.

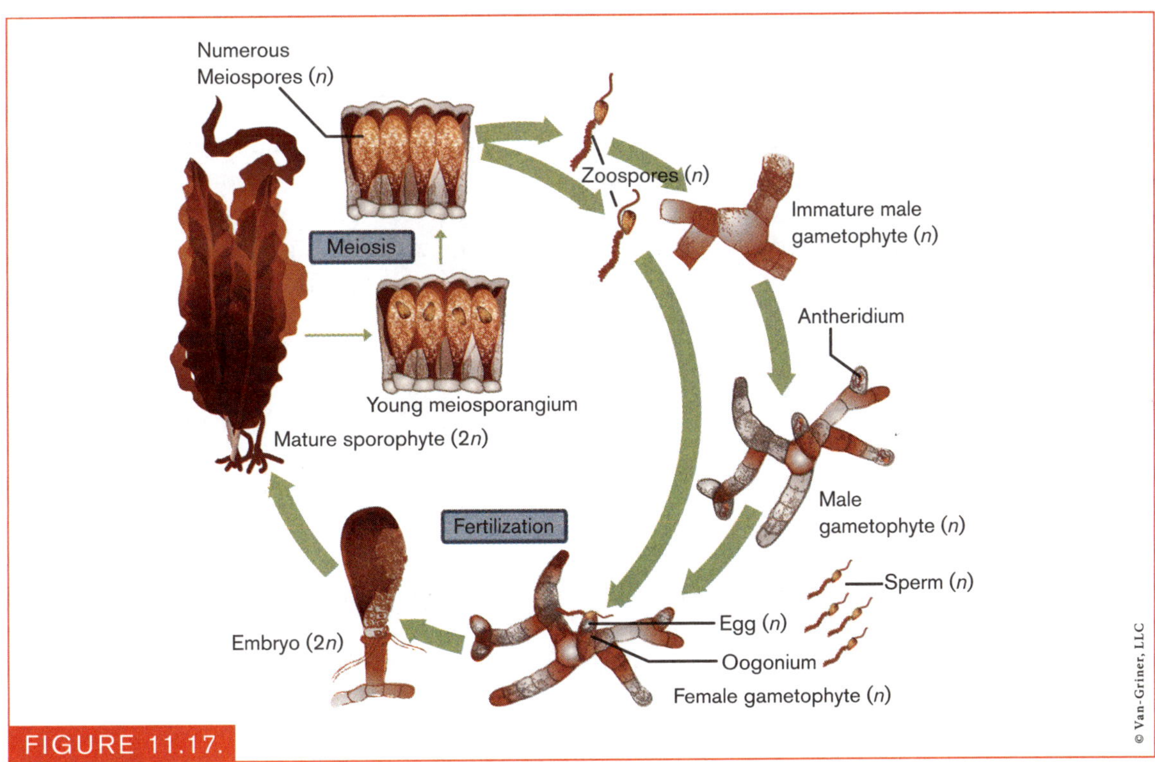

FIGURE 11.17.

The life cycle of the brown algae *Laminaria* (kelps).

FIGURE 11.18.

The basic body plan of a brown alga (a kelp).

The 'Protozoa'

We now will examine some of the typical unicellular animal-like protists that are lumped together as an artificial taxon referred to as the **Protozoa** (or 'first-animal'), or the animal-like unicellular organisms. Some organisms, like the slime molds, are fungi-like organisms, but these organisms are more closely related to amoebas. Although the terms 'protozoa' and 'algae' no longer have a formal Linnean taxonomic significance, the terms still have a generic usefulness in everyday speech.

Exercise 11.11.
Phylum Euglenophyta:
The Euglenoids

Euglena are small, perhaps several hundred microns in length. They possess typically two flagella; one of them is at the anterior end and is longer; the other is shorter and does not protrude out of the body. The euglenoids typically produce a unique form of starch called **paramylon.** Euglenoids have a **stigma** (eyespot), found next to the base of the anterior flagella. The eyespot is composed of a small amount of reddish pigment; along with some light sensitive crystals, the eyespot acts as a primitive eye. The pellicle in euglenoids is composed of proteinaceous strips beneath the plasma membrane; the pellicle supports the membrane. Euglenoids reproduce asexually by binary fission. Many of the euglenoids are photosynthetic, but they can be facultatively heterotrophic, like *Euglena* (i.e., they are mixotrophic). In the absence of light, they prey upon other small organisms.

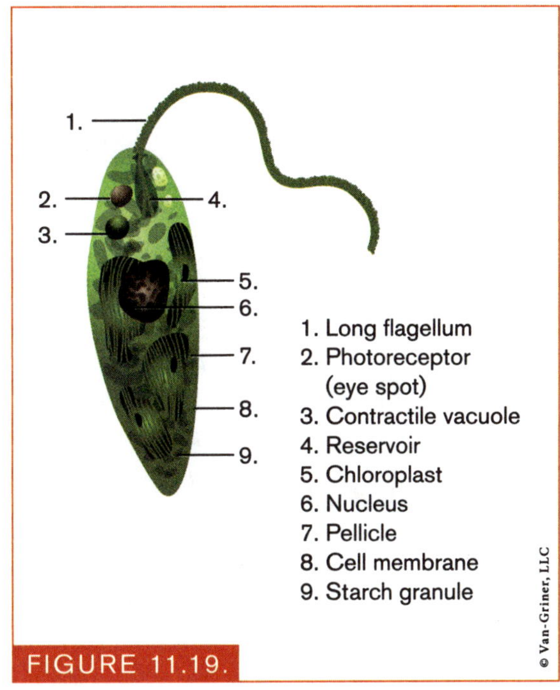

FIGURE 11.19.

The euglenoid *Euglena.*

View the preserved slide labeled "*Euglena.*" Draw what you see in the space provided below (Figure 11.20). Use Figure 11.19 to guide you.

FIGURE 11.20.

Euglena.

Exercise 11.12.

View the preserved slide specimen of *Amoeba proteus.* *Amoeba* is an example of the Phylum **Rhizopoda** (the amoebas). The amoebas are unicellular and move by using pseudopodia. They are found in freshwater and marine habitats, and in moist soils. A few are important parasites of humans and other organisms (for example, *Entamoeba histolytica*, the cause of amebic dysentery). The free-living species are predators or scavengers, feeding on bacteria, other protistans, and on detritus. Many amoebas can form cysts that allow them to withstand times of drought.

Amoeba use pseudopodia for movement and for capturing food. **Food vacuoles** form by a process of **phagocytosis,** where the cell surrounds its prey with pseudopodia, which subsequently fuse together. The prey and some water is then enclosed by cytoplasm, forming the food vacuole. Digestive enzymes are inside small vacuoles, called **lysosomes.** The lysosomes fuse with food vacuoles, and the prey are digested. Digested molecules then diffuse out of the food vacuole into the cytoplasm (this form of digestion is referred to as **intracellular digestion**). In addition, look to see if you can find any large, clear **contractile vacuoles.** The contractile vacuoles are used to expel excess water from the freshwater species. Proton pumps in the vacuole membrane pump protons by active transport, and bicarbonate (produced from water and carbon dioxide) using co-transport. Water then passively diffuses into the vacuole. The vacuole swells, makes contact, and then fuses with the outer cell membrane, expelling the water.

The amoebas have been preserved (fixed) to the slide and stained with certain dyes (thus they appear red or blue). Draw a few amoebas in the space below (Figure 11.21). Use Figure 11.23 to guide you. You should be able to see the **nucleus,** one or two **contractile vacuoles, food vacuoles, pseudopodia, and the outer cell membrane (plasmalemma).** In addition, observe the demonstration model.

FIGURE 11.21.

Amoeba.

Exercise 11.13.

View a live *Amoeba proteus* by making a wet mount. Go to the side table and obtain a slide. Use a pipette to remove a few drops of the culture medium at the bottom of the culture jar. Put a drop of the medium on your slide (use a depression side) and place a coverslip on top. View under low power (100× total magnification) and high power (400×) and view with subdued light, by adjusting the iris diaphragm to minimize the amount of light passing through the specimen. If you view live protozoans with the iris opened to maximum, you will quickly kill the organisms from the intense heat generated in the water. Draw a few amoebas in the space below (Figure 11.22). Estimate their size. Do the preserved and live specimens appear similar?

FIGURE 11.22.

Amoeba wet mount.

Watch the *Amoeba* for several minutes. You should be able to observe both the **ectoplasm** (the peripheral rim of stiff cytoplasm just under the cell membrane) and the more fluid, mobile **endoplasm.** The endoplasm should be streaming into some pseudopodia, which will then increase in length. Endoplasm is converted into ectoplasm at the tip of the pseudopodium, causing it to be anchored in place. Elsewhere, ectoplasm is converted into endoplasm.

Can you detect any moving cytoplasm? Where is it going? Are two or more pseudopodia forming? Does there seem to be a 'front' end and a 'rear' end to *Amoeba?* Do pseudopodia lead or follow? How are pseudopodia withdrawn back into the cell body? Are there any organelles in the ectoplasm?

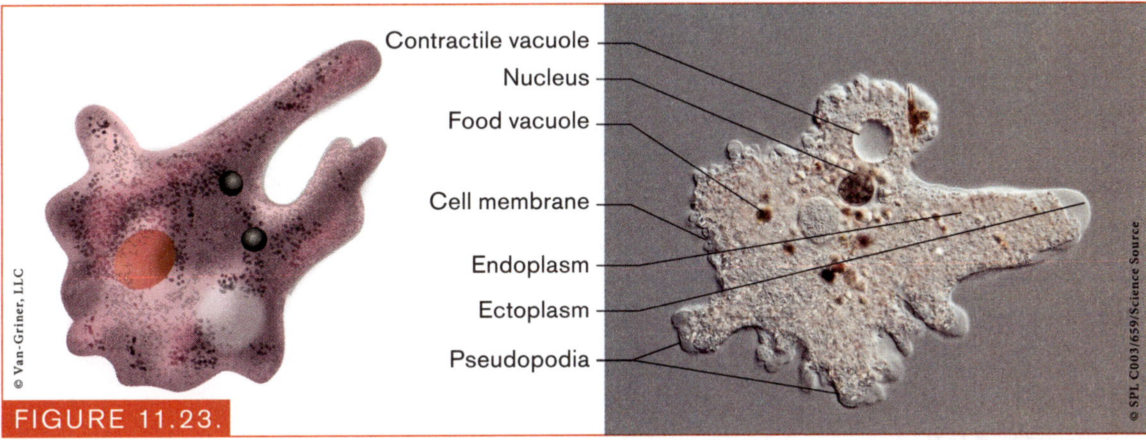

FIGURE 11.23.

The Rhizopod *Amoeba.*

Exercise 11.14.

Trypanosoma is an example of the Phylum **Kinetoplastida,** which includes the **flagellates.** Flagellates have one or more flagella. The undulation of the flagella propels the protozoan through the water.

View the prepared slide of *Trypanosoma* under high power (400× total magnification) and draw what you see in the space provided below (Figure 11.24). Use Figure 11.25 to guide you. Note the 'waviness' of the organism (the **undulating membrane**). The undulating membrane is the flagellum and portion of the cell membrane connected to the flagellum. The nucleus is centrally located. The flagellum arises from the centriole (the **kinetosome**) located at the anterior end. The **kinetoplast** is found near the kinetosome. The large single mitochondrion arises from the kinetoplast. Most of the cells in the slide are red blood cells (about 7.5 µm in diameter), but you may also find several large cells with large nuclei (white blood cells). How long is the trypanosome?

FIGURE 11.24.

Trypanosomes.

Trypanosomes cause a variety of serious parasitic diseases, especially in the tropics. *Trypanosoma gambiense* (*T. brucei gambiense*) causes the disease **sleeping sickness.** It is transmitted from one animal to another (including humans) by the bite from the tsetse fly (*Glossina*), a large biting fly that feeds on vertebrate blood. Trypanosomes live in the blood and absorb nutrients directly across their cell membranes. View the slide under high power. The lab instructor will have a slide under oil immersion at the demonstration table. You can break the objective as well as the slide, so be careful!

1. Platelet
2. Nucleus
3. Kinetosome and kinetoplast
4. Undulating membrane

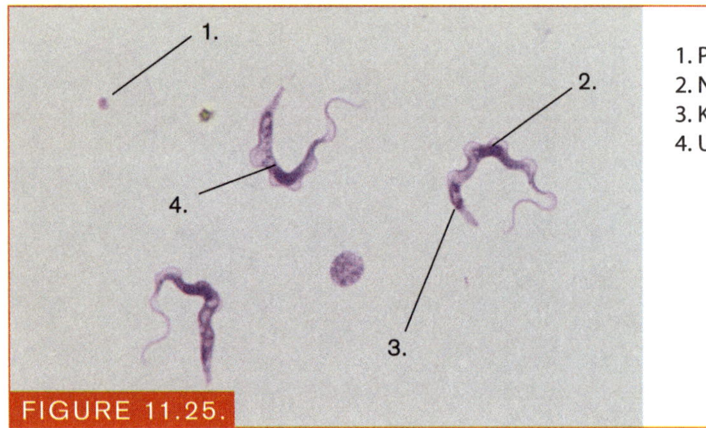

FIGURE 11.25.

The flagellate parasite *Trypanosoma*.

Exercise 11.15.

1 Observe a field of 100 red blood cells and determine the number of trypanosomes within the area containing the 100 red blood cells.

2 Divide the number of trypanosomes observed by the number of red blood cells observed (100); this gives you an estimate of the number of trypanosomes per red blood cell (rbc).

3 Determine the **total parasitic load** (the total number of parasites in the human body) from this estimate.

total parasitic load (number of trypanosomes / human) =
(number of trypanosomes / rbc) × (5,000,000 rbcs / mm³ of blood) ×
(1,000,000 mm³ / liter) × (5 liters of blood / human)

What is your estimate? _______________________________ trypanosomes per human

There are several assumptions to this technique. Make a list of what you think are the assumptions and check with your lab instructor.

Exercise 11.16.

View the *Plasmodium* slide under high power (your lab instructor will also set up some slides under oil immersion). Draw what you see in the space below (Figure 11.26). Use Figure 11.27 to guide you. **BE CAREFUL! DO NOT USE THE COARSE FOCUS UNDER OIL IMMERSION!**

FIGURE 11.26.

The malarial parasite *Plasmodium,* inside red blood cells.

Plasmodium is an example of the phylum **Apicomplexa.** The apicomplexans all have an **apical complex.** The apical complex is a group of organelles used to penetrate host cells. The apicomplexans do not have any known means of locomotion, other than perhaps a slight undulation of the cell. The apicomplexans are all parasites, different species are found in many different animals and plants. Several species of *Plasmodium* cause the most prevalent human parasitic disease on Earth: **malaria.**

Part of the life cycle occurs in the female mosquitoes of certain species (male mosquitoes feed only on plants), and part of the life cycle occurs in humans or other animals. The mosquito bites a human and injects **sporozoites** with her saliva. The sporozoites travel through the circulatory system and enter into liver cells, where they undergo mitosis (asexual reproduction) and produce hundreds of **trophozoites.** (Some malarial parasites can reside in the liver for some time, causing a relapse years later after the initial infection). The trophozoites leave the liver and enter into human red blood cells (rbcs), where the parasite feeds and reproduces asexually, forming up to two dozen daughter trophozoites mitotically. Eventually, the trophozoites cause the cell to lyse, and the trophozoites then infect new rbcs. In the rbcs, the trophozoites feed on hemoglobin. The periodic cycle of fevers and chills (occurring every two to three days, depending on species) characteristic of malaria comes from the periodic, cyclical pattern of rbc infection, lysis, and reinfection caused by the trophozoites.

Some of the trophozoites will form **gametocytes,** instead of trophozoites. If these gametocytes are sucked up by another mosquito, they are passed to the insect's digestive tract and become active, forming gametes. A female gametocyte will form an egg, while a male gametocyte will form several sperm. A sperm fuses with an egg and forms a zygote, called the **ookinete.** The ookinete undergoes meiosis and produces haploid nuclei. The ookinete embeds itself into the wall of the mosquito's stomach, forming the **oocyst.** Inside the oocyst, the zygote's haploid nuclei undergo mitosis to produce numerous haploid sporozoites. The sporozoites leave the oocyst and move to the mosquito's salivary glands, ready to be injected into another human host.

The trophozoites look like blobs or rings inside the rbc. Note that the two human parasites you have seen today live in blood, but in different microenvironments. *Plasmodium* is an **intracellular** parasite, whereas the trypanosome is an **extracellular** parasite.

There are thus two distinct hosts in the malarial life cycle: the human host (called the **intermediate host,** in which the parasite undergoes asexual reproduction) and the insect host (called the **definitive host,** in which the parasite undergoes sexual reproduction, with fertilization and meiosis).

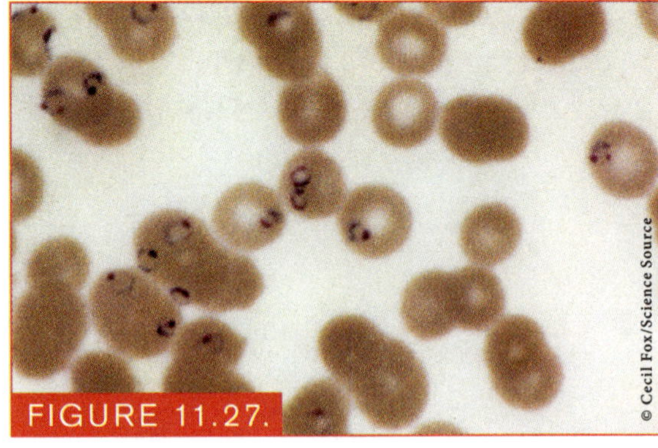

Plasmodium merozoites inside red blood cells.

Study the life cycle of the malarial parasite *Plasmodium*, at the demonstration table and in Figure 11.29 below. Draw the life cycle in the space provided below (Figure 11.28). Which host is the definitive host? Which host is the intermediate host? Why does it matter?

The malarial parasite *Plasmodium*.

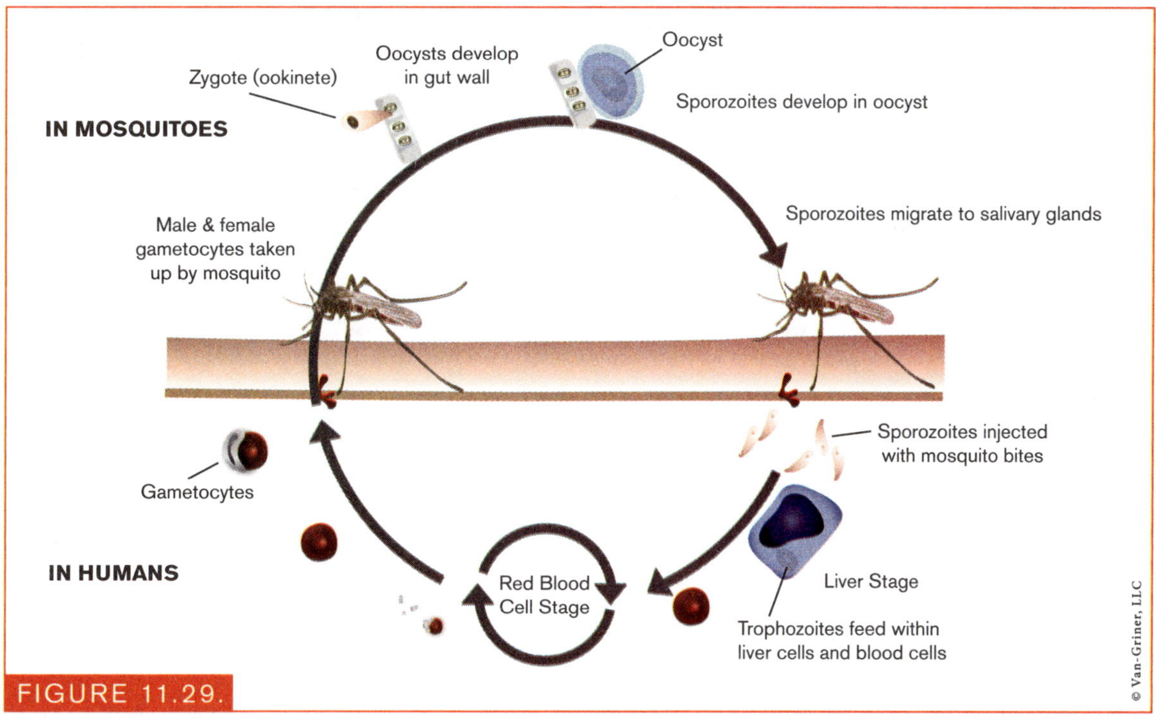

FIGURE 11.29.

The life cycle of the apicomplexan *Plasmodium*.

Exercise 11.17.

You can estimate the total parasitic load of *Plasmodium* by determining the fraction of red blood cells infested and inserting this number in the equation you used for the trypanosome infection (Exercise 11.15). For example, if 4 percent of the red blood cells are infected with a parasite, then about 1 trillion parasites (1×10^{12}) are present in the blood.

Number of malarial parasites within a human's blood: ___________________________________

There are several assumptions to this method of determining the number of malarial parasites. List these assumptions and check with your lab instructor.

Exercise 11.18.

Paramecium is the classic example of the phylum **Ciliata.** Ciliates move by **ciliary action,** where hundreds of cilia beat in a coordinated fashion, like many oars of a boat, propelling the organism. If you focus up and down through the body of *Paramecium,* you can just barely observe (by adjusting the diaphragm) the fuzzy **cilia** covering the entire body of the protozoan. In ciliates, the **pellicle** is a rigid outer covering outside of the cell membrane, providing some support and protection. The cilia protrude through the pellicle. You will be able to see one or more **micronuclei** (involved in sexual reproduction and conjugation), the large **macronucleus** (involved in asexual reproduction and control of the daily activity of the cell), and the **oral groove** (that leads to the **cytostome,** or mouth), which will not be visible. You may be able to see a **contractile vacuole,** as well **food vacuoles,** in some specimens.

View the prepared slide of *Paramecium* (either *P. caudatum* or *P. multimicronucleatum*) under low and high power (40× and 100× total magnification) and draw what you see under the scope in the space below (Figure 11.30). In addition, observe the demonstration model and make a sketch of the model, labeling the major structures.

FIGURE 11.30.

Paramecium.

Exercise 11.19.

Make a wet mount and observe live *Paramecium*. Go to the side table and obtain a small drop from the culture bottle. Place this drop on a depression slide. View under subdued light at low and high power (100× and 400× total magnification). Observe the *Paramecium* for a while and draw what you see in the space below (Figure 11.31).

FIGURE 11.31.

Paramecium.

Can you 'see' the ciliary action? Does *Paramecium* rotate as it moves? Can it back up? What happens when it encounters another object?

How long would it take for the *Paramecium* to travel across the field of view at 100×?

By using a stopwatch or your wristwatch, you can estimate the speed the protozoan moves. If the ciliate is moving too quickly for you to observe its behavior, you can add a drop of Protoslo [methyl cellulose] to the slide.

$$\frac{\text{The diameter of the field of view (in microns)}}{\text{The time (in seconds) to travel across the field of view}} = \textbf{speed} \text{ (microns per second)} = \underline{\hspace{2cm}}$$

$$\frac{\text{Field diameter} = \underline{\hspace{2cm}} \text{ μm}}{\text{time} = \underline{\hspace{2cm}} \text{ sec}} = \underline{\hspace{2cm}} \text{microns per second}$$

Exercise 11.20.

There are two distinct modes of reproduction in protozoans (and protists in general): sexual and asexual.

Fission. Asexual reproduction in *Paramecium*, *Amoeba*, *Trypanosoma*, *Plasmodium*, and other protists is often by **fission** (= binary fission). Fission is where the nucleus undergoes mitosis, and the cell subsequently divides into two by cytokinesis.

Conjugation. Conjugation is one form of sexual reproduction, where two protozoans exchange genetic material, in a fashion analogous to the fusion of two gametes in higher plants and animals. This process is also similar to the one observed in the algae. Conjugation is common in the ciliates; we will now discuss conjugation in the ciliate *Paramecium*. Two *Paramecium* of different mating strains meet, and they temporarily fuse at the oral groove. A micronucleus (originally diploid) undergoes a complex series of meiotic and mitotic events, and the cells eventually exchange haploid micronuclei. The two *Paramecium* then separate, and inside each, two haploid micronuclei fuse (one micronucleus is from that protozoan, and the other micronucleus is one provided by the partner). Each partner then eventually undergoes a series of cell divisions, producing daughter cells.

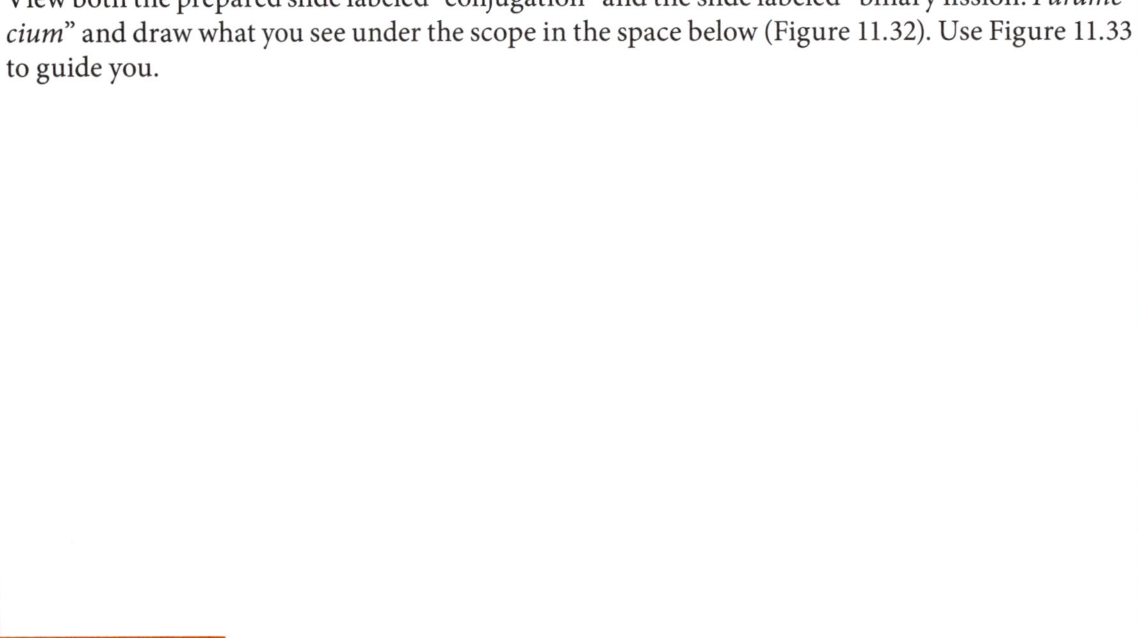

View both the prepared slide labeled "conjugation" and the slide labeled "binary fission: *Paramecium*" and draw what you see under the scope in the space below (Figure 11.32). Use Figure 11.33 to guide you.

FIGURE 11.32.

Binary fission (left) and conjugation (right) in the ciliate *Paramecium*.

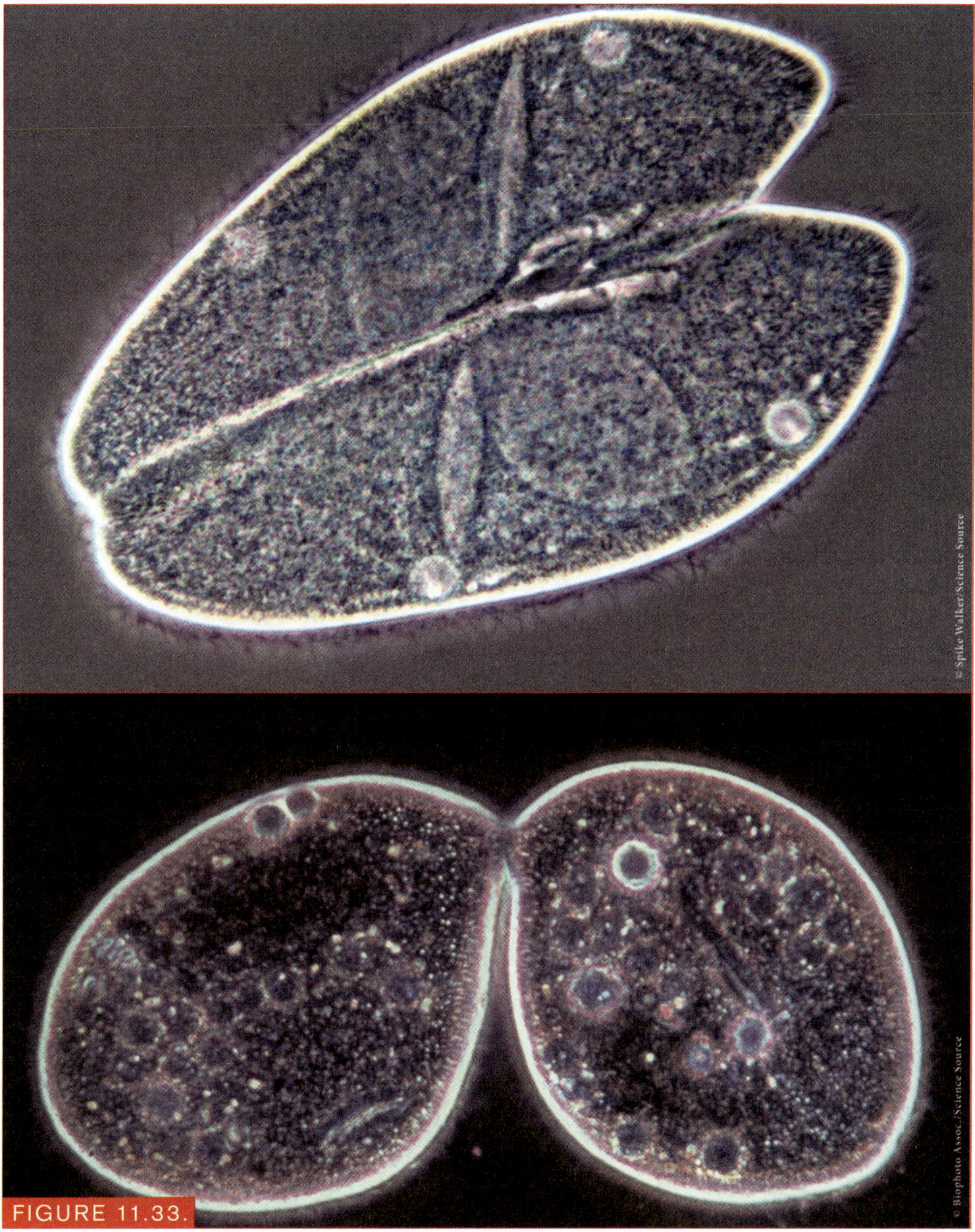

FIGURE 11.33.

Conjugation (top) and binary fission (bottom) in *Paramecium.*

Plants I. Bryophytes and Ferns

Keywords

gametophyte	phyllidium	peristome	pinna
archegonium	rhizoid	operculum	pinnule
antheridium	cuticle	chlorophyllous cells	rachis
gametangium	stoma (stomata)	hyaline cells	petiole
gametophore	foot	epidermis	fiddlehead
spore	seta	cortex	frond
gamete	capsule	xylem	sporophyll
sporangium	venter	phloem	root
sporophyte	stalk	meristems	sorus
protonema	neck	prothallium	indusium
caulidium	paraphysis	rhizome	annulus

Learning Objectives

When finished with this unit, you should be able to:

1. Discuss the concept of alternation of generations;

2. Describe the distinguishing characteristics of the mosses;

3. Describe the distinguishing characteristics of the ferns;

4. Identify representative samples of bryophytes and ferns; and

5. Describe the life cycle of a moss and a fern. Include in your description the following terms: gametophyte, sporophyte, spores, gametes, haploid, diploid, meiosis, mitosis.

Classification

Kingdom Plantae

    The nonvascular plants

        Division Bryophyta (mosses) *Sphagnum, Polytrichum*

    The seedless vascular plants

        Division Pterophyta (ferns)

The Nonvascular Plants: The Mosses

We will examine the mosses in today's lab as our example of the nonvascular plants (collectively called the bryophytes). Because they are nonvascular, most bryophytes are found in moist, shaded, terrestrial habitats. A few species are aquatic. Mosses and the other bryophytes are small; most of them are shorter than 15 cm in height, in part because they lack vascular tissues. Because they lack vascular tissues, all nonvascular plants have to be close to the water or to the ground.

Like the higher plants, the nonvascular plants have a **sporic** life cycle (see Figure 8.9 back in Unit 8) exhibiting a discrete alternation between **sporophytic** (diploid) and **gametophytic** (haploid) generations. The gametophytic and sporophytic phases of the bryophytes are easily distinguishable. The gametophyte is considered the dominant life cycle stage in the bryophytes because it generally lives longer (gametophytes live for years, while sporophytes live for a few months), and the gametophyte is somewhat larger in size than the sporophyte. Both sporophyte and gametophyte generations are always multicellular. Unlike the vascular plants, no true vascular tissues are generally found in either the bryophyte gametophytes or sporophytes, although a few mosses have some water-conducting tubes.

The **gametophytes** stay close to the ground, in part to aid the movement of the flagellated sperm to swim from the **antheridium** to the **archegonium.** Multicellular **gametangia,** an evolutionary advancement over the unicellular gametangia of the algae, are present in bryophytes. The gametangia develop on the gametophytes; archegonia and antheridia produce **gametes** by mitosis. The gametangia, particularly the archegonia, also house and protect the gametes. An **embryo** develops after fertilization within the archegonium; the embryo develops into the **sporophyte.** Throughout its existence, the bryophyte sporophyte remains attached to and is dependent upon the gametophyte for nutrients and moisture. When mature, **sporangia** form on the sporophyte. The sporangia give rise to haploid **spores** via meiosis. Released spores germinate to produce the gametophyte, thus completing the typical bryophyte life cycle (see Figure 12.1).

Similarities with the Algae

Like the green algae, bryophytes also:

1. Possess **chlorophyll *a*** and **chlorophyll *b*,**

2. Use **starch** as their main form of energy storage,

3. Use **cellulose** in cell walls, and

4. Use **motile sperm.**

Advances over the Unicellular Algae

The bryophytes exhibit several advancements over the algae. These advancements, listed below, allowed plants to colonize land:

1. **Meristems.** A plant cannot move around in the terrestrial environment. However, its roots and shoots and leaves can be produced when needed by layers of mitotically active tissues, called meristems.

2. **Alternation of generations.** Although some algae also show this trait, the alternation between separate multicellular 'adult' stages is more pronounced in the bryophytes and the higher plants. The two main adult stages are the haploid **gametophytes** (which produce gametes) and the diploid **sporophytes** (which produces spores).

3. **The nourishment and protection of diploid embryos by parent plants.** The diploid embryos are protected and receive nourishment from earlier generations. In the bryophytes, the young diploid multicellular sporophyte is retained and nourished by the female gametophyte.

4. **Multicellular sporangia.** On the sporophytes, multicellular sporangia produce many haploid spores via meiosis. The sporangia release the spores (meiospores); the spores have the capability to resist extremes in environmental conditions (like drought, extreme heat or cold).

5. **Multicellular gametangia.** Gametes are produced and stored inside these multicellular structures on the gametophytes. In bryophytes and the higher plants, the female gametophytes retain the eggs instead of releasing them into the environment.

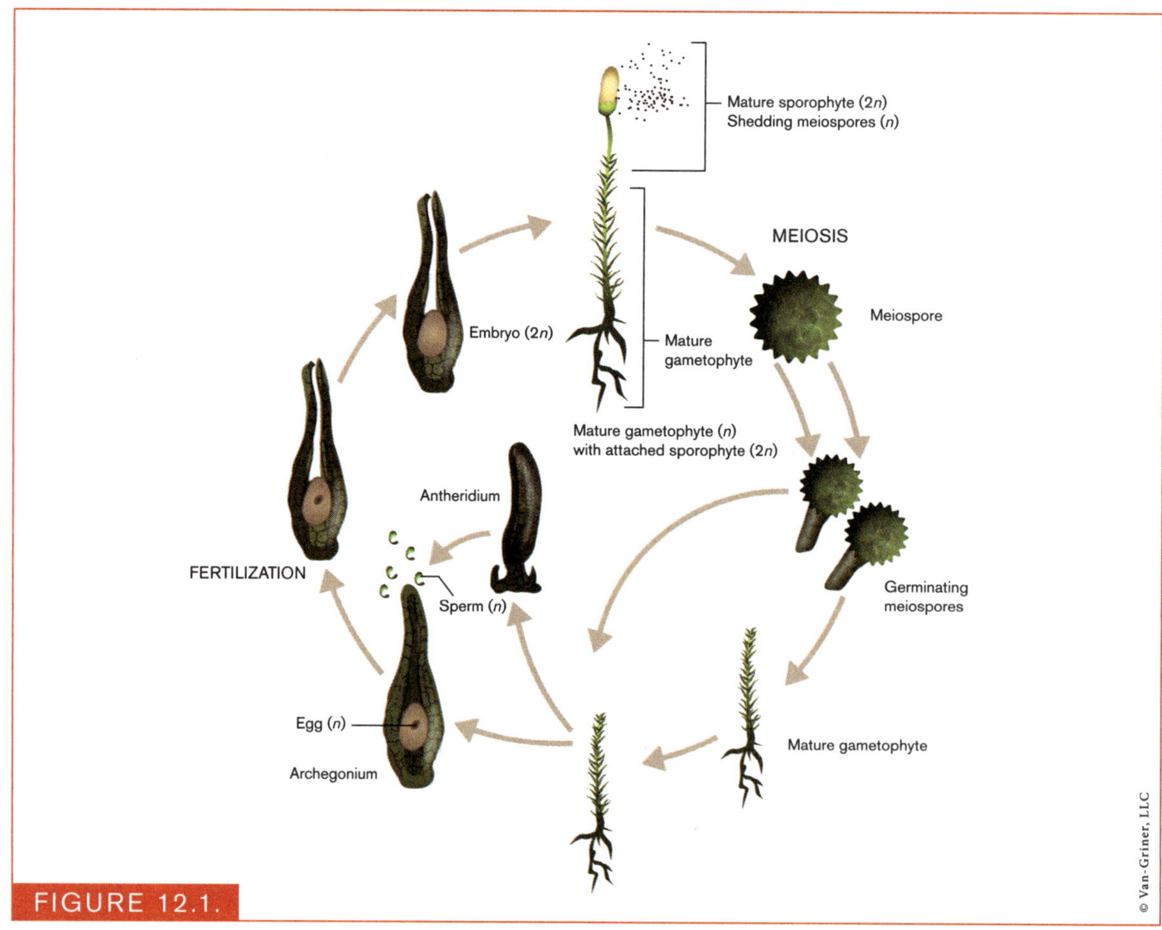

FIGURE 12.1.

Moss life cycle.

Exercises

Exercise 12.1.

Moss Phyllidia and Caulidia

Prepare a wet mount slide of phyllidia from *Sphagnum* or other live moss specimens and observe them under a dissecting scope. Make a sketch of the phyllidium in the space next to Figure 12.2 below.

You should be able to see the **chlorophyllous cells** (dark green) (see Figure 12.2 below). These cells possess chloroplasts and are involved in photosynthesis. **Hyaline cells** (light green to clear in color) are dead cell chambers that help to store water. The hyaline cells have openings or pores to the outside (these pores are not stomata). Note that the phyllidium is one or two cell layers thick.

Mosses generally lack an outer **cuticle** on the phyllidia, and they also lack **stomata** (the stomata are the pores observed in the epidermis of the leaves of higher plants). A cuticle helps in part to retard water loss, so for the bryophytes, the lack of a cuticle facilitates water absorption by the gametophyte. Mosses and the other bryophytes do not have true roots that absorb water and minerals from the soil.

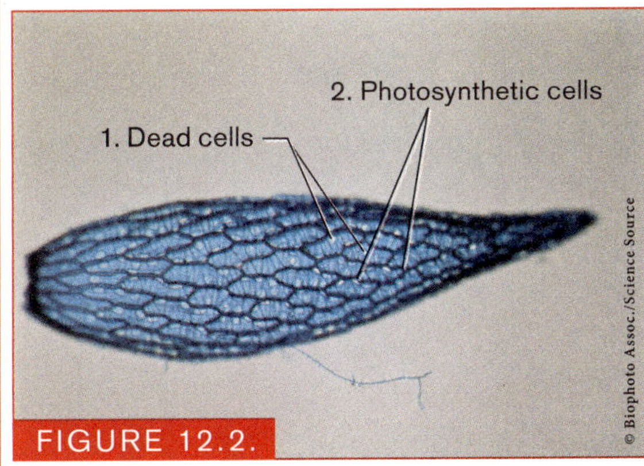

FIGURE 12.2.

Moss phyllidium.

A phyllidium is how many cell layers thick? Why is this important?

Exercise 12.2.

Moss Protonema

The germinating moss **spore** gives rise to **gametophytes.** The spore produces the **protonema** ("first-thread," Figure 12.3). The protonema is a mass of green filaments, one cell layer thick. The cells of the protonema are capable of photosynthesis (the protonema can be mistaken for filamentous green algae). A single protonema produces up to a few dozen bud-like projections (**bulbils**) that have **meristems** (mitotically active cells); these meristems give rise to the stalk-like **gametophores.** The gametophore is composed of the central stem-like stalk (the **caulidium**) and whorls of leaf-like **phyllidia.** The **gametangia** (gamete-producing structures) are on the top of the gametophores. The gametophores, rhizoids, and protonema collectively make up the gametophyte.

Examine a slide of moss protonema under low power under the microscope. Make additional sketches of the protonema in the space next to Figure 12.3 below. Bulbils, if present, are the future gametophores and gametangia. Note the numerous green chloroplasts inside the cells of a protonema.

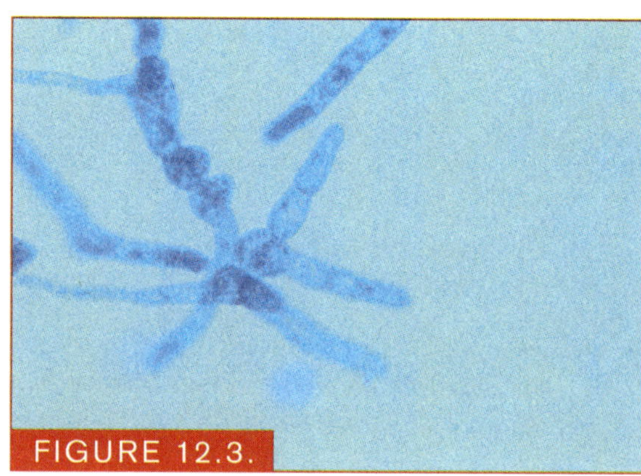

Moss protonema.

From what structures do protonema arise? Are the protonema haploid or diploid?

Exercise 12.3.

Moss Gametophytes

The gametophytes are green and photosynthetic, while the sporophytes (when mature) are not. Initially, immature sporophytes are green and photosynthetic. The mature gametophyte body is anchored in place with root-like **rhizoids** that consist of a series of cells. The rhizoids are not true roots; rhizoids are not involved in water transport. Likewise, the gametophyte caulidia and phyllidia are not true stems and leaves because they lack vascular tissues and several other structures that are found in higher plant leaves. (A few mosses possess cells that are similar in appearance to conducting tissues in vascular plants, but these cells are not considered to be either vessel elements or tracheids.) Because mosses are small and live in moist environments, basically all moss cells can absorb water from their surroundings.

Moss gametophytes normally stand upright. Phyllidia typically are spirally arranged on the caulidia. Each phyllidium is very leaf-like in appearance. The gametophores, bearing either archegonia or antheridia on the ends, generally occur on the same gametophyte (these plants would thus be called **monoecious**), although some moss gametophytes are **dioecious** (the individual gametophyte possesses either archegonia or antheridia but not both).

Examine preserved archegonial and antheridial gametophytes of *Polytrichum* under low power under the dissecting microscope. Identify the following: rhizoids, caulidium and phyllidia, antheridial head, archegonial head, antheridium, archegonium. Make additional sketches of the gametophyte in the space next to Figure 12.4 below. Note that the sporophyte is attached to the archegonial head.

Bryophyte gametophytes.

What is the function of the bryophyte rhizoids? How large are they?

Exercise 12.4.

Moss Antheridium

Several **gametangia** (gamete-producing structures) are found at the ends of the gametophores of the gametophytes. A single **antheridium** is a roundish, or sausage-shaped, structure that stands upright on the top of the gametophore (see Figure 12.1). Hairlike **paraphyses** (singular: paraphysis) are non-reproductive filaments that surround the antheridia. Several antheridia are on top of each male gametophore. A mass of cells develops in each antheridium; this mass consists of thousands of comma-shaped sperm. After absorbing water, the sperm mass separates into separate flagellated sperm that are splashed out of the antheridium with rainwater. Each sperm has a pair of flagella and can swim.

Examine the slide of an antheridial head of *Polytrichum* (moss antheridial head) under low power with the microscope. Identify the following: antheridia, stalks, and paraphyses. Make additional sketches of the antheridial head in the space next to Figure 12.5 below. Note that each antheridium consists of an outer layer of sterile jacket cells that enclose the sperm-producing tissues (Figure 12.5).

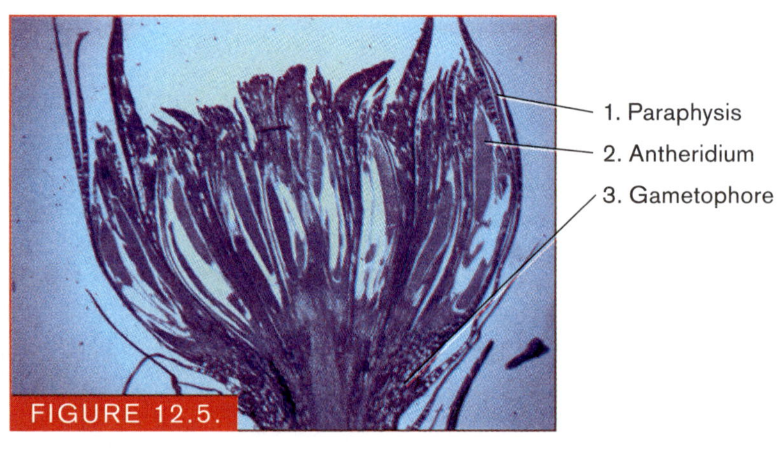

Antheridial head of a moss.

Exercise 12.5.

Moss Archegonium

The female **archegonia** are cylindrical and project upward from the base of the gametangium. An archegonium is shaped much like a long-necked vase. Certain cells in the center of the 'neck' and base of the archegonium die and break down, creating a cavity at the base of the archegonium (the **venter**), where the egg is located, and a canal that leads up the neck and to the outside (see Figure 12.1). Several archegonia are present on top of the gametophore of the female gametophyte.

A single egg is produced in a single archegonium, surrounded by tissues. Like in the antheridia, paraphyses surround the archegonia. The paraphyses absorb water and help to prevent the gametangia from drying out. Sperm swim down the neck of an archegonium and one sperm fuses with the single egg, producing a diploid **zygote.** The zygote then undergoes multiple rounds of mitosis to produce the **sporophyte.**

Examine a slide of a longitudinal section through an archegonial head of *Polytrichum* (moss archegonium) under low power using the microscope. Make additional sketches of the archegonial head in the space next to Figure 12.6 below. Identify the following: paraphyses, egg, stalk, and neck of an archegonium.

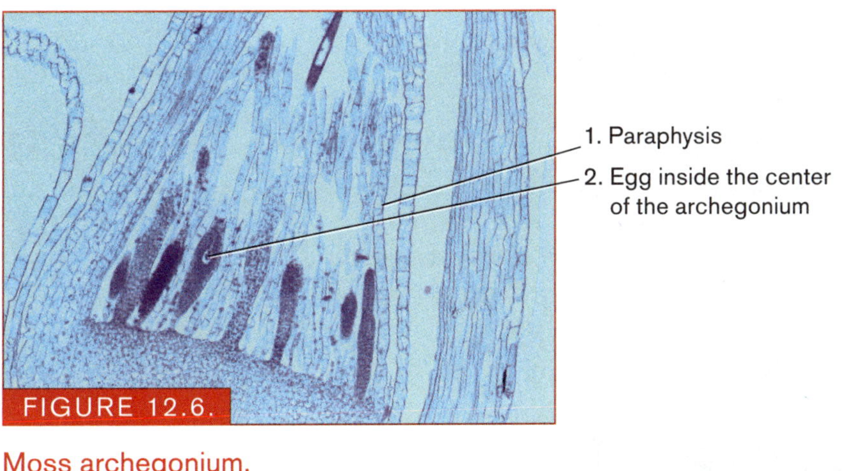

FIGURE 12.6.

Moss archegonium.

Exercise 12.6.

Moss Sporophyte

The sporophyte at maturity (Figure 12.7) is usually brownish in color and consists of a **foot,** a slender elongated stalklike **seta,** and a **sporangium** (or **capsule**). The moss sporophyte is dependent upon the gametophyte, in that the foot collects water and nutrients from the female gametophyte. In some mosses, the sporangium typically opens by the loss of a lid-like **operculum.** Millions of small spores then are released from the sporangium through the **peristome** (the terminal opening of the sporangium). The edge of the peristome of most mosses possesses one or two rows of triangular teeth. Spores are carried by the wind to other habitats. If the spore lands in a favorable habitat, the spore germinates and starts the life cycle over again. If the spore lands in an unfavorable environment, it can lie dormant for decades.

Moss sporophytes usually occur singly and are similar in size to (or slightly smaller than) the gametophyte. The capsule is elevated above the female gametophyte by an elongated seta. At the base of the seta, the foot is embedded in the gametophyte (see Figure 12.1).

Examine the preserved or dried sporophyte of mosses in the display area. Identify the following: seta, capsule, operculum, peristome. Make additional sketches of the sporophyte in the space next to Figure 12.7 below.

FIGURE 12.7.

Moss sporophyte structures.

What is the dominant phase in the life cycle of a bryophyte? How does this compare to the dominant phase of the rest of the land plants?

What process of cell division produces moss spores: meiosis or mitosis?

To what phase of the life cycle (gametophyte, sporophyte) do moss spores belong?

The Primitive Vascular Plants: The Ferns

We will concentrate on the ferns (**Division Pterophyta**) as our example of the primitive vascular plants.

In contrast to the algae, fungi, and bryophytes, the ferns and the seed plants (gymnosperms and the angiosperms) possess **xylem** and **phloem** (the true vascular or conducting tissues). Xylem cells have lignified walls (reinforced with lignin polymers) that help provide structural support to the plant. This support allows vascular plants to be much larger in size, compared to the bryophytes and algae. In addition to the presence of vascular tissues, fern and seed plant sporophytes have true roots, stems, and leaves. Ferns and seed plants also have numerous stomata, which are not generally not found in the bryophytes.

As with all plants, the primitive vascular plants have a **sporic** life cycle. However, primitive vascular plant sporophytes are larger and more conspicuous, compared to fern gametophytes. Unlike the bryophytes, sporophytes of the vascular plants are physiologically independent of the gameto- phytes, except during the embryonic stages of development. The fern gametophyte, also known as the **prothallium** (plural: prothallia) is greatly reduced in size and complexity. The fern gametophyte is not dependent upon the sporophyte at any point, but the gametophytes are restricted to moist habitats (like the bryophytes, ferns still use motile flagellated sperm that must swim to archegonia).

Division Pterophyta

The division **Pterophyta** includes the familiar present-day ferns. The ferns are the most diverse division of seedless vascular plants and number over 11,000 species. The sporophyte consists of a horizontal stem (called the **rhizome**) as well as true leaves and roots. The ferns are typically larger than the mosses; in some tropical species, the stem forms an erect trunk several meters in height. The life cycle of ferns is shown in Figure 12.8.

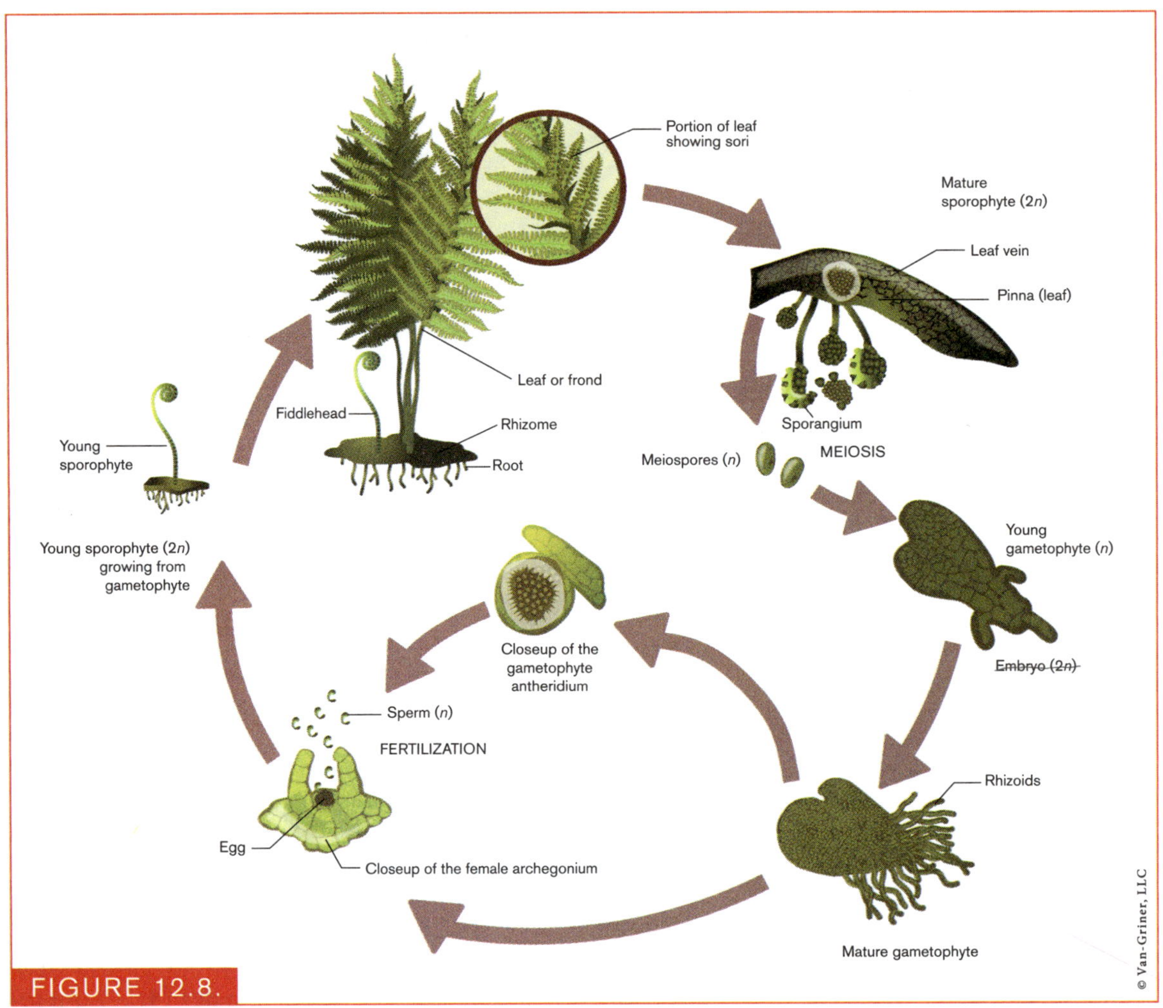

FIGURE 12.8.

Fern life cycle.

Exercise 12.7.

Living/Preserved Fern Sporophytes

Examine the living and preserved specimens of ferns. Identify the following: rhizome, roots, fronds, fiddleheads, and sori. Make additional sketches of what you see in the space next to Figure 12.9 below. Use Figure 12.8 and Figure 12.9 to guide you.

Fern sporophyte frond (leaf), with pinnae and sori.

Exercise 12.8.

Fern Gametophyte

The fern **gametophyte,** also known as the **prothallium,** is a small (several millimeters in size), green (photosynthetic), heart-shaped structure (see Figure 12.10). The fern gametophytes possess **rhizoids** to anchor the prothallia to the soil. Prothallia are usually one cell layer thick. The fern gametophyte produces **antheridia** and **archegonia.** These reproductive structures are found on the underneath side of the gametophyte. The antheridia are typically interspersed among the rhizoids, whereas the archegonia are clustered around the 'notch' of the heart-shaped gametophyte (Figure 12.10). A single egg is produced at the base of the small vase-shaped archegonium, whereas up to several hundred sperm can be present in each antheridium. On a given fern gametophyte, antheridia typically develop before the archegonia, which makes cross-fertilization more likely to occur between different gametophytes.

Like the mosses, the multi-flagellated fern sperm must swim through water to the egg in the archegonium for fertilization to occur. After fertilization, the zygote develops into a sporophyte. Only one zygote develops on the gametophyte. Like the mosses, the early embryonic fern sporophyte obtains its nourishment from the gametophyte, but the sporophyte soon becomes independent, unlike the mosses. When the sporophyte produces its own roots and photosynthetic leaves, the shorter-lived gametophyte typically dies. Therefore, both the gametophyte and adult sporophyte are green, photosynthetic, and capable of obtaining their own nutrients. Fern sporophytes can live for a number of years.

Examine the slide of a fern prothallium showing archegonia and antheridia under low power (40× total magnification). Make additional sketches of the fern gametophyte in the space next to Figure 12.10 below. Note the relative positions of the archegonia and antheridia on the fern gametophyte, as well as the rhizoids.

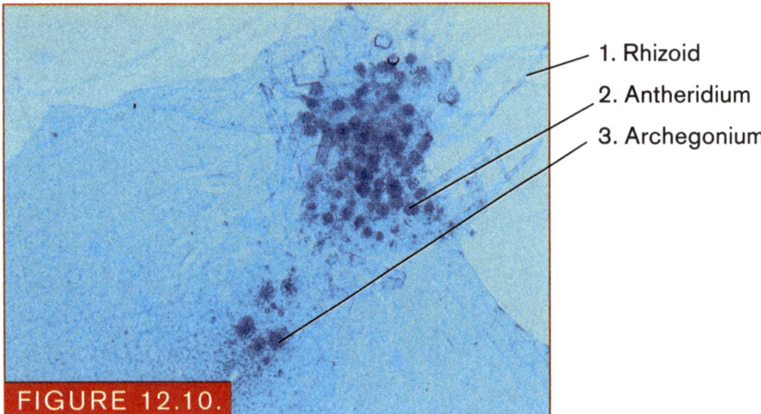

Fern gametophyte (prothallium).

What is the advantage of having the antheridia of a given gametophyte mature before the archegonia of the same individual plant?

In what type of terrestrial habitat around your home are you more likely to find ferns?

Exercise 12.9.

Fern Sporophyte

The most conspicuous part of a fern sporophyte is the leaf or **frond.** The young leaf is characteristically rolled into a tight coil, forming what is called a **fiddlehead.** As the leaf expands, the leaf unrolls from the base toward the tip. Fern leaves have a stalk-like **petiole** that attaches the leaf to the rhizome. A fern leaf may be simple or compound (compound leaves possess leaflets, called **pinnae**). If the pinnae are further divided, the leaflet subdivisions are called **pinnules.** In a compound leaf, the pinnae are attached to a central axis called the **rachis,** that attaches to the petiole. The rhizome is the horizontal stem from which the fronds and the **true roots** are attached. Unlike the bryophytes, the ferns have true roots with vascular tissues, which take up water and minerals from the soil.

Examine the slide of a young fern sporophyte (whole mount, still attached to gametophyte) under low power. Make additional sketches in the space next to Figure 12.11 below.

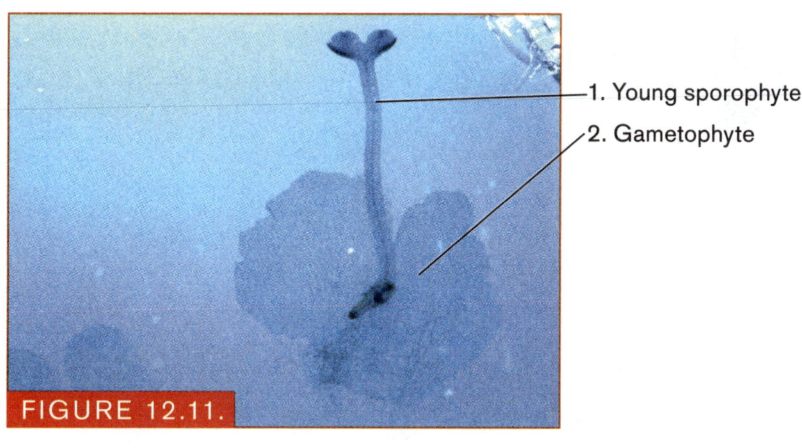

FIGURE 12.11.

Young fern sporophyte attached to gametophyte.

Exercise 12.10.

Fern Sori and Sporangia

Sporangia (Figure 12.12) commonly aggregate in clusters. The clusters are called **sori** (singular: **sorus**) and they are usually found on the undersurface of photosynthetic leafy fronds (the leaves or fronds are also called **sporophylls**). Sori may vary in shape from round to linear. The sporangia may be located from near the margin of the leaf, to a position near the center of the leaf, depending on the species. The sori of some species are covered with a thin membranous outgrowth of the sporophyll tissue (this membranous outgrowth is called the **indusium,** see the figure below). As sori mature, the indusia shrivel and expose sporangia underneath. Each sporangium is attached to the sporophyll by a short stalk. The wall of a sporangium is one cell layer thick and one side consists of a row or belt of specialized thick-walled cells (this row is called an **annulus**) that functions in the dispersal of the spores. As the capsule matures, the cells of the annulus lose water and shrink. The annulus then straightens, creating pressure on the thin-walled lip cells on the opposite side of the sporangium. The lip cells break, creating an opening to the sporangium, and further evaporation of water causes the annulus to snap back, releasing the spores. Meiosis occurs in **spore mother cells** inside the sporangium, producing the haploid spores. When these spores geminate, the spores produce a small thread-like **protonema** (similar to moss protonema) that will give rise to the heart-shaped gametophyte. Examine the slide (under low power, 40× total magnification) of the cross section of a fern indusium showing sporangia. Make additional sketches in the space next to Figure 12.12 below. Identify sori, sporangium, annulus, indusium.

FIGURE 12.12.

Fern sori and sporangia.

Plants II. Gymnosperms and Angiosperms

Keywords

homosporous
heterosporous
megaspore
microspore
megaspore
   mother cell
   (megasporocyte)
microspore
   mother cell
   (microsporocyte)
sporophyte
gametophyte
pollen cone
ovulate cone
microsporophyll
megasporophyll
pollen grain
pollen tube
tube cell nucleus

generative cell
   nucleus
sperm
strobilus
microsporangium
megasporangium
   (nucellus)
integument
micropyle
embryo
archegonia
fascicle
receptacle
calyx
sepal
corolla
petal
perianth

stamen
filament
anther
androecium
carpel
pistil
ovule
gynoecium
stigma
style
ovary
complete
incomplete
perfect
imperfect
staminate
carpellate
monoecious

dioecious
regular
   (actinomorphic)
irregular
   (zygomorphic)
cotyledons
placenta
female gametophyte
   (embryo sac)
egg
double fertilization
endosperm
fruit
pericarp
simple fruits
aggregate fruits
multiple fruits
seed
seed coat

Learning Objectives

When finished with this unit, you should be able to:

1. Identify the division of representative examples of higher plants (and if it is an angiosperm, be able to identify whether or not the example is a monocot or an eudicot);

2. Compare and contrast homospory and heterospory;

3. Describe the life cycle of a gymnosperm (the pine);

4. Describe the parts of a pine cone (male and female) and their functions;

5. Describe the cells and structures of gymnosperm male gametophytes and female gametophytes, and describe the parts of a gymnosperm seed;

6. Compare and contrast the features of monocots and eudicots;

7 Describe the structures of a flower, and identify the features of a flower that indicate whether or not it is pollinated by animals or by the wind. Be able to distinguish flowers as being monocot or eudicot, staminate or carpellate, actinomorphic or zygomorphic, complete or incomplete, perfect or imperfect;

8 Describe the life cycle of a flowering plant;

9 Describe the cells and structures of angiosperm male gametophytes and female gametophytes, and the parts of an angiosperm seed;

10 Describe the structure and function of fruits; and

11 Compare and contrast the various types of fleshy fruits and dry fruits observed in lab, and indicate the dispersal mechanisms for various fruits and seeds.

Classification:

Kingdom Plantae

  Gymnosperms (the naked seed plants)

   Division Coniferophyta (conifers, the pines and relatives) *Pinus*

  Angiosperms (the flowering plants)

   Division Anthophyta (flowering plants)

   Class Monocots

   Class Eudicots

Gymnosperms

We will examine conifers (pines and their relatives) as our example of the gymnosperms. All gymnosperms produce naked seeds (in other words, the seeds are not enclosed in a fruit, as seen in the flowering plants). All gymnosperms are wind-pollinated trees or shrubs, and most gymnosperms have unisexual male and female reproductive structures on different parts of the same plant (i.e., the plants are monoecious).

The **Division Coniferophyta** constitutes the group of gymnosperms with the largest number of present-day genera and species. One representative genus is *Pinus*. We shall use the pines to study the life cycle details of the gymnosperms.

Homospory and Heterospory
The bryophytes and almost all of the primitive vascular seedless plants (ferns and their relatives) produce one type of spore (**homospory**). The spore gives rise to the gametophyte via mitosis, and the gametophyte produces both antheridia and archegonia. This week, we will see

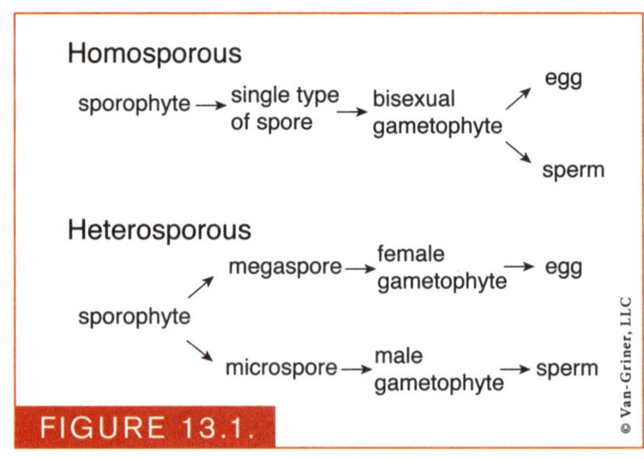

FIGURE 13.1.

The comparison of homospory and heterospory.

that all of the gymnosperms and the angiosperms show the advanced trait of **heterospory. Heterospory** is the condition where two different kinds of spores are produced by the sporophyte; these two spore types differ in size. Two different-sized haploid cells use mitosis to create two different gametophytes. The larger **megaspores** give rise to female gametophytes that have archegonia and produce eggs, whereas relatively smaller spores (**microspores**) give rise to male gametophytes that have antheridia and produce sperm (see Figure 13.1).

Pine Life Cycle

Examine the pine life cycle in Figure 13.2. A pine **sporophyte** is an evergreen tree or shrub consisting of an extensive root system and a shoot system including a trunk, branches, and leaves. Leaves of a typical pine tree are usually needle-like and occur in **fascicles** (groups) of one to eight leaves. Many conifers live in harsh environments where the soils are frozen for part of the year, making it difficult for the plants' roots to obtain water. In addition, the shoot systems of many conifers are exposed to cold temperatures and high winds. The conifers thus have evolved several adaptations to thrive in harsh cold environments.

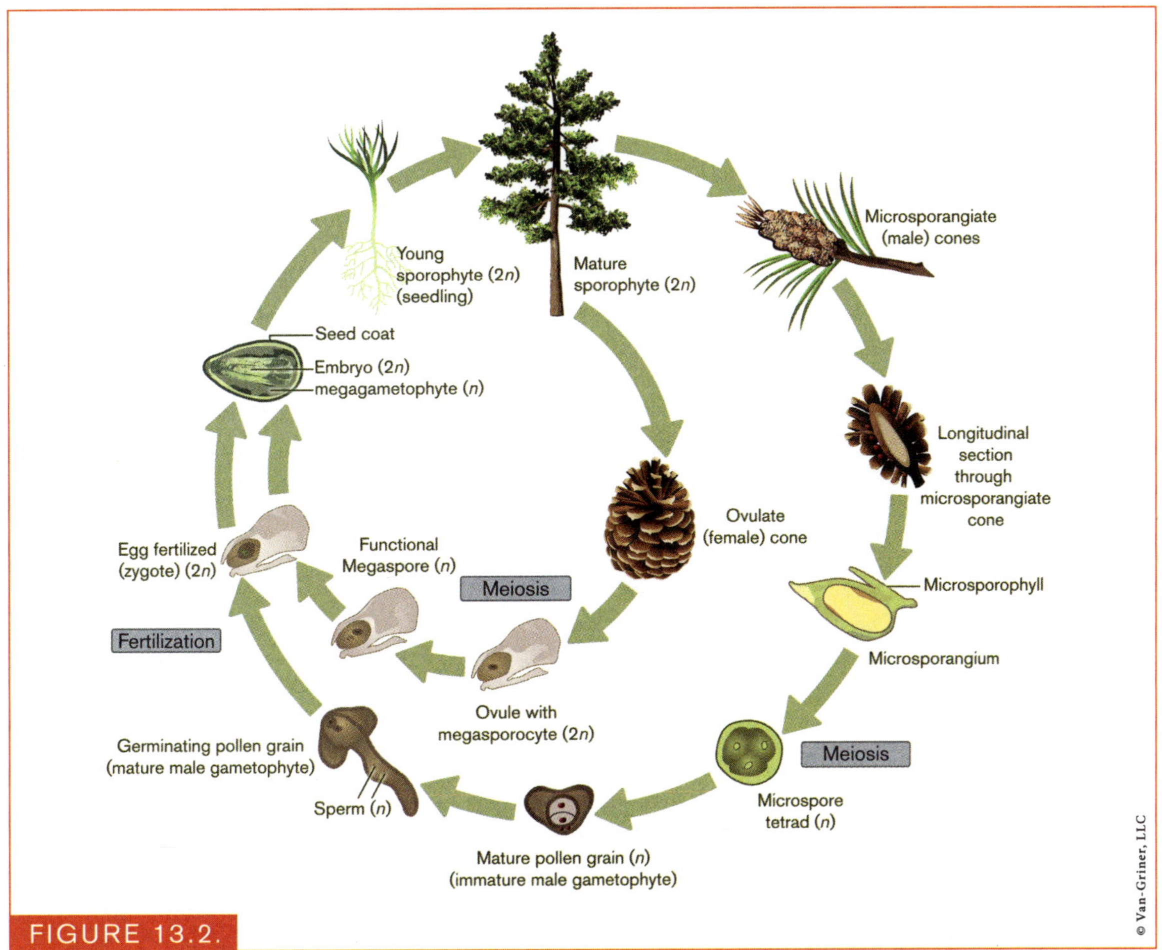

FIGURE 13.2.

The pine life cycle.

Exercises

Exercise 13.1.
Microsporangiate Pine Cone

Two kinds of cones are produced by gymnosperm sporophytes:

1 microsporangiate (pollen cones) and

2 megasporangiate (ovulate cones or seed cones or female strobili).

Microsporangiate cones (see Figure 13.2) are smaller than the megasporangiate cones and are borne typically in clusters on the lower branches of a tree. Each microsporangiate cone consists of a central axis with hundreds of **microsporophylls** (which are specialized leaves that contain sporangia) arranged in tight spirals around this central axis. **Microsporangia,** each consisting of a wall and the enclosed **microspore mother cells** (these cells are also called **microsporocytes**), are borne in pairs on the surface of each microsporophyll. A microsporocyte undergoes meiosis and produces four haploid **microspores.** Each microspore then develops into the **microgametophyte,** or male gametophyte. After the microgametophyte produces a pair of air sacs that are wing-like extensions, they are called **pollen grains** (immature male gametophytes). Thousands of pollen grains form within a single sporangium.

Under low power, examine the prepared slide of the microsporangiate cone of pine (mature male strobilus, median l.s.). Identify the central cone axis, microsporophylls, microsporangia, and developing pollen grains. Make a sketch of the pollen cone l.s. in the space next to Figure 13.3 below.

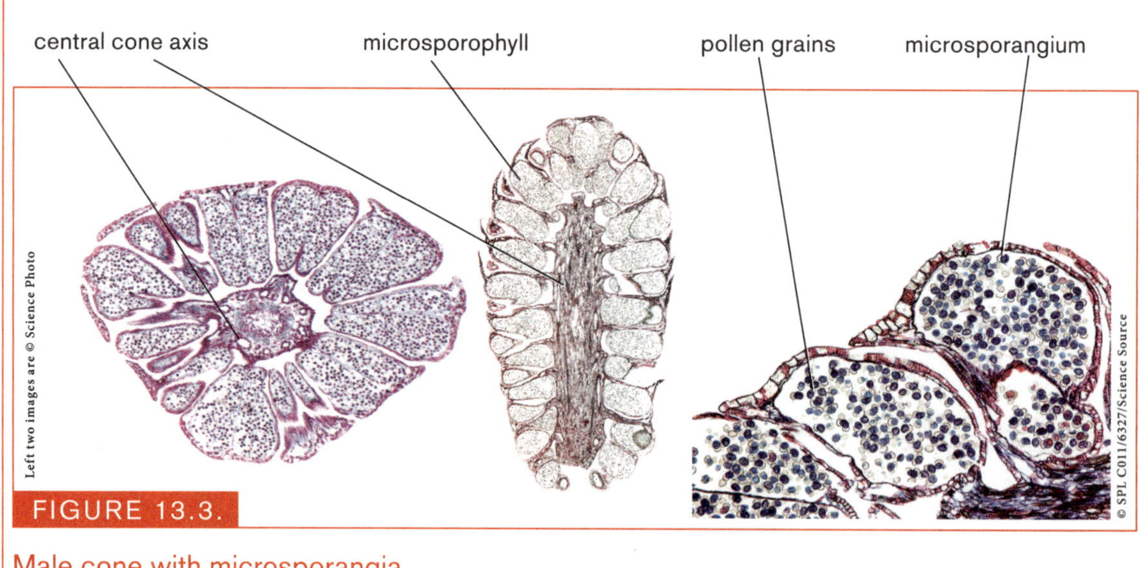

FIGURE 13.3.

Male cone with microsporangia.

What is the relationship between a microspore and a pollen grain?

What type of cell division (mitosis or meiosis) occurs in the microsporocyte?

Once the microspore has formed, what type of cell division (mitosis or meiosis) is involved in the formation of cells of the pollen grain?

Exercise 13.2.

Mature Pollen Grain

The pine **pollen grain** is made of four cells: two prothallial cells (which degenerate), a **tube cell,** and a **generative cell.** Once the pollen grain has landed on the ovulate cone (via the wind), the tube cell produces the **pollen tube,** and the nucleus enters the pollen tube. The generative cell then enters the pollen tube. As the tube develops, the generative cell undergoes **mitosis** to produce two cells (a sterile cell and a spermatogenous cell). The spermatogenous cell undergoes **mitosis** again to produce two **sperm,** which travel down the growing pollen tube. At this time, the immature male gametophyte has become a **mature male gametophyte** with sperm.

Note the extreme miniaturization that has occurred concerning the relative sizes of the gameto-phytes and sporophytes. Maturation of the pollen cones and the discharge of the pollen occur in the spring. Soon after the discharge of the pollen, the pollen cones shrivel and drop from the tree. Pollen are carried by the wind and drift to small female cones. A sticky secretion helps capture the pollen grains; as the fluid evaporates, this draws the pollen up into the cone, near the **micropyle.** After pollination, the scales grow together to protect the developing ovules.

Examine the prepared slide of the pollen grain (pine mature pollen, Figure 13.4). You may be able to see the tube cells and generative cells, if you look closely. Make a sketch of the pine pollen in the space next to Figure 13.4 below.

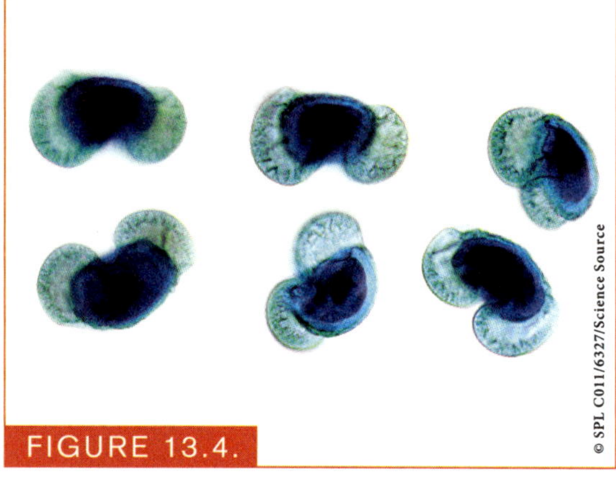

© SPL C011/6327/Science Source

FIGURE 13.4.

Mature pollen grain of a pine.

Microsporangiate cones of pine are produced in much greater abundance than the megasporangiate cones. Why?

What is the function of the inflated 'wings' (air sacs) on a pollen grain?

Why is wind-dispersed pollen an important trait for the evolution of plants?

What is the difference between "pollination" and "fertilization?"

Exercise 13.3.

Immature Pine Ovulate Cone

The megasporangiate cones (also called **ovulate cones, seed cones,** or female **strobili:** see Figure 13.2 and Figure 13.5) are also the cones commonly called "pine cones." They are found typically on the upper branches of a tree, above the pollen cones. Ovulate cones require 18 to 24 months to reach maturity. In early development, an ovulate cone is small and soft in texture, but by the end of the second year, when the seeds are mature, the ovulate cone has enlarged considerably and has become woody.

Like a pollen cone, a megasporangiate cone (also called the **seed cone**) consists of a **central axis** and spirally arranged bract scales (modified leaves) and seed scales (a modified branch). The bract scales are between adjacent seed scales. The seed scales have two **ovules** present on their upper surfaces. A pine ovule consists of an **integument** and a **nucellus.** The outer layer of diploid cells (**integument**) will eventually produce the seed coat of the mature pine seed. The integument has a small opening, the **micropyle,** which is directed toward the axis of the cone. The integument encloses the **megasporangium** (also called the **nucellus**). The **nucellus** is composed of nutritive sporophyte tissues and a **megaspore mother cell (megasporocyte).**

Under low power, examine the prepared slide of a longitudinal section of an immature pine ovulate cone showing the integuments, megasporangium, and micropyle (if visible). Make a sketch what you see in the space next to Figure 13.5 below.

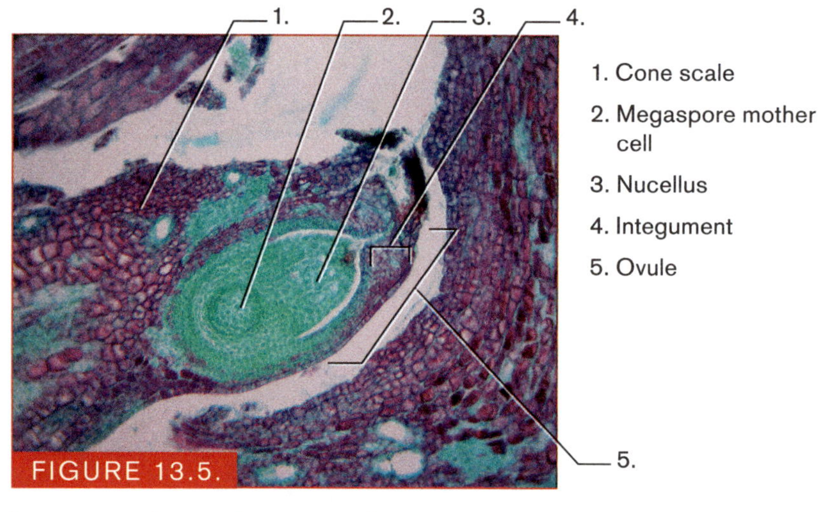

Immature pine ovulate cone, l.s.

Exercise 13.4.

The **megaspore mother cell** (also called the **megasporocyte**) undergoes meiosis resulting in a linear tetrad of **megaspores.** Three of these megaspores degenerate. The fourth megaspore undergoes mitosis; repeated rounds of mitosis eventually produces up to about 2,000 nuclei that, after cytokinesis, will form the multicellular **female gametophyte** (also called the **megagametophyte**). Two or more small **archegonia** are produced at the micropylar end of the megagametophyte during the final stages of development (see Figure 13.6); each archegonium contains a functional **egg.**

Development of the megagametophyte occurs simultaneously with the growth of the pollen tube through the megasporangial tissue. The pollen tube takes over a year to grow to the archegonium, and the megagametophyte also takes about a year to develop. The megagametophyte reaches maturity early in the second year of development, and **fertilization** then occurs following the discharge of the two sperm into one archegonium. (Note that fertilization occurs more than a year after pollination.) The two sperm nuclei enter the egg, but only one fuses with the egg nucleus; the other sperm disintegrates. The fusion of sperm and egg form the diploid **zygote.** The zygote undergoes mitosis to produce a new **sporophyte** (or **embryo**).

In the female gametophyte, all of the eggs may be fertilized, but usually only one fertilized egg completes development and produces a viable embryo. Following fertilization, the growth and development of the pine embryo occurs. The energy used for this initial growth is supplied by stored energy in the nucellus.

Under low power, examine the prepared slide of pine archegonium, l.s. (pine ovule). Identify the area included as the female gametophyte and archegonia (and egg, if one is visible. Depending on the slide, the archegonium may not contain a cross section of an egg).

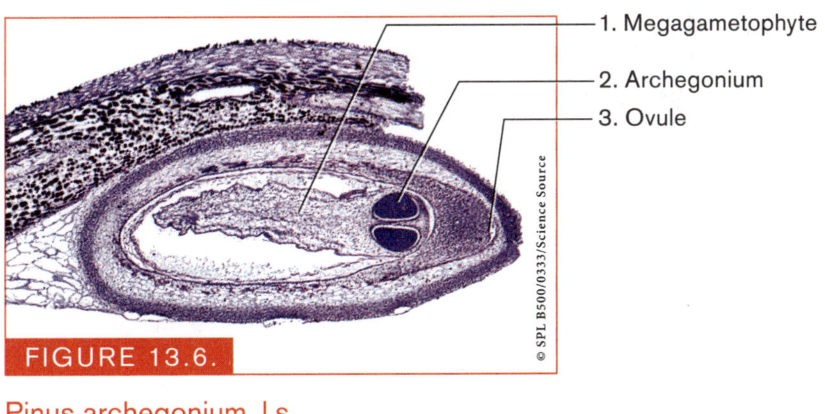

FIGURE 13.6.

Pinus archegonium, l.s.

Exercise 13.5.

The Pine Seed

Three distinct plant generations (two sporophyte and one gametophyte) are represented in a **pine seed:**

1 The seed has an outer **seed coat.** The seed coat is derived from the integuments of the parent sporophyte generation, which surrounded the remnants of the sporophyte nucellus.

2 Inside the seed coat, the remnants of the diploid nucellus and the haploid female gametophyte (both of which provide nutrition to developing embryos) are present.

3 Finally, the new diploid sporophyte embryo is within the remnants of the female gametophyte.

The pine seed also has 'wings' that form from cells of the seed cone scale of the parent sporophyte. The wings aid in the dispersal of the cone by the wind when the cone opens later. Some cones only open up to release the seeds after a fire, or after old age. Squirrels and other animals may aid the dispersal of the seeds by breaking open the cone.

Examine the display of gymnosperm seeds and cones. Look at mature old pine cones for evidence of seeds. Draw some examples of seeds and cones in the space next to Figure 13.7 below.

Gymnosperm seeds and cones.

Exercise 13.6.

Pine Seedling

Under the appropriate conditions, the pine seed **germinates.** The seed coat splits, and the young root of the **pine seedling** (the new sporophyte) comes out and anchors into the soil, followed by the shoot (Figure 13.2).

Under low power, examine the prepared slide of a pine mature embryo, l.s. (Figure 13.8). Identify the embryo. The seed coat may have been removed. The embryo is the new diploid sporophyte, with embryonic leaves (leaf primordia) and the embryonic root (root primordium). Sketch the mature embryo in the space next to Figure 13.8 below.

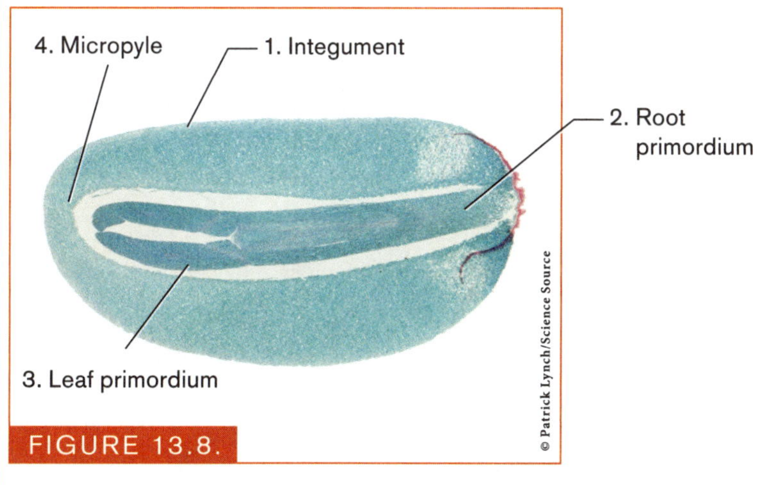

FIGURE 13.8.

Mature pine embryo, l.s.

What is the importance of the 'wing' of a pine seed? Can you think of at least two ways pine seeds can be dispersed?

How many generations (sporophyte and gametophyte generations) are represented in a pine seed? What parts of the pine seed are of each generation?

Angiosperms

The **Angiosperms** or the flowering plants constitute the largest and most conspicuous group of plants living today. They are characterized by the production of flowers that give rise to seeds enclosed in an ovary. The term "angiosperm" is an informal name for the flowering plants, all of which are included in the Division Anthophyta. Recent advances in phylogeny have suggested that the monocots diverged away from a common ancestor of the dicots. In this course, we will refer to two major clades as 'classes' in the division Anthophyta: **Monocots** and **Eudicots.** The angiosperm life cycle is depicted below (Figure 13.9).

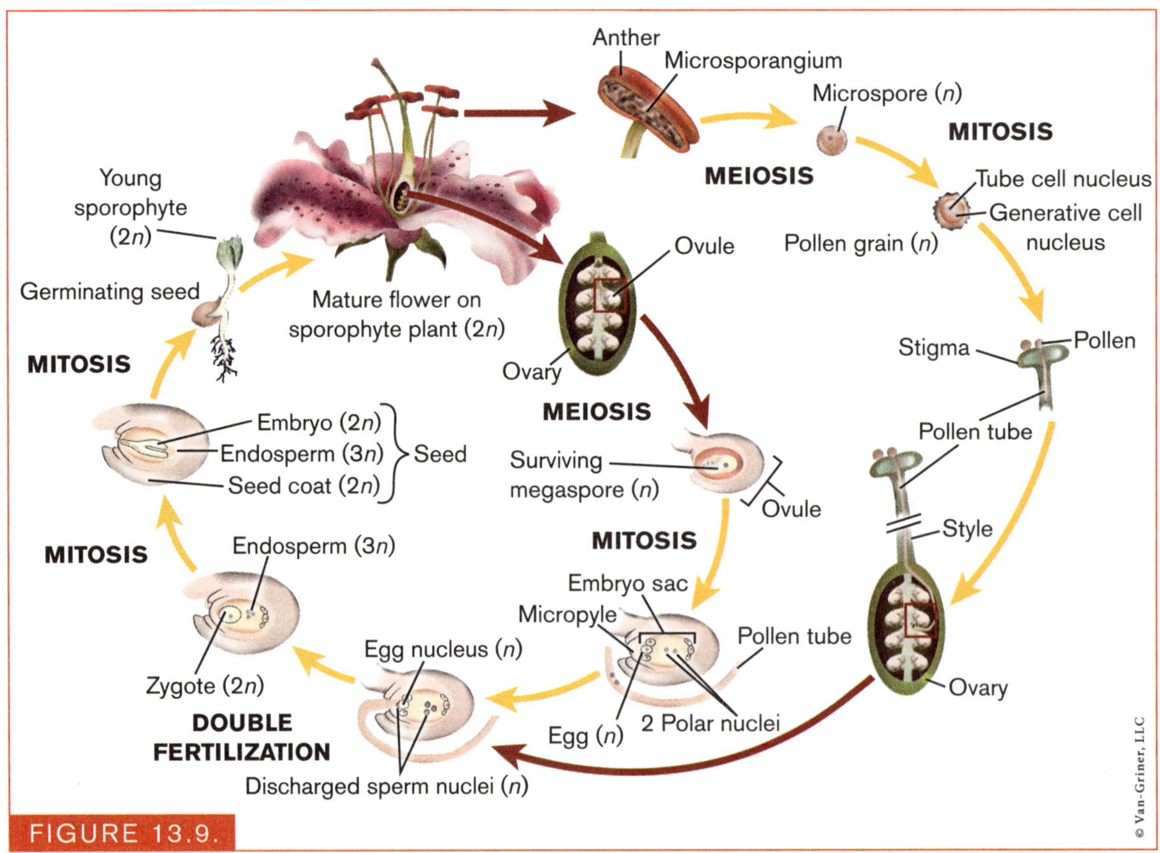

FIGURE 13.9.

The angiosperm life cycle.

Exercise 13.7.

Parts of the Angiosperm Flower

A **flower** is an aggregation of specialized leaves arranged on a stem of determinate growth. A typical flower possesses **four whorls** or rings of these specialized leaves. All of these specialized leaves attach to the stem at the site called the **receptacle.** The receptacle is the flower stalk that bears the floral organs and connects the flower to the stem. Beginning from the outside and progressing towards the inside, the names and functions of these specialized leaves are as follows (see Figure 13.11):

A The outermost whorl of modified leaves are called **sepals.** All of the sepals are collectively called the **calyx.** The sepals are often green and leaf-like in appearance (and thus look different from the petals, see below), although in a few cases the sepals are similar in appearance to the petals (in these cases, both the petals and sepals are brightly colored and conspicuous). The sepals enclose the other floral parts while the flower is still in the bud stage.

B Inside the whorl of sepals, the next whorl of modified leaves are called **petals.** All of the petals of a flower are collectively called the **corolla.** The petals are often highly colored and conspicuous.

All of the sepals and petals (the calyx and corolla) of a flower are collectively called the **perianth.**

C The third whorl is composed of a number of **stamens.** Stamens are highly modified microsporophylls. A stamen consists of a **filament** and an **anther.** The anther is the pollen-producing part of the stamen; an anther is often made up of four fused **microsporangia.** The filament is the stalk of the stamen. Pollen grains (which will produce the mature the male gametophytes) are ultimately produced in the anthers. All of the stamens of a flower are collectively called the **androecium.**

D The fourth, innermost, whorl of modified leaves are called the **carpels.** Carpels are highly modified megasporophylls, where each carpel encloses one or more **ovules.** All of the carpels of a flower are collectively called the **gynoecium.**

Pistil. The **pistil** of a flower may consist of one or more carpels, which may be separate and distinct or fused together. Whether composed of just a single carpel, or a number of fused carpels, a pistil typically consists of three distinct parts: **stigma, style,** and **ovary.**

Receptacle. The flower parts are all attached to the **receptacle.** The receptacle is the enlarged terminal portion of a stem.

Complete versus incomplete flowers. If all four whorls of the floral parts are present, the flower is called a **complete** flower. Very often one or more of these whorls may be lacking; the flower is then called **incomplete.**

Perfect versus imperfect flowers. Because stamens and pistils are essential in the sexual cycle, a flower is called **perfect** if both stamens and carpels are present. A flower that lacks either stamens or carpels is called **imperfect.** Imperfect flowers can be either **staminate** (they have stamens but lack carpels) or **carpellate** (they have carpels but lack stamens).

Monoecious versus dioecious flowers. A **monoecious** plant produces separate staminate and carpellate flowers on the same plant. A **dioecious** plant produces staminate flowers on one individual plant and carpellate flowers on another individual.

Flower Symmetry

Flowers exhibit two types of symmetry. Those that can be bisected longitudinally through many different sections such that the two halves are duplicates or mirror images of each other are radially symmetrical and said to be **regular** or **actinomorphic.** Other flowers that are bilaterally symmetrical (only one plane of division produce two mirror imaged halves) are called **irregular** or **zygomorphic.**

Angiosperm Groups

Angiosperm seeds contain either one or two **cotyledons,** or embryonic leaves. This characteristic is the basis on which the two major groups of Angiosperms are divided. Other features of plant morphology are typically associated with each class as well.

A **The Monocots** have seeds with one cotyledon and typically have flower parts occurring in threes or multiples of three. Leaf veins typically are parallel in monocots and the vascular bundles are scattered through the stem cross section. Monocots also have fibrous root systems.

B **The Eudicots** have seeds with two cotyledons and flower parts occurring in fours, or fives, or multiples of four or five. Leaf veins form net-like patterns in the leaves and the vascular bundles are arranged in a ring in the stem. Eudicots typically have taproots as root systems. There are some primitive dicots that are as closely related to the monocots as they are to the eudicots. In this course, we will discuss eudicots as a single monophyletic clade.

Obtain one of the flowers provided and determine whether it is:

monocot or eudicot   complete or incomplete   perfect or imperfect

staminate or carpellate   actinomorphic or zygomorphic

In addition, identify the various modified leaf whorls of a complete flower (sepals, petals, stamens, and carpels) and the parts of the stamens and carpels (anther, filament, stigma, style and ovary) of the flower. Sketch your flower in Figure 13.10 below. Use Figure 13.11 and the flower models on the demonstration table to guide you.

FIGURE 13.10.

Flower anatomy.

Exercise 13.8.

Examine the pictures and models of flowers, and study the parts that make up the flower. Then, without looking at the models/pictures, fill in the blanks in Figure 13.11 below. Check your answers and correct any mistakes.

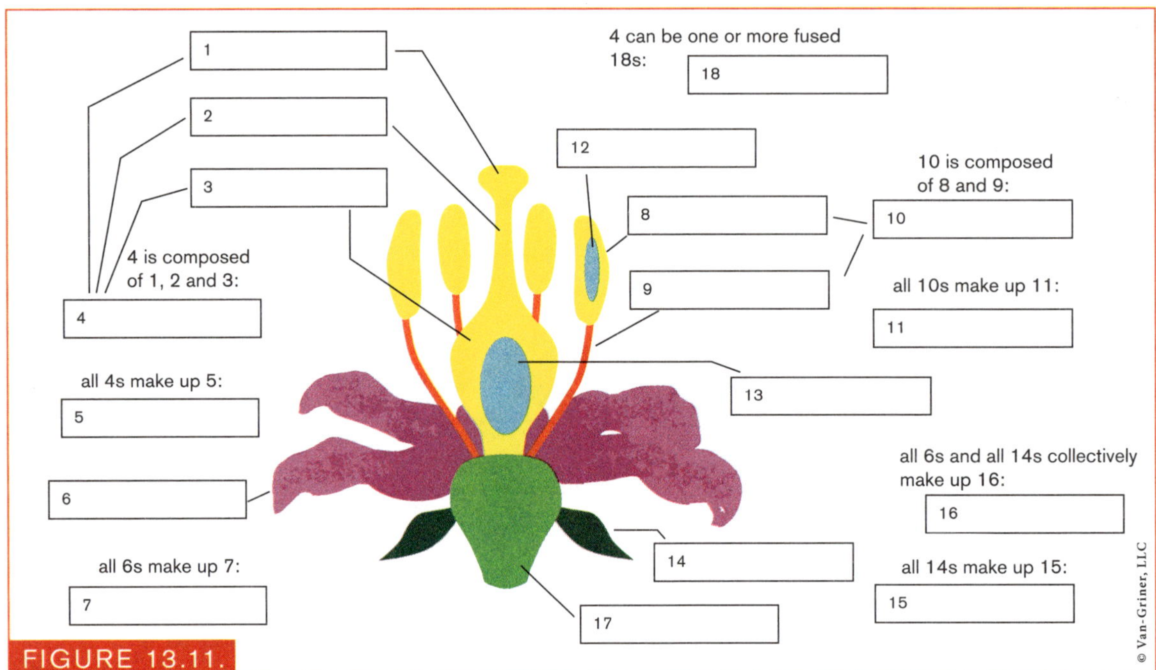

FIGURE 13.11.

The parts of an idealized flower.

Exercise 13.9.

Cross Section through the Lily Flower

The lily gynoecium is tricarpellate (the single pistil consists of three carpels). Two vertical rows of **ovules** are produced in each carpel. Each ovule consists of two **integuments** and the enclosed **megasporangium.** The integuments surround the micropyle at one end of the ovule. The **micro-pyle** is a small hole through the outer protective tissues of the ovule, through which the pollen tube can enter. Each ovule is attached to the **placenta** by a short stalk. The placenta is the part of the ovary wall to which the ovules (and later the seeds) are attached.

Cut the ovary of lily flower in cross section and determine the number of carpels. Examine the other kinds of flowers that are on display and note the variations in the number and arrangement of floral parts. Make some sketches of the cross section of the lily flower in the space provided below (Figure 13.12).

FIGURE 13.12.

Sketch of the cross section through the lily flower.

Exercise 13.10.

Lily Anther

The anther of a lily stamen is made up of four fused **microsporangia** (Figure 13.13). In each microsporangium, **microspore mother cells** undergo meiosis, forming tetrads of haploid **microspores.** The microspores of a tetrad separate from each other and each microspore divides mitotically, forming a two-celled immature male gametophyte (**pollen grain**). One nucleus will form the **tube cell nucleus.** The other pollen grain nucleus is called the **generative cell nucleus,** which will divide mitotically later to produce two **sperm** that do not have flagella. The 'sperm' in flowering plants are simply haploid nuclei.

Under low power, examine a prepared slide of lily anthers (*Lilium*: anthers x.s., late prophase) showing tetrads of microspores. You will see a cross section through four microsporangia, each with many cells undergoing meiosis. Draw what you see in the microscope's field of view in the space next to Figure 13.13 below.

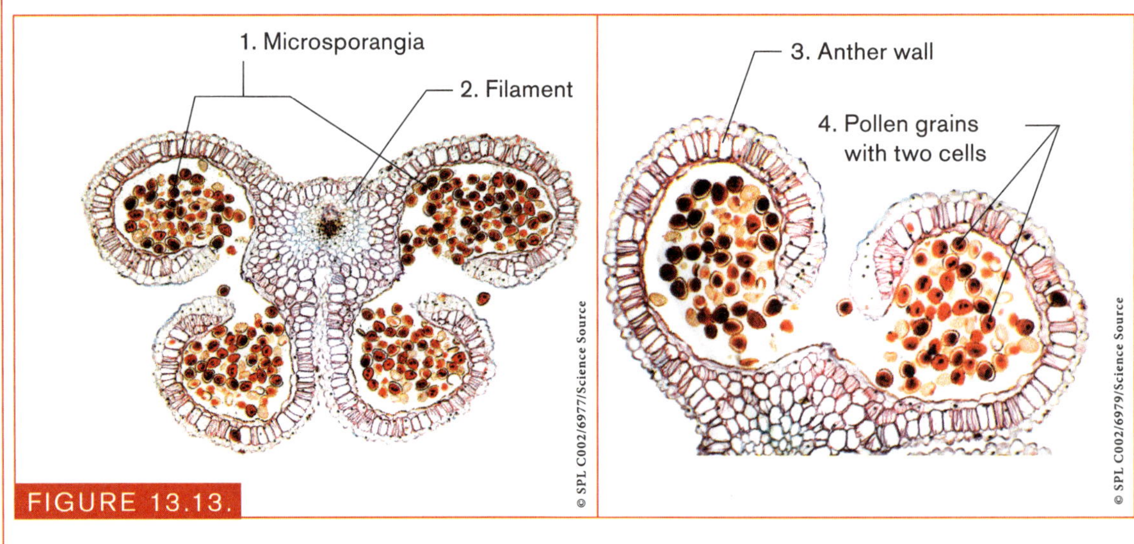

FIGURE 13.13.

Lillium anther cross section.

Exercise 13.11.

Under low power, examine a prepared slide of germinated lily pollen grains (Lily Pollen Tubes, w.m., Figure 13.14). Identify the pollen tube, tube nucleus, and the two sperm nuclei (microgametes—they may appear to be two separate nuclei, or perhaps one.) Draw what you see in the microscope's field of view in the space next to Figure 13.14 below.

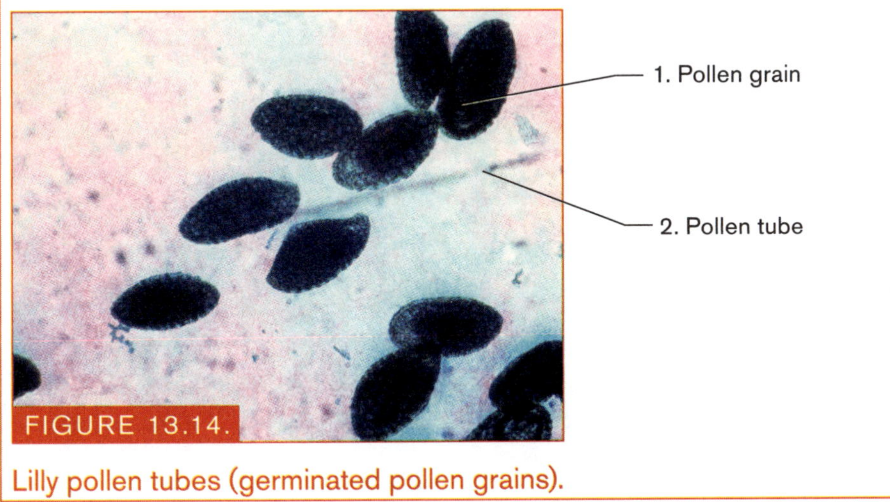

Lilly pollen tubes (germinated pollen grains).

Exercise 13.12.

Lily Ovary

Ovule development in most angiosperm species begins with the differentiation of one cell within the **megasporangium** into a **megaspore mother cell.** The megasporangia are found in the ovary of the pistil. The megaspore mother cell divides meiotically and gives rise to four **megaspores,** three of which degenerate. The remaining functional megaspore then undergoes three rounds of mitosis, giving rise to an **embryo sac** containing eight haploid cells or nuclei. Only one of these nuclei is the **egg** nucleus. The mature embryo sac is also called the **female gametophyte** or **mega-gametophyte.** In angiosperms, the female gametophyte is so reduced (eight nuclei/cells) that it lacks distinct archegonia.

Under low power, examine a prepared slide of a lily ovary (*Lilium*: megaspores) showing ovules containing megaspore mother cells. Determine how many carpels are in the lily pistil and the number of ovaries in each carpel. Identify the ovary wall, integument, megasporangium, and megasporocytes. Use Figure 13.15 and figures on the demonstration table to guide you. Sketch what you see in the space next to Figure 13.15 below.

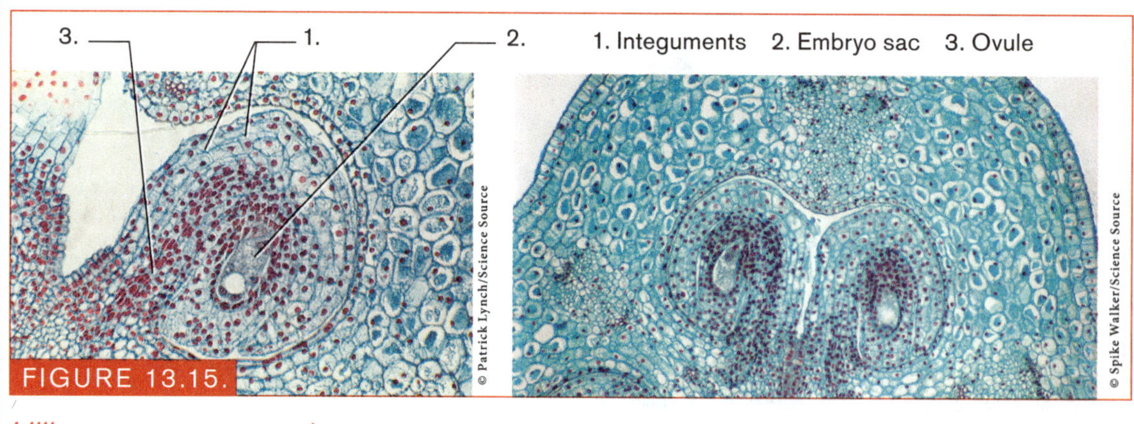

Lillium: megaspores and ovary.

Why is the internal fertilization observed in the seed plants essential for living on land?

Exercise 13.13.

Fruits and Seeds

The **fruit** is a ripened ovary. In some cases, the receptacle or other parts of the flowers, along with the carpels, make up the fruit. Tomatoes, string beans, and cucumbers are all technically fruits, in addition to apples, pears, cherries, plums, blackberries, pineapples, oranges, nuts, cauliflowers, wheat, corn, rice, and so on. **There are two main types of fruits: fleshy fruits and dry fruits.** One important distinguishing characteristic that separates the two types of fruits is the wall of the fruit, called the **pericarp.** The pericarp can be dry or fleshy at maturity.

1 There are three main types of fleshy fruits. Fleshy fruits are at least partly fleshy and moist at maturity.

A **Simple fruits** (berry, pome and drupe) are derived from a single ovary that may consist of a single carpel or a number of fused carpels.

1 **Drupes** are simple fruits with one seed (a stone or pit) surrounded by a hard outer covering (olives, cherries, peaches, plums and coconuts).

2 **Berries** are composed of an ovary with many seeds and the fleshy fruit is from the ovary (tomatoes, green peppers, bananas, and grapes are actually berries). Some berries can also possess leathery skins containing oils (lemons, limes). In addition, some berries have a thick rind (watermelon, cucumber, squashes, and pumpkins).

3 **Pomes** develop in part from the surrounding flower and stem tissues, particularly the receptacle (apples, pears).

B An **aggregate fruit** is derived from a gynoecium consisting of a number of unfused carpels. The aggregate fruit thus is made up of numerous distinct unicarpellate pistils of a single flower (strawberries, raspberries, and blackberries) and the receptacle. In some aggregate fruits, the ovules mature as dry achenes (for example, the outer 'seeds' in the strawberry).

C A **multiple fruit** is one derived from the fused ovaries and receptacles of many flowers. Each flower has its own receptacle, but they develop together into a single fruit (pineapples, figs).

2 **Dry fruits** typically are made of one ovary, with no fleshy materials around the seeds (hence they are dry at maturity, with little pericarp present). Dry fruits can be lumped into two broad groups: fruits that split when mature and fruits that usually do not split when mature.

A Fruits that split when mature:

1 A **legume** has a fruit with one cavity that splits along both sides of the ovary (beans).

2 A **capsule** is a fruit with an ovary consisting of several cavities containing seeds (lilies and irises).

B Dry fruits that usually do not split when mature:

1 An **achene** is a dry fruit with a thin pericarp with one seed. The ovary wall and seed coat are fused together (sunflowers). The single seed is attached to the pericarp only at its base.

2 **Caryopsis** fruits are single seeds that are fully attached to a thin pericarp (wheat, rice, corn, other cereal grains).

3 **Samaras** are winged seeds, where the thin pericarp forms a wing (maples, ashes, and elms).

4 A **nut** possesses a thick pericarp that is hard or woody, and the ovary wall is separated from the seed, unlike the achenes (hickories, walnuts, oaks, pecans).

A **seed** is a ripened ovule, containing an **embryo.** The external part of the seed consists of the **seed coat.** The **hilum** is a scar formed by the abscission of the short stalk by which the seed is attached to the placenta. Internally, an angiosperm seed typically includes (in addition to the embryo) the **endosperm** and any remaining megasporangial tissues.

Fruits and seeds can be transported great distances by animals, or they are dispersed by wind or water. The seeds and fruits are often ingested by various animals; however, the seeds are often not digested chemically by the animals because of the resistant outer seed coat. The seeds thus can be deposited in the animals' feces and later germinate. An angiosperm seed germinates when environmental conditions are right and the embryo develops into a young angiosperm sporophyte.

Observe the fruits displayed in the demonstration area. Look at the key provided, and determine whether each is a simple, aggregate, or multiple fruit; fleshy or dry at maturity. Determine whether there are accessory parts (particularly the receptacle) incorporated in the fruit. Sketch the fruits that you observed in the space below (Figure 13.16).

FIGURE 13.16.

Fruits.

What is the adaptive significance of a fleshy pericarp for a fruit?

Plants have developed a number of characteristics that attract animals for pollination and dispersal of seeds. With your lab partners, list a number of characteristics or traits that you think attract pollinators. What are these traits and how do they also benefit the animals? Check your list with your lab instructor.

Exercise 13.14.

Double fertilization follows pollination and germination of the pollen tube, which grows down the style of the pistil. The pollen tube enters the ovule through the micropyle. Upon reaching the embryo sac within an ovule, one sperm nucleus migrates to (and fuses with) the egg nucleus, thus restoring the diploid stage of the life cycle. The resulting **zygote** develops into an **embryo** that will be part of the mature seed. A second sperm nucleus migrates to and fuses with two polar nuclei within the embryo sac, giving rise to the **triploid endosperm** tissue.

Observe the seeds of corn (monocot) and bean (eudicot). Identify the hilum, seed-coat, endosperm, cotyledons and embryo. Use the figures at the demonstration table to guide you. Draw what you see in the space provided below (Figure 13.17).

FIGURE 13.17.

Corn and bean seed structure.

Is there a difference in the function of the endosperm and cotyledons in monocot and eudicot seeds? If so, what is that difference?

Exercise 13.15.

Comparison of the Major Plant Groups

Fill in the Table 13.1.

TABLE 13.1.

Features	Mosses	Ferns	Conifers	Angiosperms
Gametophyte or sporophyte dominant? (the other smaller or dependent)				
Sporangia present? [yes/no]				
Homosporous or heterosporous?				
Gametangia present? [yes/no]				
Water required for fertilization? [yes/no]				
Flagellated sperm? [yes/no]				
Vascular tissues present? [yes/no]				
True stems, leaves and roots present? [yes/no]				
Pollen grains present? [yes/no]				
Seeds present? [yes/no]				
Flowers and fruits present? [yes/no]				
Double fertilization and endosperm present? [yes/no]				

Keywords

apical meristem
primary meristem
protoderm
procambium
ground meristem
secondary (lateral)
  meristem
indeterminate
  growth
vascular cambium
cork cambium
cork
periderm
bark
wood
ground tissue
dermal tissue
vascular tissue
epidermis
guard cell

stoma
cuticle
cutin
xylem
tracheid
fiber
sclereid
vessel element
translocation
transpiration
vascular bundle
phloem
companion cell
sieve-tube member
parenchyma
collenchyma
sclerenchyma
node
internode

lenticel
apical bud
axillary bud
primary and
  secondary xylem
primary and
  secondary phloem
spring and
  summer wood
cortex
rays
heartwood and
  sapwood
stolons
rhizomes
tubers
bulbs
blade
petiole
spongy parenchyma

palisade mesophyll
leaf abscission
primary root
lateral root
tap root
fibrous roots
Casparian strip
suberin
endodermis
pericycle
pith
stele
vascular bundle
trichome
sieve plate
corm
hypodermis
root hairs
epidermal cells

Learning Objectives

When finished with this unit, you should be able to:

1 List the three basic types of plant organs and their functions;

2 List the three basic plant tissue types that make up plant organs;

3 Identify the three types of nonmeristematic cells, the three types of meristems (apical, primary, and lateral), the three primary meristems, and the two lateral meristems;

4 Describe the basic structure of xylem and phloem;

5 Describe the various external structures one can see on a plant stem and a plant root: node, internode, leaf scar, lenticel, buds, root cap, root hairs. List the various types of stems;

6 Compare primary and secondary growth in stems and roots;

7 Be able to identify in a longitudinal section of a young stem: apical meristem, epidermis, leaf primordia, axillary buds;

8 Be able to identify in a cross section of stem: epidermis, vascular bundles, xylem and phloem, sclerenchyma, ground tissue (pith and cortex), secondary xylem and secondary phloem, rays, vascular cambium, bark, cork and cork cambium, early and late (spring and summer) wood;

9 Compare monocot leaves with eudicot leaves;

10 Be able to identify in a leaf cross section: cuticle, epidermis (upper and lower), parenchyma (palisade and spongy), veins, xylem, phloem, collenchyma, guard cells;

11 Describe what leaf abscission means;

12 Identify the following structures seen in a longitudinal section of a young root: root cap, region of division, region of elongation, region of differentiation;

13 Describe the functions of root hairs, pericycle, endodermis, and Casparian strip; and

14 Identify in a root cross section: epidermis, cortex, pith, stele, endodermis, pericycle, xylem, phloem, lateral root.

Plant Cells, Tissues, and Organs

The multicellular plants are similar to multicellular animals in that they possess organ systems, organs, tissues, and cells. However, plants are somewhat more **modular** (made of many repeating parts) than are most animals, and on a given plant, there can be young, mature, and senescent organs present at the same time (see Figure 14.1). There are two basic **organ systems** to plants: the **root system** and the **shoot system.**

A In multicellular plants and animals, an organ system is composed of a group of organs that work together to perform a general task for the organism: for example, these general tasks include the acquisition and digestion of food, reproduction, integration of an organism's response to its environment, movement of materials through the body, and structural support. The plant organ systems are composed of many organs: roots, stems, leaves, and flowers (we examined flower structure and function last time). The stomach is an example of an animal organ.

B An organ is a specific part of the body that is composed of several layers of different tissues. An organ basically performs one or more specific functions for its organ system. The stomach, for example, stores food while mechanically breaking it down and chemically digesting it. Further down the digestive tract, the intestine is another organ of the digestive system, where most assimilation of the digested food takes place.

C A tissue is usually a mass, tube, or sheet of cells (consisting of one or a few cell types), involved in a very specific function or maintenance of an organ. For example, layers of connective tissues surround and protect the stomach, and hold the organ together, while inner layers of muscles mix food within the stomach to aid in mechanical and chemical digestion. The innermost layer of epithelium helps digest nutrients.

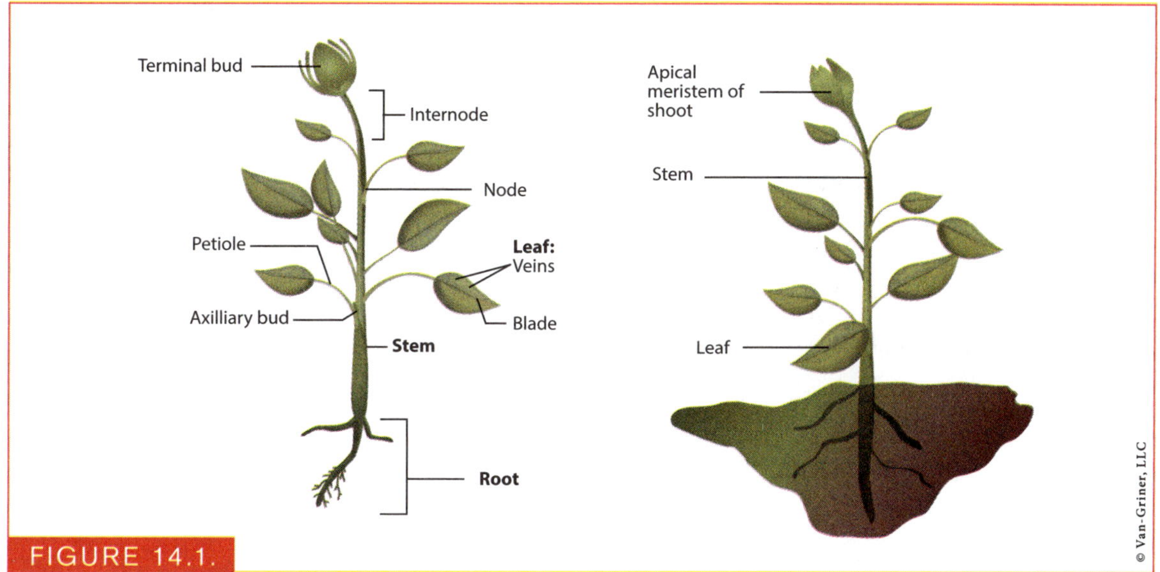

FIGURE 14.1.

The basic organs of a plant.

Plant Cell Types

There are three basic types of cells in **nonmeristematic tissues.** The cell types are **parenchyma, collenchyma,** and **sclerenchyma.**

A **Parenchyma** cells form much of the **ground tissues,** such as the **mesophyll** of leaves and the **cortex** and **pith** of stems and roots. Parenchymal cells typically are living when functionally mature and perform a variety of functions, including metabolism (photosynthesis) and storage (cortex cells). Most of the **epidermis** and much of the edible parts of fruits are composed of parenchymal cells.

Mature **parenchyma** cells have **primary walls** that are relatively thin and flexible. Primary walls allow water and other small compounds to pass through them. Parenchyma cells typically have thin primary cell walls (made of celluloses, pectins, and other polysaccharides, as well as minerals and proteins) and most lack **secondary walls.** Parenchyma come in a variety of shapes; some possess chloroplasts (for example: leaf mesophyll cells), and some do not (root cortex cells). In cross section, they appear to be polygonal or rounded, with intercellular spaces between adjacent cells (Figure 14.2). Mature parenchyma cells can also divide when needed to replace lost tissues. Parenchyma cells can elongate over time. Parenchyma cells are the least specialized cell type, but there are exceptions; the highly specialized sieve-tube members of phloem are parenchyma cells.

Developing plant cells of all types are parenchyma cells before specializing further in structure and function. Mature, unspecialized parenchyma cells do not generally undergo cell division, but many parenchyma cells can be induced to dedifferentiate (i.e., return to a less mature state), undergo mitosis, and then differentiate into other cell types. This 'dedifferentiation' occurs under special conditions, such as during the repair and replacement of organs after injury to the plant. In the laboratory, for some species, it may be possible to regenerate an entire plant from a single parenchyma cell.

B **Collenchyma** cells provide flexible support for various parts of the plant that are still growing, such as young stems. Layers of collenchyma support the vascular tissues, leaf veins, and petioles. Grouped into strands or cylinders, collenchyma cells help support young parts of the plant shoot. Young stems and leaf petioles have a cylinder of collenchyma just below their surface, which provide support without restraining growth. You have experienced collenchyma cells before: think of the 'strings' in the stalks (petioles) of celery that may have gotten stuck between your teeth. Those 'strings' of celery contain a considerable amount of collenchyma. Collenchyma cells have thicker primary walls than parenchyma cells; these walls are composed of celluloses and pectins. Unlike parenchyma cells, the primary walls of collenchyma are **unevenly thickened** (Figure 14.2).

Collenchyma cells are living when functionally mature, and they can live for a long time, like parenchyma cells. Collenchyma cells typically are longer than they are wide (allowing for bending flexibility), and they do not have chloroplasts. They can elongate as the organ they are in elongates over time.

C **Sclerenchyma cells** also function as supporting elements of the plant, with **thick secondary walls** composed of cellulose and strengthened by **lignin,** a tough alcohol polymer that provides rigidity (Figure 14.2). The secondary wall is much thicker than a primary wall and consists of a series of layers inside the primary cell wall, next to the plasma membrane. Sclerenchyma cells provide support in nongrowing regions of the plant. Sclerenchyma cells are much more rigid than collenchyma cells, and unlike parenchyma and collenchyma cells, sclerenchyma cells cannot elongate as the organ they are in elongates. The reason sclerenchyma cells cannot elongate is because they typically are dead at functional maturity; no cytoplasm is left. Instead, a small cavity or lumen is present. Sclerenchyma cells produce their rigid secondary cell walls before the cell dies. The secondary wall is less permeable to water and other small molecules, compared to the primary wall.

Vessel elements and **tracheids** in the xylem are sclerenchyma cells that function for both support and transport. Two other sclerenchyma cells, **fibers** and **sclereids,** are specialized entirely for support. Sclerenchyma **fibers** are long, slender, and tapered, and usually occur in groups. The fiber cells from hemp are used for making rope and those from flax for weaving into linen. **Sclereids** are shorter than fibers and irregular in shape. The hard shells of nuts and seed coats and the gritty texture to pears are due to the presence of sclereids.

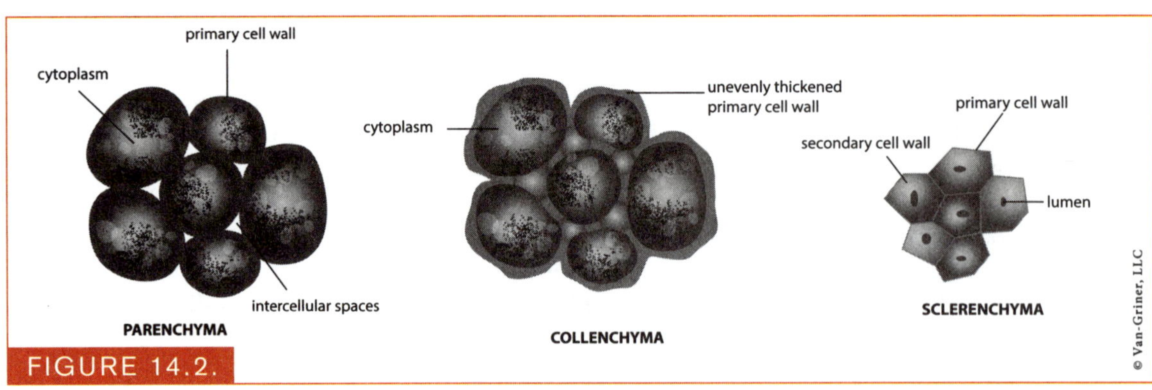

FIGURE 14.2.

Generalized depiction (c.s.) of the three plant cell types: parenchyma, collenchyma, and sclerenchyma.

Plant Tissues

Plant tissues are composed of two 'kinds' of tissues: **meristematic** and **nonmeristematic.** We will discuss the meristems first, then we will examine nonmeristematic tissues.

Meristems

Meristematic cells retain the capacity to undergo cell division (mitosis). They give rise to young cells that either remain meristematic or become specialized for other functions. Meristem cells typically are small, six-sided cells with large nuclei. Meristematic tissues come in three types: **apical meristems, primary meristems,** and **lateral meristems.** These three meristem types have different functions.

A **Apical meristems** are on the tips of young shoots and roots, which increase in length as the root and shoot grows. The apical meristems produce the primary meristems and lateral meristems.

B **Primary meristems** consist of three kinds of primary meristems and all are produced by the **apical meristem.** These primary meristems are responsible for the **primary growth** of the plant (the increase in the **length** of stems and roots). The three primary meristems are listed below.

1 The **protoderm** produces the outer epidermis to stems and roots.

2 The **procambium** produces the vascular tissues in stems and roots.

3 The **ground meristem** produces the ground tissues of stems and roots.

C **Lateral meristems** are responsible for the **secondary growth** of the plant. The lateral meristems increase the **girth** of individual stems and roots but not leaves.

There are several types of lateral meristems; the two major types are described below.

1 The **vascular cambium** produces tissues that increase the girth of the plant, particularly secondary xylem and secondary phloem. Layers upon layers of secondary xylem form over time and harden to produce the tough tissue we call **wood.**

2 The **cork cambium** acts to produce a thick covering for large stems and roots. This covering will eventually replace the epidermis. Parenchyma cells in the cortex (or in some cases from cells in the epidermis or phloem) become the cork cambium. The cork cambium develops at some distance from the tips of roots and stems. Cork cambium produces **cork cells** and **secondary cortex cells. Cork** cells have large amounts of waxy materials deposited in their cell wall; this waxy material acts as a physical barrier to damage. In stems, the cork, and cork cambium form the **periderm.** The periderm, along with the secondary phloem, form the **bark** of the tree. The bark replaces the epidermis over time. In the oldest roots, the cork cambium produces cork cells, and they combine to form the periderm of older roots. These older roots are more woody in appearance, compared to young roots, and the old roots do not absorb water.

Nonmeristematic Tissues

Other than meristematic tissue, plant organs are composed of three basic kinds of **tissues** (similar to how animals are composed of four basic tissue types). The three basic nonmeristematic tissue types are **dermal tissues, vascular tissues,** and **ground tissues.** Several different types of cells (different types of parenchyma, collenchyma, and sclerenchyma cells, see below) are found in all three nonmeristematic tissues.

A **Dermal tissues** consist of the **epidermis,** which acts as the outer 'skin' of the plant (similar to your outer epithelium). The epidermis of the leaves and young stems produces a waxy substance (**cutin**) that forms the cuticle, which helps the shoot system to retain water.

B **Vascular tissues** are involved in the transport of materials through the plant; upward from roots to stems and leaves and downward from leaves to roots. The two major types of vascular tissues include **xylem** and **phloem.** The vascular tissues will be discussed in more detail later.

> **1** Xylem typically carries **xylem sap** (water and dissolved minerals) from the roots to active tissues of the stems and leaves.

> **2** Phloem carries **phloem sap** (a solution rich in carbohydrates) from one part of the plant to another.

C **Ground tissues** are those tissues other than the epidermis and vascular tissues. Parenchyma cells are the dominant cell type in ground tissue of stems, leaves and roots, but other cell types are present as well.

Plant Organs

We will examine the three basic organs that make up plants: **stems, leaves,** and **roots.** Remember that plants are **modular organisms** that have **indeterminate growth:** many plants generally get bigger over time, adding additional parts (organs) through the year. If part of the plant is damaged (by disease, weather, or predators), the plant can respond to the loss of various organs by replacing them.

Stems

A **stem** is the main aerial stalk (or stalks) of the plant. Stems produce buds, secondary stems, flowers, and leaves (and in a few cases, additional roots). Stems support the leaves and conduct water and inorganic minerals to the leaves, and transport sugars and other products of photosynthesis to the roots. Some stems are green: parenchymal cells in the ground tissues have chloroplasts and thus can undergo photosynthesis. Some stems store water (cacti, for example) while other types of stems store food.

Exercises

Exercise 14.1.

External Features of a Stem

1 A **node** is that portion of the stem from which leaves and buds and branches arise (Figure 14.3). **Meristematic tissues** are located at the nodes.

2 An **internode** is the portion of the stem that lies between two nodes.

3 **Lenticels** (Figure 14.4) are slightly raised circular or elongated slit-like structures on the bark of young woody twigs that function in gas exchange.

4 **Buds** are undeveloped shoots in which internodes are present but generally are not elongated. Buds may be protected (covered with specialized leaves called **bud scales**) or naked (lacking bud scales). Buds found at the tips of stems are called **terminal buds (apical buds);** those buds found in the axils of leaves at the nodes are called **axillary (lateral) buds.** Buds give rise to leaves, stems, and flowers.

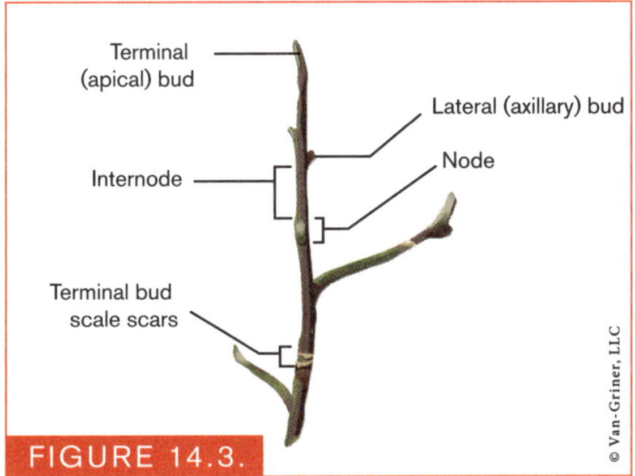

The basic parts of a woody stem.

Lenticels.

Several stem branches are at the front table; examine their basic structure using Figure 14.3 and Figure 14.4 to guide you. Identify: node, internode, leaf scar, lenticels, and buds. Draw some of the stems in the space below (Figure 14.5). Look for lenticels on these branches.

FIGURE 14.5.

Tree stems.

Exercise 14.2.

Primary Growth of Stems: Young Stems

Meristematic activity of the cells of the apical meristem results in an increase in the number of cells. Some of these cells remain **meristematic** (capable of cell division) and thus perpetuate the apical meristem (see Figure 14.6). Other cells produced by the meristem enlarge and differentiate into other plant tissues. The other cells produced by the apical meristem will become the three primary meristems, which in turn give rise to the rest of the plant cells. You can observe the outer epidermis. Also visible are **leaf primordia** and **axillary bud primordia,** which also originate from the apical meristem, and columns of developing **vascular tissues** (with xylem) running posteriorly from each young leaf.

Eudicot Stems

We will compare and contrast the monocot and eudicot stems. Tissues progressing from the outside of the stem towards the center are:

1. The **epidermis** consists of a single layer of parenchyma cells derived from the **protoderm.** The outer walls are covered with waxy substance called **cutin,** which forms the **cuticle. Guard cells** surrounding **stomata** are also present on young stems, but they are most abundant on leaves.

2. The **cortex** is a multi-layered, complex tissue. The cortex originates from the ground meristem and it consists mainly of collenchyma and parenchyma cells, but sclerenchyma fibers may also be present as well.

3. The **vascular tissue** consists of the **primary xylem, primary phloem,** and **vascular cambium.** Vascular tissues arise from the procambium. Vascular tissues typically form discrete, concentrically arranged bundles, called **vascular bundles.** The vascular cambium is found between the xylem and phloem (the vascular cambium inside a vascular bundle is also called **fascicular cambium**).

4. The **pith** (if present) is located in the center of the stem and is composed of parenchyma cells originating from the ground meristem. Pith cells tend to be large and thin-walled, and in some species, the pith cells break down after they form, creating a large cylindrical hollow area in the middle of the stem.

Monocot Stems

In monocots, the origin and development of the primary tissues are the same as those of eudicots, with a few differences.

1. The vascular bundles are scattered throughout the ground tissue of monocot stems instead of the concentric arrangement observed in eudicots.

2. Because the vascular bundles on monocots are scattered, the cortex and pith are indistinguishable, and all tissues derived from the ground meristem are collectively called **ground tissue.** The vascular bundles are surrounded by a sheath of sclerenchyma. There is no fascicular cambium in the monocot vascular bundles.

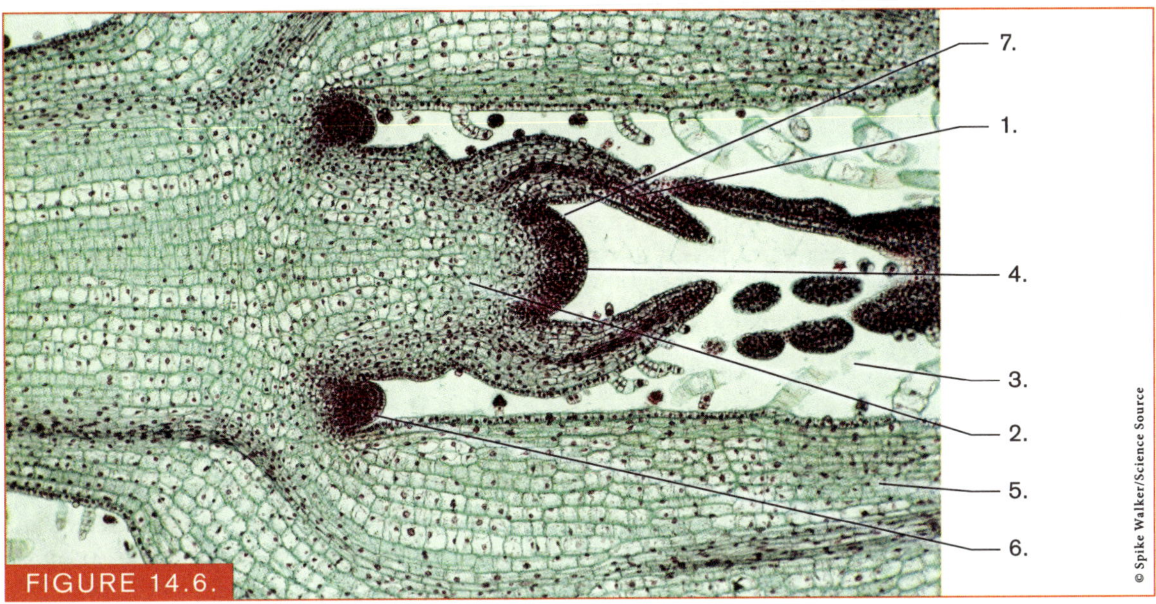

FIGURE 14.6.

The longitudinal section (l.s.) of a typical houseplant, *Coleus*.

1.	Procambrium	3.	Trichome	5.	Leaf primordium	7.	Protoderm
2.	Ground meristem	4.	Apical meristem	6.	Axillary bud		

Under low power, examine a prepared slide of a *Coleus* stem tip (l.s.). Identify the apical meristem, leaf primordia, young leaves, and axillary bud primordia. Bands of young vascular (xylem) tissues run down the length of the young leaves. **Trichomes** are small hairs extending from the epidermis. Draw what you see in the microscope's field of view in the space provided below (Figure 14.7), using Figure 14.6 as a guide.

FIGURE 14.7.

Coleus stem tip, l.s.

Exercise 14.3.

Typical Monocot and Eudicot Stems, c.s.

Phloem transports food made in mature leaves to the roots and other nonphotosynthetic parts of the shoot system. Chains of cells line up to form tube-like structures, through which phloem sap moves.

1. **Sieve-tube members.** The cells that make up a phloem tube are called sieve-tube members. Sieve-tube members are arranged end to end to form long **sieve tubes.** There are porous end walls (called **sieve plates**) between cells along the length of the tube, which allows for unimpeded movement from one cell to the next. Sieve tube members are alive at functional maturity, although they lack both nuclei and ribosomes. Sieve tube members also lack distinct vacuoles.

2. Nonconducting **companion cells** are adjacent to and connected to sieve-tube members. Companion cells retain their nuclei and are living when mature. Companion cells assist sieve-tube members in maintaining cell metabolism and function. In addition to sieve-tube members and companion cells, other parenchyma cells and sclerenchyma fibers are also present in phloem.

Phloem sap is an aqueous solution in which sugar (primarily sucrose) is the predominant solute. Phloem sap also contains minerals, amino acids, and other organic molecules, and hormones. The phloem transports the organic products of photosynthesis throughout the plant via a process called **translocation,** where sugars (in particular) are moved by active transport into sieve tube members, and water follows by osmosis. ATP thus is needed for translocation to occur. The increase in hydrostatic pressure then moves the sugary solution from one cell to the next, going from sugar sources (typically leaves in the spring through fall, and typically roots in the winter) to sugar sinks, where it is used or stored.

Xylem conveys water and dissolved minerals upward from roots into the shoots. The water conducting elements of xylem in the higher plants—the **tracheids** and **vessel elements**—are elongated cells that are dead at functional maturity. Nonconducting sclerenchyma **fibers** are also present; they function in storage and support. Some parenchyma cells are present in xylem as well. In the higher plants, both tracheids and vessel elements have secondary walls interrupted by **pits** (thinner regions where only primary walls are present). The thickened cell walls surround spaces through which fluid (**xylem sap**) flows. The process that moves xylem sap is called **transpiration** or **evapotranspiration.** Hydrogen bonds between adjacent water molecules occurs through the plant to the roots (hydrogen bonding also occurs with the cellulose walls of the vessel elements and tracheids). As a water molecule evaporates from the stomata of leaves, it 'tugs' on the next water molecule, which helps pull water up through the plant. Unlike translocation, no ATP is needed for evapotranspiration to occur.

1. **Tracheids** are long, thin cells with tapered ends. Water (the primary component of the xylem sap) moves from cell to cell mainly through pits. Because their secondary walls are hardened with lignin, tracheids are involved both in support and in transport of xylem sap. **Xylem sap** is primarily composed of water and various dissolved minerals. The sap moves generally upward through the plant (from roots to leaves).

2. **Vessel elements** are generally wider, shorter, thinner-walled, and less tapered than tracheids. Vessel elements are aligned end to end, forming long pipe-like structures called **xylem vessels.** The ends of each vessel element are almost completely perforated, enabling water to flow freely through the xylem vessel.

Under low power, examine a prepared slide of the stem cross sections of both a eudicot and a monocot ("Typical monocot and dicot stems, c.s.") and identify the primary tissues in each stem type. One cross section is that of corn (*Zea*, a monocot) and the other stem is either a bean, buttercup, sunflower, or clover (all eudicots). Note the different arrangement of the tissues found in eudicot and monocot stems. Use Figure 14.9 through 14.11 and Table 14.1 to guide you. Draw what you see in the microscope's field of view in the space provided below (Figure 14.8). Identify the phloem, xylem, vascular bundles, epidermis, the parenchyma of the pith and cortex, and sclerenchyma in the eudicot stem. Using high power, identify companion cells and sieve tube members in phloem and the large vessel elements and smaller tracheids in xylem. Make a sketch of the close-up of the vascular bundles of both the monocot (Figure 14.9) and the eudicot (Figure 14.10 and Figure 14.11) and identify the xylem, phloem, vascular cambium, sclerenchyma cells, and air spaces (formed in the monocot stem by the stretching and destruction of the primary xylem and phloem as the stem internode elongated).

FIGURE 14.8.

Monocot stem c.s. (left) and eudicot stem c.s. (right).

What can you say about the arrangement of the vascular bundles in the monocot stem versus the eudicot stem?

What is the relative position of xylem and phloem?

Note the reddish, thickened walls of cells in the eudicot vascular bundles to the outside of the phloem. What cell type are they?

What are the functions of the cortex and pith? What is the dominant cell type found in both cortex and pith?

Which cells are living when functional? Where are they in relation to the outside of the stem? How do they receive oxygen?

TABLE 14.1. Comparison of monocot and eudicots.

	Monocot	Eudicot
Cotyledons	one	two
Leaf venation	major veins parallel	major veins netlike (reticulated)
Leaf petioles	absent	present
Leaf stomata location	equally found in both epidermal layers	primarily in lower epidermis
Stem vascular bundle location	more scattered throughout cross section, more abundant near periphery	arranged in a ring near periphery
Root number	many fibrous roots (additional adventitious roots arise from stem)	single taproot arising from radicle, increased size due to apical meristem
Flower parts	three or multiples of three	four or five or multiples of four or five
Secondary growth	usually absent	usually present
Woody growth	absent	often occurs

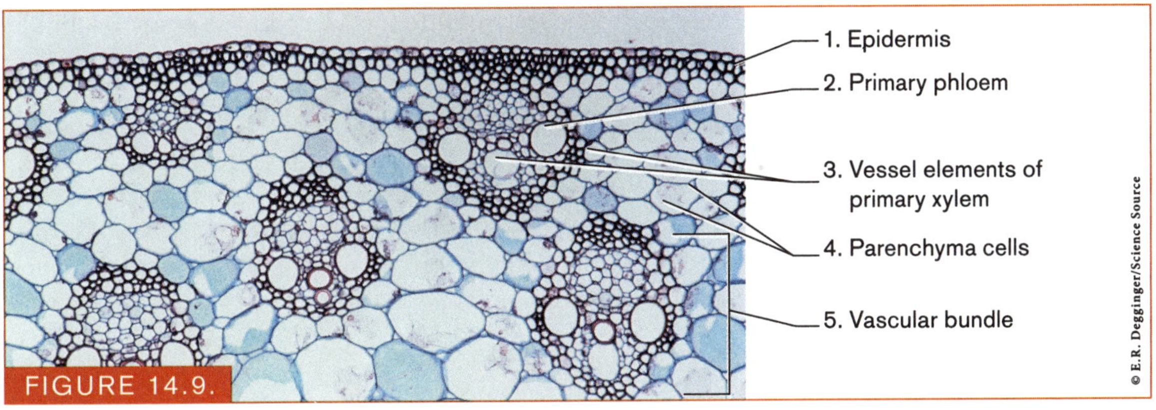

A cross section through a monocot stem, the corn plant *Zea*.

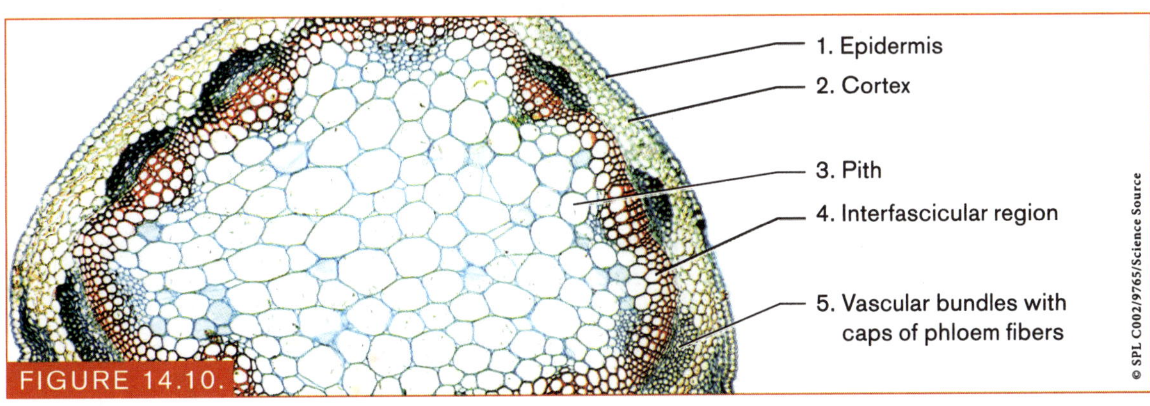

A cross section through a dicot stem, the clover *Trifolium*.

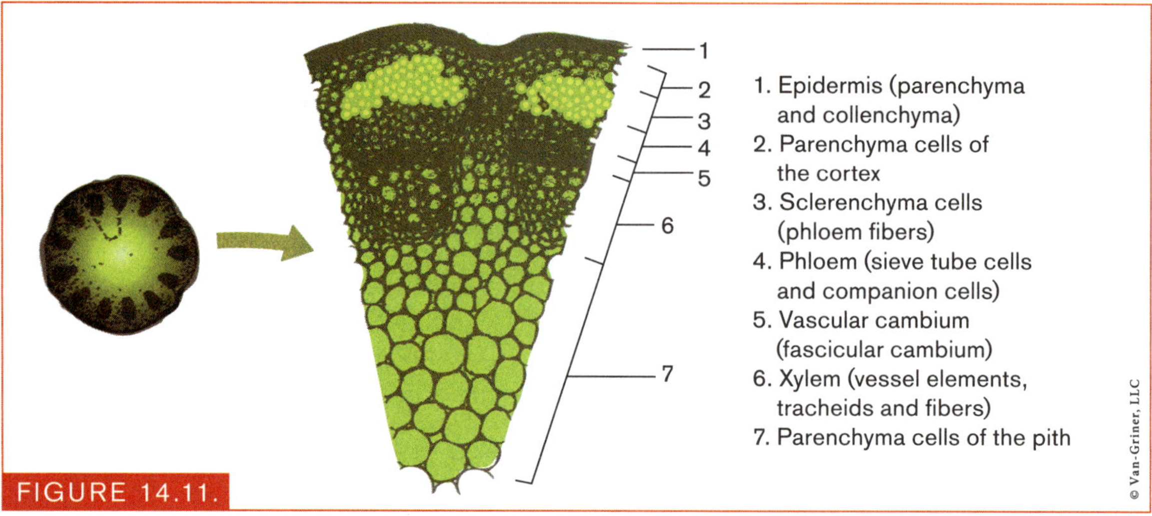

FIGURE 14.11.

The vascular bundle of a eudicot.

Exercise 14.4.

Secondary Growth of Stems

Subsequent to the maturation of the primary tissues in a eudicot stem, a meristem (**interfascicular cambium**) develops between the vascular bundles from cortical parenchyma cells. The interfascicular cambium eventually becomes continuous with the fascicular cambium within the vascular bundles. The fascicular cambium and interfascicular cambium form a complete ring or cylinder of meristematic tissue called the **vascular cambium.** Cells produced from this tissue differentiate as **secondary xylem** and **secondary phloem,** which also form as complete rings or cylinders of conducting tissue. The **cork cambium** (also called the **phellogen**) is another lateral meristem that forms from parenchyma of the cortex (exterior to the vascular cambium and its derivatives), or from epidermal cells or phloem. The cork cambium, cork, and secondary phloem form the **bark** of woody plants. **Eudicots** typically have true secondary growth, with vascular cambium, cork cambium, and bark. **Monocots** do not typically exhibit secondary growth, although a few species (such as palms) enlarge their diameters by an 'anomalous secondary growth' created by parenchyma cells (not by vascular cambia).

Woody Eudicot Stems and Annual Rings

The primary tissues of a woody eudicot stem develop in the same manner as those of herbaceous stems. However, the primary vascular tissues form a **continuous ring** (instead of discrete bundles) in most eudicots. Subsequent to the maturation of the primary vascular tissues, derivatives of the vascular cambium differentiate into components of **secondary xylem** and **secondary phloem** (Figure 14.12). The building material we call **wood** is made of secondary xylem. The continuous yearly growth in stem diameter is from the production of new secondary xylem and phloem. If there is a yearly cessation of this growth, as in the temperate regions of the world, **annual growth rings** will be formed. The yearly addition of phloem is not as conspicuous as that of xylem. The annual rings of the xylem are composed of **spring wood and summer wood.** The xylem cells produced during the wetter parts of the growing season (typically spring) is less dense (larger cells and proportionally thinner cell walls), compared to the denser summer wood, which is composed of smaller cells and thicker walls. The composition of the annual ring can include all the basic types of xylem components, i.e., parenchyma, fibers, sclereids, vessel elements, and tracheids.

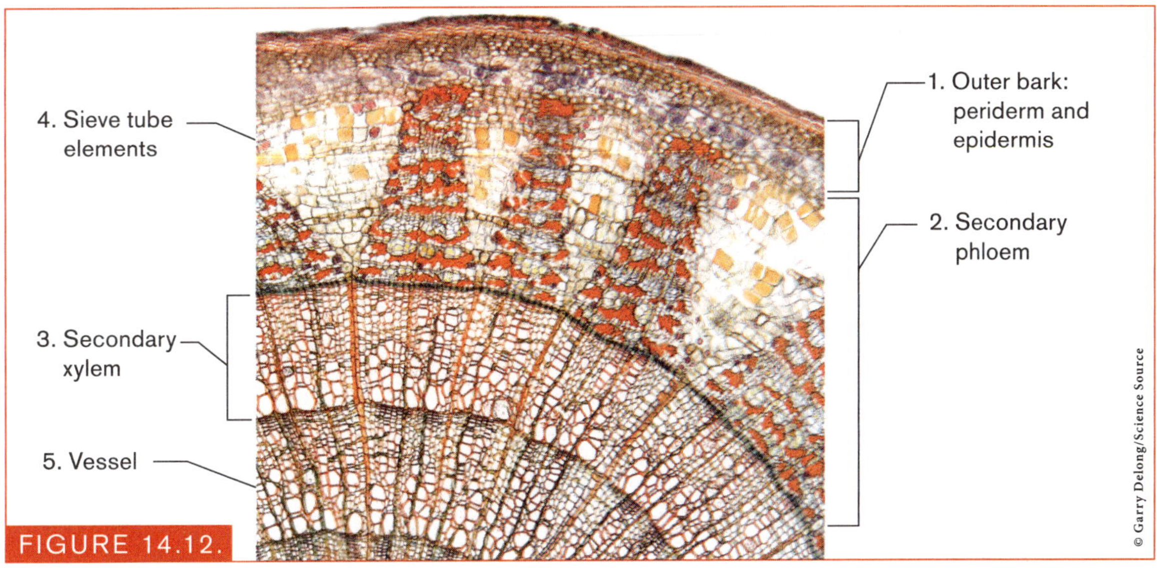

FIGURE 14.12.

A cross section through a woody stem (*Vitis* sp.), showing secondary growth.

Examine a prepared slide labeled "Herbaceous and woody dicot stems, c.s." The cross section of the herbaceous stem is identical to the one you examined in Exercises 14.2 and 14.3, and the woody stem is through a young woody eudicot tree. Use Figure 14.10 and Figure 14.11 and diagrams on the display table to guide you. Draw what you see in the microscope's field of view in the space provided below (Figure 14.13). Identify the primary tissues present in the herbaceous stem and the secondary tissues found in the woody stem. Note the periderm, annual rings, and vascular cambium in the woody stem.

FIGURE 14.13.

Cross section of herbaceous and woody stems.

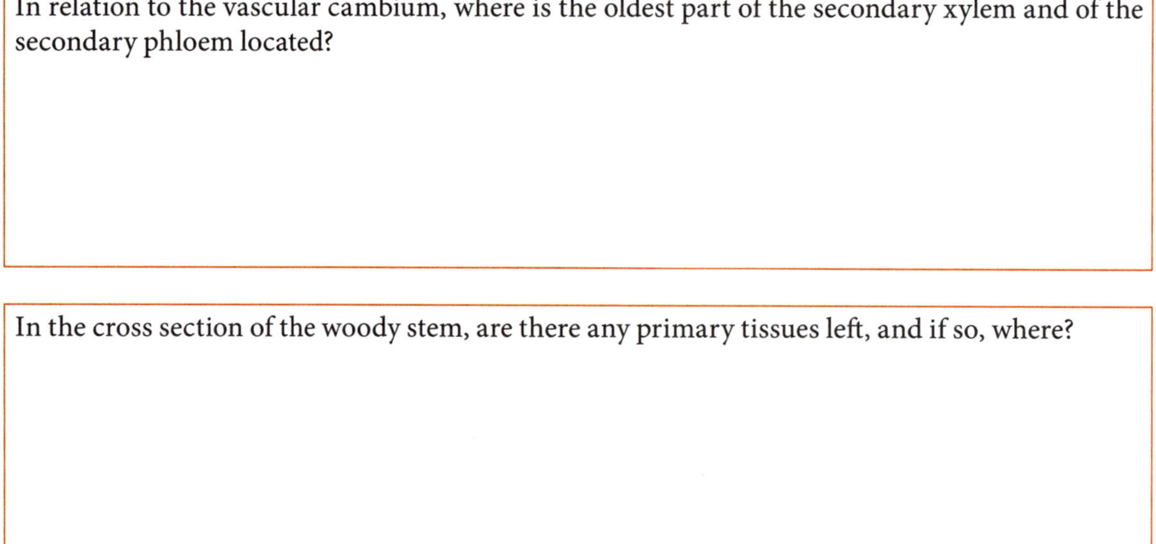

Exercise 14.5.

Secondary Growth in Stems

As secondary xylem and phloem form, a cork cambium (which gives rise to the **periderm**) arises in the outer **cortex.** The cork cambium forms the box-like **cork cells** which become impregnated with a fatty compound called **suberin.** Suberin acts as a waterproofing agent. Eventually, the epidermis and outer cortical layers are sloughed off the older stem as it increases in diameter, and the periderm becomes the outermost tissue.

Rays

Looking at the cross section of the stem, lighter streaks of parenchyma cells called **rays** can be seen radiating outward from the center of the trunk, across the annual rings. The part of the ray within the xylem is referred to as the xylem ray, while the ray's extension through the phloem is called the phloem ray. Rays allow the lateral (sideways) conduction of water and nutrients across the stem.

Heartwood and Sapwood

As most woody stems age, the older annual rings near the center become discolored by the deposition of various organic compounds. The protoplasts of some of the parenchymal cells that surround the xylem elements and tracheids grow into the pits of the dead xylem cells, protruding into and filling up the cavity of the xylem. These protrusions prevent further conduction of water. Resins, gums, tannins, and various pigments subsequently accumulate, darkening the color of this wood. This darkened central region, known as **heartwood,** functions only in mechanical support; the xylem cells are no longer conducting water. The outer lighter-colored region, the **sapwood,** functions in both mechanical support and transport.

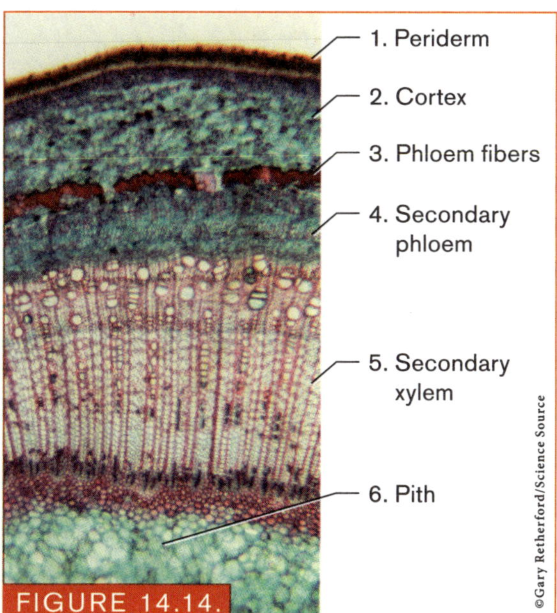

FIGURE 14.14.

Cross-section through a woody stem (*Fraxinus*), showing secondary growth.

Examine the display of a woody stem section at the demonstration table. Identify the following: bark, vascular cambial region, annual rings, spring wood, summer wood, heartwood, and sapwood. Use Figure 14.11 and Figure 14.14 to guide you, as well as any pictures or charts at the demonstration table. Draw a sketch of the woody stem section in the space below (Figure 14.15).

FIGURE 14.15.

Cross section through a large woody stem.

Bark is composed of what tissues?

What causes the cracking of the outer part of the bark?

Compared to summer wood, how thick is spring wood? Is the difference due to larger cells (diameters) or due to the presence of more cells?

What was the approximate age of this tree when it was cut down?

Other Types of Stems

Recall that not all stems are above ground or run vertically. Below ground or horizontal stems include **stolons** (the runners of strawberry plants), **rhizomes** (underground horizontal stems, like that observed in ginger), **tendrils** (threadlike stems used to attach to substrates or host plants), **tubers** (white potatoes are tubers, or modified stolons or rhizomes that are used for storing food—the 'eyes' are young stem buds), **bulbs** (consisting of a collection of modified leaves surrounding a short stem, like that of the onion) and **corms** (short underground stems used for food storage, often surrounded by a protective layer of papery leaves). Examine Figure 14.16 below.

FIGURE 14.16.

Various examples of specialized stems.

Leaves

A **External features of a leaf.** A plant's leaves are the principle organs of photosynthesis. There is essentially no secondary growth of a leaf; the primary meristems give rise to the leaf tissues (see Figure 14.17). In a few pines with long-lived needles, a small amount of secondary growth of additional phloem cells occurs over time. The **blade** is the thin, flattened, photosynthetic part of a leaf. The **petiole** is the stem-like stalk of a leaf that attaches the blade to the stem node (Figure 14.17).

FIGURE 14.17.

The basic structure of a leaf.

B **Leaf venation.** The arrangement of the **veins** (composed of the **vascular tissues** of **xylem** and **phloem,** as well as other supporting tissues) in the blade is called **venation.** There are two general types of venation (Table 14.1):

1 **Netted** (or **reticulate**) **venation** is where the leaf has one or more large veins from which smaller veins diverge. These smaller veins in turn give rise to still smaller ones, ultimately forming a network. **Eudicots** possess this type of venation.

2 **Parallel venation** is where the leaf has several veins that are more or less of equal size, which run parallel with one another down the leaf. **Monocots** have parallel venation.

C **Internal Anatomy of the Angiosperm Leaf Blade.** The **epidermis** is usually a single layer of modified parenchyma cells with a waxy cuticle, covering both the upper and lower surfaces of the blade. **Guard cells** (Figure 14.18) are specialized epidermal cells. A pair of guard cells surround a **stoma** (plural: **stomata**).

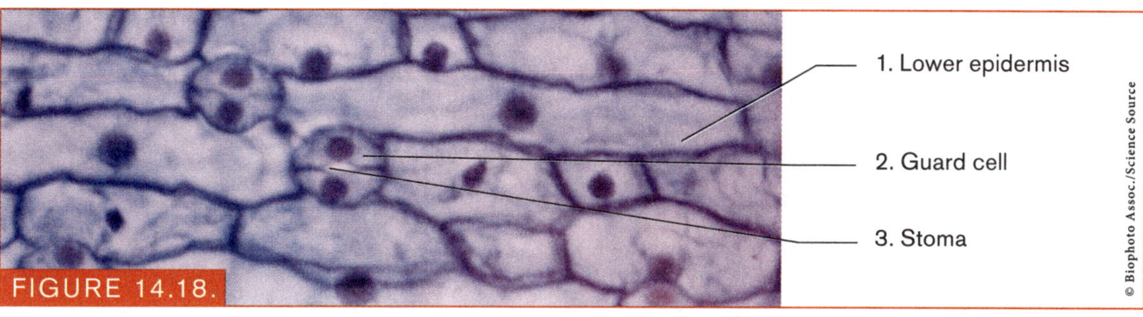

FIGURE 14.18.

Guard cells.

Eudicot leaves possess stomata located primarily on the lower surface of the blade. Monocot leaves possess stomata that are distributed more or less evenly on the upper and lower surfaces of the blade.

The **mesophyll** is the photosynthetic parenchyma between the upper and lower epidermis of the blade (see Figure 14.19). The mesophyll of eudicot leaves is differentiated into two layers:

1 **Palisade mesophyll** (palisade parenchyma), where one or more layers of elongated photosynthetic parenchyma cells lie adjacent to the upper epidermis.

2 **Spongy mesophyll** (spongy parenchyma), the loosely organized photosynthetic parenchyma cells between the palisade mesophyll and the lower epidermis.

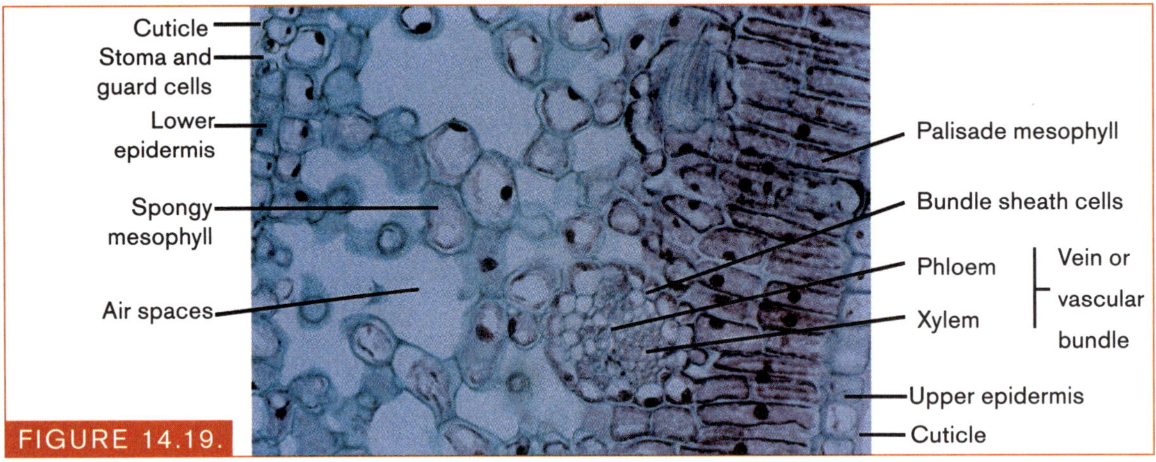

FIGURE 14.19.

Cross section of a eudicot leaf.

D **Another difference between monocots and eudicot leaves.** The mesophyll of monocot leaves is not differentiated into palisade and spongy layers (Figure 14.19).

E **Veins** constitute the vascular tissue of the leaf and are embedded in the mesophyll. Leaf veins consist of **xylem** and **phloem,** often surrounded by fibers and parenchyma. Some parenchyma cells are called **bundle sheath cells,** which forms the bundle sheath. The bundle sheath surrounds the xylem and acts in a fashion that is analogous to the endodermis of the root—no part of the vascular tissue is exposed to the air in the intercellular spaces of the mesophyll.

F **Abscission Zone.** Plants whose leaves drop periodically with the change in seasons are called **deciduous plants** (as opposed to **evergreen plants** that do not periodically drop their leaves). In temperate latitudes, the deciduous leaves are dropped in the fall and replaced the next spring; in the tropics, the leaves are dropped during the dry season. The process of leaf shedding or **abscission** is preceded by the active resorption of nutrients from the leaves. An abscission zone then develops at the base of the petiole with the formation of a protective layer of cells (on the side closest to the stem) and an adjacent **separation layer** of cells. Enzymes facilitate the dissolution of the middle lamella between the cells of the separation layer. Finally, the only intact tissue that holds the leaf to the stem is the xylem of the vascular bundles. Mechanical disturbances such as wind or vibrations will knock the leaf from the stem, leaving a protected area known as the **leaf scar** on the stem itself (see Figure 14.3). Unlike the deciduous plants, conifer needles live a few years until they are shed; a pine loses some of its needles every year.

Exercise 14.6.

Examine the prepared slide labeled "Typical monocot and dicot leaves, c.s." and identify the tissues present. Draw what you see in the microscope's field of view in the space below (Figure 14.20). Use Figure 14.19 as a guide. The v-shaped leaf cross section on the slide is the eudicot (probably a maple); the other leaf with the large number of parallel vascular bundles is the monocot (probably corn). Find the **cuticle, upper and lower epidermis, mesophyll** (distinguish palisade and spongy if both are present), **vascular bundles** or **veins, air spaces, guard cells,** and **stomates (stomata)**. For the corn vascular bundle, note the large thick-walled bundle sheath cells next to the xylem vessels. Are any collenchyma and sclerenchyma cells present? Fill out part of Exercises 14.14 and 14.15 with this information.

FIGURE 14.20.

Eudicot and monocot leaf cross sections.

Compare the structure (tissue arrangement) of a eudicot leaf with that of a monocot. Note that the vascular tissues differ (the vascular bundles have xylem and phloem on the inside, with the vascular cells surrounded by large, photosynthetic cells called bundle sheath cells). Note that the mesophyll of a monocot leaf is more uniform, without palisade and spongy layers. In monocots, a layer of meristematic cells near to the base of the leaf continue producing additional tissues by mitosis and the blade elongates (this is why you can mow your lawn and not kill the monocot grasses, unless you mow too close to the ground).

Recall the venation patterns (netlike versus parallel venation) of eudicot and monocot leaves. Can you confirm this fact from the cross sections of the two types of leaves?

Chlorophyll is most abundant in what mesophyll layer of a typical eudicot leaf? Why?

Are there any chloroplasts in the epidermis, and if so, which cells? How thick does the cuticle appear on the upper and lower epidermis of the eudicot leaf?

In what part of a leaf of a eudicot plant are air spaces more numerous? Correlate the position of the air spaces with their function. How does the distribution of the air spaces in the eudicot leaf compare to that observed in the monocot leaf?

On which surface (upper or lower) are the stomates most abundant on the eudicot leaf? Why is there a difference? How does this relate to the spongy mesophyll? Which type of tissue is near air spaces, and why?

For the monocot leaf, are there equal numbers of guard cells and stomates on the upper and lower epidermis? What does this tell you about the positioning of leaves in many monocots? Where do the chloroplasts seem to be the most abundant?

Measure the lengths and widths of some of the palisade cells and spongy cells in the eudicot leaf. Which cells are larger? Can you see the distribution of the chloroplastids within cells, and if so, how are they distributed?

Exercise 14.7.

Examine the cross sections of eudicot leaves and monocot leaves under high power. Estimate the distance between any two stomates along the lower and upper epidermis of the eudicot leaf, and fill in Table 14.2 below. (If you cannot find any stomates in the upper surface, place Xs in the column for upper epidermis.)

Do the same for the two epidermis layers of the monocot leaf. Remember, monocot leaves generally are perpendicular to the ground, so both sides of the leaf could be exposed to direct sunlight. We will call one side the 'upper' surface and the other side the 'lower' surface, just for counting purposes. Are the distances similar? How much variation appears to exist? Is there a difference between the spacing and densities of stomates between upper and lower epidermal layers?

TABLE 14.2.

Distance (mm) between:	Eudicot Leaf		Monocot Leaf	
	Upper Epidermis	Lower Epidermis	'Upper' Epidermis	'Lower' Epidermis
stomates 1 and 2				
2 and 3				
3 and 4				
4 and 5				
5 and 6				
6 and 7				
7 and 8				
8 and 9				
9 and 10				
10 and 11				
mean				

You can determine the number of stomata per mm^2 of leaf surface by squaring the average distance calculated above and divide 1 by this number (in other words, take the inverse of the squared distance) and then multiplying by 1,000,000 (the number of μm^2 in one mm^2). Fill in the following table (Table 14.3).

TABLE 14.3. Number of stomata per mm^2 = 10^6 / (average distance in μm)^2

Leaf	Average Distance (in μm) between Stomata	Number of Stomata per mm^2
Eudicot Upper Epidermis		
Eudicot Lower Epidermis		
Monocot 'Upper' Epidermis		
Monocot 'Lower' Epidermis		

Examine the results of Exercise 14.7. Are the number of stomata similar on both plants? Is there a difference between the two surfaces of the leaves for either plant? Why?

Exercise 14.8.

Examine the prepared slide of *Salix* showing the abscission layer (the slide is labeled "Abscission layer"). You can see the stem (in longitudinal section) and an axillary bud and the abscission zone. Draw what you see in the microscope's field of view in the space below (Figure 14.21).

FIGURE 14.21.

Abscission layer in *Salix.*

What is the function of the abscission zone of a leaf?

Exercise 14.9.

Examine the display of leaf specimens, models, and diagrams at the demonstration table. Draw several sketches of leaves and venation types in the space below (Figure 14.22).

FIGURE 14.22.

Leaf structure.

Roots

A Roots anchor the plant in the soil, absorb minerals and water, and store food. The first of the vegetative organs to emerge from the germinating seed is the **primary root.** As growth and development continue, a system of roots composed mainly of **lateral roots,** becomes established. If the primary root remains and enlarges, while all lateral roots are relatively much smaller; this root system is termed a **tap root system,** such as that of a carrot. A **fibrous root system,** such as that of a grass, is one composed of no distinct tap root; instead, there are many lateral roots that are all slender.

B Monocots generally have fibrous root systems. This relatively shallow and dense mat of roots increases the plant's exposure to soil water and minerals in the uppermost section of the soil and anchors it to the ground. The high surface area of fibrous roots allows these plants to rapidly take up water from rainfall. Monocot roots generally show no secondary growth because there usually is no lateral meristems present to increase the diameter of the root.

C Many eudicots have a **taproot system** consisting of a one large vertical root (the taproot) that produces many small lateral roots. The taproot anchors the plant in the soil, but it also stores food to support the production of flowers and fruits later.

D Like a stem, the development of a root (especially eudicot roots) may involve both **primary growth** and **secondary growth.** Recall that **primary growth** is the direct consequence of the enlargement and differentiation of cells produced by the **apical meristem.** It results in an increase in length, and all tissues produced by the apical meristem are termed **primary tissues. Secondary growth** is the direct consequence of the enlargement and differentiation of cells produced by **lateral meristems:** the **vascular cambium** and **cork cambium.** Secondary growth causes an increase in girth or diameter of roots, and all tissues composed of cells derived from a lateral meristem are termed **secondary tissues.** All roots undergo primary growth, but only those roots that have lateral meristems (eudicots) can undergo secondary growth.

E **Root primary growth. Young roots.** Growth in length of roots is the same as that in stems, i.e., the elongation and/or maturation of cells produced by the apical meristem. As a result of the apical meristem, a number of regions of growth can be discerned in longitudinal sections of a young root or root tip (see Figure 14.23).

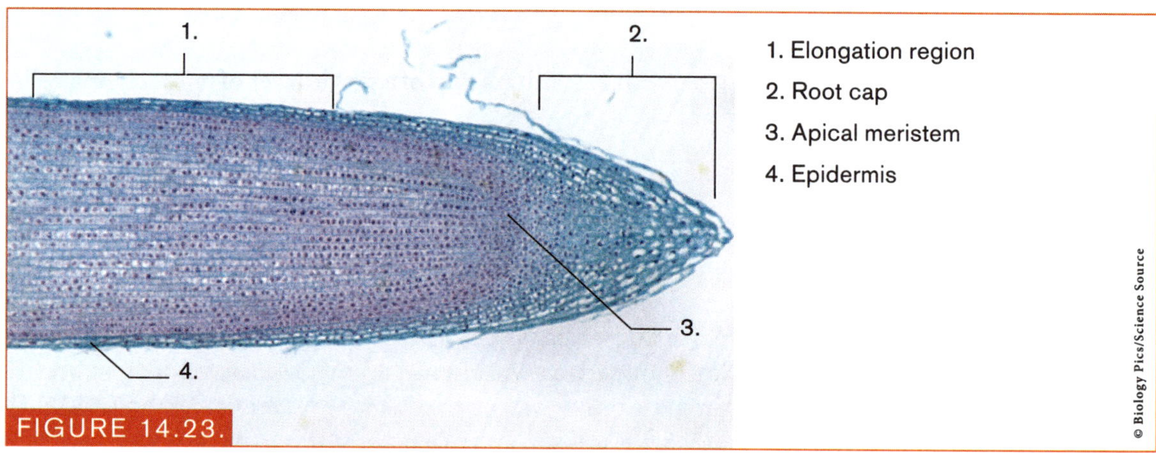

FIGURE 14.23.

Longitudinal section of a young root.

F The **root cap** is a thimble-like structure composed of rather loosely arranged parenchyma cells that covers the root apex (Figure 14.23). There is no equivalent of a root cap in stems. These special parenchyma cells are produced by the apical meristem and are sloughed off. In addition to protection of the root apical meristem, the root cap cells produce a slimy polysaccharide lubricant that facilitates the movement of the root through the soil. Cells in the root cap are able to perceive gravity.

G **Three zones to a young root/shoot:**

1 The **region of division** (or the **meristematic region,** the apical meristem is located in the region of cell division) is the compact tissue immediately behind the root cap composed of small cells (Figure 14.23).

2 The **region of cell elongation** (or enlargement) is adjacent to the apical meristem and consists of cells that are increasing in size longitudinally (Figure 14.23). Some differentiation has also begun in this region and the three primary meristems are found here:

a The **protoderm** is a single layer of cells on the outside that will differentiate into the **epidermis.**

b The **ground meristem** is several cell layers thick and extends from the protoderm to near the center. The ground meristem produces the **cortex** and the **endodermis.**

c The **procambium** is comprised of several cell layers in the central region. The procambium will give rise to the tissues of the **stele** (vascular tissue).

3 The **region of differentiation** (or **region of maturation**) is also known as the root hair zone and is adjacent to the region of elongation, further up the root.

a **Root hairs** (Figure 14.23) form and other cells differentiate into their final form in this region. After differentiation, these cells comprise the **primary tissues.**

b Externally, much of a young primary root is covered with a heavy growth of **root hairs** which indicates the region of differentiation internally. Below the root hair zone, cells are elongating and new root hairs are being initiated. The very tip of the root, covered with a root cap, includes the apical meristem.

H **Primary Tissues in Roots.** The tissues of a eudicot root are listed below, progressing from the outside in (see Figure 14.24). There are a few differences between monocots and eudicots, which are indicated below.

1 The **epidermis** is derived from the protoderm and consists of a single layer of parenchyma cells. The epidermal cells of a root normally lack a cuticle.

2 The **cortex** is a broad area of parenchyma cells derived from the ground meristem. They store starches and other materials. The cortex is located interior to the epidermis and includes the endodermis.

3 The **endodermis** is a single layer of cells (the innermost layer of cortex cells) characterized by **Casparian strips** on their transverse and radial walls. The **Casparian strip** refers to an area of cell wall that has been secondarily thickened with lignin and waterproofed with **suberin.** Suberin is a waxy material that is impervious to water and dissolved minerals. The **endodermis** surrounds the stele and regulates which minerals pass from cortex to vascular tissue. As water enters the plant roots through the root epidermis, water (and dissolved minerals and various organic compounds) could travel through the areas of the cell walls without ever entering the cytoplasm of a cell. However, the endodermis, with its Casparian strip, ensures that no minerals can reach the vascular tissue of the root without crossing at least one selectively permeable plasma membrane of a living cell. Harmful minerals may be excluded by these cells, whereas useful ones are retained.

4 The **pericycle** is a layer of cells just inside the endodermis; these cells are derived from the procambium. The pericycle is composed of one to several layers of relatively unspecialized parenchyma cells that retain a potential to undergo cell division. **Lateral roots** are created by the cells of the pericycle.

5 The **primary phloem** is a complex tissue derived from the procambium that occurs in strands between the radiating arms of the primary xylem.

6 The **vascular cambium** consists of undifferentiated procambial cells between the primary xylem and primary phloem. The vascular cambium cells appear roughly rectangular in cross section.

7 The **primary xylem** is a complex tissue derived from the procambium that occupies the center of the root, with either three, four, or more radiating arms.

8 A central **pith** region consisting of parenchyma cells is characteristic of monocot roots (see Figure 14.25).

9 The **stele** (Figure 14.24) is the central part of the root. It includes all tissues inside the cortex: pericycle, vascular tissues. In the monocots, the central pith is also found in the stele.

10 The **hypodermis** (in roots, it is also called the **exodermis**) is the outermost layer or layers of cortex cells, and it can be found in many stems and in roots. It is one to several layers of cells just under the single layer of epidermis, and in the mature roots, it may have Casparian strips and suberin, similar to the endodermis. This layer is important in preventing the outward movement of water and nutrients which have been absorbed by the region of root hairs lower down the root. The hypodermis helps the plant retain water and dissolved minerals.

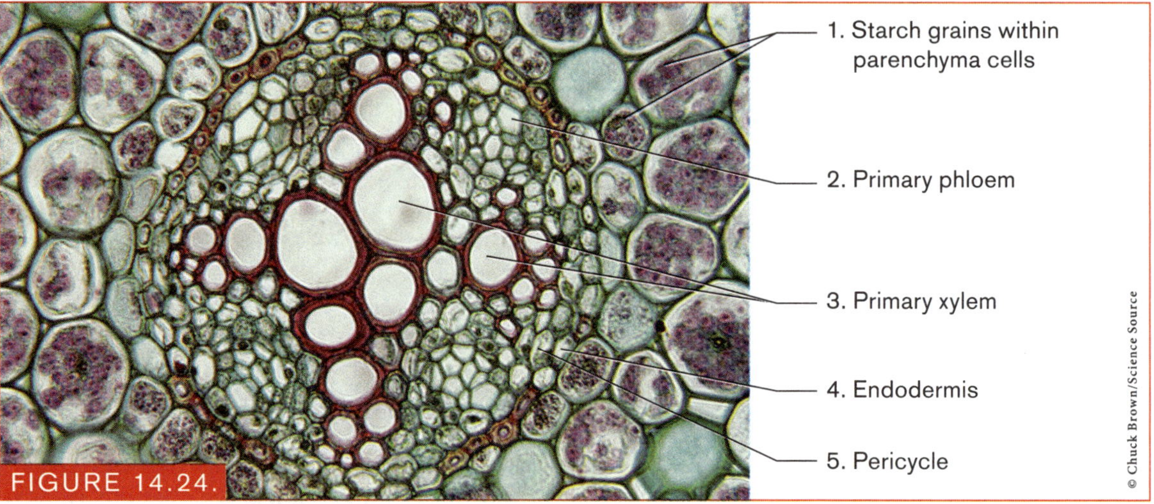

Portion of a cross section of a dicot root.

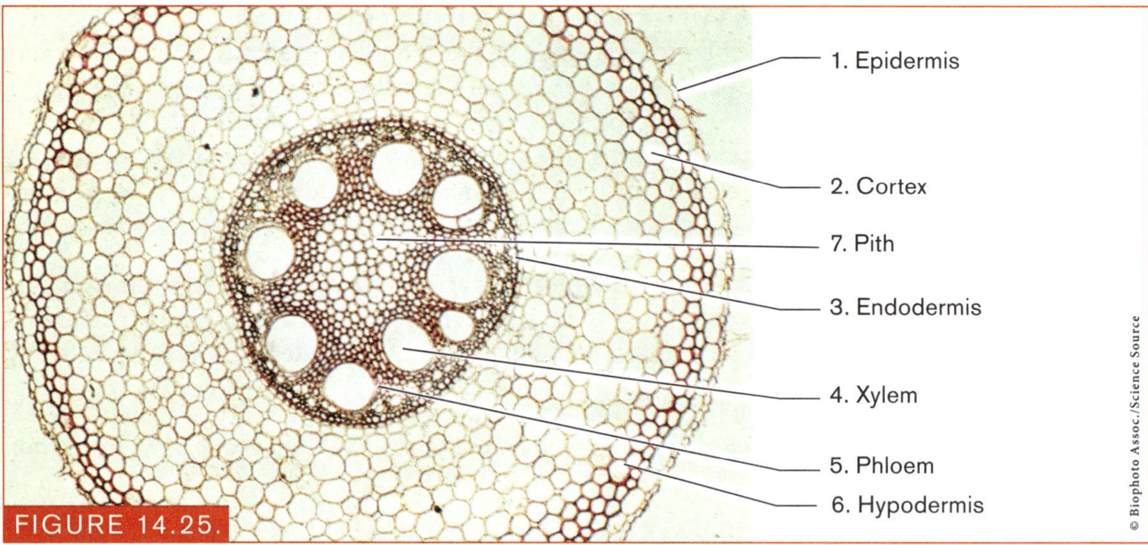

Cross section of a monocot root.

Exercise 14.10.

Go to the demonstration table, and compare the tap root of eudicots with the fibrous roots of monocots. Draw what you see in the microscope's field of view in the space below (Figure 14.26). Fill out part of Exercise 14.14 from this information.

FIGURE 14.26.

Tap roots and fibrous roots.

Exercise 14.11.

What is the function of the root cap? From what tissue are the cells of the root cap derived?

Estimate the lengths of the cells in the apical meristem and those in the region of elongation.

Exercise 14.12.

Examine a prepared slide labeled "Dicot and monocot roots, c.s." and identify the main tissues and features. The monocot is corn (*Zea*); the eudicot is the buttercup (*Ranunculus*). Note the differences in tissue arrangement between the two root types. Use Figure 14.24 and Figure 14.25 to guide you. Draw what you see in the microscope's field of view in the space provided below (Figure 14.27). Identify epidermis, vascular cylinder, xylem, phloem, pith (if present), cortex, pericycle, endodermis, exodermis (hypodermis).

FIGURE 14.27.

Monocot root (left) and eudicot root (right) cross sections.

What are root hairs? From what tissue are they derived? How many cells make up a root hair? What is the function of root hairs?

Note that the root lacks a cuticle. Why?

What is the function of the endodermis? How many cell layers are present?

What is the function of the pericycle? How many cell layers are present?

Estimate the diameters of some of the cells in the stele (xylem, phloem) and in the cortex (parenchyma). Are there any spaces between the cell walls of the cells of the stele? Between the cells of the cortex? What is the function of these air spaces?

What are the stained granules in the parenchymal cortex?

Exercise 14.13.

Soup and Salad Biology

Examine the following vegetable items found in your soups and salads, and determine what type of plant organ they are, and their function. Fill in Table 14.4 below.

TABLE 14.4.

Item	Plant Organ (root, stem, leaf, flower, fruits, stolons, rhizomes, tubers, petioles, etc.)	Function (storage, support, reproduction, photosynthesis)
tomatoes		
white potato		
sweet potato		
onion		
celery		
carrots		
broccoli, cauliflower, Brussels sprouts		
asparagus		
eggplant		
lettuce		
parsley, sage, rosemary, and thyme		
ginger		
bell peppers		
peppercorns (black pepper)		
mustard		
olives		

Exercise 14.14.

Fill out the following table, using the information from Units 13 and 14.

TABLE 14.5.

Trait	Monocot	Eudicot
Number of cotyledons		
Floral parts in multiples of:		
Leaf venation: parallel or net-like		
Location of leaf stomata, upper and/or lower epidermis		
Palisade and spongy parenchyma present?		
Distribution of vascular bundles in stems and roots		
Cortex and pith both present in stems?		
Root system: tap roots versus fibrous roots		
True secondary growth, with vascular cambium, cork cambium, and bark		

Exercise 14.15.

Fill in the following table (Table 14.6) as a study aid to master the tissues and cell types of higher plants.

TABLE 14.6.

Structure, Cell or Tissue Type	Structural Features of the Cells	Functions	Location (plant organs)
apical meristems			
primary meristems			
lateral meristems			
parenchyma			
collenchyma			
sclerenchyma			
tracheids and vessel elements			
sieve tubes and companion cells			
pith and cortex			
stele			
cork, cork cambium, periderm and bark			
epidermal cells			
guard cells			
palisade and spongy parenchyma			
endodermis			
pericycle			

UNIT 15 — The Fungi

Keywords

heterotrophic
saprobic
chitin
mycelium
hypha
septate
aseptate
dikaryotic
  (= heterokaryotic)
dikaryon
plasmogamy
karyogamy
spore

meiospore
sporangiophore
conidiophore
conidium
gametangium
sporangium
zygosporangium
ascogonium
antheridium
hymenium
ascocarp
ascus

ascospore
basidiocarp
basidium
mushroom
pileus
stipe
gills (lamellae)
basidiospore
sterigma
mold
lichen
yeast

mycorrhizae
symbiosis
soredium
crustose
foliose and fruticose
mycobiont
phycobiont
parasitism
commensalism
mutualism
sporocarp
suspensor cell

Learning Objectives

When finished with this unit, you should be able to:

1 List the basic characteristics shared by all fungi;

2 Describe the three major divisions of fungi and be able to recognize representatives of each;

3 Compare and contrast the life cycles, sexual stages, and asexual stages of the three major divisions;

4 Describe what is meant by a lichen, yeast, mold (deuteromycete or Fungi Imperfecti), and mycorrhizae;

5 Compare and contrast the three basic lichen growth forms and describe the function of soredia; and

6 Contrast plasmogamy and karyogamy.

Classification

Kingdom Fungi

Division (Phylum) Zygomycota (the zygomycetes or zygote fungi), *Rhizopus*

Division Ascomycota (the ascomycetes or sac fungi), *Morchella, Saccharomyces, Penicillium*

Division Basidiomycota (the basidiomycetes or club fungi), *Coprinus, Agaricus*

The Fungi

Fungi affect humans and all other organisms in a variety of positive ways. Like bacteria, fungi help to decompose and break down dead organic matter, recycling scarce nutrients back to the soil. Many fungi have formed mutualistic associations with other species. Lichens and mycorrhizae represent mutualistic associations between a fungus and an alga or a plant, respectively. Some fungi, like *Penicillium,* have substantial medical benefits in that they produce useful products (penicillin, for example). Many yeast are used for the production of a number of commercial foods, including bread, cheese, wine, and beer. Some fungi, like the commercial button mushrooms you buy in the store, along with exotic mushrooms such as the morels and truffles, are eaten and savored by many animals, including humans.

However, fungi can have negative effects on other organisms. A number of fungi are serious pathogens to plants and animals; for example, fungi have almost wiped out the American elms and American chestnuts. Both species once were dominant trees of the eastern deciduous forest. Some fungi, like the various rusts and smuts, are serious agricultural pests. Many people are allergic to various molds common in all homes. Fungi spoil stored food (in both the kitchen cabinet and the refrigerator) over time.

The fungi number at least 200,000 different species. (Water molds and other fungal-like protists are not currently included in the Kingdom Fungi.) The fungi colonized land at the same time as the plants, with which they have had a long symbiotic association. The **Chytridiomycota** (the chytrids) are considered the ancestral group to the fungi; until recently the chytrids were included with the protists.

The Common Characteristics Shared by Most Fungi

1 Fungi lack chlorophyll.

2 Fungi are multicellular, but a few species in many fungal groups are unicellular. These unicellular species are called **yeast.**

3 Fungi are **heterotrophic,** a trait they share with animals and animal-like protists. However, fungi do not engulf and chew up prey; instead, fungi obtain nutrients via **saprobic** nutrient acquisition. Fungi secrete digestive enzymes out of their hyphae, and the enzymes digest the organic molecules extracellularly. The fungi then absorb the nutrients across their outer cell membranes. Fungi exist either as free-living **saprobes** (absorbing dead organic matter), or as **symbionts** (absorbing liquids from living host tissues). Some symbiotic fungi are parasites (they absorb host tissues and harm the host), but other symbiotic fungi can be viewed as mutualists (they benefit from nutrients absorbed from the host, but at the same time, they provide materials to the host, and thus the host benefits as well).

4 Fungi have cells with walls strengthened with **chitin,** which is a polymer composed of many units of N-acetylglucosamine, a derivative of glucose. The body of the fungus consists of a **mycelium.**

5 The mycelium is composed of a large number of filaments, called **hyphae** (singular: **hypha**). The hyphae can be either:

    a **aseptate,** no cross walls between individual cells and nuclei, and thus they are **coenocytic** (multinucleate), or

    b **septate,** with one or two haploid nuclei in each cell. The septa are cross-walls that are incomplete: pores allow cytoplasm and organelles to move from one cell to the next.

6 Fungi possess a **zygotic life cycle** (see Figure 8.7). As in plants, the sexual life cycle of a typical fungus alternates between haploid and diploid states. However, the diploid phase in fungi is brief and unicellular. The cycle begins with **plasmogamy,** or fusion of the hyphae and cytoplasm of two genetically different mating strains of one fungal species (we use [–] and [+] to indicate the mating strains). Plasmogamy is followed by the formation of **dikaryotic hyphae.** The hyphae are composed of cells containing two genetically different haploid nuclei. The diploid phase of the cycle occurs later, when [+] and [–] nuclei fuse (the fusion of the two haploid nuclei is called **karyogamy**). Typically, karyogamy is followed quickly by **meiosis** (rather than mitosis, as in the plants). In Fungi, the haploid **spores** produced via meiosis are called **meiospores.** Meiospores are dispersed and later germinate to give rise to mycelia of genetically distinct individuals, resulting from genetic recombination of two different mating strains. The zygote (the product of the union of [+] and [–] nuclei) is the only point in the life cycle in which the diploid state exists.

7 Fungi also reproduce **asexually,** without the exchange of genetic material among individuals of the same species. **Sporangiophores** and **conidiophores** are two types of structures that arise from mitotic divisions of hyphae and give rise to asexual spores and **conidia** (singular: conidium) which germinate and form mycelia of the same mating strain.

Division Zygomycota (Zygomycetes)

These fungi are commonly referred to as the "algal-like fungi," "zygote fungi," or "conjugation fungi." They are considered to be more primitive than the rest of the higher fungi (the ascomycetes and basidiomycetes). The zygomycetes are found in terrestrial habitats and in both freshwater and marine environments.

Life cycle. The zygomycete life cycle is in Figure 15.1. Typically, the **mycelium** is composed of coenocytic **aseptate hyphae;** septa are usually formed only at the base of **gametangia** ('gamete containers') and **sporangia** (see Figure 15.2). Both asexual and sexual reproduction occurs in zygomycetes. Hyphae of mycelia of two different mating strains ([+] and [–]) come in close contact and produce hyphal extensions, called **gametangia** (see Figure 15.4). The two gametangia fuse (**plasmogamy**), forming the **heterokaryotic zygosporangium** (see Figure 15.4) containing a number of haploid nuclei from the two parental mycelia. After the gametangia fuse, another pair of septa forms on the hyphae that formed the gametangia; this creates a **suspensor cell** on either side of the developing zygosporangium (Figure 15.4). The suspensor cells support the developing zygosporangium.

Heterokaryotic zygosporangia are not diploid in the usual sense of the word 'diploid' because there are two distinct haploid nuclei present which do not immediately fuse after plasmogoamy. Sexual reproduction thus results in the formation of a unicellular resting stage, called the **zygosporangium**

(Figure 15.4). The zygomycetes do not form a distinct **sporocarp** (multicellular fruiting body) that occurs in both the basidiomycetes and ascomycetes. The zygosporangium produces a thick wall that protects against desiccation and other environmental extremes. After some time in the heterokaryotic state, **karyogamy** occurs inside the zygosporangium, forming diploid nuclei (analogous to the diploid nuclei of zygotes) that then quickly undergo **meiosis** (see Figure 15.1). The diploid phase is thus very short in duration for zygomycetes.

Later, the zygosporangium breaks open and a **sporangium** on top of a stalk (a **sporangiophore**) appears. Haploid **spores** (**meiospores**) are released away from the end of the sporangiophore (the columella) and dispersed (see Figure 15.4). The spores germinate, producing haploid **hyphae** that form a new mycelium. As you can see from this cycle, the zygote fungi spend most of the time in the haploid condition.

The mycelium can also produce sporangia **asexually** as well, generating many haploid spores (**sporangiospores**) in this fashion (see Figure 15.1). The sporangiospores germinate under favorable environmental conditions, with a hypha emerging from each spore.

Rhizopus stolonifer is the typical representative of the Zygomycetes. Commonly called the 'black bread mold,' this fungus grows readily on bread and other substrates that are rich in carbohydrates.

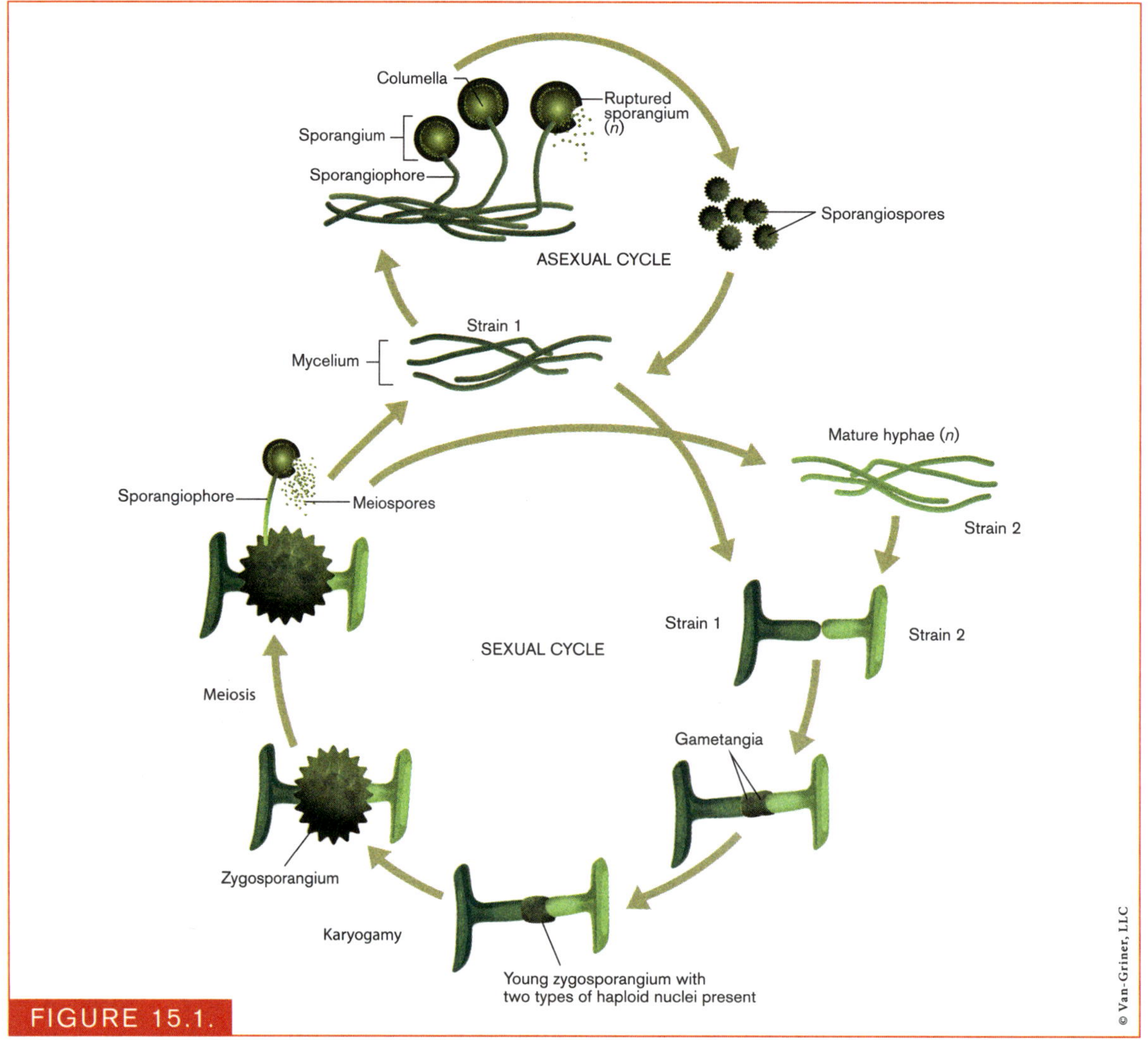

FIGURE 15.1.

The life cycle of a typical zygomycete.

Exercises

Exercise 15.1.

Examine a culture of the zygomycete *Rhizopus stolonifer* in the demonstration area and identify the mycelium and sporangia. Draw what you see in the space provided below (Figure 15.2). Use Figure 15.4 to guide you.

FIGURE 15.2.

Rhizopus.

Exercise 15.2.

Under low power, examine a prepared slide of *Rhizopus* under the microscope. Identify the mycelium, sporangia, and zygosporangia. Draw what you see in the microscope's field of view in the space provided below (Figure 15.3), using Figure 15.4 to guide you.

FIGURE 15.3.

Rhizopus.

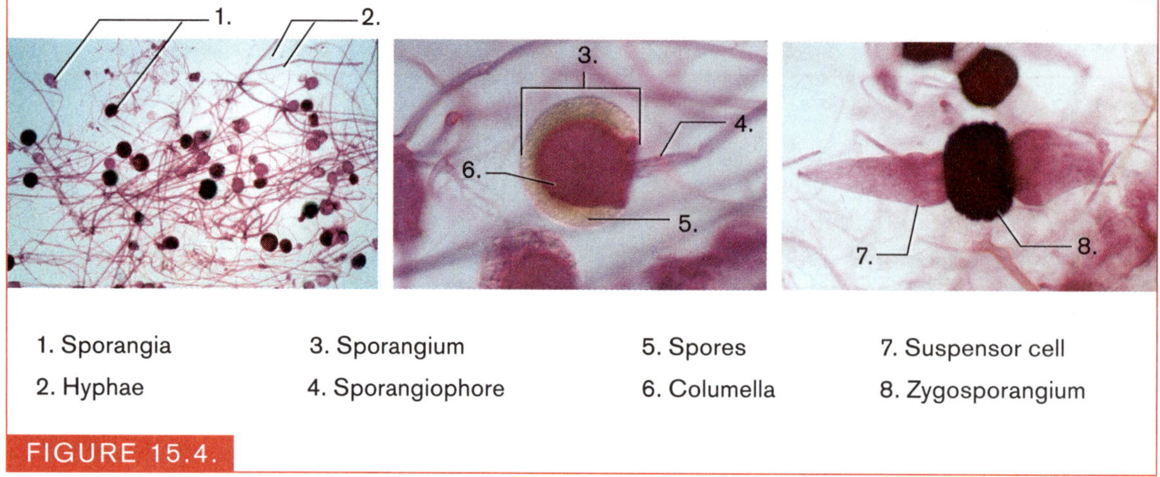

FIGURE 15.4.

Life cycle stages of a zygomycete, *Rhizopus.*

What is the difference between plasmogamy and karyogamy? In the sexual cycle of *Rhizopus* which of these processes must precede the other?

What is meant by the terms "plus" and "minus" as used in relation to fungi?

Division Ascomycota (Ascomycetes)

The "sac fungi" or ascomycetes are found in terrestrial, freshwater and marine habitats. The sac fungi are either unicellular (**yeast**) or are composed of hyphae consisting of uninucleate cells with crosswalls (the crosswalls are called **septa**).

Life cycle. The ascomycete life cycle is shown in Figure 15.5. When hyphae of two mycelia of different mating strains ([+] and [−]) come in close contact, and they form two distinct kinds of gametangia, called **ascogonia** and **antheridia,** and each gametangium contains multiple haploid nuclei. Plasmogamy of the two gametangia occurs, with the nuclei of the antheridium traveling across a cytoplasmic bridge into the ascogonium. Karyogamy does not yet occur. Many dikaryotic hyphae (containing the two different haploid nuclei) arise from the ascogonia and form a cup-like structure called the **ascocarp** (Figure 15.6). The **hymenium** is the layer of cells that contain the spore-producing cells of the ascomycetes and basidiomycetes. At the end of a dikaryotic hypha, an **ascus** forms (plural: **asci**). Karyogamy then occurs in the ascus, and the diploid **nucleus** then undergoes meiosis. In most sac fungi, each of the four haploid nuclei formed by meiosis then undergoes mitosis, forming ultimately a total of **eight haploid nuclei** (four of each mating strain) lined up inside the ascus (see the ascus of the fungus *Peziza* in Figure 15.7). Cell membranes and walls form around these nuclei to form eight **ascospores,** which then are released out of the end of the ascus. The ascospores are dispersed with the wind, landing in a new habitat and eventually germinating into a new haploid mycelium.

Asexual reproduction occurs in the ascomycetes as well. The asexual spores (**conidia**) are formed externally via mitosis at the ends of specialized hyphae called **condiophores.** Like the ascospores, the conidia are dispersed via wind and, after landing somewhere with appropriate conditions, germinate, forming new mycelia. Conidia of the fungus *Aspergillus* are depicted in Figure 15.8. *Aspergillus* recently was moved from the mold category into the ascomycetes.

Examples of Ascomycetes include *Saccharomyces cerevisiae* (a yeast, see Figure 15.9) and *Peziza* (Figure 15.7). *Peziza* is a saprophytic ascomycete that produces an apothecium or cup, which is lined with asci (sacs) containing the ascospores. Examples of preserved ascocarps may be seen on the demonstration table. Another classic example of an ascomycete is the morel mushroom *Morchella* (Figure 15.6) that is highly sought after by many North American mushroom hunters.

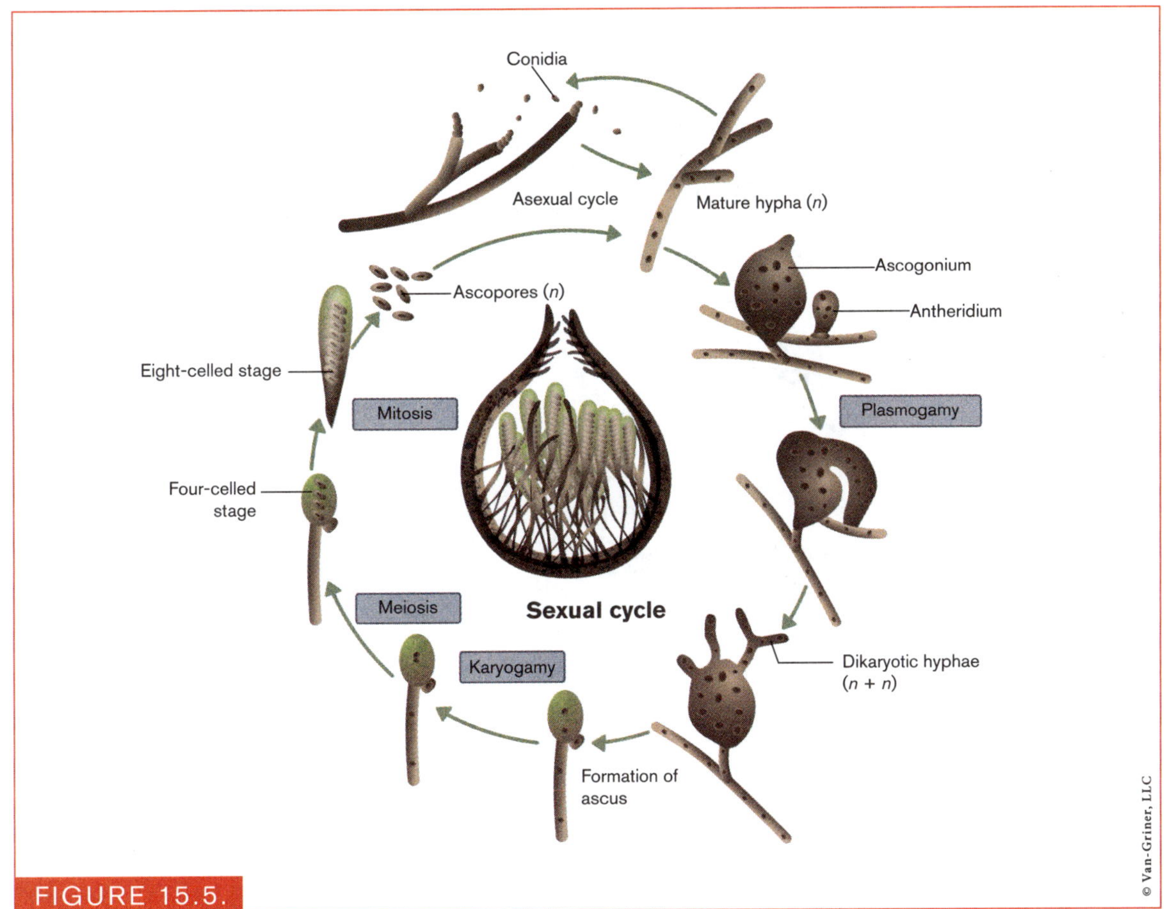

FIGURE 15.5.

The life cycle of a typical ascomycete.

FIGURE 15.6.

The ascocarp (fruiting body) of an ascomy-cete, the morel mushroom Morchella.

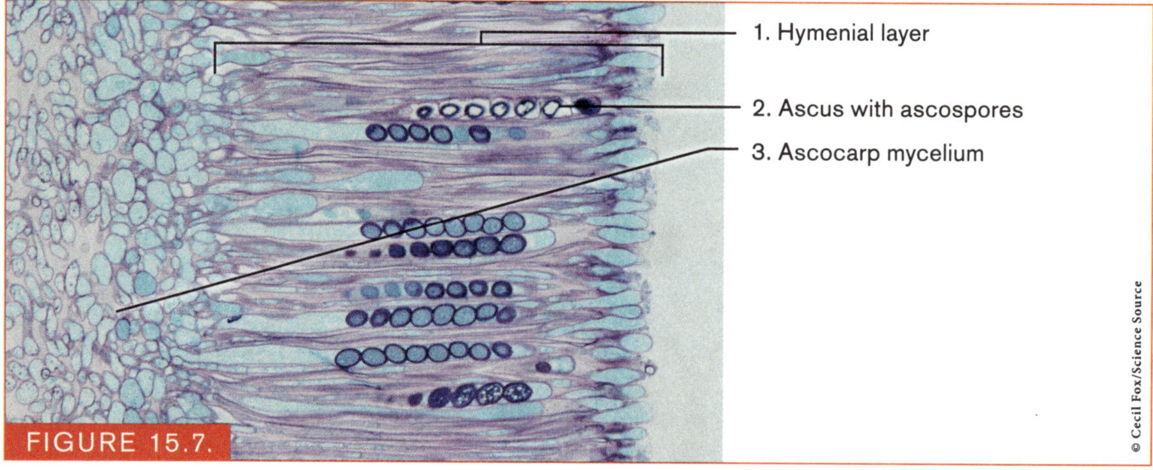

FIGURE 15.7.

The asci and ascospores of a typical ascomycete.

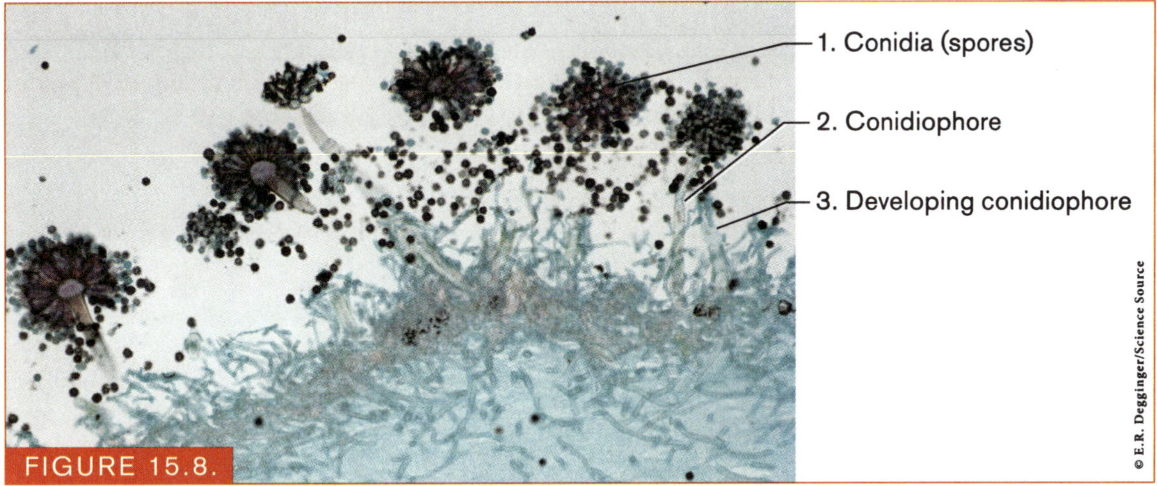

Conidiophores and conidia in the fungus *Aspergillus.*

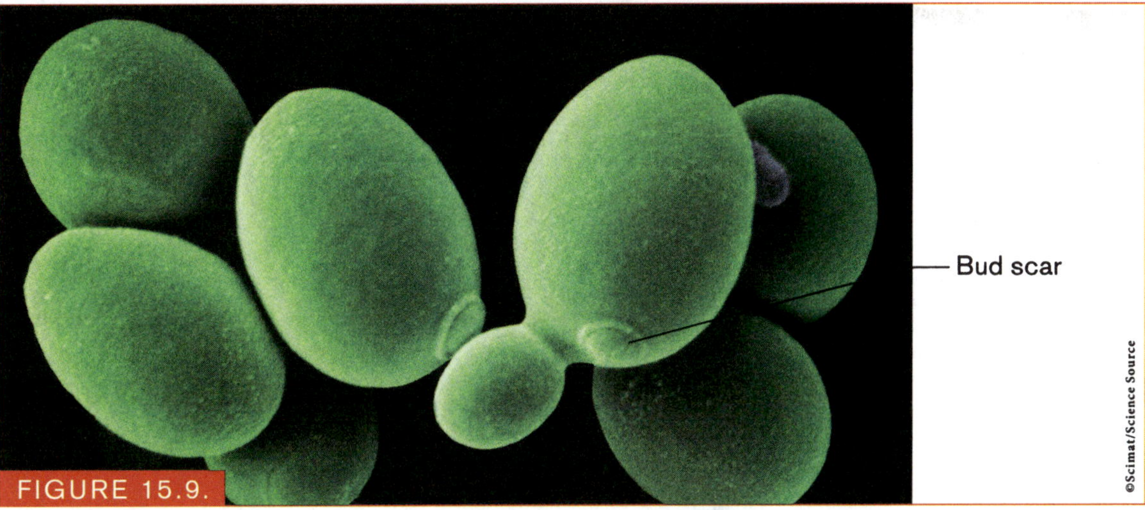

An example of a unicellular ascomycete, the Baker's yeast, *Saccharomyces.*

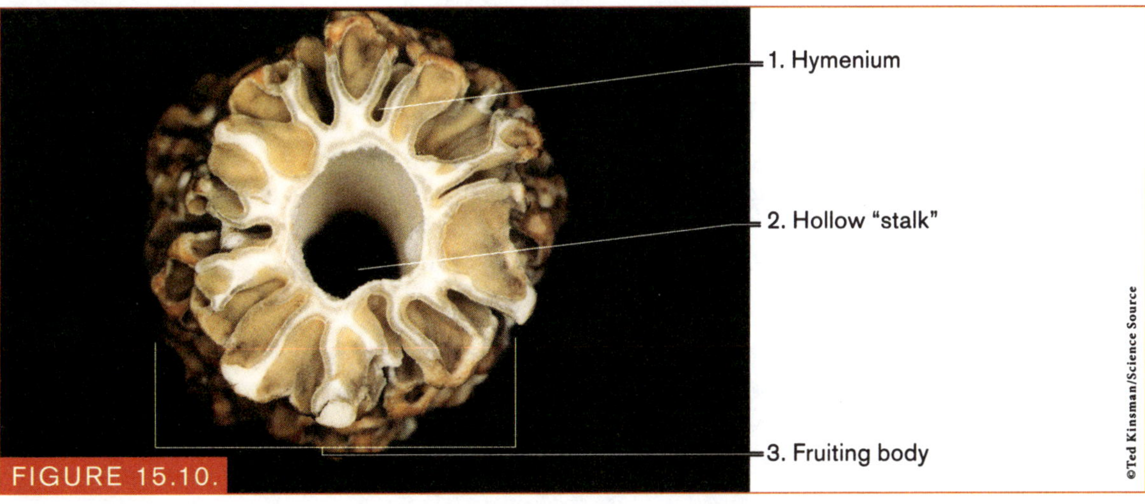

Cross section through the ascocarp of the morel mushroom, *Morchella.*

Exercise 15.3.

Under low power, examine a prepared slide of a longitudinal (or cross) section through an ascocarp of *Morchella*. Identify the hymenium, asci, and ascospores. Draw what you see in the microscope's field of view in the space provided below (Figure 15.11), using Figure 15.10 as a guide.

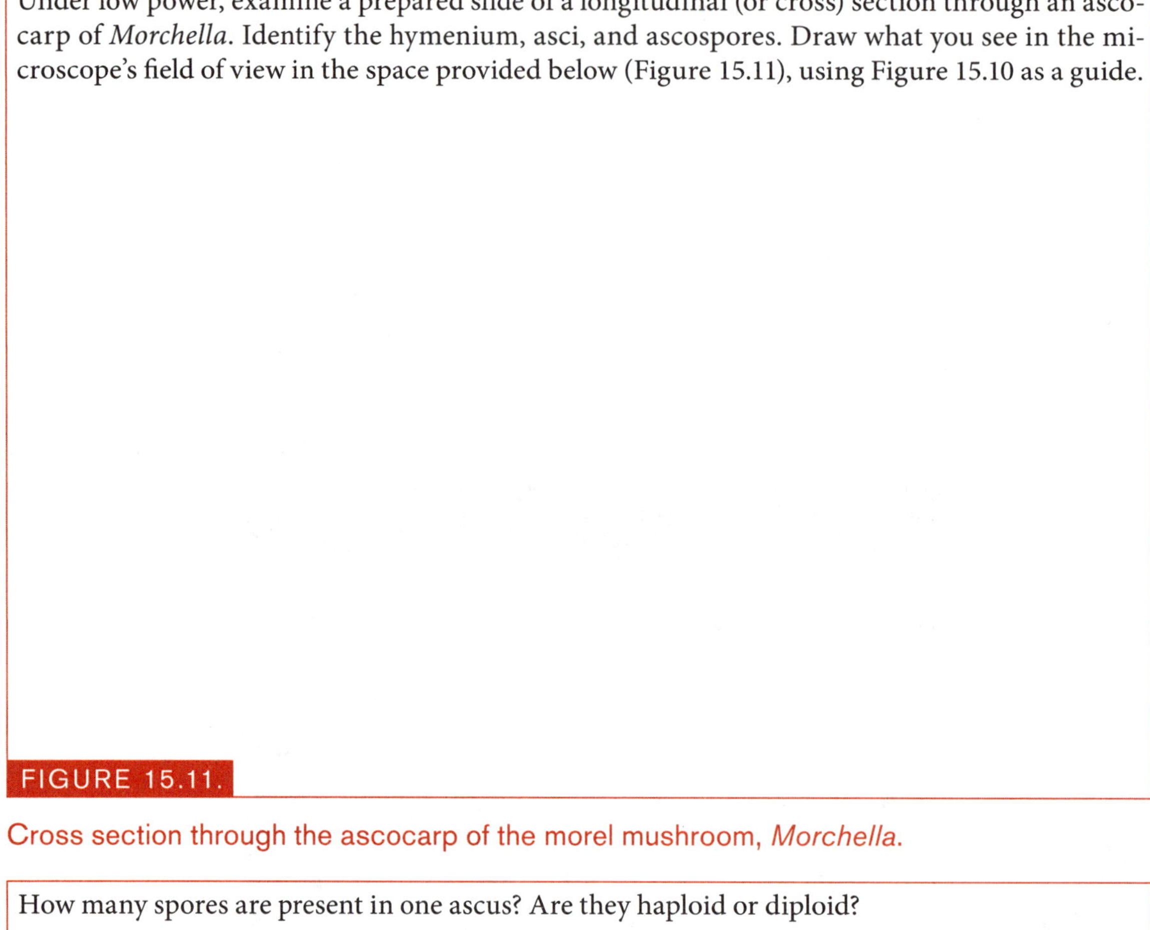

FIGURE 15.11.

Cross section through the ascocarp of the morel mushroom, *Morchella*.

How many spores are present in one ascus? Are they haploid or diploid?

Division Basidiomycota (Basidiomycetes)

The "club fungi" or basidiomycetes are a diverse group found in terrestrial habitats. Most of the fungi referred to as **mushrooms** and **toadstools** belong to this division; some, such as the field mushroom *Agaricus campestris*, are edible; others, such as the fly-mushroom *Amanita muscaria*, are quite deadly if eaten.

Many basidiomycete species, such as the wheat rust fungus and corn smut fungus, are obligate parasites. A few basidiomycetes are unicellular yeast, analogous to the ascomycete yeast. Some club fungi, such as the bracket fungi, are wood-decaying organisms commonly seen on old or dead trees, or on rotting logs. The familiar puffball fungi are basidiomycetes.

Life cycle. The generalized basidiomycete life cycle is shown in Figure 15.12. Like the zygote fungi and the sac fungi, haploid (*n*) hyphae of two mating strains of a club fungus come in close contact. The hyphae then undergo plasmogamy, forming a long-lived **dikaryotic mycelium** (*n* + *n*, which is not the same thing as a diploid state, or 2*n*). The dikaryotic mycelium can grow over time to quite large size, covering acres of soil. Specific environmental cues (temperature, rainfall) cause the dikaryotic mycelium to rapidly form large aboveground structures, called **basidiocarps** (the 'mushroom,' see Figure 15.13). Many of you have probably seen 'fairy rings' of these basidiomycete fruiting bodies (mushrooms) in your yard. Primitive basidiomycete species, such as the smuts and rusts, do not produce basidiocarps. The dikaryotic mycelia are long-lived and can produce basidiocarps every year for many years.

The **pileus** (cap) of a mushroom sits on top of the stalk-like **stipe.** The **annulus** is a ring-like band around the stipe that is the remains of a veil that had earlier covered the developing gills. There are a large number of **gills (lamellae)** (Figure 15.13) on the pileus, where the terminal dikaryotic cells form club-shaped **basidia** (singular: basidium), hence the common name of "club fungi." Inside a basidium, karyogamy occurs, and the diploid nucleus then undergoes meiosis, producing four haploid nuclei. Each haploid nucleus enters a cytoplasmic extension off of the basidium and forms a **basidiospore.** A spore sits atop an extension of the basidium called the **sterigma** (plural: sterigmata). The basidiospores break away from the basidia and are dispersed by the wind, where they land and germinate into short-lived haploid mycelia, starting the cycle over again.

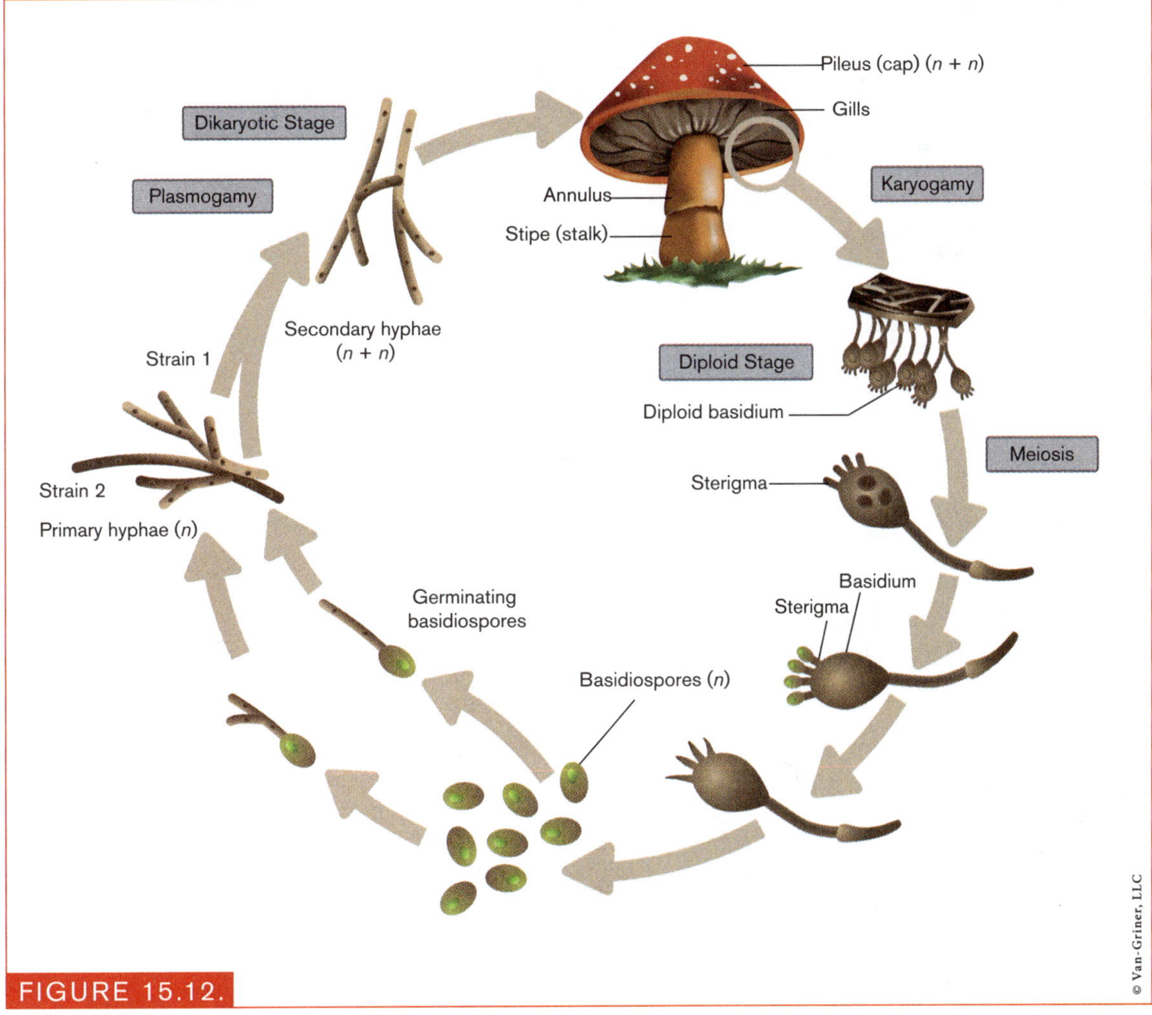

FIGURE 15.12.

The life cycle of a typical basidiomycete.

The basic structure of basidiomycete 'mushrooms.'

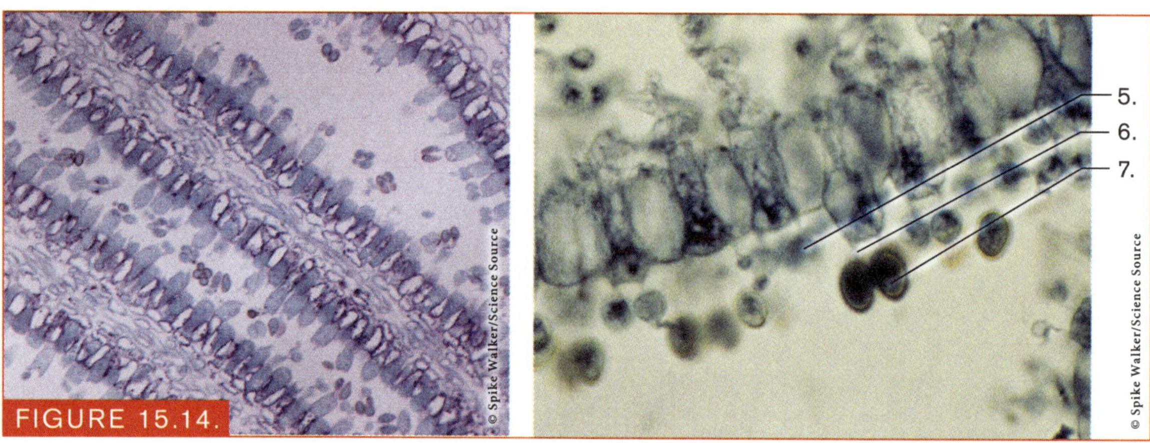

The gills of a typical basidiomycete mushroom *Coprinus.*

1. Pileus (cap)	3. Stripe (stalk)	5. Immature basidia	7. Basidiospore
2. Gills	4. Annulus	6. Sterigma	

Exercise 15.4.

Agaricus bisporus, the commercially produced edible mushroom, is an example of a more advanced basidiomycete. The general structure of the basidiocarp of the edible mushroom includes the familiar stalk (stipe) and cap (pileus) with pleat-like **lamellae** (singular: lamella) that bear the hymenium and are lined with numerous basidia. In a bracket or wood-decaying fungus, the basidia line the sides of pores; these pores are located on the lower surface.

Obtain a fresh basidiocarp of *Agaricus* and identify the stipe, pileus (cap), lamellae (gills), and annulus. You can place a very thin section of a 'gill' in water and make a wet mount. Place the slide on the microscope and examine the gill under low power. Draw what you see in the microscope's field of view in the space provided below (Figure 15.15). Use Figure 15.13 and Figure 15.14 to guide you. Can you see basidia?

FIGURE 15.15.

Agaricus basidiocarp and wet mount.

Exercise 15.5.

Under low power, examine a prepared slide of a cross section of the pileus (cap) of the basidiomycete *Coprinus* (see Figure 15.14). Identify gill lamellae, basidia, and basidiospores. Draw what you see in the microscope's field of view in the space provided below (Figure 15.16). Compare with the structure of the fresh mushroom *Agaricus*.

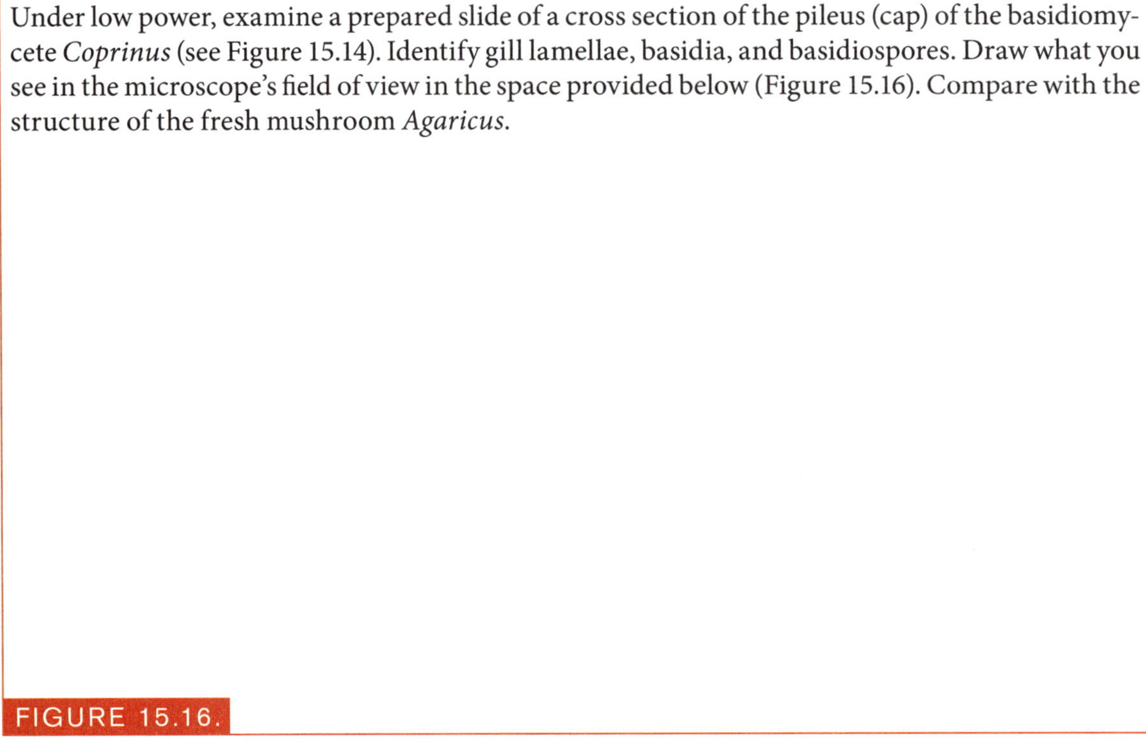

FIGURE 15.16.

Coprinus cap.

Exercise 15.6.

Examine the display of representatives of the various groups of fungi. Describe the difference between a zygosporangium, ascus, and basidium, and draw a quick sketch of each below (Figure 15.17). Use Figure 15.4, Figure 15.7, and Figure 15.14 to guide you.

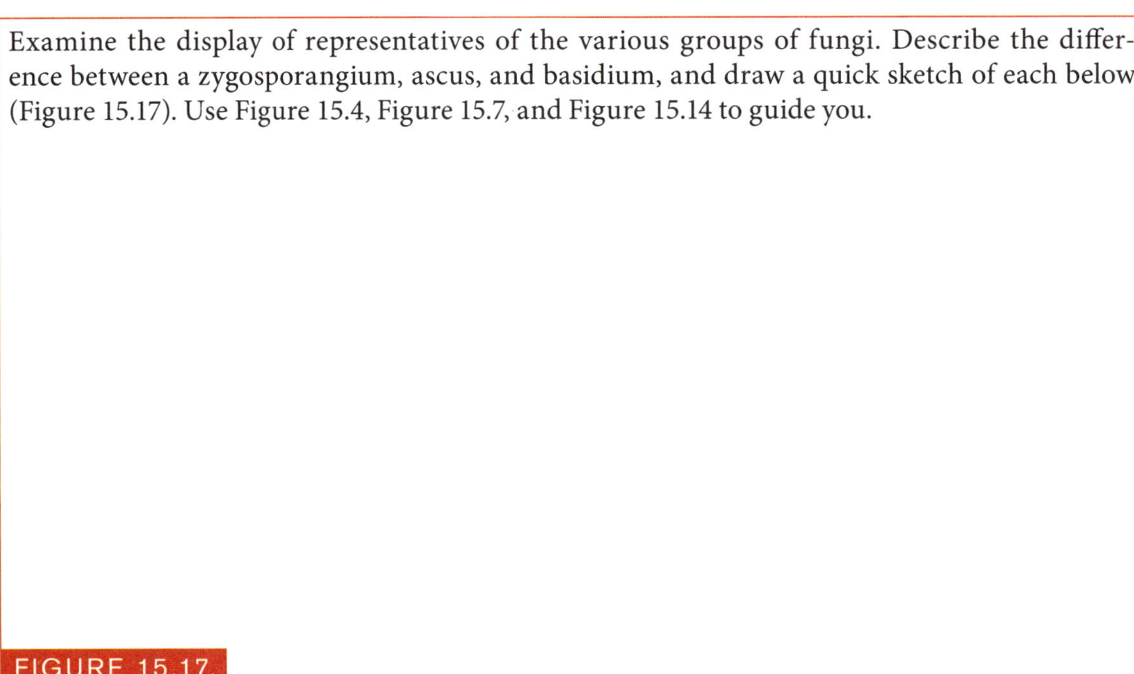

FIGURE 15.17.

Drawing of the major forms of fruiting structures (zygosporangium, ascus, and basidium).

What is a dikaryotic mycelium? Does this mean the same thing as a diploid mycelium?

The Molds (Fungi Imperfecti or Deuteromycetes)

This group, which used to be referred to as a 'division,' includes many multicellular fungi (called **molds**) that cannot be placed in any of the three previous divisions because their sexual phase is unknown. This group is polyphyletic; it is an artificial taxon without a phylogenetic basis.

The zygomycetes, ascomycetes, and basidiomycetes are grouped primarily by the type of spores produced in the sexual phase (genetic recombination of two different mating strains followed by meiosis). Because the sexual part of the cycle is not easily observed in some fungi, we lump those fungi whose sexual stages are not known into the molds, which is a mycelium that has no obvious fruiting bodies. However, just because the sexual phase for a given mold is not known does not mean that the mold has to be rare; there are many species listed in this group, and many are quite common. Well-known examples of imperfect fungi used to include the molds *Penicillium* and *Aspergillus,* although both of these species recently have been moved by taxonomists into the ascomycetes. As mycologists discover the sexual phase of an mold, the species is moved to its appropriate taxon.

In summary, a **mold** is a rapidly growing asexual fungus. Once a mold eventually produces a reproductive structure (either a zygosporangium, an ascocarp, or a basidiocarp), the fungus subsequently is placed in the appropriate division.

Yeast

Yeast are unicellular fungi that inhabit moist or aquatic habitats, and they live as commensals or parasites in or on many animals and plants. Commensal organisms live in or on another organism (host); the commensals may benefit from living on the host, but the host neither benefits nor is harmed from the association. *Saccharomyces cerevisiae*, an example of a unicellular ascomycete, is commonly called brewer's yeast or baker's yeast (see Figure 15.9). Yeast are commercially used to produce many products: bread, wine, cheese, and beer.

However, many yeast can cause disease in humans and many animals. Some yeast, like *Candida*, can be passed sexually from one human to another. The yeast *Candida* lives in the gastrointestinal tract and on moist mucus linings (like the vagina) and can be pathogenic. *Rhodotorula* is the yeast that can live on your shower curtain (a pinkish mold); this genus also can potentially cause disease.

Most yeast are in the Ascomycota (like *Saccharomyces*), but other species are in the Basidiomycota, and still others (with no known sexual stage) are lumped in the Fungi Imperfecti. Yeast asexually reproduce by **budding.**

Exercise 15.7.

Yeast

Obtain a small amount of the yeast solution at the demonstration table. Make a wet mount slide and view the slide under the microscope under low power. Draw what you see in the microscope's field of view in the space provided below (Figure 15.18). Do you observe any buds? Did you see any bud 'scars' (see Figure 15.9) on the sides of any cells?

FIGURE 15.18.

Yeast.

Lichens

A lichen is a **composite organism** consisting of a fungus (**mycobiont**) and an alga (**phycobiont**) that are mutually dependent upon each other. The phycobiont is generally a unicellular green alga, however, some phycobionts are cyanobacteria. Both algae and cyanobacteria produce organic compounds via photosynthesis. The cyanobacterium also can fix atmospheric nitrogen into forms the bacterium and fungus can use. In return for the organic compounds produced by the phycobiont, the fungus protects the algae/bacteria and provides moisture and minerals to the autotrophic phycobiont.

The mycobiont typically is an ascomycete, although a few basidiomycetes in the tropics also form associations with algae. Most of the mass of a lichen is the fungal mycelium. The phycobiont lives in a thin layer just below the lichen's upper surface (Figure 15.19).

A lichen can reproduce asexually by fragmentation and by producing structures called **soredia** (Figure 15.19). Soredia consist of a few hyphae surrounding a number of algal cells. The soredia break away and are dispersed.

The three basic growth forms of lichens are **crustose** (flattened, crust-like thallus), **foliose** (leafy looking), and **fruticose** (a collection of small branching cylinders or tubes creating a bushy appearance). All three forms may be seen in the demonstration area and in Figure 15.20. Some crustose and foliose forms can be seen on campus; they reside on the sides of rocks, buildings, and tree trunks. Foliose lichens are in the soil and on tree trunks, and some fruticose lichens hang down from the limbs of some trees in some parts of the country.

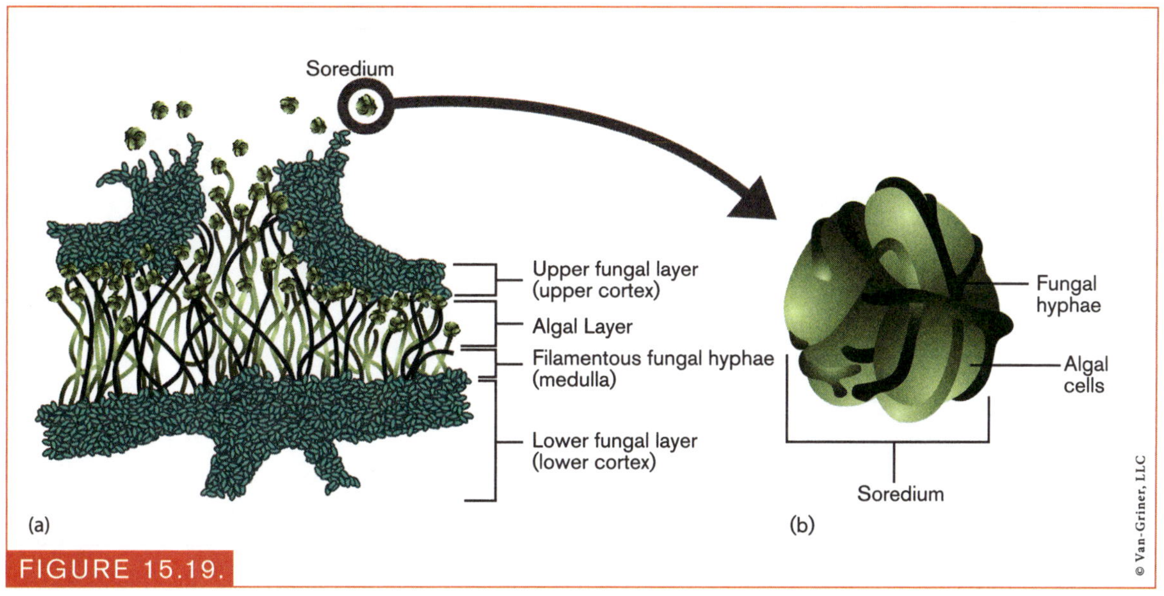

FIGURE 15.19.

Lichens and soredia.

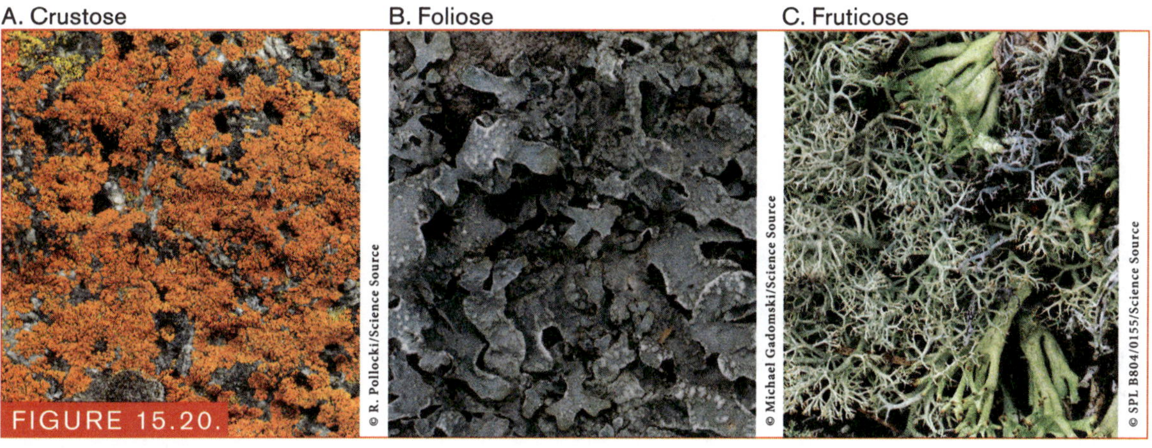

FIGURE 15.20.

Lichen examples.

Exercise 15.8.

Under low power, examine a prepared slide of a lichen thallus section. Identify the upper and lower layers of fungal mycelia containing hyphae and the inner layer containing algal cells among loosely held hyphae. Draw what you see in the microscope's field of view in the space provided below (Figure 15.21). Use Figure 15.19 to guide you.

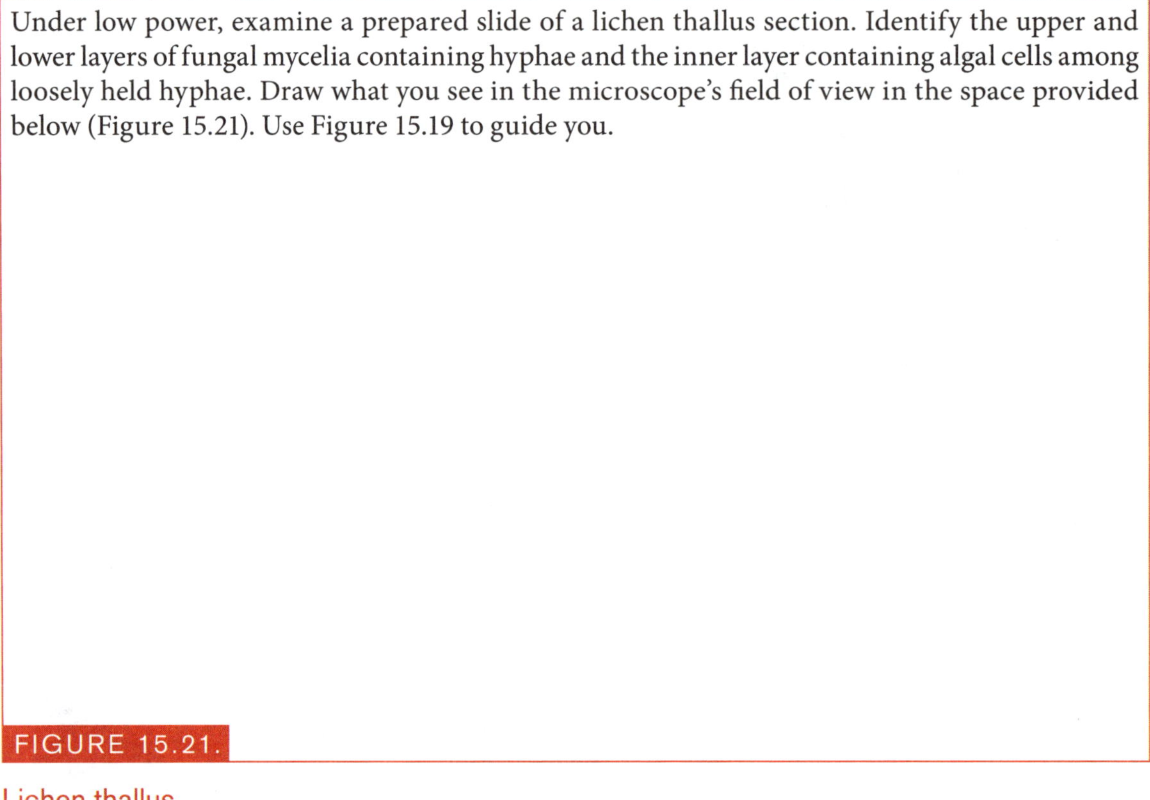

FIGURE 15.21.

Lichen thallus.

Exercise 15.9.

Examine the display of lichens and determine which are crustose, foliose, and fruticose. Make a sketch of the three types in the space provided below (Figure 15.22). Use Figure 15.20 to guide you.

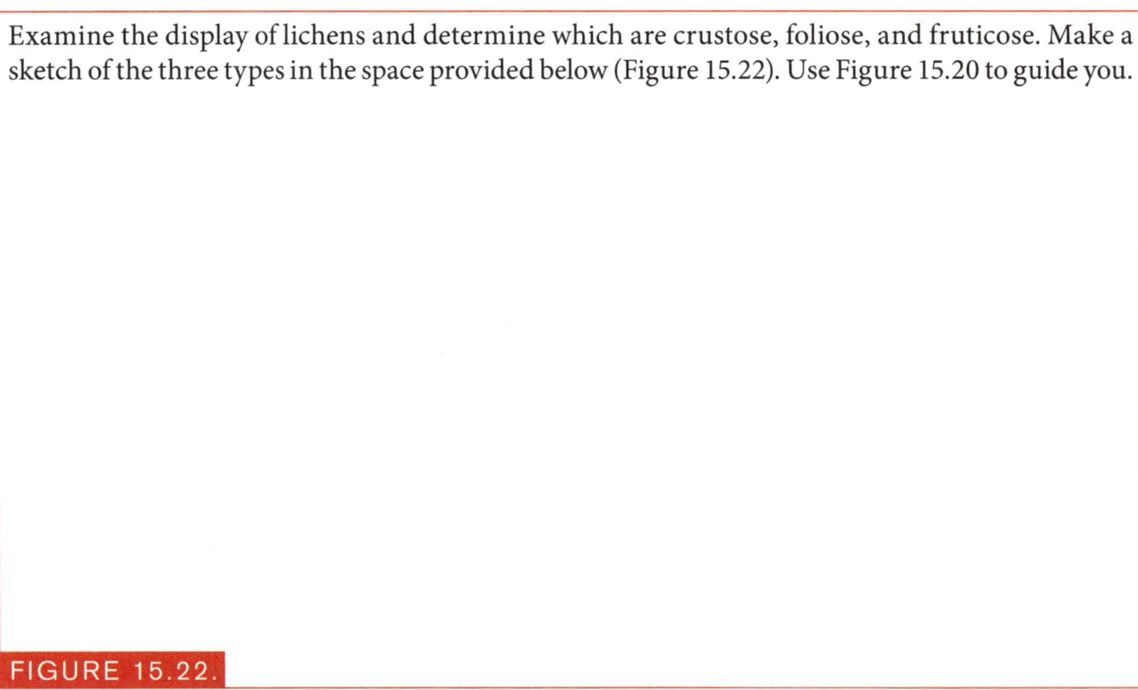

FIGURE 15.22.

Lichen types.

Why are algal cells only located on the upper side of a foliose lichen?

Mycorrhizae

Like lichens, **mycorrhizae** are composed of a **mutualistic** association of two organisms, plant roots and fungi. The mycelium of the fungus surrounds plant roots, greatly increasing the surface area over which minerals can be absorbed. The fungus trades absorbed nutrients for organic nutrients produced by the plant. Most vascular plants have associated fungi forming mycorrhizae, and many members of Ascomycota, Basidiomycota (in particular), and Zygomycota form mycorrhizal association with plants.

Exercise 15.10

Mycorrhizae

Make a sketch below (Figure 15.23) of the mycorrhizae example found at the demonstration table, showing the relationship between roots and the fungal hyphae.

FIGURE 15.23.

Mycorrhizae.

Exercise 15.11.

TABLE 15.1. The comparison of the three major fungi phyla (and molds) examined in lab.

Phylum	Examples (include genus names, if given)	Sexual Reproductive Structures	Asexual Reproductive Structures
Zygomycota			
Ascomycota			
Basidiomycota			
Molds			

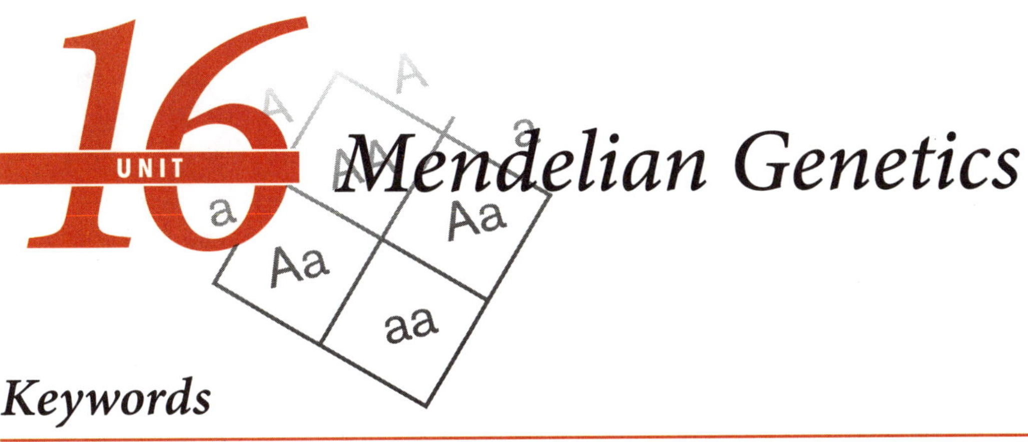

UNIT 16 — Mendelian Genetics

Keywords

gene
allele
recessive
dominant
heterozygous
homozygous dominant
homozygous recessive
genotype

phenotype
monohybrid and
   dihybrid crosses
test crosses
Punnett square
P, F_1, and F_2 generations
chi-square test
character

trait
locus
chromosome
sex chromosome
X-chromosome linked
Y-chromosome linked
autosome

Learning Objectives

When finished with this unit, you should be able to:

1 Compare and contrast blending and particulate theories of inheritance;

2 Describe Mendel's 'laws': dominance, parental equivalence, segregation, and independent assortment;

3 Describe the genotypic and phenotypic ratios expected in offspring from monohybrid and dihybrid crosses;

4 Determine the various possible gametes that could be produced from different genotypes;

5 Use a Punnett square to answer genetics questions;

6 Use the chi-square test to compare observed results with expected results from genetic crosses; and

7 Analyze a pedigree to determine modes of inheritance.

Modern genetics began in the 1850s when **Gregor Mendel** discovered the fundamental properties of heredity. He came up with the now accepted **particulate theory of heredity** that replaced the **blending theory,** a prevalent hypothesis at that time.

Biologists in the 19th century realized that both parents contribute to the characteristics of their offspring. However, before Mendel, the most favored explanation of heredity was the 'blending theory.'

Blending theory suggested that hereditary material from each parent mixes in each offspring. The assumptions of this theory are as follows.

1 The offspring's traits are typically intermediate between the two parents' traits.

2 Once traits had blended, they no longer could be separated out to appear again in later generations.

3 If blending is correct, individuals of a population should reach a uniform appearance after many generations. For example, if a population of cattle initially had black and white individuals, then over time, all cattle should appear to be grey.

However, the blending theory was inconsistent with what was often observed.

1 Offspring do not necessarily show intermediate characteristics. They may appear like one or the other parent, or they may have a completely different phenotype not predicted by the parents' phenotypes.

2 Some traits appeared to skip one generation, only to appear in the next.

3 Individuals in a population do not reach a uniform appearance. Inheritable variation is preserved from one generation to the next.

The **particulate theory** refers to an idea that parents transmit to their offspring discrete inheritable factors (these factors are now called **genes**) that remain as discrete, separable factors from one generation to the next. A **gene** is a segment of DNA that encodes for the specific amino acid sequence of a protein, such as a structural protein or enzyme. We now know that a gene is located at a specific location (a gene **locus**) on a **chromosome.** Many genes are located along the length of a single chromosome. Different plants and animals species have different numbers of chromosomes.

The contrasting forms of a gene are called alleles. For example, in peas, flower color can be purple or white; the color is dictated by the presence of a specific allele.

In the 1850s, Mendel began breeding garden peas. He used garden peas because they had several distinct properties that made them an excellent study organism.

1 They were available in many easily distinguishable varieties.

2 Strict control over mating was possible in the production of new seeds. Petals of the pea flower enclose the pistil and stamens (which produce the male and female gametophytes, which in turn produce the sperm and ova.) This enclosure of gametophytes normally prevents cross-pollination of one plant by another. In many plants, sperm and ova of the same plant in most species generally will not fuse, but in peas, that is not the case. Mendel produced hybrids by transferring pollen from one flower to another with a brush, and the flower's stamens could be pulled off before sexual maturity.

3 There were clearly defined pairs of contrasting traits for each character. Mendel appeared to have chosen seven different **characters,** each with a pair of contrasting **traits.** One character, for example, was flower color, which had two different traits: purple and white.

The peas that Mendel used turned out to be **true-breeding.** 'True-breeding' meant that the peas normally always produced offspring that had the same traits as the parents because the pea plant normally self-fertilized. Mendel started his experiments crossing two individuals from two different true-breeding varieties, which he **artificially cross-fertilized** in different experimental crosses.

The true-breeding parental plants are referred to as the **P (parental) generation.** The hybrid offspring of the P generation are the F_1 **generation (first filial generation).**

Mendel allowed the F_1 generation to self-fertilize (or he crossed two F_1 plants) to get the F_2 **generation (second filial generation).** Mendel observed the transmission of selected traits for at least three generations and arrived at several important principles or concepts of heredity. Over time, these concepts were eventually referred to as **the law of dominance, the law of parental equivalence, the law of segregation, and the law of independent assortment.** (Most biology textbooks refer to only two laws—the law of segregation and the law of independent assortment—but we will examine each of these four laws, or rules, in turn.)

One important thing you need to know about these four rules: there are observed 'exceptions' to each rule. However, the exceptions do not invalidate Mendel's laws but instead the apparent exceptions reinforce them; the basic underlying physical causes of Mendel's laws are still valid. These rules still form the basis for our understanding of the genetics of inheritance.

The 'Law' of Dominance

The law of dominance states that each inherited characteristic is determined by two heredity factors (we now call these factors 'alleles') which are inherited from the parents, one heredity factor inherited from each parent. One of these factors was considered dominant and the other recessive.

1 Alternative forms of genes (different alleles) are responsible for variations in inherited characteristics of organisms.

2 For each physical character (flower color, for example), an organism inherits two alleles, one from each parent. Mendel said that each parent contributes one factor (we now know this is an allele on a chromosome). Each gene locus (position on a chromosome) is represented twice in most animals as well as in fungi, protists, and some plants (i.e., in all diploid organisms). A diploid organism possesses two complete sets of chromosomes, composed of a specific number of homologous pairs of chromosomes. One set is inherited from each parent. In a given individual, the two alleles may be identical, or they may be two different versions (two different alleles).

3 If the two alleles differ, one is fully expressed (the **dominant allele**) and the other is completely masked or not expressed (the **recessive allele**). We will designate dominant alleles with a capital letter: P = purple, p = white. When Mendel crossed a true-breeding purple plant with a true-breeding white plant, the offspring were all purple. From this observation, one would call the purple trait dominant and the white trait recessive.

For the characters he studied, there were two contrasting traits of each character and there was no 'intermediate' or 'blended' trait. When Mendel crossed pure tall plants with pure short plants, all offspring F_1 plants were tall. They were not 'medium height,' which would be expected if some sort of blending was occurring. Similarly, crossing pure yellow-seeded pea plants with pure green-seeded pea plants produced an F_1 generation consisting of all yellow-seeded pea plants; the offspring were not 'yellow-green.' The same was true for other pea characters Mendel examined.

The 'Law' of Parental Equivalence

After Mendel carefully examined the results of his crosses, he noted that the sex of the parent was irrelevant, with respect to the dominant or recessive trait exhibited in the offspring produced by the cross. For example, all of the offspring produced by a cross between a purple-flowered 'male' plant (the plant that produced the pollen) with a white-flowered 'female' plant (the plant with the ovary) were all purple. Likewise, all of the offspring from a cross of a purple-flowered 'female' plant with a white-flowered 'male' plant were all purple. This concept is described in some textbooks as the 'law' of parental equivalence. The law of parental equivalence states that the sex of the parent does not influence the dominant or recessive trait that is inherited from that parent, and either trait (dominant or recessive) can be inherited from either parent.

The Law of Segregation

According to this law, the two alleles for each trait are packaged into separate gametes. Mendel crossed two true-breeding plants and noticed that the traits did not blend. Mendel was able to discover these laws because he used the scientific process and conducted valid, important experiments using large sample sizes. He kept accurate, quantitative records of his results.

Mendel's Experiment on Segregation

Observation. A cross between white-flowered and purple-flowered varieties did not produce an intermediate light purple or lavender flowers; the F_1s were all purple. In addition, the white trait did not appear in any of the F_1s.

Hypothesis. Mendel hypothesized that if the white-flowered trait had been lost, then a cross between F_1 plants should produce only purple flowers.

Experiment. Mendel allowed his F_1s to self-fertilize (this has the same effect as having two different F_1s mate).

Results. There were 705 purple-flowered and 224 white-flowered plants in the F_2 generation: a ratio of about 3 purple to 1 white. In all of his contrasting pairs he got roughly a 3 : 1 ratio, and in all cases the trait that disappeared in the F_1s showed up again in the F_2s. The hypothesis of the 'lost trait' was rejected, and this result was strong evidence that blending was not occurring. Both original parental traits reappeared in the F_2 generation.

Conclusion. Mendel concluded that the inheritable factor (allele) for the white trait was not lost in the F_1 generation; it must have been masked by the presence of the purple trait. Mendel said that the purple flower was the **dominant trait** (now we would say that the purple allele was the **dominant**

allele) and the white flower was the **recessive trait (recessive allele).** The dominant allele was expressed in the **phenotype** (the phenotype is the physical appearance of the plant) when both it and the recessive trait (allele) are together. When both alleles are together in the same individual, you have what are called **heterozygous individuals.**

Mendel's law of segregation (in light of what we now know):

1 The two alleles for each character separate from each other (segregate) during gamete formation. Mendel did not know about genes, chromosomes, or meiosis. However, Mendel deduced that a sperm cell or egg cell carries only one copy (allele) for each inherited trait because trait (allele) pairs presumably **segregate** from each other during gamete production.

2 All of the gametes of true breeding plants will carry the same allele. If there are different alleles in the same parent, there is a 50% chance that a gamete will receive the dominant allele, and a 50% chance it will receive the recessive allele. **This sorting of alleles into separate gametes is called Mendel's law of segregation.**

Mendel's law of segregation is quite powerful; it makes several specific predictions.

1 It predicts the 3 : 1 ratio observed in the F_2 generation of a **monohybrid cross** (one trait).

2 It predicts that the F_1 hybrids produce two types of gametes when the alleles segregate in gamete formation. Half of the gametes receive P (purple), half receive p (white).

3 It predicts that during self-fertilization, these two types of gametes will unite randomly. Ova containing the purple-flowered allele have equal chances of being fertilized by a P sperm or a p sperm. The same is true for the white-flowered ova. There are thus four equally likely combinations of sperm and ova, as shown by the **Punnett Square** (Figure 16.1):

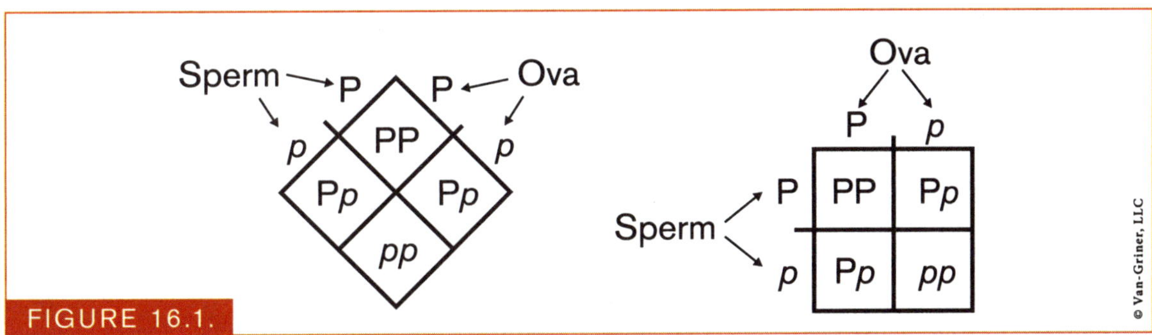

FIGURE 16.1.

Two identical depictions of a Punnett square. The Punnett square reveals possible offspring genotypes for two parental genotypes.

As shown in Figure 16.1, it does not matter if the square is a diamond or a square; use whichever one you are comfortable with using. It also does not matter if the relative positions of the ova and sperm are switched.

If a large number of F_2 offspring were produced, we should see a 3 : 1 phenotypic ratio. Why is it important that a large number of F_2 offspring had to be produced?

The F_2 progeny would include one-fourth of the F_2 with two purple alleles (PP), these would appear to be purple. About one-half of the F_2s would have one copy of each allele (Pp); because purple is dominant, these plants also would have purple flowers. About one-fourth of the F_2 plants would have white flowers because they have two white alleles (pp).

Because fertilization is essentially a random process, in a very large population, approximately ¼ of the F_2 generation would be homozygous dominant, ¼ homozygous recessive, and ½ would be heterozygous. On average, ¾ of the F_2 generation would be purple-flowered, ¼ white-flowered.

In Mendel's experiments with monohybrid crosses, he observed a **3 : 1 phenotypic ratio in the F_2s,** and a **1 : 2 : 1 genotypic ratio in the F_2s.** The ratios were always close to these, but not necessarily exactly the same, because of the random effect of fertilization.

The heterozygote may have the same phenotype as the homozygous dominants or it may have its own phenotype (thus the genotypic and phenotypic ratios were the same: 1 : 2 : 1). For example, for snapdragons, the genotype of a red-flowered phenotype would be RR, the genotype of a white-flowered genotype would be rr, and the genotype of a pink-flowered individual (which would have half of the red pigment of a red-flowered individual) would be Rr. If one of Mendel's characters had been an example of incomplete dominance, he would not have observed a 3 : 1 phenotypic ratio for that character.

The Law of Independent Assortment

According to the law of independent assortment, each pair of alleles segregates into gametes independently. In addition to various monohybrid crosses, Mendel conducted a number of **dihybrid crosses.** A dihybrid cross is between two parental varieties that had different traits for each of **two** distinct characters.

Observation. Mendel first obtained two different true breeding plants for two different characters and each character had two contrasting traits:

Tall stem, yellow seed (TTYY) plants were crossed with short stem, green seed (ttyy) plants. The resulting F_1 hybrids were heterozygous for both traits, but they all appeared to be tall-stemmed and yellow-seeded (TtYy). Both the 'short' trait and the 'green' trait disappeared in the F_1 generation.

Hypothesis. Both recessive traits disappear in the F_1s. However, if the particulate theory is true, then the recessive traits should reappear in the F_2s and four different phenotypes would occur: dominant for both traits (tall, yellow), dominant for one trait and recessive for the other (tall, green or short, yellow), and recessive for both traits (short, green). In other words, the traits of one character segregate from each other independent of what the traits of the other character do. The two dominant traits (tall and yellow) do not have to stay together in the F_2s.

Experiment. Mendel allowed the F_1s to self-fertilize. He then observed the F_2 phenotypes.

Results. Out of 556 F_2 offspring, Mendel recorded the following numbers: 315 (tall, yellow), 108 (tall, green), 101 (short, yellow), and 32 (short, green).

The F_2 phenotypic ratio is approximately a **9 : 3 : 3 : 1 phenotypic ratio.** 9 (tall, yellow); 3 (tall, green); 3 (short, yellow); 1 (short, green).

However, the phenotypic ratio roughly approximates 9 : 3 : 3 : 1—remember that fertilization is a chance event!

A Punnett square for the dihybrid cross is shown in Figure 16.2. Note that there are four possible gamete types: TY, Ty, tY, and ty.

The genotypic ratio was 1 : 2 : 1 : 2 : 4 : 2 : 1 : 2 : 1. Can you determine this genotypic ratio from the Punnett square shown in Figure 16.2?

Mendel observed the same 9 : 3 : 3 : 1 phenotypic ratio each time he examined the results of his dihybrid crosses. Mendel's conclusion: his results supported the modern hypothesis that the alleles of one gene segregate independently of the alleles of another gene locus (location on a chromosome) during gamete formation.

Mendel published his work at about the same time that Darwin published the *Origin of Species*. Darwin may have had a copy of Mendel's work, but if he did, he apparently did not read it or understand its importance. Mendel's work was ignored for about 30 years after its publication until about 1900, when three different geneticists independently came up with the same ideas. Starting in the 1930 until the 1960s, scientists tied Mendel's work with that of Darwin, and the solution to Darwin's weakest link in his theory of evolution was found. This fusion of Mendel with Darwin is an important part of what is called the 'Modern Synthesis,' one of the major theories in biology.

	Ova			
	TY	**Ty**	**tY**	**ty**
TY	TTYY	TTYy	TtYY	TtYy
Ty	TTYy	TTyy	TtYy	Ttyy
tY	TtYY	TtYy	ttYY	ttYy
ty	TtYy	Ttyy	ttYy	ttyy

*(Left label: **Sperm**; right margin: © Van-Griner, LLC)*

FIGURE 16.2.

The results of a dihybrid cross, as shown in a Punnett square. The phenotypic ratio expected among the offspring is 9 : 3 : 3 : 1.

The relationship between genotype and phenotype is rarely simple. There are many variations with respect to dominance, but the laws of segregation and independent assortment can be applied to them as well. In the 20th century, geneticists have extended Mendelian principles not only to diverse organisms, but also to patterns of inheritance far more complex than Mendel described.

Exercises

Exercise 16.1.

For each of the genotypes listed in Table 16.1, determine the phenotype using the key below.

Gene or Trait	Dominant Allele	Recessive Allele
flower color	A) purple flowers	a) white flowers
leaf color	B) purplish leaves	b) green leaves
size	C) tall	c) short
seed shape	D) round	d) wrinkled

TABLE 16.1.

Genotype	Phenotype
AA	
Aa	
aa	
AAdd	
BBCc	
AaBbCc	
AAbbccDd	
aAbBcCdD	
AABBCCDD	
AaBBccdd	
BbAADd	
ddccbbaa	

By convention, a heterozygous locus is listed with the capital letter first (e.g., Dd), but dD is also a heterozygote.

If the genotype sequence was aabbccdd, would the phenotype be different from ddccbbaa?

Exercise 16.2.

List all of the possible gamete combinations for each of the following genotypes (Table 16.2).

TABLE 16.2.

Genotype	Number of Possible Unique Gametes	Gamete Possibilities
AA		
Bb		
cc		
AAbb		
BbDD		
CcDd		
AABBCC		
AAbbCc		
AaBBCc		
BbCcDd		

Can you see the pattern to determining the number of possible gametes from a given genotype? What does it appear to be?

If you had a plant that was heterozygous for four traits (A, B, C, and D), how many possible gametes could it produce?

If you had a plant that is purple-flowered, what possible genotypes could it have?

If you had a purple-flowered, green-leaved plant, what possible genotypes could it have?

If you have a white-flowered, green-leaved, round-seeded plant, what possible genotypes could it have?

Exercise 16.3.

The Monohybrid Cross

A week or so ago, you (or your lab instructors) had planted Wisconsin Fast Plants® seeds. Today you will gather data from those plants in order to analyze a monohybrid cross. There are two alleles for leaf/stem color: green and purple. The purple stems and leaves are due to a dominant gene (called ANL). This gene codes for the expression of the purplish/reddish anthocyanin pigments in the stems and leaves. The green stems are due to the recessive allele (anl). These plants do not produce any purplish anthocyanin.

Your lab instructors will provide the summary data for all sections. You will determine if this gene segregates normally. In a monohybrid cross, all of the F_1s should appear to have the dominant trait. In the F_2s, ¾ of them should appear dominant, and ¼ should appear recessive.

Hypothesis. The traits (purplish versus green) follow the Mendelian law of segregation of alleles and the purplish trait is dominant.

Prediction 1. If the alleles for stem color are Mendelian, then we should see that all F_1s are purplish.

Prediction 2. If the alleles for stem color are Mendelian, then there should be a 3 purple : 1 green ratio among the F_2s.

Place the data that your lab instructor has provided in Table 16.3 below.

TABLE 16.3.

Generation	Number with Purplish Stems/Leaves	Number with Green Stems/Leaves	Totals
F_2 (ANL/ANL)			
F_2 (ANL/anl)			
F_2 (anl/anl)			

Were all of the F_1s the same color? Did the F_2s show a 3 : 1 ratio? You probably did not get an exact 3 : 1 ratio. However, that does not mean that Mendel's ideas are wrong; chance events and small sample sizes may skew the data.

Exercise 16.4.

Chi-Square Statistical Analysis of Your Monohybrid Cross

We can use the **chi-square (χ^2) test** to determine if the observed data differ significantly from what we expected to obtain according to our hypothesis. For example, Mendel crossed purple-flowered with white-flowered pea plants, and all of the F_1s were purple-flowered. However, in the 929 F_2s, he saw 705 purple-flowered and 224 white-flowered individuals. Prior to the experiment, Mendel predicted that 75% of these flowers should be purple (in this case, about 697), and 25% should be white (232 in this case). His observed F_2 numbers closely agreed to his predicted numbers.

However, suppose he saw 743 purple flowers and 186 white flowers (near a 4 : 1 ratio)? Could his data still support the 3 : 1 hypothesis? How about 836 purple to 93 white flowers (a 9 : 1 ratio)? How much of a deviation can occur before the scientist has to conclude that something else other than chance is at work? The chi-square test gives us an answer.

The chi-square test tests the null hypothesis, which would state that there is no significant difference between the expected result and observed result. Recall that the formula for the chi-square test is:

$$\textbf{Equation 16.1.} \quad \chi^2 = \sum \frac{(O - E)^2}{E}$$

This test is used to analyze the distribution of observations among different categories. In general, we are looking for differences in expected distributions versus observed distributions. The chi-square statistic is the sum of all of the [(Observed value − Expected value)² / Expected value] of all categories. Once we produce the chi-square value, we can use Table 16.6 and determine if the observed results vary from what would be from chance sampling.

Your null hypothesis is that there is no difference between the observed and expected values, and the alternative hypothesis is that there is a difference. The χ^2 value is looked up in a table (Table 16.6) and you look under the appropriate **degrees of freedom** (d.f.). The degrees of freedom for this test is (the number of categories − 1). We have two categories: purple and white. In this case: d.f. = (2 − 1) = 1.

If the calculated chi-square statistic is greater than the chi-square value shown in Table 16.6 below for the appropriate degrees of freedom, then you reject the null hypothesis (the flowers are in a 3 : 1 purple : white ratio) and accept the alternative hypothesis (the alleles may not act in a Mendelian way).

Let us test the actual results of Mendel's experiment (Table 16.4). He obtained 929 F_2 plants, and 705 of them were purple. A total of 224 plants were white. He would have expected (0.75)(929) = 697 of the F_2s to be purple, and (0.25)(929) = 232 of them to be white.

TABLE 16.4.

Phenotype	Observed	Expected	$(O - E)^2 / E$
purple	705	697	0.09
white	224	232	0.28
totals	929	929	$\Sigma = \chi^2 = 0.37$

In our example, the χ^2 value is 0.37, which is less than the χ^2 value of 3.84, with one degree of freedom (see Table 16.6). The results thus are not significant ($p > 0.05$) and we conclude that the observed alleles are acting in a Mendelian fashion.

However, suppose Mendel saw a ratio approaching 4 : 1 : 743 purple flowers and 186 white flowers (Table 16.5.) Does this still 'fit' a 3 : 1 ratio?

TABLE 16.5.

Phenotype	Observed	Expected	$(O - E)^2 / E$
purple	743	697	3.04
white	186	232	9.12
totals	929	929	$\Sigma = \chi^2 = 12.16$

Now the chi-square value is 12.16, which is greater than the χ^2 value of 3.84, with one degree of freedom. We see that after looking at Table 16.6, the results thus are highly significant (p-value < 0.05). We conclude that the data do **not** fit a 3 : 1 ratio.

TABLE 16.6. χ^2 test values for testing the null hypothesis of "no difference between categories" versus "significant difference among the categories" p < 0.05. If your χ^2 value exceeds the value listed below, the results are significantly different from what was expected. (Data from Zar (1996).)

d.f.	χ^2	d.f.	χ^2	d.f.	χ^2	d.f.	χ^2	d.f.	χ^2	d.f.	χ^2
1	3.84	6	12.59	11	19.68	16	26.30	21	32.67	26	38.89
2	5.99	7	14.07	12	21.03	17	27.59	22	33.92	27	40.11
3	7.82	8	15.51	13	22.36	18	28.87	23	35.17	28	41.34
4	9.49	9	16.92	14	23.69	19	30.14	24	36.42	29	42.56
5	11.07	10	18.31	15	25.00	20	31.41	25	37.65	30	43.77

TABLE 16.7.

Phenotype	Observed	Expected	$(O - E)^2 / E$
purple stems			
green stems			
totals			$\Sigma = \chi^2 =$

Place your data from Table 16.3 into Table 16.7 and perform a chi-square test of the results. Do your results 'fit' the 3 : 1 ratio that would be expected? Were your results significant? Did you accept your null hypothesis (the data fit a 3 : 1 ratio) or reject it?

Exercise 16.5.

Dihybrid Cross Analysis

Go up to the front table and observe the ears of corn. The two characters (each is controlled by a single gene) were 'seed coat color' and 'carbohydrate content.' There are two pairs of contrasting traits:

Gene 1: seed coat color: purple (Y) or yellow (y) seeds
Gene 2: carbohydrate content: starchy (smooth, Su) or sweet (wrinkled, su) seeds

(A single gene could be depicted with two or more letters or other symbols. Do not get confused. In this case, 'Su' represents only one gene, not two genes.)

An ear of both Parental (P) generations are shown for comparison. Take one of the F_2 ears back to your table and count the number of seeds in at least eight rows on your ear of corn (the more rows, the better), and fill in the following table (Table 16.8).

TABLE 16.8.

	Observed	Expected	$(O - E)^2 / E$
purple smooth (Y, Su)			
purple sweet (Y, su)			
yellow smooth (y, Su)			
yellow sweet (y, su)			
totals			$\Sigma = \chi^2 =$

Compare your results against the 9 : 3 : 3 : 1 ratio that is expected in this case and calculate the chi square statistic (3 d.f.). (Why are there three degrees of freedom in this instance?) Did your result fit the null hypothesis (9 : 3 : 3 : 1)?

Which seed color appears to be dominant: purple or yellow?

Which seed shape appears to be dominant: smooth (starchy) or wrinkled (sweet)?

Based on your observations, determine the genotypes for each phenotype observed.

Can you state the genotype of every kernel of corn with certainty? Why or why not? For what phenotypes can you state the genotype with certainty?

Exercise 16.6.

Pedigree Analysis

By using **pedigree analysis,** we may be able to determine the mode of inheritance for a given gene, whether it is autosomal or sex-linked and whether it is dominant or recessive. The pedigree indicates the parentage, marriages, sex, and birth order of the people in a family tree, and from it, we may be able to determine the mode of inheritance and who possesses various traits.

Example 1
Males (♂) are depicted as squares, females (♀) as circles.

Example 2
Marriages (or matings) are indicated by a line connecting a male and female together.

Example 3

The offspring of a marriage/mating (the sibship) are shown on the line below the marriage, in their order of birth (from left to right). In the sibship shown, the oldest is a girl, followed by a boy, and the youngest is a girl.

Example 4

Fraternal twins (from the fertilization of two eggs) are shown as two diagonal lines meeting the marriage line. Fraternal twins could both be boys, both be girls, or be a boy and a girl.

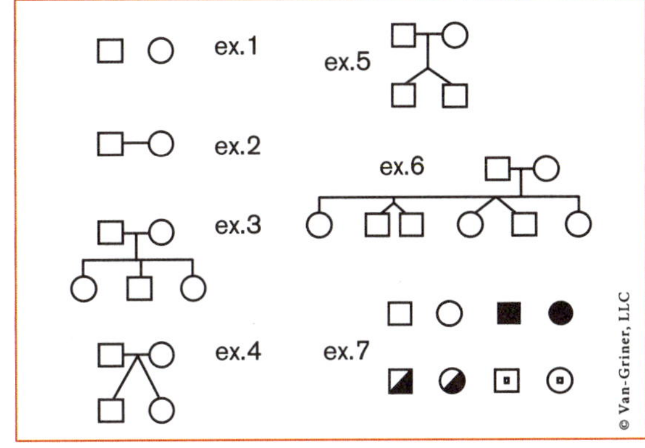

Example 5

Identical twins (from the same egg, thus the twins are always the same sex) are shown as a single line splitting into two.

Example 6

Shows a family that consists of an eldest girl, followed by identical twin boys, followed by a fraternal twin pair (a girl and a boy), and finally a youngest girl.

Example 7

The generations are labeled consecutively I, II, III, and so on, from the top of the page. An open symbol indicates a person who does not have a given trait or disease, a half-filled symbol (or a dot in the symbol) indicates one who is a carrier (heterozygous), and a person indicated with a totally filled in symbol has the trait or disease in question.

Examine each of the pedigrees on the next page. State your reasoning about which one indicates:

1 A Y-chromosome linked gene;

2 An X-chromosome linked recessive gene;

3 A dominant autosomal trait; and

4 A recessive autosomal trait.

If possible, try to figure out who must be carriers. Remember that the human male genotype is XY, and the human female is XX, with respect to **sex chromosomes.** Humans have 46 chromosomes, 23 pairs, and 22 pairs are **autosomes** (both males and females have two chromosomes of this type). The 23rd pair consists of the sex chromosomes (X and Y).

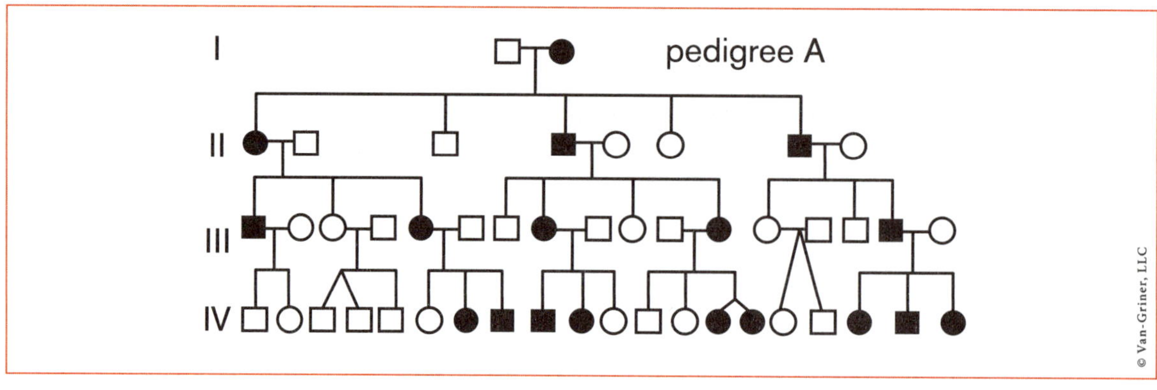

pedigree A
I
II
III
IV
© Van-Griner, LLC

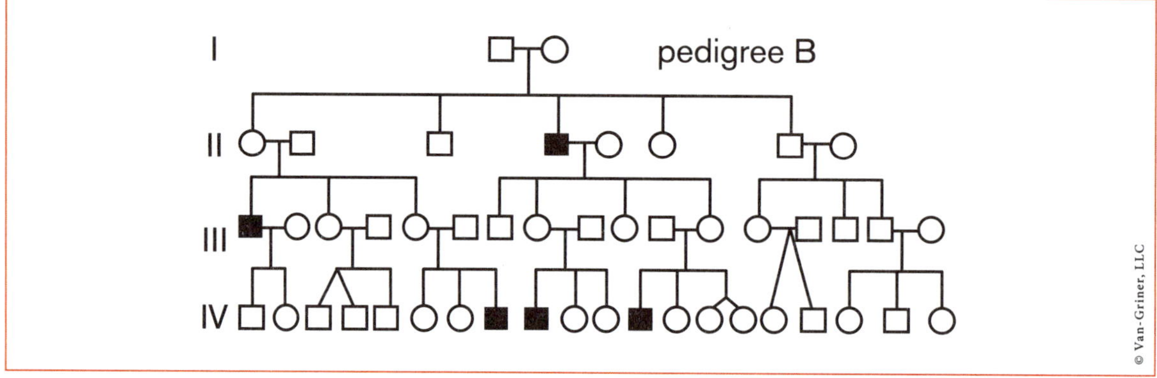

pedigree B
I
II
III
IV
© Van-Griner, LLC

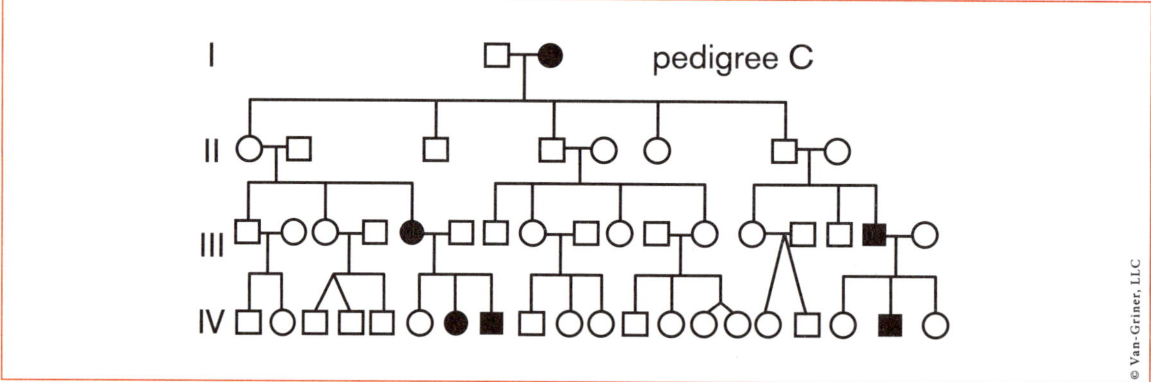

pedigree C
I
II
III
IV
© Van-Griner, LLC

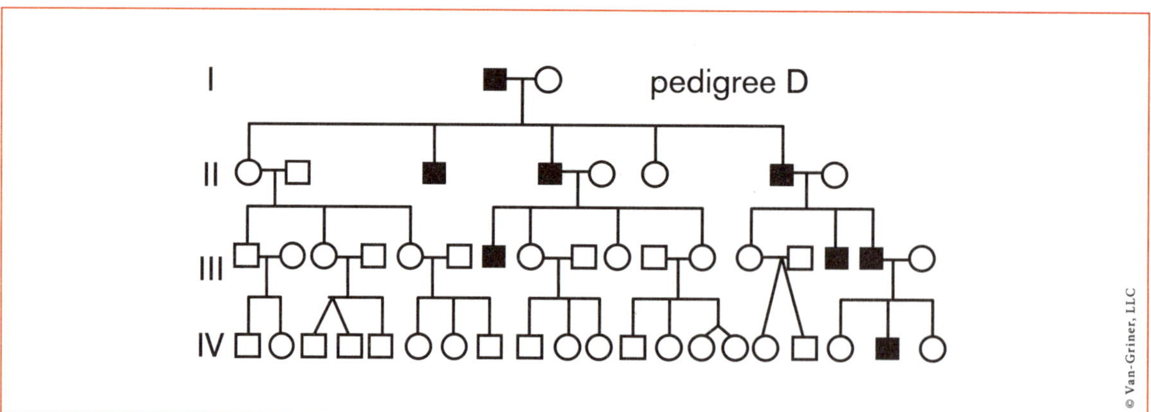

pedigree D
I
II
III
IV
© Van-Griner, LLC

DNA Structure and Function

Keywords

DNA
nucleotides
purine
pyrimidine
nitrogenous base
alpha (double) helix
DNA polymerase
replication
transcription
translation
RNA

RNA polymerase
mRNA
tRNA
rRNA
codon
anticodon
ribosome
DNA sequence
RNA sequence
amino acid sequence
start codon

stop codon
mutation
base substitution
 mutation
silent mutation
missense and
 nonsense
 mutations
base deletion
 mutation
base insertion
 mutation

inversion
restriction enzymes
electrophoresis
ribose
deoxyribose
adenine
thymine
guanine
cytosine
uracil
antiparallel

Learning Objectives

When finished with this unit, you should be able to:

1. Describe and compare the basic structure of DNA, RNA and proteins, describe the difference between a purine and a pyrimidine, and identify each nitrogen base as either a purine or a pyrimidine;

2. Describe how DNA is replicated, and list the complementary nitrogen base pairs;

3. Describe how a DNA sequence can be transcribed into a mRNA sequence, and then translated into a protein's amino acid sequence. Be able to read a DNA sequencing gel and then determine the amino acid sequence, the complementary DNA strand sequence, and the mRNA sequence that matches the DNA sequence;

4. Interpret and use the codon table to determine the amino acid sequence of a protein, given the DNA or RNA sequence, and identify the start codon and the three stop codons;

5. Describe the mistakes (mutations) that could occur during replication, transcription and translation; and

6. Understand how restriction enzymes can cut DNA, and how these DNA pieces create a distinctive pattern in an electrophoresis gel.

Today, we will examine how the genetic code in DNA is transcribed and translated into proteins. In the first exercise, you will mimic the replication of DNA and examine its structure. In the second exercise, you will determine the mRNA code from the DNA code. In the third exercise, you will determine the amino acid sequence that is encoded by a given sequence of DNA or RNA, and how various mistakes in reading or copying DNA can lead to mutations and changes in protein sequence. You will read a DNA sequencing gel, then determine the number of codons and the specific sequence of amino acids. You will also learn how DNA is isolated and 'cut' into specific segments by restriction enzymes and how these pieces are identified using gel electrophoresis.

The Basic Structure of DNA

DNA is a large molecule, containing all of the hereditary information of a cell. The DNA polymer is composed of repeating units called **nucleotides.** Each DNA nucleotide consists of three components linked together by condensation: a **phosphate,** a **five-carbon sugar (deoxyribose),** and one of four different **nitrogenous bases** (see Figure 17.1 and Figure 17.2).

The structure of DNA consists of two polynucleotide chains that are linked together by hydrogen bonds that form between nitrogenous bases. DNA consists of two strands in the form of a double helix. The sugar-phosphate backbones are on the outside of the helix, whereas the nitrogenous bases are paired on the interior of the helix (see Figure 17.1). The actual arrangement of DNA can be viewed as a ladder-like arrangement, with the sugars and phosphates acting as the sides of the ladder, and the nitrogenous bases as the rungs (Figure 17.1). A specific nitrogenous base always pairs with a specific complementary base on the other strand by forming hydrogen bonds between the two bases, and from weak van der Waals attractions between adjacent stacked bases (Figure 17.2). Each bond is very weak, but in a very large DNA molecule, millions of these bonds collectively hold the two strands together, producing a very stable structure.

There are four different nitrogenous bases in the DNA in all living things: **adenine** (A), **cytosine** (C), **guanine** (G) and **thymine** (T) (see Figure 17.2). Only certain bases are compatible to form the proper hydrogen bonds with each other. Adenine and guanine are double-ringed **purines** (two rings in the nitrogenous base structure), whereas cytosine and thymine are smaller single-ringed **pyrimidines.** In all living things, the ratio between A and T is near one. Likewise, the ratio of C : G is also near one. However, the ratio of (A + T) to (G + C) varies from species to species, and it is not necessarily 1 : 1 in any species. In Figure 17.2, the lines between letters represent covalent bonds (C—C), and the dots (O···H and N···H) represent hydrogen bonds.

The structure of one nucleotide is as follows. A phosphate is bound to the number 5 carbon [identified as 5'] on the deoxyribose molecule, and the nitrogenous base of a nucleotide is bound to the number 1 [1'] carbon of the sugar (see Figure 17.2). As the DNA molecule is formed, the enzyme DNA polymerase attaches the phosphate of one nucleotide (which is attached to the 5' carbon) to the 3' carbon of the next nucleotide via condensation, forming a sugar-phosphate backbone. In the eukaryotes, this backbone can be anywhere from millions to billions of nucleotides long. The nitrogenous bases stick out away from the backbone.

The strands in the double helix are **'antiparallel'** (see Figure 17.1 and Figure 17.2). The sugar-phosphate backbones 'run' in opposite directions. In eukaryotes, each DNA strand has two ends: a 3' end with a free hydroxyl group attached to the last deoxyribose on that end, and a 5' end with a phosphate group attached to the terminal deoxyribose. When the two strands of DNA are interacting with each other, the 5' → 3' direction of one strand runs counter to the 3' → 5' direction of the other strand. One important point to remember is that DNA has no absolute 'top' or 'bottom' or 'left' or 'right.' The terms 3' and 5' provide directionality when examining a DNA strand.

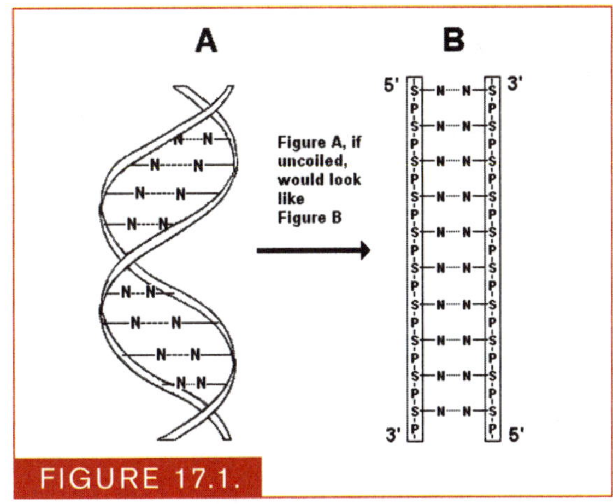

FIGURE 17.1.

The DNA double helix and the basic structure of DNA. N = nitrogenous base, S = sugar deoxyribose, P = phosphate.

DNA Replication

As mentioned above, several enzymes, including a large enzyme called **DNA polymerase,** replicate DNA prior to mitosis. One enzyme separates the two complementary strands, unlocking them like a zipper. DNA polymerase then takes free nucleotides from the cytoplasm and pairs up the nucleotides needed to match the exposed nucleotides of the strands.

When replication has finished, two identical copies of DNA have been produced. Each new DNA molecule contains one of the original strands and a newly synthesized complementary strand. This process is called **semiconservative DNA replication.** Each of the daughter cells produced in mitosis will end up with one of these copies of each DNA molecule. A chromosome is a large DNA molecule, consisting of millions to billions of nucleotides, which is visible microscopically during the G1 phase of the cell cycle in eukaryotes.

RNA

RNA (ribonucleic acid) differs from DNA in several important ways.

1. An RNA molecule is smaller than a DNA molecule.

2. **Uracil (U)** replaces **thymine (T)** in RNA.

3. The sugar component of RNA is **ribose,** not **deoxyribose.**

4. There is one major form of DNA, but there are several forms of RNA.

Transcription

DNA has one important function—it is the molecule of heredity—but RNA has several important functions and forms. One form of RNA, **messenger RNA (mRNA),** carries the message from DNA (in the eukaryotic nucleus) to the cytoplasm, where the message is read and translated into a protein. The process of making an mRNA copy of DNA is called **transcription.** Transcription takes place in the nucleus.

A large enzyme, **RNA polymerase,** transcribes DNA into RNA. It works in a fashion similar to DNA polymerase. Instead of producing a complementary DNA strand, RNA polymerase produces a complementary RNA strand from **one** of the DNA strands. The RNA molecule is complementary instead of identical to the DNA strand because the RNA nucleotides are assembled on the template using the base-paring rules (A with U, C with G).

Codons

A group of three mRNA nucleotides (a 'triplet' of nucleotides) is called a **codon.** Each codon 'word' codes for one specific amino acid, and each 'word' is composed of three nitrogenous base 'letters.'

Translation

In eukaryotic cells, the mRNA strand leaves the nucleus through a pore in the nuclear envelope and travels to the cytoplasm. Messenger RNA then meets a **ribosome.** A ribosome is an 'organelle' consisting of **ribosomal RNA (rRNA)** and various proteins. The ribosome 'reads' mRNA message, and converts this message into proteins. **Translation** is the process of combining a specific number of amino acids together in a specific sequence, as determined by the mRNA sequence. After the ribosome attaches to mRNA, another RNA molecule, **transfer RNA (tRNA),** temporarily binds to the mRNA. Specific enzymes in the cytoplasm attach a specific amino acid to the tRNA by condensation. In essentially all organisms, there are 20 different amino acids used as the monomers for proteins. Each amino acid has one or more specific tRNAs to which the amino acid is attached. On the tRNA, a group of three nucleotides comprise the **anticodon.** The anticodon of a tRNA is paired up with each successive codon along the length of a mRNA molecule, which is 'threaded' through the ribosome. If the anticodon is complementary to the mRNA molecule, the ribosome takes the amino acid away from the tRNA (by hydrolysis) and attaches the amino acid (by condensation) to the growing polypeptide chain, by forming a peptide bond.

Mutations

Any change in the DNA is called a **mutation.** Mutations can come in several forms. A **base substitution** mutation is where one nucleotide is replaced by another. In some cases, a base substitution does not cause a change in the final amino acid sequence of a protein; when this happens, it is called a **silent mutation.**

Base substitutions can cause **missense mutations** and **nonsense mutations**. A missense mutation (for example, UUU to UUA) is where the altered codon still codes for an amino acid, but for a different amino acid. A nonsense mutation occurs when the altered codon is a stop codon, and translation is stopped prematurely (for example, UGG to UGA). Nonsense mutations usually create nonfunctional proteins. A stop codon could also be altered to code for an amino acid, which also affect the protein, by making the final protein much longer than normal.

In addition to base substitution mutations, there can be other changes as well. A **base deletion** or **base insertion** mutation is when one or more nucleotides are added or removed from the DNA. Remember that the mRNA is 'read' as a series of three-letter 'words' (codons). If there is any insertion or deletion of one or more nucleotides, all of the nucleotides 'downstream' of the mutation will be improperly grouped into codons, leading to extensive missense, and, eventually, to a stop codon and termination of translation. These mutations drastically change the amino acid composition and sequence in a protein and consequently the protein often is nonfunctional.

In some cases, the replacement of one amino acid with another may not affect the three dimensional shape or activity of the protein. Replacing a nonpolar amino acid (gly, ala, val, leu, ile) with another nonpolar amino acid may not affect the functioning of the enzyme or structural protein produced. Likewise, replacing a polar amino acid (ser, thr, asn, gln) with another polar amino acid may not affect the functioning of the protein. However, replacing a nonpolar amino acid with a polar amino acid may cause a dramatic change in how the protein functions.

TABLE 17.1. The genetic code (mRNA codons, standard version).

UUU – Phe	UCU – Ser	UAU – Tyr	UGU – Cys
UUC – Phe	UCC – Ser	UAC – Tyr	UGC – Cys
UUA – Leu	UCA – Ser	UAA – STOP	UGA – STOP
UUG – Leu	UCG – Ser	UAG – STOP	UGG – Trp
CUU – Leu	CCU – Pro	CAU – His	CGU – Arg
CUC – Leu	CCC – Pro	CAC – His	CGC – Arg
CUA – Leu	CCA – Pro	CAA – Gln	CGA – Arg
CUG – Leu	CCG – Pro	CAG – Gln	CGG – Arg
AUU – Ile	ACU – Thr	AAU – Asn	AGU – Ser
AUC – Ile	ACC – Thr	AAC – Asn	AGC – Ser
AUA – Ile	ACA – Thr	AAA – Lys	AGA – Arg
AUG – Met (START)	ACG – Thr	AAG – Lys	AGG – Arg
GUU – Val	GCU – Ala	GAU – Asp	GGU – Gly
GUC – Val	GCC – Ala	GAC – Asp	GGC – Gly
GUA – Val	GCA – Ala	GAA – Glu	GGA – Gly
GUG – Val	GCG – Ala	GAG – Glu	GGG – Gly

Ala – alanine	Gly – glycine	Pro – proline	Arg – arginine
His – histidine	Ser – serine	Asn – asparagine	Ile – isoleucine
Thr- threonine	Val – valine	Asp – aspartic acid	Leu – leucine
Trp – tryptophan	Cys – cysteine	Lys – lysine	Gln – glutmine
Tyr – tyrosine	Glu – glutamic acid	Met – methionine	Phe – phenylalanine

Exercises

Exercise 17.1.

In this first exercise, you will become familiar with the components and organization of **deoxyribo-nucleic acid (DNA).** Look at the various depictions of DNA on the demonstration table. Examine Figure 17.2; it depicts the four basic nucleotides (A, T, C, and G).

You will find paper models of nucleotides at the demonstration table. Your lab instructor will assist you in producing a 2-dimensional model of a DNA strand. At your table, form a single strand of DNA, using the cutouts of nucleotides provided. Make your strand at least 9 nucleotides long.

(A) DNA and complementary strands: **At your table, using the two-dimensional paper models, connect the nucleotides together in the following sequence:**

DNA Strand

A	G	C	C	G	A	T	T	T

(B) You will then produce the complementary strand to the first strand of DNA that you made. Form the complementary strand and connect the two strands together, and have your lab instructor check your work.

DNA Strand

A	G	C	C	G	A	T	T	T

Complementary Strand

(C) Mimic DNA replication by separating the two strands that you made above and matching up new nucleotides to each. When done, you should have produced two identical molecules of DNA.

Do the strands appear to be oriented in opposite directions?

Hint: Observe the 3' and 5' ends of the nucleotides.

Can C pair up normally with A? G with G? T with T? G with A? Why or why not? Note what would happen if you try to form hydrogen bonds between two purines (A with A, G with G, or A with G), or two pyrimidines (T with C, C, with C, or T with T), or between a mismatched pyrimidine and a purine (A with C, or T with G).

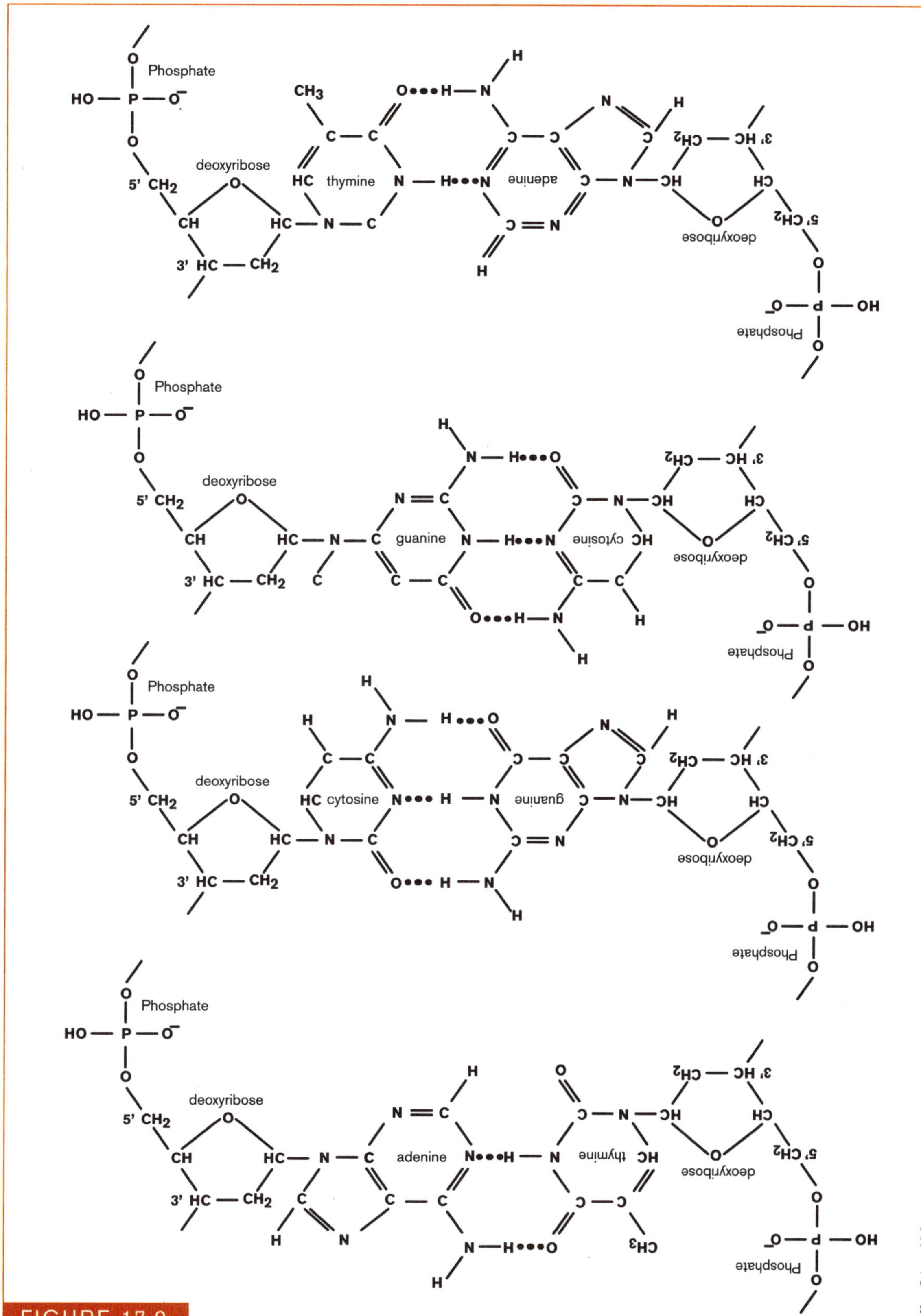

FIGURE 17.2.

The nucleotide building blocks of DNA.

© Van-Griner, LLC

Exercise 17.2.

RNA Transcription

Write the appropriate RNA strand that complements the following DNA sequence (remember: U replaces T in RNA).

DNA	A	T	T	C	C	C	G	A	T	A	G	G
RNA												

Codons. In the mRNA sequence above, how many codons are present?

Exercise 17.3.

Fill in the missing pieces of information, using Table 17.1.

DNA sequence: TAC–ACC–_____–_____–_____–CCC–_____–GAA

mRNA codon: AUG   –_____–AGU–_____–UCG–_____–_____–_____

tRNA anticodon: UAC–ACC–_____–GAC–_____–_____–_____–_____

amino acid: _____–_____–_____–_____–_____–_____–Trp–_____

How many amino acids are in this short polypeptide?

Can there be more than one codon coding for the same amino acid (examine Table 17.1)?

If the fourth codon in the mRNA is changed to CUC, would this change the amino acid? Why or why not?

If the fifth mRNA codon is changed to ACG, would this change the amino acid? Why or why not?

If the second set of DNA nucleotide triplets is changed to ATC, would this affect the protein? How?

Were there any silent mutations in the changes suggested above in questions (D through F)? If so, which one and why?

If you added a C between the second and third set of DNA nucleotide triplets, how would this change the amino acid sequence?

If you replace the last G in the DNA sequence with a T, would this affect the enzyme's function? Why or why not?

Most mutations are probably harmful. Why? Can some mutations be beneficial? How?

Your lab instructor may provide additional problems to be solved using the genetic code.

Exercise 17.4.

As a class, we will demonstrate one of the techniques in determining the DNA sequence of a gene using **gel electrophoresis.** In this exercise, we will describe how **restriction enzymes** (restriction endonucleases) work. These enzymes have been isolated and purified from various species of bacteria. These enzymes are widely used in molecular genetics for analyzing DNA and creating recombinant DNA molecules.

Restriction enzymes are bacterial enzymes that recognize a specific DNA sequence wherever it occurs in the DNA, and then cut the DNA at or near that sequence (**recognition site**). The recognition sites where the cuts occur are often palindromic (the sequences of the complementary strands are identical in opposite directions), but they sometimes are not identical. The DNA may be cut in such a way as to create a blunt end or with several nucleotides hanging off either the 3' or the 5' end (these overhangs are called 'sticky ends').

One hypothesis about the origin and function of restriction enzymes is that these enzymes act as primitive 'immune system' against viral DNA. Bacteria have many potential viral pathogens. These viruses enter and replicate inside bacteria, eventually killing the bacterial host.

Bacteria use restriction enzymes to help recognize and destroy foreign DNA. If a virus entered a bacterium containing restriction enzymes, the viral DNA is fragmented and destroyed. Bacterial restriction enzymes are very specific; they recognize short sequences on foreign DNA and cut (cleave) the DNA at those sites, producing various-sized fragments of the foreign DNA.

In addition, the enzymes do not cleave the bacteria's own DNA. The term "restriction" refers to the fact that viruses are restricted from replicating in the bacterium by enzymes that cleave the viral DNA but at the same time leave the bacterial DNA untouched. Bacteria protect their own DNA from restriction enzymes in various ways. At many points along the bacterial chromosome, the recognition sequence recognized by the bacteria's restriction enzymes may be present. By adding methyl groups to nucleotides of the bacteria's DNA that could be recognized by the restriction enzymes, this phenomenon (**methylation**) protects the bacteria's own DNA from hydrolysis.

Restriction enzymes are powerful tools in molecular biology. There are thousands of different enzymes known and hundreds are commercially available. Many restriction enzymes create 3' or 5' overhangs, which are used as sticky ends to "glue" DNA fragments from different sources together. Biologists can thus create novel genes and novel gene combinations which can be inserted into other organisms' genomes. Restriction enzymes and the DNA fragments produced by the enzymes are powerful tools in molecular biology, in medicine, and in the study of evolution.

Notice that in the piece of DNA below, two sites have the required sequence of GAATTC (in **bold**) for a particular restriction enzyme that can recognize and cut the DNA at these sites (between the G and the A of both strands).

```
GG**GAATTC**ATCCCTTAGGAAATTTGGCCC**GAATTC**CCGG
CC**CTTAAG**TAGGGAATCCTTTAAACCGGG**CTTAAG**GGCC
```

FRAGMENT 1	FRAGMENT 2	FRAGMENT 3
GG**G**	**AATTC**ATCCCTTAGGAAATTTGGCCC**G**	**AATTC**CCGG
CC**CTTAA**	**G**TAGGGAATCCTTTAAACCGGG**CTTAA**	**G**GGCC

Note that the fragments above have 'sticky ends,' or nucleotides hanging off either the 3' or the 5' end. The restriction enzyme has cut the above piece of DNA into three pieces. These pieces are smaller than the original piece and would behave differently in a **electrophoresis gel.**

A brief summary of the procedure is as follows. After the DNA is digested by various restriction enzymes, the DNA is then placed into wells (holes) in an agarose gel. An electrical current is applied to the gel for a given period of time and the DNA fragments will move through the gel. The rate of migration or distance that the pieces of DNA move through the gel is inversely proportional to their size. Nucleic acids carry negative charges and will move towards the positive electrode of the gel, but the polymers of the gel get in the way and impede the movement of the fragments. Smaller fragments will be less impeded by the various polymers of the gel, and thus smaller pieces of DNA would travel farther than larger pieces when current is applied to the gel. Placing pieces of DNA of known size in an adjacent well provides a comparison in order to estimate the sizes of the pieces of DNA that have been cut by a given restriction enzyme. After the gel has run, the DNA is usually stained or treated with a fluorescent dye that indicates the position of the DNA fragments. Different restriction enzymes have different recognition sites, thus they cut the DNA at different sites and create different-sized fragments.

The restriction enzyme cuts the DNA at the recognition sequences, creating fragments with sticky ends. A DNA ligase can then be used to rejoin the sticky fragments and seal the strands. The foreign piece of DNA may thus be incorporated into the DNA, creating what is called **recombinant DNA.** If this recombinant DNA is inserted into bacteria, the bacteria can then create the foreign gene products. See the demonstration table for more information.

The recognition sites two common restriction enzymes are depicted to the right. The sites cleaved are indicated by arrows.

*Eco*RI (from *E. coli*—*Eco*RI cuts between G and A)

*Hin*dIII (from *Haemophilus*—*Hin*dIII cuts between A and A)

*Eco*RI	G - A - A - T - T - C C - T - T - A - A - G
*Hin*dIII	A - A - G - C - T - T T - T - C - G - A - A

Examine the following hypothetical DNA sequence. Where would each enzyme (*Eco*RI, *Hin*dIII) cut the DNA? How many fragments would each restriction enzyme create?

```
G-C-A-T-G-A-A-T-T-C-C-C-A-A-T-C-G-G-A-G-A-A-T-T-C-A-A-G-C-T-T-C-T-A
C-G-T-A-C-T-T-A-A-G-G-G-T-T-A-G-C-C-T-C-T-T-A-A-G-T-T-C-G-A-A-G-A-T
```

Fragments created by *Eco*RI:	Fragments created by *Hin*dIII:

Exercise 17.5.

(This exercise was adapted and modified from a web site exercise (web link no longer active) titled 'Simulating the effects of three restriction enzymes of Lambda DNA,' devised by Colin Wood-Robinson, Centre for Studies in Science and Mathematics Education, The University of Leeds.)

1 In this exercise, each group of students (2–3 students per group) will act as a 'bacterium.'

2 You will work singly or in small groups. Your lab instructor will hand out a card to each student/group. The card represents a gene that codes for a restriction enzyme that recognizes a specific stretch of DNA which is cleaved by the enzyme.

Most restriction enzymes' names are derived from the bacterial genus, species, strain, and enzyme (in order of discovery). For example, *Eco*RI is a very common restriction enzyme; it is named after *Escherichia coli,* strain R, enzyme I (the first enzyme for this strain that was identified).

3 The bacterium (you) will be attacked by a specific **phage** (many viruses that attack bacteria are called phages), which seeks to replicate itself inside you. Your lab instructor will hand another card to you. On the card, the name of the invading phage is indicated. The phage has entered into your cytoplasm, and, if not stopped, the virus will use your cellular machinery to make many copies of itself. You, as the phage's host, provide the building blocks (nucleotides, ATP, amino acids), as well as the enzymes, ribosomes, and tRNAs, to produce many copies of both the viral genome and the viral proteins needed to create a new phage. These components self-assemble spontaneously, and then hundreds to thousands of phage leave the cell (often damaging or even killing the host as a result).

4 The phage's DNA sequence is on the lab's computers, as a Microsoft Word® file. (Phages come in several forms: single-stranded DNA, double-stranded DNA, single-stranded RNA, and double-stranded RNA. The phages we are mimicking are double-stranded viruses; however, to make this exercise easier, only one strand of DNA is represented.)

Procedure
Note: The following instructions are written using Word® with PC-based computers in mind. If you are using a Macintosh®, or if you are using WordPerfect®, your lab instructor will provide modified instructions.

Ⓐ Each phage is a separate Word® file. Open your phage's file. You are now looking at the nucleotide sequence, or genome, of the entire phage. (Remember, we are only looking at one strand of the DNA.) The genome consists of a long string of the letters a, c, t, and g (representing the four nucleotides). The sequence starts at the 5' end.

In the unlikely event that the letters are in capitalized, and not lowercase, convert all of the capital letters into lowercase letters by using the 'Change Case' command in the 'Format' pull down window on the Toolbar.

Ⓑ Next, determine the number of letters (nucleotides) there are in the genome. From the 'Tools' pull down window, click on 'Word Count.' A window pops up:

Statistics
- Pages [the number of pages to the document or selected text]
- Words [the number of words: this number should equal '1']
- Characters (no spaces) [this number is the number you want to know; it is the number of nucleotides]
- Characters (with spaces) [this number should be equal to the one above]
- Paragraphs [this number should equal '1']

<table>
<tr><td colspan="4" align="center">Note the number of characters. How many nucleotides are there to your genome?</td></tr>
<tr><td align="center">Restriction
enzyme:</td><td align="center">Genome
(phage) name:</td><td align="center">The number of
nucleotides (bases)
to the genome:</td><td align="center">The size of the
genome in kilobases
(1 Kb = 1,000 base
pairs):</td></tr>
<tr><td></td><td></td><td></td><td></td></tr>
</table>

C The names, recognition sites, and origins of commonly used restriction enzymes are listed in Table 17.5, Table 17.6, and Table 17.7. The recognition site is usually composed of 4 to 9 consecutive nucleotides. (In some cases, the nucleotides are not consecutive.) Once the enzyme finds the recognition site, the enzyme cleaves ('cuts') the DNA. The (▼) symbol in the tables refers to the site at which the DNA strand is cut by the hydrolytic enzyme.

The recognition site for a specific restriction enzyme was indicated on the card handed to you by your lab instructor. This is your 'weapon' that you will use to defend yourself!

D The phage's DNA sequence is on the computer screen. Can you readily spot the first recognition site? You will find that it is quite difficult for you to spot the sites, but the computer can do this much more rapidly and accurately than you can (the enzymes likewise work at fast speeds).

E You will perform a single digestion simulation by using the find and replace option of Word®. Perform the following steps:

Step 1 Place the cursor at the beginning of the phage sequence.

Step 2 Open the 'Edit' menu and select 'Replace.' This opens a pop up window called 'Find and Replace,' which will have three tabs: 'Find,' 'Replace,' and 'Go to.' The 'Replace' tab has been selected, with the following options:

'Find What:'

'Replace With:'

Step 3 In the 'Find What:' box, type in the recognition sequence for your restriction enzyme, without the (▼) symbol. Use lowercase letters.

For example, the recognition site for *Eco*RI is: GAATTC. Type in: gaattc.

Step 4 Move the cursor to the 'Replace With:' box and type in: g^p^paattc.

(The ^p stands for a paragraph break, or a hard return.)

Step 5 Left click on the button 'Replace All.' The program will then cut the DNA at all of the recognition sites.

Step 6 A window will pop up and it will state that Word® has completed its search of the document and has made 'X' number of replacements. The DNA sequence of the phage has now been cut 'X' times, and has created 'X + 1' fragments of various sizes. Each fragment has been separated by two hard returns.

How many restriction sites were there?	How many fragments were created?

F Now use the computer program to determine the number of the fragments created by your restriction enzyme and how large each fragment is (in bases and in Kb).

Step 1 From the 'Edit' menu, click 'Select All.' Everything will be highlighted.

Step 2 From the 'Tools' menu on the Toolbar, click 'Word Count.' Note the number of paragraphs. This number represents the number of fragments that were created.

Does the number of fragments agree with your prediction above?

Enter the number of fragments in the right-hand column of the Table 17.2. Each group of students will enter their data. Note that some of your classmates have used different restriction enzymes on the same phage, and that the class as a whole examined two or three different phages, using the same enzyme.

Did the same restriction enzyme cut different phages into the same number of fragments? Did different restriction enzymes cut the same phage in exactly the same way (i.e., were the same number of fragments produced and are they of the same size?)

G Now, determine the size of each fragment.

Step 1   Go to the top of the document and highlight the first paragraph (the first fragment produced by the digestion).

Step 2   Go to the top of the fragment, left click, and hold the button while dragging down to the end of the fragment.

Step 3   Open the 'Tools' menu on the Toolbar and select 'Word Count.' Note the number of characters (bases) in this fragment and enter it in the first column of Table 17.2. The number of words and paragraphs should equal '1'.

Step 4   Move the cursor to the next fragment and repeat Steps 2 and 3. Repeat this process until you reach the end of the genome.

Step 5   **Close the file WITHOUT saving any changes you might have made to the document!**

TABLE 17.2. Results of the restriction enzyme simulation. Fragment sizes (in bases) resulting from a simulation restriction digestion of a phage DNA.

		Fragment data								
Total Number of Fragments		4748 1,490 247 6,077 4507 2140 948 2443 29 1,159 150 1,700								
Size of Fragment (bases)	5' end	87								
		2,459								
		72								
		1,986								
		164								
		1,093								
		2,838								
		468								
		94								
		211								
		200								
		339								
		514								
		216								
		15								
		805								
		264								
	3' end	2,560								
Phage Name										
Restriction Enzyme		PST1								

H The entire class is to put their data on the board. Note that the restriction enzymes affect a given piece of DNA differently.

I Now, we will simulate the appearance of the gel if you were to isolate the fragments from the enzymatic digestion. In Table 17.3, rearrange the fragments produced by your restriction enzyme in order of size, starting with the largest. Convert the fragment sizes into kilobases (rounding to the nearest 0.1 kb).

TABLE 17.3. Phage (_________________________________) fragments produced by different endonucleases, ordered according to size.

Restriction Enzyme	(largest)			Size of Fragments (kb)									(smallest)

J The last step to this exercise is to imagine what the electrophoresis gel would look like if we digested your phage using one of these enzymes. After digesting the phage, we would add the digest to a small pit (well) in an agarose gel and then turn on a power source, applying a small electric current to the gel. The pieces of DNA then would travel towards the positive end of the gel; the speed at which the pieces move would depend upon their relative sizes. The gel then would be stained and the locations of the DNA fragments determined. Known standards of specific sizes (shown along the left-hand side of the figure on the next page) are also used, in order to estimate the size of the fragments.

Draw a sketch of what your hypothetical gel would look like. Plot where you think the fragments of your phage would appear, given the restriction enzyme you used, in lane 1 in the figure below. Plot the locations of the fragments of digests of the same phage by other restriction enzymes in the other lanes (other students would have digested the same phage). Label the lanes.

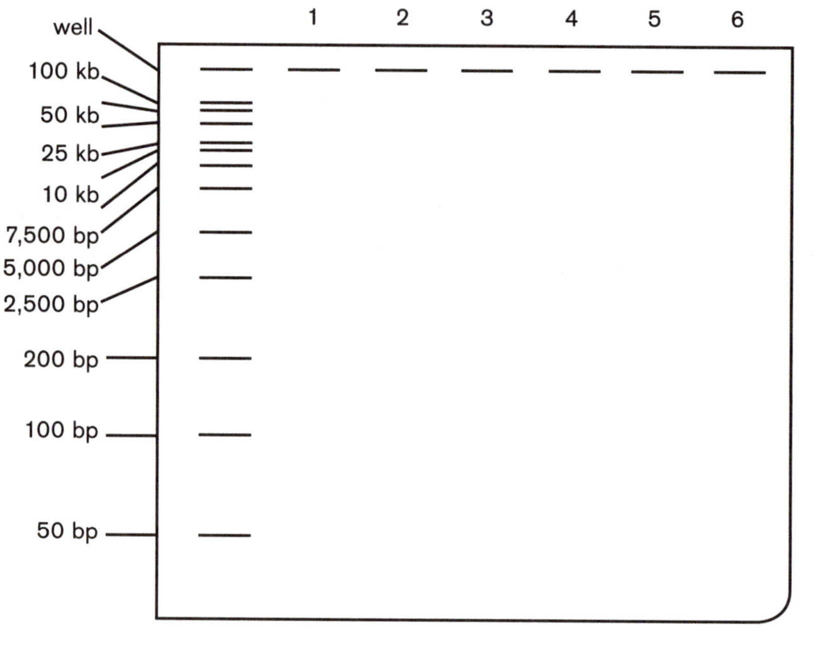

Do all restriction enzymes cut the phage at the same locations?

Are similar-sized fragments produced by all enzymes?

Examine the location of some standard DNA size markers (in 1,000 base pairs [kb] or base pairs [bp]). They indicate where DNA fragments of a given size would be located. Do DNA fragments appear to move as a linear function of their size? What is the relationship between fragment size and distance traveled?

The frequency with which a given restriction endonuclease cuts DNA depends on the recognition site of the enzyme. Table 17.5 lists several enzymes that recognize sequences four nucleotides long. Table 17.6 and Table 17.7 list enzymes with 6 and 8 nucleotide recognition sites, respectively.

You should be able to estimate how frequently your enzyme should cut your piece of DNA. Biologists examining a relatively large piece of DNA would not want to create thousands of fragments that would have to be separated on a gel, so they try to use the appropriate enzyme, given the size of the DNA, and use as small of a piece of target DNA as possible.

With the four nucleotide bases that make up DNA (A, T, C, and G), the probability of any one nucleotide occurring at a given location is ¼. If the enzyme recognizes a specific sequence four nucleotides long (assuming that each nucleotide has an equal chance of occurring at any particular site), then the number of cuts made would depend on the length of the sequence (in bp) divided by 256.

$(¼ \times ¼ \times ¼ \times ¼) = 1/256$

An enzyme recognizing a specific four nucleotide recognition sequence (a four bp 'cutter') thus should cut once every 256 base pairs, on average. The general formula for determining the number of cuts is: $(¼)^N$, where N is the number of base pairs in the recognition site. Thus, for any given piece of DNA that is X bases in length, the number of cuts that are predicted to occur would be $X/(4^N)$, and the number of fragments created would be $[X/(4^N)] + 1$. For example, a piece of DNA 33,000 nucleotides long, should be cut by a 6 bp cutter $33,000/(4)^6$ = about 8 times, creating 9 fragments.

How often should an enzyme recognizing a specific five-nucleotide sequence cut the DNA (a 5 bp 'cutter')? A six nucleotide recognition site (a 6 bp cutter)? A 7 bp cutter? An 8 bp cutter? A 9 bp cutter?

Discuss with your classmates under what conditions you would use different enzymes.

Try several enzymes (4 bp 'cutters,' 6 bp 'cutters,' and 8 bp 'cutters') on one phage and see if there is a relationship between the number of nucleotides recognized by a restriction enzyme and the number of cuts. Place the class results in Table 17.4 below.

For example, suppose your DNA fragment is 10 kb long, and you are using a restriction enzyme that has a 4 bp recognition site; then you would expect (10,000 bp/256 bp/cut) cuts, which is about 39 cuts (and thus 40 fragments). If you used an enzyme with a 6 bp recognition site on the same DNA fragment, you may get two or three fragments on average, and if you used an enzyme with a 8 bp recognition site, it is very likely the enzyme would not cut the DNA at all (why?)

TABLE 17.4. Effect of recognition site size on the number of cuts.

Size of Recognition Site	Endonuclease Name	DNA Size of the Phage (in Bp)	Number of Cuts	Mean Observed Number of Cuts	Number of Cuts Expected
4 bp					
4 bp					
4 bp					
4 bp					
4 bp					
4 bp					
4 bp					
4 bp					
6 bp					
6 bp					
6 bp					
6 bp					
6 bp					
6 bp					
6 bp					
6 bp					
8 bp					
8 bp					
8 bp					
8 bp					
8 bp					
8 bp					
8 bp					
8 bp					

Did the results in Table 17.4 fit your predicted results? If not, can you give any reasons why your results were different?

TABLE 17.5. Restriction enzyme list, 4 bp recognition site.

Enzyme	Recognition Sequence Site (5' ▼ 3') (▼ = cut)	Bacterial Source
Alu I	AG▼CT	*Arthrobacter luteus*
Cfo I (*Hha* I)	GCG▼C	*Clostridium formicoaceticum*
Cvi RI	TG▼CA	*Chlorella* strain
Fnu DII	CG▼CG	*Fusobacterium nucleatum* D
Hae III	GG▼CC	*Haemophilus aegyptius*
Hpa II (*Msp* I)	C▼CGG	*Haemophilus parainfluenzae*
*Hsp*92 II	CATG▼	*Haemophilus influenzae* 92
Mae I	C▼TAG	*Methanococcus aeolicus*
Mae II	A▼CGT	*Methanococcus aeolicus*
Mbo I (*Nde* II, *Dpn* I)	▼GATC	*Moraxella bovis* ATCC 10900
Rsa I (*Afa* I)	GT▼AC	*Rhodopseudomonas sphaeroides*
Taq I	T▼CGA	*Thermus aquaticus* YTI
*Tru*9 I	T▼TAA	*Thermus ruber* 9
*Tsp*EI	▼AATT	*Thermus* sp. IE

TABLE 17.6. Restriction enzyme list, 6 bp recognition site.

Enzyme	Recognition Sequence Site (5' ▼ 3') (▼ = cut)	Bacterial Source
Aat II	GACGT▼C	*Acetobacter aceti*
Acc III	T▼CCGGA	*Acinetobacter calcoaceticus*
*Acc*65 I (*Kpn* I)	G▼GTACC	*Acinetobacter calcoaceticus*
Acv I (*Pml* I)	CAC▼GTG	*Aeromonas caviae*
Age I	A▼CCGGT	*Agrobacterium gelatinovorum*
*Alw*44 I	G▼TGCAC	*Acinetobacter lwoffi*
Apa I	GGGCC▼C	*Acetobacter pasteurianus*
Bal I	TGG▼CCA	*Brevibacterium albidum*
*Bam*H I	G▼GATCC	*Bacillus amyloliquefaciens* H.
Bbu I (*Sph* I)	GCATG▼C	*Bacillus* sp. Bu17091
Bcl I	T▼GATCA	*Bacillus caldolyticus*
Bgl II	A▼GATCT	*Bacillus globigii*

TABLE 17.6. (continued) Restriction enzyme list, 6 bp recognition site.

Enzyme	Recognition Sequence Site (5' ▼ 3') (▼ = cut)	Bacterial Source
*Bss*H II	G▼CGCGC	*Geobacillus stearothermophilus* H3
*Bst*98 I (*Afl* II, *Msp*C I)	C▼TTAAG	*Bacillus stearothermophilus*
*Bst*Z I (*Eco*52 I)	C▼GGCCG	*Bacillus stearothermophilus*
Cla I	AT▼CGAT	*Caryophanon latum* L.
*Csp*45 I	TT▼CGAA	*Clostridium sporogenes*
Dra I	TTT▼AAA	*Deinococcus radiophilus*
*Eco*47 III	AGC▼GCT	*Escherichia coli* RFL 47
*Eco*ICR I (*Sac* I)	GAG▼CTC	*Escherichia coli* ICR
*Eco*R I	G▼AATTC	*Escherichia coli* RY 13
*Eco*R V	GAT▼ATC	*Escherichia coli* J62 pLG74
Hind III	A▼AGCTT	*Haemophilus influenzae* Rd.
Hpa I	GTT▼AAC	*Haemophilus parainfluenzae*
Kpn I	GGTAC▼C	*Klebsiella pneumoniae*
Mlu I	A▼CGCGT	*Micrococcus luteus*
Nae I (*NgoM* IV)	GCC▼GGC	*Nocardia aerocolonigenes*
Nar I	GG▼CGCC	*Norcardia argentinensis*
Nco I	C▼CATGG	*Nocardia coralina*
Nde I	CA▼TATG	*Neisseria denitrificans*
Nhe I	G▼CTAGC	*Neisseria mucosa heidelbergensis*
Nru I	TCG▼CGA	*Nocardia rubra* ATCC 15906
Nsi I	ATGCA▼T	*Neisseria sicca*
Pst I	CTGCA▼G	*Providencia stuartii*
Pvu I	CGAT▼CG	*Proteus vulgaris*
Pvu II	CAG▼CTG	*Proteus vulgaris*
Sac II	CCGC▼GG	*Streptomyces achromogenes*
Sal I	G▼TCGAC	*Streptomyces albus* G.
Sca I (*Ass* I, *Zrm* I)	AGT▼ACT	*Streptomyces caespitosus*
Sma I	CCC▼GGG	*Serratia marcescens*
*Sna*B I	TAC▼GTA	*Sphaerotilus natans* ATCC 139280
Spe I (*Ahl* I, *Bcu* I)	A▼CTAGT	*Sphaerotilus natans* ATCC 13923
Ssp I	AAT▼ATT	*Sphaerotilus natans* ATCC 13925
Stu I	AGG▼CCT	*Streptomyces tubercidicus*
Vsp I (*Ase* I, *Psh*B I)	AT▼TAAT	*Vibrio* species
Xba I	T▼CTAGA	*Xanthomonas badrii*
Xho I	C▼TCGAG	*Xanthomonas holocola*
Xma I	C▼CCGGG	*Xanthomonas malvacaerum*

TABLE 17.7. Restriction enzyme list, 8 bp recognition site.

Enzyme	Recognition Sequence Site (5' ▼ 3') (▼ = cut)	Bacterial Source
Abs I	CC▼TCGAGG	*Arthrobacter* species 7M06
Asc I	GG▼CGCGCC	*Arthrobacter* species
Fse I	GGCCGG▼CC	*Frankia* species Eul 1b
Not I	GC▼GGCCGC	*Nocardia otitidus-caviarum*
Pac I	TTAAT▼TAA	*Pseudomonas alcaligenes*
Pme I (*Mss* I)	GTTT▼AAAC	*Pseudomonas mendocina*
Sgf I (*AsiS* I)	GCGAT ▼CGC	*Streptomyces* species
*Sgr*D I	CG▼TCGACG	*Streptomyces griseus* RFL6
Srf I	GCCC▼GGGC	*Streptomyces* species
Sse 8387 I (*Sbf* I, *Sda* I)	CCTGCA▼GG	*Streptomyces* species 8387
Sse 232 I	CG▼CCGGCG	*Streptomyces* RH232
Swa I (*Smi* I)	ATTT ▼AAAT	*Staphlococcus warneri*

18 UNIT — Animals I. Introduction to Animal Diversity

Keywords

diploblastic
triploblastic
asymmetry
radial symmetry
bilateral symmetry
lateral
median (midsagittal)
frontal
medial and transverse planes

dorsal
ventral
anterior
posterior
cephalization
germ layers
endoderm
ectoderm
mesoderm

diploblastic acoelomate
acoelomate
pseudocoelomate
  and coelomate
coelom
pseudocoelom
mesenteries
monoecious and dioecious

Learning Objectives

When finished with this unit, you should be able to:

1 Compare and contrast the following concepts: body plans (diploblastic/triploblastic), body cavities (acoelomate, pseudocoelomate, and eucoelomate), planes of symmetry (median, transverse, lateral), and orientation (anterior/posterior, ventral/dorsal, lateral);

2 Describe the importance of body cavities and cephalization;

3 Describe the distinctive features of each phylum (and, in the cnidarians and flatworms, each class) of sponges, cnidarians, flatworms, and roundworms;

4 Compare and contrast the modes of sexual and asexual reproduction observed in these animals;

5 Identify the kingdom and phylum (and class in sponges, cnidarians, and flatworms) of selected specimens of the four phyla examined today;

6 Identify the following terms, structures or cell types in sponges: choanocyte, pinacocytes, amebocytes, spicules (siliceous or calcareous), spongin, ostia, osculum, spongocoel, amphiblastula, mesohyl, somatic regeneration, fragmentation, budding;

7 Identify the following structures or concepts observed in cnidarians and their life cycles: polyp, medusa, cnidocytes, nematocysts, mouth, hypostome, tentacles, epidermis, gastrodermis, gastrovascular cavity, extracellular versus intracellular digestion, mesoglea, nerve net, planula, strobilization, perisarc, strobila, ephyra;

8 Identify the following structures or concepts observed in platyhelminths and their life cycles: gastrovascular cavity, epidermis, eyes, auricles, pharynx and pharyngeal cavity, circular and longitudinal muscles, nerve cords, mouth, flame cells, protonephridia, oral and ventral suckers, gonads (testes, ovaries), scolex, proglottid, complete versus incomplete digestive tract, miracidia, sporocyst, redia, metacercaria; and

9 Identify the following structures or concepts observed in the nematodes, as shown in the roundworm cross section: cuticle, epidermis, pseudocoelom, testes, oviduct, uterus, intestine, longitudinal muscles.

Classification

Kingdom Animalia

  Phylum Porifera (the sponges)

    Class Calcarea (calcareous sponges, *Grantia*)

    Class Hexactinellida (glass sponges)

    Class Demospongiae (bath sponges)

  Phylum Cnidaria (the cnidarians)

    Class Hydrozoa *Hydra*

    Class Scyphozoa (true jellyfish) *Aurelia*

    Class Anthozoa (anemones and corals) *Metridium*

  Phylum Platyhelminthes (the flatworms)

    Class Turbellaria (planaria) *Dugesia* (*Planaria*)

    Class Trematoda (flukes) *Clonorchis*

    Class Cestoda (tapeworms) *Taenia*

  Phylum Nematoda (the roundworms) *Turbatrix, Ascaris*

Over the next few class periods, we will look at the nine most common animal phyla. All groups of animals are multicellular and presumably descended from a hypothetical unicellular flagellated protist ancestor. The simplest animals possess no true **tissues** (layers of differentiated cells) and are grouped into the **'Parazoa.'** The group 'Parazoa' currently is an artificial taxon not recognized as part of the official classification of the animal kingdom. These sponges (and the placozoans) are the only parazoan groups still alive.

Animal taxonomy continues to be in flux and textbooks vary in their definitions of the Kingdom Animalia. Not too long ago, the protozoa (see Unit 11) were lumped with the multicellular animals (the Parazoa and the Eumetazoa) and all were referred to as 'Animalia.' In this course, we will place the protozoans in with the rest of the protists and refer to the metazoans as the animals.

After the sponges, the rest of the animal phyla we will study are members of the **Eumetazoa.** The eumetazoa have differentiated cells and true tissues derived from germ layers. Like 'Parazoa,' 'Eumetazoa' is not currently an officially recognized taxon, but the two terms are useful in reminding us of the differences between the different groups of animals alive today.

Diploblastic and Triploblastic Body Plans

The simplest eumetazoans are **diploblastic** (see Figure 18.1) and have two **germ layers: endoderm and ectoderm.** After fertilization, the zygote undergoes mitotic cell division to form an **embryo.** The **ectoderm** is the outermost primary germ layer of an animal embryo; it gives rise to the outer covering of the animal, such as skin (integument) and the accessory organs associated with skin. In more complex animals, the ectoderm also gives rise to the cells of the nervous system. The **endoderm** is the innermost primary germ layer, which gives rise to the cells that line the digestive tract and its accessory organs (liver, pancreas) and the cells that line the respiratory tract in the lungs in higher animals. The major diploblastic phylum we will observe today is the **phylum Cnidaria.**

All other eumetazoan phyla are **triploblastic** and possess a **mesoderm** germ layer in addition to ectoderm and endoderm. The mesoderm lies between the ectoderm and endoderm. The mesoderm germ layer gives rise to cells between the integument and digestive tract. Mesodermally derived cells include the lining of the internal body cavity (the **coelom**), muscle cells, various parts of the circulatory system (endothelial cells of the blood vessels, and well as the cells in blood), the cells of the endoskeleton (cartilage and bones), as well as most of the cells of the excretory organs, various glands and reproductive organs.

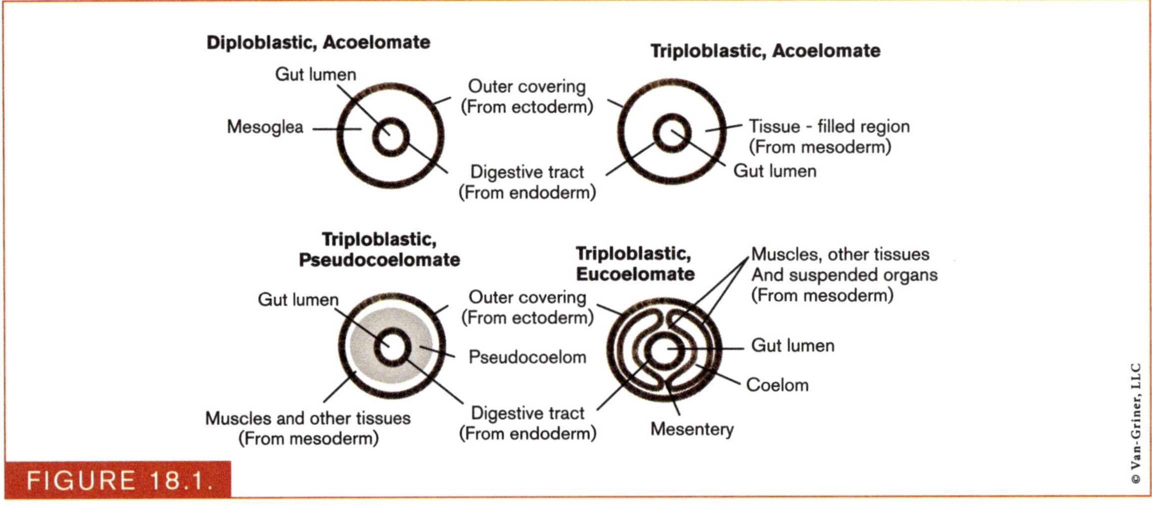

FIGURE 18.1.

Cross section through diploblastic and triploblastic body plans.

Types of Eumetazoan Body Cavities

There are four main types of eumetazoan body plans with respect to internal **body cavities (coelom).**

1 The first type includes the diploblastic animals (Cnidaria), **which do not possess an internal body cavity or coelom** (a coelom is a defined a space or cavity between the digestive tract and outer body; the space is completely lined with mesoderm-derived tissue). These groups lack mesoderm, so by definition, a true coelom could not exist (see Figure 18.1). We will refer to the cnidarians as the **diploblastic acoelomates.**

2 The **triploblastic animals** (all other phyla) have one of the three remaining types of internal body cavity arrangements (other than gastrovascular cavities, see Figure 18.1). **Triploblastic acoelomate animals** (phylum Platyhelminthes) possess the second type of body plan. The acoelomates do not possess a coelom, although they possess mesoderm. The region between the digestive tract and outer body wall is filled with mesodermally-derived cells.

3 The third type of body plan is shown by the **pseudocoelomate** phyla. Pseudocoelomate animals (phylum Nematoda is one example) possess an internal fluid-filled body cavity, but the cavity is incompletely lined with mesoderm-derived tissue (Figure 18.1).

4 The fourth type of body plan is shown by the **coelomates** (often referred to as the **eucoelomates**), which includes many of the animal phyla (arthropods, annelids, molluscs, echinoderms, and chordates are the major groups). The coelom forms during development and is a fluid-filled cavity completely lined with mesodermally-derived cells (Figure 18.1). The several organ systems are suspended within the coelom by double layers of mesodermally-derived tissues, called **mesenteries.**

Why Have Body Cavities?

A coelomic body cavity is important because it provides:

a Room for organs to grow and develop;

b An increased surface area for gas exchange and nutrient transport into and out of organs;

c A hydrostatic skeleton used for support, locomotion, and for the movement of materials within the digestive tract;

d A place to store materials; and

e A route to pass nitrogenous wastes and gametes to the outside.

Body Symmetry

In addition to the number of germ layers, animals are also distinguished according to their **body symmetry.** A **radially** symmetrical animal (examples include the cnidarians and the echinoderms) can be divided by many planes through the central axis of its body running from the top (**oral** side with the mouth) to the bottom (**aboral** side). There is no distinct head, nor are there right and left sides. These radially symmetrical animals may be divided into two mirror halves, through many different longitudinal planes (two of these longitudinal planes are depicted bisecting the sea anemone in Figure 18.2).

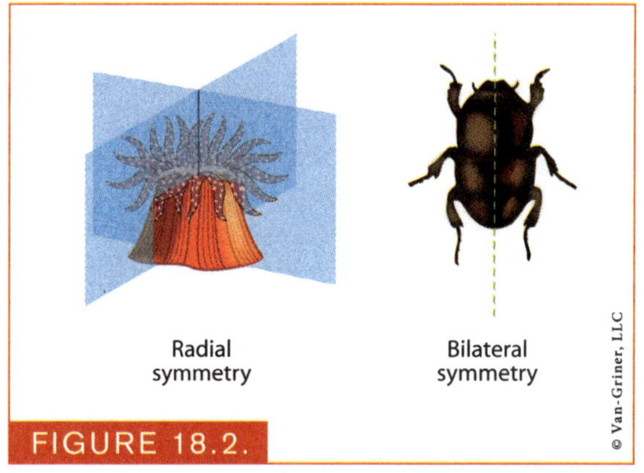

FIGURE 18.2.

Two major forms of animal symmetry.

Most sponges have no symmetry (they are **asymmetrical**) because there is no central axis that can be divided into equal halves. However, some sponges appear to have radial symmetry, similar to the cnidarians, because their body consists of a long tube-like shape.

Like the beetle in Figure 18.2, most animals are **bilaterally symmetrical,** which means that they may be divided into two mirror halves only through one longitudinal plane (the **median plane** or **midsagittal plane,** Figure 18.3). Bilaterally symmetrical animals therefore have **right** and **left sides** (lateral sides). Most animals also have a distinct head (**anterior**) and tail (**posterior**) ends, as well as an upper (**dorsal**) surface and lower (**ventral**) surface. A **transverse plane** divides the body into superior (the anterior portion of the body) and inferior (the posterior portion) parts. A **frontal plane** (also called the coronal plane) divides the body into a front (ventral) and back (dorsal) parts. A **sagittal plane** divides the body into left and right (lateral) parts. Bilaterally symmetrical animals all show distinct **cephalization,** an evolutionary trend towards concentrating sensory and nervous systems at the anterior end of the organism (which makes sense because the anterior side is what will first come in contact with the new environment). In Figure 18.3, the various planes of a bilaterally symmetrical animal (the fox) are depicted.

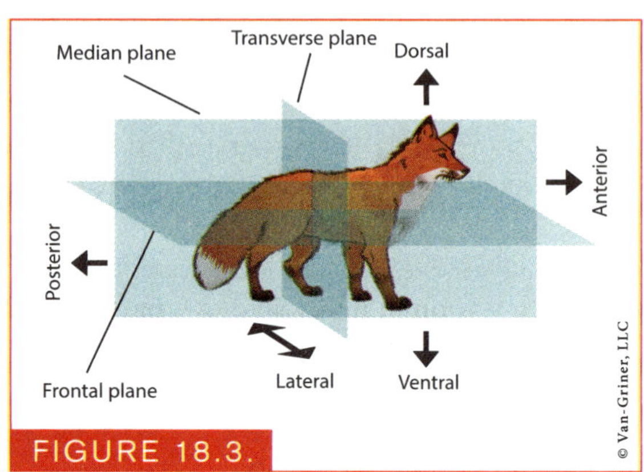

FIGURE 18.3.

The planes of symmetry in a bilaterally symmetrical animal.

Phylum Porifera

The **poriferans,** or **sponges,** are the simplest of animals. The taxonomic status of sponges (and many animal groups) are still in flux; in this class, we will treat all sponges as belonging to one phylum, with three classes.

The key characteristics (functional homologies) for all sponges are as follows:

Ⓐ Sponges are at the **cellular level of organization** because each cell is somewhat independent of other cells. There are no tissues, organs or organ systems in sponges. They generally show no obvious body symmetry.

Ⓑ **Somatic regeneration.** If sponge cells are separated from each other, the isolated cells can reaggregate and form a new sponge.

Ⓒ Most, if not all, sponge cells are **totipotent:** each cell can potentially give rise to any other cell type.

Ⓓ There are **no germ layers, digestive tracts,** or **coeloms** in sponges. Sponges thus cannot be classified as either diploblastic or triploblastic. In addition, sponges are not considered to be acoelomates, coelomates, or pseudocoelomates, nor can they be classified as protostomes or deuterostomes either, because sponges have no digestive tract (see Unit 19 for more information on protostomes and deuterostomes).

Ⓔ Inside a sponge, water moves through various pores, canals, and cavities.

F Sponges have **choanocytes,** flagellated cells that are involved in many different activities.

G The internal skeleton of a sponge is composed of many **spicules,** which can either be siliceous [glass] or calcareous [calcium carbonate]. In some species, a network of proteinaceous fibers (made of **spongin**) is present as well.

H Sponges **do not show cephalization or segmentation.** Each cell independently exchanges gases with its environment and eliminates nitrogen wastes (in the form of ammonia) via diffusion. Many sponge cells do depend on other cells for food.

I There are **no distinct muscular, nervous, or endocrine systems** present in sponges. Sponges are basically nonmoving, sessile organisms, although they do respond to touch and chemicals.

J Most sponges are marine, although a few species live in freshwater environments.

Today we will look at several sponges. One sponge is called *Grantia* (Figure 18.5), common in many shallow marine habitats along the northern Atlantic coastlines. It is a small vase-shaped sponge, with a central cavity (**spongocoel**). Water enters into **incurrent canals** through small outer incurrent pores, called **ostia** (singular: ostium). Water then moves through internal pores (**prosopyles**) that connects the incurrent canals to **radial canals.** **Choanocytes** line the radial canals. Water leaves the radial canals through small pores (**apopyles**) and enters the large **spongocoel.** Once in the spongocoel, water exits the sponge through the large single **osculum** (the outcurrent pore) on top.

Water currents are formed by the beating of flagella from thousands of **choanocytes** lining the radial canals. Saltwater, containing oxygen and food, is swept into the sponges by the beating of the flagella. Sponge cells exchange gases and expel wastes into the water as it passes by. Each choanocyte has a collar of cytoplasm (made up of small pseudopodia and mucus) that captures food particles from the water, forming food vacuoles. Digestion occurs in the choanocytes (**intracellular digestion**) when lysosomes containing digestive enzymes fuse with food vacuoles. These enzymes break down the food; the monomers created by digestion then diffuse into the cytoplasm. **Pinacocytes** are thin plate-like cells lining the outside of the sponge, as well as the spongocoel and canals. **Amebocytes** are amoeboid cells that are involved in intracellular digestion (choanocytes transfer food vacuoles to other cells, such as amoebocytes) and food transport, in spicule and spongin production, reproduction, and contraction of the sponge body. Amebocytes are scattered throughout a thin gel-like matrix (called the **mesohyl**).

Reproduction in sponges. In the *Grantia* (*Sycon*) slide, you may notice small clusters of cells in some of the radial canals. These cell clusters are sponge larvae, called **amphiblastulas.** An amphiblastula larva is formed by the fertilized egg (**zygote**) that has undergone mitosis. Eggs are retained in the mesohyl and sperm are captured by choanocytes. These choanocytes then become amoeboid and carry the sperm to the eggs for fertilization. Fertilization is thus considered a type of **internal fertilization** in these animals. Amphiblastulas break through into the spongocoel and eventually exit out through the osculum. Sponges also reproduce asexually by **fragmenting** and **budding.**

Exercises

Exercise 18.1.

Under low power, observe the prepared *Grantia* (= *Sycon*) slide: c.s. [cross section] and l.s. [longitudinal section] (Figure 18.5). Identify the amphiblastulas you can observe in the slide, if they are present. Draw what you see in the microscope's field of view in the space below (Figure 18.4).

FIGURE 18.4.

Grantia.

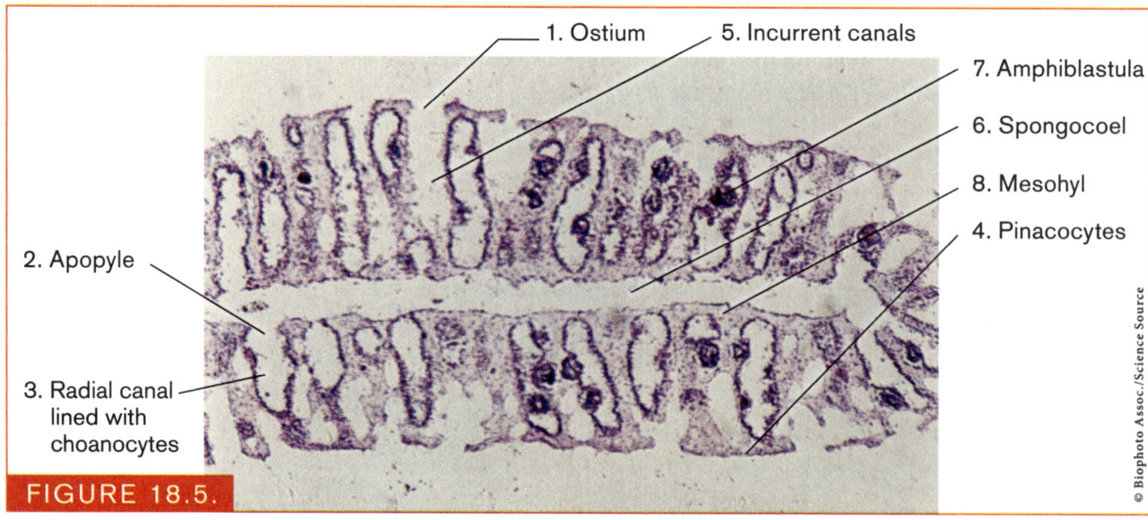

FIGURE 18.5.

Grantia transverse section.

Exercise 18.2.

Classes of Sponges

Examine the dried and preserved specimens of sponges up at the demonstration table. *Grantia* is an example of the **Class Calcarea** (Figure 18.5). They have spicules of calcium carbonate and all are marine. A few species are in the **Class Hexactinellida** (glass sponges). The glass sponges have spicules of glass and are found mostly in deep-water marine environments. Most sponges (90% of the 5,000 or so species) are in the **Class Demospongiae** (Figure 18.7). The 'bath sponge' that your grandmother used is the spongin mesh of a species in this class. These sponges have glass spicules and/or spongin fibers in their skeleton. The bath sponges are collected and compressed and crushed, releasing the cells from the fibrous spongin skeleton.

Draw a picture of the representative sponges in the space provided below (Figure 18.6).

FIGURE 18.6.

Representative sponge types.

FIGURE 18.7.

Spongin mesh of a bath sponge, Class Demospongiae.

Exercise 18.3.

Under low power, examine the spicule slide and draw in the space provided below (Figure 18.8) what you see in the microscope's field of view. Adjust the light intensity in order to see the spicules more easily. Other structures that give protection and support to a sponge are spongin fibers. In addition, go to the demonstration table and observe spongin fibers under the microscope.

FIGURE 18.8.

Sponge spicules.

How do spongin fibers and spicules differ?

Phylum Cnidaria

We will examine the three major classes of this phylum: **Scyphozoa, Hydrozoa,** and **Anthozoa. All cnidarians have the following common characteristics or functional homologies that distinguish them from other animals:**

A Cnidarians have a **diploblastic, acoelomate** body plan. Cnidarians have two dermal tissue layers: an outer **epidermis** and an inner **gastrodermis** lining the gastrovascular cavity. The **mesoglea** is an acellular gelatinous layer between the two dermal layers. The mesoglea is either thin (as in hydrozoans) or thick (as in scyphozoan jellyfish).

B The cnidarians are **unsegmented,** although some polyps undergo **strobilization** (they produce multiple medusae off of one polyp). Cnidarians show **radial symmetry.**

C The cnidarians have two distinct body forms: the sessile **polyp** and the free-swimming **medusa** (see Figure 18.9). The **hydrozoans** usually have the polyp as the only form (or the dominant form). The polyp is a radially symmetrical, cylindrical animal with a mouth surrounded by a ring of tentacles. The medusa is often the dominant life cycle stage in the **Scyphozoa;** in the scyphozoans, the polyp primarily serves as a means to produce medusae. The medusae are bell or umbrella-shaped animals with their mouths pointing downwards. **Anthozoans** (corals and their relatives) do not have a medusa stage.

Ⓓ Integumentary system. Most cnidarians have no specialized integument. The outer layer of the body is the epidermis. However, some colonial cnidarians have an protective outer covering (the **perisarc**) that is composed of proteins, polysaccharides, and chitin; the perisarc surrounds all of the polyps of the colony.

Ⓔ The cnidarian epidermis (especially on the tentacles) contains stinging cells called **cnidocytes.** These specialized cells possess a spiked, harpoon-like organelle (called a **nematocyst**) that can be discharged out of the cnidocyte very rapidly. Nematocysts pierce, entangle, and/or paralyze prey and also help defend the animal against potential predators.

Ⓕ Digestive system. In cnidarians, **digestion occurs extracellularly in the gastrovascular cavity** (an older term for 'gastrovascular cavity' is the 'coelenteron'). Digestive enzymes are secreted into the gastrovascular cavity. The digested food molecules then are absorbed by the gastrodermal cells. Fluids move through the gastrovascular cavity due to body wall contractions and to the actions of cilia of the gastrodermis. Most cnidarians are marine and carnivorous, feeding upon small planktonic animals. However, some cnidarians have **symbiotic algae** that live inside them (particularly in the corals) and the algae provide some food for the cnidarian host.

Ⓖ Respiratory system. Cnidarians have **no specialized respiratory systems.** Diffusion of gases occurs across the body wall. The gastrovascular cavity helps gases to diffuse through the body.

Ⓗ Circulatory system. Cnidarians have **no specialized circulatory systems.** Simple diffusion occurs, although ciliary action of the gastrovascular cavity helps move the contents of the digestive system (as well as food and gases) throughout the body.

Ⓘ Osmoregulatory/excretory systems. Cnidarians have **no specialized osmoregulatory/excretory systems.** Nitrogenous wastes (ammonia) diffuse from each cell and out the body wall.

Ⓙ Nervous system. Cnidarians have a simple **nerve net** (in both dermal tissues) but no brain or cephalization. Cnidarians possess sensory receptors with neurosensory cells that can respond to light, touch, or balance (gravity), depending on the receptor.

Ⓚ Reproductive system. Cnidarians can reproduce asexually (usually by budding, see Figure 18.11) and sexually (depending on the species, either polyps or medusae produce eggs and sperm). Fertilization is **external** and occurs in the water column, although the eggs are retained in numerous hydrozoans. Cnidarians generally are **dioecious** (separate sexes), although a colony may have both males and females.

L **Skeletal system.** Cnidarians generally have no major support structures; the body wall is two layers thick. However, some species (the corals) form a exoskeleton made of calcium carbonate.

M **Muscular system.** Cells found in both the epidermis (**epitheliomuscular** cells) and in the gastrodermis (**nutritive-muscular cells**) are capable of contraction. Bands of muscle in the bells of many medusae can contract, forcing water out from under the bell and thrusting the medusae forward. Some polyps either can inch along or somersault, using their oral arms.

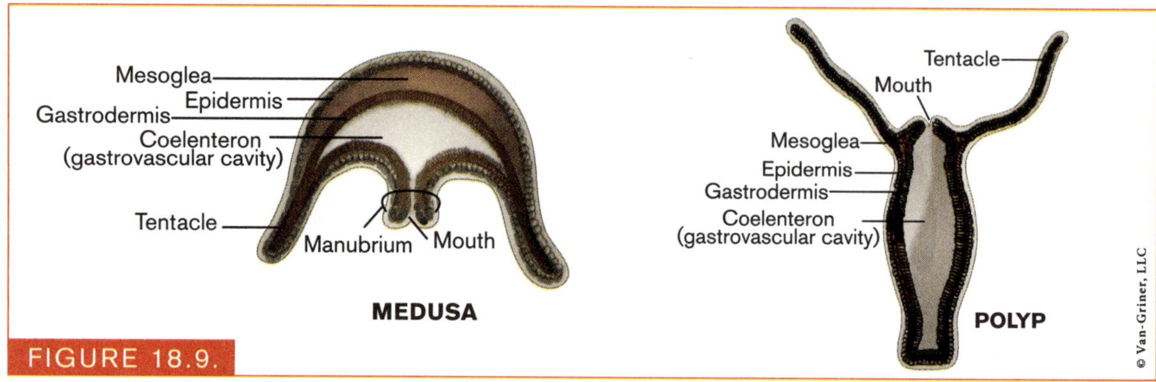

FIGURE 18.9.

Longitudinal sections of cnidarian polyp and medusa body types.

Exercise 18.4.

Examine the live *Hydra*, if available. Observe its behavior for a few minutes. If there are any *Hydra* feeding upon zooplankton prey, note how they capture them. Note the anterior end of the hydra, and use Figure 18.12 to guide you in identifying the parts of a hydra. Make a sketch of your hydra in the space below (Figure 18.10).

FIGURE 18.10.

Hydra.

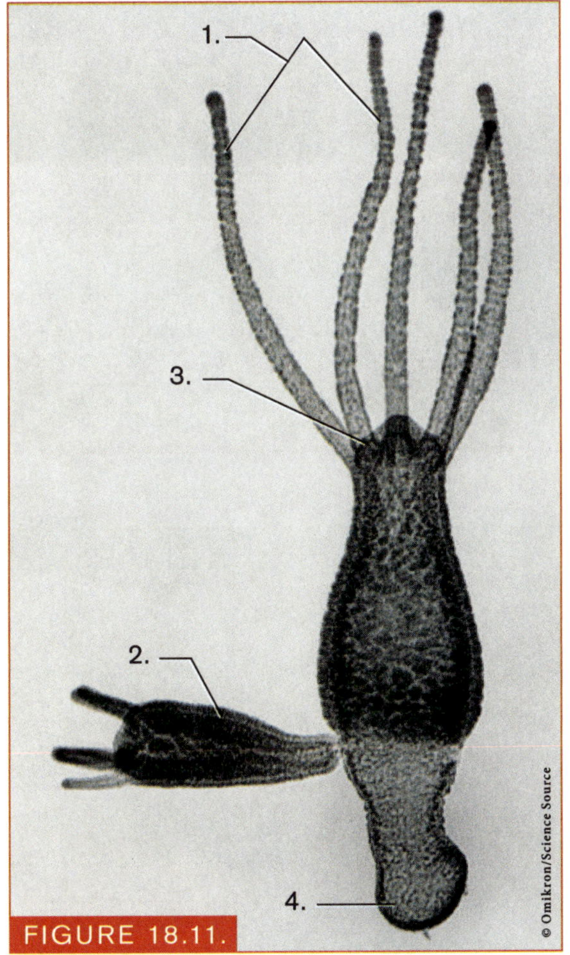

FIGURE 18.11.

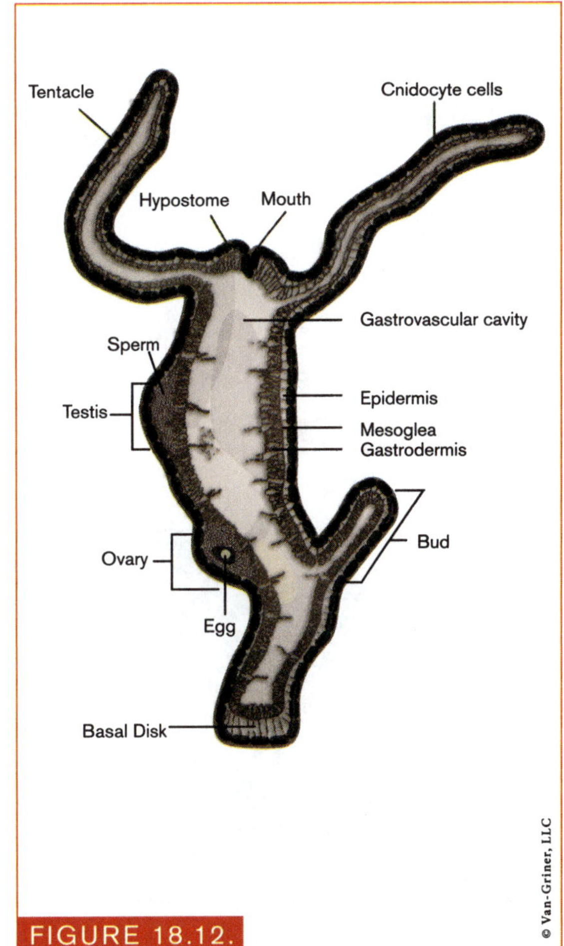

FIGURE 18.12.

Hydra bud.

1. Tentacles
2. Bud
3. Hypostome
4. Basal disk (foot)

Hydra longitudinal section.

Exercise 18.5.

Under low power, observe the following slide: *Hydra* cross section slide (see Figure 18.14). Note the gastrodermis and epidermis, and cnidocytes with nematocysts. Draw what you see in the microscope's field of view below (Figure 18.13). *Hydra* are either monoecious (an individual is both male and female) or dioecious (separate sexes); flagellated gametes produced in a testis will swim through the water and fertilize an egg inside an ovary. A young planula leaves the female and settles, producing a young adult hydra that increases in size over time. In the longitudinal section shown in Figure 18.12, the basal disk (pedal disk) contains glandular cells that help anchor the animal in place. The hypostome is the region surrounding the mouth at the oral end. Ovaries (each containing an egg) are found closer to the pedal disk, while several testes containing many small sperm are located beneath the tentacles. Figure 18.15 depicts both a male (with testes) and female (with ovary) *Hydra*.

FIGURE 18.13.

Hydra cross section.

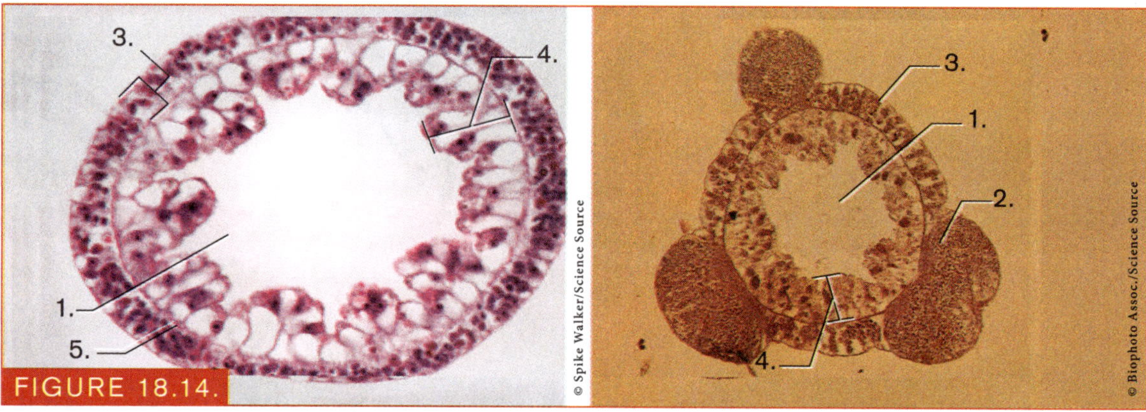

FIGURE 18.14.

Hydra cross sections.

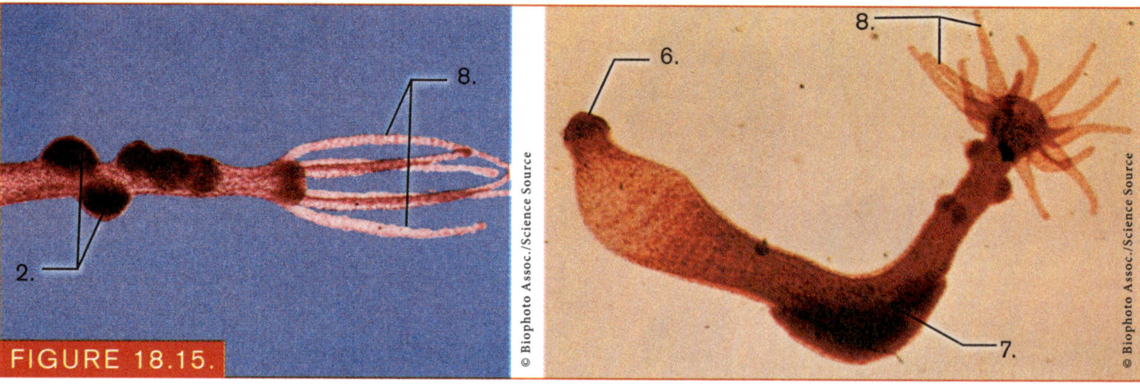

FIGURE 18.15.

A female and male *Hydra*, w.m.

1.	Gastrovascular cavity	3.	Epidermis	5.	Mesoglea	7.	Ovary
2.	Testes	4.	Gastrodermis	6.	Basal disk (foot)	8.	Tentacles

Exercise 18.6.

Under low power, examine the *Aurelia* planula, strobila, scyphistoma slides (see Figure 18.17). In addition, observe the plastomount of *Aurelia* adult medusae. Finally, using the information below, sketch the *Aurelia* life cycle in the space provided below (Figure 18.16), and make sketches of the adult, planula, scyphistoma, strobila, and ephyra.

Cnidarians use external fertilization, where sperm and eggs are shed into the water. The fertilized egg develops into a ciliated larval stage (the **planula**) that settles to the bottom. The planula develops into a **polyp.** In the *Aurelia* life cycle, the polyp (called the **scyphistoma**) eventually becomes the **strobila** (plural: strobilae). The strobila forms many **medusae** (singular: medusa) asexually, by budding. The **ephyra** (plural: ephyrae) is a young immature medusa which grows into the sexually mature adult (male or female). The adult medusae produce eggs and sperm. In *Aurelia*, like most cnidarians, the medusae are dioecious. As the adult medusae move through the open water, they shed eggs and sperm into the water column (fertilization is external). The fertilized egg forms the zygote that undergoes mitosis and over time produces the planula.

FIGURE 18.16.

Aurelia life cycle: planula, strobila, ephyra, and adult medusae.

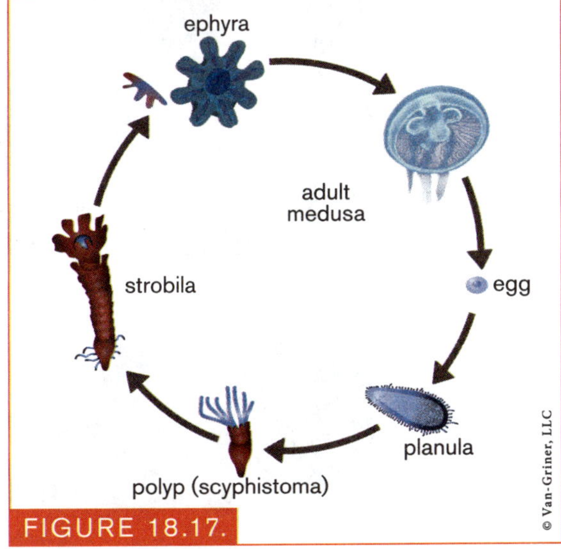

FIGURE 18.17.

Aurelia life cycle stages.

Exercise 18.7.

Observe the preserved specimens of the sea anemone *Metridium* and the corals. Preserved specimens and dried skeletons of corals are on the demonstration table. Use Figure 18.19 to guide you in identifying these animals. The mouth is surrounded by numerous short tentacles. The pharynx leads into the gastrovascular cavity. Several septa divide the gastrovascular cavity into compartments. Acontia are thread-like structures with numerous cnidocytes used for defense and prey capture; they can be extruded through the mouth. Note that anemones are solitary individuals, whereas corals form huge colonies of millions of individuals. Make a sketch in the space provided below (Figure 18.18).

All anthozoans are marine. They only have the polyp stage; there is no medusa stage. Gametes are produced by the polyps and the zygote forms a planula. The planula settles and produces a new polyp. Corals may be solitary or colonial. Many species secrete a protective outer skeleton of calcium carbonate (what you think of when you see a coral). These animals make up the largest class of cnidarians.

FIGURE 18.18.

Sketches of the sea anemone *Metridium* and corals.

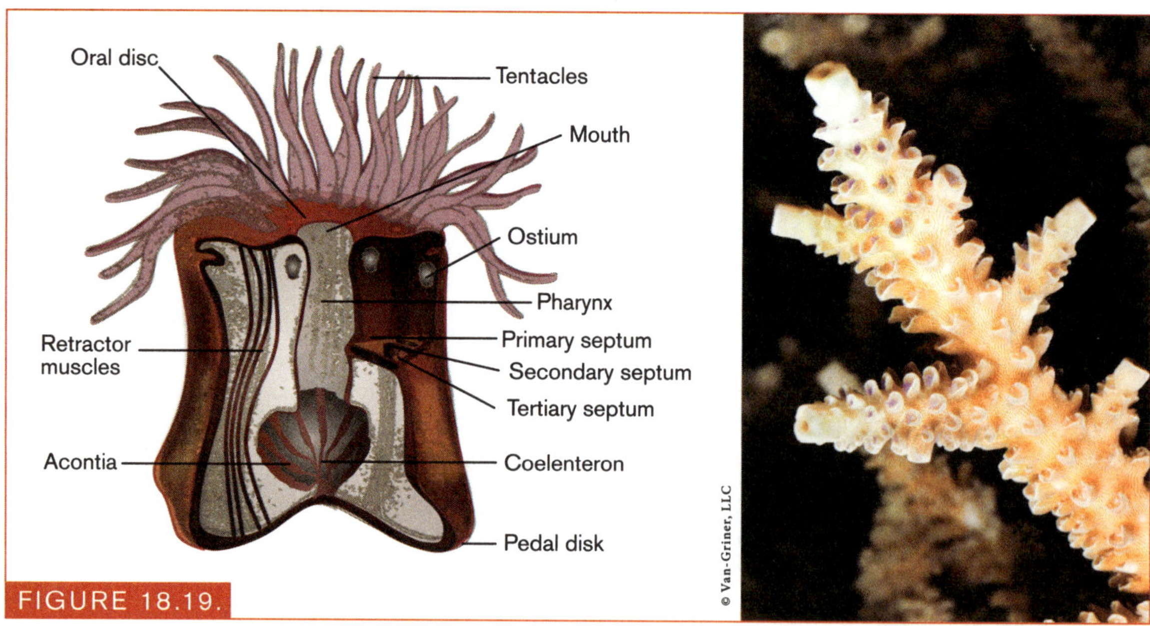

FIGURE 18.19.

The anthozoans: the sea anemone *Metridium* and Staghorn coral, *Acropora*.

Exercise 18.8.

Fill in the following table (Table 18.1) on the attributes for the three major cnidarian classes.

TABLE 18.1.

Attribute	Hydrozoa	Scyphozoa	Anthozoa
examples include (genus names)			
habitat			
medusa/polyp present in life cycle, and if both are present, which phase is dominant			
major distinguishing characteristics			

Phylum Platyhelminthes

All flatworms have the following common characteristics or functional homologies that distinguish them from other animals:

Ⓐ Flatworms have a **dorsoventrally flattened body** and **triploblastic acoelomate** body plan (ectoderm, endoderm and mesoderm). Flatworms are **unsegmented,** although the tapeworms possess proglottids, which make the tapeworms appear segmented. Flatworms also have **bilateral symmetry.**

Ⓑ Flatworms possess distinct **tissues and organs** including epithelial, muscular, and nervous tissues as well as discrete digestive, sensory, nervous, and reproductive organs. They are the first phylum we will cover that is at the **organ-system level of organization** (the animals are composed of organ systems, such as integumentary, nervous, and reproductive systems). The organ systems in turn are each composed of several organs.

Ⓒ **Osmoregulatory/excretory systems.** Flatworms have an osmoregulatory/excretory system consisting of protonephridia. Protonephridia are closed (i.e., they have no internal openings) tubes that open to the outside along the length of the body at various points; these openings are called **nephridiopores.** Small branches of a protonephridium end blindly, with **flame cells** at the end of the tubes. Fluids accumulated in the body tissues move into the flame cell and are moved out of the nephridiopore by the beating cilia of the flame cells. In most species, however, nitrogenous wastes (ammonia) diffuse out of each cell into the environment, similar to the cnidarians. The protonephridia are therefore primarily involved in **osmoregulation,** or the regulation of water and ions.

D **Respiratory system.** There is no specialized respiratory system in flatworms. Gas exchange occurs through the body wall. Parasitic flatworms typically use anaerobic respiration because they live in parts of the host's body where oxygen levels may be low.

E **Circulatory system.** There is no specialized circulatory system in flatworms. The flattened body shape permits gases and nutrients to diffuse through the body.

F **Digestive system.** Flatworms have an **incomplete digestive tract** (one opening, materials pass both ways through the mouth) consisting of a **gastrovascular cavity.** Digestion is **extracellular** initially (inside the gastrovascular cavity), followed by **intracellular** digestion inside cells lining the gastrovascular cavity, similar to what is observed in the sponges. The digestive cavity in some species is branched throughout the body, in order to facilitate the movement of food to all cells. In some parasitic species (e.g., some tapeworms), the digestive tract is much reduced or is absent; the worm obtains its food in predigested form (chemical digestion is performed by the host) across its body wall.

G **Nervous system.** Flatworms show **cephalization** (a distinct brain or concentration of ganglia in the anterior end, along with distinct sensory organs). The nervous system is more complex than the nerve-net of cnidarians. Flatworms have **cerebral ganglia** in the anterior end and several pairs of lateral nerve cords running along the length of the body. The parasitic flatworms often exhibit reduced cephalization and lack the sensory organs found in free-living species. There are distinct **sensory neurons** (carry messages to the ganglia) and **motor neurons** (carry information to muscles and other organs). Flatworms have receptor organs that can sense and respond to light, touch, chemicals, gravity, and currents.

H Flatworms are either free-living carnivores, or they exist as parasites within the digestive, respiratory, or circulatory systems of other animals.

I **Reproductive system.** Flatworms have complex reproductive systems, with testes, ovaries, and ducts associated with these organs. Flatworms are typically **monoecious,** but flatworms often have to **cross-fertilize** (exchange sperm with another flatworm). The parasitic tapeworms are able to **self-fertilize.** A few flatworm species are **dioecious.** Fertilization is **internal,** and eggs are released from the female.

J **Integumentary system.** Flatworms have a distinct skin or **integument,** which protects them from the host's digestive enzymes and the environment. The flatworms move by muscular action and by **ciliary action;** mucus serves as a lubricating slime as the animal moves. Flatworms appear to glide across the surface.

K Many flatworms can **regenerate** lost body parts. However, unlike sponge cells, a single adult flatworm cell is **not totipotent.**

L **Muscular system/locomotion. Ciliary motion** occurs by ventral cilia beating against a 'carpet' of mucus produced by the flatworm. Various circular and/or longitudinal muscles are present in the body wall. The cercaria larvae of parasitic flatworms can thrash about, propelling the infective stage.

Exercise 18.9.

Examine the live planaria (*Dugesia*), if available. Draw what you see in Figure 18.20 below. Observe its behavior for a few minutes. Determine whether they creep along inchworm style or glide. If time permits, drop a small piece of fish food on a dish containing a planaria. How does it respond to the food? How do they move?

FIGURE 18.20.

Live *planaria.*

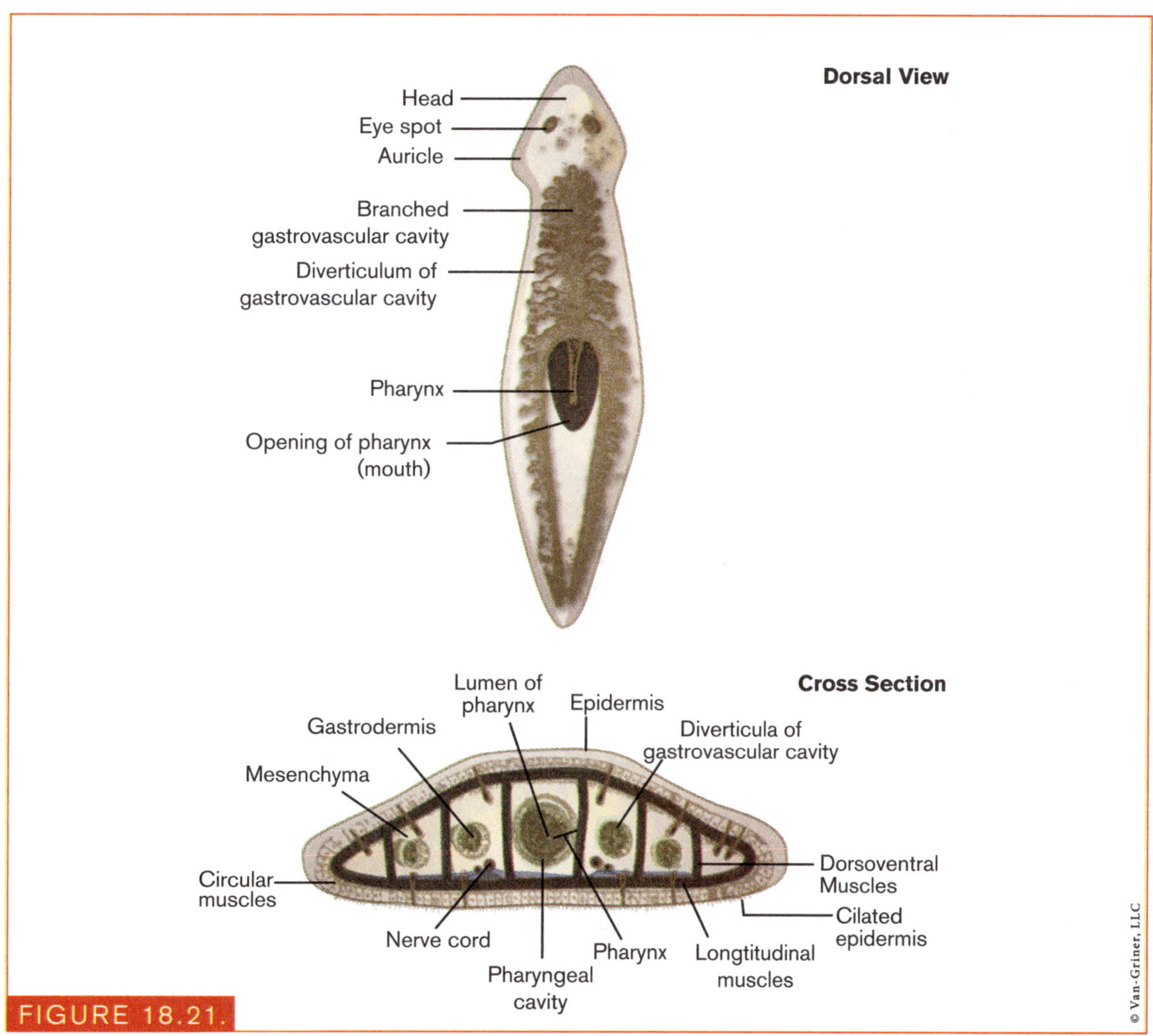

FIGURE 18.21.

The internal and external anatomy of a planarian *Dugesia.*

Exercise 18.10.

Under low power, observe the 'Planaria digestive tract' slide. Note the **eyes** or **eyespots** (that contain photoreceptors that respond to light), the **gastrovascular cavity** which is branched into one anterior and two posterior trunks; and the **auricles** (the "ears" of the planarian which possess chemoreceptors), and the muscular **pharynx** and **mouth.** On which surface (dorsal or ventral) is the mouth located? Draw what you see on the microscope's field of view in the space provided below (Figure 18.22); use Figure 18.21 to guide you. You may be able to distinguish numerous blind pouches (diverticula) of the gastrovascular cavity.

FIGURE 18.22.

The *Planaria.*

How many openings to the digestive tract are there? Is it thus a complete (one-way, two openings: mouth and anus) or incomplete (two-way, one opening) digestive tract?

Exercise 18.11.

Under low power, view the '*Planaria*, sec., three regions' slide. Note the **epidermis** (ciliated on the ventral surface), the **pharynx** and **pharyngeal cavity,** the **circular** and **longitudinal muscles** (the circular muscle layer is underneath the epidermis and the longitudinal muscle layer lies underneath the circular muscle layer), the **gastrovascular cavity,** and **nerve cords.** Note that no coelom exists and the inner part of the body is filled with parenchyma cells. Fibers of dorsoventral muscles may be seen spanning across the cross section, running between the dorsal and ventral surfaces through the parenchyma. Draw what you see in the microscope's field of view in the space provided below (Figure 18.23). Use Figure 18.24 to guide you.

FIGURE 18.23.

Planaria, c.s., three sections.

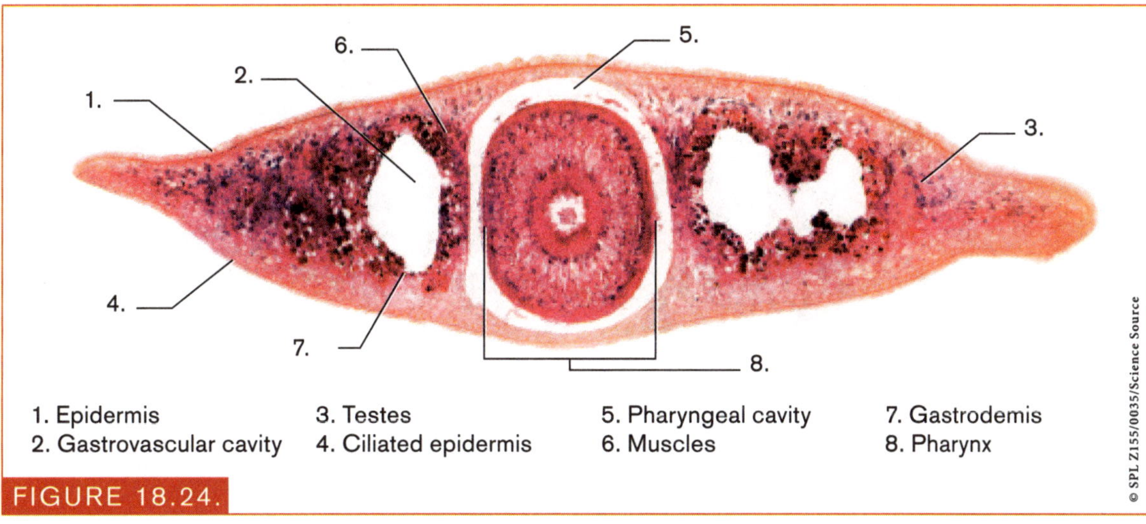

| 1. Epidermis | 3. Testes | 5. Pharyngeal cavity | 7. Gastrodemis |
| 2. Gastrovascular cavity | 4. Ciliated epidermis | 6. Muscles | 8. Pharynx |

© SPL Z155/0035/Science Source

FIGURE 18.24.

Cross section through the pharyngeal region of a planarian.

Exercise 18.12.

Under low power, view the '*Clonorchis sinensis* w.m.' (= *Opisthorchis*) slide. This species is an example of a parasitic fluke which lives in the human liver. Millions of people are infected with this parasite. *Clonorchis* is hermaphroditic and therefore possesses both testes and ovaries. Note the **testes, ovaries, oral and ventral suckers, intestine, nerve ganglia,** and **bladder and excretory pore.** Draw what you see in the microscope's field of view in the space provided below (Figure 18.25). Use Figure 18.26 to guide you.

FIGURE 18.25.

Opisthorchis sinensis, w.m.

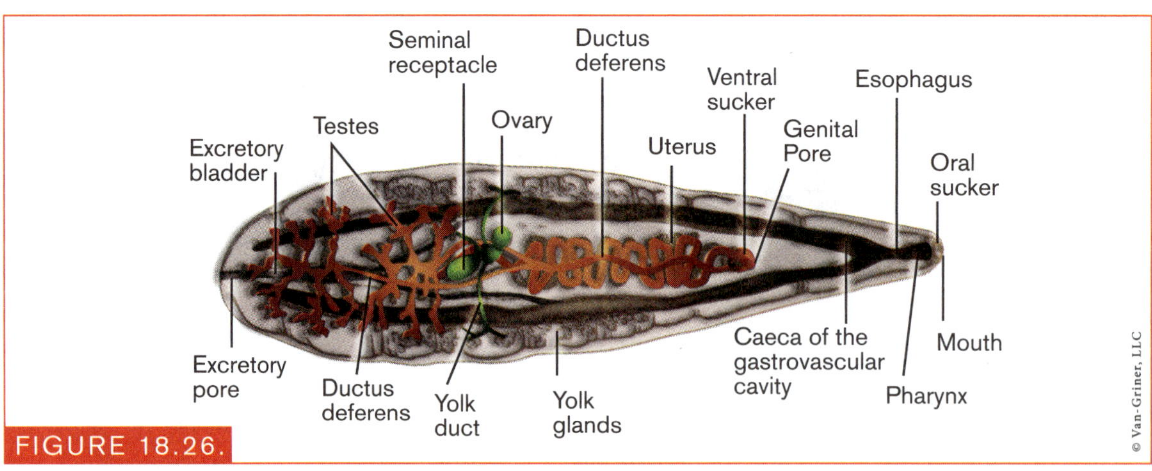

FIGURE 18.26.

Basic body plan of the Chinese liver fluke *Opisthorchis.*

Opisthorchis has a life cycle that is typical of most trematode flukes (see Figure 18.27). Adult flukes live in the host's liver. The initial, short-lived larval stage called **miracidia** (plural; singular: miracidium) hatches from the egg, and the miracidia infect intermediate hosts (various aquatic snails). A single miracidium forms a single mother **sporocyst** larva within the hemocoel of the snail. The mother sporocyst (which does not have mouthparts) absorbs nutrients form the hemolymph of the snail. The sporocyst then (asexually) forms many daughter parasites. Balls of cells (called germ balls) within the mother sporocyst will develop into larvae that possess mouths and gastrovascular systems; these larvae are called **rediae** (plural; singular: redia). One mother sporocyst produces many rediae. **Rediae** are active feeders and they digest snail tissues in their gastrovascular cavity. The rediae travel to the snail's gonad or digestive gland. All of these rediae eventually consume much of the snail's reproductive and digestive tissues. Within each redia, many germ balls develop, eventually forming distinct, short-lived larval stages called **cercariae** (plural; singular: cercaria). Each cercaria is released from the redia, and the cercariae burrow through the snail's body wall. Each cercaria has a muscular tail, which they use to swim through the water. The cercariae then travel through the water and infect a second intermediate host, a fish, where the larvae encyst as **metacercariae** (plural; singular: metacercaria). The human eats the fish, and within the human's digestive tract, the young adult liver flukes leave the metacercaria cysts. The adult Chinese liver flukes travel up the bile duct from the small intestine into the liver, where they mature and produce eggs. Eggs are carried through the bile duct back to the intestines and are passed with feces. The eggs are in water for a brief time until miracidia hatch from them, starting the cycle over again.

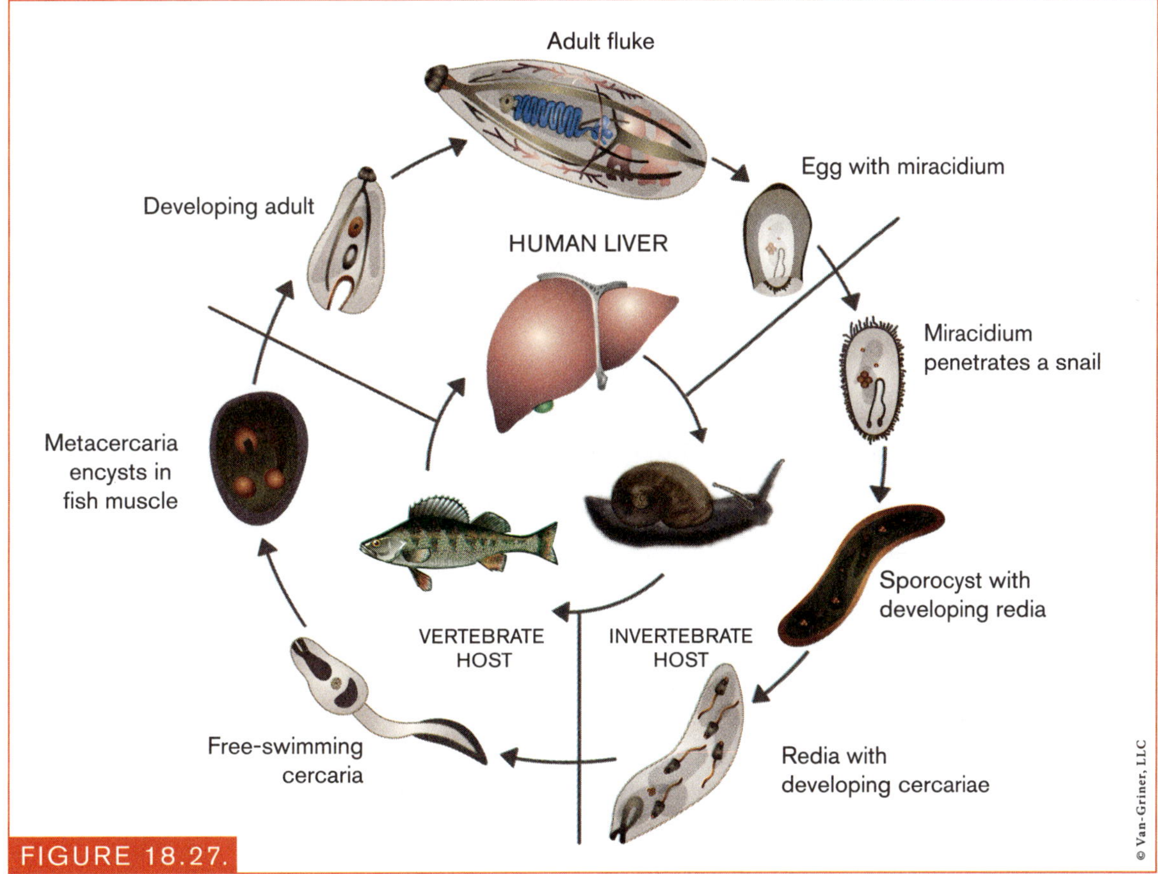

FIGURE 18.27.

Opisthorchis life cycle.

Exercise 18.13.

Under low power, view the '*Taenia pisiformis* composite, w.m' slide. This tapeworm parasitizes dogs. There are many different species of tapeworms, including many that parasitize humans. Tapeworms generally lack a digestive system; it is thought that the digestive system was lost over time because tapeworms can absorb nutrients (from the contents of their hosts' digestive systems) across their body wall. In addition to the reduction or loss of digestive systems in a number of intestinal parasites, the sensory systems are much reduced or absent.

Draw what you see in the microscope's field of view in the space provided below (Figure 18.28). Use Figure 18.29 to guide you.

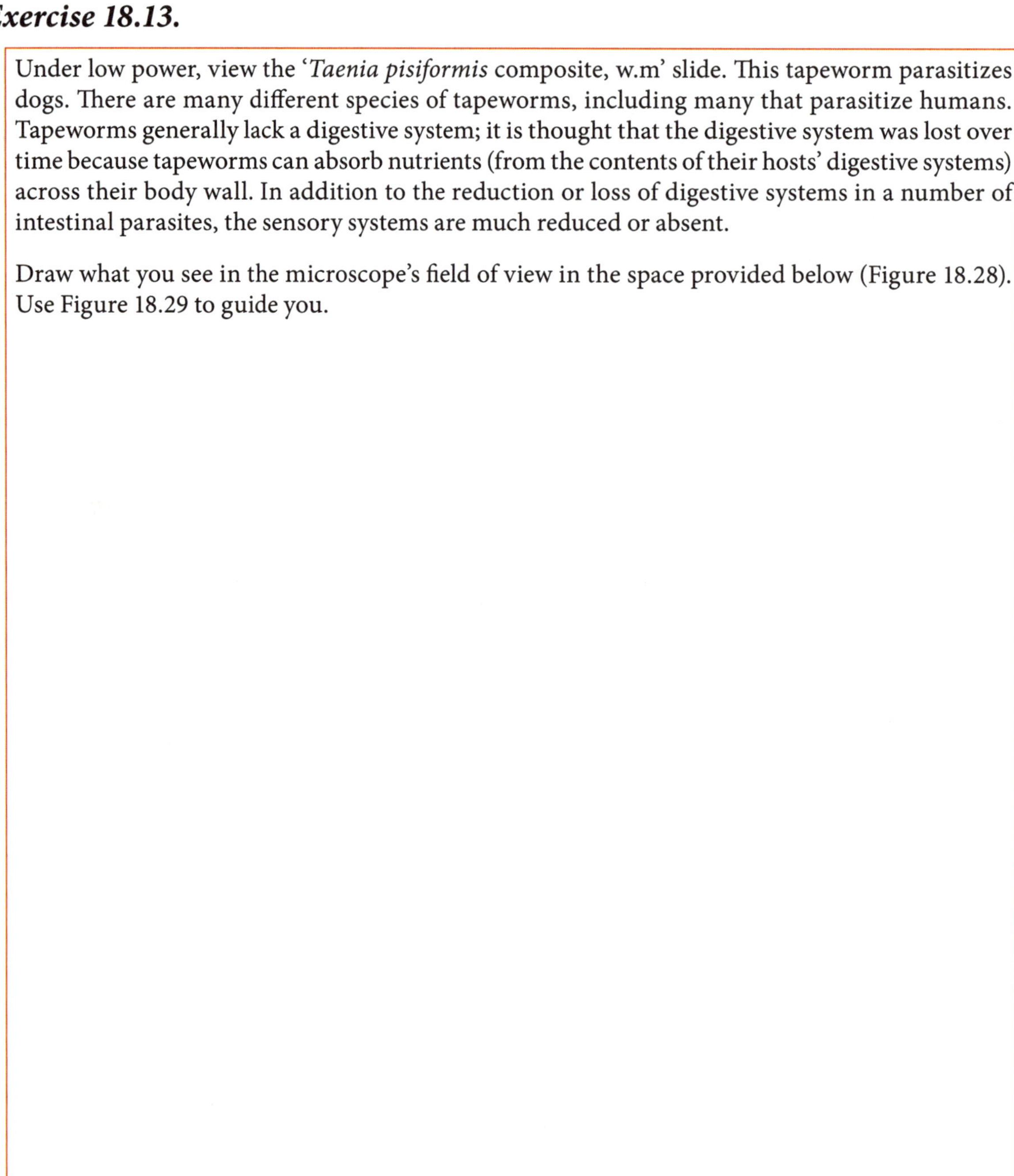

FIGURE 18.28.

Taenia.

Many tapeworms are well-adapted to living within their hosts' intestines. The **scolex** or head often contains **suckers or hooks** that allow the parasite to attach to the intestinal wall. The remainder of the body consists of segments, called **proglottids,** each of which contains both ovaries and testes. Because tapeworm can be found singly within a host, many tapeworms can self-fertilize. Many eggs fill up the proglottids, and proglottids (or eggs released from mature proglottids) are passed with the host's feces. The eggs are picked up by other intermediate hosts (such as pigs or cattle), where the eggs hatch into larvae that encyst into muscle of the host. The human (**as final or definitive host**) eats the intermediate host. The encysted larvae then hatch and the young adult tapeworm (with a scolex) attaches to the intestinal wall of the human host. Immature proglottids are produced asexually off of the scolex.

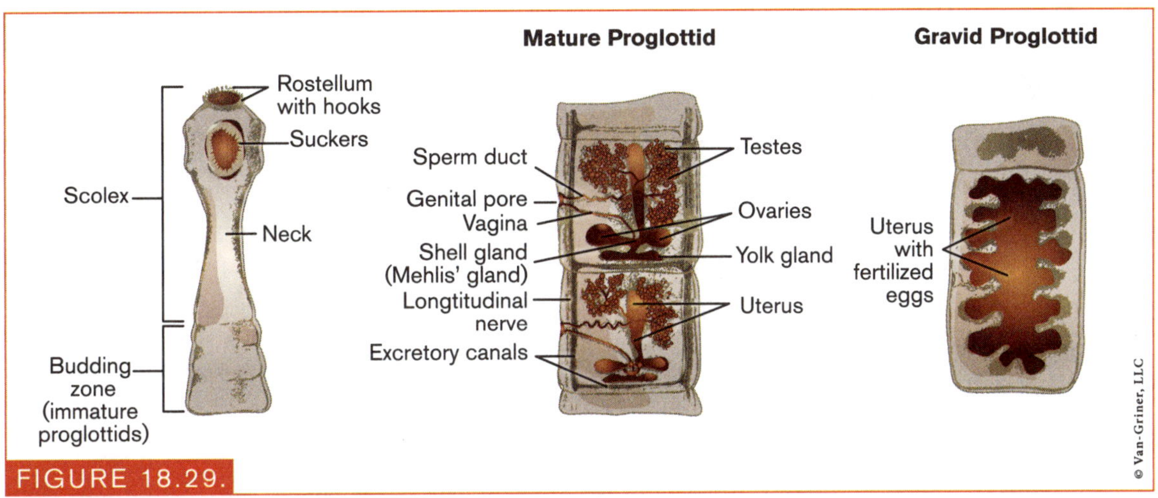

FIGURE 18.29.

The tapeworm *Taenia.*

Exercise 18.14.

List the attributes of the three major flatworm classes in the table below (Table 18.2).

TABLE 18.2.

Attribute	Turbellaria	Trematoda	Cestoda
examples (include genus names)			
habitat/lifestyle			
major distinguishing attributes			

Phylum Nematoda

A number of animals are pseudocoelomates, meaning that they have a body cavity **partially** lined with mesoderm. We will examine one pseudocoelomate phyla today: the nematodes.

All nematodes ('roundworms') have the following main characteristics or functional homologies that distinguish them from other animals:

(A) Nematodes are **roundish, cylindrical, unsegmented worms with tapered ends.** They have a **pseudocoelom.** The pseudocoelom is partially lined with mesodermal tissues. The roundworms are **triploblastic,** and they are **bilaterally symmetrical.** They also show **cephalization,** where their sensory organs and brain are in the anterior end of the animal. The brain consists of ganglia, which are distinct collections of nerve cells.

(B) Nematodes exhibit **eutely,** which means that every individual adult consists of exactly the same number of cells.

(C) **Muscular system.** Nematodes have only longitudinal muscles in their body wall. They do not possess circular or diagonal muscles that are observed in other phyla. In addition, no muscles surround the roundworm's digestive tract. Pressure is exerted on the contents of the gut by hydrostatic pressure produced by the pseudocoelomic fluids. This pressure is created by the flexing the longitudinal muscles in the outer body wall. Nematodes move in a flexing motion. **The nematodes are unique in that muscles send processes to the nerves for innervation, not vice versa.**

(D) **Digestive system.** Nematodes and other pseudocoelomates have a **complete digestive tract** (two openings to the gut, mouth to anus). Food moves in one direction through the gut. A muscular **pharynx** is present, which helps to suck food (such as host tissues in parasitic species) into the mouth. Parts of the digestive tract are specialized to process food. Like most animals, digestion is **extracellular,** occurring within the gut, followed by **intracellular digestion** (within the cells).

(E) **Integumentary system.** Nematodes have an outer, noncellular, **cuticle** (containing **chitin**) produced by the epidermis. This cuticle is shed several times as nematodes grow. Nematodes molt (typically **four molts** and four larval stages) throughout their life cycle, from egg to adult. The cuticle maintains turgor pressure, prevents the worm from drying out quickly, provides mechanical protection, and resists digestion by the host's digestive tract (particularly important for parasitic nematodes). The cuticle allows water and oxygen to move through it however, so nematodes have to stay in moist environments. The cuticle is similar to the cuticle of the arthropods.

(F) Nematodes are either free-living carnivores or detritivores (feed on dead plant and animal tissues), or they are parasites of other organisms. Nematodes are found in marine systems, freshwater systems, in moist soils, and in the tissues and fluids of essentially all plants and animals.

(G) **Respiratory system.** Nematodes have no specialized respiratory systems. Gases diffuse across the body wall. Many parasitic species can use anaerobic respiration.

(H) **Circulatory system.** Nematodes have no specialized circulatory systems. Diffusion moves materials through the animal's tissues and the pseudocoelom.

I **Osmoregulatoy/excretory systems.** Nematodes have a series of **excretory canals.** Unlike the cnidarians, **no flame cells are present in nematodes** (although flame cells are present in other pseudocoelomates). They have special excretory cells, called **renette cells,** that absorb nitrogen wastes from the pseudocoelomic fluids and these wastes can be passed through a pore outside. In addition, nematodes eliminate ammonia via the gut, in a process similar to the arthropods.

J **Reproductive system.** Most nematodes are **dioecious.** Males often have spines or hooks with which they hold onto females. After fertilization (which occurs internally), the eggs are released by hydrostatic force from the body. Soon after release, the eggs hatch into the first larval stage.

K **Skeletal system.** Nematodes use a **hydrostatic skeleton** (the pseudocoelom) and their cuticle to provide structure against which muscles work.

L **Nervous system.** Nematodes have a relatively simple nervous system, with **cephalization** and the concentration of ganglia and sensory structures at the anterior end. Several **nerve cords** (dorsal, lateral, and ventral) run posteriorly. Nematodes have several sense organs for touch, and a few species can detect light.

Exercise 18.15.

Make a wet mount of live nematodes (vinegar eels, *Turbatrix*) and observe them under low power. Observe their behavior for a few minutes. Note that the nematodes can only bend as they move—they have no circular muscles in their body wall. Draw several nematodes in the space provided below (Figure 18.30) and make an estimate of their lengths and diameters.

FIGURE 18.30.

'Vinegar eel' nematodes.

Exercise 18.16.

Under low power, view the following prepared slides: *Ascaris* adult male and females c.s. (Figure 18.33) and see Figure 18.32 as well. *Ascaris* is the human intestinal roundworm. These roundworms can grow up to 40 cm in length. While you are examining your slide, note the **cuticle, epidermis, nerve cords, longitudinal muscle cells** (which send processes to the nerve cords), the **pseudocoelom,** the **intestine,** and the reproductive organs, (**testes, vas deferens, ovaries, oviducts, and uterus**).

Although there are many variations depending on species, the complex life cycles of many nematodes are similar to that of *Ascaris*. Eggs are deposited in the host's feces. Development to the second larval stage (two molts) occurs in the egg. After getting ingested (due to not cleaning one's hands before eating), the larvae hatch from their eggs in the host's intestine, travel through the intestinal wall, and are carried by the bloodstream to the heart, and eventually through the pulmonary arteries to the lungs. The larvae burrow into the lung alveolar spaces from lung capillaries. In the lungs, the larvae typically molt for the third time. The larvae then travel up the respiratory tract and then they are swallowed back down to the stomach, eventually ending up in the small intestine once again. The larvae finally molt for the fourth and last time to become sexually mature adults in the small intestine. Nematodes harm their hosts due to the damage they cause during their complex migration through the host's body. Often, larval and even adult worms can migrate and end up in many other organs as well.

Draw what you see on the microscope's field of view in the space provided below (Figure 18.31). If there are any adult specimens, sketch them as well (see Figure 18.32).

FIGURE 18.31.

Male and female *Ascaris*, c.s.

Find the nematode intestine. Where do you see any muscle layers lining the digestive tract? Do you see muscles in the body wall? What types of muscles are present? How does this affect their movement? What is the orientation (circular or longitudinal) of the muscle cells? Compare how food is moved through your digestive tract and through the digestive tract of a nematode.

Note the extension protruding from each muscle towards the nerve cords. How does this particular type of nerve cell/muscle cell interaction differ from that seen in most animals?

In roundworms, why is the cuticle needed?

What are the advantages of having a complete digestive tract (two openings)?

What advantages are there to a fluid-filled body cavity?

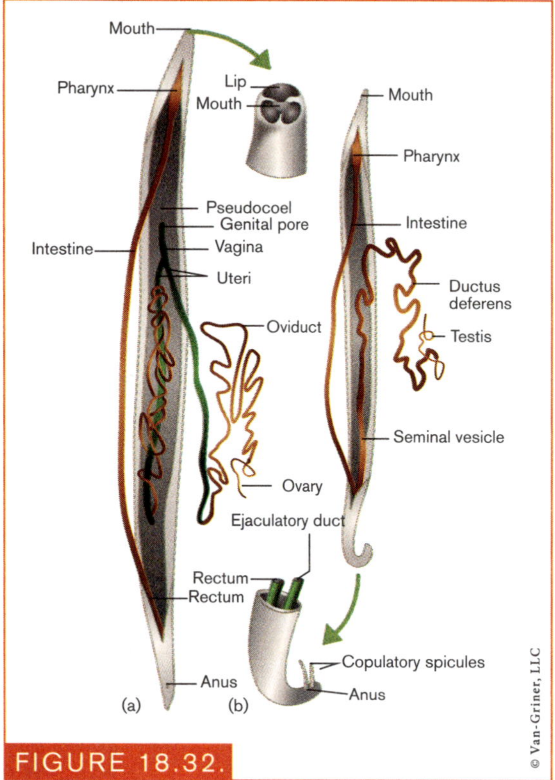

FIGURE 18.32.

Diagram of the internal anatomy of the parasitic nematode, the roundworm *Ascaris*.

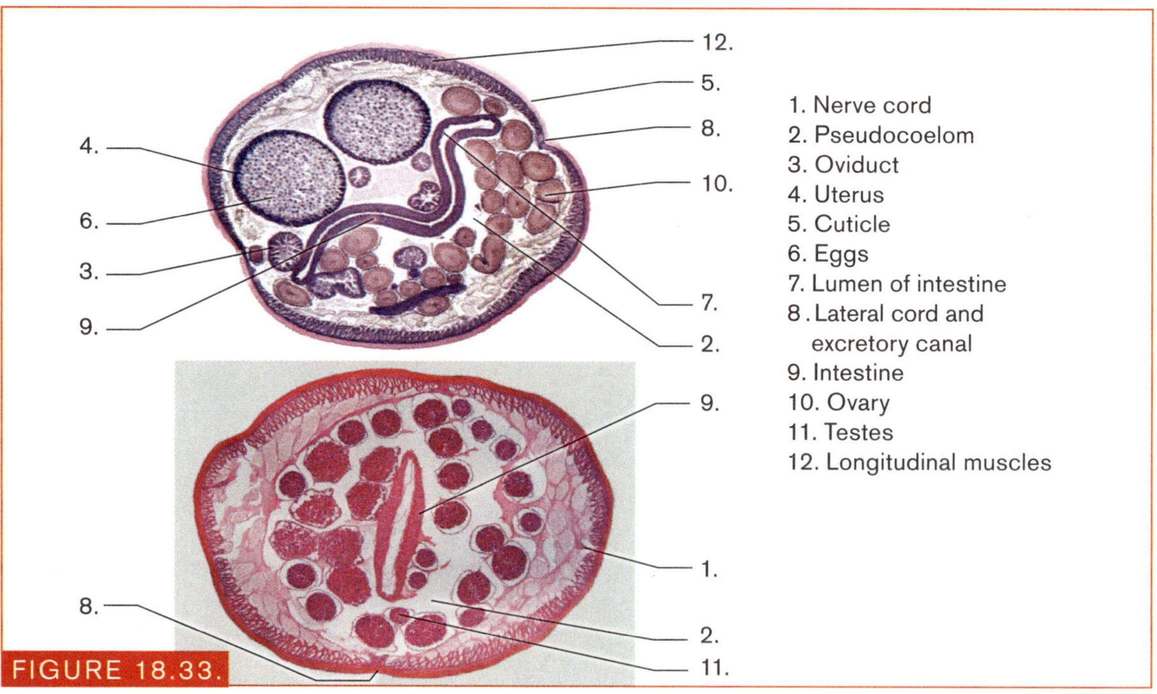

FIGURE 18.33.

Cross sections of a female and male *Ascaris*.

Exercise 18.17.

Fill in the following table (Table 18.3), adding in terms or key words that will help you distinguish each taxon from the others.

TABLE 18.3.

Character	Taxon			
	Porifera	Cnidarians	Platyhelminthes	Nematoda
diplo-/ triploblastic				
body cavity				
symmetry				
digestive				
respiratory				
circulatory				
reproductive				
excretory/ osmoregulation				
nervous				
support/ skeletons				
appendages/ integument				
groups				
other important terms, traits or key words				

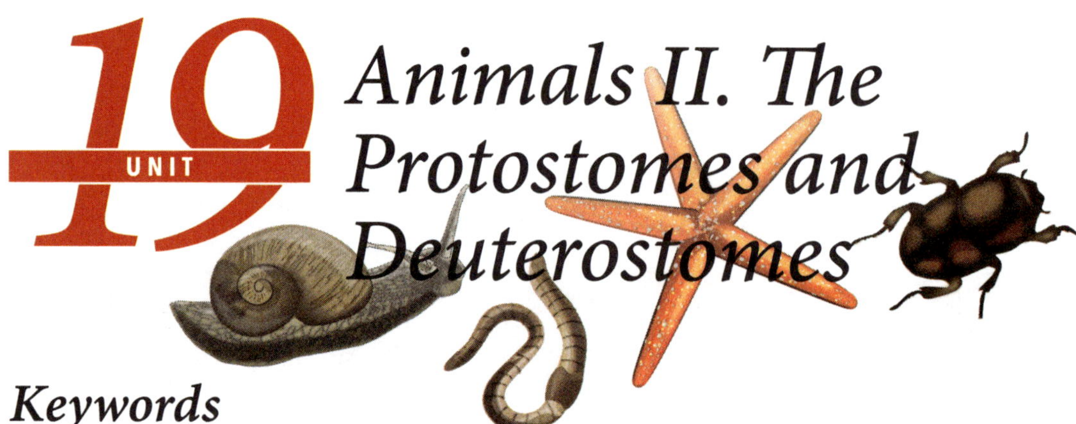

Animals II. The Protostomes and Deuterostomes

UNIT 19

Keywords

protostomes
deuterostomes
blastopore
blastocoel
zygote
embryo
blastomeres
morula
blastula

gastrula
determinate and
    indeterminate
    cleavage
radial and spiral
    cleavage
enterocoelom
schizocoelom
dioecious

monoecious
trochophore
open and closed
    circulatory systems
complete and
    incomplete
    digestive tracts
protonephridia and
    metanephridia

segmentation
metamerism
tagmata
podomeres
jointed appendages
water vascular
    system

Learning Objectives

When finished with this unit, you should be able to:

1. Describe the distinctive features for each of the three major protostome phyla (annelids, molluscs, and arthropods), as well as for the annelid classes, the mollusc classes, and the selected arthropod subphyla and classes;

2. Compare and contrast the modes of sexual reproduction observed in these animals;

3. Identify arthropod specimens to kingdom, phylum, subphylum and class. For annelids, molluscs and echinoderms, identify specimens down to kingdom, phylum, and class;

4. Identify the following structures or concepts observed in annelids and molluscs:
   * Polychaete external features: jaws, eyes, tentacles, parapodia, setae;
   * Oligochaete cross-section features: epidermis, cuticle, circular muscle, longitudinal muscle, peritoneum, typhlosole, nephridium, dorsal and ventral blood vessels, ventral nerve cord, intestine, intestinal epithelium, coelom, seta;
   * Oligochaete external features: seta, segments, clitellum;
   * Leech external features: oral and caudal suckers;
   * Molluscs: radula, shell, mantle, head, foot, gills and lungs, visceral mass;

5. Compare and contrast open versus closed circulatory systems. Compare complete and incomplete digestive tracts. Compare and contrast the nervous systems, circulatory systems, and digestive systems of annelids and molluscs to cnidarians, flatworms and nematodes;

6. Compare and contrast protonephridia (as seen in flatworms) with metanephridia (in annelids and molluscs). Discuss the advantages and disadvantages of each excretory system;

7 Describe the distinctive features of the phylum arthropoda and of each selected arthropod subphylum and class covered in this lab;

8 Identify the following structures observed in arthropods:
- Spider external features: chelicera, fangs, pedipalps, walking legs, compound eyes and simple eyes (ocelli), cephalothorax, abdomen;
- Crayfish external features: telson, uropod, carapace, cephalothorax and abdomen, antenna, antennules, compound eyes, cheliped (first walking leg), chelae, walking legs, swimmerets;
- Grasshopper external features: antenna, compound eyes, ocelli, wings;

9 Describe which arthropod subphyla possess wings, antennae, simple or compound eyes, antennal glands or malpighian tubules, mandibles or chelicerae, and describe the respiratory system type found in each arthropod subphylum;

10 List the number of legs (pairs of walking legs) and tagmata present in the representative specimens of each arthropod subphylum (spiders, crayfish, insects); and

11 Describe the distinctive external and internal features of the echinoderms (pentaradial symmetry as adults, tube feet, ossicles, water vascular system, madreporite, mouth, anus).

Classification

Kingdom Animalia

  Phylum Annelida (the annelid worms)

    Class Polychaeta (the polychaete worms) *Nereis*

    Class Oligochaeta (the earthworms) *Lumbricus*

    Class Hirudinea (the leeches)

  Phylum Mollusca (the molluscs: chitons, clams, snails, octopi, and squid)

    Class Bivalvia (the clams, scallops, and mussels) *Dreissena*

    Class Gastropoda (snails, slugs) *Physella*

    Class Polyplacophora (the chitons)

    Class Cephalopoda (octopi and squid)

  Phylum Arthropoda

   Subphylum Chelicerata (spiders, horseshoe crabs, ticks)

   Class Arachnida (spiders)

   Subphylum Crustacea (crustaceans)

   Class Malacostraca (crayfish, crabs, shrimps, amphipods) *Procambarus*

   Subphylum Uniramia (insects, millipedes and centipedes)

   Class Insecta (the insects) *Romalea*

  Phylum Echinodermata

    Class Asteroidea (the sea stars) *Pisaster*

    Class Ophiuroidea (the brittle stars)

    Class Echinoidea (the sea urchins and sand dollars)

    Class Holothuroidea (the sea cucumbers)

Today, we will continue our discussion of animals looking first at a group collectively known as the **protostomes,** which includes the phyla **Annelida, Mollusca,** and **Arthropoda.** We will distinguish this group from another group, the **deuterostomes,** which includes the phyla **Echinodermata** (which we will also see today) and **Chordata** (which we will study next time). **Protostomes** and **deuterostomes** are **triploblastic, bilaterally symmetrical, eucoelomate** animals. There is a slight exception to the previous statement: the echinoderms are bilaterally symmetrical as larvae and radially symmetrical as adults.

Protostomes and **Deuterostomes** are the two major groups of higher animals. The developmental patterns between the two groups differ in several very significant ways, although there are a number of variations and exceptions. To understand the differences between protostomes and deuterostomes, we must become familiar with their early development patterns (see Figure 19.1 through Figure 19.4).

First, the fertilized egg (**zygote**) undergoes mitosis and cytokinesis to create a two-cell stage (Figure 19.1). These two cells then quickly divide to create a four-cell stage, and so on. The cells formed by the early mitotic divisions (this cell division is also called **cleavage**), are called **blastomeres.** For most organisms, the earliest blastomeres divide fairly quickly, without much transcriptional activity occurring in between cell divisions. During the cleavage events of early development, the blastomeres become smaller and smaller with each round of cell division. Around the 16-cell stage, the developing embryo consists of a small, solid ball of blastomeres (called the **morula**). After a few more rounds of cleavage, a hollow ball of cells, called the **blastula,** is formed. The **blastocoel** is the hollow cavity of the blastula. Eventually a group of cells from the outer layer of blastomeres begins to invaginate into the blastocoel; the spherical blastula gives rise to the cup-shaped **gastrula.** The **blastopore** is the opening to a pouch-like structure called the **archenteron.** The archenteron gives rise to the gut or digestive tract of coelomate animals and is apparent in the gastrula stage.

Fate of the Blastopore

1 The annelids, molluscs, and arthropods are the dominant phyla of **protostomes.** In the protostomes, the blastopore (the opening to the archenteron or primitive gut) becomes the mouth ("protostome" means "first mouth"). The anus forms later.

2 In the **deuterostomes** ("second mouth") the anus forms first from the blastopore, and the mouth forms later. Echinoderms and chordates are the major deuterostome phyla.

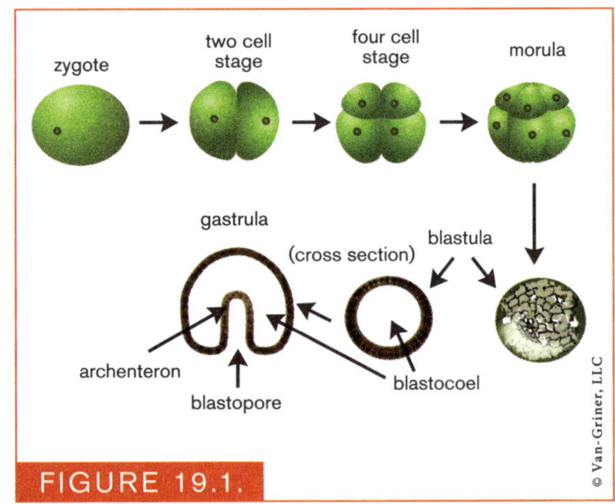

FIGURE 19.1.

Early development in animals.

Spiral versus Radial Cleavage

1 Most protostomes undergo **spiral cleavage,** where the successive planes of cell division in early development are not at right angles to the previous planes. Cytokinesis occurs diagonally to the vertical axis of the embryo. The zygote has a series of smaller cells lying on top and in the grooves of larger cells underneath (see Figure 19.2).

2 **Radial cleavage** occurs in most deuterostomes. The planes of division are at right angles to earlier planes, and the tiers of cells stack up on top of each other in the early embryo. Humans and other mammals show a variation of this cleavage type, called rotational cleavage.

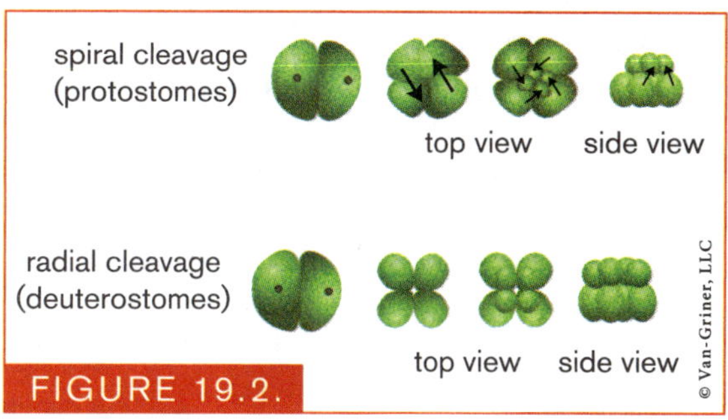

FIGURE 19.2.

Spiral versus radial cleavage.

Determinate and Indeterminate Cleavage

1 A third way that deuterostomes and protostomes differ is by the type of cell division pattern observed in the early embryo (Figure 19.3). In most protostomes, the developmental fate of each cell is determined early on (this is called **determinate cleavage**). If you divide a very early embryo of a protostome in half (for example, one that is at the 2-cell or 4-cell stage), you will not get identical twins, but two 'halves' of an embryo, or two malformed cell masses. These early cells (**blastomeres**) will give rise to different parts of the embryo.

2 However, if you divide a deuterostome embryo in half at the two-cell stage, you can end up with two identical twins. We call this ability to create identical twins from one fertilized egg **indeterminate cleavage** because the fates of these early cells do not become 'fixed' until a little later on in development.

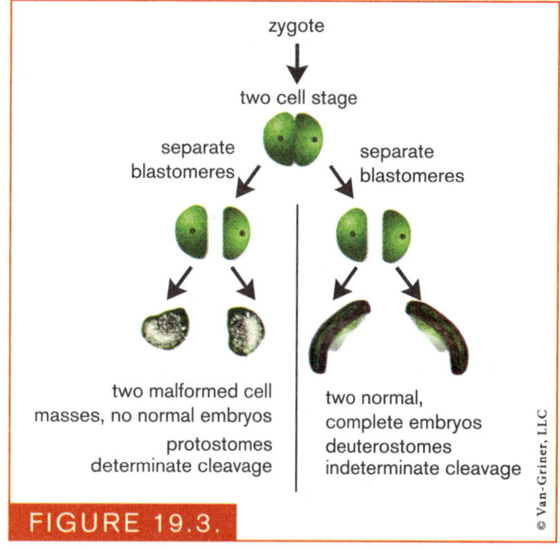

FIGURE 19.3.

Determinate versus indeterminate cleavage.

Enterocoeloms versus Schizocoeloms

1 In protostomes (and a few deuterostomes), after the archenteron forms, solid masses of mesoderm form near the blastopore (Figure 19.4). These solid masses split open, forming a fluid-filled body cavity called the **schizocoelom** ("split").

2 In most deuterostomes, the coelom forms as an **enterocoelom.** Masses of mesodermal cells 'bud' off of the wall of the archenteron to form the enterocoelom.

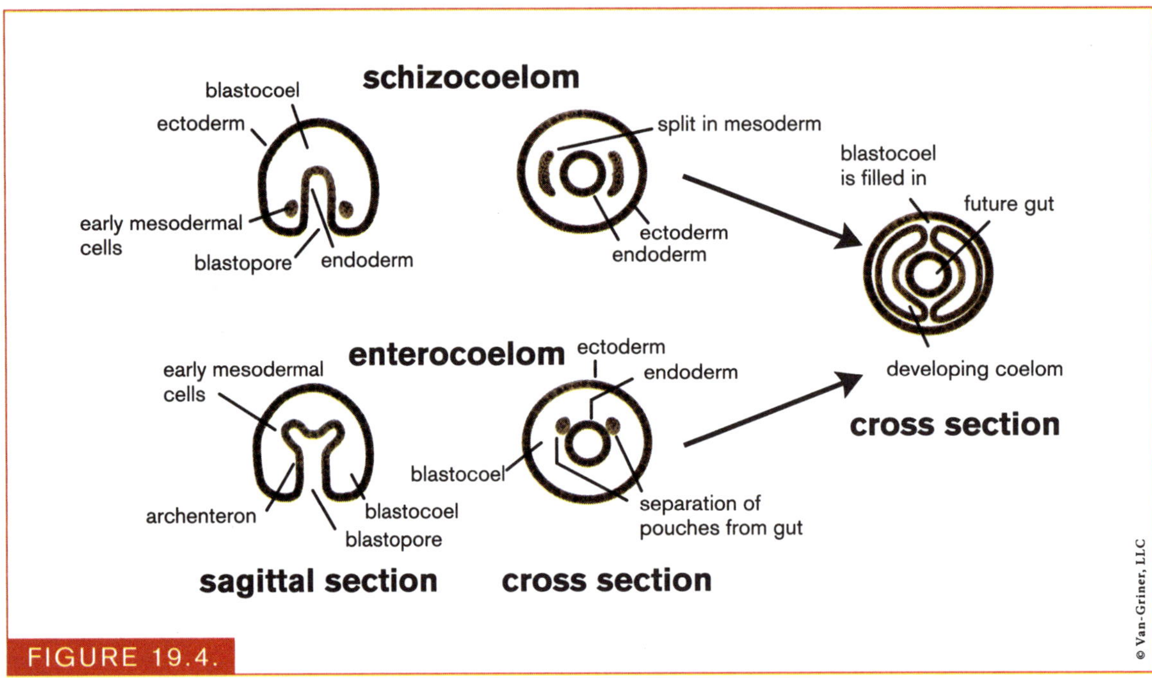

FIGURE 19.4.

Schizocoeloms versus enterocoeloms.

Phylum Annelida

All annelids have the following main characteristics or **functional homologies** that distinguish them from other animals. Many of these characteristics are shared with molluscs.

A A **triploblastic, eucoelomate** (a "true" coelom) body plan that is **bilaterally symmetrical** with distinct **cephalization.** Annelids are **protostomes.**

B Annelids show pronounced **segmentation,** where the body parts are repeated along the length of the body (this serial repetition of compartments is called **metamerism**). The identical body compartments (along with their appendages) that occur along the length of an annelid are called **metameres.**

Metamerism is considered an important evolutionary attribute because it allowed specialization of body parts. For example, metamere appendages have specific functions in higher animal taxa (food capture/gathering, locomotion, defense from competitors and predators, brooding young). Metameric compartments also allow for separate hydrostatic compartments, which in turn allow for greater behavioral complexity and locomotion.

C **Digestive system.** For all annelids, **extracellular digestion** occurs within the lumen of the gut and digested materials then are absorbed across the gut wall. The annelid digestive system is complete and many species display regional specialization of various sections for mechanical digestion, storage, chemical digestion, and absorption. The **typhlosole** is a ridge-like fold of the side of the intestine into the lumen (gut space). The typhlosole increases the absorptive surface area of the intestine.

D **Osmoregulatory system/excretory system.** Annelids (as well as molluscs) possess **metanephridia,** tubules that open at two ends: one to the outside and the other to the coelom. Filtrate from coelomic fluid is collected from the internal end of each metanephridium via the **nephrostome** and eliminated to the outside via the **nephridiopore.** Metanephridia serve both an excretory function eliminating nitrogenous waste and an osmoregulatory function eliminating excess water. Cells lining metanephridial tubules selectively reabsorb materials from the filtrate, similar to what happens in protonephridia. Compare this excretory/osmoregulatory system to that of the flatworms, nematodes, and other pseudocoelomates, which only possess protonephridia.

How do metanephridia and protonephridia differ? Flatworm protonephridia are closed tubes with an opening to the outside. There is no opening on the inside of the body. Usually, one or a few flame cells in the protonephridium cause the filtrate to move outward. In the flatworms, protonephridia are essentially osmoregulatory organs. Nitrogen wastes are removed primarily by diffusion across the body wall in the flatworms and roundworms and in many annelids as well. However, in many large molluscs (especially terrestrial snails and slugs), nitrogen waste excretion by the metanephridia is a very important advancement. Metanephridia are larger, more complex structures that often function in both excretion and osmoregulation. Metanephridia would be ineffective in acoelomate animals, due to the lack of a fluid-filled body cavity. Metanephridia also would quickly drain the body fluids of small organisms. Protonephridia (which are small and consist of a few cells) would be ineffective in filtering the larger volumes of the body fluids in the body cavities of large coelomates.

E **Circulatory system.** Most annelids have a circulatory system with **blood vessels** and **hearts.** For most annelids, blood never leaves the circulatory system (most annelids thus have a **closed circulatory system**). The leeches are the exception; they use a type of **open circulatory system,** where blood is found in blood-filled sinuses or cavities. Because blood can be put under higher pressure in closed systems, closed circulatory systems allow for more efficient and rapid transport of blood (and thus gases, food, and wastes) to and from the cells of the body.

F **Respiratory system.** For all annelids, gas exchange is through diffusion across the body wall through the skin (or gills, if present). Many annelids also have respiratory pigments (hemoglobin or chlorocruorin) in their plasma or in coelomocytes, which can help transport oxygen through the body. Capillary beds closely associated with the epidermis transport gases elsewhere.

G **Nervous system.** Annelids show **cephalization;** annelids have a well-developed nervous system with a **brain** and **ventral nerve cord.** The brain is comprised of several **ganglia** (collections of nerve cells) that have been partially fused together. **Segmental nerves** run into each body segment from segmental ganglia, innervating all organs. These advancements in nervous system structure permit more complex behaviors to occur in annelids.

H **Reproductive system.** The oligochaetes and leeches are **monoecious,** where male and female reproductive systems are present in the same individual. Reproduction is primarily sexual and fertilization is external, occurring either in the water column or inside a **cocoon.** The top-shaped larvae of marine species are called **trochophores,** which swim before settling and metamorphosing into adults. The polychaetes are **dioecious** (separate sexes).

I **Muscular system.** In all annelids, muscles are found underneath the epidermis and around the intestine. Both **circular** and **longitudinal** bands of muscles are present.

J **Integumentary system and skeletal system.** The annelid epidermis produces an external noncellular body covering called the **cuticle,** which helps prevent dessication. Layers of longitudinal and circular muscles, as well as connective tissues, are underneath the epidermis. A layer of epithelial cells lines the outside of the coelomic cavity. The epidermis is a layer of columnar epithelium. Muscles are able to effect locomotion and digestion by contracting against the fluid-filled coelom (in annelids, the coelomic compartments serve as a **hydrostatic skeleton**).

Exercises

Exercise 19.1.

Examine the live earthworms, if they are available. Observe their behavior for a few minutes. Observe their locomotion on moist soil or a moist paper towel. What happens of you use a blunt end of a probe and gently poke the anterior portion of the earthworm? What happens if you poke the posterior portion?

Exercise 19.2.

View the preserved specimen labeled *Nereis* (= *Neanthes,* or sand worm). You should be able to see the eyes and the jaws. Draw the polychaete sandworm in the space provided below (Figure 19.5). Use Figure 19.6 to guide you.

Note that the parapodium has many bristlelike **setae** made of chitin. Parapodia serve two functions: annelids use them to move and to breathe. The long dark spines are **acicula,** which are connected to body wall muscles. When the muscles contract, they pull the acicula in and out, causing the parapodium to move (see Figure 19.6).

FIGURE 19.5.

The polychaete *Nereis.*

Exercise 19.3.

Earthworm Anatomy

We will intensively study the earthworm as an example of a **eucoelomate body plan.** Compare the earthworm body plan (Figure 19.8) to that of the sponge *Grantia* (Figure 18.5), the cnidarian *Hydra* (Figure 18.14), the acoelomate flatworm *Dugesia* Figure 18.24), and the pseudocoelomate nematode *Ascaris* (Figure 18.33).

A thin **cuticle** is on the outside of the body, although you may not be able to distinguish it from the epidermis. Underneath the outer **epidermis,** you will be able to make out two bands of muscular tissues: an outer **circular muscle layer** and an inner **longitudinal muscle layer**

FIGURE 19.6.

The clam worm (*Nereis Virens*) external anatomy.

(note which direction the muscle fibers are oriented). **Setae** (two pairs per segment in an oligochaete) and their associated muscles may be visible in your slide. The setae are extruded by retractor muscles and act as anchors for movement. There is a layer of connective cells on the inside of the muscle layers (the **peritoneum**) that separates the coelom from the outer wall.

The **coelom** is inside the muscular layers. The lumen of the gut is enclosed by the **intestinal epithelium** with a small layer of circular and longitudinal muscle outside of the epithelium. Outside of the muscles, a thin visceral peritoneum then surrounds the gut. Some of the cells in the peritoneum are large yellowish **chlorogogue cells,** which may serve a variety of functions similar to the liver and kidney (for example, deamination of proteins and food and metabolic waste transport). Various **mesenteries** may be observed on the dorsal and ventral side of the gut running to the outer peritoneum. The coelom is compartmentalized by the mesenteries; the coelomic fluid of one metamere is separate from the next. The nerves and blood vessels are embedded in the mesenteries. The **typhlosole** is an invagination into the gut lumen; this invagination of the dorsal surface of the gut increases the absorptive area of the gut epithelium.

The **nephridia** may appear as a ghost-like series of membranes in the coelom. The **dorsal blood vessel** lies above the typhlosole of the gut, and the **ventral nerve cord** (which consists of a **pair** of nerves, along with an **subneural blood vessel** associated with the nerve cord) can be found ventral to the intestine.

Examine the earthworm (*Lumbricus*) cross section. Draw what you see in the microscope's field of view in the space provided below (Figure 19.7). Use Figure 19.8 and Figure 19.9 to guide you.

FIGURE 19.7.

Cross section of an oligochaete earthworm.

1. Dorsal blood vessel
2. Peritoneum
3. Typhlosole
4. Lumen of intestine
5. Intestine
6. Coelom
7. Ventral nerve cord
8. Epidermis
9. Circular muscles
10. Longitudinal muscles
11. Intestinal epithelium
12. Nephridium
13. Ventral blood vessel
14. Seta and associated muscles

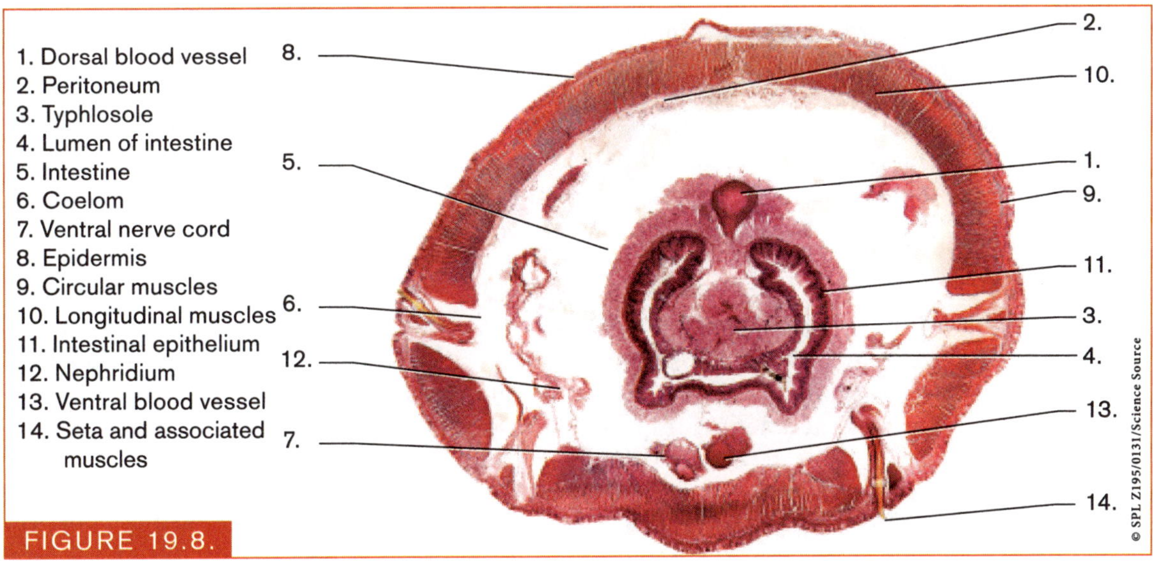

FIGURE 19.8.

Cross section of an earthworm.

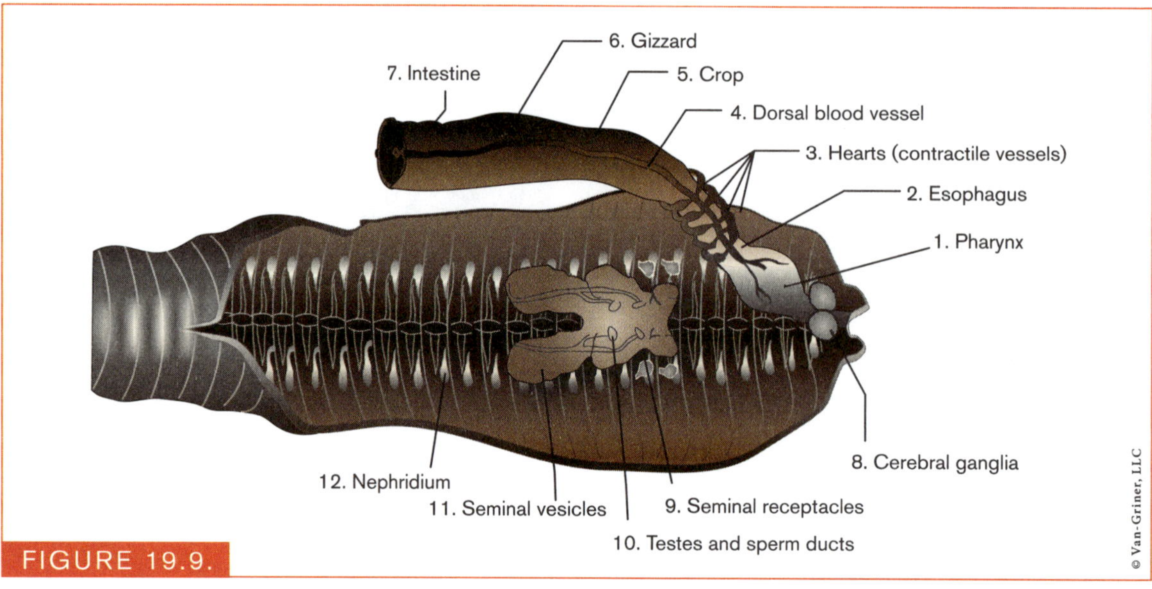

FIGURE 19.9.

Earthworm internal anatomy. The intestinal tract has been cut and partially lifted away to show ventral structures lying underneath.

Exercise 19.4.

Earthworm Internal Anatomy

The **mouth** leads to a muscular **pharynx** that leads to the **esophagus.** The esophagus leads to the **crop,** which stores ingested material temporarily. From the crop, food material moves by peristaltic contraction of muscles into the more muscular **gizzard,** where muscular contractions help grind food. From the gizzard, a long **intestine** extends posteriorly to the **anus;** digested food is assimilated across the intestinal wall.

Five pairs of **hearts** loops around the esophagus from the **dorsal blood vessel** to the **ventral blood vessel.** Both blood vessels travel longitudinally through the body. Blood flows to the anterior direction in the dorsal vessel and posteriorly in the ventral blood vessel. This blood flow pattern delivers food to the rest of the body.

The **brain** consists of a relatively large pair of **ganglia** and nerves that form a ring around the pharynx. Connecting nerves join these ganglia to each other and to the **ventral nerve cord,** which consists of a pair of nerves running longitudinally to the body. A pair of **segmental ganglia** is observed in each body segment. Nerves from a segmented ganglion innervate the organs in the segment. Large, paired **metanephridia** and their associated capillary beds can be observed in each body segment.

The terrestrial earthworms have two pairs of **testes** and one pair of **ovaries.** A small pore carries eggs to the outside of the worm. The sperm produced by the worm are stored in large **seminal vesicles,** which have a pore leading to the outside. Sperm from another worm is stored in the **seminal receptacles. A cocoon** is formed by the glandular **clitellum** on the anterior end of the worm. As the worm backs out of the mucus cocoon, it deposits its eggs as well as the sperm from the other worm stored in the seminal receptacles. Fertilization occurs inside the cocoon, and small worms hatch from the cocoon later.

Preserved earthworms are available for dissection.

Note: For the sake of time, some worms may already be opened for viewing.

First, determine the dorsal, ventral, anterior, and posterior sides. Place the earthworm on its ventral side, setae down, and pin the anterior end down. Feel the bristle-like setae on the ventral surface. Carefully open the worm on its dorsal side and observe the following structures: **pharynx, esophagus, crop, gizzard, intestine, dorsal blood vessel, aortic arches (hearts), cerebral ganglia (brain), seminal vesicles, nephridia, ventral blood vessel, ventral nerve cord.** Draw what you see in the space provided below (Figure 19.10). Use Figure 19.9 to guide you.

FIGURE 19.10.

Earthworm internal anatomy.

Exercise 19.5.

Examine the preserved specimens of leeches. Draw the external structure of the leech in the space provided below (Figure 19.11). Remember to include the **oral** and **caudal suckers.** Use Figure 19.12 to guide you.

FIGURE 19.11.

Leech external anatomy.

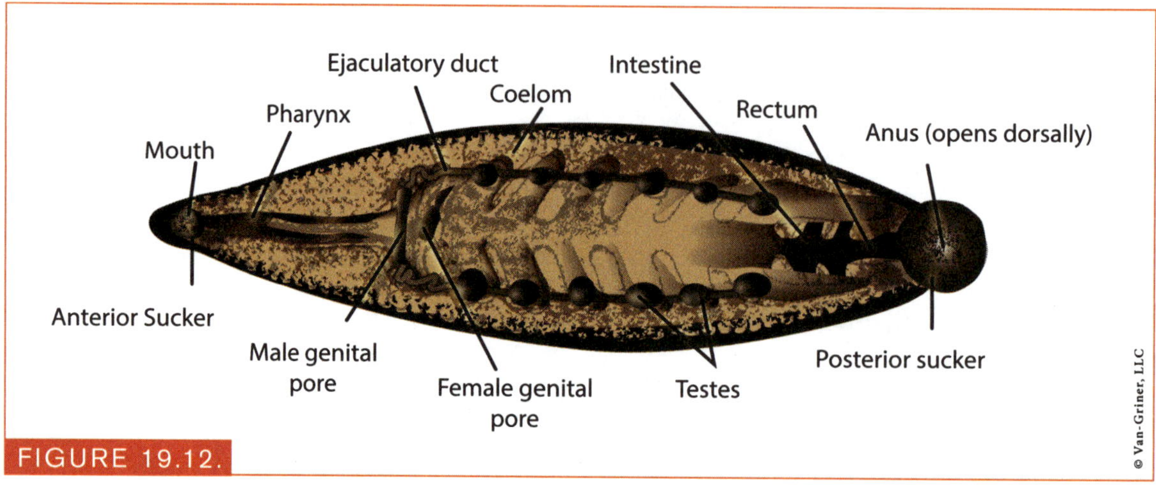

FIGURE 19.12.

Leech internal and external anatomy.

Exercise 19.6.

Examine any preserved specimens of annelids in the lab and be able to identify them by class. You may wish to make sketches of representatives of each annelid class in the space provided below (Figure 19.13).

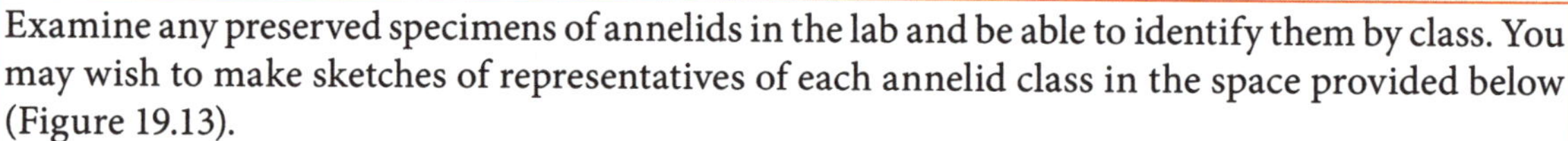

FIGURE 19.13.

Representative examples of annelid classes.

Exercise 19.7.

List the attributes of the major annelid classes in the table below (Table 19.1).

TABLE 19.1.

Attribute	Polychaeta	Oligochaeta	Hirudinea
habitat			
setae [Y/N] and if present, number per segment			
clitellum [Y/N]			
parapodia [Y/N]			
open/closed circulatory system			
monoecious/ dioecious			

Phylum Mollusca

All molluscs (or mollusks in some texts) have the following common characteristics or functional homologies that distinguish them from other animals:

A Triploblastic, **eucoelomate** body plan that is **bilaterally symmetrical** with distinct **cephalization** (with the exception of the bivalves). Molluscs are **protostomes** with spiral determinate cleavage.

B Four distinct body parts are present (see Figure 19.14). The **head,** the muscular **foot** with the **visceral mass,** and the **mantle** (which produces and maintains the shell, if present). Associated with the large and well-developed foot is the **visceral mass** containing the digestive and reproductive systems. The **coelom** is generally reduced to the area around the heart, kidney and gonads.

C **Integumentary system and skeletal system.** In molluscs, the protective calcareous **shell** is produced by a specialized part of the epidermis, the **mantle.** The mantle is part of the **skin** of the mollusc, which in some species (the land snails) is adapted to prevent excessive water loss. The epidermis is usually a single layer of columnar or cuboidal epithelial cells that are ciliated. The epidermis produces a thin proteinaceous cuticle. Three layers of muscle are underneath the epidermis: an outer circular layer, a diagonal layer, and an inner longitudinal layer. Many molluscs use a **hydrostatic skeleton** to move appendages, such as the penis or tentacles; muscular contraction forces fluid into sinuses of the penis and tentacles which causes them to evert and become erect.

The shell varies among the molluscs. Gastropods have a single coiled shell (or the shell is missing, as in the slugs); the bivalves have two valves; the chitons have eight articulated plates; and the cephalopods have either a coiled external shell, an internal shell, or in some cases, the shell is absent.

D **Muscular system and locomotion.** The large muscular **foot** is present in all molluscan species. Chitons, gastropods, and bivalves have a single large foot, while the cephalopods have multiple tentacles. Muscles are embedded into the body wall and along the gut. Some molluscs (the smaller species) glide through layer of mucus (produced by the epidermis) by **ciliary action** of the cells lining the foot. However, most molluscs move by **muscular contractions** (as waves of contractions) that sweep along the bottom of the foot. Various retractor muscles can pull the foot in and out of the shell of snails and bivalves. Cephalopods and some bivalves can use 'jet propulsion' by expelling water out of the mantle cavity via muscular contraction.

E **Digestive system.** In molluscs, **extracellular digestion** occurs within the lumen of the gut. Similar to the annelids and many other animals, digested materials are absorbed by the gut epithelium. The digestive system is complete with regional specialization of sections of the gut. Many molluscs (particularly the gastropods) have a unique, chitinous ribbon of teeth, called the **radula.** The radula scrapes food off substrates or bores holes into prey.

F **Osmoregulatory/excretory systems.** Molluscs possess well-developed, large **metanephridia,** similar to that seen in the annelids (these metanephridia are referred to as the 'kidney' in some texts). Molluscs eliminate **ammonia** as a nitrogen waste, although land snails convert ammonia to **uric acid,** which takes much less water to eliminate. Many of the marine molluscs, like all other taxonomic groups we have examined so far, are **osmoconformers;** the body fluids are iso-osmotic to seawater. However, many of the freshwater clams and snails, along with the land snails, are **osmoregulators;** their body fluids remain hyperosmotic compared to their environment. Molluscs can regulate concentrations of certain inorganic ions.

G **Circulatory system.** Most molluscs have an **open circulatory system** with a large **hemocoel** (blood-filled cavity). Cephalopods (squid and octopuses) are an exception: they have a **closed** circulatory system. Like the annelids, many molluscs have **hemoglobin** in their blood, which facilitates the transport of oxygen.

H **Nervous system.** Molluscs have a well-developed **nervous system,** similar to that of annelids, consisting of a **brain** and one or more **ventral nerve cords.** The brain in most species is composed a series of **ganglia** that encircle the esophagus, connected together by nerves. The paired ventral nerve cord arises from the brain. The gastropods and the cephalopods (in particular) have well developed brains made of a number of ganglia. The brain of bivalves is somewhat reduced. Like the annelids, many different sensory receptors (light, chemicals, and current) are found in various places of the body.

The brain and ventral nerve cord of annelids and molluscs are more complex than the nerve net in cnidarians and the ladder-like nerve cords observed in flatworms. These advancements in nervous system structure and function allow annelids and molluscs to be capable of more complex behaviors, compared to flatworms and cnidarians.

I **Respiratory system.** Most molluscs use **gills** for gas exchange, although the body wall is also important for gas exchange in some species. Some of the gastropod molluscs (those on land and some of the freshwater species) have secondarily evolved a **lung** (a vascularized part of the mantle cavity).

J **Reproductive system.** Molluscs are either monoecious or dioecious, with **internal or external fertilization,** depending upon the species. The chitons, cephalopods, and a large majority of bivalves are dioecious, while the gastropods are either monoecious or dioecious, depending on subclass. The reproductive systems are complex, with gonads and associated glands. Many marine species have a free-swimming **trochophore** larva, which develops into other larval stages before settling and metamorphosing into an adult.

K **Immune system.** Molluscs show some signs of an **immune system.** They exhibit a non-specific immunity against potential invading microorganisms. This includes the **integument** (their skin), which is a primary barrier to pathogens, and internal wandering **amebocytes** that phagocytize foreign cells and particles. If the invading organism or particle is too large, amebocytes can gather around the particle and encyst it.

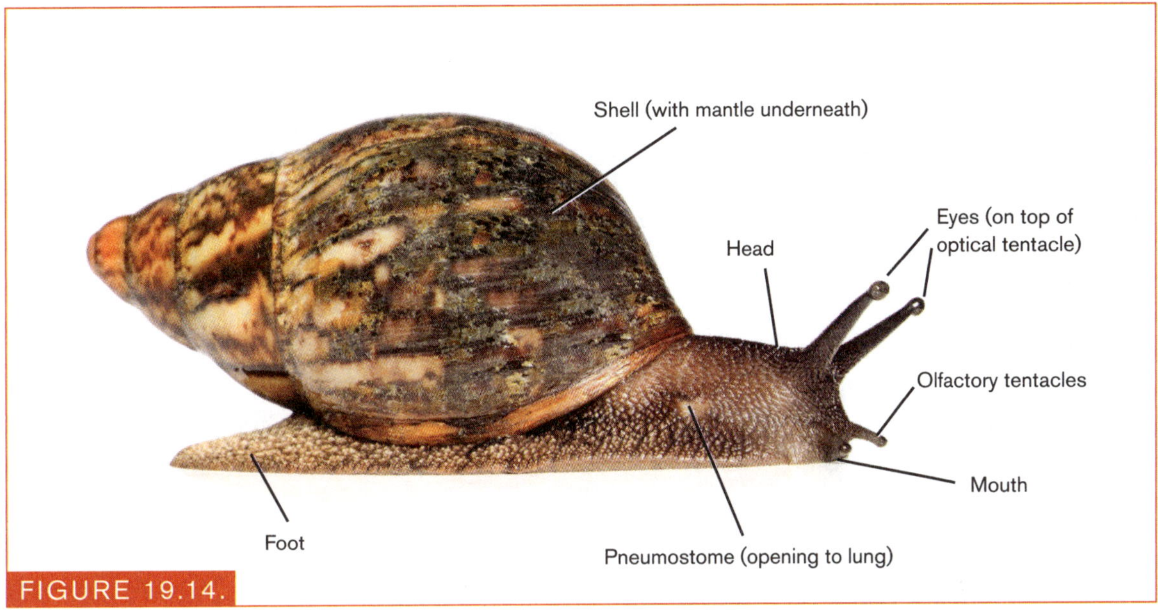

FIGURE 19.14.

The anatomy of a gastropod, showing the basic molluscan body plan.

Exercise 19.8.

Live Snails or Clams

Examine the live snails or clams. Observe the locomotion of the snails for a few minutes. Can they crawl on the surface film? What is the mucus that they secrete used for?

Exercise 19.9.

Observe the preserved specimens of chitons, snails, bivalves, and cephalopods and be able to identify them by class. Be able to identify shells, head, mantle, foot, gills. Make sketches of representatives of each molluscan class in the space below (Figure 19.15). Use Figure 19.14 and Figure 19.16 to guide you.

FIGURE 19.15.

Representative classes of molluscs.

FIGURE 19.16.

Representative specimens of molluscs.

Exercise 19.10.

List the attributes of the molluscan classes in the table below (Table 19.2).

TABLE 19.2.

Attribute	Bivalvia	Polyplacophora	Gastropoda	Cephalopoda
habitat				
respiratory structures				
circulatory structures				
head present/ absent				
foot structure				
shell present/ absent (and if present, the type)				
monoecious/ dioecious				

Phylum Arthropoda

In some texts, the 'phylum' Arthropoda has been split into several phyla, and the term "Arthropoda' (Greek for "jointed foot") used as a superphylum. We will use the classification scheme detailed at the beginning of the unit. All arthropods have the following common characteristics or functional homologies that distinguish them from other animals:

A A **triploblastic, eucoelomate** body plan that is **bilaterally symmetrical** with distinct **cephalization.** Arthropods are **protostomes** and the coelom is reduced to a body cavity called the **hemocoel.**

B A **segmented body plan** with segments that are usually fused into **tagmata** (e.g., head, thorax, and abdomen).

The creation of tagmata results in the regional formation of body parts that are specialized and highly adaptive: tagmata are involved in locomotion (thorax), sensation and feeding (head), or visceral activities of reproduction, excretion and digestion (abdomen).

Most chelicerates have two tagmata: the **cephalothorax** (sometimes called the prosoma) and the **abdomen** (sometimes called the opisthosoma, see Figure 19.20). Crustaceans also typically have a cephalothorax and abdomen (see Figure 19.22). The insects (which we will study as our uniramian representative) have three tagmata: **head, thorax, and abdomen** (see Figure 19.23).

C **Muscular system/appendages.** The arthropods possess jointed appendages that are made of segments called **podomeres.** (See Figure 19.20, Figure 19.22, and Figure 19.23). Many body segments have a pair of appendages, which can have different specialized functions. The appendages have a series of muscles associated with their movement.

D **Integumentary system** and **skeletal system.** All arthropods have an **exoskeleton** composed of the polysaccharide **chitin** and other compounds, including lipids, proteins, and calcium carbonates (crustaceans). The exoskeleton protects the animal against disease, predators, and dessication and provides sites for muscle attachment. The exoskeleton limits body size but periodic ecdyses or **molts** allows the animal to grow larger. When arthropods molt (undergo **ecdysis**), they are quite vulnerable to predators. The exoskeleton is produced by the single layer of columnar epithelium that form the **epidermis** underneath.

E **Digestive system. Extracellular digestion** occurs within the lumen of the arthropod gut. Some arthropods, like spiders and scorpions, chew upon and consume the fluids of their prey. Like annelids and molluscs, the digestive system is complete with specialization of different sections for specific functions. Mechanical digestion, storage, chemical digestion, and nutrient absorption occur in sequential sections of the digestive tract.

F **Osmoregulatory/excretory systems.** Arthropods have well-developed excretory systems, consisting of either **green (antennal) glands** or **Malpighian tubules.**

Crayfish possess **antennal glands** (also called **green glands**), which are a type of nephridium that excretes large amounts of ammonia and water. Terrestrial arthropods (e.g., insects and spiders) possess **Malpighian tubules.** The Malpighian tubules are blind tubes that dump nitrogenous wastes and water into the gut. The gut epithelial cells then reabsorb the water. The uric acid then is crystallized and is eliminated with the digestive wastes from the digestive system. Uric acid is insoluble in water and is much less toxic than ammonia or **urea,** so less water is needed to flush out uric acid. Because of this relative insolubility and subsequent savings from decreasing water loss, arthropods have much more successfully colonized land (especially dry desert areas), compared to annelids, flatworms, and other phyla that are primarily restricted to water or very moist soils. A Malpighian tubule is not strictly considered a metanephridium because the Malpighian tubules are closed at one end and develop very differently from the nephridia of the other protostome taxa. However, the green glands and Malpighian tubules are similar to metanephridia in terms of filtration and selective reabsorption.

G **Circulatory system.** Arthropods have an **open** circulatory system with a tubular heart and blood vessels that open into sinuses where food and wastes are exchanged. The fluid found within an open circulatory system of the protostomes is technically not 'blood,' but a fluid that is referred to as **hemolymph.** The composition of the hemolymph inside the blood vessels is basically identical to that of the interstitial fluids of the hemocoel.

H **Respiratory system.** Gas exchange in the smallest arthropods occurs across the body wall. The larger arthropods possess a respiratory system: **gills** (in aquatic insects and crustaceans), **tracheae** (in most insects), or **book lungs** (in spiders). However, the circulatory system is not involved in oxygen transport.

I **Nervous system.** All arthropods have well-developed nervous systems. The nervous system of an arthropod is similar to the annelids and molluscs in that they have an anterior **brain** (composed of a series of ganglia around the esophagus) and **paired ventral nerve cord.** Segmental ganglia are found in each segment, with nerves emanating from the segmented ganglia. Lateral nerves inner-vates the sensory organs, appendages, muscles, and other organs of that segment.

J **Reproductive system.** The arthropods are generally **dioecious,** with internal fertilization. **Meta-morphosis,** or a dramatic change in body plan is characteristic of some arthropods (see Figure 19.25). In many insect species, the larval stages are adapted for a different habitat than the adult.

K **Immune system.** Arthropods, like the annelids and molluscs, have a non-specific immunity con-sisting of the exoskeleton and wandering **amebocytes** that phagocytize foreign cells or particles.

Exercise 19.11.

> If any live insects or crustaceans are present in the lab, observe their behavior. Observe their locomotion on moist soil or moist paper towel. How does it differ from that of the earthworms and snails?

Exercise 19.12.

Demonstration of Insect Tracheae

Observe the insect tracheae slide. The tracheae are a series of tubes that run throughout the body of the insect. Many tracheae have small branches that are near active tissues. Oxygen diffuses from these tracheae to the muscles. Oxygen is thus "piped" to the respiring cells. Draw what you see under the microscope's field of view in the space below (Figure 19.17).

FIGURE 19.17.

The insect tracheae.

Exercise 19.13.

Preserved Specimens

Examine those animals placed on the demonstration table. You should be able to identify them to class, subphylum (if they are arthropods), and phylum. The specimens include horseshoe crabs, spiders, ticks, various insects, crabs, lobsters, crayfish, amphipods, centipedes, and millipedes. You may wish to make sketches of representatives of each arthropod subphylum in the space below (Figure 19.18).

FIGURE 19.18.

Representative sketches of arthropods.

Exercise 19.14.

Spider External Anatomy

Observe the preserved specimens of spiders. Spiders possess two tagmata: the cephalothorax and abdomen. Identify chelicera, fangs, pedipalps, ocelli (simple eyes), compound eyes, and eight walking legs. Make a sketch of what you see in the space below (Figure 19.19). Use Figure 19.20 to guide you.

FIGURE 19.19.

Spider external anatomy.

FIGURE 19.20.

Basic anatomy of the chelicerate spider.

Exercise 19.15.

Crayfish External Anatomy

Crayfish possess two tagmata: the **cephalothorax** and **abdomen.** The cephalothorax consists of 13 segments, and the abdomen consists of six segments. Each segment contains a pair of appendages, many of the appendages are branched (biramous).

The head region of the cephalothorax has five pairs of modified appendages. There are two pairs of sensory antennae on the crustaceans: the shorter **antennules** and the longer **antennae.** Both are involved in smell and touch. The strong, hardened **mandibles** (jaws) crush food. Two pairs of **maxillae** hold onto and help tear up food, as well as passing it to the mouth. The second pair of maxillae also helps to move water past the gills. The **gills** inside the branchial chamber (underneath the carapace) are attached to the base of the five pairs of walking legs. Water moves from posterior to anterior direction inside the branchial chamber, flowing past the gills.

The **carapace** is the dorsal part of the exoskeleton of the cephalothorax that protects the **gills.** There are a pair of **eyes** on the dorsal surface; the eyes are on short stalks.

The thoracic part of the cephalothorax has eight pairs of appendages. There are three pairs of **maxillipeds,** which hold onto food during eating. The next five pairs of appendages are walking legs: the first pair have the large claw-like **chelipeds** on their end. Crayfish use chelipeds for defense and capturing food, and males use them to hold onto females during mating. The other four segments contains a pair of walking legs.

In the abdomen, the first five segments each have a pair of **swimmerets,** which create water currents and function in reproduction. Males have one or two pairs of specialized swimmerets that can claps the female during mating. Females temporarily carry their eggs on their swimmerets. The sixth segment contains the **telson** (where the anus is located) and the appendages called **uropods,** which together with the telson form the fan-like tail. The tail fan can force water forward, allowing the crayfish to rapidly escape.

Observe the preserved specimens of crayfish. Make a sketch of what you see in the space provided below (Figure 19.21). Use Figure 19.22 to guide you.

FIGURE 19.21.

Crayfish external anatomy.

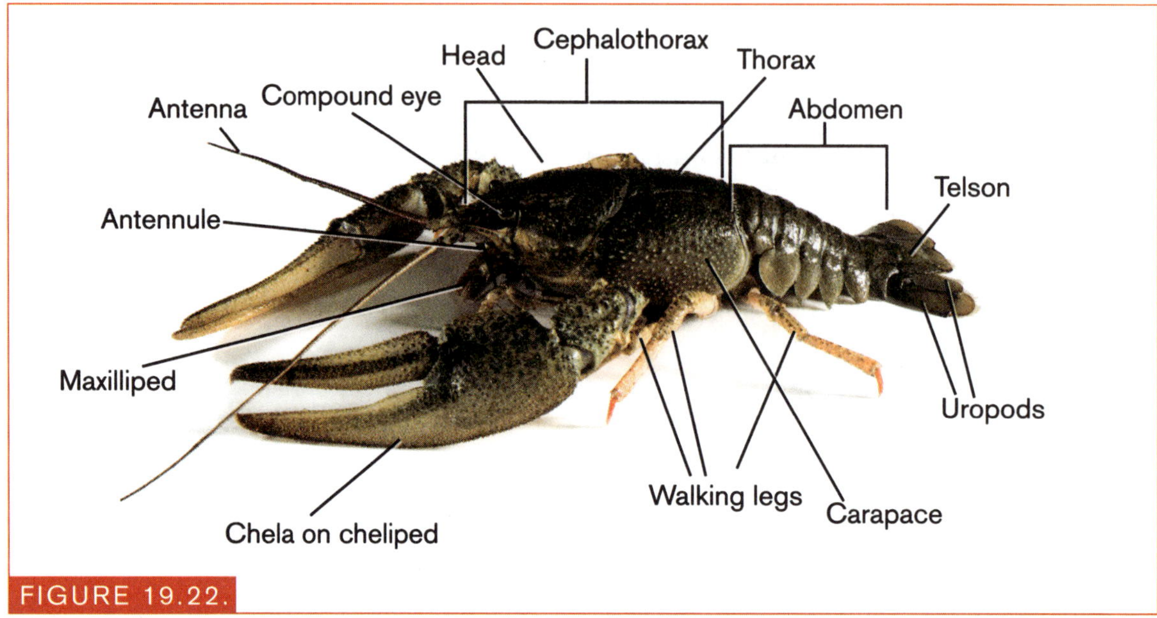

FIGURE 19.22.

Basic anatomy of a crustacean (crayfish).

FIGURE 19.23.

Basic anatomy of a uniramian insect: the grasshopper.

Exercise 19.16.

Grasshopper Anatomy

External structures (only): on preserved specimens of the grasshopper *Romalea*, observe and identify antenna (one pair), compound eyes, ocelli, wings, head, thorax and abdomen, 3 pairs of walking legs, and mandibles. Make a sketch of what you see in the space below (Figure 19.24). Use Figure 19.23 to guide you.

FIGURE 19.24.

Grasshopper external anatomy.

Exercise 19.17.

List the attributes of the three arthropod subphyla in the table below (Table 19.3). The spider will be the representative for the chelicerates, the crayfish will serve as the representative for a crustacean, and the grasshopper will serve for the uniramian insects.

TABLE 19.3.

Attribute	Chelicerata	Crustacea	Uniramia (insecta)
number of walking legs			
number of antennae			
number of wings			
mouthparts			
number of tagmata			
eyes			
respiratory structures			
excretory structures			

Exercise 19.18.

> Go to the demonstration table and examine the presentation showing the various forms of metamorphosis. There are several different types of metamorphosis. One type of metamorphosis is called **gradual metamorphosis:** egg – nymph – adult. Grasshoppers exhibit this type of metamorphosis, where nymphs are similar to adults.
>
> In other groups, there is **complete metamorphosis,** where a dramatic change in body plans occurs over time: egg – larvae – pupae – adult. See Figure 19.25 for pictures of metamorphosis.

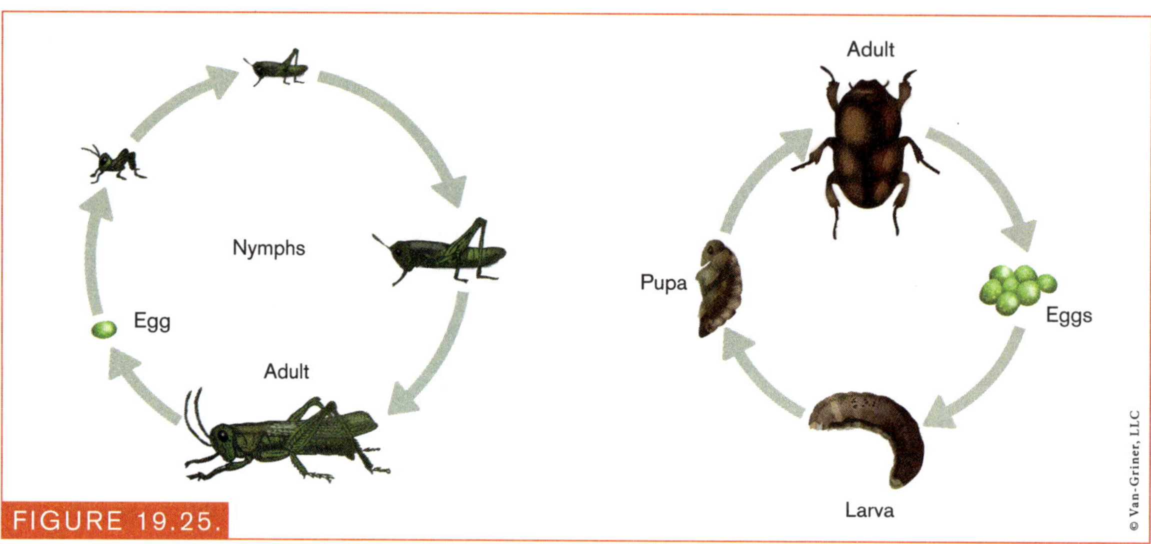

FIGURE 19.25.

Gradual (left figure) and complete (right figure) metamorphosis.

Phylum Echinodermata

Today we will look at one of the deuterostome phyla: the echinoderms. The blastopore in these animals becomes the anus the mouth forms later in development. The echinoderms are all marine. Cleavage is **radial** (as opposed to **spiral cleavage** in most protostomes). The coelom of these deuterostome phyla form as an **enterocoelous coelom** (as opposed to the **schizocoelous coelom** of the protostomes). The echinoderms are distinct from the chordates in that they have abandoned bilateral symmetry in favor of a sessile, radially symmetrical lifestyle as adults.

All echinoderms have the following main characteristics or functional homologies that distinguish them from other animals:

A **Integumentary systems.** Echinoderms have a **dermal endoskeleton** made of a series of calcareous plates (**ossicles**) and spines. Echinoderms have an epidermis that maintains the endoskeleton and protects the body. Most echinoderms are **sessile** animals. Some of the classes (Asteroidea, Holothuroidea, and Crinoidea) have small pincher-like **pedicellariae** on their outer surface that prevent small organisms from settling on the body surface. Echinoidea and Ophiuroidea do not have these pedicellariae.

B Echinoderms have a triploblastic, eucoelomate body plan. They are **bilaterally symmetrical as larvae** but they are radially symmetrical as adults (echinoderms show pentaradial symmetry, or pentamerous radial symmetry). The body plan is organized around an **oral-aboral axis.**

C Echinoderms are **deuterostomes.** The blastopore develops into the anus, and the mouth forms later.

D **Skeletal systems.** A part of the echinoderm **coelom** forms a series of water-filled canals and cavities collectively called the **water vascular system.** The water vascular system is the unique homology to all echinoderms. The water vascular system acts as a **hydrostatic skeleton,** it helps move the many **tube feet** used in prey capture and locomotion. The end of each tube foot possesses a sucker. The suckers allow the echinoderms to hold onto the substrate and to prey. Brittle stars do not have suckers on their tube feet.

E Echinoderms show **no segmentation.**

F **Digestive systems.** In echinoderms, digestion occurs **extracellularly** in the digestive system. They secrete enzymes that chemically digest their prey. The digested material is then absorbed by the epithelia of the digestive tract. The echinoderm digestive system is **complete,** except for the brittle stars, who have secondarily lost their intestines and anus and thus are considered to have an incomplete digestive tract.

G **Echinoderms do not have extensive excretory, respiratory, or circulatory systems.** Metabolic wastes (primarily ammonia) diffuse directly into the water. The water vascular system does help to distribute gases and wastes through the body, but most gas exchange is across the body wall. Small finger-like extensions off of the epidermis serve as sites for respiratory gas exchange (these extensions are called **dermal branchiae**).

H **Nervous systems.** The echinoderms do not exhibit cephalization. The nervous system is diffuse and is usually reduced to a **nerve net,** one that is analogous to the cnidarian nerve net. Compared to the arthropods, molluscs and chordates, the echinoderm sensory systems are reduced.

I **Reproductive systems.** The echinoderms are **dioecious.** Fertilization is **external,** where males and females simultaneously shed their gametes into the open water. The larvae are planktonic organisms that feed in the open waters; most echinoderm larvae metamorphose into sessile adults.

J **Immune systems.** Like many invertebrates, echinoderms also possess wandering phagocytic cells that phagocytize foreign cells or particles.

Exercise 19.19.

View the preserved specimens of echinoderms. Be able to identify echinoderm specimens to their class. Use Figure 19.28 to help you. We will see specimens of four distinct classes:

Sea stars (Class Asteroidea)
Sea urchins and sand dollars (Class Echinoidea)
Sea cucumbers (Class Holothuroidea)
Brittle stars (Class Ophiuroidea)

Sea Star External Anatomy

Place the sea star on its aboral surface (mouth down) and carefully observe the following external structures: ossicles, madreporite, anus. You will need to use the dissecting microscope to see some of the small structures, such as dermal branchiae. Turn the sea star over on its oral surface and observe the mouth, tube feet, ambulacral groove, arms. Make a sketch of what you see in the space provided below (Figure 19.26). Use Figures 19.29 and 19.30 to guide you.

FIGURE 19.26.

Echinoderm external anatomy.

Exercise 19.20.

Cross Section through a Sea Star Arm

Examine the slide of the cross section of a sea star arm. Identify the following: epidermis, coelom, tube foot, ambulacral groove, caecum, gonad. Make a sketch in the space provided below (Figure 19.27). Use Figure 19.30 to guide you.

FIGURE 19.27.

Echinoderm internal anatomy.

FIGURE 19.28.

Selected Echinoderm classes.

A. Daisy brittle-star (Class Ophiuroidea)

B. Ochre sea star (Class Asteroidea)

C. Warty sea cucumber (Class Holothuroidea)

D. Purple sea urchins (Class Echinoidea)

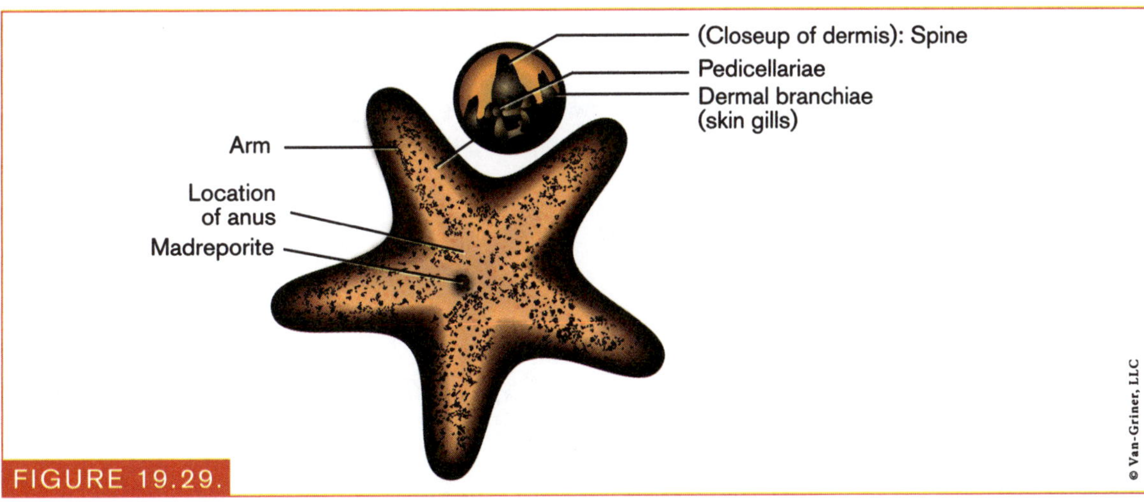

FIGURE 19.29.

External anatomy of the sea star.

FIGURE 19.30.

Cross section of the sea star arm.

Exercise 19.21.

List the major echinoderm classes and their distinguishing characteristics in the table below (Table 19.4).

TABLE 19.4.

Echinoderm Class	Common Names	Distinguishing External Features
Asteroidea		
Echinoidea		
Holothuroidea		
Ophiuroidea		

Exercise 19.22.

Fill in the following table (Table 19.5; this table is an extension of Table 18.3 of Exercise 18.17), adding in terms or key words that will help you distinguish each taxon from the others.

TABLE 19.5.

Character	Taxon			
	Mollusca	Annelida	Arthropoda	Echinodermata
diplo-/ triploblastic				
body cavity				
symmetry				
digestive				
respiratory				
circulatory				
reproductive				
excretory/ osmoregulation				
nervous				
support/ skeletons				
appendages/ integument				
groups				
other important terms, traits or key words				

Animals III. Chordates

UNIT 20

Keywords

notochord	vertebrates	yolk sac	oviparity
dorsal nerve cord	tetrapods	amnion	viviparity
post-anal tail	amniotes	ammocoete	ovoviviparity
gnathostomes	allantois	tunic	
agnathans	chorion	semicircular canals	

Learning Objectives

When finished with this unit, you should be able to:

1 Identify the chordate characteristics (notochord, dorsal hollow nerve cord, post-anal tail, pharyngeal gill slits) of representative specimens of chordates.

2 Identify the kingdom and subphylum of any chordate shown to you.

3 List the major distinguishing characteristics and recognize the key features of tunicates and lancelets:
- Lancelets: oral hood, gill bars, gill slits and pharynx, notochord, nerve cord, segmented muscles (myomeres), atrium, atriopore, anus, mouth
- Tunicates: tunic, pharynx, atrium, gill slits, incurrent and excurrent siphons

4 Identify the kingdom, phylum, subphylum and class of any vertebrate that is shown to you. In addition, be able to state if a selected vertebrate is an agnathan, a gnathostome, a jawed fish, or a tetrapod.

5 List the major distinguishing characteristics and recognize the key external features of any vertebrate shown to you. A *noncomprehensive* list of external key features follows:
- Hagfish: slime glands, gill pores, barbels
- Lampreys: ammocoete larva, gill slits, fins, and tail
- Chondrichthyes: gill slits, cartilaginous endoskeleton, dorsal, anal, pectoral, pelvic and caudal fins, spiracle, lateral line, heterocercal tail
- Osteichthyes: operculum, gills, swim bladder, lateral line, pelvic, pectoral, dorsal, anal and caudal fins
- Tetrapods: four limbs, pair of nostrils through which air can enter into the respiratory tract;
- Amniotes: amniotic egg (identify the position and function of the four extraembryonic membranes), claws
- Amphibia: cloaca, tympanic membrane, mucous glands, poison glands

- Reptilia: scales, tail, cloaca
- Aves: feathers, cloaca, wings
- Mammalia: fur (hair), mammary glands, outer ear (pinna), chewing

6 Identify the major internal structures observed in vertebrates (using the human models and any figure or picture of a human) and know their function. (The list of structures is on page 20-29).

Classification

Kingdom Animalia

  Phylum Chordata

  Subphylum Urochordata (the sea squirts)

  Subphylum Cephalochordata (the lancelets)

  Subphylum Vertebrata (the vertebrates)

   'Agnatha' (the jawless vertebrate animals)

    Class Myxini (the hagfish)

    Class Cephalaspidomorphi (the lampreys)

   'Gnathostomata' (the jawed animals)

    'Jawed fishes'

     Class Chondrichthyes (the sharks, skates and rays)

     Class Osteichthyes (the bony fish)

    'Tetrapoda' (the four-limbed animals)

     Class Amphibia (the amphibians)

     Class Reptilia (the reptiles)

     Class Aves (the birds)

     Class Mammalia (the mammals)

Phylum Chordata

The last phylum of animals that we will study is Chordata. Chordates have a **triploblastic, eucoelomate body plan.** Chordates are **bilaterally symmetrical** and show some segmentation, at least internally (for example, muscles, spinal cord ganglia, and vertebrae). All chordates are **deuterostomes;** the blastopore develops into the anus, and the mouth forms later.

All chordates possess all four of the following characteristics at some time in their life cycle. The following characteristics or functional homologies distinguish them from other animals (as shown in the tunicate larva and the adult lancelet (see Figure 20.2 and Figure 20.4).

A A slender, solid rod of cartilage-like connective tissue, called the **notochord.** The notochord lies underneath the dorsal surface. It serves as an **endoskeleton** in the primitive chordates, but it is replaced by bone and/or cartilage in the vertebrates.

B A series of paired slits along the pharynx, called **pharyngeal gill slits.** These slits serve as passageways for water to the gills, when they are present. The supporting structures, **gill arches,** are modified in higher vertebrates into the inner ear bones and the jawbone.

C A dorsal, single **nerve cord.** (Note how this differs from the ventral nerve cords typically seen in the protostomes). The brain forms at the anterior end of the nerve cord.

D A **post-anal tail.** In chordates, the tail extends past the anus.

In addition to the four key characteristics, chordates share the following features:

E Digestion occurs **extracellularly.** Chordates secrete enzymes that chemically digest their prey. The digested material is then absorbed by the digestive tract. All chordates have **complete digestive systems.** Undigested material passes out through the anus, allowing for increased specialization of the digestive tract and increased efficient one-way flow of material.

F Chordates have well-defined respiratory, circulatory, and excretory systems. The chordates possess a **closed circulatory system with a contractile heart, kidneys** with many **nephrons** (which are more advanced than metanephridia of annelids and molluscs), and **gills or lungs** for gas exchange. The muscular system of chordates are well defined, allowing rapid movement. The advanced systems allow high metabolic rates, which in turn allow for a more active lifestyle and larger body size.

G The nervous systems of most chordates are very highly developed. A large brain, along with the spinal cord, receive and send electrical signals to the muscles, glands and sensory structures located throughout the body.

H Except for the tunicates, most chordates are **dioecious,** with individuals possessing either testes or ovaries. **Fertilization is external or internal,** depending on the group.

Subphylum Urochordata

A **Integumentary and skeletal systems.** The urochordates are commonly called **sea squirts** because they expel water out their siphons if disturbed. They are also called **tunicates** because of the unique cellulose-like polysaccharide (**tunicin**) that forms the **tunic** or tough outer covering, which provides protection and support for the animal. The tunic is composed of a thin cuticle that overlies fibrous layers of tunicin and other compounds. The epidermis (consisting of a single layer of columnar epithelium) lies underneath the tunic, with connective tissues and muscle beneath the epidermis.

B The large cavity in the middle of the tunicate is called the **atrium.** The **incurrent siphon** brings in water into the atrium, the water then passes through the **pharyngeal basket,** which filters the planktonic food suspended in the water. The water then leaves out the **excurrent (atrial) siphon.**

C **Osmoregulatory /excretory systems.** The elimination of nitrogenous wastes (primarily **ammonia**) is done by diffusion across exposed body surfaces, but some species secrete uric acid. Tunicates are osmoconformers; their blood is iso-osmotic to seawater.

D **Digestive system.** The digestive system is complete, with the **mouth** leading to a large expanded **pharynx (pharyngeal basket),** where gas exchange and food capture occurs. The **endostyle,** a gland associated with the pharyngeal basket, produces mucus, which in turn entraps food. Mucus then is carried by ciliary action to the **esophagus.** The esophagus leads to a **stomach** where chemical digestion takes place, and then to an **intestine,** where assimilation takes place. Feces are expelled out the **anus,** which is located near the excurrent siphon.

E **Nervous system.** The nervous system is **reduced** in the adults, down to a series of **ganglia** found in various places in the body. Sensory systems are located in the anterior part of the animal.

F **Circulatory and respiratory systems.** Tunicates have a **heart** and **open circulatory system** in which oxygen is carried as a diffused gas. Gas exchange occurs between the water and the blood in vessels located in the pharyngeal basket. Carbon dioxide is respired with the water going out the excurrent siphon. Tunicates have no respiratory pigments, such as hemoglobin.

G **Muscular system.** Tunicate larvae are mobile, but most adults are sessile (except for several groups that are free-swimming as adults) and have lost the notochord. **Circular** and **longitudinal muscles** are found in the body wall, which allows the animals to change shape and move.

H **Habitat and lifestyle.** These animals are filter feeders (with the exception of a few deep sea forms that are carnivorous) that are found in shallow marine environments.

I **Reproductive system.** Tunicates are **monoecious** (individuals are both male and female and produce both eggs and sperm). Some species shed gametes into the water column out the excurrent siphon (**external fertilization**), but others brood the fertilized eggs in the pharyngeal basket (**internal fertilization**). For many sea squirts, the mobile larvae swim for a short period, then settle and metamorphose into sessile adults. Some species undergo asexual reproduction by budding. Tunicates can regenerate lost body parts.

Exercises

Exercise 20.1.

Using the dissecting scope, view the preserved tunicate adults. Observe the siphons, tunic, pharynx, and note that the larva has all major chordate characters. You may wish to make a quick sketch in the space provided below (Figure 20.1). Use Figure 20.2 to guide you.

FIGURE 20.1.

A tunicate or sea squirt.

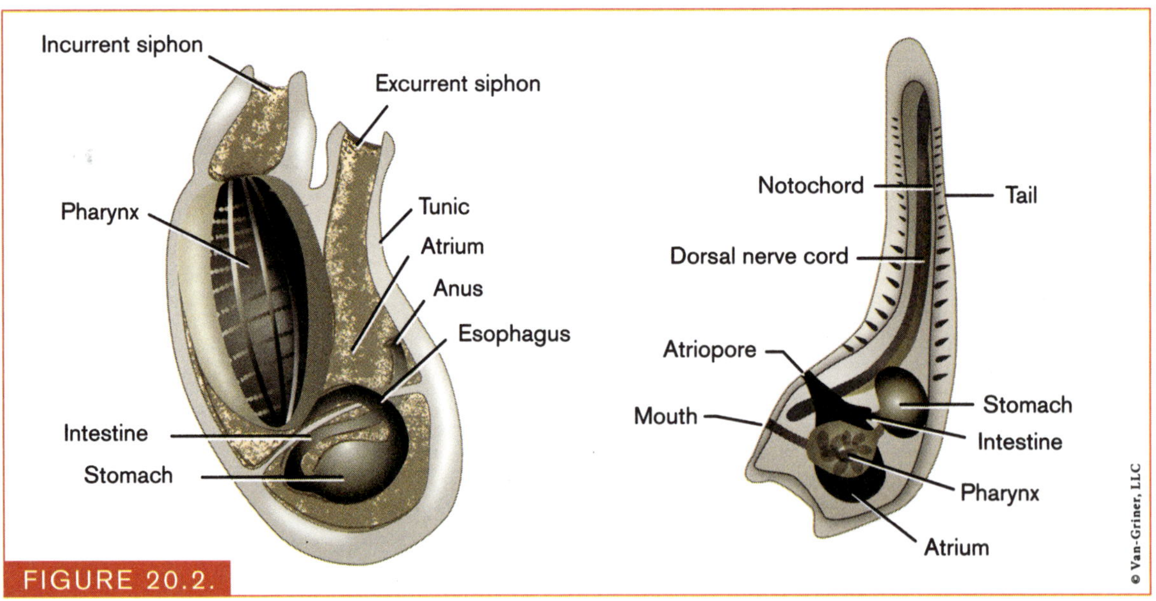

FIGURE 20.2.

Subphylum Urochordata (the tunicates).

Subphylum Cephalochordata

A **Lancelets** ("little spears") which are also called **amphioxus** ("sharp at both ends") are small (10 cm) animals that can be abundant in shallow marine sediments, feeding on a variety of foods.

B The **oral hood** is anterior, with finger-like **cirri** (tentacles) that act as both sensors and act as strainers that can sift out food from the sandy sediments.

C **Muscular system and locomotion.** The 60 or so chevron-like **myomeres** along the sides of the lancelet are **segmented muscles.** A small **dorsal fin** is on the dorsal side of the animal. The **caudal fin** is located along the most posterior part of the animal. The fins and myomeres (muscles) move the animal and bury it, tail down, into the sandy substrates.

D **Integumentary system and skeletal system.** At the dorsal side of the oral hood, a long flexible **notochord** is present. The notochord extends into the head (hence the name 'cephalochordate'). The notochord acts as a support structure for both the oral hood and provides a rigid structure for muscles to work against. The notochord is retained in the adult. The body wall (skin) is thin and somewhat transparent; it is not covered by either a test or scales. The skin is a thin layer of **epidermis** (composed of a layer of columnar epithelium), with a **dermis** (composed of connective tissues) lying underneath the epidermis.

E **Nervous system.** The **nerve cord** is dorsal of the notochord. There is **no distinct cephalization.** Sensory systems are primitive, but lancelets appear to detect light and mechanical stimuli. **Segmental nerves** leave the nerve cord to the skin and other organs all along the length of the nerve cord. An **eyespot** is at the anterior end of the animal, which may be able to detect light.

F **Digestive system.** Behind the oral hood and cirri is a cavity called the **buccal cavity,** where the mouth is located. The mouth leads into the **pharynx.** Finger-like structures, collectively called the **wheel organ,** are in the pharynx. Cilia attached to the wheel organ beat, creating a current. The wheel organ is just posterior of the oral hood. The pharynx has a series of parallel **gill bars,** through which water passes (the openings between the gill bars are called **gill slits**). This arrangement is similar to that pharyngeal basket of the tunicates. As the water passes through the gill bars, food is trapped by mucus produced by the **endostyle,** which sits on the floor of the pharynx. The mucus and food passes dorsally up to the **epibranchial groove** (also called the **hyperbranchial groove**) and then into the intestine. The water leaves out through the **atriopore.** The pharynx leads to the **intestine** and to a finger-like projection (the **hepatic cecum**) towards the head of the lancelet. Undigested material leaves via the **anus** which is located by the **ventral fin.**

G **Respiratory system.** Gas exchange occurs via primarily across the skin epithelium. There are no blood cells, nor are there any respiratory pigments.

H **Circulatory system.** Lancelets do have a **closed circulatory system,** where the colorless blood stays inside blood vessels. No distinct heart is present. The circulatory system carries digested food and respiratory gases throughout the body.

I **Osmoregulatory excretory systems.** Unlike the vertebrate nephron, metabolic (nitrogenous) wastes are eliminated via **protonephridia** located near the pharynx. Protonephridia accumulate wastes (primarily ammonia) which leaves the body through a pore in the atrium. Although the cephalochordate and flatworm protonephridia resemble each other and work in similar ways, they are considered analogous structures.

a **Reproductive system.** Lancelets have separate sexes (**dioecious**), and **fertilization is external.** Unlike the vertebrates, cephalochordates have numerous paired gonads. Gametes leave the gonads and enter the water through the atrium. The larvae stay in the plankton for a short time, until they settle out and become adults.

Exercise 20.2.

Under the dissecting scope, view the whole mount and demonstration slide of *Amphioxus*, the lancelet. Make a sketch of what you see in the space provided below (Figure 20.3). (See Figure 20.4 and Figure 20.5 to guide you.) We have a whole mount as well as a cross section of the animal. Note that all four chordate characteristics are present. **Note the oral hood, gill slits and pharynx, notochord, nerve cord, tail, intestine, and segmented muscles (myotomes).**

FIGURE 20.3.

The lancelet *Amphioxus.*

In terms of its position, how does the nerve cord of the lancelet (and the chordates) compare to the nerve cord of the protostomes (annelids and molluscs, for example)?

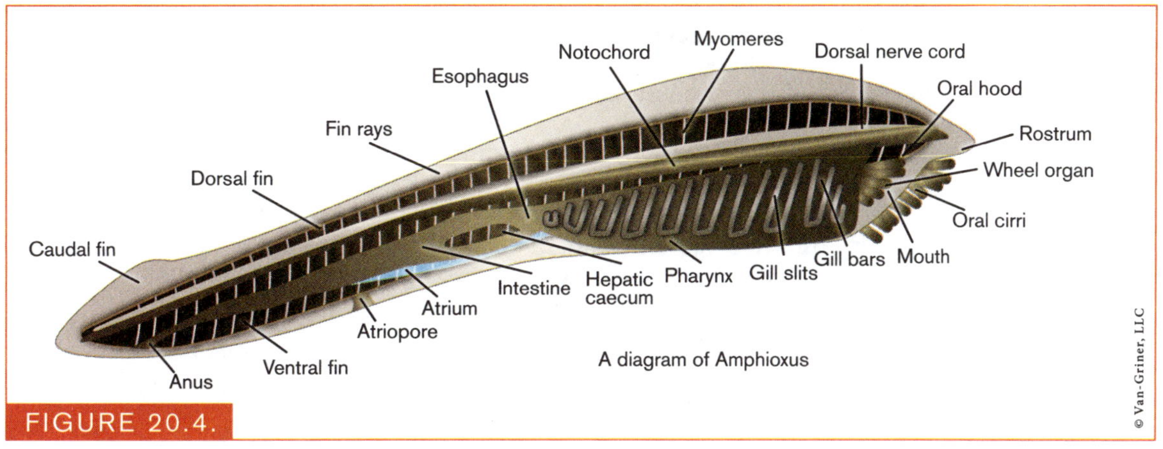

FIGURE 20.4.

Subphylum Cephalochordata (the lancelets).

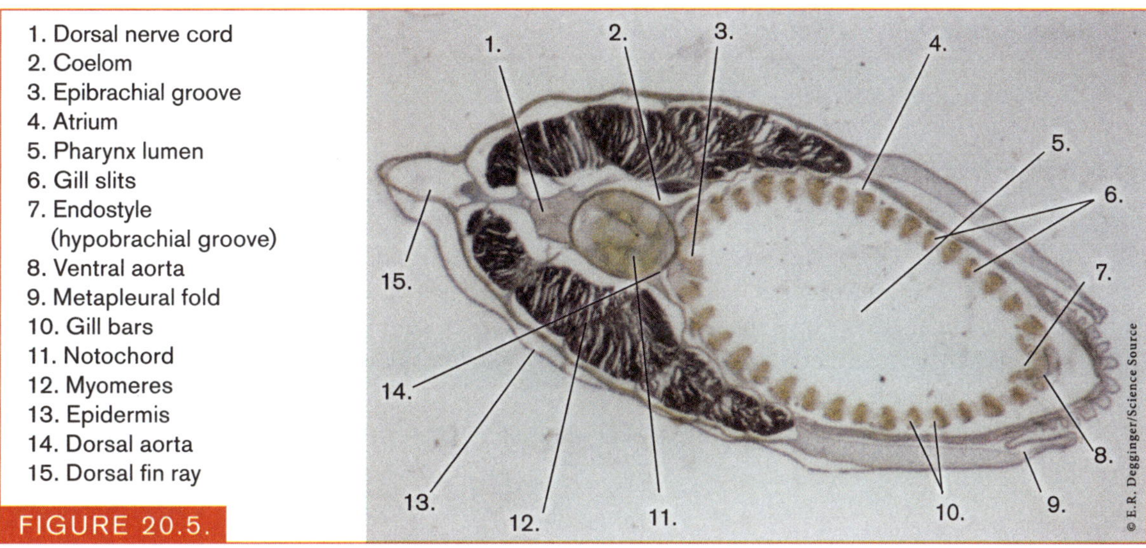

FIGURE 20.5.

Cross section of the lancelet, *Amphioxus,* showing internal structure.

Vertebrate Taxonomy in Flux: Subphylum Vertebrata

A Depending on the textbook, you will see a variety of classification schemes for the chordates. In this class, we will use the following terms and taxa. We will refer to **eight major 'groups' of vertebrates: hagfishes, lampreys, cartilaginous fish, bony fish, amphibians, reptiles, birds, and mammals.** However, the traditional Linnean hierarchical classification scheme does not easily 'fit' the cladistic scheme of the higher animals. For example: should we include birds and mammals in the reptile clade? The 'traditional' taxonomic scheme does not adequately match what we now know of the evolution of the vertebrate clade. Nonetheless, we will use the traditional classification scheme to describe the higher animals.

B **General vertebrate characteristics:**

1 All vertebrates have **vertebrae made of bone (or cartilage).**

2 All vertebrates have a **living endoskeleton** that grows with the animal.

3 All vertebrates have an integument that consists of an inner **dermis** and outer **epidermis.**

4 All vertebrates have **kidneys** with **nephrons.**

5 All vertebrates have **hearts, red blood cells, hemoglobin, and a closed circulatory systems.**

These features allow for rapid movement of materials (gases, wastes, and food) throughout the body. Red blood cells contain large amounts of the protein hemoglobin; housing hemoglobin within cells lowers the osmotic pressures and viscosity that would have to be overcome if all of the hemoglobin molecules were in the plasma. Red blood cells and a pumping heart thus allow for more oxygen to be transported to the body tissues in less time. Deoxygenated blood from the body travels to the heart, which pumps it through the gills for oxygenation. The blood then travels to the rest of the body.

The Eight Vertebrate "Classes"

The 'Agnathans'

The **'Agnathans'** (**Agnatha**) are the jawless vertebrate animals. The term 'agnatha' is an old term not used much in newer texts, but there are two groups of 'jawless vertebrates': the **lampreys** and **hagfishes.** Older texts lump the hagfishes and lampreys with the gnathostomes as a group called the 'vertebrates,' but recent books exclude hagfishes from the vertebrates. Recently, however, hagfish have been found to possess rudimetnary vertebrae, and thus the agnathans have been moved back in with the rest of the vertebrates. Authorities refer to Agnatha as either a superclass or as a subphylum.

Vertebrate Group 1. The Hagfish (Class Myxini)

'**Agnathans**' are the jawless vertebrates and are thought to be the oldest of the major taxa of vertebrates still living. They date back to the Cambrian period over 500 million years ago. These include the **lampreys** and **hagfishes.** Formally, hagfish are in the vertebrate group called **Myxini.**

A **General hagfish characteristics:**

1 Hagfish are marine benthic (bottom-dwelling) predatory/scavenging species that feed on a variety of invertebrates and dead fish. Hagfish have a **rasping tongue with teeth (made of keratin).** Hagfish use their teeth to pull of chunks of their dead prey.

2 The hagfish skeleton is composed of **cartilage.**

3 **Hagfish lack jaws and vertebrae, but they retain the notochord as a support structure.** Like the notochord of the cephalochordates, the hagfish notochord provides a stiff structure for the muscles to exert force against in order to do work.

④ Hagfish have a tubular eel-like body with a paddle-like tail, with many **slime glands on their naked skin** that produce a gooey protective slime (Figure 20.6). The large majority of the cells of the epidermis produce copious mucus, along with the slime glands found in the underlying dermis. They can 'tie' their bodies into a traveling overhand knot (anterior to posterior) to clean off the slime; the knotting behavior and slime may help them escape from predators. In the reverse direction, the knotting behavior may help them penetrate into host bodies, where they feed. Hagfish swim in a serpentine fashion.

⑤ Hagfish have **no paired appendages,** unlike the higher vertebrates.

⑥ Hagfish have a brain that is more primitive than the higher vertebrates, with small or degenerate eyes. They have keen chemosensory abilities, however. They have several sensory **barbels** around the mouth (Figure 20.26), and hagfish (and lampreys) have a single **nostril** where water can enter into a cavity containing chemoreceptors.

⑦ Hagfish possess **one pair of semicircular canals.**

⑧ Hagfish skins lack scales (Figure 20.6).

⑨ Hagfish have **pore-like gill slits.** Hagfish respire in a fashion similar to the sea squirts and lancelets, in that they take water in through their pharynx. The water then travels past internal gill pouches and then the water exists out an opening on the ventral surface. Food enters into the esophagus. Hagfish also respire through their skins, an adaptation that allows them to bury their anterior portion of their body into the host. Cutaneous respiration is important, in that hagfish do not have a muscular operculum to produce current across the gills (as in the case of bony fish).

⑩ Hagfish have a primitive circulatory systems with multiple hearts. Hagfish body fluids are **iso-osmotic with seawater** (i.e., they are osmotic conformers). The hagfish have little capacity to regulate water concentrations nor the ionic composition of their body fluids, but they live in relatively constant marine environments.

⑪ Hagfish are oviparous. They have large, yolky eggs but no independent larval stage; the juvenile hagfish hatch from the eggs.

FIGURE 20.6.

Class Myxini (the hagfish).

Vertebrate Group 2. The Lampreys (Class Cephalaspidomorphi)

A The second group of agnathans are the lamprey eels. The **lampreys** are slender, eel-like, jawless animals. Many lamprey species are found as adults in marine systems, but in a few species, the adults stay in freshwater streams and large lakes. In all species, the adults return to freshwater streams to lay their eggs. For the marine species, the lamprey larvae (the **ammocoetes**) live in freshwater streams for several years, and then return to the sea. The adults are **ectoparasites** on fish.

B **The general characteristics of a lamprey:**

1 The **ammocoete larvae of the lamprey.** The lamprey larvae show all four of the hallmarks of the chordates—a dorsal hollow nerve cord, a notochord, a post-anal tail, and gill slits. Lampreys live as **larvae for long periods** (up to seven years or more) and then develop in short-lived parasitic adults (one to several years). The larvae are suspension feeders, feeding on plankton and detritus. Biologists earlier thought the larvae were separate species. The ammocoetes have several characteristics that are homologous to the higher vertebrates, including a two-chambered heart, a three part brain, (forebrain, midbrain, hindbrain), and thyroid and pituitary glands. The kidney is similar to higher vertebrates.

2 Lampreys have a persistent **notochord** that becomes **partially enclosed by cartilage,** with extensions that surround the nerve cord. For this reason, lampreys are included with the gnathostomes as the vertebrates. The lamprey skeleton is made of **cartilage,** not bone.

3 Lampreys **lack jaws and paired appendages,** like the hagfish.

4 Lampreys have **pore-like gill slits,** like the hagfish.

5 Lampreys have a **circular mouth with keratinized teeth,** a sucker-like oral disk, and a **rasping tongue,** which they use to scrape tissue off of fish. Food (primarily blood from a host fish) enters the mouth and passes from the pharynx into the esophagus, and then into the intestine for digestion and assimilation.

6 Compared to the hagfish, lampreys have well-developed eyes and a more advanced brain. In addition, **two pairs of semicircular canals** and a single nostril (leading to a cavity with chemoreceptors) are present in the lampreys.

7 Lampreys have efficient excretory systems, with **body fluids osmotically and ionically regulated.**

8 Lampreys have **seven pairs of gills** and a **closed circulatory system** similar to bony fish (the lamprey heart consists of **two chambers:** one atrium, one ventricle). The lamprey "breathes" by extracting the oxygen present in the water. Water can enter via the mouth and through the pharynx, and proceeds a chamber (the respiratory tube) where seven gill pouches are located—each pouch is associated with gills and a gill slit. While the lamprey feeds, its mouth is attached to the host fish for long periods of time, thus water cannot enter the mouth to eventually pass by the gills for respiration. Instead, the lamprey can breathe by pumping water in and out through the gill slits.

Exercise 20.3.

The Ammocoete Larvae

The lampreys lay eggs (they are oviparous) and the larvae hatch from the egg outside of the mother. View the ammocoete (lamprey) larvae demonstration slide. These larvae are almost indistinguishable from the adult lancelets, as well as the larval tunicates. They show all four of the hallmarks of the chordates: **dorsal nerve cord, notochord, post anal tail,** and **gill slits.** Draw what you see in the space below (Figure 20.7) and compare the ammocoete larvae to the lancelet (see Figure 20.2 and Figure 20.4).

FIGURE 20.7.

The ammocoete larva of a lamprey.

In what ways are the tunicate larvae and the ammocoete larvae similar?

Exercise 20.4.

The Lamprey Adult

Examine the specimens of lampreys on display. Note the chordate characters that you can see. Examine the mouthparts and the gill slits. Make a sketch in the space provided below (Figure 20.8). Use Figure 20.9 to guide you.

FIGURE 20.8.

Class Cephalaspidomorphi (the lampreys).

Compare the lamprey to the sharks and bony fish. What characteristics are shared by both lampreys and the fish?

FIGURE 20.9.

Class Cephalaspidomorphi (the lampreys).

The 'Gnathostomes'

A Except for the hagfishes and lampreys, the other vertebrate taxa are grouped together as the subphylum (or superclass, in some texts) **Gnathostomata** (the gnathostomes or jawed animals).

B **General gnathostome characteristics:**

1 **Jaws and teeth** allow for capture and rapid ingestion of foods, as well as macerating the food prior to digestion. Most of the gnathostomes have an expansible oral cavity. Macerating the prey kills the prey and increases the surface area of the prey tissues to facilitate digestion.

2 The gnathostomes all have **paired limbs** (pelvic and pectoral limbs).

3 All gnathostomes have **three pairs of semicircular canals.**

4 The gnathostome brain is well-developed (compared to the hagfish). Gnathostomes have advanced sensory organs (eyes, ears, and other sensory organs).

The 'Jawed Fishes'

A "Fishes." Two groups make up the aquatic gnathostome vertebrates: **Chondrichthyes** and **Osteichthyes.**

1 The fish all use **gills** for respiration. Water moves past the gills, and respiratory gases are exchanged between the water and the blood inside the gill capillary beds.

2 Like the lampreys and hagfish, the cartilaginous and bony fish all have closed circulatory systems, including a **heart** with **two chambers** (consisting of one **atrium** and one **ventricle**).

Vertebrate Group 3. The Cartilaginous Fish (Class Chondrichthyes)

A The **Class Chondrichthyes** consist of sharks, skates, rays, and their relatives. They are all marine.

B **General cartilaginous fish characteristics.** The sharks and their relatives share many characteristics with the bony fishes. However, the following are the unique characteristics that all cartilaginous fish share:

1 Sharks and their relatives have a **cartilaginous endoskeleton,** which is lighter than bone. Their ancestors had a bony skeleton, thus this cartilaginous endoskeleton is a derived character.

2 Sharks typically have **placoid scales** in their skin (tooth-like scales that give shark skin a spiny feel to the touch).

3 The **shark's tail provides propulsion, and the fins (pectoral, pelvic, dorsal, and anal) are stabilizers** (Figure 20.11). The buoyancy observed in these fish is maintained in part by large amounts of oils stored in the body; sharks do not have swim bladders. The tail of many sharks is referred to as a **heterocercal** tail; the upper lobe of the caudal fin is larger than the lower lobe of the fin (see Figure 20.11). The shark's vertebral column extends into the upper lobe of the fin.

4 Almost all cartilaginous fish must **continuously swim** in order to remain in the water column and to breathe. Water enters the mouth and passes over the gills, then the water exits through the gill slits located on the side of the body (Figure 20.11). In some of the more sedentary species, a small slit behind the eye, the **spiracle,** helps these sharks pass water over their gills for respiration, without actively swimming. Unlike the bony fish, there is no operculum covering the gills and gill slits.

5 Sharks are **dioecious.** Fertilization is **internal.** All three major types of reproductive strategies observed in the jawed fishes:

> **a** **Oviparous.** A few sharks lay eggs that hatch externally.

> **b** **Ovoviviparous.** Most sharks lay eggs that hatch in the female's reproductive system. The egg yolk and glands within the reproductive tract nourish the embryos.

> **c** **Viviparous.** A few sharks bear live young; there are no 'eggs' laid initially. The young are nourished in a fashion similar to the placental mammals.

6 The blood of these marine animals is typically iso-osmotic to seawater. Sharks excrete **urea.**

Exercise 20.5.

Observe the representative cartilaginous fish we have on display, using to guide you. You may wish to make a sketch in the space provided below (Figure 20.10).

FIGURE 20.10.

Class Chondrichthyes: the sharks, skates, rays, and their relatives.

FIGURE 20.11.

Class Chondrichthyes: the sharks, skates, rays, and their relatives.

1. Spiracle	4. Posterior dorsal fin	6. Eye	9. Pelvic fin
2. Lateral line	5. Caudal fin	7. Gill slits	10. Anal fin
3. Anterior dorsal fin	(heterocercal tail)	8. Pectoral fin	

'Class' Osteichthyes

Some textbooks refer to the bony fish as a single class ('Class Osteichthyes') but in reality, what we call 'bony fish' is composed of two (or three, depending on the taxonomic authority) distinct classes, which some texts lump together as the 'Superclass Osteichthyes.'

A The first class (and the largest in terms of species) are called the ray-finned fishes (**Class Actinopterygii**). This class includes many fish that you are familiar with, such as the perches, sunfishes, and catfishes. The fins are supported by thin, parallel bony rays that stiffen the fin. There are no muscles located in the fins; instead, the muscles that move the fins are found within the body of the fish.

B The second class of bony fish are called the lobe-finned fishes (**Class Sarcopterygii**). They have long, fleshy muscular lobes to their fins, the lobes contain articulated bones that are extensions of the pectoral and pelvic areas. The bony rays are on the ends of the lobes, and the fin rays can be moved independently by muscles inside the lobe.

C The third class of bony fish are called the lungfishes (**Class Dipnoi**). In some texts, the Dipnoi are identified as a subclass of the Sarcopterygii, so in those texts, there are two classes of bony fish.

Some authorities refer to the three fishes as belonging to 'Superclass Osteichthyes.' **For purposes of this lab, we will lump the three bony fish groups together and simply refer to them as the 'Class Osteichthyes.'**

Vertebrate Group 4. The Bony Fishes

A The basic characteristics that all bony fish share are as follows:

1 The body fish skeleton is made of **bone.**

2 Bony fish are found in both marine and freshwater environments.

3 Bony fish have air-filled **swim bladders** that help them stay in the water column and conserve energy by remaining stationary.

4 Gas exchange occurs by drawing water over the **four or five pairs of gills** located in gill chambers covered by the **operculum** (Figure 20.13), a protective flap of tissue. The water enters the mouth, passes through the gills, and exits out the gill slits under the operculum by pumping action of the muscles of the gill chamber and the operculum.

5 **Tails and flexible fins.** The paired limbs of the fishes allowed for greater directional control of movement. The dorsal fins, the anal fins of the ventral surface, and the pectoral fins and pelvic fins all aid in movement and do not just serve as stabilizers, as seen in the sharks. The anterior pectoral fins and the posterior pelvic fins are analogous to the forelimbs and hindlimbs of the tetrapods, respectively. The pectoral and pelvic fins tilt the fish up or down (adjust the pitch) and allow the fish to move forward or backward, up or down, and sideways and to slow down, and stop in the water. The cartilaginous fish and bony fish have dorsal fins and anal fins (on the ventral surface) that provide stabilization from yaw (swiveling left or right) and roll (rolling left or right). The caudal fin of the tail provides most of the thrust in bony fish, but the pectoral and pelvic fins are mobile and also provide thrust (Figure 20.13).

6 The skin of bony fish are not naked, like the primitive hagfish and lampreys. The integuments of fish and amphibians is composed on an outer epidermis and an inner dermis. There are multiple layers of live cells in the fish (and amphibian) epidermis. **Scales** (that are more flattened than those of the shark) are embedded in the bony fishes' dermis; these scales help to prevent water diffusing across the skin. These scales, along with mucus glands that create a slimy **mucus,** protect the bony fish from physical damage and from bacteria and fungi.

7 Most bony fish (both the freshwater and marine species), are good **osmoregulators.** Osmoregulation is a function of both the gills and the kidneys. Most of the nitrogen wastes are eliminated in the form of **ammonia** at the **gills** and by the **kidney.** The kidney contains many **nephridia.** Nephridia filter ammonia and other wastes from the blood; these wastes are then passed out of the body.

8 Bony fish (and the cartilaginous fish) have a **two-chambered heart** (one atrium, one ventricle) and a **closed circulatory system.** The fish heart pumps blood that travels in a single loop throughout the body. The blood goes from the heart (through the aorta) to the gills, then from the gills to the rest of the body, and then back to the heart through a major vein).

9 Bony fish use **external fertilization.** The males shed sperm into the water when the females extrude eggs (**oviparous**). These eggs contain a large amount of yolk.

10 Bony fish, like all vertebrates, have a **well-developed brain, spinal cord, and a complex set of sensory organs to detect their environment.** For example, sharks and bony fish have well-developed eyes and **nostrils.** However, the nostrils of cartilaginous fish, bony fish, hagfish and lampreys do not open into the pharynx like the terrestrial vertebrates. Instead, water enters the nostrils and passes by nasal chemoreceptors, which detect chemicals in the water. Sharks and bony fish (as well as the larval amphibians) have a **lateral line organ** (Figures 20.11 and 20.13) in the epidermis that can detect small changes in water movement. The lateral line organ in some fish senses electrical fields as well.

11 Bony fish and cartilaginous fish are primarily **carnivorous,** feeding on other fish and smaller invertebrates. Their digestive system is like all other vertebrates, in that it is complete and has regional specialization. As a fish ingests its food, the food enters the mouth with the water. The water then passes through the gills (located in the pharynx). Finally, the water leaves through an opening covered by the operculum. The food enters the esophagus, which leads to the stomach and then the intestine, where chemical digestion occurs and the nutrients are assimilated. Undigested materials are expelled out the anus. Cartilaginous fish and most bony fish swallow their food whole or in chunks, using sharp teeth to hold onto prey; however, some fish have flat teeth back in the pharynx to crush shells and hard body parts of their prey.

Exercise 20.6.

Observe the representative bony fishes we have on display. Make a sketch of a representative fish in the space below (Figure 20.12), and label its external features. See Figure 20.13 to guide you.

FIGURE 20.12.

Class Osteichthyes (the bony fish).

FIGURE 20.13.

Class Osteichthyes (the bony fish).

'Tetrapoda': The Four-Limbed Animals

Some texts lump amphibians, reptiles, birds, and mammals together as one group: the 'Superclass Tetrapoda.' Tetrapods are primarily freshwater and terrestrial animals. They evolved from lobe-finned fishes that were present during the Devonian. Tetrapods have two pairs of limbs and can breathe air through two nostrils that open into the pharynx. Air passes by chemoreceptors located in the nasal cavity, in a way analogous to water moving through fish nostrils into a closed cavity. The tetrapods are divided into the Amphibians and the three **Amniote** classes (reptiles, birds, and mammals).

Vertebrate Group 5. Amphibians (Class Amphibia)

A Class Amphibia includes the frogs, toads, and salamanders. The amphibians are the oldest tetrapod group.

B **General amphibian characteristics:**

1 Amphibians generally have **four limbs** with webbed toes (digits, Figure 20.15). A few species lack legs and thus appear more snake-like. Note the elongated hind feet and the positions of the knee, ankle, elbow, and wrist of a frog.

2 Amphibians must **return to water to lay their eggs** (which lack a shell). Amphibian eggs dry out quickly and the embryos die if the eggs are left on land, or if their habitat dries up.

3 Amphibians show **metamorphosis. Eggs** of many species (but not all) hatch into larvae (tadpoles) that metamorphose into the adult, and the adult may be aquatic or terrestrial. Amphibians are generally **dioecious.** Many amphibians have **external fertilization,** with the males spreading sperm over extruded eggs by the female. In some of the more terrestrial salamanders, fertilization is internal, with the transfer of spermatophores (which contain sperm) into the female's reproductive tract.

④ Amphibian adults still have to stay moist if on land because the skin is a major respiratory organ. Even those species that possess lungs still breathe through their skin. The integument consists of an epidermis, composed of multiple layers of live cells, and an underlying dermis. They lack scales, but amphibians possess mucous glands and poison glands that are located in the dermis. Amphibians cannot travel far from water. Some amphibians retain the gills of larval stages, but some produce primitive lungs in addition to breathing through their skin.

⑤ Amphibians have **closed circulatory systems with a three-chambered heart** (two atria, one ventricle) and a separate pulmonary and systemic circulatory systems (the **double circulatory system**).

In amphibians, there are two loops to the circulatory system. One loop (the **pulmonary circuit**) travels from the heart to the pulmonary capillary beds of the surface of the body, where gas exchange occurs. Blood then is returned to the heart via veins. A second loop carries oxygenated blood to the rest of the body for gas exchange (the **systemic circuit**). As the blood leaves the ventricle, some of the blood is carried to the pulmonary circuit, some to the systemic circuit. A potential disadvantage of the three-chambered heart is that the oxygenated and deoxygenated blood may mix.

⑥ The basic **skeletal system** of the amphibians is the same as all tetrapods: four major limbs (two pairs) that support and move the body. In order to support the body on land and allow for movement, the tetrapod skeleton is modified from the basic fish plan. Amphibians do not have a rib cage or a muscular diaphragm.

⑦ The amphibians usually eliminate **urea** as their nitrogenous wastes, but some species also eliminate ammonia. Many amphibians do not 'drink' to replace water lost by desiccation, they thus minimize evaporative water loss by primarily being nocturnal and residing in humid habitats. Water is taken up across the body wall by immersing the body in water.

⑧ Amphibians generally are **carnivores,** with **complete digestive tracts.** Amphibians lack teeth, so they cannot chew; they generally swallow their food whole.

⑨ Amphibian larvae and some adults have **lateral line organs,** similar to that seen in the fish.

⑩ The larvae of the amphibians must live in water. They are referred to as **tadpoles.** Tadpoles hatch from the eggs. Tadpoles respire through their skin and through gills. As the tadpole matures, it typically reabsorbs its tail and undergoes metamorphosis by gradually growing limbs. The tadpoles develop lungs and they begin to breathe air. The tadpole's mouth enlarges, and the intestines of many tadpoles shorten (carnivore intestines generally are shorter than herbivore intestines). Larval tadpoles generally are herbivores, but a few will eat other tadpoles, including conspecifics.

⑪ Amphibians have similar senses as do the fish and the other tetrapods. They have **eyes** with lenses, corneas, and retinas. Amphibians breathe air with their mouths closed. They have **external nostrils** on top of the head in front of their eyes; air moves through the external nostrils and exits into the mouth through the **internal nostrils,** then they gulp the air to their lungs. The **tympanum** (tympanic membrane, Figure 20.15) behind each eye detects sound. They do not have the outer ear (pinna) of a mammal.

Exercise 20.7.

Observe the representative amphibians we have on display. Make a sketch of several amphibians in the space provided below (Figure 20.14). Use Figure 20.15 to guide you.

FIGURE 20.14.

Sketches of various amphibians.

What characteristics do bony fish and amphibians both share?

What characteristics do amphibians possess that are not found in fish?

FIGURE 20.15.

Class Amphibia (the amphibians: frogs, toads, and salamanders).

1. Ankle	4. Eyes	7. Brachium (upper arm)
2. Knee	5. Nostrils (nares)	8. Elbow and antebrachium (forearm)
3. Foot with digits	6. Tympanic membrane	9. Digits

The 'Amniotes': Reptiles, Birds, and Mammals

The Amniota consists of three classes: reptiles, birds and mammals. The evolution of the amniotic egg helped the successful establishment of vertebrates on land. Many adaptations had to arise for the reptiles to evolve from the amphibians. One important adaptation is the **amniotic egg.** The amniotic egg is **shelled** to prevent desiccation, and the egg has a series of **extraembryonic membranes** (amnion, chorion, allantois, and egg sac) that help the embryo develop totally inside a terrestrial egg (Figure 20.16). These membranes cushion the embryo, keep it moist, help it respire, and store food and wastes within the egg, until the young animal can hatch.

A The amniotic extraembryonic membranes

1 The **chorion** is the outermost membrane. It is involved in gas exchange from the embryo and the outside, through the shell, and it helps to cut down on water loss. In the placental mammals, the chorion helps to produce the placenta.

2 The **allantois** allows a place to store wastes (other than ammonia) and allows for water conservation. The allantois is also involved in gas exchange.

3 The **yolk sac** surround the yolk. The **yolk** and **albumin** provide nutrients.

4 The **amnion** is the fourth and innermost membrane. It immediately surrounds the embryo and the amniotic fluid. The amnion allows the embryos to be bathed in the amniotic fluid. The amniotic cavity prevents dehydration and cushions the embryo.

B **General amniote characteristics:**

1 The four extraembryonic membranes, described above.

2 All amniotes have **closed** circulatory systems with a **three-chambered or four-chambered heart.**

3 The amniotes may eliminate primarily **urea,** or other chemicals, such as **uric acid.** Because they are terrestrial, reptiles, birds, and mammals have more advanced excretory systems. They cannot use ammonia as a major form of nitrogen waste disposal because of the large amount of water required to flush ammonia from the body.

4 Another important adaptation for the amniotes is a **tough leathery skin** that protects them against desiccation and physical injury, compared to the moist, sensitive skin of the amphibians. The integument is composed of a multilayered epidermis consisting of mostly dead cells containing large amount of keratin, and a thick dermal layer where sensory organs, connective tissues, adipose tissues, and circulatory tissues are located. The amniote skin is much less permeable to water, compared to the fish and amphibians. Unlike amphibians, most amniotes also have **claws** (toenails and talons) made of keratin; claws help in locomotion, prey capture, defense, and for digging or climbing.

5 Amniotes also have **strong jaw muscles that provide more mechanical advantage** to crush or grip prey. The **jaws** come from modification of the pharyngeal slit arches.

6 The reptiles, birds, and mammals also have **internal fertilization.** This type of reproduction is required in order to have a shelled egg because the sperm must reach the egg before the egg is enclosed.

7 Amniotes also have **more efficient circulatory systems** (compared to the amphibians) with higher blood pressures in order to move more oxygen per unit time to the muscles and other organs. Amniotes are metabolically quite active.

8 In addition to possessing efficient circulatory systems that help to maintain high metabolic rates, amniotes have more efficient lungs than amphibians. All amniotes have a **rib cage** composed of rib bones and associated muscles and connective tissues; the muscles of the rib cage help to ventilate the lungs. Mammals use a negative pressure breathing system, which pulls in air like a suction pump. Mammals expand the thoracic cavity via the actions of the **diaphragm** and the rib cage muscles, whereas the amphibians (frogs, for example) use **positive pressure breathing**—'gulping' in air by the action of the oral cavity muscles.

Exercise 20.8.

Examine the depiction of the amniotic egg at the demonstration table. Make a sketch of the drawings and write down the basic functions of each membrane in the space below (Figure 20.16).

FIGURE 20.16.

The amniotic egg.

Vertebrate Group 6. The Reptiles (Class Reptilia)

A **Class Reptilia** (snakes, crocodiles, turtles and lizards). Almost all reptiles live on land.

B **General reptilian characteristics:**

1 Most reptiles have four limbs with toes (digits). However, limbs are absent in snakes and some lizards.

2 The **amniotic egg** helped reptiles (and eventually birds and mammals) to colonize land. The reptilian **egg** is covered with a **calcareous or leathery shell.**

3 There are no free-living larval stages in reptiles, birds, and mammals.

4 Most reptiles are **oviparous,** but they use internal fertilization. Reptiles have a penis to transfer sperm into the tract of the female.

5 Reptiles are **dioecious.** Because of the amniotic egg and the necessity of a shell, all fertilization in the amniotes must be internal.

6 In the dermis, reptiles have **scales** made of **keratin** that help prevent desiccation (Figure 20.18). The reptilian scales arise from the epidermis, while the scales in the bony and cartilaginous fish arise from the dermis. Some spines are elongated into distinct spikes that protrude from the skin. Some have bony dermal plates (for example, turtles). **Hair** (mammals) and **feathers** (birds) are modified scales. All reptiles periodically shed their outer epidermal layers (the shedding process is called **ecdysis**). The integument consists of an epidermis and dermis. The epidermis is composed of multiple layers of cells. Several layers of dead cells filled with keratin are on the outer surface, with a layer of living mitotically active cells underneath. Fish, amphibians and reptiles have relatively colorless skin; they all have **chromatophores** in the dermis that contain melanin or other pigments. The reptilian skin is dry with relatively few mucous glands present.

7 The reptiles evolved a distinct, efficient **lung** for gas exchange. Air enters the mouth and nostrils. Reptiles ventilate lungs by the contraction of rib cage muscles, or by buccal pumping. The crocodiles have a muscular diaphragm that is analogous to the mammalian diaphragm. The reptilian diaphragm pulls on part of the pelvis and the liver that moves posteriorly during contraction of the diaphragm. This movement provides space for the lungs to expand.

8 The circulatory plan of reptiles is based on the amphibian plan. The majority of reptiles have a **three-chambered heart** (two atria and one ventricle). However, the ventricle is incompletely divided into two, thus functionally acting as two distinct chambers. In the crocodilians, this ventricular septum is complete and they thus have four chambers. Reptiles have a double circulatory system. The red blood cells are **nucleated** when mature.

9 Most reptiles are **ectotherms** (meaning that their body temperature is dependent on the external temperature). However, some reptiles can maintain a more or less constant internal temperature via behavioral adaptations.

10 The basic skeletal plan of the reptile is similar to the ancestral amphibian plan, but with more ossification for greater support of weight. The body is supported by limbs and by girdles (pelvic and pectoral girdles), except for most snakes, who have lost their limbs over time. Air is less buoyant than water, thus the skeletal system must support the weight of the body.

11 Reptiles have efficient **kidneys** (metanephric kidneys with nephrons) and usually use **uric acid** as their metabolic wastes, thus they are able to conserve more water than the amphibians. Recall that uric acid is relatively nontoxic and requires little water to eliminate. The embryonic kidneys of reptiles are like that of amphibians and fish (remember they are in the fluid environment of the amniotic egg). Many reptiles forage and move about only at night in the hot deserts, also avoiding evaporative water loss. Because they can conserve water, reptiles were able to colonize even the harshest desert habitats. A number of reptiles also have **salt glands,** which are used to secrete excess salts while conserving water.

12 Like all chordates, reptiles have **complete digestive systems** with regional specializations for acquiring, storing, and digesting food. **Reptiles are primarily carnivores,** although a few reptiles feed on plants or carrion as well. Although they have jaws and teeth, most reptiles cannot 'chew' their food, they either swallow food whole, or swallow chunks bitten off of their food.

13 Reptiles do not have outer ears (pinnae), but they have a tympanum (eardrum or tympanic membrane) that can be covered with a thin layer of skin, a middle ear (with a single earbone) and an inner ear. Reptiles vary in visual acuity, but some can see infrared heat energy.

Exercise 20.9.

Observe the representative reptiles we have on display, and note their characteristics. Make a sketch of various reptiles in the space provided below (Figure 20.17). Use Figure 20.18 to guide you.

FIGURE 20.17.

Sketches of various reptiles.

FIGURE 20.18.

A horned lizard, *Phrynosoma platyrhinos* Class Reptilia.

Vertebrate Group 7. The Birds (Class Aves)

A **Class Aves** (the birds). The birds evolved from reptilian (theropod dinosaurs). Birds retained the amniotic egg and other reptilian characteristics. Many taxonomists now lump birds with the crocodiles and alligators.

B **General avian characteristics:**

1 Distinct characteristics include the modified scales called **feathers** (Figure 20.20), which are involved in both **flight** and in thermoregulation. The forelimbs of most birds are adapted for flight and their hind legs are still covered in scales (usually four toes, fewer in some). The bird integument is similar to that of the reptiles and mammals (epidermis and dermis), except that feathers are produced instead of plate-like scales. They have **beaks** (Figure 20.20) which are extensions of the upper and lower jaw; beaks manipulate objects, acquire and hold on to food, feed young, and are used in grooming and courtship.

2 Birds are **oviparous** (they lay eggs with a calcareous shell).

3 Birds have two sexes, male and female (they are **dioecious**).

4 The birds are primarily terrestrial and some birds walk or hop along the ground. However, most birds can **fly,** due to: a) their feathers, b) their strong breast muscles that are adapted for flight, and c) the **strong, yet light, bony skeleton.** Many of the bird bones are hollow. The bird wing acts as a airfoil.

5 The birds have a **four-chambered heart** and double circulation, and **efficient respiratory systems** with ribs (with rib bones and associated muscles), lungs, and air sacs. Birds do not have a diaphragm.

6 The birds are **endotherms.** Their body temperature stays constant over a range of ambient temperatures.

7 Like reptiles, the mature red blood cells of the birds are **nucleated.**

8 Birds possess a **single bone in middle ear.**

9 The birds' jaws (the upper maxilla and the lower mandible) are made of bone. They are covered with horny sheaths made of keratin. The jaws are called the **beak. No teeth are present** in modern birds, but some have small serrations along the edge of the beak. The strong beak is adapted for various tasks: capturing prey, crushing seeds, and holding objects.

10 Birds use **uric acid** as their main metabolic waste and have very efficient kidneys with nephrons. This allows them to be terrestrial, like reptiles and mammals, because it cuts down the amount of water needed for excretion. Like some reptiles, some birds also have **salt glands** that function in osmoregulation. These glands are located near the eyes and help excrete excess salts.

11 The birds' ureters open into the **cloaca.** There is no bladder.

12 Some birds are herbivores but many birds are carnivores, feeding upon annelids, snails, many arthropods, fish, and on reptiles, other birds, and small mammals. Birds do not have teeth, so they cannot chew their food like mammals. Instead they swallow prey whole, using their muscular gizzard to grind up food. .

13 Birds have a well-developed **brain,** with a large cerebrum. Birds are thus capable of complex instinctive and learned behaviors.

Exercise 20.10.

Observe the representative birds we have on display, and note their basic characteristics. Make a sketch of a bird in the space below (Figure 20.19). Use Figure 20.20 to guide you.

FIGURE 20.19.

A sketch of birds.

FIGURE 20.20.

A Robin, *Turdus migratorius*, Class Aves.

Vertebrate Group 8. The Mammals (Class Mammalia)

A Mammals are descended from a reptilian group called the **therapsids.**

B **General mammalian characteristics:**

1 Compared to fish, amphibians, reptiles, and birds, mammals have a leathery **skin** with modified scales called **hair** (Figure 20.21). A number of associated organs are found in the mammalian skin, including sebaceous glands and **sweat glands.** Sweat glands secrete water and the evaporation of water from the skin cools the body.

2 Mammals have **mammary glands** that produce **milk** to nourish young.

3 Mammalian **teeth** are highly modified for different functions. Mammals, as well as some of the reptiles, are referred to as the **heterodonts**—those animals that have more than one type of tooth morphology (incisors, canines, and molars, for example).

4 In mammals, modifications of bones of the ancestral reptile jaw (from the gill arches of ancient ancestors) create three **inner ear bones** or auditory ossicles.

5 Another important mammalian character is the **secondary palate** (the hard and soft palate), which separates the oral cavity from the nasal cavity. The secondary palate allows mammals (and some reptiles) to both breathe and hold things in their mouth (or chew food) at the same time.

6 Mammals have an efficient respiratory system with a muscular **diaphragm** that helps ventilate the lungs. The diaphragm separates the thoracic cavity from the abdominal cavity.

7 The mammals are **endotherms.**

8 All mammals have a **four-chambered heart** analogous to that seen in the birds. Mammals have separate systemic and pulmonary circulatory systems (double circulation).

9 Mammals have **non-nucleated, biconcave red blood cells** when mature. The mature red blood cells of all other vertebrates retain their nuclei when mature.

10 Most mammals are **dioecious** with internal fertilization. Some mammals lay eggs (the **oviparous monotremes**), and some mammals give birth to live young (the **viviparous placental** or **eutherian** mammals). The **placenta** of the placental mammals is derived from the lining of the mother's uterus and from extraembryonic membranes (the chorion) of the embryo. The placenta transfers gases, wastes, and nutrients between mother and offspring.

11 Most mammals use **urea** as their metabolic wastes. The kidneys and nephrons are highly advanced and are involved in both osmoregulation and excretion of nitrogenous wastes. Urine is stored in a muscular **bladder** prior to elimination.

12 A variety of feeding styles are found in mammals. Some mammals are herbivores, but many are carnivores. Some mammals, including humans, are **omnivores,** which eat both plant and animal matter.

13 Mammals have the most **highly specialized and advanced brains** (the largest cerebrum), with a high capacity to learning and memory. The brain's cerebrum is highly convoluted. Many mammals, except for some aquatic species, have distinct outer ears (pinnae) for collecting and localizing sound. Many mammals have sharp eyesight and smell.

A gray squirrel, *Sciurus carolinesis,* Class Mammalia.

Exercise 20.11.

Human Gross Anatomy

Animal tissues (which we will cover next time) form various layers that in turn combine to form the organs of the animals. For our discussion of mammalian internal anatomy, we will examine the major organs in a human torso. Be able to identify the following major organs of the human head, thorax and abdomen, noting their relative positions to each other:

Nervous and endocrine systems. Brain, spinal cord, pituitary, adrenal glands, gonads, thyroid, and parathyoid glands, thymus, and pineal glands (Figure 20.22).

Excretory system. Kidney, ureter, urethra, and bladder (Figure 20.23).

Respiratory system. Pharynx, larynx, trachea, bronchi, lungs, alveoli (Figure 20.24).

Digestive system and nearby organs. Mouth, teeth, tongue, salivary glands, liver, gall bladder, pancreas, esophagus, stomach, diaphragm, spleen, small intestine (duodenum, jejunum, and ileum), large intestine (cecum, ascending, transverse, descending and sigmoidal portions of the colon, rectum, and anus), sphincter muscles (Figure 20.25).

Reproductive system. Ovaries and testes, uterus, cervix, vagina, labia minora, labia majora, clitoris, penis, glans penis, oviduct (fallopian tube or uterine tube), prostate, scrotum (Figure 20.26).

Circulatory system (heart and associated major blood vessels). Heart (left and right atria, left and right ventricles), aorta, posterior and anterior vena cava, pulmonary arteries, and pulmonary veins.

Trace the route of blood as it passes through the heart and the systemic and pulmonary circulatory systems and know its status (oxygenated or deoxygenated) in each vessel or structure. Note the position of the **spinal cord,** relative to the trachea, the **esophagus,** and the major blood vessels: the **aorta** and the **vena cava.**

The Human Endocrine System

1 Hypothalamus and pituitary gland. The **pituitary gland** is composed of the **anterior pituitary** and the **posterior pituitary.** Most pituitary gland secretions are controlled by the **hypothalamus** (which is part of the brain). In humans, the pituitary is a pea-sized organ located at the base of the brain, in the center of the head.

The hormone-releasing cells of the hypothalamus produce chemicals that either affect the activity of the pituitary or are directly released in the blood as hormones. **Releasing hormones** make the anterior pituitary release its hormones. **Inhibiting hormones** from the hypothalamus make the anterior pituitary stop releasing hormones. The releasing hormones and inhibiting hormones are released into a capillary system (portal vessels) that run to a capillary bed in the anterior pituitary. Every anterior pituitary hormone has at least one releasing hormone and several have an inhibiting hormone.

2 The **anterior pituitary** produces a number of hormones that have a wide ranging effect on the human body: affecting metabolism, growth and reproduction. The anterior pituitary releases hormones from the actions of releasing hormones produced by the hypothalamus.

3 The **thyroid gland** is found in the neck in front of the trachea and consists of two lobes. The thyroid gland contains many follicles in these lobes. The follicles are fluid-filled and contain a colloid that in turn stores the thyroid hormones. Thyroid hormones are involved in the regulation of body metabolism and the concentrations of blood calcium and phosphate.

4 The **parathyroid glands** are located on the posterior surface of the thyroid. They are four small glands that are associated with capillaries. The glands produce hormones involved in blood calcium levels.

5 The **pancreas** secretes digestive juices (enzymes) as well as hormones (thus it is both an endocrine gland and an exocrine gland). The pancreas secretes glucagon and insulin, hormones that regulate blood glucose levels.

6 The **adrenal glands** are located on top of the kidneys. Some of the hormones from these glands increases heart rate, metabolic rate, blood pressure, and breathing rate, among other effects. All of these effects prepare the animal for fighting or fleeing from danger. Other hormones are involved in osmoregulation and ion regulation.

7 The **pineal gland** is in the center of the brain, attached to the thalamus. The pineal gland secretes melatonin (a modified amino acid) in response to varying light conditions (affects sleep) and is important for regulating annual cycles in many animals.

8 The **thymus** lies behind the sternum and between the lungs. The thymus secretes thymosins, which in turn affect the production of certain lymphocytes, which in turn are involved in immunity.

9 **The gonads. Ovaries** produce estrogens and progesterone (and ova), while **testes** produce testosterone and other androgens (and sperm).

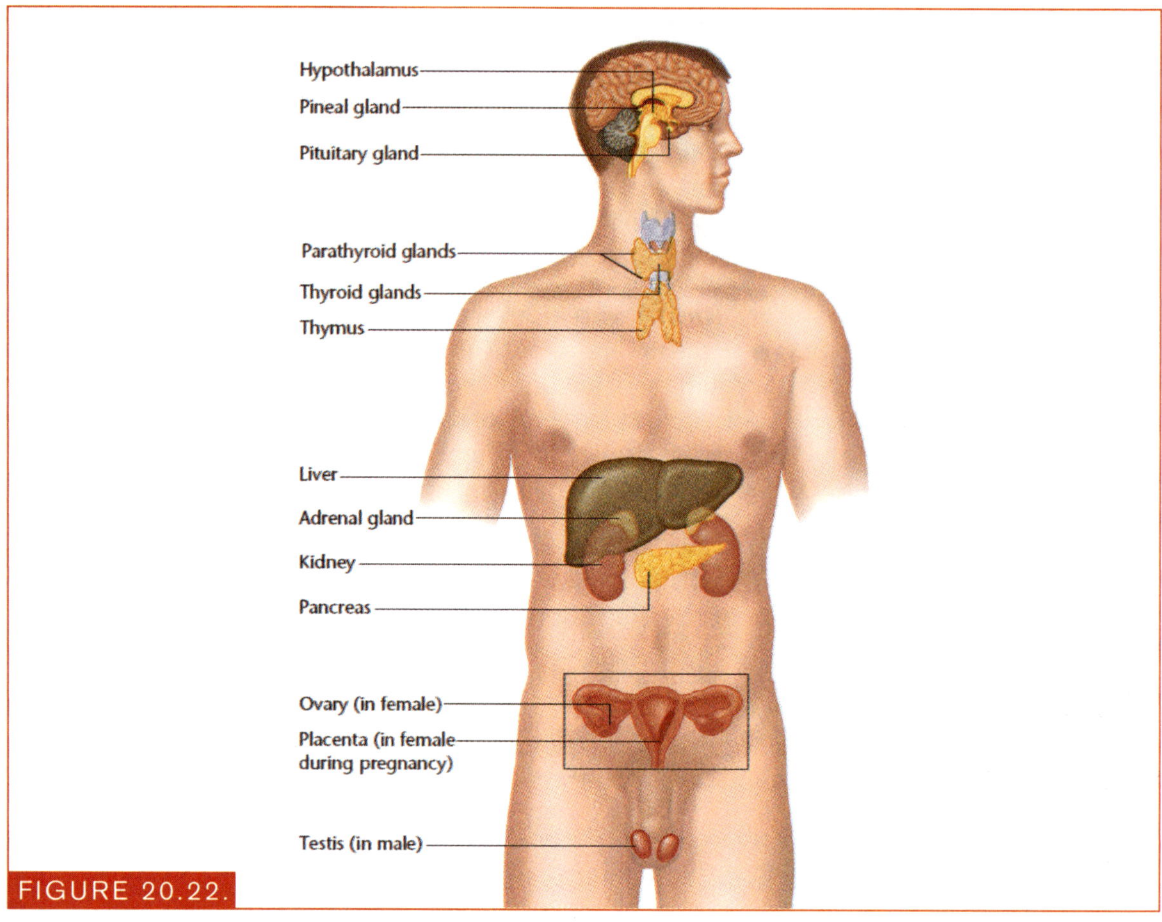

The major organs of the human endocrine system.

The Human Urinary (Excretory) System

1 The fist-sized human kidney has two distinct regions: the outer **cortex** and the inner **medulla.**

2 Numerous **nephrons** and associated blood vessels are in the medulla and cortex. Nitrogen wastes (particularly urea) and other materials are filtered and concentrated here.

3 The **ureters.** The ureter extends from kidney to urinary bladder. The ureters are about 25 cm long in humans. Peristaltic waves in smooth muscles around the ureters forces urine to the bladder. A flaplike fold of mucous membrane exists between ureter and bladder to prevent the backup of urine into the ureter.

4 The **bladder.** The spherical bladder stores urine and forces it into the urethra. A muscular sphincter prevents the emptying of the bladder via muscular contractions until a certain volume is present, then the muscle relaxes and through a **urinary reflex,** urine is allowed to leave the bladder

5 Urine leaves the bladder and enters the **urethra,** which is the short tube that leads to the outside of the body.

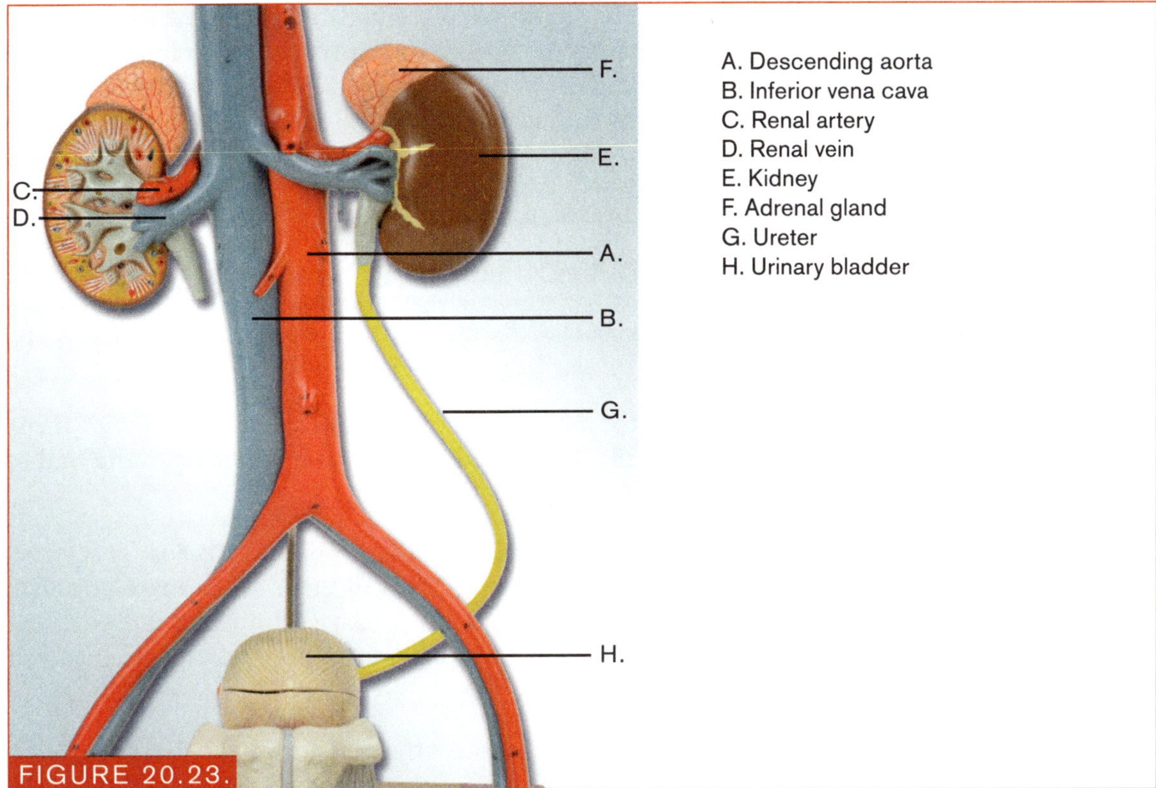

The major organs glands of the human excretory (urinary) system.

The Human Respiratory System

1 Located in the thoracic (chest) cavity, the lungs have a spongy texture and are honeycombed with a moist epithelium that functions as the respiratory surface.

2 Air enters through the **nostrils** and **mouth** and is then filtered by hairs, warmed and humidified, and sampled for odors as it flows through the nasal cavity.

3 The nasal cavity leads to the **pharynx,** and when the glottis is open, air enters the **larynx,** the upper part of the respiratory tract. The wall of the larynx is reinforced by cartilage. In most mammals, the larynx is adapted as a voice box in which vibrations of a pair of **vocal cords** produce sounds.

4 From the larynx, air passes into the **trachea,** or windpipe, whose shape is maintained by rings of cartilage.

5 The trachea forks into two **bronchi. One bronchus** leads into each lung which consists of two or three lobes. Within the lung, each bronchus branches repeatedly into finer and finer tubes, called **bronchioles.** The epithelium lining the major branches of the respiratory tree is covered by cilia and a thin film of moist mucus produced by the epithelium. The reason respiratory surfaces have to be moist is that gases (oxygen and carbon dioxide) can only cross cell membranes if they are dissolved in water. The mucus traps dust, pollen, and other particulate contaminants, and the beating cilia move the mucus upward to the pharynx, where it is swallowed.

6 At the ends of the bronchioles are short tubes (alveolar ducts) that lead to clusters of air sacs called **alveoli.** Gas exchange occurs across the thin epithelium of the lung's millions of alveoli. Oxygen in the air entering the alveoli dissolves in the moist film and rapidly diffuses across the epithelium into a web of capillaries that surrounds each alveolus. Carbon dioxide diffuses in the opposite direction.

Our lungs are ventilated by **negative pressure breathing.**

a This works like a suction pump, pulling air instead of pushing it into the lungs.

b Muscle action changes the volume of the rib cage and the chest cavity, and the lungs follow suit.

c The lungs are enclosed by a pair of membranes (the **pleura membranes**), with the inner layer adhering to the outside of the lungs and the outer layer adhering to the wall of the chest cavity.

d A thin space filled with fluid separates the two pleura membranes. Because of surface tension, the two layers behave like two plates of glass stuck together by the adhesion and cohesion of a film of water. The layers can slide smoothly past each other, but they cannot be pulled apart easily. Surface tension couples movements of the lungs to movements of the rib cage.

e Lung volume increases as a result of contraction of the rib muscles and **diaphragm,** a sheet of skeletal muscle that forms the bottom wall of the chest cavity. Contraction of the **rib muscles** expands the rib cage by pulling the ribs upward and the breastbone outward. At the same time, the diaphragm contracts and descends like a piston.

f The actions of the rib cage muscles and the diaphragm increase the lung volume, and as a result, air pressure within the alveoli becomes lower than the outer atmospheric pressure. Air thus flows into the respiratory system with an inhalation.

g During exhalation, the rib muscles and diaphragm relax. This reduces lung volume and increases air pressure within the alveoli. This forces air up the breathing tubes and out through the nostrils.

h Actions of the rib muscles and diaphragm accounts for changes in lung volume during shallow breathing, when a mammal is at rest. During vigorous exercise, other muscles of the neck, back, and chest further increase ventilation volume by raising and expanding the rib cage even farther.

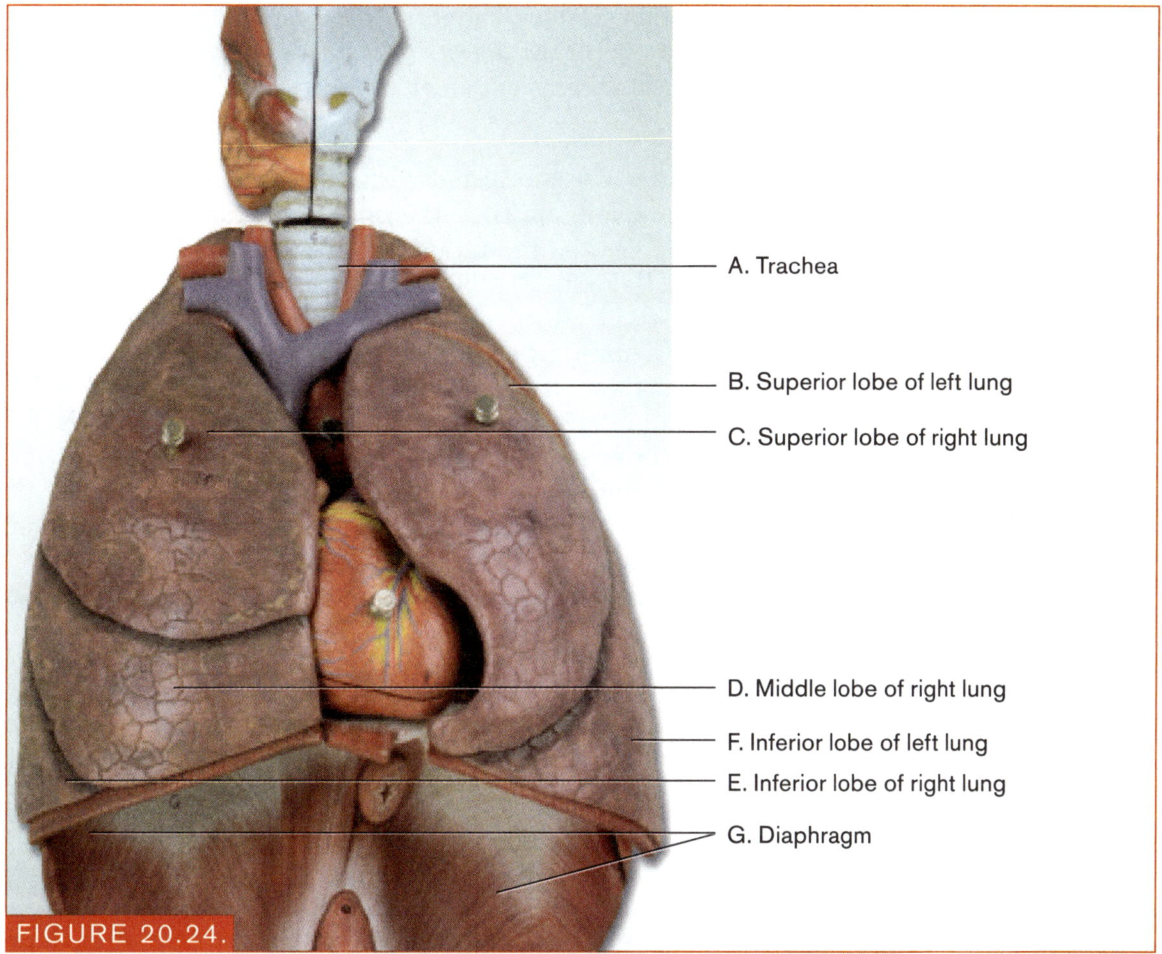

FIGURE 20.24.

The major organs and structures of the human respiratory system.

The Human Digestive System

1. The **mouth** is the opening to the oral cavity. The muscular **tongue** contains taste buds and aids in handling food. The tongue mixes food with saliva and moves food in discrete lumps (boli, singular: **bolus**) from the oral cavity to the pharynx. The **teeth** and the **tongue** are used to grind up food (and kill prey) and mix it with saliva.

2. **Salivary glands** produce saliva, which helps to aid in the movement of food and protect the epithelia from abrasion.

3. The **pharynx** is a junction that opens to the oral cavity, the nasal cavity, the **esophagus,** and the **trachea** (windpipe). Air can enter through the nostrils (and into the nasal cavity) and through the mouth into the oral cavity. When we swallow, the top of the windpipe moves up such that its opening, the **glottis,** is blocked by a cartilaginous flap, the **epiglottis.** This mechanism ensures that a bolus will be guided into the entrance of the esophagus and not down the windpipe. The trachea is ventral to the esophagus. The **esophagus** conducts food from the pharynx down to the stomach by peristalsis. The muscles at the very top of the esophagus are striated and therefore under voluntary control. Involuntary waves of contraction (**peristalsis**) by smooth muscles in the rest of the esophagus then takes over. Various **sphincter muscles** (generally composed of

smooth or involuntary muscle, although some sphincters are composed of voluntary muscles in a few places) separate major organs of the digestive tract. These muscles constrict when stimulated by the nervous system, holding material for a time in a given compartment of the digestive tract.

4 The **stomach** is a storage organ where mechanical and chemical digestion of food begins. Food leaves the stomach and enters the small intestine. The **small intestine** completes chemical digestion, absorbs the products of digestion, and transports the rest of the undigested material to the large intestine. The small intestine is about 5 to 6 meters long. The small intestine consists of three sections: the first 25 cm is the **duodenum** (anterior portion), and then the middle **jejunum,** and finally the **ileum** (largest portion, at the posterior end). **Mesenteries** (peritoneum membranes) suspend these structures from the posterior wall of the abdomen. The enormous surface of the small intestine is an adaptation that greatly increases the rate of nutrient absorption. The **large intestine** functions to reabsorb water and electrolytes and to form and store feces. The **large intestine,** or **colon,** is connected to the small intestine at the pouch-like **cecum.** The relatively small cecum of humans has a fingerlike extension, the **appendix,** which is considered a vestigial organ in humans. The **colon** has several sections: **ascending, transverse, descending,** and **sigmoid.** The sigmoidal part of the colon is connected to the **rectum,** leading to the **anus.**

5 The **diaphragm,** although not part of the digestive system, is found near the stomach. The muscular diaphragm separates the thoracic from the abdominal cavities, and it is involved in breathing. As the diaphragm contracts, the volume of the thoracic cavity increases and air is drawn into the lungs.

6 The **spleen** is the largest lymphatic organ. The spleen is next to the stomach, under the diaphragm. The spleen acts as a blood reservoir, and many lymphocytes and macrophages are located here.

7 **The pancreas** produces pancreatic juice, which is secreted into pancreatic duct that leads to the first part of the small intestine (the duodenum). Pancreatic juice contains both bicarbonates (which neutralizes the acid chyme existing the stomach) and a wide variety of hydrolytic enzymes that chemically digest food in the small intestine.

8 The capillaries and veins that drain the nutrients from the villi of the small intestine converge to form the **hepatic portal vessel (hepatic portal system),** which leads to the liver. There, the liver filters, collects, and processes the incoming nutrient-rich blood. The hepatic vein then leaves the liver, eventually joining the vena cava. The liver is the largest internal organ of the human body (the skin is the largest organ overall in size). The liver sits above and to the right of the stomach and just below the diaphragm and is composed of four lobes. The **hepatic artery** from the **aorta** carries oxygenated blood to the liver, while the hepatic vein carries deoxygenated blood from the liver to the **inferior vena cava.** The **liver** has many important functions:

a The liver metabolizes carbohydrates (especially the conversion of glycogen to glucose and vice versa), lipids, and proteins (deaminate amino acids for metabolism);

b The liver stores glycogen, lipids, proteins, vitamins, and minerals;

c The liver synthesizes albumins globulins, prothrombin, and other proteins in the blood;

d The liver filters out worn out red blood cells, white blood cells, foreign matter and bacteria from blood;

e The liver destroys or stores toxic or poisonous compounds (including alcohol);

f The liver removes or alters thyroid hormones and steroid hormones;

g The liver produces and secretes **bile.** Bile contains **bile salts,** bile pigments (from the breakdown of hemoglobin) and electrolytes. The bile comes from the bilirubin of worn out red blood cells in the blood. Bile salts emulsify fats (greatly increases the surface area so that lipases can work effectively) and help the small intestine to absorb some vitamins, cholesterol, phospholipids, and triglycerides; and

h The liver converts ammonia (from the deamination of amino acids) into urea (the less toxic nitrogen waste).

9 The **gallbladder** stores bile between meals. It stores bile salts which act as detergents that aid in the digestion and absorption of fats. Bile also contains pigments that are by-products of red blood cell destruction in the liver. These bile pigments are eliminated from the body with the feces.

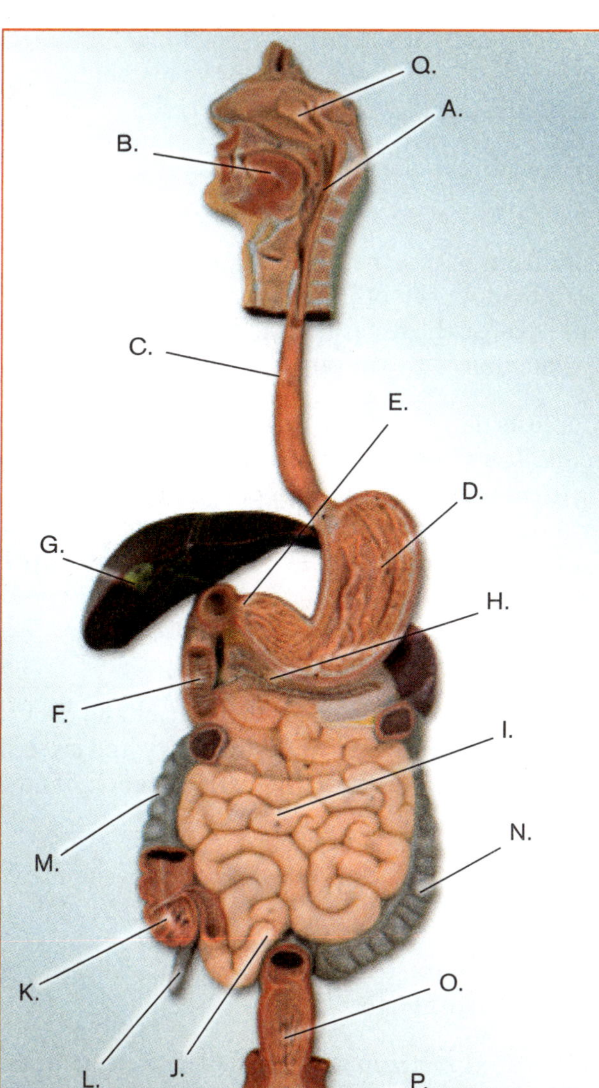

FIGURE 20.25.

The major organs and structures of the human digestive system.

The Human Male and Female Reproductive Systems

A **The Male Reproductive System**

1 **Testes** (the male gonads that produce gametes and androgens).

2 The **epididymus** is a tightly coiled tube that leads to the vas deferens. It connects to the ducts (the seminiferous tubules) within the testis. It stores immature sperm.

3 The **vas deferens** is a muscular tube about 45 cm long that passes through the lower abdominal wall (inguinal canal) and ends behind the urinary bladder. It joins with the duct of a seminal vesicle and from the ejaculatory duct, which passes through the prostate and joins the urethra.

4 The **seminal vesicle** is a sac-like structure attached to the vas deferens. The seminal vesicle consists of a number of secretory tubules. It secretes alkaline fluids (neutralize the acidic conditions of the sperm and the vagina) and contains nutrients for sperm cells.

5 The **prostate gland** surrounds the urethra just below the urinary bladder. The prostate secretes a milky fluid that neutralizes seminal fluid (which turns acidic due to the metabolic activity) and it can neutralize the acidic secretions of the vagina.

6 The **bulbourethral glands** are two small structures beneath the prostate. They secrete a fluid lubricant for the penis.

7 The **scrotum** is a pouch of skin and subcutaneous tissues that enclose the testes (a serous membrane also surrounds each testis, to allow it to move smoothly within the scrotum). The testes are outside of the body in most mammals because the testes need to be slightly cooler (about 2°C) than body temperature for sperm production.

8 The **penis** is specialized to become erect for insertion into the vagina during sexual intercourse. The tip of the penis is called the **glans penis.** The glans penis is surrounded by a hood of tissue (the **prepuce** or foreskin) and the opening to the urethra (the meatus or urethral orifice) is in the glans penis. The two **corpus cavernosum** and **corpus spongiosum** structures (which surrounds the urethra) are spongy tissues that engorge with blood during an erection. The glans penis is a bulbous extension of the corpus spongiosum.

B **The Female Reproductive System**

1 **Oviducts** (also called Fallopian tubes or uterine tubes) open near the ovaries and collect the ovum after ovulation. Finger-like projections (**fimbriae**) surround the ovary and sweep over it at ovulation, and the ovum is usually swept into the oviduct, where fertilization often takes place.

2 The **uterus** is the organ that receives the embryo and sustains its life through development. The neck of the uterus is called the **cervix,** which opens into the vagina.

3 The **vagina** receives the penis during sexual intercourse, receives the semen, conveys secretions of the uterus, and transports the offspring out during birth.

4 The vaginal opening and the opening of the urethra are in a region called the **vestibule.** The vestibule is surrounded by a pair of slender skin folds, the **labia minora** (plural; singular: **labium minus**). The labia minora are in turn surrounded by a pair of thick fatty ridges, the **labia**

majora (plural; singular: **labium majus**). At the anterior ridge of the vestibule, the **clitoris** is found. The clitoris is a short shaft of erectile tissue (similar to a penis, with a head or **glans**) that is covered by a small hood (the **prepuce**).

5 A pair of **Bartholin's glands** produce mucus into the vestibule near the vaginal opening. This mucus is used as a lubricant for sexual intercourse.

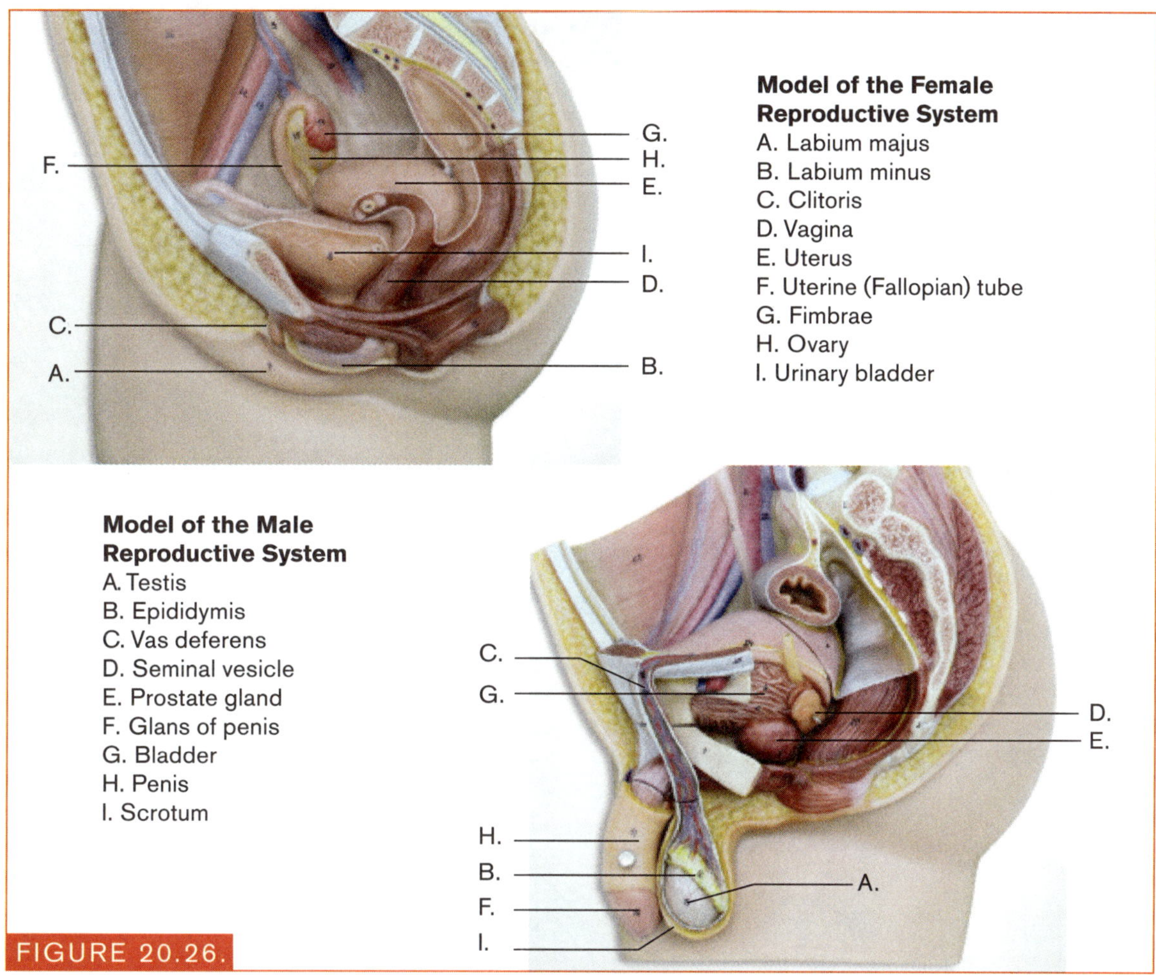

FIGURE 20.26.

The major organs and structures of the human reproductive system.

The Human Circulatory System and the Heart

Humans have a **closed circulatory system** that is actually a **double circulation system** with **pulmonary (lung)** and **systemic (to the body) circuits.** Like all mammals, humans have **four-chambered hearts.** The heart consists of two **atria** (singular: atrium; the chambers that receive blood returning to the heart), and two **ventricles** (the chambers that pump blood out of the heart). In this arrangement, the left side of the heart receives and pumps only oxygen-rich blood, while the right side handles only oxygen-poor blood. **Double circulation** restores pressure to the systemic circuit and prevents mixing of oxygen-rich and oxygen-poor blood.

The Path that a Red Blood Cell would Take through Your Body

Left atrium – left ventricle – aorta – body capillaries – vena cava – right atrium – right ventricle – pulmonary artery – lung capillaries – pulmonary veins – left atrium. Note that the pulmonary artery carries unoxygenated blood, whereas the pulmonary vein carried oxygenated blood.

Heart valves. There are four valves in the mammalian heart, each consisting of flaps of connective tissue, that prevent back-flow and keep blood moving in the correct direction. Between each atrium and ventricle is a set of **atrioventricular (AV) valves** which keeps blood from flowing back into the atria when the ventricles contract. Two sets of **semilunar valves** exist between the left ventricle and the aorta and between the right ventricle and the pulmonary artery. These valves prevent back-flow from the blood vessels back into the ventricles when the ventricles relax. The heart sounds we can hear with a stethoscope are caused by blood recoiling against the closing of the valves ('lup'—the AV valves close—and 'dup'—the semilunar valves close).

Go to the demonstration table and examine the path of blood as it travels through the double circulatory system of a mammal. Draw the figure in the space provided below (Figure 20.27).

FIGURE 20.27.

The mammalian circulatory system.

Exercise 20.12.

Fill in the following table (Table 20.1), which is an extension of Table 18.3 (Exercise 18.17) and Table 19.5 (Exercise 19.22).

TABLE 20.1.

Character	Phylum Chordata
diplo-/ triploblastic	
body cavity	
symmetry	
digestive	
respiratory	
circulatory	
reproductive	
excretory/ osmoregulation	
nervous	
support/skeletons	
appendages/ integument	
groups	
other important terms, traits or key words	

UNIT 21 — Animals IV. Higher Animal Form and Function

Keywords

tissue
histology
simple epithelia
stratified epithelia
pseudostratified epithelia
ciliated epithelia
mucus
squamous
cuboidal
columnar
basement membrane
keratin
ground substance

matrix
lacunae
canaliculi
lamellae
collagen
elastin
ligament
tendon
osteocyte
chondrocyte
erythrocyte
biconcave
leukocyte

phagocytosis
fibrin
albumin
globulin
microfilaments
actin
myosin
uninucleated
multinucleated
intercalated disks
soma
axon
dendrite

neuron
glial cell
synapse
endoderm
mesoderm
ectoderm
zygote
morula
blastula
blastocoel
blastopore
gastrula
archenteron

Learning Objectives

When finished with this unit, you should be able to do the following:

1 List the four major types of animal tissues;

2 Describe the examples of epithelial tissues and list their structures and functions. Compare and contrast simple, stratified, and pseudostratified epithelia;

3 Describe the examples of connective tissues examined in lab (areolar, dense regular and dense irregular, adipose, cartilage, bone, and blood), and list their structures, functions, and locations in the body. Discuss the three components (cells, matrix, fibers) in each major type of connective tissue;

4 Describe the examples of muscle tissues (stratified, smooth, cardiac). Discuss where each muscle type is found, and describe its function. Compare and contrast each muscle tissue in terms of structure, speed of contraction, and the time it takes for each muscle type to fatigue. Discuss the relationship of muscle fibers to muscle bundles and muscles;

5 Describe the examples of nervous tissues;

6 Understand and identify on pictures and slides, the following terms, structures, or stages in sea star development: unfertilized egg, fertilized egg (zygote), 2-, 4-, and 8-cell stage;

7 morula, blastula, blastocoel, blastopore, gastrula, archenteron, coelomic vesicles; and

8 Describe the three germ layers and list the adult structures that arise from each germ layer.

Animal Tissues: Structure and Function

Like the multicellular plants, animals are made of several basic kinds of **tissues.** Cells in both plants and in animals are arranged into tissues that perform specialized structural and functional roles.

Tissues are aggregations of cells; usually one of a few types of cells are present in a tissue. These aggregations are usually in the form of sheets, tubes, or small masses within animal organs. In a tissue, the cells have similar structure and origin and have the same function (secretion, contraction, protection, and so on). In the human body, there are over 200 different tissues; however, they fall into one of four basic types: **epithelial, connective, muscular,** and **nervous** (Figure 21.1). You will be examining and drawing one or more examples of each type in lab today.

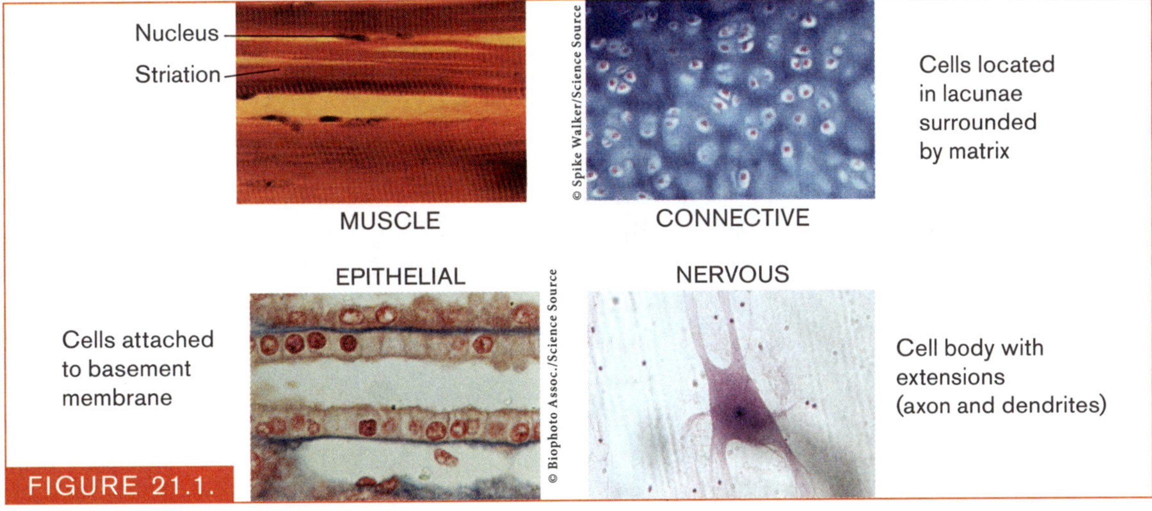

The four basic types of animal tissues.

Epithelial Tissues

A **General characteristics of epithelial tissues:**

1 Epithelial tissues arise from sheets of tightly packed and tightly connected cells of several shapes, depending on their function.

2 Epithelial tissues come from all three germ layers: ectoderm, endoderm, and mesoderm.

3 Some epithelial tissues are **simple epithelium,** meaning that they consist of one cell layer (see Figure 21.1). This is opposed to **stratified epithelium,** which is composed of multiple layers (Figure 22.2). **Pseudostratified epithelium** consists of usually one layer, but because of the location of the nuclei, it appears that more than one layer of cells are present.

4 Epithelial tissue (epi- "= outer" or "= upon") cover the outside of the body and cover all internal organs and body cavities. These tissues cover all of the free body surfaces and are the major tissue of glands.

5 The epithelium is anchored to connective tissue by a **basement membrane** (the extracellular matrix secreted by the epithelial cells, see Figure 21.1). The basement membrane separates the epithelial cells from the connective tissues (such as loose connective tissue or fat) lying underneath.

6 Epithelia function in protection, secretion, absorption, excretion, and sensory reception. Specifically, epithelial tissues function against bacterial invasion, fluid loss, and mechanical damage from forces such as abrasion. Some epithelial tissues stretch, allowing the organ (such as the bladder) to expand.

7 Some epithelial layers are ciliated. Ciliary movement sweeps material across the surface of the epithelium. In the mammalian respiratory tract (nose, pharynx, trachea), ciliated epithelia typically produce copious amounts of **mucus.** Dust particles, spores, bacteria, pollen, and other materials in the inspired air are trapped by the mucus, and the action of the cilia dislodges and transports the mucus out of the respiratory tract. Mucus protects the epithelium (collectively called **mucous membranes**), either by moistening or waterproofing the epithelia (for example, ear wax).

8 There is no direct blood supply to epithelial tissues. Diffusion of gases and other materials occurs between epithelial cells and nearby capillary beds.

B **Major Types of Epithelium**

1 **Simple squamous epithelium** consists of a single layer of thin or flattened cells (Figure 21.2). Simple squamous epithelium often are 'leaky,' thus allowing for diffusion of gases across their surfaces or between adjacent cells. The pancake-shaped squamous cells are found in the capillaries, veins, and arteries (these epithelia are called endothelia), as well as in the skin, the mouth cavity, and the lungs.

2 **Simple cuboidal epithelium** consists of a single layer of cube-shaped cells. Simple cuboidal epithelium carries out secretion and adsorption. Examples include the cells lining the kidney tubules, and the cells in various glands. They primarily are involved in excretion (secretion or absorption) of materials.

3 **Simple columnar epithelium** consists of elongated, column-shaped cells whose nuclei are located near the basement membrane. Columnar cells are often involved in absorption, lining the uterus and the digestive tract (where they secrete the enzymes and also absorb the digested nutrients).

4 **Stratified squamous epithelium** (strat- "layer") is composed of many cell layers (Figure 21.3). Stratified squamous epithelium covers the skin and lines the mouth, throat, vagina, and anal canal. Proteins fibers made of **keratin** are found in skin cells, nails, and hair. Keratin is waterproof, and protects the skin from microbial invasion and injury.

5 **Pseudostratified columnar epithelium** consists of a single layer of cells attached to the basement membrane, but because the location of the nucleus differs from cell to cell, the tissue takes on the appearance of multiple cell layers. Pseudostratified epithelium line the trachea and other parts of the upper part of the mammalian respiratory tract.

6 **Glandular epithelium** is composed of cells that are specialized to secrete substances. Mammary glands, sweat glands, and endocrine glands are examples or organs composed of these specialized epithelia.

Exercises

Exercise 21.1.

Squamous Epithelium

Examine the simple squamous (lung tissue) slide under low and high power. Draw what you see in the field of view in the space provided below (Figure 21.2). Use Figure 21.1 and Figure 21.4 to guide you.

FIGURE 21.2.

Squamous epithelium.

You are observing these cells in cross section. Draw what you think the three-dimensional shape of the squamous cells would be in the space above, if you were looking at the cells if you were standing inside the air filled alveolus.

If you observe a capillary cross section, or a small blood vein or artery, look at the squamous epithelium that composes the side of the vessel, and make a sketch in the space above.

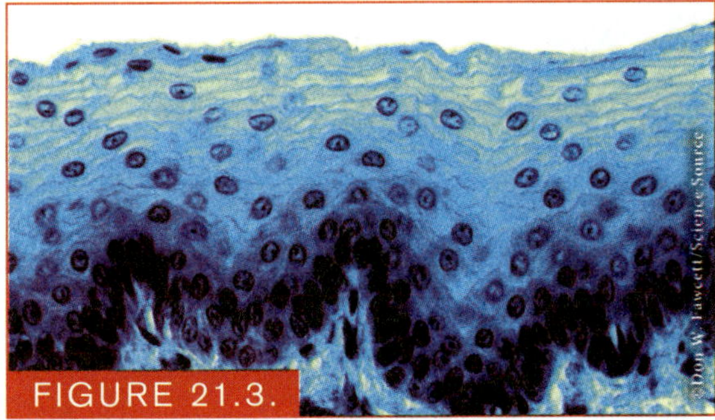

FIGURE 21.3.

Stratified squamous epithelium.

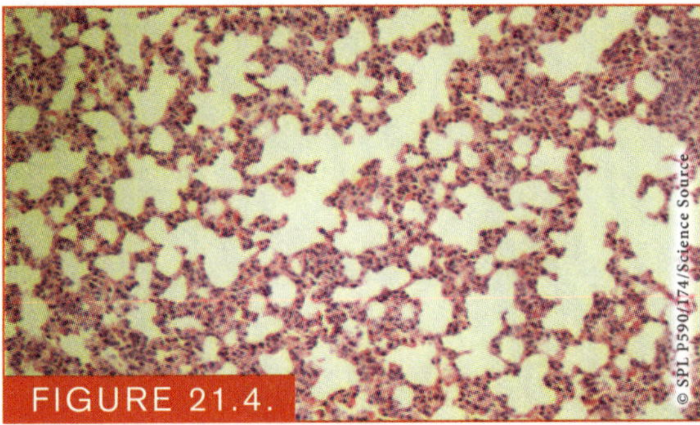

FIGURE 21.4.

Lung Alveoli. Simple squamous epithelium in the lung alveoli. The flattened cells lining the air spaces (alveoli) in this figure are simple squamous epithelium.

Exercise 21.2.
Cuboidal Epithelium

Examine the simple cuboidal tissue (kidney slide) under low and high power. The cuboidal cells will be the cells lining the various tubules; they are the cube-shaped or box-shaped cells. Draw what you see in the field of view in the space provided below (Figure 21.5). Use Figure 21.1 and Figure 21.6 to guide you. Draw the three-dimensional shape of the cuboidal cells as you imagine seeing them lining a tubule. You may see other tissues in this slide: what tissue types are also present?

FIGURE 21.5.

Cuboidal epithelium.

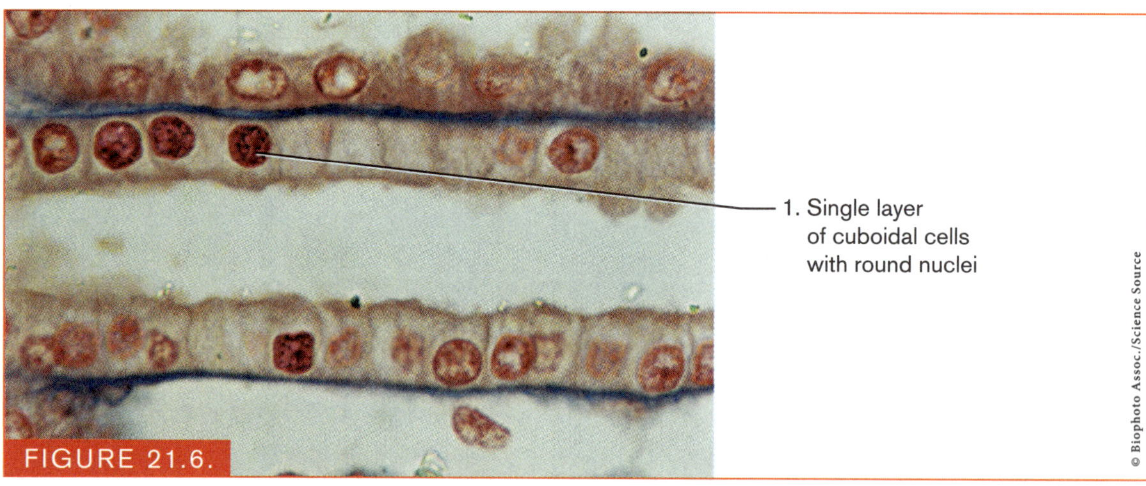

FIGURE 21.6.

Simple cuboidal epithelium.

Exercise 21.3.

Columnar Epithelium

Examine the simple columnar slide (gut) under low and high power. Draw what you see in the field of view in the space provided below (Figure 21.7). Draw the three-dimensional shape of these columnar cells, if you were looking at a thick section of the gut cross section. Use Figure 21.1 and Figure 21.8 to guide you. You may see other tissues in this slide: what tissue types are also present?

FIGURE 21.7.

Columnar epithelium.

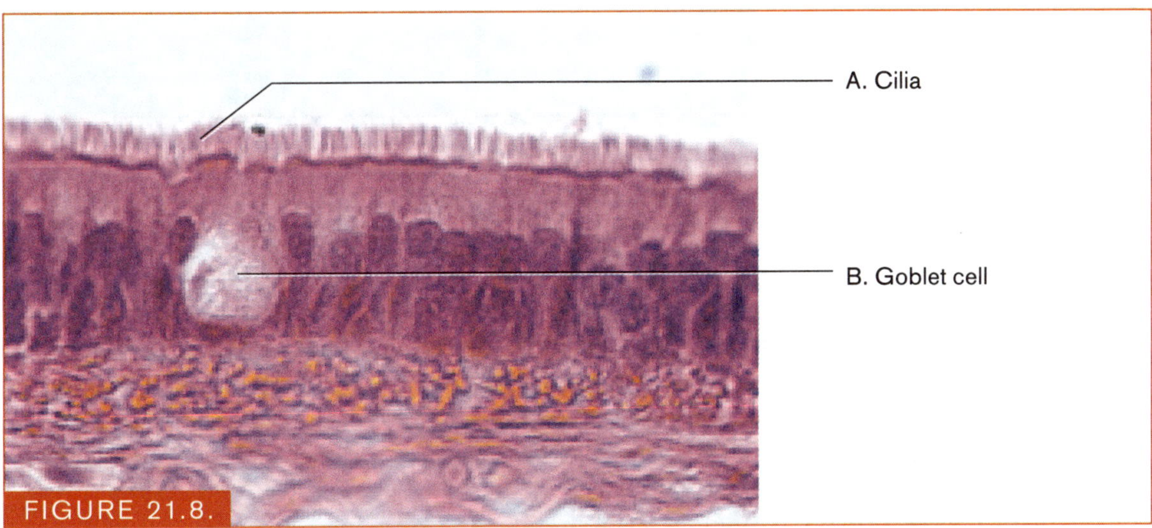

FIGURE 21.8.

Simple columnar epithelium.

Exercise 21.4.

Stratified Epithelium

Examine the skin c.s. slide (stratified epithelium) under low and high power. Draw what you see in the field of view in the space provided below (Figure 21.9). Use Figure 21.3 to guide you. Note the many layers of dead keratin-filled cells that are sloughing off of the surface. These cells protect the body by producing a waterproofing layer (they are more tightly connected than the squamous epithelium of the capillaries), as well as protection against abrasion and bacterial invasion. Note that adipose tissue and other connective tissues are underneath the basement membrane.

FIGURE 21.9.

Skin c.s. and stratified epithelium.

Connective Tissues

A **General characteristics of connective tissues:**

1 Connective tissues join, support and protect other tissues. Connective tissues provide a framework for other tissues. Connective tissues fill space, store fat, produce blood cells, provide defense against infection, and repair damaged tissues.

2 Connective tissues are characterized by a **sparse population of cells** inside an extracellular **ground substance** (see Figure 21.1). The cells are found as single cells or as a small number of cells in clusters (in bone, these clusters are in small 'pockets' called **lacunae**), surrounded by a **matrix.** The composition of the matrix varies with connective tissue type, but it consists of the ground substance and protein fibers. In some connective tissues, many **fibers** are present (primarily **collagen,** but other protein fibers can be present as well). The ground substance is composed of a variety of materials, depending on tissue type. The ground substance consists of different noncollagenous proteins, water, salts, metabolites, and other materials. The ground substance can vary from fluid to solid. Connective tissue cells produce both the fibers and the ground substance.

3 Connective tissues are of mesodermal origin.

4 Most connective tissues have a direct blood supply (capillary beds are present within the connective tissues), although a few connective tissues do not have a direct blood supply. For those tissues that do not, diffusion to and from nearby capillary beds must suffice for movement of gases, food, and wastes.

B **Major types of connective tissues:**

There are two major categories of connective tissues: **proper connective tissues** and **specialized connective tissues. Proper connective tissues** generally bind other tissues together, with a considerable amount of collagen fibers. **Specialized connective tissues** have a variety of support, storage, transport, and protective functions.

1 **Proper Connective Tissues**

I **Areolar** (also called **loose**) **connective tissue**

a Areolar connective tissue binds epithelial tissues to underlying tissues.

b Areolar connective tissue forms the membranes found between organs. Loose connective tissue also is found beneath the skin.

c Areolar connective tissue is composed of spindle-shaped cells (**fibroblasts**) that produce the fibers.

d In addition, some immune cells (**macrophages**) are present in connective tissues, as well as in other tissues. The immune cells defend the body against foreign cells. This tissue is vascularized.

e There are smaller **elastin fibers** and larger **collagen fibers** present, embedded in a viscous liquid matrix. Collagen fibers give strength to resist stretching, but elastin fibers are flexible, allowing for some distortion. The elastin fibers allow a rapid return to the original shape of the tissue if it is distorted.

II **Dense** (sometimes referred to as **fibrous**) **connective tissue**

a Dense connective tissue often binds different materials together. There are two main kinds: **dense regular connective tissues** and **dense irregular connective tissues.**

b **Dense regular connective tissues** are found in **tendons** (connects muscle to bone), **ligaments** (connects bones to bones at joints), as well as surrounding bone and other organs. The collagen fibers form parallel bundles, with the spindle-shaped fibroblasts running parallel with the fibers.

c **Dense irregular connective tissues** form capsules around many organs and are found in the deep layers of the skin. The collagen fibers have a complex arrangement that resists tensile stress (stretching) from any direction.

d Dense connective tissue is composed mostly of strong **collagen fibers** and relatively few cells. Dense connective tissues of ligaments and tendons have a blood supply, but bone is more vascularized and relatively simpler in structure, compared to tendons. This is why torn tendons often take longer periods of time to heal than do broken bones.

❷ Specialized Connective Tissues

❶ Adipose tissue (fat)

a Adipose tissue is a specialized form of connective tissue that stores fat (energy storage), cushions organs and joints against physical force, and is used for insulation against cold.

b Adipose tissue is found beneath the skin, in abdominal membranes, and around the heart, kidneys, and joints.

c **Fat cells** are the major cell type in adipose tissue. Fat cells are large cells that are filled with lipids. The lipids are stored in a large vacuole, called the **fat droplet.** The fat cell nuclei are pressed to the sides of the fat cells. In Figure 21.15, small strips of connective tissues are scattered among the fat cells; these interstitial areas contain fibroblasts, small arteries, veins and capillaries, and nerves.

❷ Cartilage

a Cartilage provides support and a framework for various parts (nose, ears, ends of bones, trachea, vertebral discs).

b Most vertebrates replace cartilage with bone, another connective tissue. Cartilage is the skeleton of all vertebrate embryos, and cartilage makes up the adult skeleton in the Chondrichthyes (sharks).

c In cartilage, the cells (**chondrocytes**) are present in small 'island-like' cavities called **lacunae.** The intercellular material of cartilage is largely composed of collagen fibers and a gel-like ground substance (made of hyaluronic acid and chondroitin sulfate).

d Cartilage does not have a blood supply (bone and many other connective tissues do have a direct supply), thus cartilage damage takes time to heal.

❸ Bone

a Bone protects vital organs (such as the brain, lungs, heart) and provides a tough endoskeleton for muscles to work against. Bone also stores vital ions (such as calcium and phosphate) and is the main site where blood cells are produced (by the **marrow,** the tissues found in the hollow interiors of long bones).

b Bone has cells (**osteocytes**) in a hardened matrix. The intercellular matrix (ground substance) of bone consists of mineral salts (Ca and P) and some collagen fibers. Bone is the strongest connective tissue. The fibers help bone to resist tensile forces (stretching), and the matrix also resists compression (crushing forces).

c Osteocytes are found in small pockets or cavities in the bone (**lacunae,** = "islands"). The material of bone is often arranged in concentric circles (**lamellae**) around the **Haversian canals.** The Haversian canals contain the blood vessels and nerves. Small **canaliculi** are observed crossing the lamellae (canaliculi = "little canals"). Osteocyte processes extend into the canaliculi. Osteocytes are found in small lacunae, and canaliculi connect these islands to the blood supply in the central Haversian canals.

d **Osteons (Haversian systems)** are the fundamental unit of bone. An osteon consists of the large central Haversian canal surrounded by a number of concentric lamellae.

IV Blood

a Blood transports substances (food, wastes, oxygen and carbon dioxide, hormones, immune cells) and helps maintain homeostasis.

b Blood consists of cells in a watery ground substance or matrix called **plasma.** The cellular components of blood include **red blood cells (erythrocytes), white blood cells (leukocytes)** of various types, and **platelets.** The plasma contains water, salts, hormones, wastes, gases, and food.

c No protein fibers are present normally in blood, although fibers can form if blood clotting is stimulated to form a blood clot. The protein is in the form of inactive **fibrinogen,** which is soluble. **Fibrin,** when formed, is insoluble and makes up much of the blood clot.

d In addition to fibrinogen, large amounts of two other proteins (**globulins** and **albumins**) are present in blood.

e A substantial number of **platelets** are found in blood. Platelets are fragments of cells; they are involved in blood clotting.

f Red blood cells (erythrocytes) contain packed hemoglobin molecules and are involved in carrying most of the oxygen to the body. In mammals, the normal red blood cell is **anucleated** (no nucleus) when mature and is shaped like a doughnut. They are **biconcave** cells: there is actually no hole in the middle; instead, a thin membrane is stretched across the center. These cells are very distortable, allowing them to squeeze into capillaries that are thinner in diameter than the red blood cells themselves.

g Several types of white blood cells (leukocytes) are involved in immune responses. Some of the white blood cells produce antibodies, some produce toxic chemicals, and others use **phagocytosis** against dying or worn out cells and against foreign cells and cell products, such as proteins and toxins. Many of the invertebrate animals have ameboid cells in their blood or plasma that perform similar functions.

Exercise 21.5.
Areolar Connective Tissue

Examine the areolar (loose) connective tissue slide under low and high power. Draw what you see in the field of view in the space provided below (Figure 21.10). Use Figure 21.11 to guide you.

FIGURE 21.10.

Areolar (loose) connective tissues.

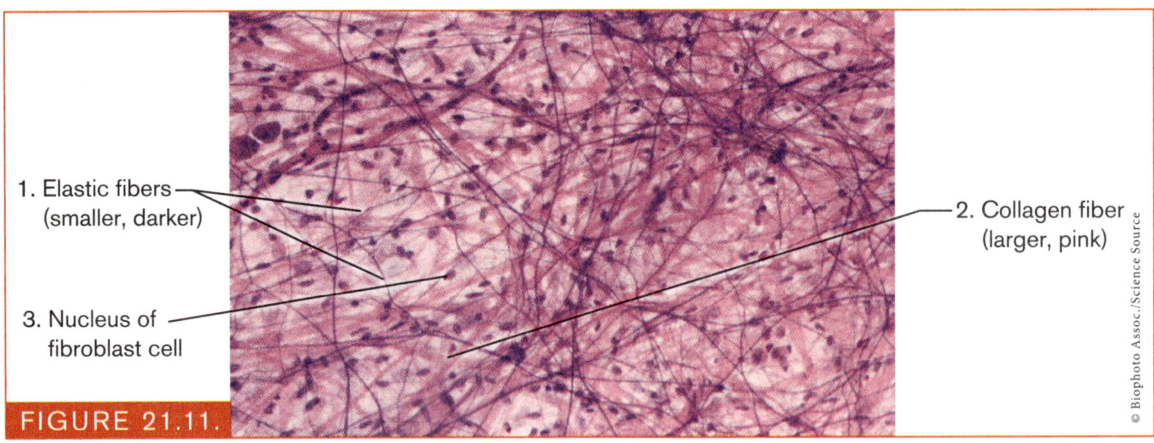

FIGURE 21.11.

Areolar connective tissues.

Exercise 21.6.

Dense Connective Tissue

Examine the slide of dense connective tissues (longitudinal section of a tendon, and/or the dense irregular connective tissues underlying skin). Draw what you see in the figure below (Figure 21.12). Use Figure 21.13 to guide you. Note the patterns of fiber orientation. Based on this observation, can tendons resist stretching and bending forces from all directions equally, compared to areolar tissues?

FIGURE 21.12.

Dense connective tissues.

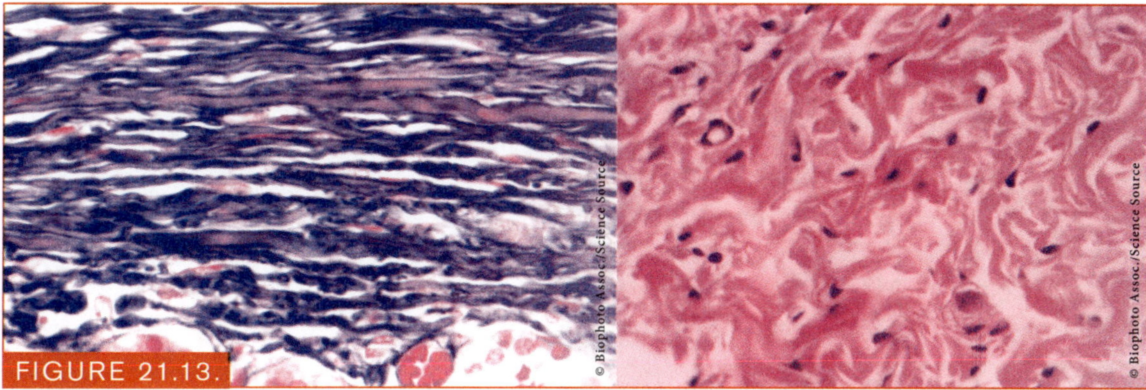

FIGURE 21.13.

Dense connective tissues—regular (left) and irregular (right).

Exercise 21.7.

Adipose Tissue

Examine the adipose tissue (fat) under low and high power. Draw what you see in the field of view in the space below (Figure 21.14). Use Figure 21.15 to guide you.

FIGURE 21.14.

Adipose (fat) connective tissue.

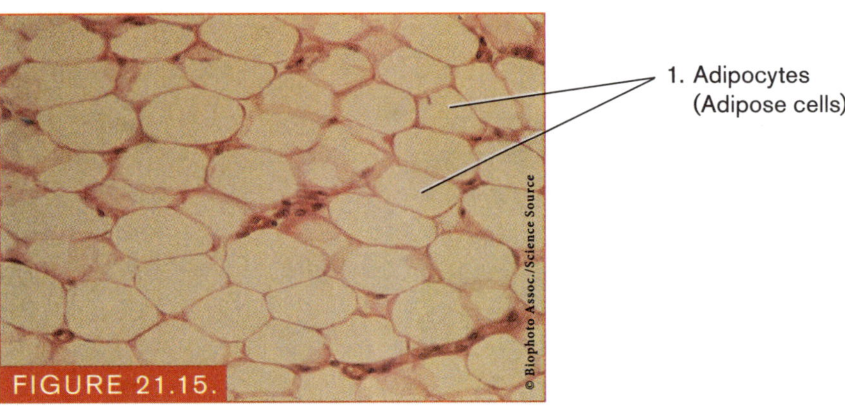

FIGURE 21.15.

Adipose tissue.

Exercise 21.8.

Cartilage

Examine the hyaline cartilage slide under low and high power. Draw what you see in the field of view in the space provided below (Figure 21.16). Use Figure 21.17 to guide you. Note that you see multiple tissues on this slide: what other tissues are present?

FIGURE 21.16.

Hyaline cartilage slide.

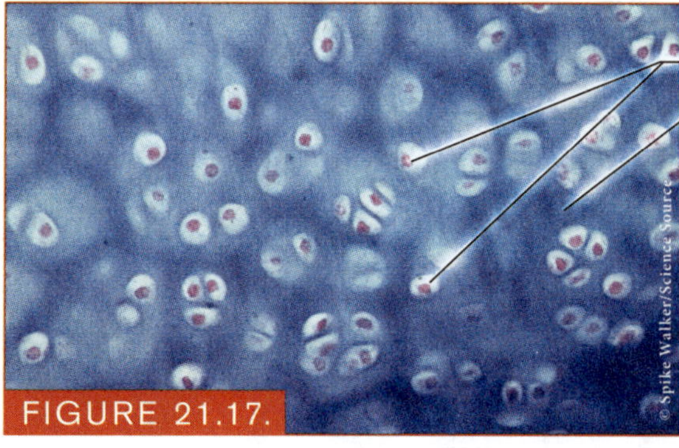

FIGURE 21.17.

Hyaline cartilage.

Exercise 21.9.

Bone

Examine the bone (bone, ground, human) slide under low and high power. Draw what you see in the field of view in the space provided below (Figure 21.18). Use Figure 21.19 to guide you.

FIGURE 21.18.

Bone.

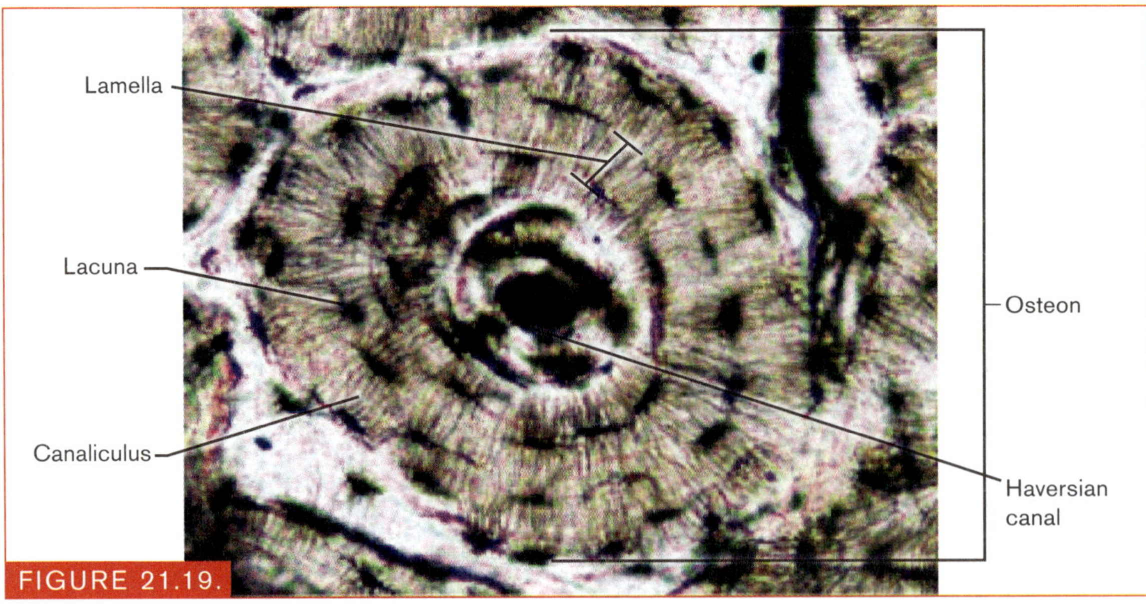

FIGURE 21.19.

Bone: the osteon.

Exercise 21.10.

Blood

Examine the human blood slide under low and high power. Draw what you see in the field of view in the space provided below (Figure 21.20). Use Figure 21.21 to guide you. Draw and identify the various types of cells.

FIGURE 21.20.

Blood.

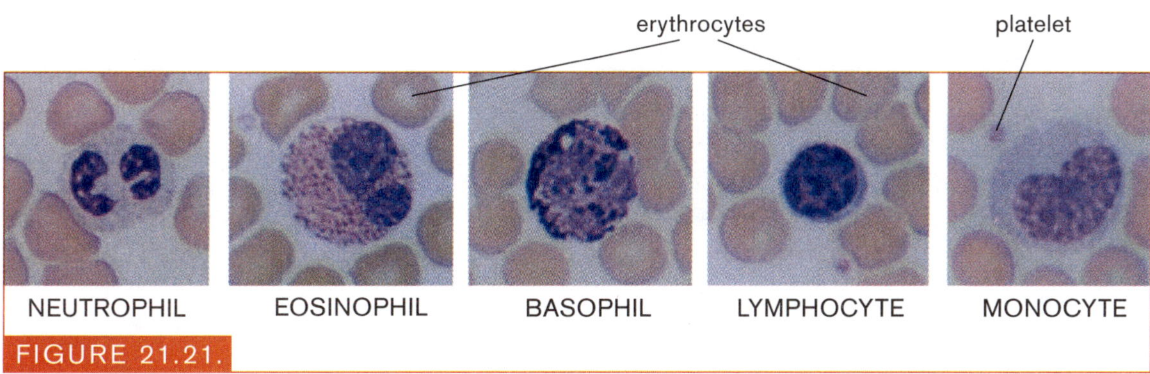

FIGURE 21.21.

Blood cells. The anucleated cells are erythrocytes.

Exercise 21.11.

Avian Blood Cells, Sickle Cell Anemia

Examine the demonstration slides 'chicken blood' and 'sickle cell anemia' under high power. Draw what you see in the field of view in the space below (Figure 21.22).

FIGURE 21.22.

Sketches of avian (chicken) blood (left) and blood from a person with sickle cell anemia (right).

How does bird blood differ from mammal an blood, in terms of the red blood cell shape and nucleus?

What problems (physiological, biochemical, behavioral) could these sickle-shaped cells cause?

Muscle Tissues

A **General muscle tissue characteristics:**

a Muscle tissue is usually the most abundant type (in terms of weight) in most large animals. Muscle tissues are composed of elongated cells that are capable of contraction upon simulation (see Figure 21.1).

b Muscle tissues are contractile tissues that move parts of the body.

c There are **three types:** skeletal, smooth, and cardiac muscle.

d The three types of muscle tissues vary in terms of their structure, their speed of contraction, and their time to fatigue, and whether or not they are under voluntary control.

e Muscle cells are of mesodermal origin.

f Muscle cells contain many parallel bundles of **microfilaments** made of **actin** and **myosin.**

B **Types of muscle**

1 **Skeletal muscle (voluntary** or **striated** muscles)

a Skeletal muscle is the most abundant type of muscle in higher animals. Skeletal muscle cells are very large cells in the human body (up to 40 mm long or more).

b Skeletal muscles are under **voluntary** control (you can flex these muscles consciously). They usually are attached at both ends to bones. Muscles are attached to bones by dense connective tissues called **tendons.**

c The skeletal muscle cells (fibers) are large cylindrical cells. The voluntary muscles have very prominent **striations,** and each cell is **multinucleated,** with the nuclei pressed to the sides of the cell.

d The skeletal muscle fibers contract immediately when stimulated, and they relax immediately when not. They also fatigue most rapidly, compared to the other muscle types.

e The skeletal muscle cells (**muscle fibers**) are grouped into muscle **bundles,** which in turn are grouped into muscles. Muscle cells are metabolically quite active, so they are heavily vascularized. In verterbates, individual motor nerves connect to many individual muscle cells in a muscle bundle.

2 Smooth muscles (involuntary muscles)

a The smooth cells are long and spindle-shaped (fat in the middle, tapered at both ends). **No striations** are visible; the myofibrils and the sarcomeres are not lined up as they are in skeletal muscles.

b There is only one nucleus in each smooth muscle cell (located in the center). The cells are referred to as being **uninucleated.**

c Smooth muscle tissue is found in the walls of hollow internal organs (gut, bladder, blood vessels, and the uterus). Smooth muscle cells do not form bundles; instead, they form sheets or small layers of cells.

d Smooth muscle is under **involuntary control** (because of this, it is sometimes referred to as **involuntary muscle**). Smooth muscle cells are innervated by nerves from the autonomic nervous system; in addition, smooth muscles respond to nonnervous stimulation, from mechanical stretching and hormones. Gap junctions between cells coordinates activity by allowing ions to flow from one cell to the next, causing simultaneous contractions. The smooth muscle cells contract relatively slowly when stimulated, but they can stay contracted longer than can voluntary muscles (smooth muscle does not fatigue as rapidly as skeletal muscle).

3 Cardiac muscle

a Cardiac tissue is found only in the heart and in the walls of the large vessels attached to the heart.

b Cardiac muscle is under involuntary control and are adapted to rhythmic contractions. Nerves from the autonomic nervous system innervate cardiac muscle cells.

c The single nucleus (in some species, two nuclei can be present in some cells) is located in the center of each cardiac muscle cell (like involuntary muscle cells), but the cells are distinctly striated (like skeletal muscles).

d Cardiac muscle cells are often branched.

e Cardiac cells are connected by **intercalated disks,** and the cells are arranged in branching networks. These structures help to coordinate contraction of adjacent cells; gap junctions that cross the intercalated discs allow ions to flow from one cell to another and thus cause the cells to contract rhythmically.

f Cardiac muscle cells are intermediate in terms of fatigue and contraction speed. Cardiac muscle cells rest between heartbeats.

Exercise 21.12.

Smooth Muscle

Examine the **smooth muscle (involuntary muscle, visceral muscle)** slide under low and high power. Draw what you see in the field of view in the space provided below (Figure 21.23). Use Figure 21.24 to guide you. You will see various connective tissues and perhaps small blood vessels interspersed among the individual muscle fibers. Note that there are two bands of smooth muscle cells, one group of cells in cross section (the longitudinal muscle band) and one group in longitudinal section (the circular muscle band). Draw what you believe is the three-dimensional shape of smooth muscle cells, based on what you see.

FIGURE 21.23.

Smooth muscle.

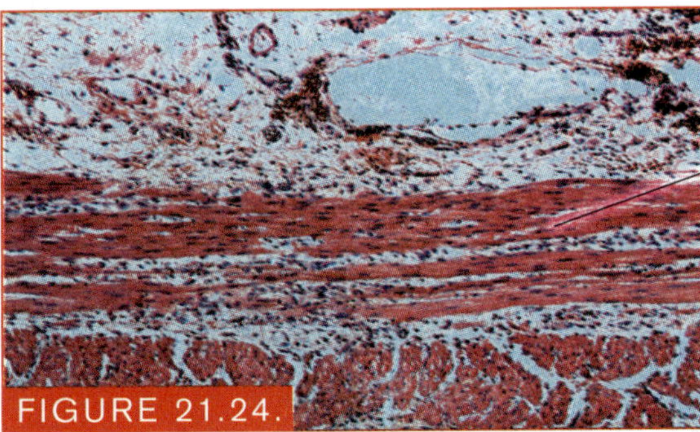

FIGURE 21.24.

Smooth muscle.

Exercise 21.13.

Skeletal Muscle

Examine the **skeletal muscle** (= **voluntary muscle**, = **striated muscle**) slide under low and high power. Draw what you see in the field of view in the space provided below (Figure 21.25). Use Figure 21.26 to guide you. You may see connective tissues, adipose cells, and small blood vessels scattered among the skeletal muscle fibers. How much larger are the skeletal muscle cells, compared to smooth muscle cells? Draw the three-dimensional shape of a skeletal muscle cell. Do you see any cells in cross section?

FIGURE 21.25.

Skeletal muscle.

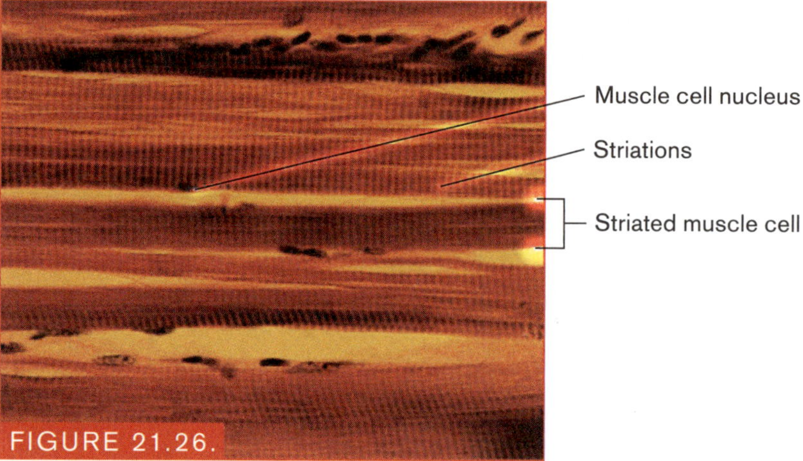

FIGURE 21.26.

Skeletal muscle.

Exercise 21.14.

Cardiac Muscle

Examine the cardiac muscle slide (look at the "3 muscle types" slide and the slide marked inter-calated disk, monkey) under low and high power. Draw what you see in the field of view in the space below (Figure 21.27). Use Figure 21.28 to guide you. As in the other two muscle cell types, you may observe different connective tissues and blood vessels among the cardiac muscle fibers. Draw the three-dimensional shape of a cardiac cell, based on what you see.

FIGURE 21.27.

Cardiac muscle.

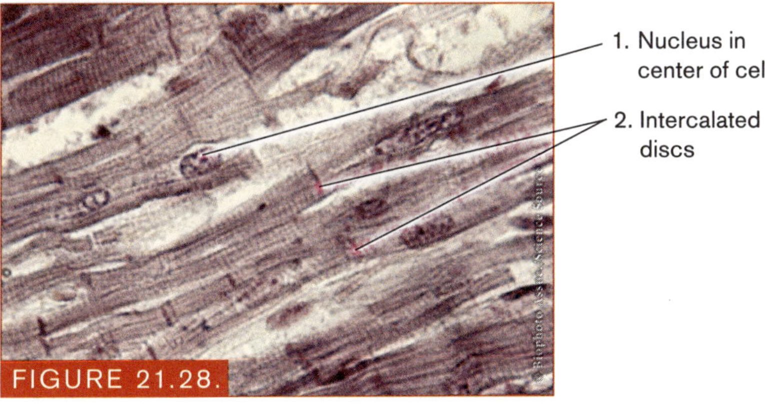

FIGURE 21.28.

Cardiac muscle.

Exercise 21.15.

Fill in Table 21.1 below (the comparison of the three muscle types).

TABLE 21.1.

	Skeletal Muscle	Cardiac Muscle	Smooth Muscle
location			
striations present?			
basic shape and relative size			
number and location of nuclei			
relative speed of contraction			
relative length of time before fatigue			
special features			

Fill in Table 21.2 below (the various structural protein fibers present in different structures).

TABLE 21.2.

Organ or Tissue	Structural Protein
skin (epithelium)	
blood	
bone	
cartilage	
proper connective tissues	
muscle	

Nervous Tissues

A **General nervous tissue characteristics:**

1 Nervous tissues are found in the brain, spinal cord, and peripheral nerves. **Nervous tissues** (see Figure 21.1) sense external and internal stimuli. They send signals to each other and to various parts of the body, such as the **effector organs** (glands and muscles).

2 Nerve cells are of ectodermal origin.

3 **Neurons** are nerve cells and the functional unit of the nervous system. They are very sensitive to changes (they are very irritable) and respond by transmitting nerve impulses to other neurons or to other cells such as muscles.

4 Nerve cells function in coordinating, regulating, and integrating body activities.

5 These cells in higher animals often send action potentials in a unidirectional direction (from **presynaptic cells** to **postsynaptic cells**). The connection between adjacent nerve cells is called the **synapse.** Nerve cells make synapses to muscles, receptors, and glandular cells.

B **Types of Nervous Tissues**

1 The basic type of nerve cell is called the **neuron.** The neurons are uninucleated cells that are composed of a cell body (**soma**), an **axon,** and one or more **dendrites,** through which they receive inputs from other cells.

2 Other supportive cells in nervous tissues are called **neuroglial (glial) cells.** Some glial cells surround nerves (axons of nerve cells), others support neurons in other ways.

Exercise 21.16.

Neurons

Examine the nerve cell (motor neuron) under low and high power. Draw what you see in the field of view in the space provided below (Figure 21.29). Use Figure 21.30 to guide you. Note the cell body or **soma** (where the nucleus and most organelles are located) and various cellular extensions, or processes. One or more of these processes are called **dendrites,** which receive information from other cells. Each nerve cell sends information on to the next cell through the single **axon.**

FIGURE 21.29.

Motor neuron.

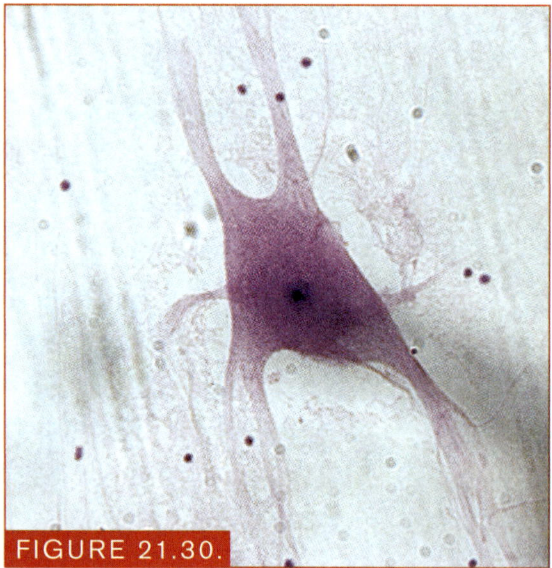

FIGURE 21.30.

Motor neuron from spinal cord.

Exercise 21.17.

Neuromuscular Junction

Examine the motor nerve cell ending slide (at demonstration table under high power). Do not change the objective; use fine focus only. Draw what you see in the field of view in the space provided below (Figure 21.31). Use Figure 21.32 to guide you. (**Be careful!** This slide is very expensive.) Note the synapse that a nerve has made to several muscle fibers (cells). In mammals, one motor nerve innervates several muscle fibers. Are you observing an axon, or a dendrite?

FIGURE 21.31.

Motor cell ending: the neuromuscular junction.

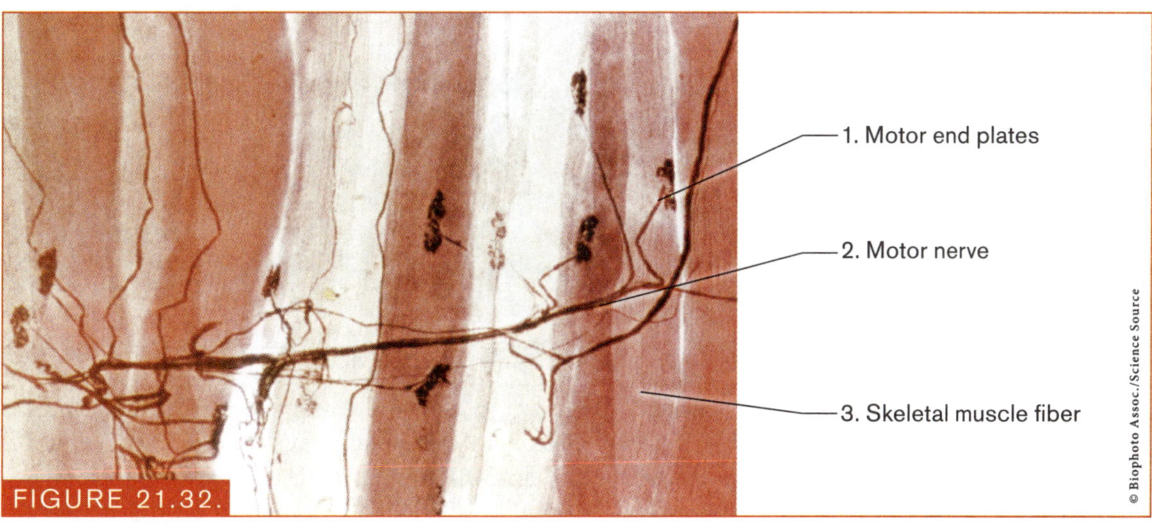

FIGURE 21.32.

The neuromuscular junction.

Exercise 21.18.

How Many Oxygen Molecules are in Your Circulatory System Now?

Divide into small groups and answer the following problems.

Stem cells, located in bone marrow, produce the cells that eventually give rise to erythrocytes (red blood cells, rbcs), leukocytes (white blood cells, the majority of which are neutrophils), and thrombocytes (platelets). Adult human males have about 5 to 6 million red blood cells per cubic millimeter (mm^3), and adult women have about 4 to 5 million rbcs/mm^3. We will take the average for humans as about 5 million/mm^3.

Recall that one liter (1 L) is equal to 1 cubic decimeter (dm^3). In addition, 1 L = 1 million millimeters (mm^3) or 1 million microliters (μl). One liter of water weighs 1,000 grams (g), or one kilogram (kg).

> Convert the conventional number "five million per mm^3" into a scientific number, using scientific notation:

The total amount of blood in the human body varies (in adult males, the blood volume is somewhat larger than in females), but the total blood volume (in milliliters or cubic centimeters, cm^3) of an average human can be roughly estimated using the following equation:

Blood volume (in liters) = 0.07 × (your weight in kilograms).
(Recall that one pound = 0.4536 kilograms.)

The estimate is based on several lines of reasoning, including the fact that the total amount of blood is about 7% of your body mass, and we are also assuming that one liter of blood weighs the same as one liter of water.

> How many oxygen molecules (O_2) can be carried by a single hemoglobin molecule, if it is fully oxygenated?

> Hemoglobin is packed inside each mature red blood cell. There are roughly 270 million hemoglobin molecules per erythrocyte. How many oxygen molecules are carried in a single red blood cell if all hemoglobin molecules inside the cell are fully oxygenated? Convert this number into scientific notation.

In addition to red blood cells, there are about 150,000 to 400,000 platelets present (we will use a rough average of 250,000 or 2.5×10^5) present in 1 mm^3. There are approximately 5,000 to 10,000 leukocytes per mm^3 of blood (mean = 7,500), with the most common cell (neutrophils) comprising about 70% of the total.

Based on the information above, fill in Table 21.3, using scientific notation. Assume the average number of red blood cells, white blood cells, and platelets. For the last column, assume that all hemoglobin molecules are fully saturated with oxygen.

TABLE 21.3.

	Cell		
	Erythrocyte	Neutrophil	Platelet
your blood volume (L)			
number of cells per mm^3			
number of cells per L (dm^3)			
total number of cells or platelets in your body			
total number of hemoglobin molecules in your body			
total number of oxygen molecules carried in your blood			

The life span of a typical red blood cell is about 120 days. The life span of the neutrophils is about 8 hours, and the life span for platelets is about 1 week. Worn-out cells are phagocytized by white blood cells in the liver. If the number of red blood cells stays constant through time, how many red blood cells are destroyed/produced per year? Per day? Per hour? Per minute? Per second? During the time you have been sitting in lab?

Exercise 21.19.

Animal Development

Go to the demonstration table and examine the demonstration slides and other materials of the *Asterias* mature, egg, starfish development composite, bipinnaria, and brachiolaria larval stages. Draw each of the following stages in the space provided below (Figure 21.33).

FIGURE 21.33.

Sea star development.

A **The major stages of sea star development:**

1 **Unfertilized egg.** You will be able to see the nucleus and nucleolus in the unfertilized egg.

2 **Fertilized egg.** After fertilization, the large nucleus and nucleolus are no longer seen because the sperm and egg **pronuclei** are about to combine. A wrinkled **fertilization membrane** may be seen in some zygotes; this prevents other sperm from penetrating the egg.

3 **2-cell, 4-cell, and 8-cell stage.** The fertilized egg soon begins mitosis (the process of producing daughter cells is called **cleavage**), producing 2-, then 4- and 8-cell stages. After about an hour, the zygote divides into two identical daughter cells (**blastomeres**). Several hours later, the blastomeres have divided again, producing first the 4-cell stage, and after the third division, the 8-cell stage. Note that the planes of cell division are at right angles to each other.

4 **Morula stage.** About 6 hours after fertilization, the larva has reached the **morula** stage. It is a solid ball of cells, consisting of 16 to 64 cells, but it does not have a definite blastocoel (central cavity).

5 **Blastula stage.** Once the blastocoel appears (about 9 to 11 hours after fertilization), the larva is at the **blastula** stage of development. The larva has reached this stage once a cavity appears inside the solid ball. This is the beginning of the **blastocoel.**

> How big are individual blastomere cells, as well as the morula and blastula, compared to the fertilized egg?

6 **Gastrula stage and the three germ layers in higher animals.** The embryo begins to elongate and the **archenteron,** or primitive gut, develops. The opening to the archenteron is the **blastopore.** At the blastopore, cells start to stream inward to form the archenteron. These cells that line the archenteron will form the **endoderm.** In most animals, the endoderm forms the gut epithelia and part of the associated digestive organs, such as the liver and pancreas. In mammals, the lungs are also primarily of endodermal origin. The outer layer of cells of the gastrula form the **ectoderm.** In most animals, ectoderm forms the skin and its associated organs, and the nervous system.

Coelomic vesicles can be observed forming off of the end of the archenteron. These pouches will eventually form the **coelom.** These cells are part of the **mesoderm.** Mesoderm is the germ layer that gives rise to the lining of the coelom; to muscles; to bone, blood, and other connective tissues, and to the reproductive and excretory systems.

> Can you see the blastopore? What do the archenteron and blastopore become in the adult deuterostomes, such as echinoderms and chordates? What does the blastopore become in the protostomes (annelids, molluscs, and arthropods)?

7 **Bipinnaria larva.** in echinoderms, the next stage in development is the **bipinnaria larva.** The mouth develops, and the larva can begin to feed. The final stage is the **brachiolaria.** After the brachiolaria stage, the larva settles to the bottom and metamorphoses into the adult echinoderm.

Animal Senses

Keywords

sensation (perception)
receptor
effector
chemoreceptors
pain receptors (nociceptors)
projection
thermoreceptors
photoreceptors
mechanoreceptors
sensory adaptation
interneuron
motor neuron
sensory neuron
blind spot
rods and cones
sclera
cornea
conjunctiva
bipolar cells
ganglion cells
retinal pigmented epithelium
Müller fibers
tapedum lucidum
iris
pupil

lens
anterior chamber
aqueous humor
posterior chamber
vitreous humor
retina
macula
fovea
choroid
optic nerve
retinal vein and artery
Meissner's corpuscle
Pacinian corpuscle
Merkel's cells
root hair
 plexus nerves
organ of Corti
auditory hair cells
vestibular duct
tympanic duct
cochlear duct
basilar membrane
tectorial membrane
exocrine
endocrine

epidermis
dermis
hypodermis
papillary layer
reticular layer
keratinocytes
sweat glands
sebaceous glands
arrector pili muscle
hair
muscle spindle
taste buds
papillae
microvilli
pinnae
external auditory canal
ear drum (tympanic
 membrane)
malleus, incus, and stapes
 (auditory ossicles)
cochlea
semicircular canals
auditory nerve
Eustachian tube

Learning Objectives

When finished with this unit, you should be able to do the following:

1 Describe the basic kinds of sensory receptors and their functions;

2 Discuss why sensory adaptation is important;

3 Describe the basic structure of the eye, the ear, and the skin, and identify the structures and receptors for touch, taste, smell, sight, hearing, and pain;

4 Describe the structures and functions of the integumentary system;

5 Compare and contrast exocrine and endocrine glands; and

6 Describe and identify the cell types and structures of the eye (retina), the ear (cochlea), and the skin.

Sensory Perception

In today's lab, you will be conducting a series of simple experiments examining your sensory systems and perception. Animals can detect and respond to internal and external stimuli; these stimuli include light, heat, cold, sound, touch, pain, chemicals, gravity, and electromagnetic fields.

Sensory receptors are categorized into five types, according to the stimulus to which they are most sensitive. In general, each type of receptor is very sensitive to one type of stimulus, yet is relatively insensitive to other stimuli. **Chemoreceptors** respond to changes in the chemical concentrations of body fluids, ingested materials and the outside environment. **Pain receptors** (also referred to as **nociceptors**) respond to tissue damage from a variety of causes. **Thermoreceptors** respond to changes in the external or internal temperatures. **Photoreceptors** respond to the presence of and changes in electromagnetic radiation, particularly in the visible light portion of the spectrum. Finally, there are many kinds of **mechanoreceptors** that respond to changes in touch and pressure. Mechanoreceptors sense mechanical forces that deform or displace tissues/organs in the body. The receptor cells may be neurons, but often they are specialized epithelial cells.

Sensory receptors typically have receptor proteins in the outer plasma membrane that respond to a specific stimulus. Once the stimulus is detected, the receptor proteins generally cause the opening or closing of ion channels, which then affects the resting potential of the receptor. This eventually causes the creation of action potentials (or the prevention of actions potentials) by the receptor cell or by a sensory cell one synapse away. The change in action potential frequencies traveling down a nerve towards the brains is interpreted by higher order brain cells as a sensation.

A **sensation (perception)** occurs when the brain receives information from sensory cells and interprets them. Although the brain typically is the organ involved in perception, it projects the sensation back to the apparent source (for example, it appears that the eyes see and the ears hear). This phenomenon is called **projection.**

TABLE 22.1. Sensory receptors: the types of receptors that respond to certain stimuli.

Receptor	Stimulus	Location (and specific receptor examples in humans)	Sense
photoreceptor	light (electrognetic radiation)	eyes (rods and cones)	vision
chemoreceptor	food chemicals and odors	taste buds, mouth, nose, tentacles, antennae, auricles (olfactory receptors, gustatory receptors)	taste, smell
chemoreceptor	carbon dioxide and hydrogen ions	brain, circulatory system	blood chemistry
auditory receptor (a mechanoreceptor)	sound (air or water vibrations)	ears, tympanic membranes (auditory hair cells)	sound
touch mechanoreceptor	light force exerted by an object	skin (Meissner's corpuscles, Merkel's cells, root hair plexus nerves)	touch
pressure mechanoreceptor	heavy force, pressure	skin (Pacinian corpuscles)	deep pressure
rheoreceptor (a mechanoreceptor)	current (force transmitted from water or air currents)	auricles of flatworms	water currents
baroreceptor (a mechanoreceptor)	blood pressure	circulatory system	blood pressure
proprioreceptor (a mechanoreceptor)	pressure exerted by changes in body position and by gravity	limbs, muscles, tendons, statocysts (muscle spindles, Golgi organs)	kinesthetic sense
pain receptor	pain	skin, cornea, much of the internal body, except in the brain	pain
temperature receptor	temperature of the body and the outside	skin (heat receptors, cold receptors)	temperature

Some of the cells are specialized for conduction of nervous impulses to and from the brain. Some cells of the **central nervous system** (the brain and spinal cord) integrate the information sent from sensory cells in the **sense organs** and send signals to the cells that elicit some response to the stimulus (the **effector organs,** such as muscles and glands). In many cases, your brain integrates information received from your sensory cells and then executes a complex response. In higher animals, a large number of cells may be involved in sensing and responding to a stimulus. In humans, we see a great range of complex responses; some responses are under conscious control, and some are not.

Exercises

Exercise 22.1.

The Blind Spot

In the eye, at the point in which the optic nerve joins the retina, there are no light receptors present. This area is called the **blind spot.** Place your hand over your left eye. Look with the right eye at the circle above. Move the manual slowly away from your face until one of the 'x's disappears. This is your blind spot.

Once the 'x' has disappeared, continue moving the manual slowly away from your face. Does the spot reappear? Observe closely. How does it reappear?

Close your right eye and use your left eye to stare at the filled circle as before. Do you have a blind spot with your left eye? Use your left eye and place the 'x' into your blind spot, and then open and close your right eye, keeping your left eye open. What happens? You have binocular vision (the area is seen by both eyes) directly in front of you. Relate the field of view for binocular vision with the locations of your blind spots.

Did you see a hazy area or dark area in your vision? Why not? Does your brain 'see' something that is not there? How does your brain do this? The **blind spot** occurs because there are no photoreceptors over the point at which the optic nerve leaves the back of the eye. Repeat the experiment, but keep both eyes open. Does a blind spot exist when both eyes are open?

Exercise 22.2.

Color Vision: Rods and Cones

There are two groups of sensory cells in your retina: **rods** and **cones.** Rods are more sensitive to light (they can detect the presence of fewer photons than can cones); this is why we can see under low light levels, and this is also why we can see dim astronomical objects (like a faint star) with our peripheral vision. When we attempt to view the star directly, our cones may fail to detect it. However when only rods are stimulated, your perception is 'white' light, not color, and the vision is 'grainier.' Cones predominate in the area of the **fovea;** the fovea is responsible for the sharp color vision in daylight. At the peripheral portions of your visual field, rods are much more abundant. In humans (and in our closest primate relatives), there are three distinct populations of cones. One population of cones is sensitive to blue light, one population is sensitive to green light, and one population is sensitive to red light, although the spectrum range detected by all three cone types overlap. In addition, the portion of the light spectrum sensed by the rods overlaps that detected by the three types of cones, but the rods need fewer photons to respond.

Perception of Color under Bright Light and Low Light

Do our eyes resolve all colors equally well? The entire class will perform this exercise simultaneously. The class will stand at one end of the lab with the lights on. The lab instructor has a series of cards with various colored disks on them. The lab instructor will randomly shuffle the cards and ask you to write down the color of each card's disk in turn. Write your answers on another sheet of paper. After the test, your lab instructor will tell you the color of each card in order. For each color, determine how many you guessed correctly, and provide the instructor your results (the percentages of each color correctly identified). Your lab instructor will tally up the results for the class.

Next, turn off the lights. During the daytime, the room will be dimly illuminated from the windows. At nighttime, the lab instructor will have a small nightlight plugged in to provide low illumination. Your lab instructor will again show the cards from across the room one at a time in random order. Again determine how many of each color you correctly identified. Tally your scores (or the lab's scores) in Table 22.2.

TABLE 22.2. Color perception

Color	Percent Correctly Identified under Well-Lit Conditions	Percent Correctly Identified under Dark Conditions
white		
grey		
black		
violet		
red		
orange		
yellow		
green		
blue		
blank (no disks)		

Which colors can you easily see in the light and in the dark? What is the purpose for the 'blank,' white, and black cards? Look at your scores: did you get progressively worse over time in the dark?

Is there any pattern to the overall responses of the class that you can determine? What colors may have been misidentified as what other colors? To what color are the cones most sensitive? The least sensitive? Think about the color of light used by pilots, submariners, astronomers, and other persons who have to read instruments under low light. Scientists observing invertebrates and other mammals under dark conditions also use the same color of light: the animals are less sensitive to it and behave as if they are in the dark. What color is this light?

Exercise 22.3.

Color Blindness

Color blindness is a color vision deficiency due to the deficiency or total absence of certain color-sensing cone populations. The most common color-blindness is due to a deficiency of red and green cones, thus people who are red-green color blind have difficulty distinguishing these two colors. Someone who is blue-yellow color blind cannot easily distinguish these two colors. Someone who is totally color blind only sees in shades of grey.

Examine the chromatic plates for detecting defective color vision. **DO NOT TOUCH THE COLOR PLATES WITH YOUR FINGERS!** Turn the pages at the edges. Do you show any type of color blindness?

Males are more likely than females to be color blind. Why do you think this is so?

Exercise 22.4.

Eye Dominance

Many of you have a preference for using one or the other hand for throwing and writing. You may also have a dominant eye preference as well. With both eyes open, extend your arm and hold your index finger (forefinger) up several feet in front of your face, with a distant object behind your raised finger. Focus on your finger. Close one eye, then reopen it. Do this several times. Do this procedure with the other eye. Opening and closing which eye causes your finger to appear to move relative to the background object: your left eye, your right eye, neither eye, or both eyes? If the object seems to jump back and forth when you close one eye, the eye that is closed is your dominant eye. It is possible that neither eye is dominant.

If you are having difficulty with determining eye dominance by the blinking method, look at the figure above. Hold the page between 2 and 12 inches from your nose, staring at the two circles with both eyes open. Cross your eyes slightly until you see a third circle appear between the other two circles. The word that you see in the central circle indicates your dominant eye. If you cannot cross your eyes, hold the page about a foot from your nose and slowly bring the page to your face, until you see the inner circle.

If you have difficulty with the methods described above, try the following method. Place your hands together at arm's length in front of you. Make a small triangular 'window' between your thumbs and forefingers, and stare at someone else's face through the 'window.' Bring your hands toward your face, and continue staring at the face through the 'window.' If you bring the 'window' towards one eye, that eye is your dominant eye. Likewise, as you move your hands away from your face towards the person, often they will see only one of your eyes through the window; that eye is the dominant eye.

If a person only uses the input from one eye, how could that affect their vision, compared to a person using both eyes equally?

Exercise 22.5.

Visual Near Points

Many of you have noticed that as people age, their vision changes. The shortest distance that an object is in sharp focus is called the **near point.** The closer the distance, the greater the ability of your eyes to focus on objects at various distances. This distance increases with age (Table 22.3). As you get older, you eventually need assistance to read fine print. You will know this because you need to move books away from your face in order to focus on the print. Time for bifocals!

If you wear glasses, take them off. Hold this page at arm's length. Close one eye and focus on the phrase below.

Biology is fun!

Slowly move the page towards your face until the words become blurred. Then move the page away until the words are in sharp focus again. Your lab partner should then measure the distance from your eyes to the page. This distance is your near point for that eye.

Try this with your other eye.

Your near point: Left eye: _________ cm; Right eye: _________ cm

Are you 'showing your age,' as compared with the following table?

TABLE 22.3. Estimated near points as a function of age.

Age (years)	Near Points (cm)
10	7
20	10
30	20
40	40
50	55
60	80
70+	100

Exercise 22.6.

Visual Acuity

Stand 20 feet away from the visual eye chart, behind the tape mark on the floor. Your lab partner will ask you to close one eye. Read the letters that your lab partner points to on this chart, and work your way down the chart. Note the lowest row of letters that you can accurately read. The number next to that row is the farthest distance (in feet) that a person with normal vision can read the letters of that row. For instance, if you can read accurately down to the row of letters marked "20/20," this means that your visual acuity is considered 'average.' The average person can read this line from 20 feet away. If you can read the 20/20 line, try reading the 20/10 line (if you can read that line accurately, you can read a line at 20 feet that most people can only read from 10 feet). If you cannot read the 20/20 line, can you read the 20/40 line?

First look at the chart with one eye (close the other), then look at the chart with the other eye, and then look with both eyes open. How good is your vision?

Without glasses or contacts: Right eye: _________; Left eye: _________; Both eyes: _________

With glasses or contacts on: Right eye: _________; Left eye: _________; Both eyes: _________

Exercise 22.7.

Structure of the Eye

A dense fibrous connective tissue sheath called the **sclera** surrounds the eye (Figure 22.1). Skeletal muscles that attach to the sclera move the eyeball around in its socket. In the front, the sclera becomes an thin transparent layer of cells, called the **cornea,** that allows light to penetrate into the eye. The cornea has a thin layer of epithelial cells and a layer of collagen fibers that allows the unimpeded passage of light. No blood supply is present, but many free nerve endings (nociceptors) are present. The **conjunctiva** is a layer of stratified epithelia that is found exterior to the sclera. It lubricates and protects the eye. Behind the cornea, light enters the fluid-filled **anterior chamber** filled with a less viscous, watery **aqueous humor.**

Within the anterior chamber is the **iris,** which is a layer of pigmented muscles (this pigmentation causes your eyes to be called 'blue,' 'brown,' or some other color). The hole in the center of the iris is the **pupil** (the black central portion of your eye). The diameter of the pupil increases and decreases in size as the muscles of the iris contract or relax, which allows more light (enlarged pupil diameter) or less light (decreased pupil diameter) to enter the eye.

Behind the pupil is the single clear **lens** of the eye (Figure 22.1). The ability to focus light comes from muscles that can cause the lens to become more spherical or more flattened, allowing the eye to focus on near (or far objects). Behind the lens is the fluid-filled **posterior chamber** filled with a viscous **vitreous humor.**

Light enters the pupil from all angles; the light must be bent in towards the photoreceptors that are located at the back of the eye (in the **retina**). The cornea and the lens accomplish this bending. As the light reaches the photoreceptors in the back of the posterior chamber, the image is upside down, due to the bending of the light. The brain, however, adjusts for this and the image is perceived right-side up.

The **retina** (Figure 22.1) is the innermost layer at the back of the eye where the photoreceptors and other nerve cells are located. The photoreceptors (**rods** and **cones**) transduce the light into electrical signals that the brain will interpret as vision. The rods and cones are named because of the shape of the outer segment of these cells.

The actual parts of the rods and cones that respond to light are at the outer edge (the back) of the retinal layer, embedded into the **retinal pigment epithelium** (the outer layer of the retina next to the choroid, see Figure 22.2). The retinal pigmented epithelium helps nourish the photoreceptors. Behind the retinal pigment epithelium is a layer of blood vessels and connective tissues (this layer is called the **choroid**) that nourishes the retinal cells. Behind the choroid is the sclera. About 130 million rods are found throughout the cup-shaped retina; the roughly 6 million cones are also found in the retina, with many of them concentrated around the **fovea centralis.**

The **macula,** or **macula lutea,** is a small yellowish region of the retina in which the sharpest color vision occurs. In the center of the macula, the **fovea,** or **fovea centralis,** is a small spot (about 1 mm across) in the central part of the retina where many cones (and no rods) are located. The fovea is responsible for the sharp, colorful images we see when we are standing in bright sunlight. The density of rods is greater in the periphery of the retina than in the central part of the retina near the fovea. As darkness settles in, you may have noticed that your color perception disappears and your vision is not as sharp.

At the **optic disk (optic disc)**, axons from the ganglion cells exit the eye to form the optic nerve that travels to the brain. No photoreceptors are located at this spot (hence the **blind spot**). The **retinal artery** and **retinal vein** also enter the eye at the optic disk (Figure 22.1).

You will notice that the choroid contains a dark pigment, **melanin** (Figure 22.2). In humans and the primates, this pigment helps prevent excess reflection of light. For many other animals, including dogs, cats and other groups who can be active at night, there is less melanin, which in part explains their superior night vision. In many nocturnal animals, a portion of the choroid has a highly reflective tissue, the **tapetum lucidum,** which helps collect additional light that is then detected by the receptors. You may have noticed the **red-eye effect** in photographs taken of you and your friends in dim light; this is due to the partial reflection of light (especially red) from the choroid. You may have also noticed a strong **eyeshine** occurs when you shine a light on your dog, cat, or wild animal who has turned their head and looked back at you from the darkness; this eyeshine is due to the controlled light reflection by the highly reflective tapetum lucidum.

Eye Model

Observe the general model of the eye at the demonstration table and identify the parts of the eye listed below. Use Figure 22.1 to guide you.

Sclera, cornea, iris, pupil, lens, anterior chamber, aqueous humor, posterior chamber, vitreous humor, retina, macula, fovea, choroid, optic nerve, retinal vein, and **artery.**

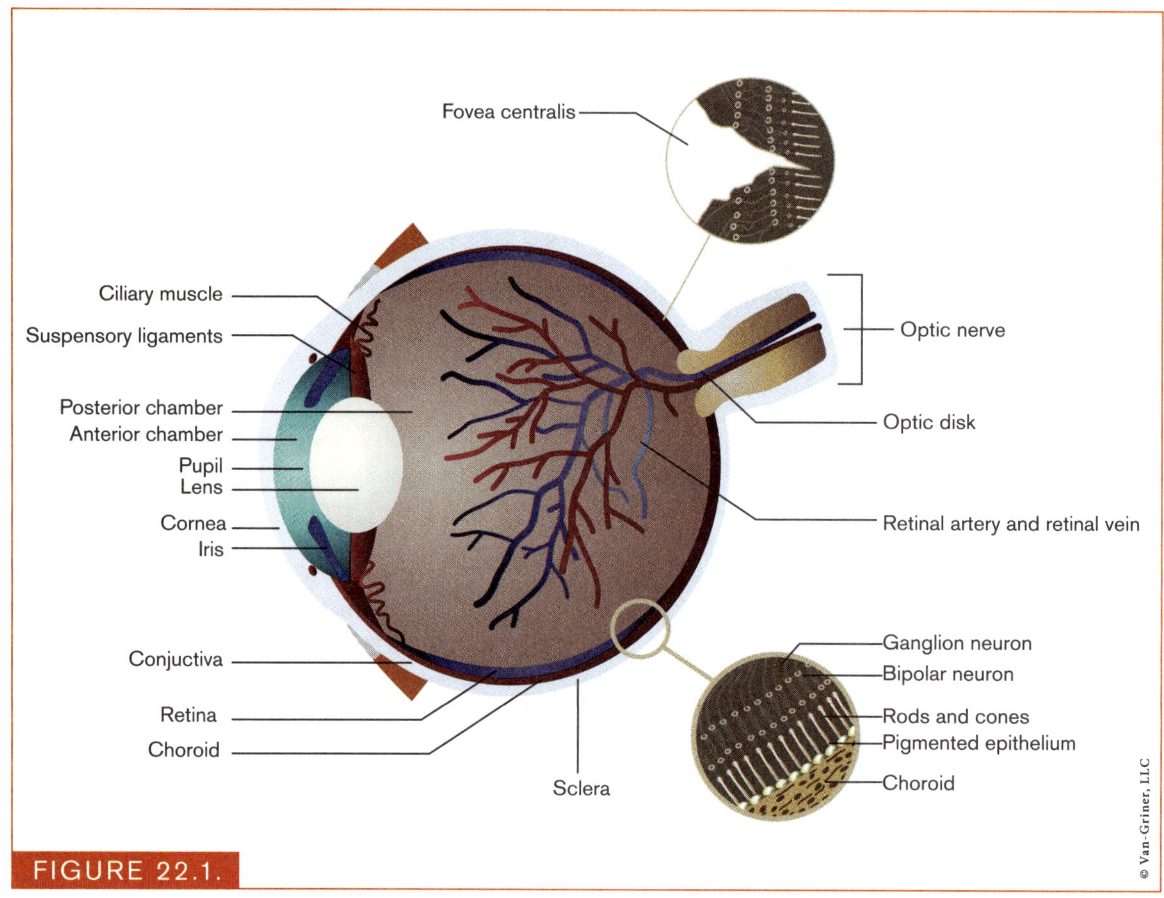

FIGURE 22.1.

Cross section through the mammalian eye.

Exercise 22.8.

The Retina

The **rods** and **cones** are the photoreceptors (they are called 'rods' and 'cones' because of the shape of the outer segments of these cells). In Figure 22.2, the thick band of darkly stained nuclei are the nuclei of the rods and cones. The smaller band represents the nuclei of the **bipolar cells** and other interneurons involved in the initial processing of the visual information gathered by the photoreceptors, before the information is sent to the brain. The bipolar cells make synapses with the rods and cones. The bipolar cells also make synapses with the **ganglion cells,** which are the innermost layer of cells of the retina, next to the posterior chamber. The ganglion cells axons conjoin and form the **optic nerve** that leaves the eye and sends signals to the brain for further processing. There are about 6 million ganglion cells. Perhaps as many as a thousand rods (through their connections to bipolar cells) send information to a single ganglion cell; for cones, particularly in the fovea, a single cone and bipolar cell makes contact with a single ganglion cell, thus providing sharper detail.

In addition to bipolar cells and ganglion cells, several other types of interneurons are present in the retina and are involved in the processing of visual information in the eye. **Horizontal cells** and **amacrine cells** are interneurons. Horizontal cells regulate and integrate the output from photoreceptors to the bipolar cells, and the amacrine cells integrate and regulate the output of the bipolar cells and the ganglion cells. You may be able to identify a few of the horizontal cell and amacrine cell nuclei in the outermost edges of the thin band of nuclei of the bipolar cells. The nuclei that you see in the innermost region of the retina are those of the ganglion cells. The Muller fibers are glial cells that recently have been shown to act as 'optical fibers': they are funnel-shaped cells that are oriented parallel to the direction of light striking the retinal surface. They collect and pass light back to the photoreceptors, minimizing the distortion of light as it passes through the retinal cell layers.

The Retina and Retinal Processing

Observe the prepared slide of the retinal cross section at the demonstration table and identify the parts of the retina listed below. The retina consists of the parts of the eye labeled 3 through 13 in Figure 22.2. Use Figure 22.2 to guide you. Note the layers of the cross section that represents the **photoreceptors** (**rods** and **cones**), the **bipolar cells,** the **ganglion cells,** the **retinal pigmented epithelium,** the Muller fibers, the **choroid,** and the **sclera.**

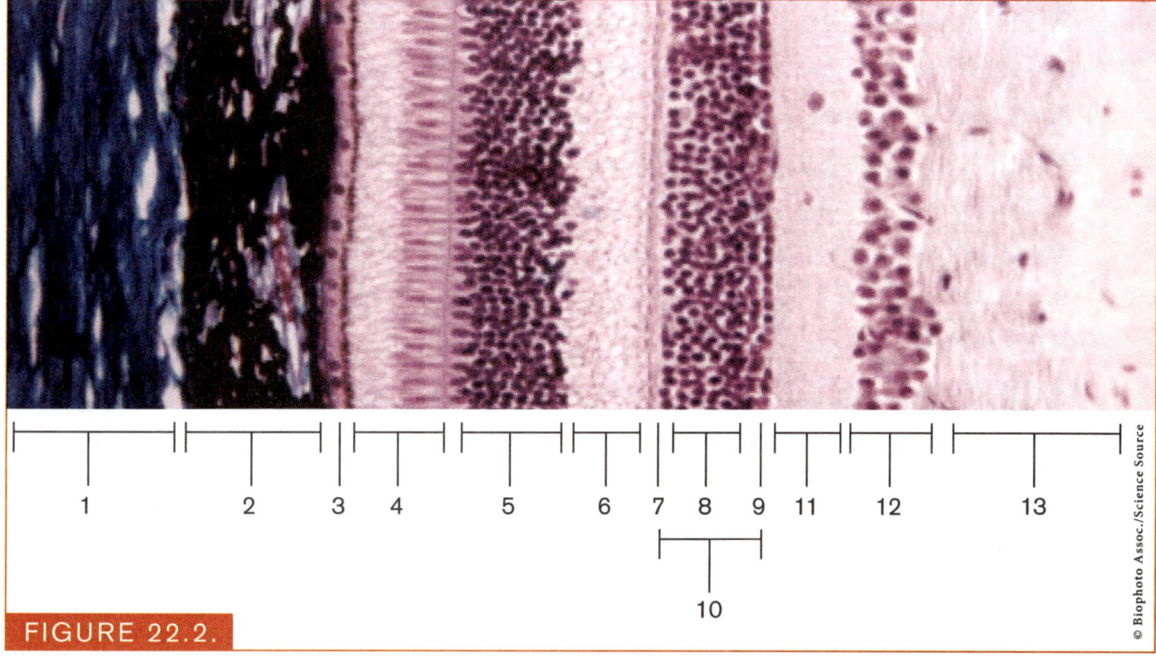

FIGURE 22.2.

Cross section through the retina of the mammalian eye.

1. Sclera (connective tissues and blood vessels)
2. Chloroid
3. Retinal pigmented epithelium
4. Photoreceptor layer (inner and outer segments of the rods and cones)
5. Outer nuclear layer (nuclei of rods and cones)
6. Outer plexiform layer (synapses among photoreceptors, horizontal, and bipolar cells)
7. Horizontal cell nuclei
8. Bipolar cell nuclei
9. Amacrine cell nuclei
10. Inner nuclear layer (7, 8, and 9 combined)
11. Inner plexiform layer (synapses among bipolar, amacrine, and ganglion cells)
12. Ganglion cell nuclei
13. Muller fibers and blood vessels

Exercise 22.9.

Density of Touch Receptors and Two-Point Discrimination

> Touch receptors vary in their densities on various parts of the body. We can estimate the relative densities of these touch receptors by the following exercise. Have the subject close their eyes while seated. You can make a homemade 'touch caliper' that is a paper clip refolded into a U shape, so that both ends are parallel to each other and are separated by a certain distance (1 to 40 mm). Touch one or both ends of the paper clip to each of the the locations listed below in Table 22.4. If the subject felt two points, write 'Yes' in Table 22.4 below. If the subject perceived only one point, write 'No.' Touch each area at least three times.

TABLE 22.4. Two-point discrimination data.

Location Tested	Distance between the Two Points (in mm)						
	0 (1 pin)	1 mm	2 mm	5 mm	10 mm	20 mm	40 mm
fingertip							
back of hand							
back of neck							
upper arm							
tip of nose							
palm of hand							
forehead							

In locations where there are more touch receptors, the skin is more sensitive to touch and thus it can provide more information about the number of touches (one or two pins) pressed against the area. The smallest distance that the subject reliably felt two pins applied means that two different touch receptors have been stimulated separately.

You can determine the number of receptors per cm^2 of skin by squaring the smallest distance (in mm) where two distinct points were perceived (the smallest distance where the subject said 'Yes' reliably in Table 22.4) and dividing this into one (take the inverse of the squared distance), and then multiplying that number by 100 (the number of mm^2 in one cm^2). Fill in the following table (Table 22.5) with your results.

number of receptors per $cm^2 = [1 / (distance)^2] \times 100$

TABLE 22.5. Estimated receptor densities of different parts of the body.

Location Tested	Shortest Distance Two Points Were Perceived (in mm)	Number of Receptors per cm^2
fingertip		
back of hand		
back of neck		
upper arm		
nose		
palm of hand		
forehead		

Do all parts of the body appear to have touch receptors in equal densities? Where are touch receptors concentrated?

A sensory receptor senses the pressure exerted by a point and sends information through several relay cells to a cell in the central nervous system (CNS) in the brain. In order to discriminate two points pressing in on our skin, we have to have two different receptors sending two different signals, which the brain interprets as two points. Neighboring receptor cells connect to different CNS neurons. A CNS neuron involved in the perception of pressure interprets all of the information sent to it (from the area of the skin around the sensory receptor) as coming from one point. This area of the skin is called the **receptive field** for the neuron. If the two points are pressing in the same receptive field, the CNS neuron would interpret the sensory information as coming from one point on the skin, not two. In order for you to sense two different points of pressure, two separate CNS cells must be activated by stimulation to their respective receptor fields. At the fingertips, the denser concentration of sensory cells (and the smaller receptive fields for the CNS neurons) allows you to distinguish two distinct points at a distance of a few millimeters, whereas the sparse distribution of pressure receptors on your back may require a distance of 30 to 70 mm in order for you to sense two distinct pressure points.

Exercise 22.10.

Temperature Adaptation

Place your left hand in very warm water and your right hand in ice water (or vice versa). Leave your hands in the water until you get used to the temperatures (sensory adaptation has occurred). Does the sensation change with time? After a few minutes, place both hands in a pan of water (whose contents are at room temperature). Note the sensation. What do you now perceive?

Exercise 22.11.

Sensory Adaptation: Touch

In addition to perception and projection, another phenomenon of sensation is called **sensory adaptation.** You experienced this phenomenon in Exercise 22.10. Have the subject rest their forearms with the palms facing up on the table. Have them then close their eyes. Place a penny on the inner surface of the forearm. Note the time. The subject will soon notice that the initial pressure sensation will disappear. Tell them to tell you when the sensation disappears. Record the time interval (in seconds) between the time you placed the penny to the time they no longer sense it on their arm. This is called **adaptation time.**

Your adaptation time:

The pressure receptors adapted to the stimulus. After they are stimulated, these receptors do not continue sending signals to the brain, unless there is a change in the intensity of the stimulus. To show this, add three or more pennies on top of the initial penny. Record the time it took for the sensation to disappear. What happened? Why is sensory adaptation important

Hint: Do you always feel your clothes, or the floor, or your seat?

Now, sit on the stool and think about a part of your body that is in contact with clothing (arm, leg, etc.) Do you now feel your clothes?

Exercise 22.12.

The Skin (Integumentary System)

In some texts, the human 'skin' is thought of as an organ; however, it represents a large **organ system.** The **integumentary system** includes the epidermis and dermis, and the associated **accessory structures,** such as hair, nails, and numerous **exocrine glands.** Exocrine glands that have a duct that leads to an outer or inner body surface, as opposed to **endocrine glands,** which are ductless and whose secretory products (hormones) are released directly into blood or interstitial fluids. A number of sensory structures are present in the integument as well. Throughout the animal kingdom, the outer integument includes calcareous shells, chitinous exoskeletons, feathers, hooves, spines, and scales of various types, in addition to epithelial and associated connective tissue layers.

The integumentary system has a variety of functions that help to maintain homeostasis.

❶ It is involved in respiration (cutaneous respiration) in many animals.

❷ It is involved in the excretion of nitrogenous wastes.

❸ The integument is important in water and salt balance (osmoregulation and ionoregulation).

❹ In humans, vitamin D_3 is produced in the integument.

❺ The integument stores different materials for different animals, including salts, water, and fat.

❻ The integument also supports and protects the body from microbial infections and ectoparasites.

❼ The integument protects against physical (abrasion, ultraviolet radiation) and chemical damage.

❽ It is involved in temperature regulation for many animals.

❾ Finally, the integument is a major site for the sensory reception of chemicals, food, light, temperature, pain, and pressure.

The mammalian skin is composed of two components: the outer **epidermis** and the inner **dermis.** There are several layers of epithelial cells, most of the cells are **keratinocytes.** From the outside in, there are four (or five layers, if we are referring to the **thick skin** of the soles of the hands and feet). **Thin skin** covers most of the human body (this thickness is only referring to the epidermis, not the entire integument). The surface layer is composed entirely of dead keratinocytes; this layer is called the **stratum corneum.** The dead skin cells continuously flake off the surface (the source of much of what you call 'dust' on floors and carpets). In the thick skin of the palms and soles of the feet (but not in thin skin), there is a thin layer of dead, clear cells that are called the **stratum lucidum.** Below the stratum lucidum (or corneum of thin skin), a thin layer of living cells called the **stratum granulosum** helps waterproof the skin. Below the stratum granulosum is a thicker layer of living cells called the **stratum spinosum;** filaments of keratin in these cells helps hold the cells together and resist abrasion. Below the stratum spinosum is the **stratum basale.**

Keratinocytes in the deepest layer of cells (the **stratum basale,** which are connected to the **basement membrane**) undergo mitosis and the resultant daughter cells move up the strata to the outside. The cells eventually die (they lose their nuclei and other cellular components), but they produce large amounts of keratin, lipids, and other compounds that give mechanical strength to skin. **Melanocytes** are located in the deepest layer of the epidermis; they manufacture the pigment **melanin** that is transferred to keratinocytes inside small vesicles (melanosomes). Melanin helps protect the deeper tissues from UV radiation.

There are no blood vessels in the epidermis; the living keratinocytes are nourished by diffusion of oxygen and food from blood capillaries of the underlying dermis. The deepest layers of the epidermis form extensions that penetrate into the dermis, called **epidermal ridges. Dermal papillae** (containing loose areolar connective tissues) extend from the dermis into the epidermis. The dermal papillae and the epidermal ridges interdigitate with each other. These ridges increase the surface area of the skin; the ridges form the unique 'fingerprint' patterns of whorls and spirals on your fingers and palms.

The **dermis** is the layer of cutaneous membrane beneath the epidermis. It is composed of several types of connective tissues, whose collagen fibers (along with elastin and other fibers) give skin elasticity and tensile strength. The connective tissues also support the epithelial cells of the epidermis and cushion the underlying organs from physical damage.

The outer **papillary layer** of the dermis is composed of areolar connective tissues, including the dermal papillae. The inner **reticular layer** of the dermis is made of dense connective tissues and is composed of collagen and other protein fibers.

Many of the **mechanoreceptors** involved in temperature sensation and touch are present in the dermis. **Tactile (Meissner's) corpuscles** are small sense organs just beneath the epidermis in the ends of the dermal papillae that stick up into the epidermis. These small organs respond to light touch and adapt rapidly, as discussed in Exercise 22.11. The **Pacinian corpuscles** are larger and deeper in the dermis (in the reticulated layer), compared to tactile corpuscles. The Pacinian corpuscles detect stronger pressure changes (for example, someone pokes you in the arm) and especially to vibration of the skin (due to the skin of your finger passing over a surface with fine striations or bumps that are less than a mm in size). Like Meissner's corpuscles, they adapt rapidly. The epidermis contains many free nerve ending that are associated with pain or temperature. The stratum basale of the epidermis has many specialized epithelial cells, called **Merkel cells,** that have contact with nerve fibers; these cells also sense fine contact with the skin.

The **hair follicles** and their associated smooth muscles (**arrector pili muscle**), nerves (**root hair plexus**), and **sebaceous (oil) glands** are in the dermis. The root hair plexus responds to light touch when the hair moves. Blood vessels, lymphatic vessels, and nerves are all found in the dermis. In humans, many **sweat glands** are also present; sweat glands produce copious amounts of a watery **sweat** that rises to the skin's surface through small pores. The evaporation of this sweat is a major method of heat loss from the human body.

The **hypodermis** or **subcutaneous layer** lies below the dermis. It is composed of loose connective tissues, including **adipose** (fat) tissue. The hypodermis attaches to the integument and separates the integument from the underlying connective tissue layers of the bones, muscles, and other organs. Some texts refer to the hypodermis as part of the integument, others do not. For this class, we will include the hypodermis in our discussion of the integument.

Touch or bend a single hair on various parts of your body (head, face, neck, arms, legs) without touching or pressing into your skin. What do you feel?

Go to the demonstration table and use Figure 22.3 to guide you. Examine the skin model slide and be able to identify the following structures on the model and on any figure: **hair follicle, sebaceous gland, epidermis, dermis, hypodermis, sweat gland, lamellated (Pacinian) corpuscle, tactile (Meissner's) corpuscle, artery, vein.**

Discuss the following with your classmates and the lab instructor. Your skin contains collagen fibers, which are strong and resist stretching, but can be bent, whereas the elastin fibers permit some stretching of the skin to occur, and both the fibers and that portion of your skin will return to their original length after stretching. This allows your skin to stretch somewhat, particularly in some directions. The arrangement and orientation of the collagen and elastin fibers tends to be in parallel bundles (which establishes the lines of cleavage for the skin). These fibers are aligned to allow some stretching of the skin along directions of normal movement of the body parts. A cut in the skin that parallels the fibers' orientation can remain closed, but a cut perpendicular to the orientation will stay open as the elastin fibers recoil. Does this fact matter to surgeons and surgical procedures?

The superficial layer of the hypodermis (the portion next to the dermis) is rich with capillaries and small arteries and an extensive number of veins. Explain why this fact is important to the dermis and epidermis. The deeper portion of the hypodermis has fewer capillaries and blood vessels and no vital organs that can be damaged. Think about the long hypodermic needles used to give **subcutaneous injections,** where the drug is administered (or water) deep into the hypodermis. Discuss why hypodermal injections are a useful way to administer drugs.

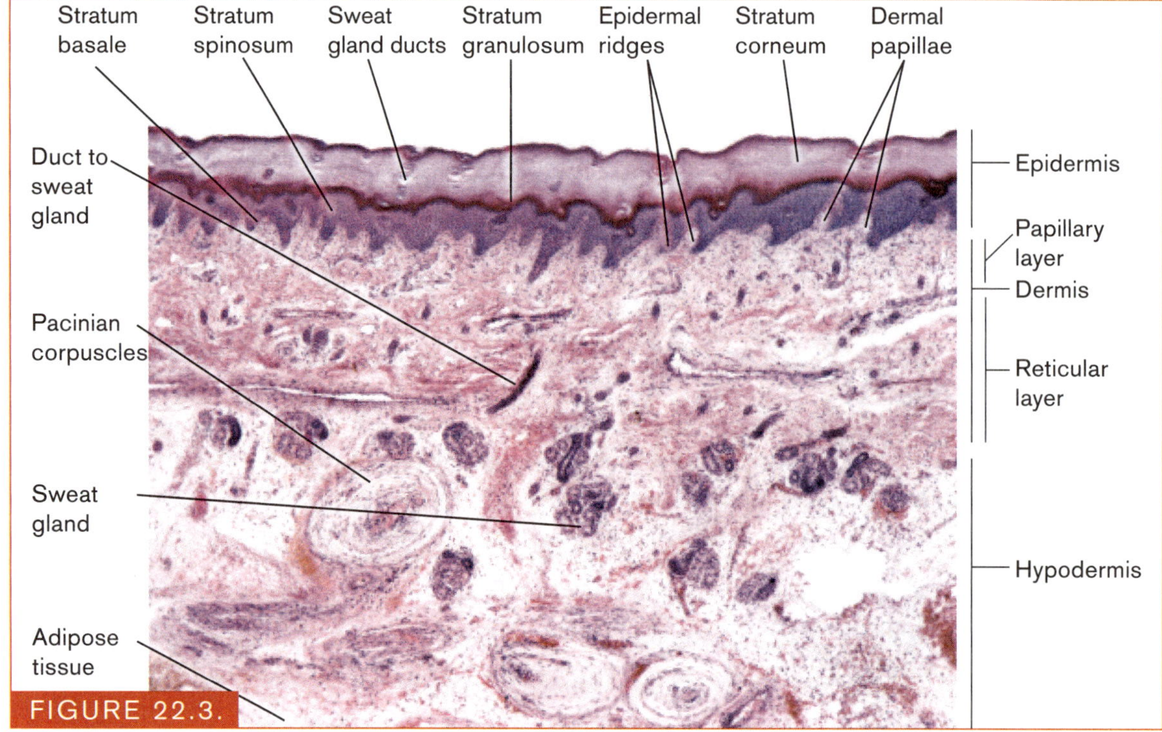

FIGURE 22.3.

General structure of the human skin.

Mechanoreceptors

Observe the prepared slides of the Meissner's corpuscle and the Pacinian corpuscle at the demonstration table. Make a quick sketch of what you see in the space provided below (Figure 22.4).

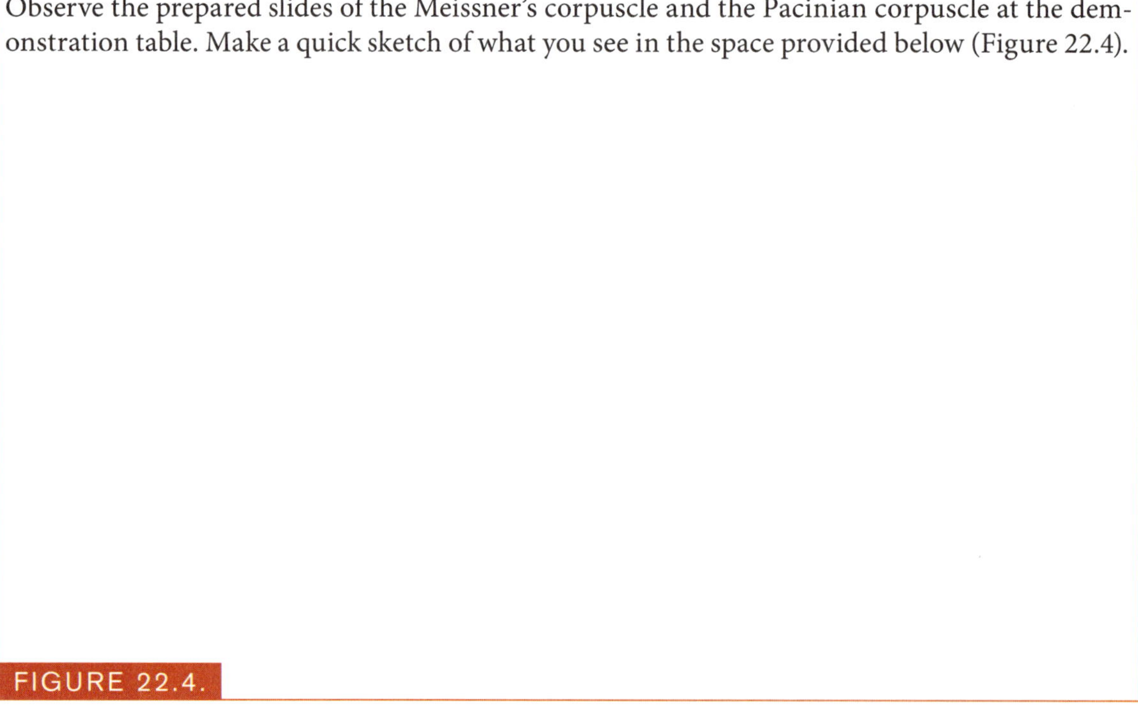

FIGURE 22.4.

Meissner's corpuscle and Pacinian corpuscle.

Exercise 22.13.

Discrimination of Weight

Sensory receptors are associated with special muscle fibers embedded within skeletal muscles that detect changes in the length of the skeletal muscles. The special muscle fibers and the associated mechanoreceptors are referred to as a **muscle spindle.** The muscle spindle sends information to the brain central nervous system via a sensory neuron; the brain can interpret the information to determine the position of body parts and the amount of gravitational force acting on the muscles. The muscle spindles can affect the contraction of muscles, activating motor neurons to resist the muscle stretch.

Each student can act as the test subject, with one or two other students acting as experimenter. Have the subject close their eyes; they are to keep their eyes closed for the duration of the test. Hand them two of the partially-filled water bottles (one of the bottles labeled 'X' and one of the bottles labeled 'A' through 'J'). Do not tell the subject which bottles are being handed to him/her. The subject will always have 'X' in one hand (randomly place 'X' either in the left hand or the right, and be sure to randomize which bottle is handed to the subject first: either 'X' or the other bottle). The subject is to determine quickly (within three seconds, without hesitation) which bottle feels heavier. They cannot say "both are equally heavy": this opinion will count as an incorrect answer. The subject cannot shake the bottles or look at them. If they cannot tell which is heavier, they are to make a guess, as best as they can. The recorder notes in Table 22.6 below whether or not the subject was correct (✓) or incorrect (✗). Take the two bottles back, and then hand back one of the bottles labeled X back to them with another bottle (A–J), until the subject has been tested with all 10 bottles. If time allows, repeat several times. (The bottles have a precise amount of water in each. Recall that 1 ml of water weighs 1 gram).

TABLE 22.6. Weight discrimination.

Bottle (weight)	The number of times the subject (class) correctly identified if the other bottle (A–J) was heavier than X (200 g). Use a check (✓) for a correct answer, and an x (✗) for an incorrect answer (or for a "I cannot tell" or "I do not know" answer).
A (205 g)	
B (210 g)	
C (215 g)	
D (220 g)	
E (225 g)	
F (230 g)	
G (235 g)	
H (240 g)	
I (245 g)	
J (250 g)	

Examine the results above. What seems to be your threshold for correctly distinguishing weight? Provide the lab instructor your estimate of your threshold weight. He or she will post the threshold estimates on the front board.

Examine the class data. What appears to be the typical threshold, under these conditions, for the ability to sense differences in weight?

Exercise 22.14.

Ear Model

The **ear** is involved with detecting acoustic stimuli (sound waves, which is vibration of the air), which then are interpreted as sound. The **outer ear** consists of the **pinna** (what you call your 'ear') and the **external auditory canal,** which is about 2 cm long. The pinna collects sound waves and directs sound into the external auditory canal. Glands in the canal produce wax, which resist microbial growth and helps to prevent foreign objects passage into the ear.

What we call 'sound' is energy in the form of air pressure waves of alternating high and low pressure. The **eardrum,** or **tympanic membrane,** is at the end of the external auditory canal. Behind the eardrum is a small air-filled cavity called the **middle ear.** A air-filled tube, called the **Eustachian tube** or **auditory tube,** leads from the middle ear to the back of the pharynx. Normally, the four cm long Eustachian tube is closed, but it can expand to let a small amount of air through from the pharynx. As you have gone up in an airplane, you may have noticed 'pressure' building up in your ears; your ears 'pop,' especially as you swallowed, to equalize the air pressures on either side of the eardrum.

Attached to the other side of the eardrum are three tiny bones (the **auditory ossicles**). The first ossicle, attached to the eardrum, is the **malleus** (hammer); the malleus attaches to the **incus** (anvil), which in turn attaches to the **stapes** (stirrup). The stapes then makes contact with the **oval window** of the **inner ear.** The vibrational energy of air pressure waves is transduced into mechanical movements of the ossicles. Small muscles (the tensor tympani and the stapedius) prevent the middle ear bones from vibrating too strongly against the oval window. Contractions of these muscles dampen the movement of the inner ear bones, so that sounds created by chewing and speaking, along with loud external sounds, are lessened, protecting the inner ear from loud noises. As the stapes moves, it vibrates against the oval window, which causes the fluid (perilymph) in the cochlea to generate pressure waves.

Observe the general model of the ear at the demonstration table and identify the parts of the ear listed below. Use Figure 22.5 to guide you.

Pinna, external auditory canal), eardrum (tympanic membrane), malleus, incus and stapes (auditory ossicles), cochlea, semicircular canals, auditory nerve, Eustachian tube.

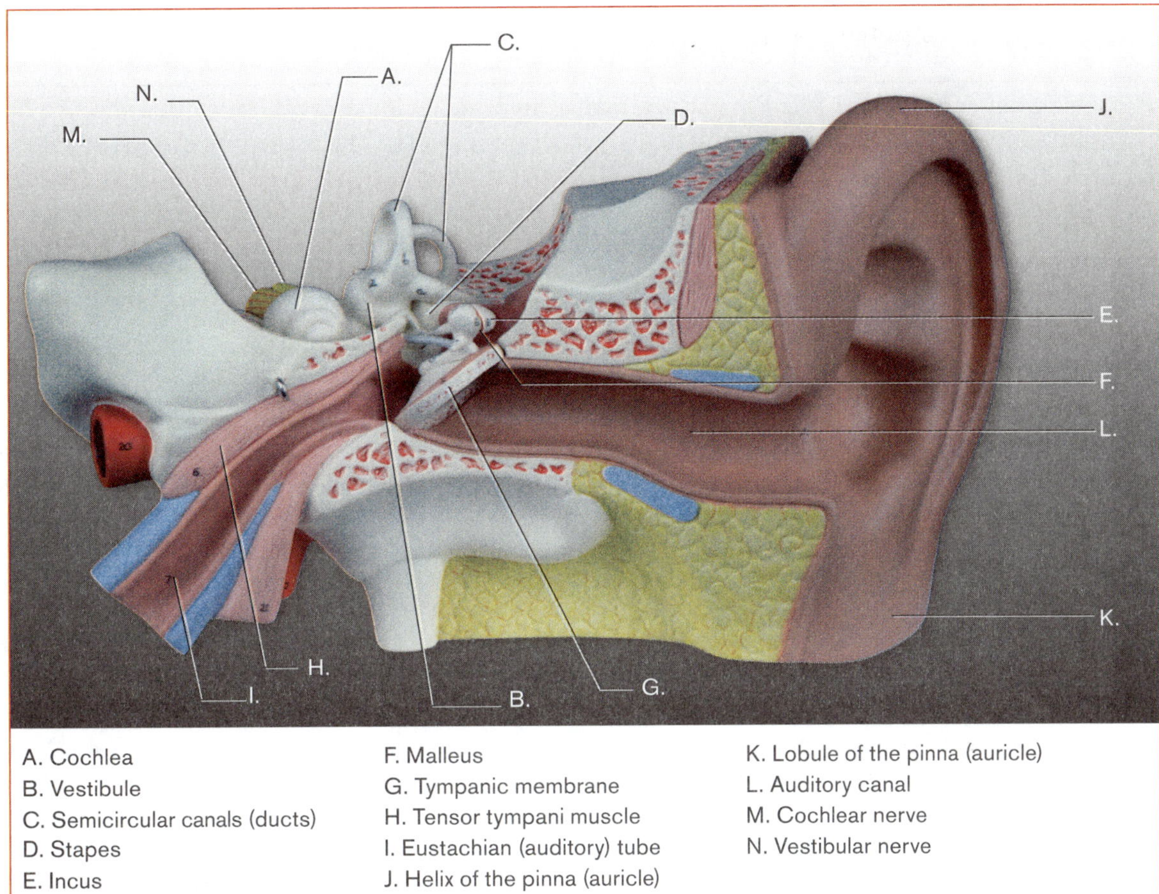

A. Cochlea
B. Vestibule
C. Semicircular canals (ducts)
D. Stapes
E. Incus
F. Malleus
G. Tympanic membrane
H. Tensor tympani muscle
I. Eustachian (auditory) tube
J. Helix of the pinna (auricle)
K. Lobule of the pinna (auricle)
L. Auditory canal
M. Cochlear nerve
N. Vestibular nerve

FIGURE 22.5.

General structure of the human ear.

Exercise 22.15.

The Cochlea and Auditory Perception

The inner ear is a fluid-filled structure encased in bone; it consists of the **cochlea** and the **three semicircular canals** (also referred to as semicircular ducts). The three semicircular canals are involved with equilibrium. It is in the cochlea that the vibrations transmitted from the eardrum through the ossicles are converted into signals sent along the auditory nerve to the brain.

The cochlea is like a tapered tube. The **basilar membrane** divides the tube lengthwise into two fluid-filled canals (the vestibular canal [or duct]), and the tympanic canal [duct]), which are joined at the tapered end. Pressure waves move through the perilymph down the vestibular canal and into the tympanic canal. At the end of the tympanic canal the waves dissipate against the **round window,** a membranous structure separating the inner ear from the middle ear. The pressure waves of the perilymph distort the basilar membrane on their way to the round window. The location of the distortion at a particular place in the inner ear is a function of the frequency of the pressure waves. High-frequency sounds (short wavelengths) vibrate the basilar membrane near the oval window, while low-frequency (long wavelength) waves vibrate the basilar membrane farther from the oval window.

The mechanoreceptors of the inner ear (**hair cells**) at a given point on top of the basilar membrane respond to the vibration. There are about 20,000 hair cells in the cochlea that are found along the length of the cochlea; the hair cells and associated cells make up the **organ of Corti.** The hair cells sit inside a third canal that is called the middle canal (or **cochlear duct**). A small membrane (the **tectorial membrane**) sits on top of the hair cells. Hair cells have special sensory cilia that are displaced against part of the tectorial membrane. This deflection causes potentials in the hair cells which will stimulate the sensory neurons synapsed with the hair cells. The sensory neurons then generate action potentials. The axons of the sensory nerves form the **auditory nerve** that travels to the brain.

Observe the prepared slide of the cochlea at the demonstration table and identify the parts of the cochlea listed below. Use Figure 22.6 to guide you. Note the position of the **hair cells** and the basilar membrane.

Organ of Corti, hair cells, vestibular duct, tympanic duct, cochlear duct, basilar membrane, tectorial membrane.

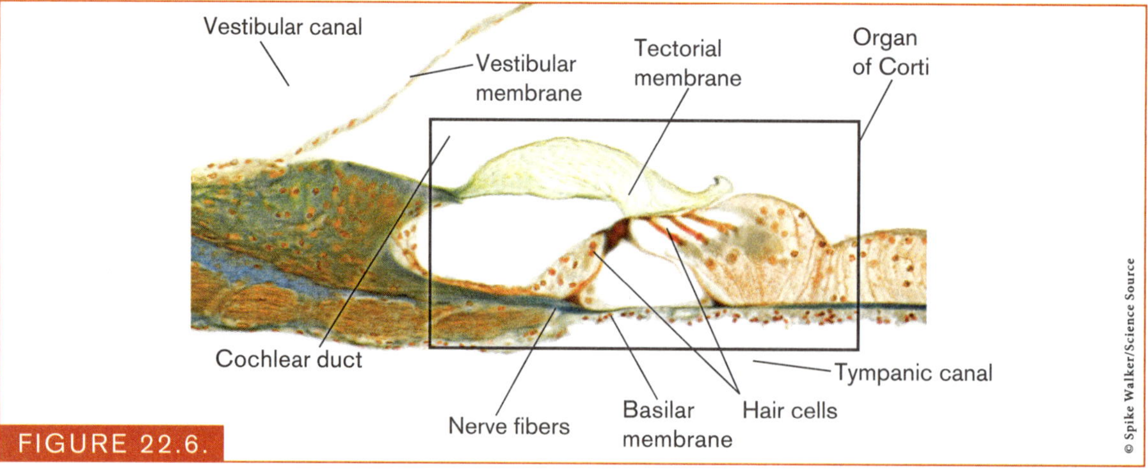

FIGURE 22.6.

Cross section through the spiral organ (the organ of Corti) in the cochlea of the mammalian ear.

Exercise 22.16.

Hearing Acuity

To point out the function of the pinna and the auditory canal, go out into the hall. Have another student stand at the other end of the hall and drop a pin or coin or some small object onto the floor, from a height of a couple of inches. Face directly at them, and close your eyes. If you heard the object drop, note how loud and clear the sound was. Then, cup your hands to your ears, and listen again for the object to drop. Can you hear it more loudly or clearly when you cupped your ears?

Exercise 22.17.

Determination of the Number of Cells Involved in the Reaction to Stimuli

A Your lab instructor will describe one of several ways that you can determine your 'reaction time.' Fill in Table 22.7 below.

TABLE 22.7. Reaction time calculations.

Trial	'Reaction Time' (sec)
1	
2	
3	
4	
5	
average	

B Measure the distance from the eyes to the back of the head (the visual centers are in the back). (You can use string to hug the head closely, then measure the length of the string). Add this to the distance from the head to the shoulder. Add this to the distance from the shoulder to the middle of the forearm (the muscles used to react to the stimulus are located here). Measure the total length in meters.

'Distance for nerve transmission': _________________ m

C Divide the total length measured in part B by 100 m/sec (the average nerve conduction rate). This provides you the 'time' it takes for the signal to be transmitted from eye to brain and from the brain to the muscles.

'Time for signal transmission from receptors to effectors': _________________ sec.

D Subtract the 'signal transmission time' from part C from the 'reaction time' calculated in part A to give the 'thinking time.' The thinking time is the total of all time involved in sending the signal from one cell to the next via synapses.

'Thinking time': _______________________ sec.

E Now divide the 'thinking time' calculated in part D by 0.005 sec/synapse. The 0.005 sec is the average length of time it takes for a synaptic signal to cross the synaptic cleft and be received and transduced into a nerve impulse. This last calculation gives a very rough estimate of the average number of synapses involved in seeing, perceiving, thinking about, and reacting to the visual stimulus. Does your estimate surprise you?

Your estimate of the number of synapses involved:

_______________________ synapses

Exercise 22.18.

Pain. A number of pain receptors exist in the body. They respond to various forms of tissue damage or to excessive stimuli. For obvious reasons (!), we will not be hitting each other over the head with mallets. However, we can perform a harmless exercise that allows us to experience a mild discomfort on one body part, where the pain appears to be located elsewhere. This phenomenon is called **referred pain.** Some of the sensations called referred pain are highly predictable and occur in most people. This allows physicians to diagnose certain ailments from the location and types of referred pain.

Referred pain. Immerse one of your elbows into the bowl of ice water and keep it immersed for several minutes. As you keep the elbow immersed, have another student/lab partner record your sensations of pain, and the perceived location of this pain.

Note the location of the perceived pain. Do you sense pain at the elbow? Where does the referred pain often appear for a person who has suffered a mild heart attack?

Exercise 22.19.

Smell

Our smell receptors (olfactory receptors) are found in our noses. You have probably watched your pet cat or dog rouse from a nap, raise their head, and sniff in air. You have probably sniffed the air at times as well, which causes you to look for the location of the food (or some other odorous material!). Sniffing forces more air in through the nose and across the nasal epithelium in the roof of your nasal cavity, where olfactory receptors are located. Olfaction (the sense of smell) is where molecules of the substance you are detecting interact with your 10 million or so olfactory receptor cells.

The **olfactory receptor cells** are neurons that have special sensory **cilia,** which protrude out of the cell and into a layer of **mucus** (which is produced by other cells). The molecular receptors on the surface of these olfactory receptors interact with specific airborne molecules (called odorants, which first diffuse into the mucus). The olfactory receptors then send signals to the brain via the **olfactory nerve.** The brain interprets the signals and creates a perception of smell. In addition, a substantial part of the 'tastiness' of food is actually due to the olfactory receptors in our nose reacting to odorants emanating from the food.

Observe the prepared slide of the olfactory epithelium at the demonstration table. Make a quick sketch of what you see in the space provided below (Figure 22.7).

FIGURE 22.7.

Olfactory epithelium.

Exercise 22.20.

Spice Identification

Work in pairs or small groups. One of the secrets to being a good cook is the understanding of the appropriate use of spices. Spices enhance the attractiveness (flavor and smell) of our food. Your lab instructor will give you a number of marked (but unlabelled) bottles, each of which contains a single common cooking spice. Open each bottle, one at a time, and everyone take a whiff of the odor. Write down in Table 22.8 below what you think is the identity of the spice.

TABLE 22.8. The results of the spice identification experiment.

Bottle Number	What You Think the Spice Is	The Correct Answer
1		
2		
3		
4		
5		
6		
7		
8		
9		
10		
11		
12		

How many spices did you get correct? How does this compare to the responses of the other students? Determine if students who have had a lot of experience with cooking had higher scores.

Exercise 22.21.

Taste

Smell and taste work together for the perception of taste. We have **taste receptors** found in several places in our mouth. Most receptors are located on our **tongue,** but a few of them are found on the soft palate, epiglottis, pharynx, and elsewhere. There are up to 40 sensory neurons (**gustatory receptors**) located in each of roughly 3,000 **taste buds** in the adult human. The taste buds are located primarily on the sides of the various **papillae** of your tongue. These specific **chemoreceptors** respond to chemicals that have been dissolved in saliva. The receptors have small **microvilli** that extend through a small pore (opening) to the taste bud; the cells depolarize when specific chemicals react with specific receptors on the microvilli. Three **cranial nerves** (facial, glossopharyngeal, and vagus nerves) carry signals from these cells to the brain, which interprets the incoming signals as a taste sensation. The chemicals may also interact with smell receptors found in the nose, thus the nose is almost as important as the tongue for the perception of taste. There are six known taste sensations, each with a specific receptor: **salty, sweet, sour, bitter, umami,** and **water.** Umami is the pleasant taste we perceive when eating certain foods; the umami receptors appear to be sensitive to the presence of the amino acid glutamate. It is one of the reasons monosodium glutamate (MSG) is added to foods, making them more 'savory.'

Observe the prepared slide of the gustatory epithelium (taste buds) at the demonstration table and identify the taste buds on the slide. Make a quick sketch of what you see in the space provided below (Figure 22.8).

FIGURE 22.8.

Taste buds and gustatory epithelium.

Recall the times you have had a head cold. Were your sensations of food different then? Why?

The receptors that sense acidic (sour) tastes are about a 1,000 times more sensitive than the salty and sweet receptors, and the receptors for bitter tasting compounds are about 100,000 times more sensitive that the salty or sweet receptors. Discuss among your lab mates and your lab instructor why that difference in sensitivity may be of adaptive value to humans.

23 UNIT Populations

Keywords

gene	homozygous	fitness
allele	homozygous dominant	selection pressure
genotype	homozygous recessive	census
phenotype	genetic drift	sample
genotypic ratio	mate selection	mark-recapture
phenotypic ratio	mutation	Lincoln Index
gene pool	migration	quadrat techniques
dominant	natural selection	exponential growth
recessive	evolution	logistic growth
complete dominance	adaptation	carrying capacity (K)
incomplete dominance	fitness	growth rate (r)
heterozygous	speciation	environmental resistance

Learning Objectives

When finished with this unit, you should be able to:

1 Define the theory of Hardy-Weinberg equilibrium and list the Hardy-Weinberg equations;

2 List the five simplifying assumptions of Hardy-Weinberg equilibrium;

3 List the five fundamental assumptions of Hardy-Weinberg equilibrium and how these fundamental assumptions can be violated by natural populations;

4 List the five basic evolutionary forces (genetic drift, natural selection, mate selection, mutation, net migration) and how these evolutionary forces can cause evolution in a population. Relate these evolutionary forces to the five fundamental assumptions of Hardy-Weinberg equilibrium;

5 Discuss the effects that meiosis, fertilization, and random mating have on Hardy-Weinberg equilibrium;

6 Calculate expected genotypic ratios from Hardy-Weinberg equations and determine if evolution has occurred in a population;

7 Compare and contrast censusing and sampling a population;

8 Estimate population sizes using mark-recapture and quadrat techniques, and list the assumptions to each method;

9 Describe exponential and logistic growth; and

10 Use exponential and logistic population growth equations.

Hardy-Weinberg Equilibrium

First, a few basic definitions:

An **organism** is the fundamental unit in understanding biology. Evolutionary processes work at the level of the individual (via survival and reproduction of individual organisms). An organism is a single living individual (composed of one or more cells) of one species.

A **species** consists of all individuals in an area that potentially can mate and produce fertile offspring (recall that this definition is the biological species concept). There are several types of species definitions, but the biological species concept is the one we will use here.

A **population** is a group of interbreeding individuals of one species that lives in a defined area at a particular time. This defined area may be naturally described by clear geographical landmarks and formations (such as all of the smallmouth bass in a particular lake), or the area may be arbitrarily delineated by the investigator. This definition of a population emphasizes both the geographic limit to a population, as well as the temporal limit to a population. Populations are dynamic in that they do change in their sizes and locations through time.

In the early 20th century, G. Hardy and W. Weinberg independently devised several mathematical equations that we now use to predict the **allele** and **genotype** frequencies in a population. These equations and their assumptions became the basis of a theory that demonstrates the evolution of populations. The basic premise of the theory (**Hardy-Weinberg equilibrium**) is that in the absence of evolutionary forces, both allele frequencies and genotype frequencies of a given population remain constant (i.e., in equilibrium) from generation to generation. This constancy is maintained if only segregation and fertilization occurs (i.e., alleles separate from each other during the meiotic production of gametes, and the subsequent fusion of two gametes restores the original ploidy, or chromosome number, of that species).

To determine if a population is in equilibrium, one must know how many alleles are involved and their dominance relationships. An **allele** is an alternative form of a **gene** (a segment of DNA that encodes for a particular trait). For simplicity, we'll use simple Mendelian traits that have two contrasting alleles, 'A' and 'a'. We first determine the number of all of the 'A' and 'a' alleles in the population's **gene pool** (the total number of alleles present in the population). Because many organisms are diploid (possess two complete sets of genes), the population's gene pool is twice the number of individuals in that population. We'll define 'p' as the relative frequency of the dominant 'A' allele, and 'q' is the relative frequency of the recessive 'a' allele.

Suppose we had a total of 50 snapdragon plants. Red ('A') is **incompletely dominant** over white ('a'). The **phenotype** is the outward appearance of the organism; it refers to the expression or effects of the organism's genes. The phenotype of the **heterozygous** ('Aa') plants are pink, the phenotypes of the **homozygous** 'AA' plants are red, and the phenotypes of the homozygous 'aa' plants are white. We have 8 red plants, 24 pink plants, and 18 white plants. The **genotypic ratio** and **phenotypic ratio** are the same: 8 red ('AA') : 24 pink ('Aa') : 18 white ('aa'). Because we have 50 diploid individuals, there are 100 alleles in this population's gene pool. We can determine the number of 'A' and 'a' alleles by using the following analysis.

Eight of the plants are red ('AA'), therefore 16 alleles are 'A'. The 24 heterozygous plants (pink) represent another 24 'A' alleles. The relative frequency of the 'A' allele is therefore $16 + 24 = 40$ alleles, divided by the total number of alleles ($50 \times 2 = 100$), or $40 / 100 = 0.4 = p$. We can determine q by multiplying the total number of white individuals ('aa') by 2, and adding the product to the 24 'a' alleles from the heterozygotes: $((18 \times 2) + 24) / 100$ or $60 / 100 = 0.6 = q$.

The **first Hardy-Weinberg equation** (Equation 23.1) is quite simple: it is the sum of the two relative frequencies of the two alleles:

> **Equation 23.1.** $p + q = 1$

The sum of the two frequencies should equal 1. We can check this result by adding p and q together: $0.4 + 0.6 = 1$. Now, if both sides of the equation $p + q = 1$ are squared $[(p + q)(p + q) = (1)^2]$, we derive the **second Hardy-Weinberg equation** (Equation 23.2):

> **Equation 23.2.** $p^2 + 2pq + q^2 = 1$

Why did we square the first equation to get the second? Examine the following **Punnett square**. The Punnett square is useful to show all of the possible genotypes of any potential offspring of any two individuals. The cross of two heterozygous individuals and the possible allele combinations that could be found in their offspring are shown below:

		Male Gametes	
		A	a
Female Gametes	A	AA	Aa
	a	Aa	aa

The expected genotypic ratio is 1 'AA' : 2 'Aa' : 1 'aa', which is the same as the coefficients of Equation 23.2 above. Notice that if we allow 'p^2' to equal 'AA', '$2pq$' to equal 'Aa', and 'q^2' to equal 'aa', we come up with the same result.

We can add in the values for the proportions of 'A' and 'a' into the Punnett square, and by multiplying the relative frequencies, come up with the expected genotypic frequencies for the offspring:

		Male Gametes	
		p (A) = 0.4	q (a) = 0.6
Female Gametes	p (A) = 0.4	0.16 AA	0.24 Aa
	q (a) = 0.6	0.24 Aa	0.36 aa

In our snapdragon example above, what is the expected genotypic frequencies (in percent of the total population) for 'AA', 'Aa' and 'aa' genotypes?

_______% 'AA', _______% 'Aa', _______% 'aa'

If our population size remains stable at 50 individuals for the next generation, we would expect:

_______ plants to be red, _________ plants to be pink, and _________ plants to be white.

Over time, we would expect a large population of snapdragons to consistently maintain 'p' = 0.4 and 'q' = 0.6 from one generation to the next, if there are no forces affecting the relative gene frequencies of the two alleles.

We can use these same equations for other traits in which we have **complete dominance.** For example, purple flowers ('W') are dominant to white flowers ('w') in pea plants. In a population of 24 plants, 16 plants are purple and 8 plants are white. We do not know how many of the purple-flowered plants are heterozygous ('Ww') or homozygous dominant ('WW'). But, because we know how many plants are **homozygous recessive** ('ww' or white), we can calculate p and q. If 8 out of 24 are white (q^2), then the square root of 8/24 = q, or approximately 0.58. The value for p therefore is $1 - q$, or $1 - 0.58 = 0.42$. The proportion of homozygous dominants in the population would be expected to be $(0.42)^2 = 0.18$ or 18%. Out of 24 individuals, we would expect 18% ((0.18 × 24) or approximately 4) to be 'WW', and 2(0.58)(0.42)(24) = approximately 12 plants to be 'Ww'.

The Hardy-Weinberg equations can be used to determine if evolutionary forces are acting upon the population. Hardy and Weinberg theorized that the frequencies of the alleles and the frequencies of the genotypes should not change from one generation to the next in the absence of evolutionary forces such as natural selection or genetic drift. Alleles that have a very low frequency can be maintained within a very large population for a long period of time, and are not lost simply because they are rare. Therefore, the basic null hypothesis of the Hardy-Weinberg equilibrium is that once equilibrium has been reached (and as long as no evolutionary forces are acting on the population), the frequencies of alleles and genotypes should not change through time.

There are five **simplifying assumptions** about Hardy-Weinberg equilibrium that many texts do not cover, but they are implied in the discussion of the theory:

1 **The species in question is diploid.** The species is not a haploid or polyploid (triploid, tetraploid, or hexaploid).

2 **There are only two alleles involved.** We will identify the two alleles as 'A' and 'a'.

3 **The species has discrete generations.** In other words, once one generation reproduces, the entire parental generation dies before its offspring become reproductively mature.

4 **The species is reproducing exclusively sexually.** The species can be either monoecious or dioecious, but it is not using asexual reproduction.

5 **The gene for the trait under consideration is autosomal.** The gene is not on a chromosome that has a different number of copies in different sexes. For example, the gene is not located on either an X or a Y chromosome.

These simplifying assumptions are important in order for the equations to work properly, but the equations for Hardy-Weinberg equilibrium can be expanded or altered in order to allow exceptions to all of these simplifying assumptions to occur (i.e., multiple alleles and polyploidy can be taken into account). You will perform one exercise examining Hardy-Weinberg equilibrium in a gene with three alleles today (see page 23-10).

The null hypothesis has been tested repeatedly in natural and laboratory populations. In general, when scientists examine populations and ascertain the gene frequencies, the results generally do not support the null hypothesis of Hardy-Weinberg equilibrium. In order for the Hardy-Weinberg equilibrium to be maintained, certain assumptions must be met. **The five fundamental assumptions of Hardy-Weinberg equilibrium are listed below.** These five fundamental assumptions are assumed to be true if the population is in equilibrium (i.e., the population is not evolving). These assumptions are related to the potential forces that could change the relative frequencies of either alleles or genotypes.

1 **There is an infinite (or at least a very large) population size.** Large populations reduce the possibility that random processes (such as genetic drift) affect gene frequencies.

2 **No mate selection occurs.** All individuals in the population must have an equal chance to mate with any other individual; organisms cannot selectively mate with other individuals based upon traits influenced by the gene in question. Within a single population, all mating should be random.

3 **No net mutation occurs.** The likelihood of allele 'A' mutating to 'a' must equal the mutation rate of allele 'a' mutating to 'A'.

4 **No net migration occurs.** The likelihood of either allele entering or leaving the population must be equal. Individual organisms that carry these different alleles must be equally likely to migrate out of (or into) the population.

5 **No natural selection occurs.** One phenotype cannot be more successful in surviving and reproducing than any other phenotype.

Usually, one or more of these fundamental assumptions are not met in natural or laboratory populations. The population thus is said to be evolving when the population's gene pool changes over time (i.e., the relative frequencies of 'A' and 'a' change over time).

What can cause a change in the Hardy-Weinberg equilibrium (in other words, what forces can cause evolutionary change to occur in a population)?

1 **The population size is small, allowing for random fluctuation in allele frequencies to occur.** Genetic drift and other related phenomena occur, due to small population size.

2 **Mate selection (nonrandom mating) has occurred.** Organisms select for or against certain phenotypes to be potential mates. Mate selection may not necessarily change allele frequencies, but it can change genotype frequencies.

3 **Net mutation occurred.** One allele changes into the other more often than the reverse mutation. In other words: 'A' → 'a' is more likely than 'a' → 'A'.

4 **Gene flow occurred.** A change in gene frequency due to selective migration of alleles into or out of the population has been observed.

5 **Natural selection occurred.** A differential survival and reproduction of individuals (phenotypes) has occurred. Because of this selection at the level of the individual organism, some alleles have increased in frequency in the population, and other alleles have decreased.

Note that the processes of meiosis, fertilization, and random mating do not change allele frequencies, by themselves. These processes help to randomly recombine and 'expose' alleles or allele combinations to evolutionary forces.

Examine Figure 23.1. It depicts the Hardy-Weinberg equilibrium frequencies for two alleles: 'A' and 'a'. The abscissa (*x*-axis) shows the allele frequencies (*p* and *q*), whereas the ordinate shows the genotype frequencies of the three possible genotypes: 'AA', 'Aa,' and 'aa'.

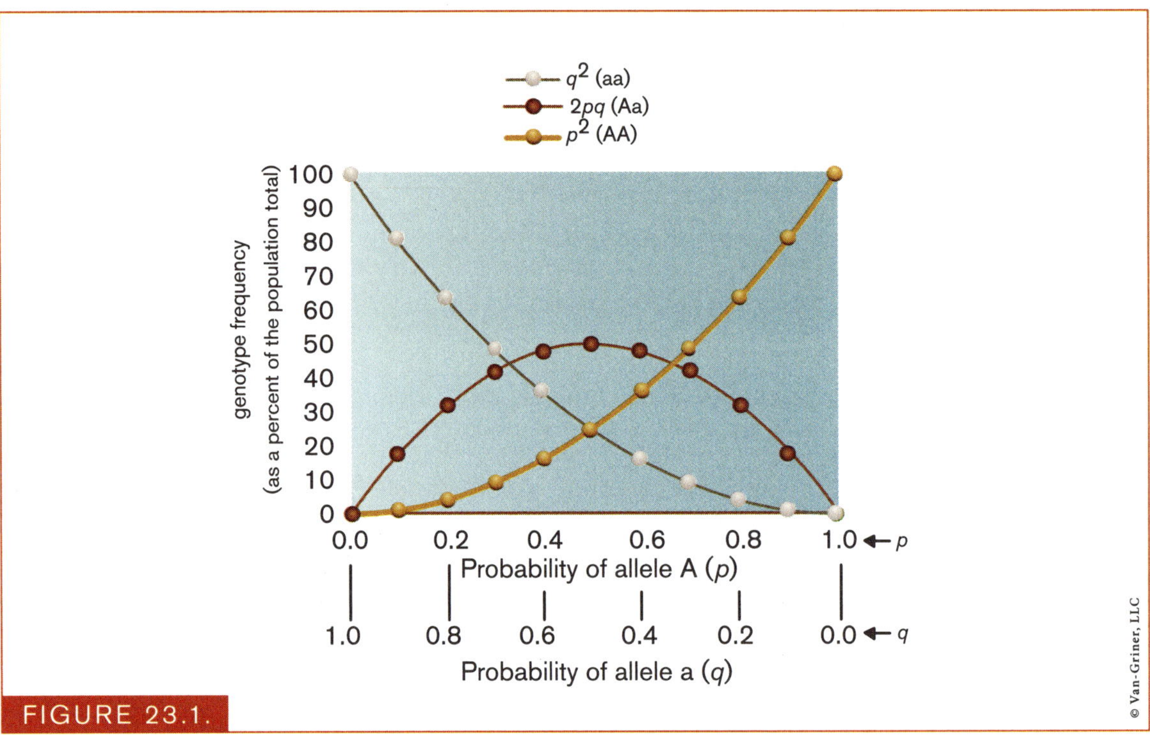

FIGURE 23.1.

Hardy-Weinberg equilibrium: the relationship between allele frequencies and genotypic frequencies, if the population's gene pool is in equilibrium.

Exercises

Exercise 23.1.

Hardy-Weinberg Equilibrium

Suppose there are 100 grey squirrels (*Sciurus carolinensis*) on campus, and four of the squirrels are white albinos and 96 are of the typical grey color. Albinism is an inherited trait where there is a lack of melanin pigment in the skin, fur and eyes of many animals, including humans. This lack of melanin pigment is due to a defective enzyme (or the total absence of the enzyme) involved in the production of melanin. The albino allele is recessive to the normal melanin-producing allele, which codes for a functioning enzyme. The recessive albino allele (white coat color) is denoted by the letter 'a'; the dominant wild type allele (grey) is 'A'. Assume the population is in Hardy-Weinberg equilibrium.

Are all of the 96 grey squirrels homozygous 'AA'?

What are the allele frequencies p (the frequency of 'A') and q (the frequency of 'a')? Show how you arrived at your answer.

In this population, there are 200 alleles. Are most of the albino alleles present in the albino squirrels, or in the heterozygotes? How many heterozygotes are present, if the population is in Hardy-Weinberg equilibrium? Show how you arrived at your answer.

Examine Figure 23.1. If a population is in Hardy-Weinberg equilibrium, can heterozygotes ever be a majority (greater than 50%) of the population? Why or why not? Can either homozygote be the most prevalent genotype? What does p and q have to be for the genotype 'AA' to be the most prevalent genotype (i.e., more than 50% of the population has this genotype)?

What must the allele frequencies (p and q) be, if the relative frequency of heterozygotes equals the frequency of one of the homozygotes? Show your reasoning.

If the population is in Hardy-Weinberg equilibrium, the relative frequencies of the genotypes, and the relative allele frequencies (p and q)

____

from generation to generation. (Fill in the blank).

If gene frequencies, as predicted by Hardy-Weinberg equilibrium, change over time in a population, then what can definitely be said in all cases?

Suppose there are three alleles found at a gene locus in a diploid mammal population: A, a, and ä. Allele A is dominant to both a and ä, and allele a is dominant to ä. Allele A codes for black fur, allele a codes for orange fur, and allele ä codes for white fur.

1 List all possible genotypes and their phenotypes.

2 Modify the Hardy-Weinberg equations to take into account the presence of the third allele (p = allele A frequency, q = allele a frequency, and r = allele ä frequency). Have your lab instructor check your results.

Estimation of Population Size

Understanding the abundance and distribution of a population is an important biological question. It is essential to know how many individuals there are in a population and how they are distributed in space before the causes that affect population size and distribution can be investigated.

There are two major methods to determine the animal densities in a given area: 1) a direct count (census) and 2) indirect estimates (sampling). A **census** is a direct count of all individuals of a given species in an area. Although a census can be accurate, it is often impractical to count all individuals because they are either: a) too mobile, b) too rare, c) too abundant, or d) too difficult to observe and count accurately.

A census is the most direct and accurate means of determining population size, but a census is often impractical to do for many populations. For example, when we attempt to count all humans in the USA every decade, there are many people who are not counted, for various reasons. Taking a census in remote areas is often not done due to time or budgetary constraints. A population that consists of a few individuals per square mile is very difficult to count, particularly if they are timid (afraid of humans) or they are cryptic. Counting even sessile organisms such as trees is too time-consuming; there may be thousands to millions of individuals. In some instances, the individuals of certain size or age classes may be difficult to count. For example, it is impractical to count the eggs and larva of various insects that inhabit the insides of fruits and bark of trees.

Sampling a Population:
An Example of Proportional Reasoning

The second method involves taking **indirect estimates** of abundance, where the population size is estimated from a smaller part (a **sample**) of the population. A series of samples usually are taken from a population, and from these samples, we infer some generalizations about the population as a whole (such as population size, density, dispersion, age structure, or sex-ratio). If done correctly, sampling can tell us something about these parameters, without having to undergo a costly, labor-intensive census of the population. There are two main types of sampling techniques: **mark recapture** (best for mobile animals) and **quadrat sampling** (best for immobile animals and plants).

First, we need to talk about an important concept in biology, called **proportional reasoning.** Proportional reasoning involves the ability to compare **ratios.** The simplest definition of a ratio is that a ratio is a comparison of two numbers or quantities. In a ratio, the two numbers usually are separated by a colon (:) or forward slash (/), if you are referring to fractions. For example, suppose your dog had a litter of five puppies. Two puppies were male, and three were female. The ratio of male to female puppies thus is 2 : 3, which is read or said as "two males to three females." This means that for every two male puppies, there were three female puppies. Compared to the total number of puppies in the litter, 2/5ths (40 percent) of the puppies were male, and 3/5ths (60 percent) of the puppies were female.

Two quantities are called **proportional** if they have a constant ratio, which means that one quantity varies as a constant multiple of the other. For example, the amount of water you need to properly cook rice (according to many cookbooks) is one volume of dry rice to two volumes of water.

This means that if you want to cook a cup of dry rice, you add a cup of uncooked rice to two cups of water. If you want to cook two cups of dry rice, then you need four cups of water. The amount of uncooked rice is proportional to the amount of water needed.

Back in elementary school, you were taught that a proportion was the equality of two ratios (Equation 23.3).

> **Equation 23.3.** $\dfrac{a}{c} = \dfrac{b}{d}$

Suppose 'a' = 4, 'c' = 5, and 'b' = 12, but 'd' was unknown. Given the values of any three of the terms of the proportion, you can determine the fourth, unknown term. In this case, you could determine 'd' by **cross multiplication:** simply multiply 'b' $\times$ 'c', and then divide the answer by 'a'. The unknown term 'd' is thus $[(12 \times 5) / 4] = 15$.

Mark-Recapture Method

One of the most commonly used sampling methods in animal ecology involves proportional reasoning. This method is called the **Mark-Recapture Method** (also known as the **Lincoln Index**). The mark-recapture method is the ratio of two proportions (Equation 23.4):

> **Equation 23.4.** $\dfrac{N}{F} = \dfrac{S}{R}$ or $N = \dfrac{FS}{R}$

At the initial time (T_1), there are 'N' individuals of the species in the area. At time T_1, a certain number of animals are captured and marked by some method ('F' for 'first' sample), and released in the area they were captured. At a later time (T_2) the population is sampled again, the total number of individuals in the new sample is ('S' for 'second' sample). Some of animals in S are unmarked ('U') and some are marked and thus recaptured a second time ('recaptured,' 'R'). The total of the second sample equals the number of marked and unmarked individuals ($S = U + R$). The ratio of marked individuals to the total captured at T_2 ($S : R$) will equal the ratio of the population size at T_1 to the number initially captured ($N : F$), provided that certain assumptions are met.

As an example of the utility of mark-recapture: suppose you wish to know the number of dragonfly larvae in a pond. At T_1, you captured and marked 75 dragonflies ($F = 75$). At time T_2, you captured 50 dragonflies ($S = 50$), and 25 of them were marked ($R = 25$). Therefore, you estimate that there are $[(75)(50)] / (25) = 150$ dragonfly larvae in the pond at that time.

The Lincoln Index is the simplest of the numerous mark-recapture models that ecologists, wildlife biologists and fisheries managers use in estimating population size. However, sampling a population provides only an estimate of the population size. Because the individuals sampled are determined largely by chance, successive sampling can provide very different estimates. As described earlier, multiple sampling will tend to even out the variation in the samples due to chance.

Exercise 23.2.

Mark-Recapture Sampling

We have a container with an unknown number (N) of bottle caps that represent individuals of a given species. At time T_1, you will reach in with one hand and collect a number of the bottle caps. Your lab instructor will tell you how many handfuls you may collect (in other words, each of you will have a different sampling effort). Count these caps and set them aside. Now, place an equal number of different colored caps back into the container. The different colored caps represent marked individuals. The number of marked caps = F. Put the lid on the container and shake the container for about 10 seconds; this simulates the time it takes for the organisms to disperse and redistribute themselves through the sample area. Next, you are to collect a second sample (S) at time T_2 by reaching in and collecting bottle caps. Collect the same number of handfuls that you collected the first time. Record the total number of caps captured (S) this second sampling time, as well as the number that are of the second color (the recaptured 'marked' organisms, R). Once you know the values for the variables you know (F, S, and R), you can solve for N.

Important note: After you have finished sampling, please return all bottle caps to their original places!

Determine your estimate of N, and place the data on the front board. After your classmates have all conducted the exercise, record the class data in Table 23.1 below. In addition, plot N as a function of sampling effort (F) in Figure 23.2.

There are a number of important assumptions about any model in science. With respect to mark-recapture, what do you think are important assumptions to the method? Confer with your table mates and list what you think are important assumptions to mark-recapture sampling below.

Later in the lab, your lab instructor will place on the front table a list that most ecologists would view as important assumptions to mark-recapture sampling. Write them down below. Were you and your table mates able to identify them all? Did you come up with an assumption not listed?

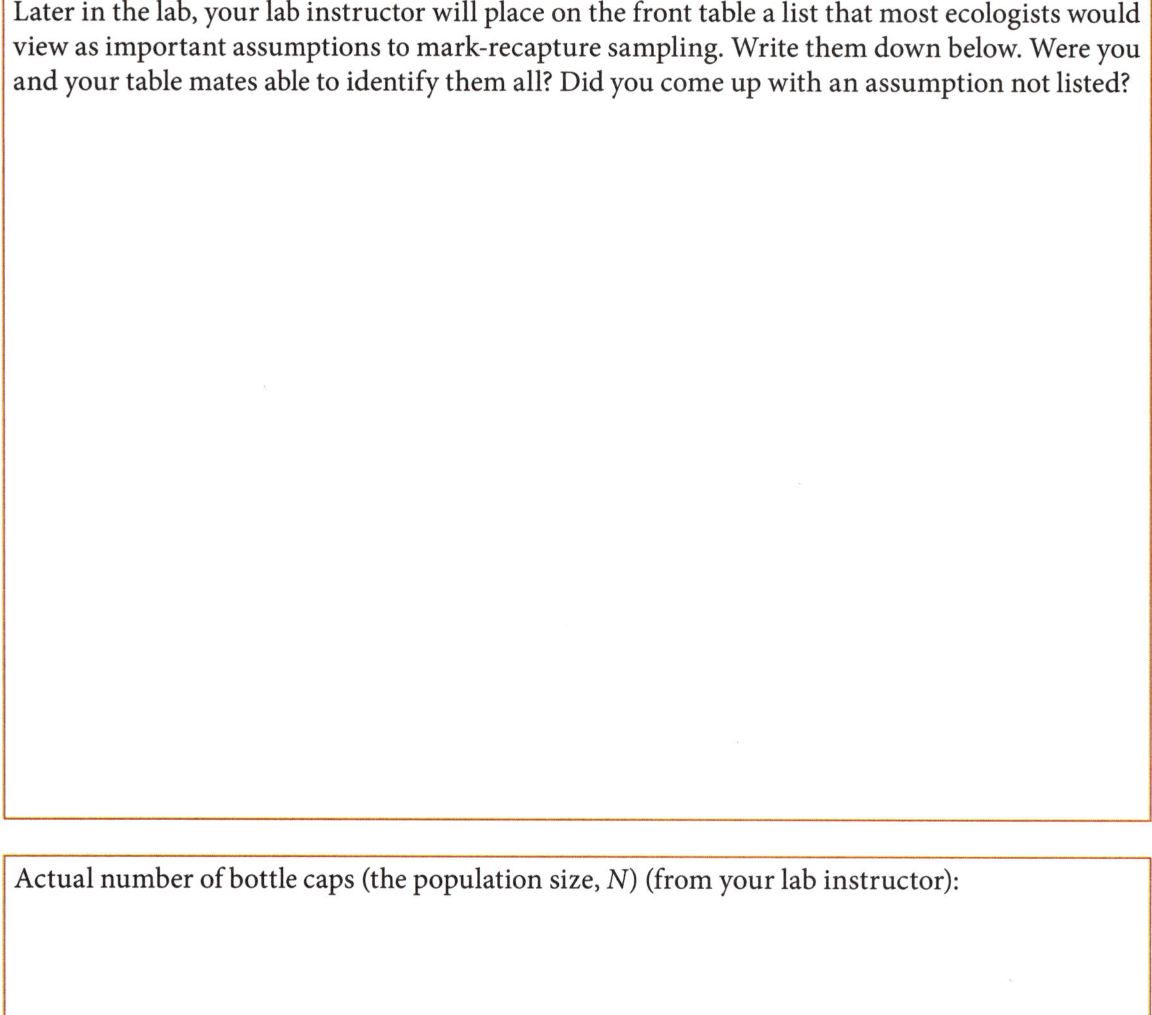

Actual number of bottle caps (the population size, N) (from your lab instructor):

The population estimate N is only an approximation. The accuracy of these statistics depends upon the initial number of marked individuals in the population; if the number of marked animals in the population is small, then the chance of obtaining the correct answer is small.

You will discover that your estimate of the population size is probably quite different from the true population size. Ecologists usually do not have enough time to count every single animal in the population. The variability in the estimates made by you and your classmates represents the **sampling error**—where the estimates cluster about the true population size (recall this discussion from the first chapter). Sampling errors can be reduced by increasing sampling intensity (gathering more animals per sample), taking replicate samples, standardizing the sampling procedure, and not violating any of the assumptions mentioned above.

This exercise gives us the opportunity to observe the difference between **accuracy** and **precision.** Recall that accuracy is an indication of how closely a measurement (sample) agrees with a true value (in this case, the actual population size). Precision is a measure of how closely repeated measurements of the same thing agree with one another (i.e., how your estimate of the population size agrees with that of your classmates). Scientists strive for high accuracy and high precision. High accuracy is obtained by using the correct method or procedure; high precision is obtained by using a method or procedure correctly and consistently.

Was your estimate accurate?

Can replication improve the accuracy? Replication involves making repeated standardized samples. You must standardize the sampling procedure (i.e., you and all other students must use the same technique in order to compare estimates).

Can increasing the period of time allowed for mixing improve the accuracy? What would happen if you did not shake the container?

What could happen if you waited too long between the two sampling periods? How would it affect your estimate?

Hint: Instead of thinking about bottle caps, think about real animals.

Examine Figure 23.2. What is the effect of increased sampling effort on the population estimates? Do the results fit what you expected to see?

TABLE 23.1. Mark-recapture data for the bottle cap exercise.

Number in First Sample (F)	Number in Second Sample (S)	Number Recaptured (R)	Estimated Population Size (N)

FIGURE 23.2.

Effect of increased sampling effort (*F*, abscissa) on population size estimation (*N*, ordinate).

Exercise 23.3.

Quadrat Sampling

Quadrat sampling works well for sessile (immobile or very slow-moving) animals and for plants. The total area of the population is divided into a known number of units (quadrats) of which a proportion is sampled.

Suppose you want to know the number of oaks in forest, which is 100 acres in size. You would first divide forest into number of sections (quadrats). Next, you would randomly choose a number of quadrats, and then you would count the number of oaks in each quadrat. You then would determine the mean number of oaks per quadrat ($\bar{x}$). Finally, you would multiply the mean number of oaks/quadrat by the total number of quadrats (T); this final number would be your estimate of the total number of oaks in the forest (N) (see Equation 23.5).

> **Equation 23.5.** $N = T\bar{x}$

For example, there are a number of white oaks in a 100 acre forest. You divided the forest up into 100 one-acre quadrats. You chose ten 1 acre quadrats and counted the following number of white oak trees in each quadrat: 0, 2, 1, 6, 0, 5, 2, 2, 4, and 10 trees. The mean = 3.2, standard deviation = 3.12, sample variance = 9.73. Thus, you estimate that there were 3.2 white oaks/acre × 100 acres/forest = 320 white oaks in the forest. (Note that as you multiply the average number of oaks per acre by the number of acres in the forest, the unit 'acre' cancels out.)

Up at the front table, there is a large sheet of paper. On the paper, there are a large number of three species of tree which are represented by different colored dots: red maples (*Acer rubrum*, red dots), white oaks (*Quercus alba*, blue dots), and green ash (*Fraxinus pennsylvanica*, green dots). It would take you some time to count all of them. However, you will note that the area is divided into 100 equal-sized quadrats. If you sample properly, you should be able to give a reliable estimate using a relatively few sample quadrats.

Work in small groups. Your lab instructor will tell you which tree you will sample. In your group, discuss how many samples you need to take and which quadrats you will sample. After you have determined your sampling approach, talk to your lab instructor. If your lab instructor has agreed to your approach, count the number of trees in each quadrat you selected, and place the number of trees counted in Table 23.2.

A random number generator is on the next page (Table 23.3). There are pairs of letter/number combinations [from a0 to j9] that are arranged in a random order. Note that the grid is labeled a through j on one axis and 0 through 9 on the other.

For example, suppose you sampled quadrat 'c0' (the third column, the first row) and you observed that two sugar maple trees were present. Write 'c0' in the quadrat box below, and write the number of sugar maple trees that were in the quadrat in the adjacent box labeled 'number of trees.' After you have finished your sampling, calculate the mean number of trees per quadrat. Finally, multiply the mean number of trees in a quadrat by the total number of quadrats (100) to estimate the tree's population size.

TABLE 23.2. Quadrat results. Tree species sampled: ___________________________

Quadrat	Number of Trees	Quadrat	Number of Trees	Quadrat	Number of Trees	Quadrat	Number of Trees

TABLE 23.3. Pairs of random quadrat coordinates (to be used for Exercise 23.4). A list of 100 pairs of random letter/number coordinate pairs is below. Each combination is used only once. You may start at any point and read numbers from that point in any direction, up, down, across, or diagonally. You may also read every other pair, or every third pair, or use some other method.

i7	d6	j3	h6	e0	b2	j8	a5	i8	b1
c0	f8	h4	a1	d0	b4	f0	g2	c8	c9
j5	a2	e8	c7	f5	h0	d7	f7	b0	g6
c6	h9	h3	e5	d8	f3	i1	a7	d4	i3
e7	g3	f9	a3	g8	i0	e3	j9	g7	a6
f6	g9	e2	h5	g4	j4	a0	i6	j6	d9
i2	g5	c1	h1	b3	j2	j0	i9	h2	h8
j7	b9	e9	g1	f4	a4	e6	d3	f2	b8
b6	g0	c5	f1	d2	a8	b7	a9	b5	c2
h7	c3	c4	d1	i4	d5	e1	e4	i5	j1

What is your estimate? $N =$ ________________ trees.

Species:

The actual population size (from your lab instructor):

$N =$

With respect to quadrat sampling, what do you think are important assumptions to the method. Discuss with your table mates and list what you think are important assumptions to quadrat sampling below.

Later on in class, your lab instructor will place on the front table a list that most texts would view as important assumptions to quadrat sampling. Write them down below. Were you and your table mates able to identify them all? Did you come up with an assumption that was not listed?

Examine the entire forest. Do you see any pattern with respect to the distribution of the trees within the area? What reasons do you think could be responsible for the overall distribution that you see?

Population Growth

Exponential Population Growth

Once individuals of a species successfully colonize a new habitat, they begin to reproduce and increase their numbers. The new habitat must supply all of the resources (food, water, nutrients, nest sites, and so on) needed in order for the population to grow.

One potential population growth pattern is that of **linear or arithmetic growth** (Figure 23.3). The numbers of individuals increases at a linear rate over time: 1, 2, 3, 4, 5, and so on. The same number of individuals are added during each time period.

However, populations rarely, if ever, grow in a linear fashion. Instead of linear growth, a different pattern of growth usually is observed. During the early phase of the successful colonization of a new optimal habitat, the population can initially grow at a rapid pace. This phase is called **exponential growth,** the time when the population is increasing rapidly (see Figure 23.3). As an example, imagine that a small group of rats 'jumped ship' onto a lush tropical island. Our hypothetical rat population may increase in numbers in an exponential fashion, in the absence of competitors, disease, inclement weather, or predators, and in the presence of lots of food.

A population that is growing exponentially adds a number of individuals over a time period that is in proportion to the population size N at the beginning of the time period. For example, if a population grows at 200% per year, a population of size $N = 10$ individuals would add 20 organisms in a year, but if the population size was 10,000, then 20,000 new individuals would be added over the same time interval.

To appreciate the power of exponential growth, imagine the exponential population growth in a protozoan that splits by binary fission.

Time (X) in hours	0	1	2	3	4	5	6
Number of cells	1	2	4	8	16	32	64

The data are plotted in Figure 23.3. In the figure, you see a J-shaped or **exponential curve.** We can model this type of growth using a differential equation of calculus (Equation 23.6). (Don't panic!)

> **Equation 23.6.** $\delta N / \delta t = rN$

What does Equation 23.6 mean? It states that over the change in time (δt), the change in the population size (δN) is equal to the difference between in birth and death rates, times the initial population size (N) at the beginning of the time interval (Equation 23.7).

b = **birth rate:** the number of births per time interval per individual

d = **death rate:** number of deaths per time interval per individual

i = **immigration rate:** or the number of immigrants moving into the population from outside per time interval per individual

e = **emigration rate:** the number of individuals leaving the population per time interval per individual

> **Equation 23.7.** $r = b + i - d - e$

The statistic r is called the **reproductive rate, or growth rate, of the population.**

For the moment, we will ignore immigration and emigration (i and e) because if they do not differ from each other, they would have no impact on r. We can predict what the growth rate is by knowing the birth rates and death rates:

$r = 0$ No growth ($b = d$)   (No change in N will occur over time.)

$r < 0$ Negative growth ($d > b$)   (A decrease in N will occur over time.)

$r > 0$ Positive growth ($b > d$)   (An increase in N will occur over time.)

Under optimal conditions, bacteria can divide about every 30 minutes. A single bacterium could create a colony of 1.4×10^{14} bacteria (140 quadrillion) after 24 hours! This is why health experts tell you to put away any food as soon as possible in the refrigerator, to allow frozen meats to thaw in the refrigerator, to cook your food thoroughly, and to wash and clean used cutting boards and other utensils with soap and hot water. Refrigeration slows down bacterial growth, making it less likely for you to get sick from eating food containing large numbers of bacteria.

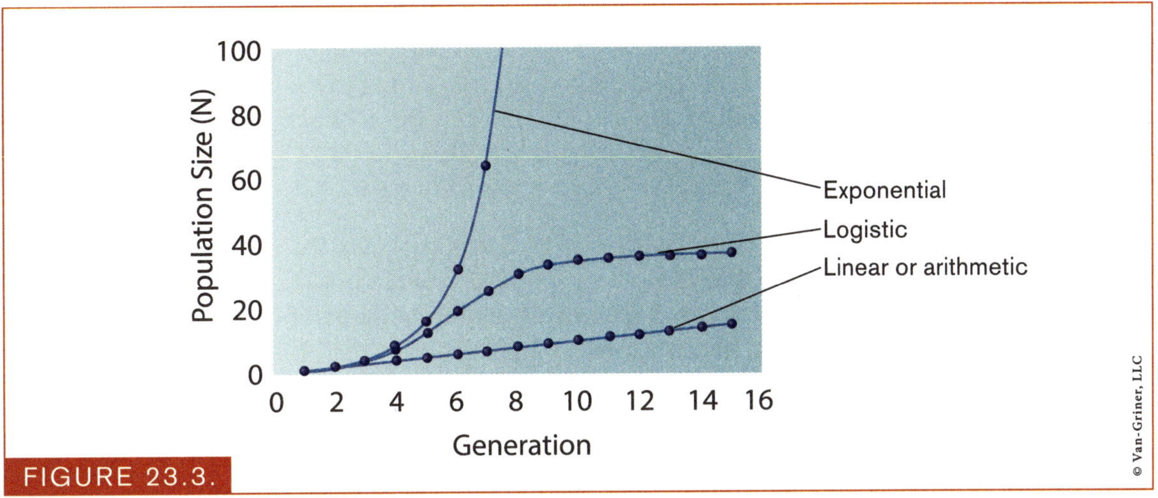

FIGURE 23.3.

Linear, exponential, and logistic growth curves.

Populations cannot grow exponentially for long. Populations tend to level off or fluctuate around a certain size because the environment has only so many resources. Predators, parasites, competitors, disease organisms and the physical environment itself may dramatically affect the population through mortality and birth rates (increase d and decrease b). All of these factors that limit the exponential growth of a population collectively are called the **environmental resistance** to the population increase.

Logistic Population Growth

For most populations, *N* does not continue to increase exponentially; *N* tends to level off after a certain population size has been reached. There are limits to growth imposed by the environment. Eventually, some resource or resources (for example, food, water, nest sites) becomes limiting to the expanding population. There simply is not enough of the resource left to support a rapidly expanding population. The population growth observed under conditions of limited resources is called **logistic growth. The logistic growth curve is S-shaped, or sigmoidal, when population density is plotted over time** (Figure 23.3).

The carrying capacity (*K*) is the maximum sustainable population size for that particular environment. We can add the dampening effect of resource limitation to our exponential growth equation of Equation 23.6 and produce the **logistic growth equation** (Equation 23.8):

Equation 23.8.
$$\frac{\delta N}{\delta t} = rN \left(\frac{K-N}{K} \right)$$

The '$(K - N) / K$' term in Equation 23.8 reduces the rate of unrestricted growth (the 'rN' term). In other words, '$(K - N) / K$' represents the unutilized opportunity for population growth. Initially, N is small and not near K, so the population at first grows exponentially (examine Figure 23.3 again). As population size (N) approaches the carrying capacity (K), the population growth rate ($\delta N / \delta t$) slows down. When $N = K$, $\delta N / \delta t$ equals zero, the growth rate r at that time also equals zero because b and d are then equal.

The following scenario will help you visualize what $[(K - N) / K]$ means. Imagine you are in a theater, and there are 200 seats. The total number of seats in the theater (200) is equal to K. Suppose 100 people bought tickets before you did, and they are already sitting in some of the seats (N). Therefore, the $(K - N)$ term equals the number of seats (200) minus the number of seats already taken (100). This number (200 – 100), divided by the total number of seats initially, gives the proportion of available seats left $[(200 - 100 / 200] = 0.5$. One-half of the theater's seats are still available.

Populations can exceed K temporarily, but when this happens the population size eventually declines. Again, let's imagine that the theater management sold 210 tickets for the show, but there are 200 seats available. This would mean that ten people would be standing, and the fire marshal (if he/she was present) could force them to leave the theater.

Exercise 23.4.

Exponential Growth

Each group of students will have a board (similar to a checkerboard) and a number of beads. The board represents the environment, and each square represents the amount of resources needed for survival and reproduction of a single individual (bead). Start with a single bead (the beads represent individuals belonging to a hypothetical species of the genus *Beadus*) on the board. Each bead reproduces one offspring each time period. Place a second bead on an unoccupied square. In this exercise, no beads die over time. At the end of the second time period, there are now two beads on the board. For the next time period, place one additional bead for each bead currently on the board (for time period three, you would place two additional beads separately on unoccupied squares, for a total of four *Beadus* individuals). You can continue doing this manually, but you will rapidly run out of beads and spaces, so think of this as a mental exercise, once you understand what is going on here. Continue filling in Table 23.4 and plot the data on graph paper provided on the following page (Figure 23.4).

TABLE 23.4. *Beadus* exponential growth data.

Time Period	Population Size N
1	1
2	2
3	4
4	
5	
6	
7	
8	

FIGURE 23.4.

Exponential and logistic growth. The population size *N* (ordinate, *y*-axis) is plotted as a function of generation or time period (abscissa, *x*-axis).

Exercise 23.5.

Logistic Growth

Perform the following experiment by following the rules listed below. Write your data down in Table 23.5.

1 You will start the exercise with one bead. Place a 1 in the second column. Roll one die. Then roll a second die. The two numbers tells you which square in which to place the bead. For example, if you had rolled a 3 then a 5, place the bead in the square located in the third row, fifth column. (To speed up things, you may use the table of random numbers [Table 23.6], so you can do this exercise quickly, without having to roll any dice.)

2 At the start of each time period, count the number of *Beadus orangii* (represented by the orange beads) that are alive (on the board) at the beginning of the time period. Write that number in the column labeled "*N* at Start of Time Period" in Table 23.5 for the appropriate time period.

3 You will roll the dice each time before you place a bead on the board.

4 Each individual *Beadus orangii* alive at the start of the time period will reproduce one offspring during the time period. Double the number in the second column in Table 23.5 and place this number in the third column (the column labeled "Total *N* after Reproduction"). For each bead on the board at the start of the time period, roll and add one additional bead on the board. At the end of the 'birth phase' of the time period, you should have a number of beads on the board that is equal to the number in column 2.

5 If any bead or beads land on a square that is occupied, go ahead and place the bead in the square alongside any other bead(s) present.

6 At the end of the 'birth phase' (after you have placed **all** of the beads on the board), if you see that two or more beads occupy any one square, all of the beads in that square are 'killed' (by environmental resistance, in this case, starvation). Remove all beads from any square that has two or more beads in it. Add up the number of beads 'killed' that time period and write that number in the third column in the Table 23.5 (the column labeled "*N* Killed"). This is the 'death phase' for that time period.

Only one *Beadus orangii* can occupy any given square. Remember, that square represents all of the resources needed for survival and reproduction of one individual. If two or more beads are 'sharing' that square, there is not enough resources to keep two or more alive and so all of them in that square will 'die.' **Intraspecific competition** occurs when two individuals of a single species compete for resources.

7 Count the beads that are left on the board. Write that number in the last column of Table 23.5 (the column labeled "*N* for Start of Next Time Period"). That is the number at the start of the next time period's 'colonization phase.' Some beads may live for several time periods, while others die quickly.

8 Repeat Steps 4 through 7 and continue gathering data until you reach at least 10 time periods.

TABLE 23.5. Logistic population growth of the hypothetical population *Beadus orangii*.

Time Period	*N* at Start of Time Period	Total *N* after Reproduction	*N* Killed	*N* for Start of Next Time Period
1	1	2		
2				
3				
4				
5				
6				
7				
8				
9				
10				

Plot the results (in the second column, labeled "*N* at Start of Time Period") on the same graph with the exponential growth (Figure 23.4). Label your two curves. Did you draw an S-shaped curve (logistic curve)?

Compare that curve with one where the population is doubling each time period (the exponential growth curve on the same figure). How do the curves compare?

The logistic growth curve represents logistic growth. You should notice a curve that erratically fluctuates around a relatively constant plateau. Estimate the 'plateau level' for the population's *N*; that number will provide you an estimate of the carrying capacity *K* for *Beadus orangii* in this model.

> What is your estimate of *K* for *Beadus orangii*?
>
> *K* =

> Actual theoretical estimate of *K* for *Beadus orangii* (from your lab instructor):
>
> *K* =

> What happened to death rates and population growth over time (were they constant)? Did the numbers added each successive generation change?

Exercise 23.5 is based on a similar exercise described in G. Summers (1984) *Laboratory Exercises in General Biology*, second edition. Burgess Publishing Co, Minneapolis, MN.

TABLE 23.6. One thousand pairs of random numbers (from 1 to 6).

To use this table, simply start at any random point and read consecutive pairs of numbers either left or right across the row, or read up or down the column, or read in any diagonal direction. Each pairs represents the *x,y* coordinates for placing individuals on the board in both Exercises 23.5 and 24.1.

32	21	14	52	45	66	36	14	63	52	42	36	61	55	53	16	31	11	66	13	66	64	65	42	26
61	64	66	11	45	14	51	36	55	61	43	63	33	66	14	24	44	16	45	11	21	12	54	16	32
52	46	25	55	14	13	12	42	56	14	45	23	51	41	42	51	13	62	55	61	32	64	32	15	52
23	21	43	54	35	64	32	56	14	13	21	41	63	15	24	52	64	36	36	26	16	44	41	26	36
44	45	32	65	33	24	44	23	11	21	65	66	34	34	63	26	26	62	22	32	32	63	51	12	14
52	34	65	55	66	45	15	12	13	32	52	26	32	33	26	13	64	23	41	51	45	34	22	46	66
46	61	16	11	11	54	45	26	65	53	15	11	33	53	22	25	46	13	36	41	23	13	56	61	43
41	34	46	44	32	36	12	33	45	11	31	15	35	26	62	13	21	65	62	45	35	53	42	36	42
34	62	46	51	21	22	33	44	41	33	14	54	44	24	25	33	55	51	36	11	44	35	44	26	63
23	66	56	43	31	55	46	52	31	64	66	23	53	56	65	24	55	16	56	21	23	62	63	53	51
63	25	61	22	14	15	54	65	23	16	55	26	35	62	53	62	35	45	54	12	64	43	15	66	33
22	16	25	62	55	26	16	15	53	43	23	53	42	44	56	24	26	63	54	32	64	15	14	34	36
14	51	41	33	53	14	43	25	41	51	25	26	64	43	53	63	51	66	16	64	42	63	26	31	46
53	34	34	16	44	54	42	13	11	64	43	54	24	56	25	56	22	12	42	21	34	62	36	31	56
45	45	65	61	52	12	12	31	43	11	11	25	11	21	64	53	61	44	31	55	31	52	15	61	22
15	46	61	35	45	54	32	33	56	31	23	56	66	51	21	34	51	35	35	41	31	63	43	33	21
35	43	22	42	43	11	33	13	32	62	22	15	55	63	46	14	25	46	56	61	32	61	12	46	24
54	55	65	46	31	21	64	22	26	22	25	44	16	24	53	33	54	25	16	15	11	31	46	51	45
21	35	54	26	35	22	36	15	65	35	34	23	11	22	33	14	41	53	52	54	12	31	11	63	55
26	22	55	66	42	61	46	31	42	61	23	41	56	11	51	46	41	65	65	41	23	13	25	66	66
25	21	32	52	66	24	44	44	34	44	32	51	43	51	31	64	46	25	64	53	35	51	25	15	61
32	16	25	13	63	54	26	31	55	55	15	56	13	42	34	14	53	22	36	15	46	65	41	24	22
42	23	24	66	65	63	45	25	42	23	53	34	26	33	36	66	61	62	15	12	52	16	34	61	22
43	15	66	43	25	26	21	11	55	66	16	54	26	22	11	16	42	65	42	32	55	65	65	14	21
13	56	41	64	56	12	22	16	63	54	62	11	24	33	22	41	24	25	11	44	24	54	23	65	56
44	12	43	14	55	55	33	36	33	62	32	33	23	56	43	13	16	35	21	15	23	52	64	42	15
42	51	35	21	22	34	53	42	15	36	22	44	26	34	31	65	56	13	12	46	15	34	63	62	15
35	65	11	52	22	41	52	54	25	13	65	56	12	24	46	46	34	45	12	11	42	23	33	42	41
61	13	63	21	25	35	41	46	32	41	35	52	45	13	65	33	24	32	61	24	64	32	41	62	54
45	11	15	54	14	64	25	14	63	41	33	25	55	22	45	14	61	35	51	12	52	45	62	64	51
46	52	23	14	63	65	34	24	35	31	66	64	26	46	22	24	13	63	24	43	61	66	35	52	41
44	16	61	66	44	51	12	53	53	65	11	13	12	55	12	36	65	32	21	46	43	16	21	41	21
24	42	51	21	51	14	16	34	12	45	25	45	31	55	62	23	16	24	21	34	46	24	23	16	36
13	62	62	31	13	52	53	46	63	12	53	64	22	26	31	45	43	36	62	31	54	36	56	15	63
51	31	44	45	41	35	61	36	14	66	52	33	31	61	53	52	64	62	64	63	61	56	16	43	66
46	21	41	21	25	44	34	43	32	14	13	62	54	52	24	34	16	15	24	55	43	62	52	35	34
35	64	33	35	63	23	12	36	56	44	51	13	14	62	36	23	36	41	24	12	64	16	36	13	54
12	64	36	33	33	45	54	56	53	26	53	65	63	15	16	34	35	61	43	51	54	56	25	44	21
32	44	52	24	66	62	42	51	25	42	62	32	63	43	56	42	62	42	52	23	35	52	66	43	45
11	12	22	36	23	31	53	61	44	56	14	55	53	14	12	31	54	54	23	55	44	26	34	11	45

Communities and Ecosystems

Keywords

species
community
ecosystem
watershed
competition
competitor
predation
predator
prey
mutualism
symbiosis
mutualist
obligate

facultative
commensalism
commensal
parasitism
parasite
host
intraspecific competition
interspecific competition
habitat
niche
competitive exclusion

competition coefficients (α and β)
trophic level
food chain
food web
ten percent rule
producers
consumers
autotrophs
heterotrophs
carnivore
herbivore

detritivore
decomposer
pathogen
top carnivore
bioaccumulation
biomagnification
biotic
abiotic
pollutant
pollution
compartment
flux
residence time

Learning Objectives

When finished with this unit, you should be able to:

1. Compare and contrast the key words listed above;

2. Examine the impact of competition and predation on communities, and use the equations concerning competition;

3. Describe the concept of competitive exclusion;

4. Describe the basic structure of food chains, food webs, and the concept of the ten percent rule;

5. Discuss the processes of bioaccumulation and biomagnification, and describe the attributes of chemical compounds that causes them to bioaccumulate and biomagnify;

6. Describe the basic parts of an ecosystem; and

7. Determine the flux rates of nutrients, determine the reservoir (compartment) sizes in an ecosystem, and calculate the residence times of nutrients.

Communities

Species Interactions

There are many interactions between species, some are beneficial (+), some are antagonistic or detrimental (–) to one or both species. In some cases, there is no direct benefit or detriment (0) (Table 24.1).

TABLE 24.1. Species interactions.

Interaction	Direct Effects of One Individual of One Species upon the Other	
	Species 1	Species 2
competition	(–) competitor	(–) competitor
predation	(+) predator	(–) prey
parasitism	(+) parasite	(–) host
commensalism	(+) commensal	(0) host
mutualism	(+) mutualist	(+) mutualist
detritivory/decomposition	(+) detritivore/decomposer	(0) detritus

Symbiosis (Greek, "living together"). In a broad sense, a 'symbiosis' is any interaction between two species (both referred to as **symbionts**); in the narrow sense, 'symbiosis' is a synonym for 'mutualism.' When you use the term, make it clear which definition of 'symbiosis' is implied. An **endosymbiont** is one organism that lives within another organism's body.

Effects at different levels. The pluses, minuses, and zeroes in the table above are only referring to the direct interactions between two individuals of the two populations. In many cases, a species interaction may be positive at one level, but negative at another. For example, a predator kills one prey (an obvious negative for that prey individual), but the predator may benefit the entire prey population indirectly by removing a diseased individual from the prey population.

A **Competition** is an interaction between two or more species where a **limiting resource** causes a reduction in reproduction and survival for (usually) both competing species. No competition can occur if resource is not limiting.

B **Predation.** Predators catch individual prey and eat them. Most authors view predators as only including the animals that eat other animals. However, some animal-eating plants are well-known (the Venus fly trap, for example) and many plant-eating animals kill their plant prey. For this course, we will view predators as any organism that kills and eats another (the predator removes the prey from the prey population). Predators generally kill and consume all or most of their prey. In addition, predators are usually larger than their prey, and they usually kill solitary prey one at a time (a lynx preying upon a hare), although some predators kill perhaps millions in one attack (whales feeding on planktonic krill). Some exceptions exist where prey are larger than individual predators—wolves and lions, for instance, may hunt in groups after prey much larger than themselves.

C **Parasitism. Parasites** are animals (or, in some cases, protistans, plants, or fungi) that consume tissues of (or steal food from) their living hosts. A **host** is any organism on which (or in which) another organism lives; the host provides nutrients, shelter, or transport to the other organism (be it a parasite, mutualist, or commensal). Hosts are usually larger than parasites. Parasites generally harm hosts, but often do not kill them; the harmful effect may be small. However, some parasites may directly kill their hosts at times, or they may make the host susceptible to the host's predators.

D **Commensalism** occurs when one species (the **commensal**) benefits from the association and the other (the **host**) is neither harmed nor benefitted by the presence of the commensal. For example, many commensal organisms are those that live on the surface of another organism.

E **Mutualism.** Both interacting species benefit from a mutualistic association. Some mutualistic associations are **facultative** (where the two interacting species may live independently of each other), and other associations are **obligate** (where the two interacting species must be together for one or both to exist). This facultative/obligate dichotomy also pertains to parasitic and commensalistic associations as well.

There are many examples of mutualism. Almost all major plants of forests and grasslands have mutualistic endosymbionts (fungi and plant roots combined form mycorrhizae) or blue-green bacteria (endosymbionts) that help plant obtain nutrients from the air and soils. Corals (the major builders of coral reefs) have large numbers of unicellular algal endosymbionts that assist them in building up the calcium carbonate of the reef. Many flowering plants rely on insects or birds as pollinators. Lichens are associations of blue-green bacteria (or green algae) with fungi.

F **Detritivores** ("detrit-" = wear off). Animals that eat dead organic matter, such as leaves and sticks (detritus). However, detritivores may be actually consuming the bacteria and fungi that have colonized the dead organic material, and possibly very small animals living on the detritus are eaten as well. Detritivores are sometimes depicted to form a separate food web, with connecting links to the predatory food web. Although detritivores and decomposers consume dead top carnivores, we usually do not think of detritivores as 'supreme' carnivores above the top carnivores. In this course, we will distinguish between two groups of organisms that feed upon dead organic matter: detritivores and decomposers.

Decomposers consume dead organic matter, and they reconvert nutrients back to forms useful for plants (for example: nitrogenous compounds such as proteins and amino acids are converted to nitrates). Bacteria and fungi usually are considered to be the major decomposer taxa. In addition to breaking down dead organic matter, some decomposers may feed upon living hosts as well and thus act as **pathogens.** Pathogens are generally defined as the bacteria and other microbes (such as viruses) that cause disease in a host. 'Decomposer' and 'detritivore' are used interchangeably in some texts, but most make a distinction between the two terms based on: 1) size and taxonomy (animals versus microscopic bacteria and fungi); 2) consumption (ingesting chunks of dead organic matter followed by chemical digestion in the gut, versus extracellular digestion and absorption of molecules from the environment); 3) the microbes' abilities to chemically digest large compounds that deteritivores typically cannot process (such as lignins and celluloses); and 4) microbes break down complex molecules completely into simpler molecules that autotrophs can use, such as nitrates and ammonia. However, it has been shown recently that plants are able to take up proteins and simple carbohydrates from their environment, without the help of decomposers.

Exercises

Exercise 24.1.

Population Interactions: Competition

Follow the directions of Exercise 23.5 (the *Beadus* exercises for logistic population growth). However, in this exercise, you will be place individual beads of two different colors (representing two different species) on the board. If two beads of any color (with one exception described below) land on the same square, remove all of the beads in the square at the **end** of the reproductive phase. The exception is where one bead of *Beadus verdantae* (green beads) is with one or more beads of *Beadus orangii* (orange beads). Remove the orange bead(s) only, leaving the green bead behind. However, if two or more green beads are in the same square, either with or without orange beads, remove all of beads from that square. **Interspecific competition** occurs when individuals of two or more different species compete for resources.

1. Count the number of *Beadus orangii* (orange beads) and *Beadus verdantae* (green beads) that you have alive at the beginning of the time period. Write that number in the first column for each species in Table 24.2 for the appropriate time period. You will start the exercise with one bead of each species.

2. Roll one die. Then roll a second die. (Or, instead, use Table 23.6.) The two numbers tell you on which square to place the bead. Like the logistic growth model, this is the 'colonization phase' of the competition model.

3. Roll each time you place a bead on the board. Place the *B. orangii* beads first, then the *B. verdantae* beads.

4. Each individual *B. orangii* and *B. verdantae* alive at the start of the time period will reproduce one offspring during the time period. Double the number in column one and place this number in the second column in the data sheet for each species. For each bead you just placed on the board in the 'colonization phase,' roll and add one additional bead on the board. At the end of the 'birth phase' of the time period, you should have placed a number of beads on the board that is equal to the number in second column for a species.

5. If, during rolling the dice, any bead (regardless of species) lands on a square that is occupied, go ahead and place the bead in the square alongside any other bead(s) present.

6. If, at the end of the 'birth phase' (but **ONLY** after you have placed **ALL** beads of both colors on the board), two or more orange beads occupy any one square, all of the orange beads of that square are all 'killed' due to crowding. Remove all orange beads from the square.

7. If two or more green beads occupy a given square, remove all of the beads (both green and orange) from the square.

8. If one green bead occupies a square with one or more orange beads, remove all of the orange beads from the square but leave the green bead on the board.

At the end of the 'death phase,' only one bead can occupy a square. Remember, that square represents all of the resources needed for survival and reproduction of one individual. If two or more beads are 'sharing' that square, there is not enough resources to keep two or more alive and so all of them in that square will 'die' during the 'death phase,' unless it is one green bead and one or more orange beads. In that case, only remove the orange bead(s).

9 Count the beads that are left on the board for each species. Write that number in the fourth column of Table 24.2. That is the number of individuals of that species alive at the start of the next time period's 'colonization phase.' Some beads thus may live for several time periods.

10 Repeat Steps 4 through 9 and continue gathering data until you reach at least 10 time periods.

TABLE 24.2. Interspecific competition results.

Time Period	*Beadus orangii*				*Beadus verdantae*			
	N at Start of Time Period	Total *N* after Reproduction	*N* Killed	*N* for Start of Next Time Period	*N* at Start of Time Period	Total *N* after Reproduction	*N* Killed	*N* for Start of Next Time Period
1	1	2			1	2		
2								
3								
4								
5								
6								
7								
8								
9								
10								

Plot these data (the first column for each species) on graph paper provided in Figure 24.1.

What happened when *B. verdantae* and *B. orangii* competed?

In the 1920s, A. J. Lotka (American) and Vito Volterra (Italian) independently added additional variables to the logistic equation (Equation 23.8). Lotka and Volterra added **competition coefficients α and β** (alpha and beta), which are used to help determine the impact of **interspecific competition** (see Equations 24.1 and 24.2):

Equation 24.1.
$$\frac{\delta N_1}{\delta t} = r_1 N_1 \left(\frac{(K_1 - N_1 - \alpha N_2)}{(K_1)} \right)$$

Equation 24.2.
$$\frac{\delta N_2}{\delta t} = r_2 N_2 \left(\frac{(K_2 - N_2 - \beta N_1)}{(K_2)} \right)$$

where r_1 and K_1 are the growth rate and carrying capacity for species N_1, and r_2 and K_2 are the growth rate and carrying capacity for species N_2.

αN_2 = the equivalent number of species 1 (N_1) individuals. The alpha coefficient allows you to determine what the equivalent individual impact of species 2 on the change in population size of species 1.

βN_1 = the equivalent number of species 2 (N_2) individuals. The beta coefficient allows you to determine what the equivalent individual impact of species 1 on the change in population size of species 2. Remember that both species are using the same resources (the same squares).

In most cases, one of the competing species is more adapted to the local climate, or can extract more nutrients, or can reproduce more offspring, or is more aggressive or territorial than the other species. In these cases, if the species compete long enough, the better competitor can drive the other species into extinction locally. This phenomenon is called **competitive exclusion. The competitive exclusion principle states that in any one habitat, two species cannot coexist in the same niche indefinitely.**

Niche versus habitat. An organism's **niche** is its functional role in the community. Examples of the niches found in a deciduous forest would include seed predators, insectivores (eats insects), and so on. In other words, the niche is the organism's 'job or profession.' The **habitat** for an organism is the 'address' of the organism, or in other words, the physical location in which it lives. An organism's habitat is defined as the place or environments in which the individual or species resides. While you are on campus, your niche is 'student,' while your lab instructor's niche is 'instructor,' and the habitat where both of you reside would be the classroom building.

FIGURE 24.1.

Results of the *Beadus* competition experiment. Population size (ordinate, *y*-axis) is plotted as a function of generation or time period (abscissa, *x*-axis).

Can you estimate what the alpha and beta values should be for *Beadus orangii* and *Beadus verdantae*?

Your lab instructor will tell you the carrying capacities (*K*s) and the alphas and betas for each species (Table 24.3).

TABLE 24.3. Results of the competition experiment.

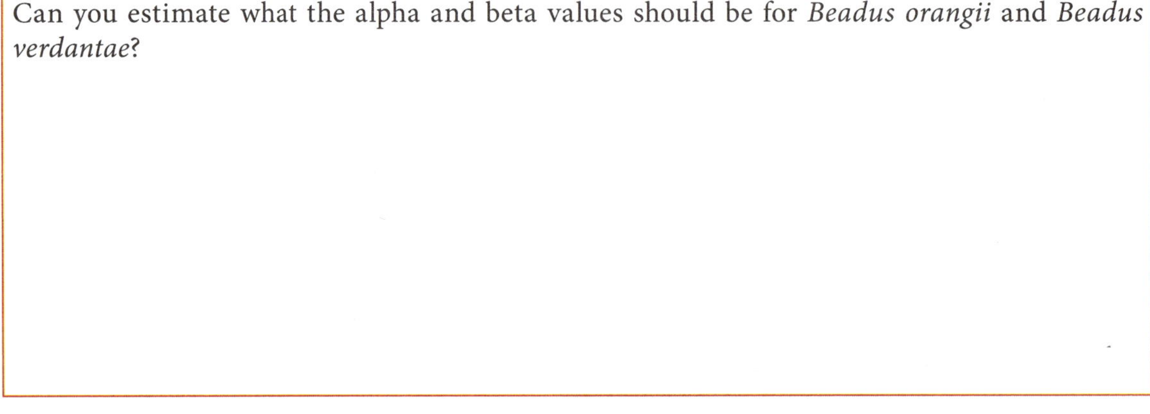

Species	*K*	Competition Coefficient
B. orangii (N_1)		$\beta =$
B. verdantae (N_2)		$\alpha =$

Given the *K* values and the competition coefficients above, can you see why *B. verdantae* is a better competitor in this model?

The Structure of a Community

An ecological community consists of all interacting populations in a defined area. There may be no rigid geographical boundary to a population, community, or ecosystem, so boundaries are sometimes arbitrarily determined by the scientist. Communities often are depicted as having a definite **trophic structure,** where there are 'layers' of organisms grouped according to their mode of nutrition: producers, herbivores, carnivores, and so on. Examine Table 24.4. It shows the relative positions (trophic level) for several species in a grassland community and in a lake community. In Table 24.4, the 'flow' of energy would be from the bottom towards the top. The energy source (in most cases, the sun) is not considered to be a trophic level.

TABLE 24.4. The trophic structure of a community.

		Lake Food Chain	Grassland Food Chain
consumers or heterotrophs	4th trophic level	lake trout	hawk
	3rd trophic level	minnow	robin
	2nd trophic level	zooplankton	insect
producers or autotrophs	1st trophic level	phytoplankton	grass
(energy source)		(sunlight)	(sunlight)

Food chains are linear chains of who eats whom in a community. In the lake community (in Table 24.4 above), sunlight is captured by phytoplankton and converted into the chemical bond energy of carbohydrates and other compounds. Small crustaceans, rotifers, and insects eat the phytoplankton, and the zooplankton in turn are eaten by the planktivorous ("plankton-eating") minnows. The small minnows are eaten by the piscivourous ("fish-eating") trout. Food chains are the pathways through which energy and transfer of nutrients (food) passes from one organism to another.

A food web is a series of interconnected food chains. Ecologists have published a variety of food webs of a number of communities. A food web is a summary of known feeding relationships in a biological community. The food web illustrates how each organism in a community is consumed by (or consumes) other organisms. The food web also can suggest which species would be in competition for the same food sources. See Figure 24.2 as an example of a food web.

The average number of steps in a food chain, from the producers to the top carnivores, is around three to six. Some of the food chains in a complex food web may be longer than six levels, but the average length of all food chains in a complex food web is six or less. There is a decrease in available energy that can be transferred to the next level at each step because much of the energy consumed by an organism (perhaps as much as 90%) is used for respiration and maintenance. On average, ecologists estimate that about 10 percent of the chemical energy available at one trophic level is transferred and stored in usable form in the bodies of the organisms at the next trophic level. In reality, the number can vary from less than 1% to perhaps 30% or more, but 10% is a rough average. This general observation about food webs is called the **ten percent rule.** Because much of the energy at one level is not available to the next level, that fact helps explain why three to six trophic levels exist for most food webs; there simply is not enough energy to sustain a viable population of carnivorous animals residing exclusively at a very high trophic level. Suppose that you had a 10th trophic level consumer; only 0.00000001% of the energy fixed by the plants would be available to such a high level consumer.

A community's food web consists of a series of feeding levels, called trophic levels. The first level consists of all of the **autotrophic** plants, who are called the **producers** of the food web. Producers capture sunlight and convert it into chemical energy stored in the chemical bonds of glucose and other compounds. Instead of sunlight, some autotrophs in a few places can use a high energy chemical source for synthesis of organic molecules. For example, consider the bacteria that live in deep sea vent communities in total darkness: they cannot rely on light, instead, they use hydrogen sulfide and other energy-rich molecules from the vent for their energy source. This process is called chemosynthesis, to distinguish it from photosynthesis.

In addition to the producers, there are a number of **consumers** present in food webs. Consumers are also called **heterotrophs** because they consume at least some of their food 'prefabricated' in the form of organic matter created by other living organisms.

Consumers are divided into several groups:

1. **Primary consumers** (herbivores "herb-" = grass, "-vore" = to devour). Animals that eat primarily plants (many herbivores may incidentally be consuming small insects and other organisms that are on the plant material, but the plants are thought to be the primary material being consumed). The herbivores compose the second trophic level of the food web.

2. **Secondary consumers** (carnivores "carn-" = flesh). Animals that eat animals that eat plants. Secondary consumers make up the third trophic level of the food web. Some plants (producers) can be considered carnivorous! Pitcher plants and Venus flytraps capture insects and other small organisms in traps; these traps contain digestive enzymes that break down animal tissues. These plants are also autotrophs, but they live in nitrogen-poor habitats and thus need animal protein as a nitrogen source.

3. **Tertiary consumers** (carnivores). These animals consume the carnivores and often sit on top of the food webs, at the fourth level. Tertiary consumers may not be the end of the chain; there may be higher levels above the tertiary consumer. The final organisms that sit on top of the food web are called the **top carnivores:** no higher trophic level predator kills and eats them (although when top carnivores die, decomposers and detritivores consume their dead bodies).

4. **Omnivores** ("omni-" = all). Omnivores are heterotrophs that eat both plants and animals. Omnivores thus reside at several trophic levels, both as herbivores and as carnivores. (Some texts may define omnivores as feeding on several trophic levels, but the most precise definition of omnivory is that plants and animals both are consumed as primary food sources.)

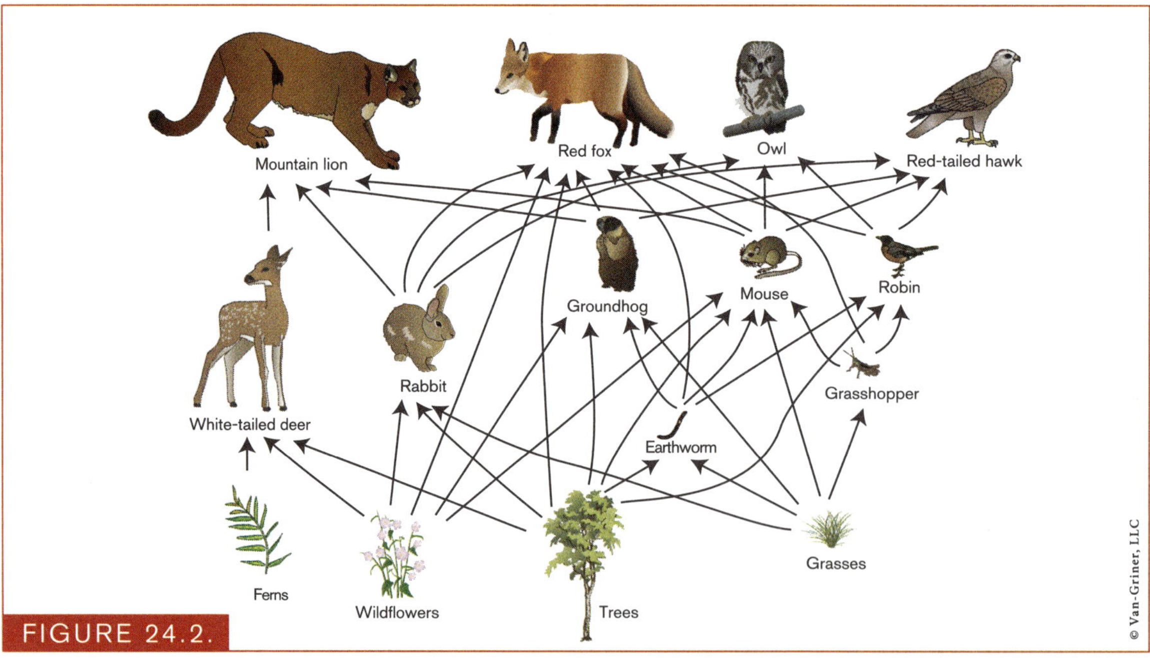

FIGURE 24.2.

A food web. The producers (plants) are eaten by a variety of primary consumers which in turn are eaten by higher trophic level consumers. The arrows indicate the flow of energy (predation) from one organism to another.

Exercise 24.2.

Which of the animals in the food web depicted in Figure 24.2 would be considered herbivores? Carnivores? Omnivores? Do they sit on more than one trophic level?

What is the maximum number of trophic levels in the food web depicted in Figure 24.2 (i.e., what is the longest food chain)?

If there were 5 tons (10,000 pounds) of energy fixed at the level of the plants, how much biomass would you predict would be present in the animals at the top of the web? Explain your answer.

First, what is meant by "Energy flows through ecosystems, but nutrients cycle within ecosystems." Could energy 'cycle?' Why not?

Bioaccumulation and Biomagnification

For many years, humans have been searching for new ways to increase crop yields and eliminate pests that compete for our food or spread disease. Pesticides were developed in order to eliminate agricultural pests and disease-carrying organisms such as weeds, biting flies, and mosquitoes, and several compounds have been quite valuable in controlling various pest species, thus increasing food supplies and saving many lives. However, pesticides also can have undesirable effects. One major problem with pesticides is nontarget toxicity: in addition to killing mosquitoes and other pests, some pesticides have long-term deadly effects on other species, such as songbirds and large birds of prey that are at the top of food chains (eagles, hawks, and falcons). These species were not targeted. In addition, the insect pests have become partially or totally immune to the pesticide's effects. Finally, toxic compounds may build up over time in soil and water, particularly if neither living things nor the physical environment can degrade them. Some pesticides are very persistent and mobile, thus they can travel long distances from their application site, by wind and water.

Bioaccumulation occurs because most organisms do not have the biochemical ability to metabolize, detoxify, or excrete pesticides, heavy metals, and other toxic compounds. Instead, these chemicals are stored in fat, bone, or other parts of the body. Bioaccumulation is the accumulation of toxic, non-metabolizable, non-excretable compounds in the bodies of all living things over time. The process of bioaccumulation is shown in Figure 24.3. The toxin can increase in concentration over time, as more and more of the compound is absorbed by the organism from the air, water, or its food. The concentration of the toxin may be at very low levels in the environment, at concentrations that may be barely detectable. The toxic effects of the pesticide also may not be apparent in the small concentrations found in the small, short-lived organisms at the base of the food web. However, if the toxin is not excreted or broken down, the levels of the toxin will increase over time in their flesh. Because higher trophic level consumers generally are longer-lived and eat many prey over their lifetimes, the amount of the toxin thus will accumulate to a point where the toxin's concentration could affect the health, reproduction, and survival of higher trophic level consumers.

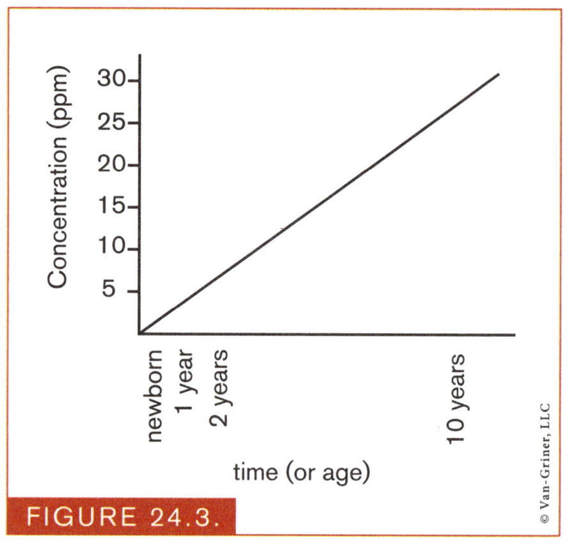

FIGURE 24.3.

Bioaccumulation.

Compounds that may bioaccumulate and biomagnify have the following attributes:

a They are stable chemically; they are not broken down by weathering forces of the physical environment (chemical degradation, light degradation, and so on),

b They are not easily detoxified or metabolized by bacterial activity, or by organismal metabolism,

c They are fat soluble and/or they can be sequestered in bone or other tissues,

d They are not be easily excreted by the excretory systems,

e They are able to pass up through the food chain from organism to organism through predation.

Biomagnification (**biological magnification**) occurs when organisms accumulate these toxic compounds over time in their tissues, and when predators eat them, the predators end up with greater levels of toxic compounds accumulating in their bodies. **Biological magnification** (or **biomagnification**) thus is the increase in the concentration of toxic compounds within the body tissues of successively higher trophic level consumers in a food web. (Figure 24.4).

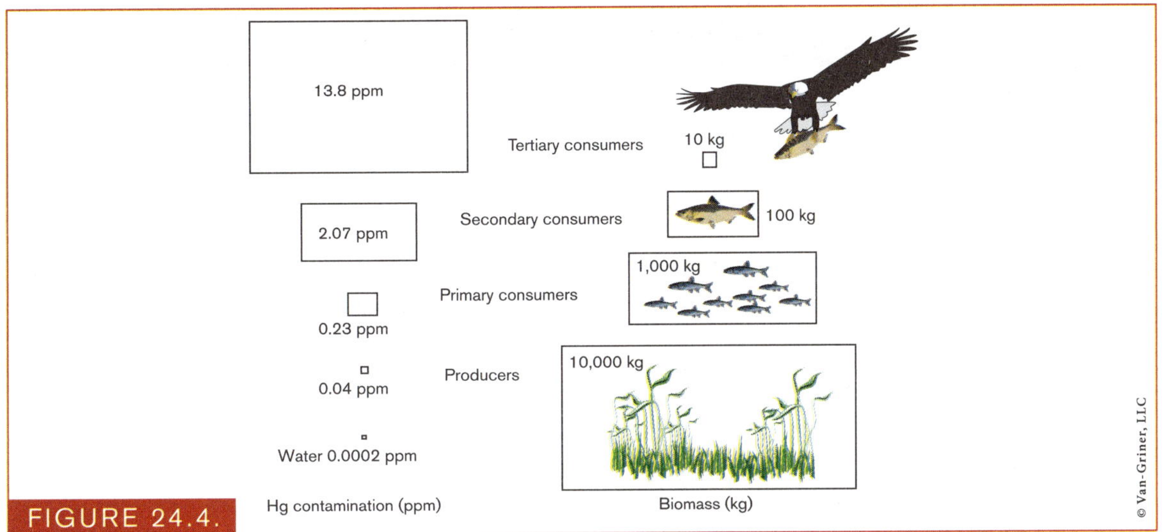

FIGURE 24.4.

Biomagnification.

Exercise 24.3.

1 Biomagnification demonstration. Your lab instructor will hand you a lanyard attached to a name tag. Place the lanyard around your neck. You become the organism listed on the name tag. You will be either: a lake trout *Salvelinus* (5), a cisco fish *Coregonus* (4), a shrimp *Mysis* (3), a water flea *Daphnia* (2), or phytoplankton (1). The food chain is depicted in Figure 24.5. The lab instructor and possibly several students will take on the role of "Environment" (0).

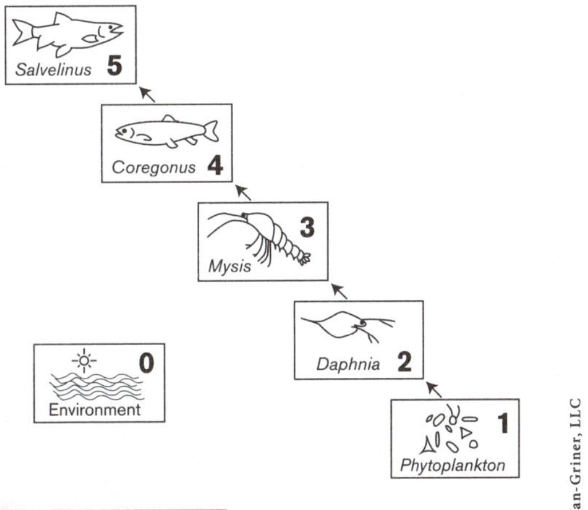

In addition, your lab instructor (who will play the part of the 'physical environment') will hand to each of you 20 3″×5″ index cards. On the back of each card, there will be either the letters "CHONP" (representing "Carbon-Hydrogen-Oxygen-Nitrogen-Phosphorus") or "Hg" ("Mercury"). Note the number of each type of card in your hand in the table below (Figure 24.5) in the row labeled "initial." Calculate the percentage of your total cards that are mercury (Hg) by dividing the number of cards that are Hg by the total number of cards (and then multiply by 100).

Shuffle up your cards and do not look at the backs. Hold the stack of cards in your hand, face down, so that you do not see the letters.

FIGURE 24.5.

Lake food chain. The arrows indicate the flow of energy from prey to predator (i.e., the trout *Salvelinus* eats the cisco *Coregonus*, and so on). The plants (phytoplankton) receive energy from the sun.

TABLE 24.5. The initial setup of the biomagnification exercise.

Your Level (0–5):	The Number of Cards in Your Hand of Each Type			
	'CHONP'	'Hg'	Total Number of Cards	'Hg' Load (%) 'Hg'
initial number of cards				
final number of cards				

3 Now, for the next 10 minutes or so, you are to mingle around the room, meeting other students. You are to meet as many of the others you can. You may interact with the same person several times, but after a given interaction, you must meet at least one other person in the room before interacting with someone you previously had an interaction. If the two of you are more than one trophic level apart [for example, a *Coregonus* (trophic level 4) meets a *Daphnia* (trophic level 2)], there is no interaction; each goes off to meet another student. However, if you come in contact with a student whose species is one trophic level lower than your species (for example, you are a *Daphnia* (trophic level 2), and you come into contact with "phytoplankton" (trophic level 1), the student who is the lower trophic level (the "prey") hands over the top three cards from their stack to the other student (the "predator"). The "predator" must accept all cards handed to them by placing them on the bottom of their stack. The "prey" cannot pick and choose which cards to hand over to the "predator." These three cards represent the act of predation—the transfer of prey biomass to the predator.

4 When any "phytoplankton" (trophic level 1) meets the "environment" (0), the person playing the role of "environment" will hand ten cards face down to the producer, who will place the cards at the bottom of their stack. This represents the process of photosynthesis and the intake of water by the plant.

5 The lab instructor (and possibly several students) will act as the "environment." Each "environment" person will have a large number of cards. When any 'organism' that resides at trophic levels 2 through 5 (i.e., animals) comes in contact with the "environment," the two will trade five cards by taking the top five cards of their stacks and handing the cards to the other. Each will place the cards on the bottom of their stack. This act will mimic the effect of respiration and excretion by the "organism" and the intake of water and air from the "environment." The "organism" cannot look at the cards handed to them, nor can they choose which five cards they will give to the "environment." However, the "environment" person will look at the cards handed to him/her, and will hand back any cards labeled "Hg" back to the "organism," who will place any cards handed back on the bottom of their stack.

6 If you run out of cards (because you handed all of them over to your "predators"), find an "environment" person who will hand twenty additional cards to you. If you are an "environment" person, periodically hand your cards to the lab instructor and obtain fresh cards. If your class size is low, your lab instructor will have you do the following. There will be a number of piles of cards (each pile with a lanyard) lying around the room. You will pick up one pile and its lanyard. Travel from one pile to the next, leaving or removing cards from the piles following the instructions above. Periodically, your lab instructor will ask you to place your current pile an lanyard on the table, pick up another pile of cards, and continue as before.

7 At the end of the time period allotted by the lab instructor, he or she will tell each student to sit down. Tally the total number of cards in your hand and the number of cards of each type. Place these data in Table 24.5.

8 Tell your lab instructor your trophic level and initial and final mercury loads for Hg from Table 24.5. Place your data on the front board. Copy the information placed on the front table in Table 24.6, and calculate the average initial and final mercury loads for all five trophic levels and place the results in Table 24.7. (To speed up the exercise, the lab instructor may assign each student or small group of students the job of calculating one average for a given trophic level.)

Alternative instructions: If your class size is too small, your lab instructor may use the following instructions. Piles of cards are scattered around the room, with associated lanyards and name tags. Pick up one pile of cards (and its name tag and lanyard) and travel through the room, interacting with each pile of cards in turn. Follow the instructions as outlined above. Your lab instructor will periodically tell you to stop; when this happens, put your pile of cards and name tag/lanyard down and pick up a nearby pile of cards with its name tag/lanyard, and continue. After several rounds, your lab instructor will tell the class to stop. The class then will calculate heavy metal loads for each pile of cards as before.

Do the results support what you thought you would see as the outcome of this exercise?

TABLE 24.6. Data from the bioaccumulation/biomagnification exercise.

Trophic Level (1–5) or Environment (0)	Initial Hg Load (%)	Final Hg Load (%)

TABLE 24.7. The results for the bioaccumulation/biomagnification exercise.

Trophic Level/Environment	Average Heavy Metal Load (%) for Mercury (Hg)	
	Initial	Final
lake trout *Salvelinus* (5)		
cisco *Coregonus* (4)		
shrimp *Mysis* (3)		
water flea *Daphnia* (2)		
phytoplankton (1)		
physical environment (0)		

In some lakes, the shrimp and the cisco are missing. Under those conditions, the lake trout feed upon *Daphnia* directly, and there are only three trophic levels. In other lakes, the shrimp are missing, and the smaller fish are feeding on zooplankton, such as *Daphnia*. What would happen with respect to the level of biomagnification that would be observed? What would you predict is the effect of **food chain length** on biological magnification? Can you imagine a scenario where humans can use this process of bioaccumulation for our benefit.

Hint: What do you think the term 'phytoremediation' may mean?

In the biomagnification exercise, although the data you collected are hypothetical, they are based on actual research. The following paper provides some further information on the subject:

Cabana, G. and J. B. Rasmussen. 1994. Modelling food chain structure and contaminant bioaccumulation using stable nitrogen isotopes. Nature 372: 255–257.

Ecosystems

Ecosystems can be viewed as the sum of all interactions between the living community and the nonliving physical environment. In Figure 24.6, four compartments: the hydrosphere (oceans, lakes and rivers), the atmosphere, the lithosphere (soils, rocks), and the biosphere (the living biological community) are depicted.

A key feature of ecosystems is the **cycling of nutrients** between living and nonliving compartments of the ecosystem, and the **flow of energy** (primarily from the sun) into and eventually out of the ecosystem.

The environment refers to the world around a given organism. The environment thus is all of the **abiotic** ("nonliving, physical") and **biotic** ("living") factors that a single organism is exposed to at any point in its life.

One example of an ecosystem is a large pond. There is a distinct boundary (the water's edge), and there are places where inputs (any streams emptying into the pond) and outputs occur (any streams that drain away from the pond). One commonly studied terrestrial ecosystem is called the **watershed.** A watershed is an area of land drained by a single stream or river.

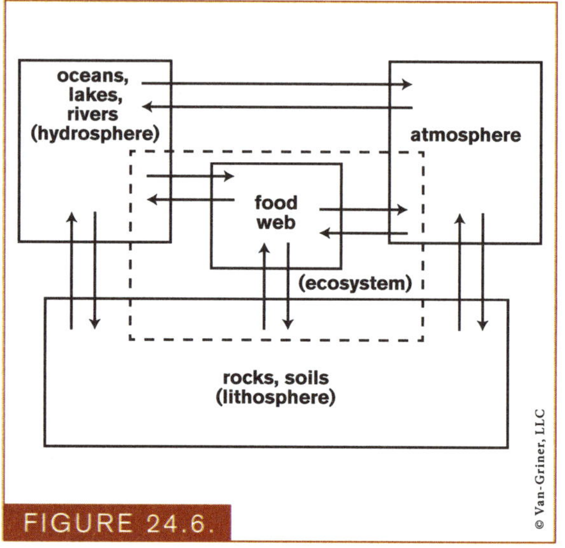

FIGURE 24.6.

The major compartments of the ecosystem. An ecosystem is enclosed within the dotted box.

Energy flow in ecosystems is linear, or one-way. Energy can move along a food web from one organism to the next as long as it is not used for respiration and it is in a form the next consumer can digest (bone and fur is not easily digested by many animals). When energy is used for metabolism and other forms of work, it is turned into thermal energy (heat) and is then unavailable for use by any other organism in the ecosystem. Nutrients (such as nitrates and phosphates), on the other hand, may be retained within a given ecosystem to be reused again and again.

Nutrients tend to stay within their ecosystems. Each element follows a unique pathway, due to the transformations that occur along the way. For example, N_2 in the atmosphere ammonia (NH_3 or NH_4^+, in the water or soil, along with nitrates (NO_3^-) and proteins and urea in animals.

The Earth and its ecosystems are resilient. Ecosystems can dilute, break down, and recycle many of the chemicals we add to the air, water, and soil, as long as we do not overload an ecosystem's abilities to process pollutants. The Earth can replenish topsoil, water, air, forests, grasslands, and wildlife, as long as we do not use these resources at a rate that is faster than they are renewed.

All nutrient cycles have the same overall structure. First, let's discuss several terms concerning systems and nutrient cycles:

Compartments (= **reservoirs**). Compartments are components of the cycle, such as the atmosphere, the soils, the water and the various living organisms of the food web.

Flux. A flux is defined as the movement of nutrients between compartments and their magnitudes.

Residence time. The residence time is calculated as the amount of nutrient in compartment divided by the flux into or out of the compartment (assuming that the compartment size stays the same and flux in = flux out).

A **system** is a part of the universe that can be isolated and studied. We could talk about the entire Earth, a watershed, a population, or an organism. To a parasite, the human digestive tract is the system in which it lives. On the tundra, water in a depression formed by a footstep is a system for microscopic organisms. Systems have inputs and outputs, and we can study how systems are connected and how they work internally.

Steady state is a term that describes a system in equilibrium, with inputs balancing outputs. Any change either inputs or outputs may disturb the equilibrium of the system. Thus inputs must equal outputs for the system to stay in equilibrium. Remember our discussion earlier about the responsiveness of systems. A system can respond, yet appear to stay relatively constant, depending on its inputs and outputs.

On a global scale, the solar input (ultraviolet, visible, infrared) roughly equals the outgoing radiation (reflected visible light and outgoing infrared heat energy) leaving Earth. Thus the temperature of the atmosphere, the land, and the oceans (temperature is a function of the difference between heat output and solar input) stays constant through time (over the course of thousands of years). However, if the sun increases its output, or we decrease the ability of heat to leave the planet by increased CO_2, and other pollutants, then the temperature will rise (we call this increase in temperature of the Earth 'global warming').

What is **pollution?** Pollution is defined as the excessive, unwanted inputs of chemicals or energy into the environment as a result of human activity. When pollution occurs, the resource that is polluted (air, water, etc.) may become no longer useful. Most **pollutants** are solid, liquid, or gaseous chemicals, or they can be energy emissions (excessive heat, noise, light, or radiation). It is true that pollutants are produced in nature (for example, ozone is produced by trees), but the relatively small amount of naturally produced pollutants typically is small, compared to the additional amounts produced by human activity. Natural ecosystems are capable of dealing with the small amount of "pollution" produced by organisms. However, ecosystems may not be able to handle the additional pollutants produced by human society.

The **average residence time** is a measure of the time it takes for any or all of the resource in a pool (= reservoir) to be moved through the system. To determine the average residence time, divide the total size of the pool by the average rate of transfer into and out of the pool (i. e., the average flux rate). Say you have a small lake containing 1,000 cubic meters of water (the reservoir), and on average 100 cubic meters of water enters and leaves the lake every day (the average rate of transfer, because inputs = outputs, the lake level stays constant). Thus $1,000 \text{ m}^3 / 100 \text{ m}^3 \times \text{day}^{-1} = 10 \text{ days} =$ average residence time (the average time a molecule of water stays in the lake).

Exercise 24.4.

Examine Figures A through D in Figure 24.7. The clear circles represent units of water; the filled circles represent units of water that contain a pollutant. Assume that in each system that the source of the pollutant was discovered and stopped, so that no additional pollutant is entering. Systems A and B are small systems (small reservoirs), containing 10 units of water at any one time. Ecosystems A and C have a flux rate of 5 units per hour (5 units in and 5 units out per hour). Systems B and D have a flux rate of 1 unit per hour. Systems C and D are larger systems (larger reservoirs) with a total of 30 units.

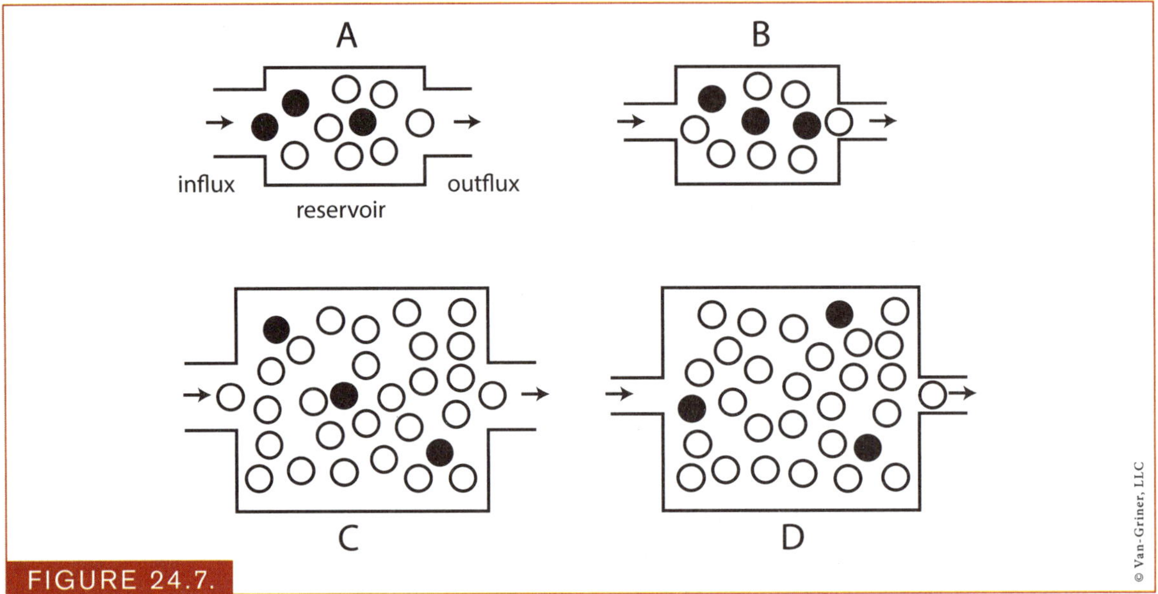

FIGURE 24.7.

Four ecosystems.

TABLE 24.8. Calculate the following results from the data in Figure 24.7 above.

System (Figure 24.7)	Reservoir Size (units)	Flux Rate (units/hour)	Residence Time (hour)
A			
B			
C			
D			

Think about a local ecosystem, such as a large river, a small stream or an underground aquifer. How would it respond to pollution?

With respect to the systems shown in Figure 24.7, which system would be most easily polluted (in other words, in which system would you see the effects the presence of pollutants the fastest)? Which system would be most easily flushed out? Which system would take the longest time, once polluted, to be cleared of pollutants?

Exercise 24.5.

The figure below (Figure 24.8) is a depiction of the global carbon cycle. The numbers refer to reservoir sizes in gigatons of carbon (GtC) and the flux rates of gigatons of carbon per year (GtC/yr).

Note that the flux rate from the atmosphere to the food web is missing. If both compartments remain constant in size, and the flux rates (in and out) are balanced, what must be the yearly flux rate from the atmosphere to the food web?

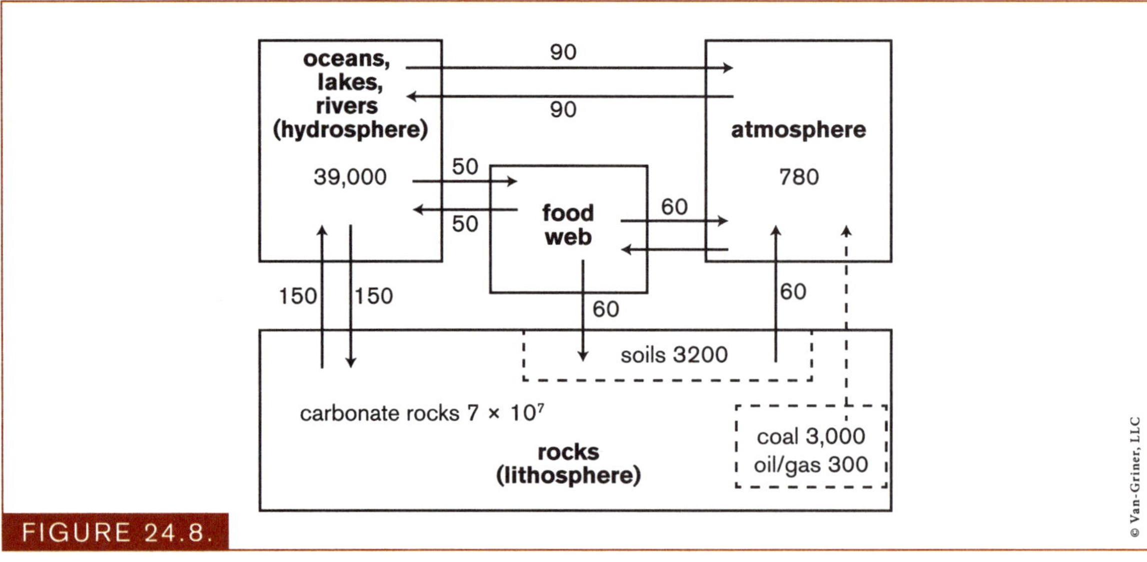

FIGURE 24.8.

The global carbon cycle.

If the average residence time for an atom of carbon is about 4 years in the food web, how much carbon must be present in the food web?

TABLE 24.9. Calculate the carbon flux rates and residence times for each compartment.

System (Figure 24.8)	Reservoir Size (GtC)	Flux Rate (GtC/year)	Residence Time (years)
hydrosphere (oceans, lakes, rivers)	39,000		
lithosphere (carbonate rocks)	7×10^7		
atmosphere	780		
biosphere (food webs)			4

Note the dotted line from oil and coal to the atmosphere. If the flux rate of fossil fuel burning is about 7 GtC per year, what could happen to the global carbon cycle?

Proper Microscope Usage and Care

I. The Compound Microscope

Study the parts of the microscope. If you have any questions concerning use of a microscope or dissecting scope, please see your lab instructor. Microscopes are fragile and expensive; even if you have used one before, please refresh yourself on their proper use. If you break one through carelessness, you will be asked to pay for its replacement.

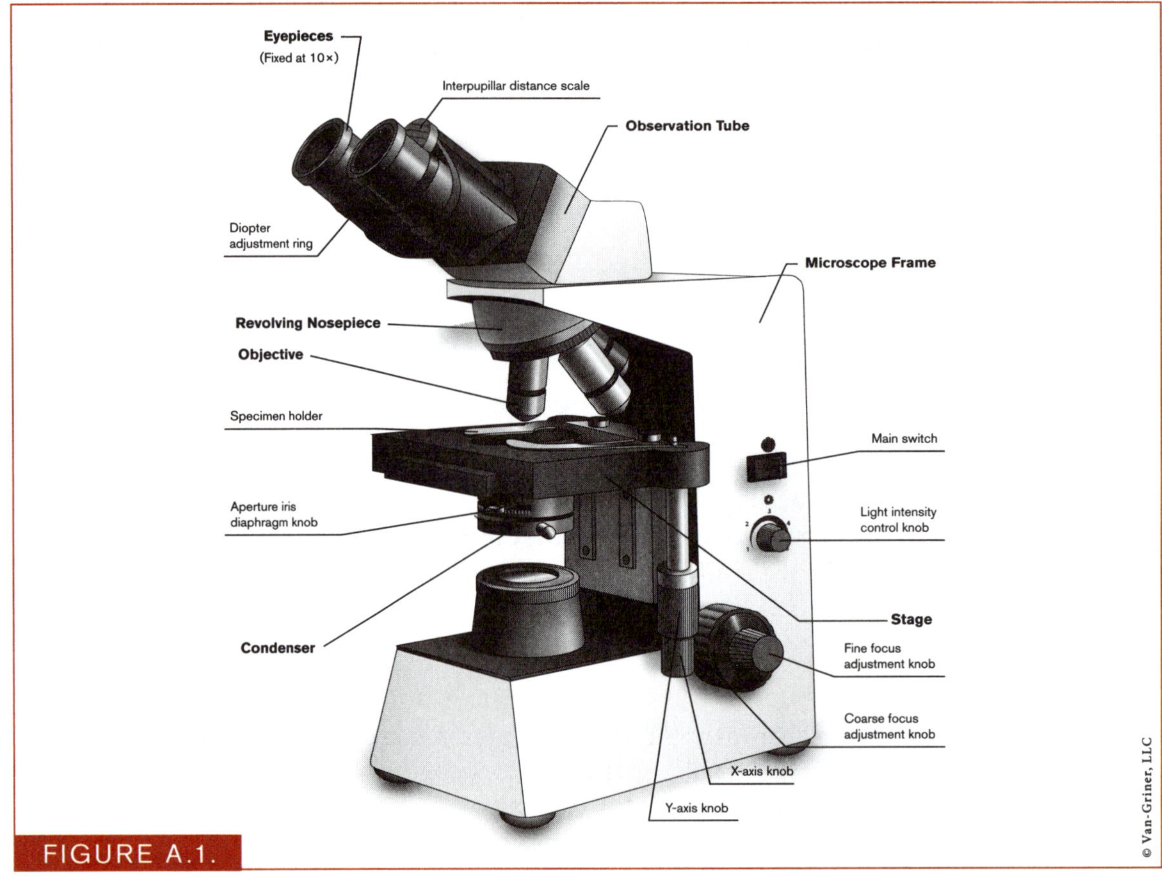

FIGURE A.1.

The parts of a microscope.

Base. The horizontal platform that supports the microscope. The light source is located in the base.

Arm or microscope frame. The vertical frame of the microscope on which the stage, body tube and nosepiece are attached. On the arms, there is a **main** switch that toggles back and forth, turning the light source on and off and a **light intensity knob** for adjusting the light intensity.

Stage. The horizontal platform on which specimen slides are placed. Some of the microscopes have **slide clips** that hold the specimen slide in place; others have a **specimen holder** or **mechanical stage,** with adjustment knobs (Y-axis and X-axis) that are geared to allow fine movement of the slide.

Ocular (eyepiece). The lens through which one looks at the specimen. The eyepiece sits on top of the body tube. Newer microscopes are binocular: they have two oculars. The lenses inside the ocular magnify objects by ten times (10× = the **power** of the lens inside). The magnification power is usually etched on the side or top of the ocular as well as on the side of the objectives. A built-in **pointer** is usually present in the ocular.

Objectives. At the bottom end of the body tube is a rotating **nosepiece** that acts as a turret with anywhere from two to four **objective lenses (objectives)** attached to it. The smallest lens (present on some of the scopes) is the **scanning lens.** It has a power of 4×. Other objectives attached to the nosepiece are 10× (**low power**), 40× (**high power**) and 100× (**oil immersion lens**). The total magnification of the object when a given lens is in alignment is calculated as the power of the objective times the power of the eyepiece (see Table A.1)

TABLE A.1. Determination of total magnification.

	Objective Lens	Eyepiece (Ocular)	Total Magnification
scanning	4×	10×	40×
low power	10×	10×	100×
high power	40×	10×	400×
oil-immersion	100×	10×	1,000×

Most microscopes are **parfocal,** in that the image focused under low power should also be nearly in focus at higher power. Most microscopes are also **parcentered,** meaning that the image should stay in the center of the field of view under higher magnification. Some are not in perfect alignment, so you will need to do minor refocusing and repositioning of the slides.

Iris diaphragm. The iris diaphragm is located just below the stage. Most microscopes have an **iris diaphragm,** where the aperture of the iris is controlled by an adjustable lever. By adjusting the size of the opening, you adjust the amount of light that passes through the specimen and the microscope. The **substage condenser lens** (and its adjustment knob) is located under the stage. The lever controlling the diaphragm is projecting from one side of the condenser lens. The condenser focuses light onto the specimen.

As you use successively higher magnifications, the area you are magnifying gets smaller, and the amount of light passing through to the ocular is decreased. You will need to adjust the iris and the light intensity (the light intensity knob) accordingly.

Coarse and fine focus adjustment knobs. These knobs are on the side of the microscope arm. The larger knob (coarse) moves the entire stage away from or towards the slide. The smaller knob sticking out from the coarse adjustment knob is the fine adjustment. The fine adjustment knob changes the distance from specimen to objective very slightly with each turn of the knob. You use these knobs to bring the object into focus. There is a lever next to the coarse adjustment knob (**coarse adjustment knob tension ring**) that when depressed, 'locks' the distance that the objective can move towards the specimen. This is to prevent you from ramming the objective into the slide with the higher power objectives. When not needed, leave this ring unlocked.

Because each person is different with respect to their eyesight, the dissecting scopes and compound microscopes are adjustable. Place an object on the stage and view it under reflected light. As you look through the oculars, adjust the oculars to fit the distance between your eyes so that you can see one image (**interpupillary adjustment**). Some students (because of astigmatism, or because they have a dominant eye) may have difficulty in adjusting the scope to see one image. If this happens, view the image using only your dominant eye.

For those students who can see a single field of vision, but the focus is not sharp, you may have to adjust for each eye separately. You can use the **diopter adjustment** to help bring the views of both eyes into focus. One of the oculars is fixed in place, and the other is adjustable. Bring the image into focus using the coarse adjustment knob for the fixed ocular first to suit that eye; then by rotating the diopter adjustment on the adjustable ocular, you should be able to bring the image into sharp focus while viewing with both eyes.

General Rules of Proper Microscope Use

1 **Always carry the microscope with both hands.**

2 When unplugging your microscope, please firmly grab the microscope's **plug** when pulling it out of the socket. **Do not pull the plug out of the electrical socket by pulling on the cord.**

3 When putting the microscope away, **make sure that the lowest power objective (4×) is in alignment with the body tube.** Do not keep any higher powered objectives in alignment.

4 **Never touch the lenses with anything except lens paper.** Do not use paper, paper towels, cloth, or your fingers to clean any of the objectives or oculars.

5 When putting the microscope away, clean any immersion oil off of the objectives. Never use oil on any objective except the 100× (oil immersion) lens. In addition, please remove any microscope slides and place them back into their appropriate containers.

6 **You should never use the coarse adjustment knob while using high power or oil immersion objectives.** Always focus first using low power, then switch to higher power objectives.

7 Turn off the power switch, and turn the light intensity knob to an intermediate level to maximize bulb life.

8 As you adjust from one objective to the next, **use the gnarled ring on the nosepiece.** Do not swing the nosepiece around by pulling or pushing on the objectives.

9 You can move the slide back and forth and up and down by using the **slide manipulator** (*X*-axis and *Y*-axis) knobs.

10 When you are done using the microscope, make certain to do the following:

    a Swing the scanning (4×) objective into place.

    b Carefully wipe up any oil or water that is on the microscope. In addition, remember to take the microscope slide that you were looking at off the stage, and put it back into its box!

    c Turn the light intensity knob downward, and turn the power off.

d Unplug the cord, wrap up the cord and carefully cover the microscope with its cover.

e The lab instructor will tell you if you are to put the scope away or to leave it on the table.

Microscope image. Due to the optics of the microscope, when you look at an object and move the slide around, you will note that the object appears upside down and that it moves in the opposite direction as you move the slide.

The **depth of field** refers to the thickness of an object in sharp focus and depends in part on the level of magnification. As you move the fine focus knob, you are focusing at different planes through the object.

How to measure size of microscopic objects. Although many cells and objects you will be observing this semester are small, we can estimate the average sizes of cells and organelles by comparing their sizes with the diameter of the field of view or with the size of the pointer. The pointer has an apparent length and width that changes with each successive magnification. Examine the chart below. A micron (micrometer, μm) is $1/1,000^{th}$ of a millimeter (mm) or 10^{-3} m. A mm is $1/1,000^{th}$ of a meter (m).

TABLE A.2. Estimated lengths of the pointer and the diameter of the field of view.

	AO Sixty Microscopes (blue-grey)			Olympus CH 30 Microscopes (beige)		
Magnification	Pointer Length (μm)	Pointer Width (μm)	Diameter of the Field of View (μm)	Pointer Length (μm)	Pointer Width (μm)	Diameter of the Field of View (μm)
40×	1,400	200	4,200	2,500	60	4,500
100×	560	80	1,600	1,000	24	1,800
400×	140	20	420	250	6	450
1,000×	55	8	160	100	2.5	180

For example, let's say you are looking at an organism under the microscope at 100× with an Olympus scope. It is a little over twice as long as the pointer base width, at 100×. Therefore the organism is approximately 50 μm long. Your lab instructor will provide you with the length and width of the pointer, if you are using a different brand of microscope.

II. The Stereoscopic Dissecting Microscope

Go over the various parts of a stereoscopic dissecting scope. Note that the there are several differences between the compound microscopes and the dissecting scopes.

1 All dissecting scopes are also **binocular.** They have two eyepieces and thus you can use both eyes.

2 Unlike the compound microscopes, the image is not inverted when using a dissecting scope. (Check out this fact by moving a specimen around while examining it under the dissecting scope.) The dissecting scope is used for specimens that are too large for the compound microscope.

3 You can also see a three-dimensional view of the object at low magnification, with a total magnification of up to 60×.

4 There are two different sources of illumination for many dissecting scopes. **Incidental (reflected) light** illuminates the object from above; the light bounces off the specimen and into the scope. **Transmitted light** passes through the object from below, like the compound microscopes. You can look at objects using either or both of the light sources. Often, these dissecting scopes have either a frosted translucent plate (for transmitted light) or a black/white sided contrast plate (for reflected light only). These plates can be removed and switched with the other, depending on the light source.

5 The dissecting scope is used to look at larger specimens, or at objects that are too opaque to look at under the compound microscope. A compound microscope has a small **working distance,** or the distance between the object and the objective lens. The dissecting microscope has a lower resolution and magnification than the compound microscope, as well as a much larger working distance.

When done, remove the specimens, turn the power switches to 'off,' unplug the dissecting scope, and place the protective cover over the top of the scope. **Like the compound scopes, carry the dissecting scopes with both hands back to the cabinet if you are asked to put them away.**

Acknowledgements

Unit 6	Figure 6.4	http://www.yellowtang.org/cells.php
Unit 13	Figure 13.5	Shutterstock
	Figure 13.14	CMSP
Unit 14	Figure 14.17	iStock
Unit 15	Figure 15.4	CMSP
Unit 18	Figure 18.7	iStock
	Figure 18.19	iStock
	Figure 18.33	Shutterstock
Unit 19	Figure 19.14	Bigstock
	Figure 19.22	Bigstock
	Figure 19.23	Bigstock
Unit 20	Figure 20.15	Bigstock
	Figure 20.18	Bigstock
	Figure 20.20	Bigstock
	Figure 20.21	Bigstock
	Figure 20.22	Jeff Spencer & Van-Griner, LLC
	Figure 20.23	Jeff Spencer & Van-Griner, LLC
	Figure 20.24	Jeff Spencer & Van-Griner, LLC
	Figure 20.25	Jeff Spencer & Van-Griner, LLC
	Figure 20.26	Jeff Spencer & Van-Griner, LLC
Unit 21	Figure 21.1	Photoshelter
	Figure 21.8	Photoshelter
	Figure 21.26	Photoshelter
	Figure 21.30	Photoshelter
Unit 22	Figure 22.3	Phototake
	Figure 22.5	Jeff Spencer & Van-Griner, LLC

Literature Cited and Suggested Additional Readings

Chappell, M. A. and L. R. G. Snyder. 1984. Biochemical and physiological correlates of deer mouse α-chain hemoglobin polymorphisms. Proceedings of the National Academy of Sciences USA 81: 5484–5488.

Chappell, M. A., J. P. Hayes and L. R. G. Snyder. 1988. Hemoglobin polymorphisms in deer mice (*Peromyscus maniculatus*): physiology of beta-globin variants and alpha-globin recombinants. Evolution 42(4): 681–688.

Clausen, J., D. D. Keck and W. M. Hiesey. 1940. Experimental studies on the nature of species. I. Effect of varied environments on western North American plants. *Carnegie Institution of Washington Publication* 520, 452 pp.

Clausen, J., D. Keck, and W. Hiesey, 1958. Experimental studies in the nature of species, vol. 3: Environmental responses of climatic races of *Achillea. Carnegie Institution of Washington Publication* 581, 129 pp.

Crowl, T. A. 1990. Life-history strategies of a freshwater snail in response to stream permanence and predation: balancing conflicting demands. Oecologia 84: 238–243.

Crowl, T. A. and A. P. Covich. 1990. Predator-induced life-history shifts in a freshwater snail. Science 247:949–951.

Findlay, C. S., R. F. Rockwell, J. A. Smith and F. Cooke. 1985. Life history studies of the lesser snow goose (*Anser caerulescens caerulescens*). VI. Plumage polymorphism, assortative mating and fitness. Evolution 39(4): 904-914.

Huff, D. 1954. How to Lie with Statistics. W. W. Norton and Company, New York.

Lack, D. 1947. Darwin's Finches. Cambridge University Press, Cambridge, England.

Magnusson, W. E. and G. Mourão. 2004. Statistics Without Math. Sinauer Associates, Inc., Sunderland, Massachusetts.

Nunez-Farfan J. and C. D. Schlichting. 2001. Evolution in changing environments: the 'synthetic' work of Clausen, Keck, and Hiesey. Quarterly Review of Biology 76(4):433–57

O'Brien, S. J., D. E. Wildt, D. Goldman, C. Merril and M. Bush. 1983. The cheetah is depauperate in genetic variation. Science 221:459–462.

Paulos. J. A. 2001. Innumeracy: Mathematical Illiteracy and its Consequences. Hill and Wang, New York.

Smith, T. B. 1987. Bill size polymorphism and intraspecific niche utilization in an African finch. Nature 329: 717–719.

Smith, T. B. 1990. Natural selection on bill characters in the two bill morphs of the African finch *Pyrenestes ostrinus*. Evolution 44: 832–842.

Snyder, L. R., J. P. Hayes and M. A. Chappell. 1988. Alpha-chain hemoglobin polymorphisms are correlated with altitude in the deer mouse *Peromyscus maniculatus*. Evolution 42(4): 689–697.

Zar, J. H. 1996. Biostatistical Analysis. Prentice Hall, Inc., Upper Saddle River, NJ.